V

LL

WW

010

Spitfire

Spitfire

Portrait of a Legend

LEO McKINSTRY

JOHN MURRAY

First published in Great Britain in 2007 by John Murray (Publishers)
An Hachette Livre UK company

1

© Leo McKinstry 2007

The right of Leo McKinstry to be identified as the Author of the Work
has been asserted by him in accordance with the Copyright, Designs and
Patents Act 1988.

A CIP catalogue record for this title is available
from the British Library.

ISBN 978-0-7195-6874-9

Typeset in Bembo by M Rules

Printed and bound in Great Britain by William Clowes Ltd, Beccles, Suffolk

John Murray policy is to use papers that are natural, renewable and
recyclable products and made from wood grown in sustainable forests.
The logging and manufacturing processes are expected to conform to the
environmental regulations of the country of origin.

John Murray (Publishers)
338 Euston Road
London NW1 3BH

www.johnmurray.co.uk

To Christopher Foyle, a hero of books and aviation

Contents

Illustrations

Photographic credits: RAF Museum: 1, 7, 11, 22, 24, 25, 36, 45; Imperial War Museum: 4, 10, 14, 16, 18, 19, 27, 28, 29, 30, 32, 33, 35, 37, 38, 39, 40, 42, 43, 44; Getty Images/Hulton Archive: 5, 13, 17, 20, 23, 34; Corbis Picture Agency: 9, 12, 46; Vickers Archives: 8, 15; Science Photo Library: 6; National Portrait Gallery: 21; Frank Sanders: 31; Sarah Quill (The Jeffrey Quill Estate): 41; Vintage Magazine Company: 26. Every effort has been made to clear permissions. If permission has not been granted please contact the publisher who will include a credit in subsequent printings and editions.

Introduction

Flying over the coast of France with 611 Squadron on a sweltering June afternoon in 1941, Pilot Officer Wilfrid Duncan Smith was feeling hot. The sun was beating through the canopy of his Spitfire, and the burden of flying four combat missions a day was beginning to take its toll. On this scorching afternoon he was part of a Spitfire formation providing a high escort to twelve lumbering Blenheim bombers, which had been instructed to bomb the railway marshalling yards at the coastal town of Hazebrouck. Having crossed the French coast at 28,000 feet, Duncan Smith's section suddenly came under attack from a wave of Messerschmitt 109s. His section broke, and, through expert turning, he and his section leader, Flight Officer P. S. C. 'Polly' Pollard, managed to latch on to the tails of two of the 109s, closing on them fast from 200 feet above. 'As the 109 filled the width of my windshield I opened fire with everything I had. I was that close I could not miss. I blasted into the side of the cockpit and engine. Bits flew off and thick smoke gushed; the 109 rolled slowly over and plunged vertically.'

At that moment, Duncan Smith came under fire from another pair of 109s, tracer streaking past his cockpit. He broke sharply into a right-handed climbing turn, trying to catch up with Pollard, whom he had seen in the sky above. But as they met up and then moved to rejoin the rest of their squadron they were confronted by a formation of at least nine Messerschmitts. 'I saw the guns of the lead 109 wink at me and tracer flew past. There was a loud bang somewhere along my fuselage. The next second I was fighting for my life. As I turned my Spitfire in a tight circle, wings shuddering in the agonizing grip of high "G", my eyeballs in a grey mist, doing their best to pop out, I heard Polly's voice from a great distance, "Look out behind, dive for the deck." My radio subsided into a high-pitched squeal.' Duncan Smith now saw Pollard locked in bullet-strewn combat with a German fighter. The Luftwaffe plane caught fire, falling to earth in a ball of flame, but soon afterwards Duncan Smith lost sight of Pollard, who had gone into a tight spiral. Just then he himself came under fire again from one of the 109s. As the enemy dived away,

Duncan Smith caught a glimpse of the pilot's black-helmeted head. 'I think it was at this point that I lost my temper. I was thoroughly frightened and fighting mad. I went after the Hun hell-bent on murder. I wanted to kill that black-helmeted man more than anything else in life. I meant to get him even if it took me all the way to Berlin.'

Following the German into a dive, his Spitfire gradually caught up with the Messerschmitt. 'Now I was ready, ready to make the kill. I eased the stick forward a little and at 50 to 100 yards range I pulled the nose of my Spitfire up sharply, lined up my reflector sight, and opened fire, pouring cannon shells into the enemy's belly. There was a sheet of flame, the Me 109 flicked over on to its back and dived straight into the ground.'

Duncan Smith made his way back to Kent, flying at low level and with dangerously little fuel left in his tank. On landing, he found he had been hit by two cannon shells in the fuselage and the radio. But there was even worse news. Flight Officer 'Polly' Pollard, his leader and close friend, was missing. He was never seen again.[1]

In this tale of heroism and tragedy, so typical of the experience of RAF pilots throughout the war, the robust fighting qualities of the Spitfire are graphically illustrated. The same character shines through the accounts left by Pilot Officer John Allen, who won the Distinguished Flying Cross for his exploits in his Spitfire during the evacuation of Dunkirk in May 1940, but was killed in action two months later. During a mission on the first day of Dunkirk, flying at 4,000 feet 'looking for trouble' over the beaches, his squadron was met by a large German formation of 60 machines, made up of 20 bombers and 40 fighters. 'The fighters, mostly Messerschmitts, heeled over and came screaming at us, and the next second we were in the thick of it. That attack, like most dogfights, developed into individual scraps,' recalled Allen. Chasing an Me 109 in a dive, he soon got the German in the centre of his sights:

> When you get them there they stick. Once there you can hold them for ever. I thumbed the trigger button just once, twice. I smelt the cordite fumes blowing back from my Brownings as 1,200 squirts a minute from each of them went into him. I saw the little spurts of flame as the tracers struck. For a fraction of a second I saw the back outline of the pilot's head half-slewed around to see what was after him, before presumably he ceased to know. I saw a burst of flame and smoke from his engine, and then he was going down in a twirling spin of black smoke.

Allen and his squadron landed back at their station, refuelled, reloaded, and were back in the air within little more than fifteen minutes. Soon they were mixing it with more Germans, this time the formation including Junkers 88 bombers as well as Me 109s:

> I picked out a Junkers Ju 88 whose tail gunner got on to me as soon as I engaged. The tracers of his guns sheered past me, seeming to curve lazily past my clear-vision window. You watch them quite calmly. They never look as if they are going to hit you, even when they are practically dead on. Again there was that lovely feeling of the gluey controls and the target being hauled into the sights. Then thumb down on the trigger again and the smooth shuddering of the machine as the eight-gun blast let go. This time I must have cut him in two. His tail folded back on his wings and there was a great smoke and flash of flame as he went down.[2]

More than sixty years after the end of the Second World War, the Spitfire continues to grip the imagination of the public. Its unique blend of elegance, beauty, power and speed have made it the most cherished symbol of Britain's heroic struggle against Nazi Germany. Its unmistakable elliptical wings and the reassuring beat of its Rolls-Royce Merlin engine immediately conjure up images of dashing aerial combat in the Battle of Britain. It is rightly still regarded as the greatest British fighter aircraft ever built, a plane whose revolutionary design and supreme manoeuvrability helped to ensure our national survival. Thanks to the Spitfire, what could have been our darkest hour became our finest. And the Spitfire continued to play a vital role in helping to rebuild Allied supremacy in Europe, North Africa and the Far East, whether in mounting a heroic defence of the besieged island of Malta in 1942 or in destroying Germany's deadly V-1 rockets in 1944.

The Spitfire's grace and fighting qualities meant that it was adored by the pilots who flew it. 'It was so sensitive on the controls. There was no heaving or pulling or pushing and kicking. You breathed on it,' said George Unwin, who flew with 19 Squadron at Duxford in Cambridgeshire, which was the first unit to receive the Spitfire in 1938. 'If you wanted to turn, you just moved your hands slowly and she went. She was really the perfect flying machine. I've never flown anything sweeter.'[3] These are sentiments echoed by Wing Commander H. R. 'Dizzy' Allen, 'I have no words worthy of describing the Spitfire. 'It was an aircraft quite out of this world. There was certainly no love/hate relationship between me and my Spitfires; there was only love on my account and on not one occasion did any of these aircraft let me down.'[4] Reflecting the reputation of the plane within the RAF, Bill Rolls, posted to a Spitfire squadron in early 1940, was thrilled when he and a fellow pilot first caught sight of the fighter on their arrival at their new base: 'As we went by the grass mound, we saw a Spitfire only a few yards away. It was fantastic to see one so close. We looked for as long as we could and then hugged each other in sheer joy. We had arrived.'[5]

Flight Lieutenant Godfrey Ball, a member of the Royal Australian Air Force, was another young pilot instantly captivated by the Spitfire. He gave this vivid description of his first time in charge of the plane, when he was based at RAF Heston, just west of London, in the autumn of 1941: 'I was going to fly the world's greatest fighter, the fabulous Spitfire. Surely this was the greatest honour that could be conferred on an aspiring pilot. I felt that I had reached the top of my profession. It certainly was the height of my ambition.' Ball climbed into the cockpit and, with the help of the ground crew, was strapped into his seat. After a final check, he gave the motor several strokes of its priming pump and secured it in the locked position:

> I held the control column back with my knees clasped around it and grasped the throttle lever with my left hand. I switched the two magnetos to the 'on' position and then pressed the twin start buttons, one for the starter motor itself and the other for the booster coil. The huge propeller turned slowly with a jerky motion as it overcame the compression of each cylinder. Then a couple fired weakly and, next moment, the engine had burst into life. I was positively awed by the predicament. For just a moment I felt it was all beyond me. Then with that fatalism which suppresses fear I waved the chocks away, released the brakes, increased the power gingerly, and allowed the magnificent creature to ease its way forward.

Ball was granted clearance for take-off. Because of the length of the Spitfire's nose, forward visibility was poor, and he had to keep swinging the plane from side to side as he taxied across the field. 'As I gathered speed, I had hardly got the throttle open before the tail lifted and my forward view improved greatly. I only had to breathe on the control column and the plane lifted off the ground.' Soon he was climbing through the air, at an angle steeper than anything he had previously experienced. As he practised his aerobatics, this initial flight lived up to all his expectations: 'It was such a clean aeroplane, with its graceful thin wings, that it seemed to slice through the air.' The sound of the Merlin only enhanced the appeal of the machine. 'It seemed to have a definite beat, almost like a twin-engined aircraft when the motors are not perfectly synchronized.' After forty-five minutes of exercises, Ball returned to the base, using the long, curving approach that was needed with a Spitfire because of its restricted view. 'I put down the flaps, re-trimmed the aircraft to keep a constant speed of 90 miles per hour, and floated gently to the ground. The elevators were wonderfully light and effective and I was quite confident as I eased the stick back and felt all three wheels run along the grass together before I rolled to a gentle stop.'[6]

Another pilot from overseas, Lee Gover from California, also had his first experience of a Spitfire in late 1941, after joining the RAF in the USA and then enduring a long, nauseating sea voyage across the Atlantic. In the diary he kept during the war years, he too conveyed his sense of awe at the aircraft. 'Had my first look at the Spitfire this afternoon. What an airplane! It is much bigger than I thought it would be – over 30 feet long and I can almost stand under the wingtip. I just stood there and looked and couldn't say a word. This is the best fighter in the world, and I am going to fly it. Every moment of the training and the trip are worth it to me.' Of that first take-off, he wrote:

> I gave a little throttle and she started moving forward toward the open field ahead. I had trimmed her to take-off settings, so I slowly opened the throttle to full power and how that beautiful Rolls-Royce engine screamed. It was easy to keep her straight down the field with a little rudder pressure, and as the tail came up it was just a matter of getting enough airspeed to lift her off. At 80 miles an hour, I eased back ever so gently on the control stick and up she went . . . As I turned and banked, climbed and dived, the aircraft made me feel that I was built right into her. She was just part of me and no matter what you asked her to do, she did it. She was very, very sensitive on the controls but a dream to fly. Some aircraft do unexpected things when they stall or you try to do certain manoeuvres, but not the Spit. She was so smooth and held no sur-prises in any way. I often marvelled at how this plane could be so easy and civilized to fly and yet how it could be such an effective fighter, able to hold its own with any plane in the world.[7]

It was precisely this ability in combat that made the Spitfire so devastating. Aesthetics and speed would have been nothing without the raw power to destroy the enemy. The Spitfire could not have lasted so long or won such deep respect from its pilots if it had not been such an effective aerial weapon. In war, there is no room for sentiment. Results are all that matters. From the first moment it went into prolonged action against the Luftwaffe, in May 1940 over the shores of northern France, the Spitfire showed that it could inflict serious losses. Even the Germans came to admire the plane, having initially been dismissive of the RAF's capabilities. In October 1939 an analysis of Britain's air defences carried out for the German High Command argued that the RAF's front-line fighters would 'not reach the same level of technical capacity as their German counterparts'.[8] But that view had changed dramat-ically after the experiences of 1940. At the height of the Battle of Britain, the Luftwaffe's greatest fighter ace, Adolf Galland, was called into a meeting with Reichsmarschall Hermann Göring to discuss Germany's failure to win the air war. Tempers grew frayed as Galland highlighted the Spitfire's defensive excel-lence. Finally, Göring turned to Galland and asked what he wanted for his squadron. 'I should like an outfit of Spitfires,' replied the ace.[9] Galland later claimed that he had not really meant his words, since he was still attached to the Me 109, and had only blurted out the remark because of his frustration at Göring's lack of any strategic understanding. Nevertheless, his bold statement reflects how fear of the Spitfire dominated the Luftwaffe's thinking. Another German veteran, Heinz Knoke, had no doubt about the Spitfire's superiority: 'The bastards can make such infernally tight turns. There seems no way of nailing them.'[10]

This ability to hit back at the enemy was retained throughout the war, as the Spitfire went through continuous development, with the addition of more firepower, bigger engines and better equipment. That the original design could be so drastically exploited was a tribute to its inherent aerodynamic qualities. In total there were no fewer than 19 different marks and 52 variants, as the Spitfire was used for everything from fighter-bombing to photoreconnaissance. Following D-Day in 1944, some Spitfires even delivered beer to RAF personnel, the bomb racks under the wings carrying barrels. The final version of the Spitfire, called the Seafire 47, designed for naval carrier work, was radically different from the first Mark I of 1938. Its huge Griffon engine had 2.3 times the power of the original Merlin, while its cannon fired twice the weight of projectiles per second as the Mark I. As Jeffrey Quill, the outstanding test pilot of Supermarine Aviation, which built the plane, pointed out, 'The maximum gross weight of the Seafire 47 was equivalent to the Mark I carrying 32 airline passengers each with 40 lb baggage allowance.'[11] So effective was the Spitfire's development that when production finally came to an end, in 1948, more than 22,000 had been built – a record unmatched by any other British plane.

Like production, public affection for the Spitfire, first sparked by the Battle of Britain, remained undiminished throughout the war. The little aircraft was as much an icon of national defiance as Winston Churchill himself, the very name 'Spitfire' becoming synonymous with courage and airborne triumph. The mood of popular goodwill was most clearly demonstrated in the establishment of Spitfire funds throughout the country during the dark days of 1940, with the aim of raising money for the Ministry of Aircraft Production. It is the only time in British history that vast numbers of citizens have voluntarily, even enthusiastically, donated money directly to the government. Young boys gave pennies, industrial tycoons thousands. Cities and villages, local councils and major companies joined in this outpouring of national determination to build more Spitfires. By the time the funds closed, in mid-1941, over £13 million had been raised.

Even when the nation was safe from invasion, the Spitfire's reputation continued to be enhanced, not only by exploits in battle, but also by official propaganda, articles, books and films, such as *The First of the Few*, starring Leslie Howard and David Niven, a 1942 biopic about Reginald Mitchell, the Spitfire's brilliant designer. Though it owed more to romantic imagination than to historical accuracy, the film captured the heroic spirit of the Spitfire, particularly because genuine Battle of Britain pilots were used in its production. Another stimulus to the Spitfire's growing appeal was Richard Hillary's book *The Last Enemy*, published in the same year, a haunting evocation of the realities of war for a young pilot. A handsome Oxford graduate, Hillary was shot down and suffered severe burns after a dogfight with a Messerschmitt in September 1940. The experience formed one of the most compelling passages of his book, in which he described how, after taking off from Hornchurch, in Essex, and reaching 12,000 feet, his Spitfire squadron came under attack.

> I was weaving and turning in a desperate attempt to gain height, with the machine practically hanging on to the airscrew. Then, just below me and to my left, I saw what I had been praying for – a Messerschmitt climbing and away from the sun. I closed in to 200 yards and from slightly to one side gave him a two-second burst: fabric ripped off the wing and black smoke poured from the engine, but he did not go down. Like a fool, I did not break away, but put in another three-second burst. Red flames shot upwards and he spiralled out of sight. At that moment, I felt a terrific explosion which knocked the control stick out of my hand and the whole machine quivered like a stricken animal. In a second, the cockpit was a mass of flames: instinctively, I reached up to open the hood. It would not move. I tore off my straps and managed to force it back; but this took time and when I dropped back into the seat and reached for the stick in an effort to turn the plane on its back, the heat was so intense that I could feel myself going. I remember a second of sharp agony, remember thinking 'So this is it!' and putting both hands to my eyes. Then I passed out.

Hillary regained consciousness as he fell through the sky. Fortunately he was able to open his parachute before he plunged into the North Sea. It was then that he became aware of the full extent of his injuries. 'For the first time, I noticed how burnt my hands were: down to the wrist, the skin was dead white and hung in shreds. I felt faintly sick from the smell of burnt flesh.'

After a long time floating in the water, sustained by his lifejacket, he was rescued by sea launch and then taken to hospital, where he felt himself 'floating on a great sea of pain'. The agony continued in the months that followed, as he had to endure extensive plastic surgery to his ravaged face and hands. With the iron will typical of the wartime RAF, he regained sufficient physical fitness to fly again, but tragedy struck once more when he was killed in an accident on a routine training flight in January 1943.

The Last Enemy had been published only months earlier, and had instantly been hailed as a classic. Apart from the author's descriptions of combat and of coping with his injuries, what was also absorbing about the book were his accounts of the thrill of flying the Spitfire, such as this moment in his training, when he climbed to 12,000 feet to test his skills at aerobatics. 'With one or two very sharp movements on the stick I blacked myself out for a few seconds, but the machine was sweeter to handle than any other I had flown. I put it through every manoeuvre I knew of and it responded beautifully. I ended with two flick rolls and turned back for home. I was filled with a sudden exhilarating confidence. I could fly a Spitfire.'

For many in Britain in early 1943, Hillary's personal strength was reflected in his aircraft, that fine-looking but rugged machine which had saved the nation in time of peril. But it had not been easy to achieve this iconic status, for the Spitfire saga was filled with setbacks. On many occasions before the victory of the Battle of Britain it seemed that the plane was doomed. The prototype flew in March 1936, but there followed long years of frustrations, political wrangling and bitter recriminations between Supermarine and the government. By the outbreak of war, the credibility of the Spitfire within the corridors of the Air Ministry had dwindled so badly that the aircraft's long-term prospects were dismal. Exasperated senior figures in the Air Staff considered concentrating their efforts on other fighters, such as the twin-engine Westland Whirlwind, rather than wasting more time on the troubled plane.

If the Spitfire was an emblem of the nation's resolution in the Battle of Britain, then two years earlier its crippling production difficulties were a clear indicator of the crisis engulfing the aircraft industry as manufacturers struggled to cope with the demands of the government's RAF expansion programme in the face of Nazi Germany's phenomenal military growth. So serious was this mess that it prompted angry debates in the House of Commons and turmoil in the Cabinet in early 1938, with the failure to deliver the Spitfire seen as one of the worst examples of the Air Ministry's incompetence. The political maelstrom led to resignations from the Cabinet, and Winston Churchill – at the time a backbencher – played a vital role in piling the pressure on the Neville Chamberlain government over the weakness of the nation's air defences. But enforced Cabinet reshuffles provided no solution to the Spitfire fiasco. Renewed pledges on delivery proved worthless. By the summer of 1938, as Hitler cranked up the language of menace against Czechoslovakia, not a single RAF squadron had been provided with any Spitfires. In fact it was only in August that year, a month before the Munich Agreement, that the very first Spitfires arrived for operational duty, going to 19 Squadron at Duxford. There is little doubt that this chronic shortage of modern fighter planes heavily influenced Neville Chamberlain in his negotiations with Hitler. Given that the RAF could provide little protection if Germany were to unleash a bombing offensive against Britain in the event of war, Chamberlain viewed a belligerent stance as irresponsible. In fact Sir Hugh Dowding, the head of the RAF's Fighter Command, welcomed Munich precisely because it bought more time for Spitfires to be produced, though it is now known that Hitler had no intention of bombing Britain in 1938. Not only were all his energies focused on Czechoslovakia, but, just as importantly, the Luftwaffe had nothing like sufficient long-range bombers to mount such a campaign. Munich bought time for Germany as well.

Right up to 1940, despite a renewed drive for rearmament, the RAF was still deficient in Spitfires. Two-thirds of the front-line strength of Fighter Command were made up of slower, less manoeuvrable Hawker Hurricanes, while there was also a dangerous absence of reserves and planes for training units. The limited numbers forced Dowding and his key group commander, Keith Park, to husband their resources with delicacy. This they did with rare skill, assisted by the sophisticated defence organization which Dowding had built up over the previous four years, but they would not have been forced into this predicament if the Spitfires had been delivered in the quantities needed.

The conventional narrative of the Spitfire story pins most of the blame for these problems on the Tory-dominated 'National' governments of the 1930s. Through a cocktail of ineptitude, military ignorance, and the ideology of appeasement, the political rulers of the decade are supposed to have disastrously restricted production of new types and undermined the strength of the RAF. Chamberlain, his Chancellor of the Exchequer Sir John Simon and the Defence Co-ordination Minister Sir Thomas Inskip are regularly portrayed as the villains, starving the aircraft industry of funds and preferring to surrender to Hitler's demands rather than build up Britain's fighting forces. They were allegedly supported in this approach by the officials of the Air Ministry, who lacked the will to ensure that the Spitfire moved from the drawing board into the squadrons.

Conversely, the heroes were the Supermarine company, other parts of private industry, and a few lone figures in the RAF – especially Dowding – who spent their time trying to overcome the indifference and hostility of the supine political establishment. Central to this version is the claim that the Spitfire was essentially a private venture from Supermarine, developed by Reginald Mitchell when he was liberated from the enervating influence of the Air Ministry. One of those assiduous in putting forward this claim was Sir

Robert McLean, the former chairman of Vickers Aviation, owners of Supermarine in the 1930s. In an interview in 1960, McLean said that the Air Ministry's specification for a new fighter, issued in October 1931, was 'unduly restrictive', preventing Mitchell from designing the killer aircraft he wanted. So McLean decided to give him a free hand by embarking on a private venture in co-operation with engine-maker Rolls-Royce. According to McLean, as the project moved forward, the Air Ministry 'was advised in no circumstances would they be allowed to interfere with its design. The Air Ministry naturally resented this and initially refused to supply equipment, though they later agreed to do so.' In the same interview, McLean was equally scathing about the Air Ministry's role in production once the prototype had flown. 'They turned the job over to their own production department, who began by taking away from Supermarine's the order for the construction of the wings and going out to a woodworking firm. This was a disastrous decision and subsequently led to great delays.'[12]

Politicians and civil servants often make easy scapegoats, but in his caustic recollections McLean tried to rewrite history in the most cavalier manner. The same could be said of all those who have propounded the myth that the government of the 1930s should bear sole responsibility for the Spitfire crisis. As an analysis of contemporary official and private papers reveals, the truth was very different. In reality it was the government that was the essential driving force behind the creation of the Spitfire, constantly pushing for improvements in fighter design and increased levels of output. In many ways, private industry lagged badly behind the Air Ministry, hence the constant friction between them. And the senior politicians – particularly the much derided Chamberlain and Inskip – were instrumental in forcing the RAF to adapt their strategic thinking in favour of fighter defence, instead of remaining trapped in the old belief that the only method of waging an air war was through bomber attacks on the enemy's terrain.

McLean's claims were wilfully misleading, aimed at putting himself in the best possible light. The Spitfire could never remotely be described as a private venture. The Air Ministry archives show that officials and senior RAF personnel were involved in every stage of the design process, while the government actually paid for the prototype. Moreover, far from taking away production, the Ministry gave Vickers Supermarine continual encouragement, only to be let down by the firm's lack of capacity, inexperienced management, and chaotic subcontracting arrangements – a desperate situation that McLean tried to cover up with soothing words and wildly optimistic forecasts. The Ministry's sense of mounting vexation shines through the minutes of the meetings held between 1935 and 1938 by the Secretary of State for

Air, Lord Swinton. At one such meeting, in February 1937, Swinton launched a scathing attack on Supermarine: 'It really was a disgraceful state of affairs and he felt that if this sort of thing went on it might be necessary for the Air Council to see the whole Vickers Board and tell them that they must take immediate and practical measures to put an end to what can only be described as an intolerable situation.'[13]

An abrasive, highly efficient Yorkshire squire, with the attitude and balding looks of a retired pugilist, Viscount Swinton was perhaps the most important politician in the entire Spitfire saga. His decisiveness as Air Secretary gave the impetus to the development of the final prototype and the placing of the first order. He was also vital in urging the mass production of the Merlin engine. Without his constant drive, the programme might have slid into paralysis. But because he loathed publicity, often acting more like a business executive than a party figure, his role has been barely acknowledged. In all the wealth of literature about the RAF in this period, there is hardly a mention of his name. Nor did the government of the time recognize his contribution, as the crisis over production ultimately ended in his political exile. He deserved a better fate.

Yet it is equally unfair to give no credit to Neville Chamberlain and other key members of his Cabinet, including Inskip. After the fall of France in mid-1940 they were lambasted as the architects of disaster, the 'guilty men' who had brought the nation to the brink of ruin through their misguided policies. But it was thanks partly to the political emphasis that Chamberlain and his circle gave to fighters that Britain was able to defend itself later that year. Since 1934, Chamberlain had been stressing the need to concentrate on fighter defence at home instead of spending the money on expensive bomber fleets, expeditionary forces, and grandiose imperial projects overseas. His outlook was shared by Inskip, who, in a memorandum to the Air Staff in December 1937, argued that defensive fighter capability was the first requirement of the RAF. In this prophetic document, Inskip said that

> what we want to do in the first weeks of a war is to knock out as many German aeroplanes as we can, with a view to upsetting the morale of their Air Force . . . They must come to this country to damage us. They are likely to concentrate on the great centres, such as London, which provide an irresistible target. In fact, it would seem in accordance with strategical principle that the decisive place and the decisive time for the concentration of our own air forces would be somewhere over our own territory.[14]

Inskip, an overweight lawyer, had predicted the progress of the air war in western Europe with far greater accuracy than many of the uniformed air marshals. It is no exaggeration to say that the Battle of Britain was fought in 1940 along the lines that Chamberlain and Inskip had forecast, with the type of air force they had provided. Indeed, Chamberlain wrote bitterly to his sister Ida in July 1940, after he had been replaced by Churchill in the wake of mounting criticism over the conduct of the war, 'If I am personally responsible for deficiencies in tanks and guns, I must equally be personally responsible for the efficiency of the RAF.'[15] In contrast, Churchill, for all his energetic campaigning for rearmament throughout the 1930s, demonstrated a shaky grasp of what the RAF would actually need to take on the Luftwaffe, pinning his faith not in the Spitfire but in slower, two-seater fighters. He wrote in 1938:

> We should now build, as quickly and in as large numbers as we can, heavily armed aeroplanes designed with turrets for fighting on the beam and in parallel courses. The urgency for action arises from the fact that the Germans must know we have banked upon the forward-shooting plunging 'Spitfire' whose attack must most likely resolve itself into a pursuit which, if not instantly effective, exposes the pursuer to destruction.[16]

A plane such as he envisaged was already being built. It was called the Boulton-Paul Defiant, and it was to prove a disaster, providing little more than target practice for the Me 109.

Nor does the Air Ministry fit the narrow-minded image promulgated by McLean. Though there were many on the Air Staff who clung to the doctrine of the bomber offensive, there were others who throughout the 1930s recognized the need for new fighters. Innovation was not the prerogative solely of aircraft-industry designers. Officials and experts were continually experimenting with new ideas, trying out new weaponry and equipment, urging industry to be more daring. A department that developed the radar network in the late 1930s was not one hidebound by conventional thinking. If anything, complacency was the hallmark of large sections of private manufacturing, as illustrated by a note from Sir Charles Burnett, the Deputy Chief of the Air Staff. Increasingly irritated by the way fighter design was following 'purely orthodox lines', in July 1932, just when the Spitfire was first being developed, he expressed the wish 'to get out of this rut. We tell the designer what we want, show how we want to get away from stereotyped tactics and we leave him to make the best suggestions we can.'[17] In an Air Ministry paper written two years later, the anger at private industry's inertia over producing new fighter models was all too obvious. Having pointed out that the Supermarine prototype was months behind schedule, the document continued, 'The aircraft firms can, of course, produce innumerable excuses for late deliveries but it does appear that they are inclined to play fast and loose with us . . . The time has come when we must apply the screw. The position will go from bad to worse unless something fairly drastic is done to impress on the trade that there is a limit to our credulity and our patience.'[18] That patience continued to be stretched well into the war.

By far the darkest episode in the Spitfire's history was the disastrous start to production at the Castle Bromwich aircraft factory in Birmingham. This massive plant, which would eventually employ over 13,000 workers at its wartime peak, was first conceived in 1938, when the RAF's expansion programme was rapidly accelerating and a major increase in industrial capacity was needed. In May that year the motor magnate Lord Nuffield, the founder of Morris Motors, reached an agreement with the government to construct and run the factory. Yet by May 1940, two years after the deal had been struck, not a single Spitfire had come off the production line. In fact much of the basic building work had not even been completed. The shambles was to leave the RAF woefully short of fighters for the looming conflict with Germany. The full extent of the Nuffield debacle can be revealed from an examination of Air Ministry papers and documents in the Vickers archives, many of which have not previously been studied.

The early Castle Bromwich interlude, in all its grimness, is a reminder of the troubled times the Spitfire experienced before it reached its wartime position at the centre of the government's plans and the nation's hearts. But none of this detracts from the greatness of the plane itself. Indeed, it only makes the ultimate triumph of the Spitfire more appealing. To have emerged successfully from such struggles and then go on to victory against the world's mightiest air force is a tribute to its excellence. And, like character tested in adversity, the Spitfire saga is all the more powerful because of these trials.

There were to be further troubles during the war, such as destruction of the Supermarine factory at the height of Blitz, which led to the dispersal of Spitfire manufacturing across the south of England. Laundries, university buildings, garages, bus depots, even a stately home were requisitioned in the drive to re-establish production – another of the fascinating episodes in this story. In the air, a new crisis beckoned in the autumn of 1941 with the arrival of the deadly Focke-Wulf 190, which for a time outclassed the Spitfire and sank the morale of the fighter squadrons until the Supermarine design team came up with a new high-powered version, the two-stage supercharged Mark IX. The siege of Malta in 1942, when the Spitfire pilots had to fight against overwhelming odds while living on pitifully limited rations, was another exhausting but inspiring chapter. The same is true of the blood-soaked Dieppe landings in the same year, the air campaign in Sicily and Italy from 1943, and the brutal fight against Japan in Burma. The cold reality of war can be seen in this extract from the unpublished diary of Flight Sergeant 'Dobbie' Dobbins, in which he describes strafing Japanese boats near Rangoon in early 1945:

> Unless you have flown, you will never know the thrill of going past your objective at 1,000 feet, turning over on your side and peeling straight for the target. I switched my gunsight on and turned my 'fire and safe' unit to 'fire'. As I straightened out in the dive, I placed my lead on the boats and when I was at about 400 feet I opened up with cannons. What a wizard sight. There were bags of explosions and bits of boats blew up everywhere. I went in twice and gave a couple of busters on each dive. I know that I made a mess of them, for two sank and the other was blown to hell.[19]

The richness of the Spitfire story is made all the greater by the sense of paradox that runs through it. The plane bristled with aggression, yet it was essentially a defensive weapon: its greatest moments were not in attack, but in the protection of Britain. It was the most sophisticated fighter of its day, yet it was initially built in the most primitive conditions at Supermarine, where machine tools were scarce and a hairdryer and a cardboard box had to serve as a wind tunnel. Its designer, Reginald Mitchell, was a supremely practical Midlander, trained in the locomotive industry, yet he built the most aesthetically pleasing aeroplane of his era. Mitchell and Sir Hugh Dowding, the architect of fighter strategy, were deeply conservative men who became revolutionaries in aviation. The Spitfire's finest hour confounded national stereotypes: the RAF was highly professional, efficient, disciplined and technologically advanced, while the Luftwaffe was daring but ill-prepared, aggressive but disorganized. The reverse of the traditional imagery of the British and Germans was epitomized by the difference between the characters of Dowding and Göring. The former – universally known as 'Stuffy' – was cautious, unemotional, brilliant at the detail of planning, but difficult in company, whereas the latter was noisy, reckless, amateurish and moody, but not without a certain bombastic charm. The same contradiction can be seen in the politicians. Neville Chamberlain and his ministers were portrayed as the enemies of effective military defence, yet their decisions gave the nation the Spitfire, the finest guardian of Britain. Similarly, Lord Beaverbrook was one of the loudest supporters of appeasement right up to 1939, but few on the production side did more to foster national spirit and help defeat Germany in 1940. Similarly, in the mid-1930s, when peace campaigns were at their height, no company was more unpopular than Vickers, because of its link with armaments. Labour leader Clement Attlee captured this mood of hostility by sneering at 'the Vickers crowd' in his condemnations of militarism.[20] But it was Vickers that built the most popular aircraft of them all.

Speed was one of the primary virtues of the Spitfire, but its early development and production were anything but fast. As war began to seem inevitable, there was a desperate race against time to ensure that the RAF had anything like sufficient numbers. But when it did arrive with the squadrons, it soon won the admiration of pilots and the public. As the Vickers test pilot Alex Henshaw wrote, the Spitfire 'probably had a greater impact on the will of the people to survive, and put more heart into their morale when it was at its lowest ebb, than anything created in modern times. At the same time that it sustained and encouraged every man, woman and child in a small island under attack, it struck not only a physical blast but a strange psychological terror into its opponents as they heard its name over the radio.'[21]

It was impossible not to be moved by the plane. 'My good Spitfire behaved beautifully and the engine purred with a regularity that gladdened my heart,' said the Belgian-born pilot Jean Offenberg in his journal when describing a dogfight with two Me 109s over France in 1941.[22] Even the vanquished could not suppress their appreciation. In a lecture on the Spitfire in 1976, the former Vickers engineer D. E. Holmes recounted this memory of an occasion when he was working on the restoration of a Spitfire Mark 21 in the late 1960s at the South Marston airfield in Wiltshire. At the time, a number of German businessmen were making regular trips to their Swindon factory, using South Marston as a landing base for their private plane. The two captains of this executive jet were both ex-Luftwaffe pilots. 'After each landing,' recalled Holmes, 'these two German pilots, having dismissed their passengers and fitted their control brakes to the Turbo Commander, would make their way to the hangar and pay homage to their one-time adversary. They left only after having given the engine cowling a fond pat of admiration and with the usual remark, "Wunderbar."'

I

'The supremacy of the monoplane'

'THE CULT OF the Clitoris' was one of the more controversial obsessions of the Honourable Noel Pemberton Billing, right-wing politician, prolific inventor, theatrical impresario, magazine publisher, and aeronautical pioneer. His fixation did not reflect some clinical priapism within his personality; indeed, like most men born in the Victorian era, he was rather ignorant about the female anatomy. When he first heard the word 'clitoris' he had to ask a doctor what it meant. But as a self-appointed guardian of public morals during the First World War he was consumed with the idea that the British political establishment had been undermined by a vast network of 47,000 sexual deviants, whose perversions had led to their being blackmailed into giving clandestine support for the German cause. One of the figures at the centre of this lurid conspiracy, claimed Billing, was the exotic dancer Maud Allan, who had won international fame before the war with her daring performances in Oscar Wilde's notorious play *Salome*, dancing on stage in a costume consisting of little more than a few beads and a transparent black chiffon skirt. 'A delicious embodiment of lust,' read one breathless advertisement for her act in 1908.[1]

Allan spent most of the First World War in Hollywood, but late in 1917 she announced that she was returning to London to perform again in *Salome*. This was too much for the monocle-wearing, strait-laced Billing, who took this as another sign of the degeneracy sweeping through London society. The independent MP for East Hertfordshire since 1916, Billing also ran an extreme nationalist magazine called *The Vigilante*, aimed at rooting out any unpatriotic sentiments in public life. It was through this publication that he now launched his attack on Maud Allan, hoping to goad her into a libel action which he could then exploit to highlight his theories about rampant sexual decadence. In February 1918 he placed a large notice in *The Vigilante* accusing Allan of using her renewed performances to spread the 'The Cult of the Clitoris', by which he meant lesbianism. Allan swallowed the bait and sued, and so, in March 1918, began one of the most sensational trials of the First World War.

Ever the showman, Billing was in his element, filling the Old Bailey with talk about German agents and widespread homosexuality. He provided not a shred of evidence to support his charges, but, in the feverish atmosphere of war, Maud Allan and her fashionable circle were a convenient target for the anger felt by the British public after four draining years of military stalemate. In a verdict that reflected emotion rather than objectivity, the jury found in his favour. But it was to be a short-lived triumph. In 1921 he had to leave the Commons because of poor health, and subsequent ventures into film-making and the promotion of his many inventions proved equally fruitless. Cantankerous and unbalanced, he continued to make frequent, often expensive, appearances as a defendant in libel trials before his death in 1948.

His had been an energetic, eccentric, but strangely unfulfilled life. His creative mind flitted from one project to another without ever making a success of any of them. During his lifetime, he took out no fewer than 2,000 patents, including those for a self-lighting cigarette, a miniature camera, and a clothes-measuring contraption. His brief political career saw him wallowing in aggressive puritanism and flirting with neo-fascism, while his failed adventures in the theatre seem only to have fed his neurotic homophobia. His mind was fertile yet strangely foolish: he started a magazine entitled *British South African Autocar* without realizing that, at the time of the launch, there were no motor cars in South Africa. But Billing did give one priceless gift to Britain: the Supermarine Aviation company, which, twenty years after its foundation, was to build the Spitfire.

Aeronautics were perhaps the greatest fascination of Billing's early life. In the Edwardian era, he had been quick to see the potential of air power, and in 1908 he became the editor of the magazine *Aerocraft*. In the same year he built three light monoplanes at his own airstrip in Essex, two of which he managed to get off the ground. His real interest lay in seaplanes; he believed that they represented the future of flying, since three-quarters of the earth was covered in water. In 1913 he acquired a waterfront site at Woolston on the river Itchen near Southampton, where, in a converted shed and old coalhouse, he planned to develop his first commercial aircraft. His aim, he told the press, was 'to build a boat that will fly rather than an aeroplane that will float',[2] Reflecting this purpose, the name of his company was to be Supermarine, the opposite of submarine. The first Supermarine craft to emerge from the Pemberton Billing works, the distant ancestor of the Spitfire, was the PB1, exhibited at Olympia in March 1914. Though widely praised for its clean lines and 'exquisite workmanship',[3] it is doubtful whether this plane actually ever flew. At the outbreak of war he was engaged in a number of projects, including a single-seat scout, which he claimed to have designed, constructed and tested in just nine days. Another of his early designs was an ingenious flying boat which in the event of a crash could discard its wings and turn into a motorboat, since the engine was mounted in the hull. But neither this nor the scout was ordered by the government. Even more ambitious was the mighty Zeppelin-killer, a quadruplane known as the Nighthawk, which carried cannon, a sleeping berth and a searchlight, and was supposedly able to idle at 28 mph, waiting for the enemy. Again, it never went beyond the prototype stage.

By mid-1916 Billing, as restless as ever, was hearing the call of politics, partly because he was eager to make the case for a stronger air force. One of his electioneering stunts was to drag the PB9, the nine-day wonder, around the streets as he made his harangues. On his election to the Commons, where he took to describing himself as 'the first air member', he handed his company over to his close friend Hubert Scott-Paine, who continued in the same spirit of 'extreme unorthodoxy'.[4] Typical of this approach was a machine with folding wings which could be stowed in a submarine, though this was too audacious an idea for the Admiralty. Far more successful was the small, single-seat, wooden-hulled biplane called the N1 Baby. Effectively it was the first flying-boat fighter, proving that Supermarine could be practical as well as innovative.

Scott-Paine – known as Ginger because of his red hair – also gave an early inkling of Supermarine's enthusiasm for speed, for he was a large man with a taste for fast planes and motorboats. His own origins may reflect the ill-disciplined atmosphere of the early aircraft industry. According to Denis Webb, a Supermarine employee who spent his entire career at the company from 1926, Scott-Paine had once been a boxer, earning his living at fairs around the country. As a keen amateur pugilist himself, Billing had originally hired him as a chauffeur, so that he himself could practise his art whenever he wanted. Webb had little time for Scott-Paine's methods. 'I cannot help feel that Scott-Paine treated the whole outfit more like an expensive hobby than a serious business and with no proper concentration on either running it as an air service or as a design and construction firm.'[5]

A year after the transfer of the company by Billing, an event of far greater significance occurred. In 1917, just as the new MP for East Hertfordshire was beginning to work himself into a frenzy about lesbian-inspired treachery, a shy, blond-haired twenty-one-year-old engineer from the Midlands arrived at Supermarine. Reginald Mitchell had no professional experience of aviation, but he had been 'mad about aeroplanes' since his childhood.[6] Born in 1895, Mitchell was the son of a Yorkshireman who had begun his working life as a teacher but had moved to Stoke-on-Trent to begin a new career running a printing business. Young Reginald was a bright child: inquisitive, excellent at mathematics, and also good at art – a rare combination of gifts that was to be invaluable in the creation of the Spitfire. The predominant theme of his early years was his passion for aircraft – an unusual interest, since flying was still in its infancy. Using their own designs, since no model kits were available, he and his younger brother Billy made model planes from bamboo cane, paper and twisted rubber. There were, however, few openings in the Midlands for an adolescent obsessed with aviation, so when he left school, in 1911, at the age of sixteen, Mitchell became an apprentice at the locomotive firm of Kerr, Stuart & Co., receiving instruction in the basic aspects of engineering. He also supplemented his training through attendance at night school in Stoke, studying mechanics, drawing and higher mathematics.

Throughout his life, Mitchell was never at ease with either authority or workplace routine. His imaginative side recoiled at restrictions on his freedom. For all his shyness, he always had a rebellious streak. This trait was apparent even in his spell at Kerr, Stuart & Co. One of his first allotted tasks was to make tea for his fellow apprentices and the foreman, to whom Reginald had taken an intense dislike. When this foreman complained one morning about Reginald's tea, saying 'It tastes like piss' and spitting out a mouthful on the ground, Reginald decided to take his revenge. As his son recalled in his affectionate biography of his father, 'The next day he went off to the wash-room as usual to fill the kettle with water, but this time, instead of tap water, he peed in the kettle. Having boiled it he made the tea and handed the mugs round, having first warned his fellow apprentices not to drink any. The foreman took one sip, then a larger one and said, "Bloody good mug of tea, Mitchell, why can't you make it like this every day?"'[7]

When war broke out, Mitchell twice tried to enlist in the armed forces, but on both occasions he was told that his engineering skills were too valuable. Finally, three years into the conflict, he spotted an advertisement for a job at Supermarine. At last there was a chance of working in the one field that truly excited him. Having been invited for interview, Mitchell impressed Scott-Paine with his enthusiasm and practical outlook. To his delight, he was appointed Scott-Paine's personal assistant – a post that would mean involvement in all aspects of Supermarine's operations. It was a big change in his life, for Mitchell had rarely ventured outside Stoke before. But he quickly proved himself, and within a year he had been promoted to assistant works manager.

His improved pay and status meant that he felt secure enough to marry Florence Dayson, a headmistress from Stoke, who was eleven years his senior. Despite the substantial age gap, it was to prove a generally happy marriage, even though Mitchell, often wrapped up in his work, could be a distant, volatile husband. Placid and intelligent, Florence tried to tolerate Reginald's often unpredictable behaviour. 'He'd be talking to you one moment and then the next he'd be miles away,' she recalled in an interview in 1940.[8] But their only son, Gordon, born in 1920, confessed that domestic harmony did not always reign in the Mitchell household. 'He was a damned difficult man to live with sometimes. He had a very short temper. He got very angry at times and occasionally we had some pretty awful rows.'[9] Typical of his explosiveness was the time he was sent some dodgy oysters by the local fishmonger. 'Immediately father was on the phone to the fishmonger and subjected him to a barrage bordering very close to pure rage. I had little doubt that father had concluded that the fishmonger was an incompetent fool and in consequence let him have it with all guns firing.'[10]

At Supermarine, Mitchell's obvious capabilities meant he was given increasing responsibility for major projects. Soon after arriving at the company, he assisted with the design of the tail for the huge Nighthawk anti-Zeppelin prototype, while he also produced some of the drawings for the N1 Baby flying-boat fighter. With the end of the war, the growing diversity of ideas being developed by Supermarine provided more scope for Mitchell's talents. Part of the impetus for this expansion was inspired by Commander James Bird, a dashing former naval pilot and architect, who became Scott-Paine's partner in running Supermarine, though he was the one with the sharper business brain. His naval background gave him a natural authority, and he was highly respected by the workforce. Like Billing, he was a colourful enthusiast for flying boats, though he shared none of the eccentric MP's prurient moral zealotry. 'He was loved by his men and he certainly attracted the ladies,' wrote Denis Webb:

> What went on in his steam yacht in Southampton Water during the summer was anybody's guess. One time a lady turned up asking to be ferried out to this yacht. Later in the day another woman arrived saying that she was his wife. The caretaker did quite the wrong thing by saying that there must be some mistake as Mrs Bird was already on board! However, he ferried this person out and then 'retired to prepared positions', as the Navy might put it.[11]

Reflecting his strong confidence in Mitchell's talent, Commander Bird made him Supermarine's chief engineer and designer in 1920. Mitchell was still only twenty-five years old, but he soon justified the directors' faith. His first design was for a new single-engined biplane amphibian, powered by a Rolls-Royce Eagle VIII engine. Entered into an Air Ministry competition at the Aeroplane and Armament Experimental Establishment at Martlesham Heath, near Ipswich, the plane finished in second place, but was judged by the Air Ministry to be so good that the value of its prize money was doubled to

£8,000. This aircraft later evolved into the Seagull, a model produced in large quantities for the RAF and the Royal Australian Air Force.

The Seagull was just the start in a long line of successes produced by Mitchell's genius. During his twenty years at Supermarine, he designed twenty-four different planes, ranging from ultra-reliable flying boats to record-shattering high-speed seaplanes. His productive versatility resulted from his instinctive understanding of aeronautical engineering, his highly practical nature, his enormous capacity for work, and his gift for leadership. 'There was a sort of direct and shining common sense which illuminated his approach to all problems,' said the test pilot Jeffrey Quill, who recalled that one day Mitchell had said to him, 'Jeffrey, if anyone tries to tell you something about an aeroplane which is so damned complicated that you can't understand it, then you can take from me that it's all balls.'[12] But what elevated him to a higher level was the originality of his mind. Though he often seemed a hard-nosed pragmatist, there was also an air of the artist, of the visionary, about him. Joe Smith, the man who succeeded him as the chief Supermarine designer, thought that his creative flair was the 'driving force of his life. No other man in my experience produced anything like the number of new and practical fundamental ideas that he did during his relatively short span of working life.'[13] As Sir Robert McLean of Vickers once put it, 'He was a curious mixture of dreams and common sense.'[14]

Known throughout Supermarine as 'RJ', Mitchell inspired awe and affection. Recalling the first time he met him at the Southampton factory, Cyril Russell, one of the staff, later wrote, 'There was something about him that immediately left an indelible impression, a fine forehead, fair hair brushed straight back, a strong-featured face and an aura of quiet unassuming authority.'[15] Those who worked with him were always struck by his ability to get to the heart of any problem. Arthur Black, Supermarine's metallurgist, gave this recollection:

> I remember how RJ's well-built figure, medium height with fair colouring, could be seen in the workshop each morning, studying with complete concentration the developing shape of the aircraft being built. He would walk round it and study it from all angles, now and then examining a detail minutely. I sometimes wondered if he was aware of how closely he was watched for some clue as to what his reactions were going to be. If he was satisfied, he would pass on to the next job; but if he was not satisfied, then much of the design work and manufacture might well have to be done again.

Black also recalled the fear that Mitchell could provoke:

> There were, however, things one didn't do. His best work arose from a power of concentration, and in the picture of him which most springs to mind he is

seated with his elbows on the drawing board, face cupped in hands, thinking out the latest problem. Woe betide the unwary but enthusiastic technician who broke in on that concentration.[16]

Jack Davis, who joined Supermarine as a draughtsman in 1925, had similar memories:

We often saw him in the workshops and noticed his keen interest in structures. On one occasion he picked up a rudder and without weighing it decided that it was too heavy. It had to be redesigned from scratch. Later as a junior draughtsman I saw how he spent hours alone in his office and did not like to be disturbed. On occasions he would sally forth into the drawing office, surrounded by an entourage of senior men, then sit at a drawing board, pencil in hand, and make positive suggestions before reaching a decision . . . In short, he kept everyone on their toes. Some people preferred to stick with the well-trodden path and repeat earlier design work, but he made it clear that we had to adopt new ideas because aeronautical science was moving so fast you could not risk being left in a rut.[17]

Mitchell's successor, Joe Smith, gave this description of his working method:

He was an inveterate drawer on drawings, particularly general arrangements. He would modify the lines of an aircraft with the softest pencil he could find and then re-modify over the top with progressively thicker lines, until one would finally be faced with a new outline of lines about three-sixteenths of an inch thick. But the results were always worthwhile and the centre of the line was usually accepted when the thing was re-drawn.[18]

Despite his achievements, Mitchell remained a modest man throughout his career. He avoided the limelight and disliked public speaking, not least because of self-consciousness about a slight stammer. Entirely lacking in vanity, he was driven by professional pride, not the desire for public adulation, though he did enjoy some of the material fruits of success, including a good salary, a series of high-class motor cars, and a large house in Southampton built to his own specification. The Supermarine seaplane pilot Richard Atcherley said of him, 'He set his sights deliberately high, for he had little use for "second-bests". Yet he was the most unpompous man I ever met.'[19] On one occasion Mitchell turned up late for an official dinner, having been working in his office. Instead of going to the top table, where a place had been reserved for him, he sat among his own employees.

Mitchell often appeared to be shy, especially in the company of strangers or women, but he could also be charming, with 'an engaging smile which was often in evidence and which transformed his habitual expression of concentration', according to Joe Smith.[20] Though devoted to his work, he was no monomaniac. He was keen on sport, especially cricket, golf and tennis, and later also took up sailing. Unlike many driven men, he was a surprisingly good loser, since he played for relaxation rather than competition. His boyishness came out in his enthusiasm for practical jokes, and he was often the ringleader for pranks after official functions. One night in the early hours he gathered a group of staff outside the bungalow of the humourless Supermarine commercial manager A. E. Marsh-Hunn, and proceeded 'to serenade him in a raucous and unmelodious manner.'[21] Denis Webb, as a young Supermarine trainee, experienced Mitchell's lack of self-importance at their first meeting:

> He was reputed to have a shortish fuse at times so I was in somewhat of a stew. I need not have been. He was friendly and pleasant and put me completely at ease and made me almost forget that I was just a humble apprentice. It was quite obvious that RJ's success had not gone to his head and never did. Later, if he saw me foot-slogging over to Southampton and he was making his stately way in his Rolls-Royce, he would not be above offering me a lift. He was a man in a million.[22]

It would be wrong, however, to pretend that Mitchell was a paragon. He could be brusque, moody and insensitive. His temper was often just as bad in the office as at home, particularly when he was under pressure. 'If you went into his office and found that you could only see RJ's back bending over a drawing, you took a hasty look at the back of his neck. If that was normal, you waited for him to speak, but if it rapidly became red, you beat a hasty retreat,' remembered Joe Smith.[23] Mitchell could be a strict, sometimes unreasonable taskmaster. Eric Lovell-Cooper, another Supermarine worker, saw this side when Mitchell asked him to undertake a large redesign job on the fuselage and wing surfaces of a seaplane. 'The whole exercise took little more than a week. I remember asking RJ when he returned after the test flight if they had performed satisfactorily. He rather curtly replied, "Of course they did, why shouldn't they?" which I thought was a bit hard after all the long hours I and others had worked in order to produce them.'[24]

Mitchell may have been a brilliant designer, but he was a woeful organizer. Routine meant nothing to him. Hopelessly unpunctual, he would often disappear in the middle of the day for a round of golf or a trip in his sailing boat. He disliked seeing visitors. Staff knew that when he barked from his office, 'I'll see him in ten minutes,' that was Mitchell's code for 'Get rid of him.'[25] He loathed dealing with administration, especially written correspondence. When his long-serving secretary Vera Cross first went to work for him, she found it difficult to cope because of his unpredictability and the chaos of his office. He had no filing system, and piles of letters sat unanswered on his desk. This would not have mattered if Supermarine had remained just a minor enterprise on the south coast. But from the early 1930s, the company was engaged in one of the Air Ministry's most vital contracts, and Mitchell's careless approach was reflected in the lack of effective administration at Supermarine for much of that decade. According to Denis Webb, the running of the company was still in a mess as late as 1935: 'We had absolutely no kind of organization which helped keep track of what was happening in the shops. There was no proper recording system and parts were not stored in any order.' As for the management, said Webb, 'running around like a bluebottle in a dustbin was no substitute for organization.'[26]

All Mitchell ever really wanted to do was design planes, and as soon as he had taken over as chief engineer in 1920 he had proved remarkably good at it. His initial success at Martlesham was followed by the Sea Eagle, a six-passenger commercial amphibian, and the twelve-seater, twin-engine Swan, of which the Air Ministry ordered a military version. But his two great successes of the 1920s were the Southampton flying boat and the series of fast seaplanes which brought Britain international victory in the Schneider racing contests.

The Southampton Mark I, which first flew in 1925, was a large, wooden-hulled plane with an unorthodox triple fin. Admired for its reliability, ease of maintenance and long range, it was soon in service with the RAF, working around Britain's coast and venturing as far afield as Greece and Egypt. The affection it engendered in the crews and the public, who liked its image of stately power, greatly enhanced the name of Supermarine and R. J. Mitchell. This growing reputation was further magnified by the Southampton Mark II, Mitchell's first metal-hulled flying boat. In October 1927 the plane captured international attention when a formation of four gleaming-white Southamptons made a historic voyage all the way from Plymouth to Australia, via stops in the Middle East, India, Hong Kong, Japan and Singapore. Again, despite the unprecedented length of the journey, Mitchell's Southampton had proved its utter dependability. 'So far as dangers were concerned, the cruise was as prosaic as a P&O steamer plying between Tilbury and Bombay,' ran a contemporary account.[27] In the context of the Spitfire, what has always been ignored about the England–Australia flight was that it was led by Group Captain Henry Cave-Brown-Cave, who became Director of Technical Development in the Air Ministry in 1931. In this position, he was to have a primary role in pushing forward the early Spitfire project. His experience of the Southampton can only have given him a favourable opinion of Mitchell's work.

But even more important for the future of the Spitfire was Mitchell's development of world-beating speed planes. This was an entirely different field for Supermarine, with the emphasis on sleek aerodynamism rather than rugged simplicity. In 1913, the very year when Billing had founded his works at Southampton, the French industrialist and aviation enthusiast Jacques Schneider had established an international competition to find the fastest seaplane in the world. Schneider, whose wealth came from the armaments industry, hoped that his contest would spur technological progress in marine aviation, and he put up an annual prize of £1,000, along with an elegant silver trophy. The first event, held in Monaco, was won by Schneider's compatriot Maurice Prévost in a Deperdussin, averaging a speed of just 45.75 mph. The next year, again in Monaco, Britain had its first victory, as Howard Pixton was the victor in his Sopwith Tabloid. 'In a country where the Navy is held in great honour, the triumph of an English hydro-plane will be well-noted,' said the French paper *Le Temps*.[28] The Schneider contests were suspended throughout the First World War, during which aircraft technology made rapid advances, especially in the power of engines. When the competition resumed, in 1919, Supermarine entered for the first time. But the event, held at Bournemouth, was turned into a farce by foggy conditions and mistaken application of the rules by the judges. The only pilot to complete the course, Sergeant Guido Janello of Italy, was disqualified because he was said to have followed the wrong route. Supermarine's own Sea Lion Mark I, a development of the N1 Baby, was one of the many entrants forced to retire, having sustained damage in practice.

The fiasco of Bournemouth discredited both English management and the Schneider Trophy itself for the next couple of years. The contests of 1920 and 1921, in Venice, were won by Italians against almost non-existent foreign competition. Under the Schneider rules, if Italy were to win a third successive time in 1922, it would have a permanent hold on the trophy. Working up a lather of patriotic sentiment, the British press urged the aircraft industry to stop this eventuality and restore some pride after the humiliations of the post-war years. Supermarine, absent since 1919, responded to the appeal. Commander Bird and Hubert Scott-Paine decided to finance an entry as a private venture, with the help of the Napier Company, which provided the Lion engine. Mitchell then went to work, developing the Sea Lion biplane from the 1919 entry into a new Mark II streamlined version, with the wingspan reduced and superfluous fittings and landing gear removed.

The 1922 contest was held over a triangular course in the Bay of Naples. The competition was also triangular, Italy, France and Britain taking part. The Italians, the acknowledged world leaders in aviation design, were confident of victory, but they faced a real test in Mitchell's Sea Lion II, flown by the charismatic Supermarine test pilot Henri Biard, a native of Guernsey. Amid thrilling scenes in the final laps above the blue of the Mediterranean, Biard managed to retain a narrow lead over his three Italian rivals, averaging 145.7 mph – just 2.5 mph ahead of the nearest Italian pilot. When the Supermarine team returned to Southampton there were, according to *Flight*'s report, 'remarkable scenes' of celebration.[29] Large crowds lined the water's edge at Woolston, while later there was a civic reception led by the mayor. True to his nature, R. J. Mitchell, the real architect of this triumph, remained in the background. Indeed, the local press did not even mention his name in its coverage.

The Sea Lion's win had not only boosted the company; it had also given a new stature to the Schneider Trophy, which now began to attract major public interest on both sides of the Atlantic. As the international competition intensified, the event grew into one of the biggest fixtures in the sporting calendar. Press speculation created an atmosphere of feverish excitement in the build-up to the contests. Newsreels in the expanding cinema network allowed audiences to catch glimpses of the high-speed action. Eager to raise their prestige, the French, American and Italian governments put money into their national entries, while encouraging their air forces to provide pilots and expertise. The significance of the Schneider Trophy reflected the mounting public fascination with aviation. At the time of Supermarine's victory in 1922, it was less than twenty years since the Wright brothers had first flown. But during the war interest had been stimulated by tales of the fighter pilots' daring exploits. In the period after the Armistice awareness had been further heightened by pioneering adventures such as the first direct flight across the Atlantic, made by Alcock and Brown in 1919, as well as the start in 1920 of the annual RAF pageants at Hendon, which allowed thousands to see live displays of aerobatics, formation flying and mock dogfights.

The 1923 Schneider race, at the Isle of Wight, was the biggest air event held in Britain at the time. Supermarine's entry was a further refinement of the Sea Lion, the Mark III, with a modified hull and a more powerful Napier engine. But on the day, despite more heroics from Captain Biard, it proved no match for the swift Curtiss biplanes of the United States Navy, which attained speeds of over 173 mph. The Sea Lion, essentially a souped-up flying boat, looked outdated by comparison to the Curtiss, with its floats and its compact D-12 engine. Yet the defeat of 1923 turned out to be a blessing in disguise for Mitchell, for it forced him to adopt radically different thinking. Mitchell recognized that if he were to regain the Schneider Trophy he would have to come up with a new design based entirely on the goal of achieving the maximum possible speed. And that meant replacing the biplane with a monoplane structure. There had, of course, been monoplanes from almost the beginning of powered flight: Blériot had flown the English Channel in one in 1909, and the winning French entry at Monaco in 1913 had been one. But in the first decades of the century biplanes had been generally preferred, because they provided large lifting surfaces while allowing aircraft to remain lightweight. Their disadvantage was the large amount of drag they produced.

In the quest for speed, Mitchell decided it was time to move away from recent tradition. The aircraft he eventually produced was the S4, a near-revolutionary monoplane. It still contained the Napier 12-cylinder Lion engine, but in other ways it could have hardly been more modern, from the fully cantilever construction of the wings, without any external struts or wires, to the ultra-streamlined fuselage. When it was first unveiled to the press, in September 1925, it caused a sensation. *Flight* magazine commented:

> One may describe the Supermarine Napier S4 as having been designed in an inspired moment. That the design is bold no one will deny and we think the greatest credit is due to R. J. Mitchell for his courage in striking out on entirely new lines. It is little short of astonishing that he should have been able to break away from the types with which he has been so intimately connected and not only abandon the flying boat type in favour of the twin float arrangement but actually change from the braced biplane to the pure cantilever wing.[30]

The S4 soon showed that its power matched its arresting looks. During trials on Southampton Water, the plane shattered the world speed record, reaching 226 mph. In early October it was taken over to Baltimore in the USA for the eighth Schneider race, where it instantly made a big impression. 'One cannot help feeling a certain amount of surprise that a British designer has had sufficient imagination to produce such a machine,' said one condescending US journalist.[31]

But almost from the moment of its arrival in Baltimore, the S4 was plagued by ill luck. At the site of the race, at Chesapeake Bay, the machine was housed in a makeshift canvas hangar. During a storm shortly before the contest, a pole collapsed across it, causing serious damage to its tail. Fortunately, Mitchell was quickly on the scene to organize repairs, and with typical energy he had the S4 ready by the day of the race. Misfortune continued in the event itself. When Captain Biard took the plane to 8,000 feet, it appeared to develop such a violent wing flutter that spectators thought he was performing a stunt. But this was no stunt. The S4 went into a spin, and, though Biard managed to flatten out the angle of its fall, it still plunged into the sea with such force that the floats collapsed, the fuselage was ripped apart, and Biard was knocked unconscious. As his body, still trapped in the wreckage of the cockpit, sank beneath the waves, the icy water suddenly revived him. His frozen fingers managed to undo the straps and, with pain coursing through every limb, he clawed his way to the surface. He had sustained two broken ribs and severe injuries to his stomach muscles. But it was a miracle that he had survived.

For all his brusqueness, Mitchell was a sensitive, compassionate man, deeply concerned about his pilots. In fact this was the one of the reasons why he became so intense when working on a new design. 'He could never escape the sense of responsibility for the safety of the pilot,' recalled Arthur Black.[32] This burden had been all the greater with the S4 because Mitchell was pushing the boundaries of aerodynamics as they were understood at the time. Later research suggested that the S4's wing flutter might have been caused by over-large ailerons, though it may also be possible that Biard, unused to such an innovative machine, misjudged a turn and stalled it.

Despite this setback, Mitchell was certain that his design was the way forward. The Air Ministry agreed. The 1925 contest was the first time that the government had, as part of its development programme for high-speed aircraft, given its backing to a Supermarine entry in the Schneider Trophy – further evidence that officialdom was   always as backward-looking as is often claimed. The company itself was equally supportive of Mitchell: in December 1924 he was given a ten-year contract, with the promise of a directorship within three years. When he signed this document he was still in his twenties – a remarkable testament to his talent. He now started work on improving the S4, particularly dealing with the lack of stiffness in the wings and poor visibility. He did not have time to complete these changes by the next Schneider contest, in 1926, which was won by Italy in the USA, but by 1927 he was ready with his latest creation, the magnificent S5. This had a low wing, supported by wire braces to overcome the flutter problem, while the fuselage, made largely of metal, was much narrower than on the S4, which meant that the fuel had to be carried in the floats. Further streamlining was achieved by removing the obtrusive radiators of the S4, replacing them with double-skinned surface coolers made of copper sheet.

By now the government was heavily involved with the British entry, despite the reservations of the bomber-minded Marshal of the Royal Air Force, Sir Hugh Trenchard, who regarded Schneider planes as mere 'freak machines'.[33] Finance was put up for the development of the S5, and the RAF provided the pilots for the race. Against the dreamy backdrop of the Venice skyline, Flight Lieutenant Sidney Webster powered the S5 to victory at 281 mph. To reinforce the dominance of Supermarine, another S5 finished in second place. Awarding the trophy to Webster, Prince Scalea, President of the Aero Club of Italy, said that the English pilots 'had won a victory which has stirred the imagination of the whole world'.[34] When Mitchell and the Supermarine team returned to Southampton and alighted at the city's main station, there were huge crowds to greet them. At the inevitable municipal reception which followed at the civic centre, the Mayor turned to Mitchell and said, 'You have done something for England that will live through generations to come.'[35] Despite his dislike of public oratory, Mitchell could not avoid delivering a response, but with characteristic modesty he gave most of the praise to the Supermarine staff and the RAF.

Thanks to the two Scheider triumphs and the Southampton flying boat, Supermarine and Mitchell were now highly regarded in the world of aviation. In 1927 Commander Bird turned the firm into a public limited company, and in the following year the entire share capital was bought by Vickers Aviation, a subsidiary of the giant Vickers Armstrong armaments and shipbuilding group. Reflecting the soaring reputation of Mitchell, one of the conditions of the purchase was that he would not be able to terminate his contract with Supermarine before 1934. Sir Robert McLean, the austere, imperious chairman of Vickers Aviation, later explicitly stated that 'the object of acquiring the Supermarine Company was primarily to acquire the services of Mitchell, who was recognized to be an outstanding designer.'[36] Even if it meant expansion, much of the Supermarine workforce was unhappy with the change, for Vickers had a name as a second-rate employer, as Denis Webb remembered: 'We naturally considered that we built rather better aircraft than Vickers and the idea of being bossed about by them did not appeal to us at all. A rather crude joke went round the workshops in the form of a question: "Why are we like a bunch of choirboys? Because we're being buggered by Vickers."'[37]

Indirectly, the Vickers takeover led to one of the less edifying episodes of Mitchell's career. Worried about the poor organization of Supermarine, Sir Robert McLean sent the renowned designer Barnes Wallis, who was based at the Vickers plant in Weybridge and was later to create the bouncing bomb of the Dambusters Raid, to Southampton to improve the administrative efficiency of the company. Wallis, an even more austere man than McLean, arrived at Woolston during the Christmas holidays of 1929 and immediately installed himself in Mitchell's office. He then embarked on an overhaul of the design department, tightening up on the time-keeping by staff. In the New Year of 1930 Mitchell arrived back at Supermarine and was outraged at what he perceived to be Wallis's presumption. Having turfed him out of his office, he gave Wallis an old desk and chair in a disused loft on a remote corner of the Woolston site, telling his staff, 'Don't make him too comfortable.'[38] For a time Wallis accepted the situation, hoping it might improve. But the tension between the two great designers became unbearable. Wallis went to McLean, who took the problem to the board of Vickers Aviation. Meanwhile, Mitchell was threatening to resign if Wallis remained on the Supermarine staff. Eric Lovell-Cooper recalled, 'Mitchell said, "It's either him or me!" I heard him say that, "You can make your own choice."'[39] It is a measure of the esteem in which Mitchell was held that the board came down in his favour. Wallis was asked to return to Weybridge, and was not seen again at Woolston during Mitchell's time. He later commented after Mitchell's death, 'He resented the Vickers takeover and naturally hated my inspection, but the truth was that his design team was weak on structure.'[40]

Wallis's view was hardly borne out by events. In the mid-1920s, certain self-styled experts had claimed that 260 mph was the maximum speed at which man could fly. Mitchell had proved them wrong, but, like all pioneers, he was not a man to rest content with his achievements. The search for ever greater speed drove him to seek further improvements to the S5. He now decided that no more power could be extracted from the Napier Lion engine, so he turned to Rolls-Royce. It was the start of the partnership that would ultimately have a huge influence over the development of the Spitfire. In mid-1928 he went to visit Sir Henry Royce, the outstanding engineer and founder of the firm, who was living in semi-retirement in West Wittering in Sussex following a near fatal illness, though he still exerted a close control over all design work at the Rolls-Royce factory in Derby. Henry Royce had risen from an impoverished background and, like Mitchell, had worked for a time in the railway industry. His success stemmed from his belief that far higher standards of performance and reliability could be achieved in combustion engines by the application of precision engineering and better design. The Rolls-Royce Eagle, which powered much of the Royal Flying Corps's equipment in the First World War, was one of his many triumphs. At the time of Mitchell's first visit in 1928, he was working on a new engine called the Buzzard, which offered a substantial increase in performance over previous models. After discussions with Mitchell, he agreed to adapt the Buzzard for use by Supermarine. What he built, after just six months of redesigning, was the potent 37-litre 'R' engine, which featured a large supercharger and gave over 1,900 horsepower.

Mitchell's next Schneider seaplane, the S6, was designed around the 'R' engine. The aircraft had to be larger, to accommodate the power plant's greater size, and the wings were made of the lightweight alloy duralumin, but otherwise its layout was similar to that of the S5. And, like the S5, it was to prove a world-beater, as on 7 September 1929 Flying Officer H. R. D. Waghorn raced to victory at 328 mph – almost 43 mph faster than the Italian who finished second. The supremacy of the S6 was reinforced only a few days after the race, when Squadron Leader A. H. Orlebar raised the world speed record to 357.7 mph – a speed that would have been unthinkable only five years earlier. Such was the gap between Supermarine and its competitors that Britain looked likely to win again when the contest would next be held, in 1931 – a third consecutive triumph which would mean permanent possession of the trophy.

But then Supermarine hit a political obstacle. The Labour government of Ramsay MacDonald, beset by economic crisis, announced that it would not provide any funds to support the British entry. According to the Air Minister, Fred Montague, the Schneider Trophy was 'in the nature of a sporting contest', so private enterprise would have to meet the costs.[41] The decision outraged the aviation world. 'If we let the Schneider Trophy go aeroplane trade will go too. Government blunder. Public astounded,' screamed the headlines of the Daily Mail.[42] But the government refused to move. Financial expediency was dressed up in the moral language of internationalism: in the view of the Chancellor, Sir Philip Snowden, the Schneider competition encouraged 'pernicious rivalry between nations'.[43] Given the estimated six-figure bill for participation, Supermarine's bid looked doomed. But then, at the eleventh hour, rescue came in the form of a £100,000 cheque from Dame Fanny Houston, reputedly the richest woman in England,[44] who was appalled at what she regarded as Labour's lack of patriotic spirit. 'My blood boiled with indignation, for I know every true Briton would rather sell his last shirt than admit that England could not afford to defend herself against all-comers,' she declared.[45] The daughter of a Camberwell box-maker, Fanny Radmall had come into her fortune through her marriage to the shipping magnate Sir Robert Houston, who died in 1926. Combative and generous, she used her wealth to support an eclectic range of causes, including oppressed Russian Christians, women's rights, coalminers, and a rest home for nurses. Now Mitchell's Supermarine seaplanes were added to the list.

Lady Houston's gift was well spent, allowing Mitchell to improve the S6. More power was derived from the 'R', raising its output to 2,350 horsepower, and the dimensions of the airframe were extended to accommodate more fuel and provide more cooling surfaces. This modified plane, the S6B, had to be built under tremendous pressure of time because of the delays over funding, but it was finished shortly before the contest. In the end the event, held in September 1931 at Calshot, near Southampton, was an anticlimax. The French and Italians were forced to withdraw because of engine trouble, and Britain enjoyed an uncontested victory. Nevertheless, the S6B would almost certainly have smashed any competition that took to the air. During the

Schneider week, it reached a world record speed of 379.05 mph. Two weeks later, with Flight Lieutenant George Stainforth at the controls, the plane broke the 400 mph barrier, flying at 407.5 mph – an astonishing speed in an era still dominated by biplanes.

R. J. Mitchell had shown himself to be the most innovative mind in the British aircraft industry. It was inevitable that the Air Ministry would want to utilize his talents for military purposes. Yet, for all the glory of the Schneider wins, these were bleak days for British aviation, especially the Royal Air Force. Funding was scarce, ministerial support absent. Successive governments, desperate to balance their budgets, were reluctant to fund new types of plane. Memories of the wholesale slaughter of the First World War made military spending unpopular. Since 1918, there had been drastic cuts to the RAF. At one stage in the early 1920s the Tory Prime Minister Andrew Bonar Law even pressed for the abolition of a separate air force, eager to see it subsumed within the navy and the army. Sir Hugh Trenchard, the domineering head of the RAF, fought a heroic rearguard action against such a move, but he could not halt the decline. Once the possessor of the world's largest air force, Britain had sunk to the position of a third-rate air power, its aircraft increasingly obsolete, its squadrons denuded.

Yet the potential for the future was not as dire as this picture suggests. Heavy spending in the 1920s would only have been wasted on models which would have been outmoded almost as soon as they had gone into service. The gigantic leaps in aircraft design and technology meant that any major European nation with the political will could now create a modern force. What was missing in Britain was this political will. All three major parties were struggling to cope with the fallout from the 1931 economic crisis, which saw the downfall of Labour and the creation of the National government, headed by Ramsay MacDonald and Stanley Baldwin. But, aside from the politicians, there were figures in the Air Ministry and the RAF who did recognize the urgent need for modernization. They included men such as Sir Hugh Dowding, a former fighter pilot, who became the Air Council's Member for Supply and Research in 1930, and Group Captain Henry Cave-Brown-Cave, the Director of Technical Development, and his deputy, Major J. S. Buchanan. The simplistic numbers game of trying to build as many aircraft as possible had no appeal for them. What they were interested in was the effectiveness of the air force rather than its mere size. In particular, they rejected the fashionable dogma about the primacy of the bomber.

The Italian army officer General Giulio Douhet had given this theory widespread currency in the 1920s through his influential book *The Command of the Air*, which argued that the invention of flight had transformed the rules of war. According to Douhet, military power now depended on the ability of air forces to inflict devastation on enemy territory. No longer would military campaigns be conducted by armies across a battlefront. Air power had inaugurated the era of total war, where civilian populations were at the mercy of strategic bombardment. 'Nothing man can do on the surface of the earth can interfere with a plane in flight, moving freely in the third dimension. All the influences which had conditioned and characterized warfare from the beginning are powerless to affect aerial action,' he wrote.[46] In this new world, the side which could mount the most brutal aerial assault would prevail. In certain English military circles, the idea of the so-called 'knock-out blow' became fashionable, victory being seen as swiftly achievable with a massive air attack. Sir Hugh Trenchard, Chief of the Air Staff, was a passionate believer in this creed; indeed, within the RAF, the strategy became known as 'the Trenchard doctrine'. One consequence of this approach was the dismissal of any role for fighters. They were seen as an irrelevance, incapable of doing anything against the might of the bomber. As Trenchard himself put it in 1916, 'The aeroplane is not a defence against the aeroplane.' And he was still sticking rigidly to this opinion seven years later: 'Fighter defence must be kept to the smallest possible number.'[47]

But Trenchard's views were by no means universally shared. Throughout the 1920s there were enthusiasts for a strong fighter force, and, as technology advanced, their arguments gained greater weight. If the speed of the latest seaplanes could be harnessed by fighters, it was possible that a credible threat could be mounted against the bomber. As early as 1927, Robert Brooke-Popham, the RAF's head of fighter operations, could be found complaining that 'there is no doubt that the speed of our fighters today is too low. I feel quite certain that we must go on asking for what are stated to be impossibilities.'[48] At the time, reflecting the neglect of the government and the indifference of Trenchard, the RAF's fleet of just thirteen fighter squadrons had barely advanced since the First World War, being made up largely of sluggish biplanes like the Gloster Grebe and the Armstrong-Whitworth Siskin, with fabric-covered wings and exposed radial engines. The pitiful inadequacy of the fighters was exposed time and again during RAF exercises, when they could barely outpace the heavier bombers they were supposed to be attacking. The next generation of fighters, led by the Bristol Bulldog and the Hawker Fury, were still biplanes with fixed undercarriages and limited armaments. The advocates of a realistic air defence knew that something had to change.

From the beginning of the 1930s, pressure began to mount for a radical departure. 'For years past our technical experts have been following purely orthodox lines without variation,' said one memorandum from Sir Charles Burnett, the Deputy Chief of the Air Staff.[49] Another Air Ministry paper of the time argued that a fast, single-seater fighter was vital, using the lessons from Mitchell's success: 'The Schneider Trophy definitely proved the supremacy of the monoplane for pure performance.'[50]

Burnett was also concerned to see an end to the anachronistic nature of British weaponry: 'I would like to see provision made for four .303 guns . . . and these should be fitted clear of the propeller disc. For a long time we have been pressing to have the gun power of our fighters increased. It seems to me that we are not making any advance at all in the armament of our fighters if we allow the same armament that was carried in 1917.'[51]

In an attempt to inspire fresh thinking in the aircraft industry, in October 1931 the Air Ministry issued Specification F7/30, calling for a new day and night fighter to replace the Bristol Bulldog. The essential requirements of the plane were that it should have a minimum speed of 195 mph in level flight at 15,000 feet, be entirely of metal construction, contain four .303 machine guns, provide good visibility for the pilot, have a landing speed of around 60 mph and a minimum service ceiling of 28,000 feet.

These were demanding conditions, calling for higher all-round level of performance than any contemporary fighter, and the Air Ministry was keen to support any attempt at innovation. The new urgency was reflected in a note about the specification from Sir John Salmond, who now held Trenchard's old position of Chief of the Air Staff and had far less tunnel vision than his predecessor:

> There remains one point to which I attach importance: that is encouraging novel types so as to get away from the tractor biplane. Past experience shows that we can depend upon plenty of 'private venture' entries of the stereotype design to select from but that firms are reluctant to risk their money on highly speculative ventures of novel design. If we are to get serious attempts at novel types to meet this specification we shall have to provide the incentive.[52]

Those words blow apart the idea of the entire Air Staff remaining trapped in the past. But then myth-making has long enveloped Specification F7/30, a vital document which ultimately led to the creation of the Spitfire. Its critics have claimed that it shows the air establishment at its worst. One author, David Divine, wrote, 'It epitomized once again the weakness of the administrative machine of the Air Ministry: its timidity in progress, the poverty of imagination, the stultification of its bureaucracy.'[53] Such charges are unjust. Contrary to what the detractors say, F7/30 did not stipulate any particular design or engine. It referred only to performance. In fact at one stage the Air

Ministry had considered specifying a monoplane, but abandoned the idea, fearing that it might stifle the competition between the air firms. Even Eric Morgan and Edward Shacklady, in their monumental, prodigiously researched history of the Spitfire, now the standard technical reference work on the subject, made an error in writing that F7/30 'called for a maximum speed of 195 mph', when this was actually the minimum.[54]

The greatest myth of all is that the specification was so restrictive that it stifled Mitchell's creative vision, causing a troubled early period for the fighter. This was the line put about by Sir Robert McLean of Vickers after the war, and it has been repeated in histories ever since. In an interview in 1959 McLean claimed that 'from the day he received it, Mitchell had no faith in the F7/30. The whole conception of this aircraft was hostile to the concept of speed.'[55] McLean was backed up by the Vickers sales director, R. C. Handyside, who recalled:

> Mitchell had no confidence in F7/30 at all and it was Mitchell who impressed on McLean that it would be no good. Mitchell did not do this directly but he used the Supermarine test pilot to keep niggling at McLean. It was particularly irksome to Mitchell because he knew that he was capable of extending the Schneider Trophy aircraft to war-winning fighters. I once heard him say, 'God. If I ever had a free hand I would design a winner.'[56]

But Supermarine design staff, who worked directly with Mitchell at the time, were dismissive of the idea that Mitchell greeted F7/30 with disappointment. Alan Clifton, who was assistant designer to Mitchell, remembered a very different attitude. 'In the early days at least, the F7/30 seemed to Mitchell quite reasonable and even quite forward – for example, the design allowed for a ceiling higher than the world's existing record.' Clifton believed that any uneasiness on Mitchell's part may have arisen from the fact that this would be 'his first venture into military aircraft' and he recognized that he was 'no expert' in the field.[57] Beverley Shenstone, the Canadian-born aerodynamicist who worked with Mitchell throughout the development of the Spitfire, expressed some exasperation with the distortion of history. 'As far as my experience of the design of the F7/30 is concerned, no dismay was expressed by anybody . . . We may have found it difficult to fulfil but that was quite clearly – looking backwards – our own fault.'[58] Indeed, Shenstone argued that the real problem was that the phenomenal success of the Schneider aircraft had bred a mood of complacency at Supermarine. 'My own feeling is that the design team had done so well with the S5 and S6 series of racing floatplanes which in the end reached speeds of over 400 mph that they had thought it would be child's play to design a fighter to fly at little over half that speed. They never made that mistake again.'[59]

The Schneider experience made Supermarine the favourite to win the F7/30 contract. But the Air Ministry's hopes that Mitchell, or any of the other top British aircraft engineers, could produce a major breakthrough in fighter design were not realized. This was not for lack of commercial interest. Like the rest of the country, in 1931 the aircraft industry was in the middle of a slump, with most of the companies desperate for new work. As a result, F7/30 generated more activity than any previous RAF fighter specification. Yet the intense competition tended to produce variety rather than quality. At the initial stage, eight companies submitted no fewer than twelve different designs, though only half were monoplanes. Among the biplanes was the unusual Westland PV4, with its power plant buried in the fuselage, and the Gloster SS37, powered by a Bristol Mercury engine, which eventually became the Gloster Gladiator, the RAF's last operational biplane. One of the mono-planes was the Vickers Jockey, a pet project of Sir Robert McLean's, which evolved into the unwanted Vickers Venom and was regarded by many at Supermarine as a direct rival to their fighter.

Of the other monoplanes, the Supermarine entry, named the Type 224, was the most advanced. After a conference on the tendered designs in May 1932, chaired by Air Commodore Cave-Brown-Cave, it was agreed to instruct Supermarine to proceed with the prototype of the Type 224. Two of the biplane designs were also approved. Yet this decision in favour of Supermarine could not conceal a sense of dissatisfaction with Mitchell's design, for his proposed plane had none of the elegance or excitement of the later Schneider models. It was an awkward, ungainly beast, with an exposed cockpit, an ugly cranked wing spanning 46 feet, and a large fixed undercar-riage enclosed within voluminous trouser fairings. The graceful streamlining that had made Mitchell's reputation was wholly absent.

Almost from the start, Mitchell sensed that he was on the wrong track. His doubts about his approach were reflected in the interminable delays in building the mock-up and then the prototype, as Mitchell tried to make alterations to the design. The limited progress began to cause frustration within the Air Ministry. 'I note that the construction of the mock-up is pro-ceeding very slowly,' wrote an official from the Directorate of Technical Development to Supermarine in December 1932, seven months after the design was first approved. The mock-up conference was finally held on 20 April 1933, at which further modifications were discussed. At last it seemed that Supermarine was moving. A sense of optimism was conveyed by Flight Lieutenant Boswell, who visited the factory in July 1933 to look at the Type

224 design from the viewpoint of repair and maintenance: 'Very little experience on this type of construction in service exists but as it represents progress, and possesses advantages over other types, we are prepared to override the existing doubts of its capability of repair and maintenance by the service.'[60] But then there followed more months of hold-ups. 'Any comments which you may have to make on the reasons for the relative lateness of the firm's programme will be of interest,' the Air Ministry wrote sarcastically to Supermarine in October 1933.[61] It was the same story at the start of 1934, when an internal Ministry paper complained that progress on the F7/30 had been 'most disappointing'.[62]

The biggest technical problem for Mitchell's team was the need to accommodate the new Rolls-Royce Goshawk engine, a supercharged plant which was supposed to deliver high power without being too heavy. But it used a complex evaporative cooling system, whereby steam from the engine was piped through a series of condensers running the whole length of the wing. The condensed water was then collected in tanks in the trousers of the undercarriage, before being pumped up to the header tank at the front of the engine. All this complexity ran counter to Mitchell's ideas about streamlining. Apart from this difficulty, there may have been other factors at work to account for the delays. Ernest Maybridge, another member of the design team, felt that the near-fatal crash of Captain Biard in 1925 was an influence. 'We were a bit over-cautious with the wing and made it thicker than it need have been. We were still very concerned about possible flutter, having encountered that with the S4 seaplane.'[63] Denis Webb had this interesting comment on Mitchell's own attitude: 'My impression was that RJ, who had always been more of a practical engineer than a technician, had allowed himself to be lured by some of his bright boys into trying to follow other people's ideas instead of his own.'[64]

Yet what was perhaps more significant than any of this was the collapse of Mitchell's health, just at the time when the Type 224 was being built. In the summer of 1933, after he had been feeling poorly for some months, he underwent a medical examination. The outcome could hardly have been more traumatic. It was found that he was suffering from cancer of the rectum, and needed urgent surgery. He underwent the operation in August, which involved the removal of his rectum and the routing of his severed colon through a hole in his abdominal wall. For the remainder of his life he would have to wear a colostomy bag. But Mitchell was a tough man, both mentally and physically. He refused to let his disability stop him from working at Supermarine. After a period of recuperation, he was back at his desk in early 1934. Ever the engineer, he devised his own appliance, made of wool and an aluminium ring, to secure his colostomy bag, and this was so practical that it featured in medical textbooks.

Understandably, those with a condition like Mitchell's often led reclusive lives, out of embarrassment or fatigue. Sir Henry Royce's departure from his company's works in Derby had been prompted by the onset of intestinal cancer, which, as with Mitchell, forced him to wear a permanent colostomy bag. What is remarkable about Mitchell's case is not just that he went back to Supermarine, but that no one there actually knew of his condition – not even Alan Clifton, who worked beside him. His was as great a feat of stoicism as those of the pilots who later flew in his Spitfires. For all his bravery, however, there was no doubt that his life-threatening illness exacerbated his natural traits of moodiness and abruptness, especially because he had been warned by his surgeon that the cancer might well return. The events of the summer of 1933, wrote his son Gordon, 'had an indelible effect on my father's character'.[65] From the day of his diagnosis he was living with the prospect of an untimely death, yet he still had so much to do. Instead of retreating into a domestic sanctuary, he was more impatient than ever. Moreover, he was in frequent discomfort. Denis Webb recalled, 'None of us knew at the time about the trouble, and a year or so later, when I was working in Marsh-Hunn's office, Hunn would come back from a meeting with RJ and complain about his ill-humour. Little did we realize the pain he must have been in.'[66] Eric Lovell-Cooper said, 'He used to have terrible tempers as you can imagine. He was in shocking distress a lot of the time.'[67]

Mitchell's return in early 1934 did not bring any improvement in the prospects of the Type 224. On 10 February the prototype was ready for its first flight. But shortly before take-off, problems developed with the evaporative cooling system, all the water having been ejected into the wing condensers, leaving the engine and the header tank dry. Repairs were carried out, and on 20 February the plane finally took to the air. All the worst fears were confirmed, as it struggled to just 230 mph – far below the predicted speed of 245 mph. The absence of wing flaps meant that it failed to meet the required landing speed. Just as disturbingly, the cooling system again proved unreliable: 'The low-level warning device for the water header tank was showing throughout although the gauge showed the tank to be full of water. One wing-tip warning light was also showing although no steam was issuing,' stated the report from S. Scott-Hall, Supermarine's resident technical officer.[68] As the Air Ministry commented sardonically at the end of the month, the plane's systems 'do not seem to be all that might be desired'.[69] Jeffrey Quill later flew the Type 224 as an experiment in 1936 and recalled, 'It was not a good aeroplane. It was disappointingly slow and had a poor rate of climb. The evaporative cooling was a dog's breakfast. It was just not a very good design. By hindsight the wing was too thick and big, the all-up weight too high and the drag too great.'[70]

Specification F7/30 had been a failure for Mitchell – the first of his career. But he knew a better fighter could be created out of the mess of steam, flashing warning lights, and trousered undercarriage.

2

'I don't want anything touched'

B RITISH AIR POLICY in 1934 was schizophrenic. On the one hand, there
was still a powerful mood of pacifism in the country, a legacy of the hor-
rors of the First World War. The hopes invested in the Geneva Disarmament
Conference, which had dragged on since 1932, were indicative of this attitude,
as was the belief that all international problems could be solved through
negotiations at the League of Nations. Because of anxiety about the devastation which could be wreaked by the bomber, air forces were at the centre of
disarmament talks, reflected in an array of proposals for restrictions on the size
and payload of military aircraft. On the other hand, there was a growing realization that the rise of the dictators in Germany and Italy had made the
disarmament talks an irrelevance. Two of Hitler's first acts on coming to
power in 1933 had been to withdraw from the Geneva Conference and the
League of Nations. His determination to turn Germany into an aggressive
military power was all too obvious. And the recognition of this threat led to
the first tentative moves towards rearmament, even while the National government's Labour Prime Minister, Ramsay MacDonald, was still indulging in
the hollow rhetoric of peace across the Geneva negotiating table.

The Conservative leader Stanley Baldwin was MacDonald's nominal
deputy in the National government, though in practice, as Lord President of
the Council, he was really joint Prime Minister. His pose as a bluff English
countryman disguised his gifts as a canny, even cynical, political operator.
Pragmatism was seen as his greatest political virtue, though this could often
mean little more than enthusiasm for short-term expediency, especially when
it came to foreign and defence policy. One of his fellow ministers, Lord
Winterton, later wrote, 'I was devoted to Stanley Baldwin but he had very bad
faults, the worst of which was leaving decisions as long as possible. I doubt if
anyone, except perhaps his wife, knew whether it was mental inertia or weakness of character that impelled him to avoid difficult decisions.'[1]

By far the biggest decision of the time was how to respond to the threat of
Germany, and Baldwin had a key role in formulating air policy, both as Lord
President and, from 1935, as Prime Minister, having succeeded MacDonald.

Characteristically, he managed to face both ways, combining a weary fatalism about the nightmare of war with an unconvincing pledge to rebuild the national air forces. In one of his most famous speeches, he warned, 'I think it is well for the man in the street to realize that there is no power on earth that can protect him from being bombed. Whatever people may tell him, the bomber will always get through . . . The only defence is offence, which means that you have to kill more women and children more quickly than the enemy if you want to save yourselves.'[2]

This was the Trenchard doctrine in its crudest form, holding that security could be achieved only through the threat of massive bomber retaliation. But if Baldwin really believed that, he was, like most of the government, unwilling to provide the means to achieve such security. There were no moves to create an intimidating RAF bomber force. Interminable discussions were held in endless committees, but few new planes were built. Half-measures, confusion, endless penny-pinching and a yearning to avoid the whole nasty business were the hallmarks of government policy under Baldwin and MacDonald. The absence of clarity and purpose was worsened by the two figures at the top of the Air Ministry, the Ulster peer Lord Londonderry, the Secretary of State for Air, and, from 1933, the painfully inarticulate Chief of the Air Staff Sir Edward Ellington.

Londonderry, ironically, was one of the few senior politicians with any direct experience of aircraft, having qualified as a pilot. Fabulously wealthy, with majestic homes in Northern Ireland and Mayfair, he was renowned as one of London society's leading hosts. But his social attainments were not matched by his political stature. Lacking any weight in Cabinet, he provided little direction for the air force. The Tory politician John Davidson called him

> a rather soft, Regency-beau type of man. Although he had a certain amount of cunning and capacity, he was not really equipped for thinking. His association with the Air Force, though keen, was rather on the social than the technical side. He hadn't got the capacity to deal with the Air Council or give them a positive lead. But Londonderry took himself very seriously and this was in a sense a tragedy because others did not take him seriously at all.[3]

Almost as unimpressive was Sir Edward Ellington, whose conservative views, awkward personality and verbal hesitancy were exactly what the Air Staff did not need in this period of mounting crisis. A former artillery officer who transferred to the RAF on its creation in 1918, he had risen to the top through hard work and ambition, but he was badly exposed in the highest job. Sir Wilfrid Freeman, who served on the Air Council with Ellington and in the late 1930s was to be one of the architects of the Spitfire programme, described him as 'the worst Chief of the Air Staff we ever had. He never pulled a single unofficial string. He was not only a misanthrope but he never made the least attempt to do his job or get to know politicians. He pretended to despise them but was, in fact, frightened of them.'[4] Ellington showed little appreciation of the pace of German militarization or the concept of fighter defence. Typical of his orthodoxy was his rigid adherence to the Trenchard doctrine; he even opposed training fighter pilots in the use of radar (then known as Radio Direction Finding), because he feared that if the technique were successful the vulnerability of the bomber might be exposed.

Contempt for both Londonderry and Ellington shines through the diaries of Sir Henry Pownall, who served with them from 1933 on the Committee of Imperial Defence when the debates about the first steps towards RAF expansion began in earnest. 'Londonderry was quite hopeless and was on the verge of getting the Air Ministry's requirements for the odd aerodrome turned down with a bang through his own sheer ineffectiveness,' reads one entry for April 1933. Another, for December 1934, records that 'the Chief of the Air Staff is unconvincing and, from the point of view of the Secretary, difficult to deal with. And he is a cheerless cove. In eleven meetings I have never once seen him smile nor heard him make a cheerful remark to anyone. He and Londonderry must be a pretty bad half-section.'[5]

The lack of leadership meant there was little coherence about the rearmament proposals which began to wend their way through the labyrinthine structure of Whitehall from late 1933, following alarming reports from Germany that Hitler planned to increase military spending by at least 33 per cent. In December 1933 Pownall wrote in his diary, of the Foreign Office chief Sir Robert Vansittart, 'He has got the German danger very much on his mind and refuses to believe their pacific intentions.'[6] Yet Vansittart's concerns were hardly reflected in the subsequent discussions about the need to strengthen the RAF. In addition to the usual emphasis on the bomber, there were calls for more support for the air force in the wider reaches of the empire, especially in the Far East, where Japan was now regarded as a threat. Sniping could also be heard from the other two services, the navy and the army, about too much attention being paid to the RAF.

But there was one senior politician who rose above this bureaucratic paralysis. Neville Chamberlain, Chancellor of the Exchequer in 1934, has usually been painted as a dangerous defeatist because of his policy of appeasement in the late 1930s. His alleged narrow provincialism led to Lloyd George's famous accusation that he always looked at foreign affairs through the wrong end of a municipal drainpipe. But earlier in the decade Chamberlain had a stronger understanding of Britain's defence needs than most of his colleagues. A clear-sighted realist, he had no time for grandiose talk about war with Japan or colonial force or large bomber fleets when Britain was still incapable of defending itself in the event of a European conflict. To the consternation of Londonderry, Ellington and most of the military chiefs, he pressed for a far greater concentration on home defence through fighter squadrons. Funding for the RAF should be increased, he argued, offset by reductions in the budgets for the army and navy. Chamberlain felt that the need for a substantial rise in fighter expenditure was made all the more urgent by the news that Germany was now producing 500 airframes per month. Yet his approach prompted the bizarre spectacle of the political and military chiefs of the Air Ministry seeking to resist a substantial expansion of their service. There was no need to overreact, stuttered Ellington, and especially not at the expense of the Far East. It would be quite sufficient, he claimed, to expand the RAF to 52 homebased squadrons during the years up to 1940. Vansittart at the Foreign Office was outraged at this complacency, particularly because the plan for 52 home squadrons had originally been agreed as long ago as 1923 but had never been implemented. 'The execution by 1940 of a scheme approved in 1923 is no deterrent. Such a measure would probably be treated in Europe as the mountain's mouse. Events in Germany are leaving it far behind,' he wrote.[7] Londonderry, too, ended up in the strange position of criticizing the Chancellor for proposing too rapid a growth in the RAF at home. He said he 'regarded the Chancellor's proposals as being better designed for public consumption than for real utility,' adding that 'the Air Ministry themselves were not in any great hurry.'[8] Pownall thought that Londonderry's stance showed him at his worst, writing of an Imperial Defence Committee meeting in June, 'Charlie Londonderry was as wuffly as ever and fairly tied the Committee up in figures which he obviously did not himself understand.'[9]

It was Chamberlain, however, who was in control of spending, and he forced the expansion scheme on the reluctant Air Minister and Chief of the Air Staff, providing for an increase in the Metropolitan Force, the RAF's front-line service in the south-east, to 84 squadrons by 1939, or 1,252 aircraft. Agreed by the Cabinet in July 1934, this was called 'Scheme A', the first in a series of thirteen RAF expansion programmes during the 1930s. It was hardly on the level of what Hitler was doing, but it was a start. 'I am on the whole well-satisfied with our discussions on the subject. I have really won all along the line,' Chamberlain wrote to his sister Hilda, though he added that the menace of Germany meant that defence spending had to remain focused on the RAF. 'If we are to take the necessary measures of defence against Germany, we cannot afford at the same time to rebuild our battle fleet.'[10]

Chamberlain's focus on fighter defence might not have been welcomed by Ellington and other followers of Trenchard, but it was exactly in tune with the views of Sir Hugh Dowding, the Air Member for Supply and Research. Cold, unsentimental and far-sighted, Dowding had long believed the primary duty of the RAF was to protect Britain. As with Chamberlain, his outlook might have been described as insular in its suspicion of foreign adventures and cautious in its reluctance to launch strategic offensives. But it was an approach that offered more real safety than theories about bomber fleets. In one of his more perceptive moments as Prime Minister, Ramsay MacDonald told Londonderry of the fundamental flaw in Trenchardism. 'Your weakness is that you cannot secure us against bombardment though you can make a mess of the other fellow.'[11] Dowding believed that a modern, sophisticated defence network, led by the latest fighters, could provide precisely that security.

Like Reginald Mitchell, Hugh Caswall Tremenheere Dowding was the son of a schoolmaster. His father, who married the daughter of the governor of Aden, ran a preparatory school in Scotland, where Dowding was born in 1882. After education at Winchester, he joined the Royal Engineers, serving in the Far East and India, before signing up for the Royal Flying Corps, the predecessor of the RAF, in 1912. Tellingly, as a flying officer during the First World War, he several times clashed bitterly with Trenchard over fighting equipment and pilot casualties. Trenchard described him as 'a dismal Jimmy' because of his perceived lack of aggressive spirit – a deeply unjust charge given that Dowding had demonstrated incredible bravery by flying under fire behind German lines.[12] But Trenchard succeeded in having him removed from the front line by putting him in charge of RFC training. During the 1920s, after Trenchard had again tried to organize his departure from the RAF, Dowding held a series of unrewarding appointments at the Air Ministry and overseas before reaching the rank of Air Member for Supply and Research in 1930.

Ever since his schooldays he had been seen as unapproachable – hence his nickname 'Stuffy'. Rigid and self-critical, lacking in warmth and humour, there was an air of the puritan about him. He once said that he had been drunk on only two occasions in his life, and had enjoyed neither experience. Some saw him as merely old-fashioned; others found him impossibly prickly. Air Marshal Sir Philip Joubert de la Ferté said that he could be 'extremely exacting and tiresome' towards subordinates.[13] 'Stubborn as a mule' was the verdict of Sir Arthur Harris, head of Bomber Command during the war.[14] Dowding's natural remoteness was deepened soon after the First World War by the personal tragedy he experienced when his wife died after only two years of marriage, leaving him to bring up their infant son on his own. He fell back on his immediate family for comfort, living first with his father and later with his sister.

Despite his image, Dowding was unconventional in his thinking. During the First World War, for instance, he had advocated the use of radio communications between pilots and ground controllers. 'I was the first person in England, if not the world, to listen to a wireless telephone message from the air,' he recalled.[15] But the War Office considered his idea impractical – a rejection that aggravated his dislike of official bureaucracy. Dowding had also been the prime mover behind the R101 airship project, which ended in disaster when the dirigible crashed in northern France on its way to India, killing all its occupants.

As one of the leading members of the Air Council, he had broad scope for his originality, especially regarding fighter development. He had been among those pushing for new types to capitalize on the Schneider successes, though, with characteristic foresight, he saw little future for marine aviation. Now that Britain held the trophy permanently, there had been talk in the Air Ministry of hosting a new international competition like the Schneider. Dowding was strongly opposed to this, because 'there was absolutely no value in floatplanes as a combat machine.' Instead, as he later recalled, he wanted firms 'to cash in on the experience that had been gained in aircraft construction and engine progress so that we could order two of the fastest machines which it was possible to build with no restriction except landing speed, and that had to be on grass airfields.'[16] After much negotiation and redesign, those two machines would turn out to be the Spitfire and the Hurricane.

Dowding had been involved with the F7/30 specification from its inception, and had shared in the disappointment over Mitchell's product. He was particularly irritated by the drag-inducing trousered undercarriage. 'There is no reason why Supermarine should not have included retractable undercarriage and flaps in their original design,' he wrote to Air Commodore Cave-Brown-Cave in August 1934.[17] On a deeper level, Dowding was so exasperated with the air industry's failure to produce effective prototypes within a reasonable period that, according to one 1934 Air Ministry report, he believed that 'the time has come when we must apply the screw.'[18] Early that year the Ministry even looked into purchasing the PZ24 fighter from Poland, which had the potential to exceed the F7/30 types. 'The PZ24 is 4 mph faster than the Supermarine and climbs 15,000 feet in two and a half minutes less,' ran a paper on the suggestion.[19] But the Air Ministry did not pursue the idea: it thought the Polish plane insufficiently advanced, and also had ethical doubts about buying a Polish plane to meet British fighter requirements.

By this stage Mitchell, also dissatisfied with his first stab at F7/30, was working on a series of radical alterations to the Type 224 – so radical that it would evolve into a very different aircraft. Knowing that he needed something less bulky, he cut the wingspan by almost 6 feet, reduced the wing's thickness, installed wing flaps and a new tailplane and elevator, placed the oil and cooler tanks under the engine, enclosed the cockpit, installed four guns operating outside the propeller, and fitted a retractable undercarriage, with the legs folding outward. This new model, styled the Type 300, was said to have a top speed of 265 mph. It is often claimed in Spitfire literature that the Air Ministry was dismissive of these changes, hence the need for a private venture. But this is far from the case. What the Air Ministry really believed was that the changes were too far-reaching to be accepted under the F7/30 contract, for such a move would have been unfair on other bidding companies. But the Director of Technical Development, Air Commodore Cave-Brown-Cave – the one-time hero of the England–Australia flight – was actually so favourable towards Mitchell's new plane that he decided to avoid the contractual problems by suggesting that it might be ordered as an experimental aircraft, separate from F7/30. 'I think it would be a wise precaution to order one of these modified F7/30s from Supermarine if they will quote a reasonable price and delivery. It will be a suitable type on which to overcome many of the problems we shall have later . . . It will also be a most interesting experiment with wing flaps on a high-performance plane,' he wrote to Dowding in August 1934, showing a resourcefulness for which he has never received much credit.[20] Equally keen on innovation, Dowding agreed. So on 4 September 1934 the Contracts Section of the Air Ministry wrote asking Supermarine to submit a quotation for the modified fighter: 'The Department requests that you will inform them as soon as possible what will be the cost and time for the delivery of the new aeroplane. I am to add that the request for a quotation must not be taken as indicative of any intention on the part of the Department to order such a plane.'[21]

Given that the Ministry had already spent £18,000 on Supermarine's F7/30 model, this was another indication of official support for Mitchell. He now pressed on with his redesign, making the wing even thinner, further reducing the wingspan, and adopting a stressed-skin construction. Yet these alterations were likely to yield only slight improvements. The central problem remained the 660-horsepower Goshawk engine, not just because of its complexity, but also because of its limited power. Supermarine considered the alternative of the new Napier Dagger engine, but, at only 700 horsepower, it did not seem the answer. But now, after almost three years of personal and professional setbacks, Mitchell enjoyed a stroke of good fortune. While he was redesigning his fighter, Rolls-Royce began work on a new aero engine – one that had far greater potential than the Goshawk.

This engine, unlike Supermarine's fighter, was a genuine private venture by Rolls-Royce, as shown by its initial name, the PV12. The 27-litre power plant, in development since 1932, already offered 800 horsepower at 12,000 feet, and looked likely soon to go past 1,000 horsepower with further work. Mitchell sensed he finally had the solution. There was now a real chance that his fighter, further cleaned up, could exceed 300 mph. Thanks to the Schneider planes, Mitchell had an excellent relationship with Rolls-Royce, and the company reached an agreement with Supermarine for the PV12 – soon known as the Merlin – to be installed in the redesigned fighter.

Sir Henry Royce had died in 1933, and the creative force behind the Merlin was Ernest Hives, the company's chief engineer and later to be general manager at Derby throughout the Second World War. Like Royce, Hives came from a humble background. The son of a factory clerk in Reading, he began his career as a mechanic and driver at the Napier Engine Company. In 1908 he joined Rolls-Royce, where he was to remain for the next fifty years. The Eagle, the power plant behind the Royal Flying Corps, was his first great success, and it was followed by the Kestrel, the Schneider 'R' series, and then the Merlin. Practical, self-confident and innovative, Hives was not unlike Mitchell in combining a gift for leadership with a reserved personality. 'I do not think anyone knew him well,' wrote Alec Harvey-Bailey, who worked with Hives at Rolls-Royce. 'He was a private and somewhat self-protective person; his dinner-table conversation was light and amusing but if anyone crossed his invisible boundary he would instantly grow cold. One could feel the ice-crystals forming in the atmosphere and the formality would be instant.'[22] Hives could also be waspish. Once, when asked how many people worked at Rolls-Royce, he replied, 'About half of them.'[23]

Hives's PV12 engine greatly improved the prospects of the Type 300, as did another element of the redesign which occurred in the autumn of 1934. Tinkering by Supermarine on the 224's wing had removed its inverted-gull lines and made it thinner, but Mitchell and his team were still dissatisfied. So they decided to go for an elliptical shape, which was both more aerodynamic and more practical, as Beverley Shenstone of Supermarine later recalled: 'Aerodynamically it was the best for our purpose because the induced drag, caused in producing lift, was lowest when this shape was used; the ellipse was an ideal shape, theoretically perfection.'[24] The other advantage of the ellipse was that it had a wide chord (the distance between the leading and the trailing edge) at the wing root (where the wing joined the fuselage) and tapered only very gradually towards the tip, which meant that it had enough space for guns and a retractable undercarriage. In contrast, the chord of a straight-tapered wing, as originally proposed on the 224, started to reduce as soon as it left the root. Furthermore, a slight twist in the new wing meant that any stall began at the root rather than the tip, thereby giving pilots advance warning in tight turns and allowing them to retain aileron control. This was a virtue that in the Spitfire would later save many lives, as the hugely experienced test pilot Jeffrey Quill explained in a 1976 interview:

> The Spitfire's extremely docile behaviour in the stall was one of its greatest features. You could pull it well beyond its buffet boundary and drag it round with full power and little airspeed; it would shudder and shake and rock you from side to side, but if you handled it properly it would never get away from you. Whether they knew it or not, there are many pilots alive today who owe their survival to this remarkable quality in the Sptifire – and I am one of them.[25]

The ellipse was to become the most distinctive feature of the Spitfire, adding to its beauty and instantly recognizable charm. But such aesthetics appear to have been of little consideration to Mitchell. According to Shenstone, 'He was an intensely practical man and he liked practical solutions to problems. I remember once discussing the wing shape with him and he said jokingly, "I don't give a bugger whether it's elliptical or not, so long as it covers the guns."'[26]

It is often claimed that, in adopting elliptical wings, Mitchell was influenced by his appreciation of the German He 70, a beautifully clean transport plane designed by the German engineer Professor Ernst Heinkel. In fact, after the war, Heinkel himself liked to trumpet his role in creation of the Spitfire. But there is little evidence to support this. Mitchell was well aware of the He 70, which was exhibited at air shows across Europe and at one point was even used by Rolls-Royce as a test bed for the Merlin. But, as Shenstone pointed out, the He 70 had little relationship to the Supermarine fighter: 'Our wing was much thinner and had a quite different section. In any case, it would have been simply asking for trouble to have copied a wing shape from an aircraft designed for an entirely different purpose.'[27] Alan Clifton, who was intimately involved with the entire Spitfire project, once said, 'I don't think that RJ cared at all about what the Germans were doing. He did care about the shape of his wings but he never copied anything. I think all of us at the time realized that the thinnest wing can often be the best, whereas earlier people were afraid of very thin wings in case they broke off.'[28] Besides, Mitchell had long understood the aerodynamic qualities of the elliptical wing. He had proposed one on the experimental Type 179 flying boat, designed in 1930. And the Crusader seaplane, an entry for the 1927 Schneider Trophy from the firm of Short-Bristow, also had an elegant elliptical wing, though engine trouble meant that it could not compete in the race. The reality is that Mitchell turned to this shape on his own initiative. Jack Davis of Supermarine said that it was essentially a compromise: 'the logical result of integrating aerodynamic and structural requirements.'[29]

By the end of 1934 the beauty of the Spitfire was starting to emerge from the beast of the 224. Mitchell's continued work on the fighter late in that year had been approved by the Vickers Aviation board, headed by McLean. But it would be wrong to take this as indicating a 'private venture', as McLean often did in later years. Throughout this entire process, the Ministry were closely involved, and Mitchell was in constant communication with officials from the Air Staff and experts from the Aeroplane and Armament Experimental Establishment at Martlesham Heath. As Dowding himself said after the war, 'Mitchell was a genius in his own line but it is ridiculous to regard the Spitfire as the child of his fancy forced upon a reluctant and obstructive Air Ministry.'[30]

In two fascinating letters written in 1960, Beverley Shenstone not only dismissed the ideas of a private venture but implied that McLean was actually lukewarm about carrying on with Mitchell's fighter, preferring another Vickers monoplane design, the Venom, for which he was seeking government support. 'The idea of taking the F7/30 and improving it was certainly a Supermarine idea, so you can say it was a private idea, but the venture was by no means private, considering that the whole thing was paid for by the Ministry under a Ministry specification.'[31] In his second letter, Shenstone wrote, 'Without seeming to lack respect for Sir Robert McLean's ability and energy, in my opinion the Spitfire would not have been born if Mitchell had not been willing to stand up to McLean, particularly in the era when McLean quite clearly preferred the Venom concept to the Spitfire concept because it was cheaper and lighter.'[32] This is borne out by private correspondence in the summer of 1937 between McLean and the Vickers director Sir Archibald Jamieson. 'The Venom is a much smaller machine than the Spitfire,' wrote McLean on 26 July, 'and would of course be much cheaper to build. The pilots also say that she is probably a better bit of equipment than either our Spitfire or the Hawker Hurricane.' On this letter, now in the Vickers Archive, Jeffrey Quill scribbled in the margin, obviously with some annoyance, 'I never said that!'[33] McLean's gift for presenting a distorted version of reality would become more apparent as the Spitfire's development reached its nadir.

Almost as soon as Mitchell had put forward his further revamped design, with new wings and the alternatives of a PV12 engine or the Goshawk, the Air Ministry was enthusiastic. Dowding once more took the lead, visiting McLean and Mitchell to discuss the project. He immediately saw its potential, and on 8 November 1934 sent off this hurried note to the Deputy Director of

Technical Development at the Air Ministry, Major James Buchanan: 'Spoken to McLean. Do not press the Dagger engine on this new F7/30. Let them use the Goshawk or the PV12. Give them an ITP [Intention to Proceed] as soon as possible.'[34] Within three weeks the Air Ministry had given Supermarine a provisional contract, worth £10,000, to develop the new prototype during the next ten months. Mindful of past experience, the Ministry's contracts director warned Mitchell, 'I am to remind you that delivery is urgently required. Please proceed.'[35]

Events were now moving fast. On the 5 December a full design conference was held at the Air Ministry, headed by Buchanan and Dowding. At this meeting it was formally agreed that the Rolls-Royce PV12 engine should be used and four guns should be installed in the aircraft's wings. Some concern was expressed by the RAF about the limited forward visibility because of the plane's long nose – something that would later become one of the serial complaints about the Spitfire – but Mitchell said the proposed position of the cockpit 'represented the best possible compromise having regard to the importance of performance' and that 'a subsequent appreciable alteration would be likely to delay the delivery.'[36]

By September the Air Ministry had agreed that the Mitchell's blueprint had now moved too far away from F7/30 to be covered by that specification, not least because there was now increasing interest in the Gloster Gladiator biplane, seen as a potential stopgap fighter after the early failures of the more advanced monoplane designs. In fact, the Gladiator – which first flew in September 1934 and had a speed of 253 mph – was eventually awarded the F7/30 contract in June 1935, going on to see wartime service right up to 1942. But it is another sign of the Air Ministry's co-operative, forward-looking attitude that a new specification was devised, purely to cover the new experimental Mitchell design. This was called F37/34, and was issued on 5 January 1935. Then, as work on the prototype continued, another major development occurred, whose effects were to be just as far-reaching as the creation of the Merlin. It had been envisaged that the Type 300 would have four guns – two in each wing. But continuing studies by the Air Ministry, aimed at future fighter development, began to suggest that such firepower might not be sufficiently lethal against modern, fast-moving, heavily armoured bombers. What was really needed, said the experts, were eight guns firing at least 1,000 rounds per minute if the enemy target were to be destroyed.

A key advocate of the need to shift to an eight-gun fighter was Squadron Leader Ralph Sorley of the Ministry's Operational Requirements Branch. Not overburdened by modesty, Sorley wrote after the war about the influential role he had played in changing orthodox thinking on fighter weaponry, thereby paving the way for the Spitfire. 'As the individual who was (I think without controversy) responsible for the original eight-gun fighter,' he began a *Times* article in 1957, before going on to explain how, in 1933, 'my whole waking hours were devoted to one problem: what fighter could be evolved which would stand the highest chance of defeating the fast bomber.' In his account, Sorley told how, in his quest for the answer, he had made a visit 'in great secrecy' to the Hispano-Suiza cannon factory in the 'bowels of a fort near Paris' to watch an impressive 20-mm gun in action. He had also arranged for tests of the new Browning .303 gun on ranges at Shoeburyness, firing short bursts from eight guns at a range of 400 yards. 'After much arithmetic and burning of midnight oil, I reached the answer of eight guns as being the number required to give a lethal dose in two seconds of fire.'[37] In another record, Sorley said that the 20-mm cannon were highly attractive in terms of lethality, but were unreliable in the air because of their supersensitivity. 'They were in continuous trouble with stoppages. The broad conclusion was that the Hispano gun would not fire successfully unless the mounting was extremely solid.' He admitted that the choice between cannon and machine guns was 'something of a nightmare. It was a choice on which the whole conception of the aeroplane would depend.' But the trials with the .303 Browning, he said, proved 'sufficiently convincing and satisfying to enable eight guns to carry the day.'[38] Sorley, who confessed to 'becoming a fanatic' over this issue,[39] had been heavily influenced in his support for wing-mounted multi-gun installations by a series of articles in the French aeronautical magazine *Les Ailes* ('Wings') in 1934. These articles dismissed the idea of inevitable bomber pre-eminence, but warned that a new breed of modern fighter would need the right weaponry to be effective. 'The single-seater fighter should be able to fire as many rounds as possible during the time favourable for attack, which can only be accurate at close range,' declared one piece.[40]

Sorley was certainly the central figure in pressing the case for eight guns. But it would be wrong to claim that his stance was unique. As the historian Colin Sinnott has pointed out, there were others in the Air Staff who were pressing for the same as Sorley. Hugh Dowding, typically, had argued in August 1931, before Specification F7/30 was even issued, that 'the multi-gun type of fixed-gun single-seater fighter is more likely than is the two-gun single-seater fighter to produce the density of fire necessary to ensure a hit on a vital part of the target.'[41] Air Marshal Edgar Ludlow-Hewitt, the Deputy Chief of the Air Staff, and Wing Commander A. T. Williams, Head of Flying Operations, were both supporters of eight guns, while in 1932 Wing Commander R. Collishaw had even proposed a ten-gun plane. However, Sir Edward Ellington, true to the inept nature of his leadership, was concerned about too much priority being given to fixed-gun single-seaters, and felt that what the RAF really needed were two-seater fighters. It was a view shared by Group Captain R. E. C. Pierse, the Deputy Director of Intelligence. In a memorandum that now looks absurd, with the benefit of hindsight, Pierse argued that the 'the single-seater, however many guns it carries, is, I think, the least useful for a fight . . . The movable multi-gun multi-seater fighter is beyond doubt the right answer . . . It is so far in advance of the single-seater that the latter must be considered obsolescent now.'[42]

In the spring of 1935, as a result of pressure from Sorley and the other multi-gun enthusiasts, the Air Ministry issued a new specification, F10/35, calling for a fighter with a speed of at least 310 mph and an armament of at least six guns, though preferably eight. This was meant to provide the new type of fast, well-armed monoplane that F7/30 had ostensibly failed to deliver. But, as Mitchell progressed with his prototype, it soon dawned on some at the Air Ministry that they might not need to go through the whole laborious tendering process. The answer to F10/35 could already be in existence, at the Supermarine works in Southampton. What was more, another new eight-gun fighter was emerging from the Hawker company, where the designer Sidney Camm was working on a prototype in response to a separate, recently issued specification, F36/34. Suddenly, after years of biplane-dominated paucity, it looked as if the Air Ministry might finally be able to start modernizing the RAF.

It was Ralph Sorley who first recognized the potential for Mitchell's new machine to fulfil all the requirements of F10/35. On 26 April, he visited the Supermarine works to inspect a wooden mock-up, having previously been to the Hawker factory. As he explained in a report to the Air Staff, he was deeply impressed by what he had seen. 'Both aircraft look to be excellent and in the hands of Mitchell and Camm, I suggest they are likely to be successes.' He had discussed with Mitchell the increase in guns as set out in F10/35. 'He is naturally desirous of bringing the aircraft now building into line with this specification. He says he can include four additional guns without trouble or delay.' Mindful of the deepening threat from Germany, Sorley argued that the Hawker and Supermarine fighters should be ordered immediately, without all the usual delays caused by waiting for prototypes to be tested. 'I say this because I foresee in these two aircraft the equipment we should aim at obtaining for new squadrons and re-equipping Bulldog squadrons in 1936 *if* we commence action *now* to make this possible . . . I suggest that we must for 1936 make every endeavour to commence production of the new monoplane types instead of always ordering the last type which is verging on obsolescence,' he continued, giving the example of the Gloster Gladiator.

To do this I suggest we should *now* speculate the cost of jigs and tools for both the Hawker and Supermarine aircraft so that while the prototypes are being completed and flown the necessary production for the squadrons in the 1936 programme may be completed . . . I am aware that this is an unorthodox method but with the political situation as it is and the possibility of increased expansion close upon us we should take steps to produce the latest design in the shortest possible time.

Sorley concluded with this warning: 'I feel quite sure that unless we make our preparations for next year's programme early we shall again find ourselves in the same unfortunate position as we are now in and may miss the opportunity of introducing really modern aircraft which are available.'[43]

After further discussions, on 4 June the Air Ministry agreed to ask Supermarine to bring the Type 300 into line with specification F10/35, the tendering process for which was now suspended.[44] But Sorley's other proposal, of ordering of the Hawker and Supermarine monoplanes immediately, was a step too far. Air Commodore R. H. Verney, who had succeeded Cave-Brown-Cave as Director of Technical Development, wrote that, while he accepted there were 'special circumstances' about the prototypes of these two monoplanes, there was also a risk of wasting jigs and tools if major alterations had to be made; hence 'I would rather say that directly the aeroplanes have been flown, and we know the best or the worst, as the case may be, that then would be the time for a production gamble.'[45] Even a progressive like Dowding agreed. He minuted, 'Personally I think the DTD's suggestion to wait till the machines have taken to the air is sound.'[46]

With full Whitehall backing, if not actual production orders, the development of the prototype accelerated. Apart from the addition of the four extra guns, which necessitated some modifications to the wings, other important changes arose from the installation of the Merlin engine. The first stemmed from Rolls-Royce's decision to improve the Merlin's cooling system by using ethylene glycol, which had a much higher boiling point than water and therefore greatly reduced the amount of coolant required. As a result, a system using glycol could be up to half the weight of one using water. In turn, this also meant that the plane needed a much smaller radiator, and here the Royal Aircraft Establishment at Farnborough was of critical assistance to Supermarine. A young scientist there, Frederick Meredith, had been experimenting with a new type of ducted radiator, in which air was compressed and heated before being expelled at high speed. This radiator reduced the drag, not only because much of its structure could be buried within the airframe, but also because the expulsion of the heated air acted like a rudimentary jet engine, giving a small amount of thrust to the plane.

A less technical but more emotive change was the widespread acceptance of the word 'Spitfire' to describe Mitchell's plane. It is astonishing to think, in retrospective, that two of the alternatives considered were 'Shrew' and 'Snipe' – ideas which, fortunately, won no backing. For once Sir Robert McLean, so full of overblown claims about other aspects of the plane's history, seems justified when he said that the name originated with him, for he was in the habit of calling his young daughter Ann 'a right little Spitfire'. McLean had actually urged that the early Type 224 be called the Spitfire: in December 1933 the Air Ministry received a cable from Supermarine, in reference to the Type 224, 'Would you kindly reserve the name "Spitfire" for our day and night fighter now being built in Southampton?' The Air Ministry showed no interest in this appellative discursion: 'Until it is accepted for supply to the RAF, you will continue to refer to this aircraft by the title Supermarine F7/30.'[47] Nor, beyond McLean, did the Supermarine workforce have any initial enthusiasm for the name. At Woolston the plane was generally known as the 7/30 or just 'The Fighter'.[48] Mitchell himself had little time for the title: 'Just the sort of bloody silly name they would think of,' he is reputed to have said.[49] But, at McLean's insistence – and to Mitchell's regret – the name was retained for the redeveloped plane.

The indifference over the name indicated a wider unconcern about the fighter at much of the Supermarine plant. Mitchell, his design team and the Air Ministry were engrossed by progress of the Spitfire, but their attitude was not shared across the workforce, as Denis Webb recalled: 'Many of us were not frightfully interested in it. We had recently produced another similar machine which had been a flop and for all we knew this might be the same. In any case, it hadn't the majesty or dignity of a flying boat. We were a professional crowd and to us it was just another bloody aeroplane.'[50]

To the more alert politicians, the Spitfire was certainly not 'just another bloody aeroplane'. It was part of the vital process of air rearmament to cope with the threat of Germany, which was now casting an ever larger shadow over Europe. At the beginning of March 1935, less than two months before Sorley had seen the wooden-mock up at the Supermarine factory, Göring had announced to the world that Germany had created an air force, in direct contravention of the terms of the 1919 Versailles Treaty. Worse followed weeks later when the Foreign Secretary, Sir John Simon, on an official visit to Berlin, was told by Hitler, 'We have achieved air parity with Britain.'[51] Like much of Hitler's bluster, this claim may have been exaggerated. Nevertheless it sent a shiver down the spine of the government. The feebleness of the expansion schemes for the RAF was now exposed, as was the complacency of Londonderry and Ellington. 'Things look very black. I feel we are drifting on a tide whose destination is perfectly obvious,' wrote Sir Henry Pownall in his diary, adding that the Foreign Office felt that the rate of expansion needed at least to be doubled.[52]

In classic Whitehall fashion, the government's response to the crisis was to set up yet another committee. This one, entitled the 'Sub-Committee on Air Parity', was itself an offshoot of the Ministerial Committee on Defence Requirements. As so often before and since, the politicians proved better at expanding the administrative machinery of the state than at strengthening its front-line operations. But the chairmanship of this committee was to signal a new, more resolute, direction of government policy. It is a measure of how low the Air Secretary Lord Londonderry had fallen in prime-ministerial esteem that Ramsay MacDonald did not ask him to take on the job. This was an obvious snub, given that air policy was his portfolio, but one deserved because of Londonderry's disastrous failure to grasp the magnitude of the task. Shortly before Christmas 1934, for example, Londonderry had attacked the very notion of rapid RAF expansion: 'Demands of this kind may be inspired by patriotism but they are certainly not inspired by statesmanship. We have no need of an enormous fleet of aircraft.'[53] And soon after Hitler's announcement he circulated to Cabinet colleagues a paper drawn up by Ellington attacking the 'panic' over German air strength.[54] Reeking of torpid negligence, this document openly admitted that Germany might have air superiority over the home-based RAF by 1937.

The man that the ageing MacDonald, in one of his last acts as Premier, chose as the committee chairman was of a very different calibre. Sir Philip Cunliffe-Lister, the Colonial Secretary, was a tough-minded, aggressive Tory politician, who preferred executive action to political manoeuvring. His quick temper and dislike of self-publicity meant that he had not risen as far up the Westminster ladder as his talent should have deserved, but his strong-willed determination was exactly what the government needed at this moment of crisis. His vigour was immediately reflected in the way he conducted his business. His committee held its opening meeting on 1 May 1935, and within a fortnight it had issued two hard-hitting reports to the Cabinet, calling for the government to place orders for another 3,800 aircraft by 1937 in order to reach parity with Germany – a plan that would soon evolve into RAF expansion Scheme C.

Cunliffe-Lister's committee laid particular emphasis on the need for quality as well as quantity, and this led to the first references to the Spitfire and the Hurricane at ministerial level. At a meeting on 13 May, Cunliffe-Lister directly asked Ellington about 'the existing position regarding experimental orders'. Ellington replied that, in the case of Hawker, the prototype was expected to be flown in June, while for the Supermarine the earliest would be November 1935. He continued, with his usual pessimism, 'Both these types could be produced within twelve months of the order being given. It was anticipated, however, that with this new type trouble must be anticipated, particularly aerodynamic troubles in connection with controls. The Americans were experiencing considerable trouble in this matter and it was not considered safe to jig-up these machines without further test.' He concluded, in something of an understatement about the two planes' proposed new firepower, 'The new types of fighters were an advance on the old, in that they carried four or more guns instead of two.'[55] This analysis was then set out in the committee report of 17 May to the full Cabinet, with a small change in the dates of prototype deliveries:

> The firms Hawker and Supermarine are designing low-wing monoplanes with retractable undercarriages, flaps for slow landing and an estimated speed of 300 mph. Prototypes may be expected in July and October 1935 respectively. In the case of these types, however, the Air Ministry anticipate that trouble may be experienced, owing to the fact that they are low-wing monoplanes, and difficulties must in consequence be expected. It is unsound, in view of these possible difficulties to count on them for the two-year programme but if the tests are satisfactory orders could and we think should be placed for some of these types.[56]

The Cabinet endorsed this position.

Sir Philip's impressive chairmanship soon resulted in his elevation. When Baldwin succeeded MacDonald as Prime Minister in June 1935, he removed Londonderry from his post, replacing him with Cunliffe-Lister. Baldwin told Londonderry that the reason for the change was that, given the mounting importance of RAF expansion, the Air Secretary had to sit in the Commons. The dishonesty of this justification was soon exposed by Baldwin's decision to make Sir Philip a peer, precisely so that he would be freed from the demands of handling Commons business and could concentrate on air policy. Cunliffe-Lister, who was bored by the rhetorical debates of the Lower House, welcomed the move and took the title of Viscount Swinton, the name derived from his wife's estates in Yorkshire.

The arrival of a new Secretary of State radically changed the atmosphere of the Air Ministry. There was a sudden animation about the place. The reluctance of the Air Staff to embrace expansion disappeared. Swinton reinforced this sense of urgency with two important decisions that he made within weeks of taking up office. The first was to appoint the Scottish industrialist William Weir as his chief, though unpaid, adviser. An engineer by background,

Weir had enjoyed a long career in public life but had made few enemies, partly because he had no political ambitions himself. Though his outlook was that of a wealthy, orthodox Conservative, he remained ferociously independent and preferred to use his enterprising mind for major national projects rather than for personal advancement. He had first risen to public prominence during the First World War, when his success in running the family engineering and munitions firm led to his appointment in 1917 as Controller of Aeronautical Supplies. He immediately proved his managerial skills by presiding over a phenomenal increase in aircraft production. By March 1918, monthly output was exceeding the entire annual output of 1915. So dazzling was his achievement that he was soon made Secretary of State for Air and raised into the peerage as the 1st Viscount Weir of Eastwood. But Lord Weir had no wish to stay in a formal political position and resigned almost as soon as the war was over. During the 1920s and early 1930s he served as a kind of general consultant to government and industry. It was his initiative that led to the creation of the National Grid, Great Britain's electricity supply network, while he also played a vital part in the growth of civil aviation and public housing. As a symbol of his independence, when he took on the job with Swinton he refused to base himself in the Air Ministry, but instead used an office in his rooms at the Adelphi Hotel in the West End, with his own brother J. G. Weir acting as his assistant. Like many of those in the Spitfire story, including Swinton and Dowding, he lived for his work. Though married, he ensured that his wife stayed in his native Scotland, and he seems to have had no private or social life.

Swinton's second decision, again at variance with the lethargic regime of Londonderry, was to establish a series of frequent progress meetings with the leaders of the Air Staff. During the years building up to war, these meetings were to be Swinton's main vehicle for keeping up the pressure for modernization and growth. Their minutes form an absorbing commentary on the development and production of the Spitfire, showing just how close the programme almost came to complete breakdown. At the fifth such progress meeting, on 30 July 1935, the subject of the Spitfire and Hurricane was raised when Dowding responded to concern about the new generation of fast German bombers. The Gloster Gladiator, he said, 'would clearly be of no use against 270 mph machines, but the new experimental fighters should have an adequate margin'.[57] Then in October Dowding reported on the progress of the Spitfire prototype: 'This aeroplane promised well and should be flying any day now.'[58] His words were a sign of the growing confidence within the Air Ministry about the plane. In late November 1935 the Director of Technical Development, Air Commodore Verney, made a visit to Supermarine and subsequently told the Ministry, 'The fuselage is nearly completed and the engine installed. The wings are being plated and some parts of the undercarriage still have to be finished. I like the simple design of the undercarriage very much. Also the flush riveting of the surfaces of the fuselage and wings . . . As far as I can see it cannot be flying this year but it should be early in January. In many ways it is a much more advanced design than the Hawker and should be a great deal lighter.'[59]

When 1936 dawned, the Spitfire prototype was still not flying. The delay was reported to a progress meeting on 6 February, during which there was also a wider discussion of the qualities of the plane:

> Lord Weir asked when the Supermarine fighter was likely to be flying. The Air Member for Research and Development [Dowding] replied that the firm said it would be flying by 20 February but he thought himself that it could hardly do so before April. The firm had a good designer, Mr Mitchell, but they were very slow. In reply to a further question from Lord Weir, the AMRD said that the aircraft looked fairly promising and, being an improved version of an earlier low-wing monoplane, the prospects of success were not so problematical as in the case of an entirely new type.[60]

Nearly three weeks later, on 25 February, it was reported that the maiden flight was imminent. The meeting was told that, if production trials were successful, an order could be placed in May and Supermarine would be able to start production in September 1937, turning out the Spitfire at the rate of five a week. As a result, it would be feasible to deliver 380 planes by the end of March 1939 – a forecast that was to prove hopelessly optimistic.

At the beginning of March 1936 Supermarine made the final adjustments to the Spitfire as the plane was prepared for its first flight, which was to take place at Eastleigh aerodrome in Southampton. Overseen by foreman Gerry Scrubby, the prototype had been built in a corner of the Woolston works under strict security, hidden from the rest of the factory by a tarpaulin screen. Supermarine were particularly anxious to avoid the prying eyes of German Lufthansa pilots, who regularly landed their seaplanes on the waterfront nearby to have their mail cleared by British customs based at Woolston. Denis Webb, in his memoir, left this account of the final tests at the factory before the prototype was taken to Eastleigh:

> The first engine run was carried out at night for security reasons, with the tail skid lashed to a holding-down ring on the quay normally used for tethering down flying boats. Scrubby, recalling the occasion, said that the flames from the exhaust were spectacular, as was the noise. After the runs were completed, the wooden fixed-pitch airscrew and the wings were removed and the aircraft

loaded on to lorries for the journey to Eastleigh aerodrome and re-erected there in our hangar, where, incidentally, the S6B was stored, less engine.[61]

For many years there was a controversy over the date of the first flight, for until recently the documentary evidence was surprisingly sparse. Mitchell made no note of it in his personal engagement diary, and Jeffrey Quill at one stage thought it must have taken place on 6 March, since this was the day that he flew Mutt Summers, the Vickers chief test pilot, to Eastleigh. But then a set of faded Supermarine reports was found at Hursley House, the stately home to which the company's headquarters was moved during the war. Among these papers, now lodged in the Southampton Hall of Aviation, was the Spitfire's test-flight record, which showed categorically that the prototype first flew on 5 March 1936.

Joseph 'Mutt' Summers was the ideal pilot for the maiden flight. Thirty-two years old, big, ebullient and self-assured, he was renowned for his lightning-quick reactions. It was joked that if a kitchen table had a propeller fixed to it, he could fly it.[62] Not only did he revel in his glamorous image as a top pilot, he was also popular at the Air Ministry because of his fluent German, which meant that he was in regular contact with Luftwaffe pilots and officials. But he was not so well liked at Supermarine, as Denis Webb recalled: 'I think part of the dislike stemmed from a rather supercilious smile which seemed to be permanently affixed to his face as if he was rather condescendingly visiting poor or humble peasants.'[63]

In the late afternoon, Summers strode across the Eastleigh airfield towards the Spitfire. Now accorded the official registration of K5404, the plane was unpainted, its metal surfaces having been given only a protective treatment. It had no guns or ammunition, and had been fitted with a special fine-pitch propeller to improve take-off. At 4.35 p.m. Summers strapped himself into the cockpit and started up the engine. A light breeze was blowing across the aerodrome. Summers taxied over to the far side of the airfield, turned into the wind, and then opened the throttle. 'The new fighter fairly leapt off and climbed away,' recalled Jeffrey Quill, who was standing beside Mitchell to watch the event.[64] While in the air, Summers cruised gently and performed some checks on the stalling characteristics and landing flaps. Throughout, he kept the undercarriage down. Denis Webb gave the reason for this, contradicting the usual explanations:

> The undercarriage was not retracted and some books state that this was a deliberate policy, presumably to avoid any chance of a chassis malfunction with the one and only prototype on its first flight. Retractable undercarriages were still very new and not always reliable. However, according to Gerry Scrubby, who

helped prepare the machine for the flight, they had some trouble with the 'up' locks in the wings and so to avoid any delay it was decided to carry out the first flight with the undercarriage locked down.[65]

After eight minutes, Summers came in to land, put the aircraft down on three points, and taxied towards the hangar. By the time he had shut down the engine, a small crowd had gathered round, eager to hear his verdict. According to one account, provided by Quill:

> Mutt pulled off his helmet and said firmly, 'I don't want anything touched.' This was soon destined to become a widely misinterpreted remark. What he meant was that there were no snags which required correction or adjustment before he flew the aircraft again. The remark has crept into folklore implying that the aeroplane was perfect in every respect from the moment of its first flight, an obviously absurd and impracticable idea.[66]

Summers took the plane up for a longer flight the next day, lasting twenty-three minutes, and completed two more trips before he handed over the testing to Jeffrey Quill. In his report after the fourth flight, on 14 March, Summers wrote, 'The handling qualities of this machine are remarkably good.' The elevators, rudder and wing flaps were all described as 'very effective', and the ailerons 'powerful and quite light'.[67] Interestingly, he called the plane the 'Spitfire II', to distinguish it from the failed 224.

Reports of the success of the initial flights reached the Air Ministry, creating a mood of exhilaration, as the intelligence officer Group Captain Frederick Winterbotham later described: 'Some of my friends from the Air Ministry went down to the first test flight and they were so excited about the Spitfire. All through the Air Ministry it was terribly secret. Nobody had known anything about it but it really looked as if we were going to have something which would match up to anything the Germans could build.'[68] Dowding, in his understated way, was also buoyant, telling Swinton on 10 March that 'the flying was highly satisfactory.'[69] At Swinton's progress meeting on 17 March he elaborated on this, following a visit to Eastleigh: 'He was glad to report that it was flying remarkably and the firm, who were very pleased with it, said that it would probably be much faster (350 to 360 mph) than the Hawker fighter. Its only drawback was that it had a very poor downward and forward view. He had tried the retractable undercarriage, the flaps and the other gadgets and they seemed to be very efficient.'[70] Some of the first RAF Spitfire pilots might have disputed that point about the undercarriage, since it could be operated only by a heavy hand pump, which led to scraped fingers and, for the inexperienced, an awkward, porpoise-like movement in the initial climb.

It was towards the end of March that Jeffrey Quill became the leading Spitfire pilot, and his advice proved crucial in the development of the plane in the coming years. The son of an Irish engineer, he was just twenty-two years old when he joined Vickers as principal assistant to Mutt Summers in January 1936, having previously been an exceptional pilot with the RAF. One of his primary reasons for joining Supermarine was because Summers persuaded him that he would have the chance to fly an exciting experimental fighter.

Jeffrey Kindersley Quill was physically a smaller man than Summers, but he had perhaps an ever bigger character. Highly intelligent and courageous, he had an instinctive mastery of aeroplanes and a deep integrity that inspired confidence. The author Larry Forrester wrote of him, 'His puckish face always seemed to have a half-smile and with his soft casual voice and sporting clothes, you might have taken him for an indolent and spoiled youth – until you noticed his eyes: bright, alert and dominating.'[71] His fellow Spitfire test pilot Alex Henshaw felt that 'what set him apart from many in his field was a very thorough grasp of aerodynamic and technical engineering at a very high level. But perhaps his greatest gift to those technicians with whom he worked was his concise analysis and the articulate manner in which he could explain problems to the design team in a language they clearly understood.'[72] Mitchell, in particular, relished hearing Quill's views after any test flight in a Spitfire, and when parked near an aerodrome he would often invite him for a chat in the back of his Rolls-Royce. 'He made me see that the most valuable contribution which I could make was to concentrate on becoming a better and better pilot and to try to absorb a natural understanding of the problems of engineers and designers,' wrote Quill in his autobiography.[73]

Quill's first flight in the Spitfire took place at Eastleigh on 26 March, and every detail became etched in his memory:

> With the seat in the fully-up position there was very little headroom but at once I felt good in that cockpit. I primed the Merlin engine carefully and it started first time. I began taxiing out of the north-east end of the airfield which was, of course, entirely of grass. Never before had I flown a fighter with such a very long nose; with the aircraft in its ground attitude vision directly ahead was completely obscured so I taxied slowly on a zig-zag course in order to ensure a clear path ahead.

After reaching the end of the airfield, Quill, performed his final cockpit checks, turned into the wind, and opened the throttle. The torque of the propeller tended to pull the plane to the left as it sped over the grass, and Quill had to apply a lot of right rudder to keep it straight. But soon he was airborne and climbing. Then he had to raise the undercarriage with the hydraulic pump, using his right hand while keeping his left on the control column, inevitably leading to an oscillating movement. After that obstacle was cleared, however,

> the aircraft began to slip along as if on skates with the speed mounting up steadily and an immediate impression of effortless performance was accentuated by the low revs of the propeller at that low altitude. The aeroplane just seemed to chunter along at outstandingly higher cruising speed than I had ever experienced before, with the engine turning over very easily, and in this respect it was somewhat reminiscent of my old Bentley cruising in top gear.

Quill flew to several thousand feet, performed some gentle rolls and dives, and then started the descent to land. As became the standard procedure with all Spitfires, he approached the airfield in a sweeping curve to improve his visibility.

> As I chopped the throttle on passing the boundary hedge the deceleration was hardly discernible and the aeroplane showed no desire to touch down – it evidently enjoyed flying – but finally it settled gently on three points and it wasn't until after the touch-down that the mild buffeting associated with the stalling of the wing became apparent. 'Here', I thought to myself, 'is a real lady.'[74]

The Air Ministry were gratified by the news of the Spitfire's impressive start. Again, Swinton showed his sense of urgency, eager to place a provisional order – though he seemed even more taken with the Hawker Hurricane. The minutes of his progress meeting of 31 March recorded this exchange with the Air Member for Supply and Organization, Sir Cyril Newall, shortly to become Chief of the Air Staff: 'The Secretary of State asked how many of the Supermarine fighters it was proposed to order. The AMSO replied that an order for 300 had been provisionally agreed. In reply to a question from the Secretary of State, the AMSO said that it would not be correct to say that the Hawker was a much better aircraft, though it certainly had a much better forward and downward view.'[75]

The day after this meeting, 1 April 1936, a major change occurred at the top of the RAF's structure – one that would have far-reaching implications for the Spitfire and the Battle of Britain. In one of his more constructive moves, Sir Edward Ellington divided the air force into a series of functional commands, dealing with fighters, bombers, coastal operations, and training. Dowding was now elevated to the post of commander-in-chief of Fighter Command; having presided over the creation of the Spitfire, he would now be in charge of deciding how it would be used. His place as Air Member for Research and Development was taken by the sophisticated Sir Wilfrid Freeman, who was the very opposite of Dowding in personality. Urbane and cultured, he possessed striking good looks and had a reputation as something of a lothario. Having married for a second time, he feared that his divorce from his first wife had held back his career. But now, as the new AMRD, he was quickly to form a vital partnership with Swinton and Weir. From April 1936 they became a forceful triumvirate at the heart of air policy, driving through the expansion of the RAF and continually pushing for more output from industry. Major G. P. Bullman, head of the Air Ministry's Engine Research section, painted this portrait of Freeman in action:

> His magnetism attracted the industry and made them feel a sense of relief that there was now a key man at the Ministry, urging and pulling them along with unusual panache, a man of piercing perception, ready to play for high stakes, to take instant decisions, by no means always on the advice of his civil service staff or indeed of his service colleagues. He was a man who walked alone, sometimes withdrawn into himself, apt to suffer migraines, but generally sparkling, most penetrating in conversation, often delighting in playing the devil's advocate to see how one would respond: in my case often with fury but ending in a mutual chuckle. He could be wickedly mischievous and impish in his comments and as often most generous and understanding. He was a wonderful boss, though sometimes I could have killed him. Beyond doubt, he was the most inspiring man I ever served.[76]

Amid all the enthusiasm for the new plane, Mitchell was one of the few to experience a feeling of disappointment. He had been hoping for a speed of 350 mph, but it had reached only 335 mph – not much faster than Sidney Camm's Hurricane, which was well ahead of the Spitfire in development and, being of a more conventional design, was much easier to produce. The official prototype trials at the RAF testing base of Martlesham were imminent, and Mitchell sensed they would be crucial to the Spitfire's future. As Jeffrey Quill wrote, 'Unless the Spitfire offered some very substantial speed advantage over the Hurricane it was unlikely to be put into production. Thus the disappointing speed performance of our prototype at that early stage was something of a crisis and Mitchell was a very worried man.'[77] He need not have been so anxious. Over the next few weeks a number of improvements were made, including a change in the balance of the rudder, new cowlings and fairings, and the installation of a new propeller. Perhaps most important was the application by a Rolls-Royce subcontractor of an ultra-smooth finish, in a high-gloss pale grey-blue colour. Jeffrey Quill flew the restyled plane, and found that he could reach 348 mph in level flight and 380 in a dive without any problems. 'I think we've got something here,' he said to the Spitfire engineers after landing.[78]

Mitchell was now happy for the prototype to be taken to Martlesham for its official Air Ministry tests. On 26 May, Mutt Summers flew K5404 over to the RAF base, where the commander of RAF Martlesham's A Flight, Humphrey Edwardes-Jones, was due to hold the first trial in the late afternoon. Though the station usually closed at five o'clock, it is a sign of the excitement engendered by the Spitfire that a large group of officers, civil servants and staff were still there at five thirty when Flight Lieutenant Edwardes-Jones stepped into the cockpit and started the engine. 'Usually the first flight of a new aircraft did not mean a thing at Martlesham; they were happening all the time. But on this occasion the buzz got around that the Spitfire was something special and everybody turned out to watch – I can remember seeing the cooks in their white hats lining the road. I took off, retracted the undercarriage and flew around for about 20 minutes. I found that she handled very well,' he remembered. But when he was making his final curved approach towards the grass of the airfield, 'I had a funny feeling that something was wrong. Then it suddenly occurred to me. I had forgotten to lower the undercarriage!' Fortunately he managed to operate the hand pump just in time.

> It came down and locked with a reassuring 'clunk'. Then I continued down and landed. Afterwards people said to me, 'You've got a nerve, leaving it so late before you put the wheels down.' But I just grinned and shrugged my shoulders. In the months that followed I would go quite cold just thinking about it: supposing I had landed the first Spitfire wheels-up! I kept the story to myself for many years afterwards.[79]

Edwardes-Jones had been instructed to telephone Sir Wilfrid Freeman at the Air Ministry as soon as he landed, giving his initial opinion of the plane. He went into the office and was immediately put through to the Air Member for Research and Development. 'I don't want to know everything and obviously you can't tell me,' said Freeman. 'All I want to know now is whether you think the young pilot officers and others we are getting in the Air Force will be able to cope with such an advanced aircraft.' After taking a deep breath and pondering his own near disaster – which reflected how novel a retractable undercarriage still was in 1936 – Edwardes-Jones replied, 'Yes, provided they are given adequate instruction in the use of flaps and retracting undercarriage.'[80] This was good enough for Freeman. On the strength of this oral message, he confirmed a production order for 310 Spitfires to be delivered by March 1939. The total price of the contract for 310 planes was £1,395,000, or £4,500 per aircraft, excluding the engine, radio and guns. The contract for the planes was issued on 3 June, just eight days after Edwardes-Jones's first flight. That the Air Ministry had acted with unprecedented swiftness showed the invigorating unorthodoxy of Sir Wilfrid Freeman, who loathed long-winded Whitehall protocol.

After Martlesham, K5404 was displayed to the public for the first time in the summer of 1936. With its unrivalled speed and clean lines, it immediately created an enormous stir. The press had already been building up the mood of excitement with tantalizing news stories about a world-beating aircraft that had just been produced at Woolston, as in this report of 26 March from the *Southern Evening Echo*:

> Keen observers in and around Southampton have recently been interested in the high-speed performances of a remarkable plane which has made occasional flights from Eastleigh Airport. The machine is the very latest type of single-seater fighter, designed and built for the RAF by The Supermarine Aviation Works (Vickers) Ltd. Produced amid great secrecy, the plane is one of the fastest of its category in the world . . . Even the uninitiated have realized when watching the streamlined monoplane flash across the sky at five miles a minute (300 mph) and more, that here is a plane out of the ordinary.[81]

On 18 June at Eastleigh aerodrome, K5404 made its debut in public, at an open day organized by Vickers to show off their latest types, whose number included not just the Spitfire but also the Wellington bomber, designed by Mitchell's old adversary Barnes Wallis.

Jeffrey Quill took off normally, but had only just become airborne when he saw to his horror that he was rapidly losing oil pressure. He knew the engine would soon seize up if he carried on, but he could not land immediately because the Eastleigh railway works were straight ahead. With the consummate skill that made him such an outstanding pilot, he climbed a few hundred feet, took off as much power as he dared, put down the undercarriage, and swept round in a slow left-hand turn. With one final burst on the fading engine, he was able to land normally. Quill was disappointed that he had not been able to give the public the display he had rehearsed. On the other hand, he had learned how safe the Spitfire and the Merlin could be, even in a crisis. 'At the end of it all I felt a very friendly disposition towards the new Merlin engine,' he wrote. 'It started for me a process of confidence in that remarkable piece of machinery which was to grow ever stronger as my hours in the air with it increased.'[82]

Despite the oil leak, the press corps, fuelled by champagne provided by Vickers, were still impressed. It was 'the fastest military aeroplane in the world,' reported *The Times,* in an article which eulogized K5404's modern features:

> There are no bracing wires above or below the wing. There are no corrugations on the smooth surface of the fuselage. There is a clean, unbroken cowling over

66

the upper part of the engine . . . It may also be as surprising in construction as in design, for it has a comparatively small wing area and though it carries a big military load is not heavily loaded, as its easy manoeuvres today showed. It took off and climbed admirably and when it had to land it came in with the flaps down at so low a speed that it seemed not to belong to the fighter class.[83]

The fault in the oil pressure, caused by a loose pipe, was soon fixed, and within less than a fortnight the plane was on display again, this time at two much bigger public events, the first at the RAF Pageant in Hendon, and the second at an airshow at Hatfield organized by the Society of British Aircraft Constructors. After the latter, *Flight* magazine was full of praise:

> It is claimed – and the claim seems undisputable – that the Spitfire is the fastest military plane in the world. It is surprisingly small and light for a machine of its calibre (the structure weight is said to have been brought down to a level never before attained in the single-seat fighter class) and its speed and manoeuvrability are something to marvel at. Tight turns were made at high speed after dives and the control at low speeds was amply demonstrated. The demonstration was cramped by low clouds but after the main flying display the machine was taken up again and gave one of the smoothest displays ever seen in this country.[84]

Mitchell had come through the ordeal of cancer surgery to see his prototype gloriously take to the skies. It had required a superhuman effort, working long hours and dealing with a multitude of technological problems while coping with pain and worry. Moreover, he had been told by his doctors that, despite the operation in 1933, there was a strong likelihood that the cancer would return. Yet the knowledge that he might be living on borrowed time only strengthened his determination to complete his task. And even in the shadow of death he was not concerned just with the Spitfire. In 1936 he was also working on the redesign of one flying boat and proposals for another, as well as on the radical development of a heavy bomber for the RAF, specification B12/36. His initial designs showed that, like the Spitfire, this bomber was far ahead of other contemporary types.

It was an awesome workload, made even more draining by the fact that, by the autumn, he was an increasingly sick man. It was all too apparent that the cancer had returned. Heroically, he carried on at the Supermarine works, often irritable and exhausted, but never less than wholehearted in his commitment. But from the turn of the year he was forced into taking periodic absences from work. Then in February 1937 he went into a London hospital for more tests, retaining the faint hope that a second operation might halt the cancer. He was told that there was little prospect of that: he was unlikely to live to see the summer. Mitchell took the news with characteristic fortitude, as Joe Smith of Supermarine movingly testified:

> In the whole range of human emotions there can be nothing as terrible as the realization that an incurable disease makes one's death inevitable within a short space of time. To have the courage to face such a tragic fate unflinchingly must be the hope of every man, adding a fervent prayer that it will never happen to him. It did happen to Mitchell and I can personally vouch for the fact that he behaved in a way which was beyond praise. To talk to him during this period was to see the highest form of courage, and the memory must always remain an inspiration.[85]

Mitchell demonstrated not a moment of self-pity, but instead spent much of his time settling all his affairs, such as his will, so that his wife and teenage son would suffer no financial hardship. His focus on the needs of his immediate family was demonstrated in a letter that he sent to his solicitor in Stoke on 20 March 1937, in which he reiterated his desire to leave his estate to them rather than put some of it in a trust or distribute it more widely among his other relatives. His words were made all the more poignant by their candour:

> I have very great confidence in my wife and son so I feel quite safe in leaving matters as they stand. I have already discussed this very fully with my wife and to a certain extent with Gordon, as I have now told him that there is a very good chance that I shall not get better. I have explained to him, to the best of my ability, the various points. I feel quite confident that he will respect these all his life and will act accordingly. It must be remembered that I am leaving my wife and boy at a time when heavy expenses will be incurred and there will be no income except from the capital I leave them.[86]

He accepted his fate with dignity, but not without regret at the tasks he would have to leave unfinished. 'They think the end will probably be about June . . . I – who have so much to do – have only until June,' he told a visitor to his Southampton home of Hazeldene.[87] The news of his illness caused sorrow at the Air Ministry, mixed with a desire to express gratitude for all he had achieved. Sir Edward Ellington wrote to him, 'I think I have never told you before how your great services to the RAF and aviation as a whole are valued. I am fully aware, as are all the other members of the Air Council, of the unsparing manner in which you have devoted your great abilities to the task of design and I wish you to realize that, however incomplete you may feel your work to be at present, we know that you have always given us of your best.'[88] Wilfrid Freeman told him of the department's 'grief at the illness of a personal and greatly respected friend'.[89] In reply, Mitchell again was unsparing in his honesty: 'I am very pleased to say that I have always trained my staff to be thoroughly up to date with all new ideas and proposals being carried out at Supermarine. I feel very confident that they will be able to carry on without me.'[90]

By the end of March, Mitchell's condition was rapidly worsening, his pain only partly lessened by the morphia he was given. He spent much of his time in his garden, looking out on his pond and the first blooms of spring. Though not a devoutly religious man, he derived comfort from his talks with the local Anglican vicar, the Rev. Stretton Reeve, who later recalled, 'What stands out in my memory is the indomitable courage that he showed. He was only young and did not want to die but he faced the situation in which he found himself with bravery and steadfastness. He was obviously suffering much, but he refused to give in and fought in a way that was truly remarkable.'[91] One sign of that fight was his decision to try one last remote chance of a medical cure. Despite his crippled condition and the advice of English experts that there was no hope, at the end of April he travelled to Vienna to visit the renowned clinic founded by Professor Freund, one of the pioneers of cancer treatment. Escorted by his wife and a nurse, he looked a gaunt figure as he was helped into the De Havilland Rapide private plane at Eastleigh. The affection in which he was held was all too obvious, as Jeffrey Quill wrote: 'A large number of design staff from Woolston somehow found it necessary to visit Eastleigh that morning and I well remember the scene as RJ's plane taxied in front of a crowd of his devoted staff who had assembled on the tarmac to wave him good luck and God speed.'[92] Mitchell spent a month at the Austrian clinic, but the specialists, led by the centre's American director, F. Pearson, could do little. The cancer had progressed too far.

Mitchell returned to England to spend his last days at Hazeldene. He lapsed into unconsciousness on 6 June, and died at two o'clock on the 11th. He was just forty-two years old. Following the funeral in his local parish church in Highfield, Southampton, his body was taken to be cremated and his ashes were then interred at a private ceremony in South Stoneham Cemetery near Eastleigh. At the moment of interment, three RAF planes flew past in formation and dipped their wings in salute at his passing. It was a gesture that encapsulated the debt that the air force and the nation owed RJ. As Viscount Swinton put it in a letter of condolence to Mitchell's widow, 'His was real genius, a flair of his own and an infinite thoroughness. His work is his memorial.'[93]

3

'A disgraceful state of affairs'

～～

'**E**VERY DAY COUNTS,' WROTE Winston Churchill to Lord Swinton in August 1935:

> The Germans are spending £1,000 million this year on military preparations direct and indirect. Can you doubt what this portends? Their lead in the air is growing hourly greater. For eighteen months or more we shall only be falling further behind the Air Parity we were assured would be maintained and was necessary for our safety. We are moving into dangers greater than any I have seen in my lifetime and it may be that fearful experiences lie before us.[1]

Swinton was in a more encouraging frame of mind, partly because of the designs for the Spitfire and Hurricane. 'We have some remarkable developments in equipment which are probably in advance of anyone,' he replied.[2]

The positive outlook created by the Spitfire prototype grew with the success of the maiden flights and the plane's dramatic performances in the air shows of the summer of 1936. The mood of elation was further reinforced in September by the glowing RAF report into the handling trials of K5404 at Martlesham. In its summary of flying qualities, the report stated:

> The aeroplane is simple and easy to fly and has no vices. All controls are entirely satisfactory for this type and no modification to them is required . . . The controls are well harmonized and appear to give an excellent compromise between manoeuvrability and steadiness for shooting. Take-off and landing are straightforward and easy . . . In general the handling of this aeroplane is such that it can be flown without risk by the average fully trained service fighter pilot.[3]

In fact Swinton was so impressed with the first appearances of the Spitfire that he considered the possibility of ordering it in even larger quantities than the Hurricane. Alongside the contract for 310 Spitfires from Supermarine, the Air Ministry had already asked Hawker to produce 600 Hurricanes. Swinton was concerned by the difference in these two orders, given that the Spitfire had now proved itself to be 35 mph faster. He raised the subject at his progress meeting on 16 June, and was told by Air Vice-Marshal Christopher Courtney, the Deputy Chief of the Air Staff, that 'it would be desirable to wait until more was known about the Supermarine fighter.' Somewhat defensively, Swinton said 'he entirely agreed and had no wish to dictate on such a question. He felt bound to raise it, however, since the expected speed of the Spitfire was a factor which had only just come to light.'[4] But he had not given up. At another meeting, on 22 June, he pointed out that, if the two contracts stood, then the Air Staff would effectively be ordering twice as many of a plane that they knew to be slower. In reply, Ellington, the Chief of the Air Staff, showed his predictable complacency: 'It was hardly possible to judge the two types properly until each had been flown by an ordinary service pilot but he did not think the difference in speed would be so great when the official performance figures for the Supermarine were known. But in any case a fighter with a top speed of 315 mph would give a reasonable margin of speed over any known bomber.'[5] He was badly mistaken. Fighter speed was to be a crucial factor of the air war.

Yet, amid all this optimism, there was one nagging doubt about the Spitfire, which would eventually make irrelevant all the discussions about the size of orders. At the progress meeting on 16 June, Sir Cyril Newall, the Air Member for Supply and Organization, had warned that the plane 'could not easily be produced in quantity because of its stressed skin construction', adding that 'the numbers required could not possibly be obtained from the Supermarine company', though he hoped that 'the production difficulties would be got over one way or another.'[6] The robust Scot Lord Weir, Swinton's adviser, was not happy with these vague attempts at reassurance. At the end of July he told the Air Staff that 'Supermarine's programme was very large in relation to the size of their works and he would like to be sure that their capacity had been carefully examined before their scheme of orders under the new programme had been decided on.'[7]

Little such scrutiny had been made, and by the end of the year increasing concerns were being raised about the slow start to production. Sir Robert McLean had promised the Air Ministry that deliveries could start from September 1937, but that had already started to look improbable. In January 1937 Swinton asked the Air Staff 'if the Spitfire was behindhand'. Sir Cyril Newall reported that 'he was rather alarmed by something he had heard the previous day. The new Air Attaché had paid a visit to the Supermarine Works at Southampton and had come back with the information that we should probably only get a few of this type during the present year, instead of 60, as shown in the firm's latest estimate of deliveries.'[8] Shortly afterwards, Weir said that reports from Southampton confirmed all his worst fears. 'The trouble which he had anticipated over the production of the Spitfire had now come to a head.'[9] Three days later, at another progress meeting, Sir Cyril Newall painted an even bleaker picture. 'The firm had frankly miscalculated the magnitude of their task . . . The situation was most disquieting.'[10] And it was going to become worse in the coming months.

There were two factors at the heart of the production problems: one lay in the nature of the aircraft itself; the other in the running of the Supermarine company. Because the Spitfire was a far more advanced plane than any fighter previously built for the RAF, the techniques used in its manufacture were often highly complex, sometimes untested. An array of engineering problems was created by everything from the hydraulics for the undercarriage to the pneumatics for the guns. The Supermarine engineer Eric Lovell-Cooper recalled that, when the Spitfire had been on display at the show in Hatfield in 1936, he had talked to a technical expert who had worked on the Hurricane. 'Well, I like the Spitfire to look at but you'll never get it into production,' said this technician.[11] What exacerbated the difficulties was that Supermarine did not always have the sophisticated technology for mass production and had to farm out some of the work. Cyril Russell, who began working for the company in 1936, left this record of the frustrations in dealing with the top rear panel on the Spitfire fuselage, described by Russell as 'a little beast' and officially registered in the factory as part 363: 'Originally it was considered that this panel for production could only be a power-press job and Woolston, in those days, did not have anything in the machinery line that could handle that class of work. Whoever pressed out those early 363s did not make a very good job of it and our section was left with the task of altering these pressings to get some sort of fit. Not an easy task and probably expensive as well.'[12]

The Spitfire's most celebrated feature, the elliptical wing, was also its most troublesome to produce. The key component of the wing was its curved leading edge, which comprised a D-shaped torsion box attached to the main spar. It was a brilliant design, giving the wing its strength, lightness and excellent aerodynamic qualities. But it was complicated to make, again beyond the capability of Supermarine. The alloy skins of the leading edge were shaped and fused by the Pressed Steel Company in a process requiring a high degree of accuracy, as Supermarine worker Bert Axell recalled:

> I remember visiting the Pressed Steel Company to witness the operation on their stretch presses of the formation of the top and bottom skins. The sheets, fifteen feet by five feet, were placed on the apparatus. Various automatic things moved in and pulled and shoved in various directions. The die tools rose and fell and within minutes an accurately formed leading edge section was rolled off. Quite incredible. I remember asking the boss man if it would be possible to produce the leading edge in one piece. 'No problem at all' was his answer – except for the basic width of the steel which at the time was beyond rolling mill capacity.[13]

Equally intricate were the two booms of the main spar. These consisted of a series of concentric square tubes which were tightly telescoped inside one another. The number of these tubes decreased along the length of the wing towards its outer end, with the innermost and longest tube stretching the entire span from root to tip. To form the main spar itself, these two booms were then attached to a metal plate, which was stiffened by vertical channels. It was another feat of precision engineering, this time carried out by Reynolds Tubes, and it was vital to the structural strength of the wing. But again its production was far removed from that of the biplane wings which were still being built. And the dimensions of the Spitfire did not help with output, according to Denis Webb: 'Our main problem was the smallness of the Spitfire and the large amount that had to be built into it as well as the electrical wiring and hydraulic, fuel and other pipework. With a large flying boat you could have forty or more men working on it without getting in each other's way, but on the Spitfire there would be a crowd.'[14]

The complications of the plane were increased by the frequent modifications which arose after the first flight of the prototype. These included a new oil-cooler and gun mountings, the installation of a reflector gunsight, wireless and a more advanced Merlin engine; and the thickening of the gauge on the alloy sheets for the leading edge. At one stage Air Commodore Verney, the Director of Technical Development, even suggested that the petrol tanks be moved from the fuselage to the wings in order to provide greater safety for the pilot from burns. Such a proposal showed no appreciation of the thinness of the Spitfire's wings; nor would it have been feasible without a total redesign of the entire aircraft.[15] The endless alterations put severe pressure on the Supermarine draughtsmen, already struggling to cope with the need to supply drawings of components to the subcontractors as well as complete other projects. Jack Davis of Supermarine felt that this workload led to severe delays: 'The task of redoing the drawings took about a year. One couldn't conveniently use prototype drawings for the production aircraft; there were so many changes. Though some of the production drawings might have looked the same as those for the prototype, it was much better to redraw and renumber the whole lot.'[16] Cyril Russell further explained that, on the prototype, 'occasionally a sketch would be sufficient information for work to be done by hand or very primitive tooling', but this could never be 'as comprehensive as production drawings for general issue would need to be'.[17]

Supermarine had to subcontract much of the manufacture not merely because of technological requirements, but also because the Woolston factory lacked the capacity and the labour. Still operating from the site that Noel Pemberton Billing had opened in 1913, Supermarine had a workforce of only

1,370 in 1936. It was short of facilities, space, equipment and staff. For all Mitchell's innovations, its prime source of income since its foundation had been small orders for flying boats. Even in 1936 the company had only two tracers in the drawing office and, according to Cyril Russell, 'a ridiculously small design team'.[18] It was, in Denis Webb's words, 'a low key set-up'.[19] To meet the demands of the biggest order in its history, Supermarine embarked on a programme of expanding its works and payroll. Nevertheless, it had to sub-contract over 70 per cent of the initial production run. By 1938, almost eighty firms were involved in the contract, including General Aircraft and Pobjoy Motors working on the wings, Folland Aircraft on the tail, Singer Motors on the engine mountings, and G. Beaton on the wing ribs. These arrangements turned out to be a recipe for chaos, with the subcontractors complaining about the late delivery of drawings and material, and Supermarine grumbling about the slow manufacture and poor quality of vital parts.

Bill Newton, one of the Supermarine design team, thought that inexperience was at the centre of this friction. 'All the engineering firms got involved in this subcontracting. One of them knew nothing about aircraft and put in 15,000 queries in 18 months. Another sub-contractor used to aircraft work put in just 57 queries in the same 18 months.'[20] A glimpse of these troubles was revealed in the dry official prose of the company's first quarterly report of 1937:

> The manufacture of a large proportion of the major components of the 310 Spitfires has been allocated to sub-contractors. In many cases the sub-contracting firms had no previous experience of aircraft work which necessitated a high standard of supervision on Supermarine's part. This, together with the difficulty in obtaining prompt supplies of material by many of the sub-contractors, had put back Spitfire deliveries by three months.[21]

Serious faults could also be found in the Spitfire management. At the top of the parent company, Vickers Aviation, was Sir Robert McLean, a cold, determined Scot. An engineer by background, he had made his name – and gained a knighthood – by reorganizing the Indian railways in the early 1920s, before joining Vickers in 1927. 'He was a pretty fearsome chap to have to deal with,' says Eric Lovell-Cooper.[22] But, for all his Caledonian ferocity within the company, McLean's greatest weakness during this period was his reluctance to be honest with the Air Ministry about Supermarine's problems. His wilfully misleading forecast had led the Ministry to believe that the first Spitfires would be coming off the production line in the autumn of 1937, and even when it became obvious that the delivery date had badly slipped he continued to make optimistic noises about an impending tidal wave of new planes that somehow never materialized. Thus in the second quarter of 1937, even as the problems worsened, his Supermarine report stated, 'Production at the works is proceeding satisfactorily. The greater number of tools and jigs are near completion. Most sub-contracts are proceeding satisfactorily and no outstanding difficulties have yet arisen likely to make impossible the realization of the production programme.'[23] This was an absurd gloss to put on the situation. If he deserves some of the credit for the birth of the Spitfire under Mitchell, he also deserves censure for provoking such a mood of disillusion at the Air Ministry towards the Spitfire programme that it was almost abandoned before the war started.

The death of Mitchell cannot be directly blamed for the troubles over production, for he was always a designer rather than a manager, and indeed by late 1936 he was more interested in the development of the B12/36 bomber than in the Spitfire. He was briefly succeeded as head of design by Major Harold Payn, a former First World War fighter pilot, who had been brought in by McLean to assist Mitchell after the Vickers takeover. But, in a pre-war climate of heightened sensitivity over espionage, 'Agony' Payn, as he was known at Supermarine, did not last long. A divorcee, Payn was refused security clearance for his new job by the Air Ministry, on the ground that his second marriage was to a foreigner. Having been kicked out of Supermarine, he then struggled to find work. His place was taken by Joe Smith, Mitchell's balding, benevolent chief draughtsman, who was to preside over the Spitfire programme for the next decade.

A former apprentice with Austin cars, Smith had nothing like Mitchell's originality, and the only plane he designed from scratch, the Swift jet, was a failure. But he was a solid, reassuring figure, hugely respected by his workforce, and, more than anyone else in British aviation, he saw the potential of the Spitfire for almost unlimited redevelopment. 'We never regarded him in the same league as Mitchell as a designer,' wrote Harry Griffiths, a Supermarine engineer, 'but Mitchell would have been a difficult act for anyone to follow. Joe was perhaps more accessible and drew on the experience and advice of his staff in great measure.'[24] Jeffrey Quill, who worked closely with him throughout the war, described Smith as 'a thoroughly practical engineer of great determination and tenacity, with a strong personality and an ability to impose his authority'.[25] Like Mitchell, he was a modest man with a liking for practical jokes. Beside his desk he had a papier-mâché replica of a Spitfire drop tank, which looked as heavy as the real thing even though it weighed only a few ounces. When any unsuspecting visitors turned up in his office, he would pick up this object with a great show of effort, and then hurl it at them with the word 'Catch!', revelling in their looks of terror. He could also laugh at himself. Once, at a Supermarine dinner, a nervous tongue-tied worker in his post-prandial speech meant to refer to him as 'the Master', but ended up saying 'the Bastard'. Smith was the one who laughed the loudest.

The most significant executive figure at Supermarine during the initial period of production was the Woolston works manager, Trevor Westbrook, a human volcano who would later find a place for his explosive personality in Lord Beaverbrook's unconventional wartime regime at the Ministry of Aircraft Production. Westbrook had arrived at Woolston with the Vickers takeover in 1928, and by the mid-1930s he had the responsibility for preparing the company for its daunting job on the Spitfire. If boiling energy alone could have transformed an organization, then Westbrook would have been Britain's finest manager then, but in reality his youthful ferocity could sometimes be counterproductive. Furthermore, the complexity of the task required more than fiery exhortation. One of the recurrent themes of the Spitfire saga is the bad-tempered nature of many of its key players, including Mitchell, Swinton and Beaverbrook, and pilots like Bob Stanford-Tuck – a reflection of their desperate urge to see that Britain was equipped for war. But Westbrook exceeded them all. 'He always managed a scowl and a few barks when anyone else was present,' recorded Denis Webb, who worked as his assistant manager from 1935. 'An extraordinary character, he seemed to be almost terrified of appearing human.'[26] Cyril Russell gave this insight into his personality: 'He was a bachelor, lived in the Botleigh Grange Hotel, played rugby and flew his own small aircraft. He had strong, rugged features and an athletic body. Add to this his open sports car and his position, it was no wonder that many a female heart fluttered in his presence.'[27]

Westbrook was only in his late twenties when he went to work at Supermarine, and some detected immaturity behind his bullishness. 'Many of his decisions were far too hasty. He undoubtedly had drive and initiative but would have been better working under someone older,' wrote Denis Webb, who claimed that Mitchell himself became 'rather browned off with his childish ways'. One example occurred during an expansion of the works, when Mitchell was fed up with the continuous racket from pneumatic drills outside his office. He phoned up Westbrook, asking that the building work be done during the night shift. Westbrook refused. 'Right, I'm going home,' said Mitchell, 'and I won't return till the job is finished. If Sir Robert wants to know where I am, you can tell him.'[28] Westbrook instantly capitulated. Roger Dixon, a Supermarine technician, known as 'Deafy' because of his hearing problem, also saw his combustible impatience at work during the preparations for the last Schneider contest. 'He tried to speed up two fitters who were gently easing on the propeller boss of the first S6B. In the end, he grabbed the big wrench and gave it a big pull and the thread seized. The whole front of the Rolls-Royce engine had to come off and be sent back to Derby.'[29] According to Dixon, Westbrook cruelly sacked one employee for the simple offence of having a glass eye.

But such methods were far from proving successful. By early 1934, wrote Webb, the commercial manager A. E. Marsh-Hunn was 'frothing at the mouth in sheer frustration' at the lack of progress on all fronts, including the prototype. 'Trevor Westbrook seemed to think that running around like a demented cat and expecting others to do likewise got things done quicker. In fact it resulted in things taking longer. In his early days we all hated his guts.' But Webb, having taken up his post in Westbrook's office, began to under-stand the reasons for his boss's near permanent apoplexy. The Woolston works had no proper recording systems. Parts were just dumped in the nearest bin. An air of chaos hung over the place. 'What the situation would be like when we had the Spitfire in production with about ten thousand individual parts just didn't bear thinking about.' Westbrook, aided by Webb, set about a wholesale reorganization, doing all this while the works were being rebuilt and massively extended. 'The place reminded me of Dante's inferno except that in winter it was bloody cold with at times no roof and at other times no walls.'[30] But the need to modernize frequently led to bitter clashes with the Supermarine board over funding for new equipment and buildings. Westbrook even bought one machine tool with his own money, eventually recouping the sum from his expense account. The restrictions on workspace were also an inhibiting factor. At one point, before work began on a new factory by the river Itchen, Westbrook considered moving the whole operation to Oxford.

He was still struggling to implement this reorganization when, in early 1937, he was promoted by Vickers to take over its Weybridge factory, which was engaged in the troubled Wellington bomber project. He left a legacy of improved facilities for Spitfire production, particularly at the Itchen works. Yet the programme was still hopelessly behind schedule. His place as Supermarine manager was taken by the far less intimidating, less forceful H. B. Pratt, a highly strung individual who had worked for Vickers on airships and was later, in 1940, to commit suicide, overwhelmed by his responsibilities. On his arrival, Pratt could do little to turn around the deepening crisis over the Spitfire, which was now alarming the Air Ministry. As Jeffrey Quill put it, 'The early history of Spitfire production was traumatic.'[31] At Swinton's progress meetings throughout 1937, complaints about Supermarine grew ever more embittered. In February it was reported that Sir Robert McLean had been urged to break the logjam in output by using more subcontractors. But, to the outrage of the Air Ministry, he had refused such an idea, and instead had suggested that Supermarine divert resources from the production of the

Walrus flying boat. Sir Cyril Newall said that the proposal was 'totally unacceptable. What Sir Robert was obviously trying to do was to keep the whole of Spitfire production under his own control. He had, for instance, said that it would be impossible to get fuselages made outside without a great deal of confusion and difficulty.' Swinton described this as 'a disgraceful state of affairs', and warned that, if it carried on, he would summon the entire Vickers board in front of the Air Council. His adviser Weir agreed, and felt Supermarine should be 'compelled' to make more use of subcontractors.[32]

That month, the deepening shambles over the Spitfire prompted the government to demand that Vickers restructure its aircraft division, with the result that McLean's Vickers Aviation company lost its semi-independent status and had its operations taken over by Vickers-Armstrong, headed by the former naval officer and baronet Commander Sir Charles Craven, who hid his toughness beneath a coating of charm. Weir confirmed the move to Swinton. 'Sir Charles Craven has just left me. I explained to him that the magnitude of the work we had entrusted to Vickers was so great and the results up to now so unsatisfactory that we had come to the conclusion that the management must be improved and strengthened. He agreed with me.'[33] With his easy social grace, Craven was a much more co-operative figure for the Air Ministry to deal with than the hostile McLean. But McLean was not forced out completely. While Craven took over as chairman, he was given the job of managing director of Vickers Aviation as well as a seat on the board of Vickers-Armstrong. The arrangement did not work out, and within a year McLean had left to become chairman of the music and entertainment group Electrical and Musical Industries, better known as EMI – a somewhat incongruous post for such a dour Scot.

The Air Ministry recognized that Vickers' corporate reshuffle could not work an instant miracle with the Spitfire: 'Sir Charles Craven must be given time,' said Newall in March 1937.[34] But, with German militarization gaining pace, time was precisely what the Air Ministry did not have. Within a month, Newall was again expressing his anger at the latest figures from Supermarine, which predicted that only 4 Spitfires would be delivered in December 1937, and 14 in the whole of the first quarter of 1938. This forecast, said Newall, 'clearly demonstrated how fantastic was the programme of estimated deliveries previously given by the firm'. In addition, McLean had written to the Air Ministry warning that even this paltry level of output could not be met without improvements in the supply of labour and raw material, and greater efficiency from subcontractors. Newall saw this as another attempt by Supermarine to evade responsibility. 'It was incumbent on the management to exercise effective control and see that things did not go wrong.'[35]

The eagerness to blame subcontractors intensified the disenchantment of the Air Ministry:

A meeting of these sub-contractors had recently been held by the Air Ministry in order that these allegations made by Supermarine that all the sub-contractors were behindhand could be investigated. The result of the meeting had been to establish beyond any possibility of doubt that in the case of General Aircraft and Beaton and Sons, the allegation was entirely without foundation, except in regard to the delivery of raw material, for the ordering of which Supermarine were themselves responsible.[36]

By June it had emerged that the first Spitfire would not even be delivered by the promised date of December, and by the early autumn delivery had retreated still further, to February 1938. Swinton's impatience was almost palpable: 'The firm themselves admitted that the Spitfire deliveries were incapable of achievement,' he said in September 1937. 'If the position was as stated, the situation in the fighter squadrons early in 1938 would be extremely serious, as they would have practically no up-to-date aircraft.'[37]

At the end of 1937, just six Spitfire fuselages had been completed and were awaiting the delivery of wings from the subcontractors, led by General Aircraft. The Vickers Aviation board was told that the delays with the wings were 'primarily due to the sub-contractors' inexperience of this kind of work', which meant the 'first aircraft would not be delivered until the end of March 1938'.[38] McLean explained to Sir Charles Craven in November 1937 that the workmanship of the outside firms had been shoddy:

There has been great disappointment over Spitfire progress during the last month. It was planned that General Aircraft and Pobjoy would receive from us complete spares and leading edges and would, on those, erect the trailing edge ribs manufactured by Westland and Beaton and then complete the wing by riveting and sheeting. Unfortunately the ribs supplied by both these subcontractors have proved defective and have had to be rectified before the work can proceed. It is difficult at the moment to say what additional delay will be caused by this contretemps.[39]

Again the Air Ministry refused to tolerate this scapegoating. 'The main source of the trouble', Swinton was told in January 1938, 'appeared to be the failure of the parent firm to supply accurate drawing to the various sub-contracting firms.' Sir Wilfrid Freeman added that he too had heard 'bitter complaints from the sub-contractors about the poor quality of the drawings they had received from Supermarine.'[40] The Air Ministry was equally aggrieved that, after all these delays, Supermarine were now quoting a price of £7,000 per aircraft for the whole of the contract – far in excess of what was expected. It was pointed out that the Hurricane was being built for just £4,000 per plane. On 12 February 1938, Swinton learned that there was still no sign of a production Spitfire ready to fly. A Ministry official had been to the Supermarine works, whose labour force had now grown to 2,200 employees, but 'had seen only one Spitfire in the course of erection'.[41] A few days later Swinton had to report to the government's key armed-services body, the Committee of Imperial Defence, that the 'production position of the Spitfire was unsatisfactory and there had been serious delays'. But, sensing that he would be the target of criticism from his political colleagues, Swinton tried to absolve his department of blame. 'He would like the Committee to note that the Air Ministry had made exceptionally few modifications and that Vickers had been given a free hand.'[42]

The Spitfire's problems may have been damaging for the Air Ministry, but they were hardly unique. Throughout this period, the aircraft industry was desperately trying to cope with the twin demands of supplying the RAF's expansion programme and introducing new technology, but its structure was ill-suited to these two objectives. It was an anomalous industry, neither nationalized nor based on the free market. Around 90 per cent of its work depended on government contracts, and Air Ministry officials were closely involved with every major company. Ostensibly the firms were in competition with each other in bidding for work, but in practice the government tried to keep them all viable by parcelling out its projects. The Air Ministry often spoke of its 'family' of aircraft companies, reinforcing this image of responsibility. Yet, because the fig leaf of competition had to be maintained, the government liked to pretend that it might place orders overseas if British designs or production were not up to scratch – as when a Polish fighter was briefly considered as an alternative to the woeful Type 224.

The outrage provoked in the industry by any suggestion of foreign purchases only demonstrated how utterly reliant the aircraft companies were on the state. And this culture of dependency had the negative effect of encouraging a spirit of conservatism. The cosy contracting arrangements bred a safety-first attitude, devoid of real enterprise or ambition. Mitchell himself had been guilty of this lack of daring when he first began work on his fighter. It was telling that when he had been in genuine competition with overseas rivals, in the Schneider Trophy, he had been far less inhibited about taking risks. Lord Weir pointed out that, unlike in most other industries, the government itself was the driving force behind change, particularly through its selection of prototypes and aeronautical research. Moreover, the instinct to spread projects around the industry militated against preparations for mass production, since no one firm gained experience in delivering a major contract or training a large workforce. Economic experts argued that the resulting shortages in skilled labour were the central cause of the industry's failure to deliver on its contracts.

For all its criticisms of industry, however, the Air Ministry was itself guilty of promoting wastefulness, through its bureaucratic methods and its lack of clear direction. The push for innovation and rearmament meant that officials could lose their focus, swamping companies with demands for new projects and new types: in October 1936 there were no fewer than 55 experimental designs in progress. The Ministry's civil servants also had the traditional Whitehall fault of regarding a new committee as the solution to every problem. 'I have for some time been gravely concerned with the vast numbers of com-mittees, sub-committees, and conferences which have to be attended by members of my department,' wrote Sir Wilfrid Freeman in March 1937. In one extreme case, one of his officers was a member of thirteen different commit-tees and had attended thirty-seven conferences in the previous four months.[43] All these meetings, Freeman argued, left little time to implement decisions.

Some felt the way to cut bureaucracy and industrial inefficiency was to establish a much stronger, more rigorous form of state control, an idea made attractive by the astonishing results apparently being achieved by the Nazi regime. After visiting Germany in 1937, Roy Fedden of the Bristol Company wanted a virtual dictatorship by the Air Ministry, governing every aspect of production, to 'cut out for once and for all the soul-destroying procrastination and pin-pricking delays with which the whole organization is at present hidehound'.[44] But both sides – the Air Ministry and industry – shied away from such a drastic step. Co-operation, not con-trol, was the theory. In the absence of a dictator, Lord Swinton had to suffice as the national leader. But his problem was that he had responsibil-ity without real power. When it came to aircraft deliveries, he could encourage but not demand, exhort but not decree. As the Spitfire crisis worsened at the beginning of 1938, his political credibility began to fade, his decline made all the worse because of the fanfare which had greeted the prototype in the summer of 1936. The mutterings against him were heard not just in Cabinet but in Parliament as well, where the Labour Opposition was starting to ask questions about the delay in the Spitfire programme.

To Swinton's supporters, these mounting criticisms were cruelly unjust, for no politician had been more energetic in pressing for the Spitfire. In 1935, he had seen its potential far earlier than any of his colleagues – certainly earlier than the incumbent Air Secretary, Lord Londonderry. In 1936 he had given Supermarine a large contract only days after the plane had flown at

Martlesham, just as he had bravely ordered the Merlin before it had completed its official tests. In doing so, he realized he was taking a risk, as he wrote later: 'We felt that existing aeroplanes, which could have been built in quantity, would prove death traps. We knew we should have countless difficulties and setbacks, but we firmly took the decision. If we had not done so we would have lost the Battle of Britain.'[45] Executive decision-making had long been at the centre of Swinton's political career – one reason why he was so admired by Weir and Freeman, who both despised the normal run of politicians. The son of a Yorkshire landowner, he had been born in 1884 and qualified as a barrister before entering politics, where he enjoyed a strong ministerial record if not public recognition. Aggressive, hard-working, sometimes intolerant, he was described by Sir Stephen Luke, his private secretary at the Colonial Office, where Swinton was Secretary of State in the early 1930s, as 'the most dynamic minister I served in thirty years in the public service, exuding energy and vitality combined with great personal charm (when he chose to exercise it)'.[46] The contemporary journalist Harold Begbie once wrote that 'like all true experts he is an enthusiast. His mind seems to rejoice in the smoothness and decision with which it works, in the unerring deductions it makes from the facts it has so thoroughly accumulated.' Of Swinton's appearance, he said, 'He is tall and powerful, but with a slight stoop of head and shoulders. He is boyish-looking, but prematurely bald over the forehead. His clean-cut and well-bronzed face is chiefly noticeable from a structural point of view for a jowl which a prize-fighter would regard as a stroke of genius.'[47]

Yet by March 1938 Swinton's brusque urgency had not brought a single Spitfire out of the Supermarine factory. Across the government, the absence from the RAF's front line of its much vaunted new fighter was felt all the more keenly because of the emphasis on rearmament and home defence. The year 1934 had marked a turning point in air policy, when ministers, led by Chamberlain, had finally woken up to the threat of Germany and the scandalous neglect of the RAF. But Scheme A, providing for a Metropolitan Force of 1,252 aircraft by 1939, had made little progress towards implementation because of the problems of the industry. In the four years that followed, the government had drawn up an increasingly desperate series of expansion schemes aimed at strengthening the RAF and deterring Germany. With each new announcement, however, the list of schemes lengthened into a grim alphabet of failure. By February 1936 the letter F had been reached, calling for 1,736 aircraft in 124 front-line squadrons. This was meant to lead to some form of air parity with Germany, but the scale of Nazi militarization made the plan look pitifully inadequate. On 7 March, just two days after the Spitfire prototype had first flown, Hitler had signalled his sinister intentions by sending in his troops to reoccupy the Rhineland, the zone along the border with France demilitarized by the Treaty of Versailles. The advent of the Spanish Civil War, in which the Luftwaffe saw highly effective action against the Republican forces, reinforced the need for rapid modernization of the RAF.

In 1937 Air Commodore Douglas Evill of the Air Staff visited Germany and saw for himself the growing might of the Luftwaffe. 'The main impression was one of a regime determined at all costs to have a large air force of the highest efficiency and allowing no considerations other than that of military requirements to influence their preparations,' Evill wrote in his report. One sign of that drive for efficiency was the new Messerschmitt 109 fighter, 'which is of high performance and very similar in appearance to the Spitfire'. Evill concluded, 'Progress towards air strength is rapid. We have a great deal to learn.'[48] Schemes G and H were put forward in a forlorn attempt to catch up, swallowing ever larger sums of public money. In March 1938, Weir rightly complained of 'the intolerable load placed on democratic countries by what is, in truth, definite aggression through the incidence of the German cult of super-efficiency in armament strength and the planning and widespread sacrifice imposed on the nation by all this'.[49]

If Britain were to remain a great international power, its government had no choice but to continue with air-force expansion. But, beyond mere numbers and level of expenditure, an argument still raged over the nature of that expansion. The Trenchard doctrine had not yet expired within the Air Staff. The new Chief was Sir Cyril Newall, who succeeded Ellington in 1937 and was described by one colleague as 'sound, level-headed and decisive'.[50] For all his greater competence, however, he continued to adhere to the RAF's traditional attachment to the bomber offensive – as to some extent did Swinton, who was always better on detail than on strategy. The opposing position was held by Neville Chamberlain, Prime Minister from May 1937, who had long believed that home defence was the primary duty of the air force.

During his political battle for the fighter against the bomber, Chamberlain had a key ally in the well-fed form of the Minister for Defence Co-ordination, Sir Thomas Inskip. The appointment of Inskip to this post in March 1936 had been greeted with widespread astonishment. A rotund lawyer, he had no previous experience of military issues. Until his elevation, his only notable public achievement had been his successful campaign to defend the Anglican prayer book from reform. Baldwin had deliberately chosen such an apparently colourless, second-rate figure in order to keep out Winston Churchill, whom he feared would create mayhem in his Cabinet and stir up feeling against Germany. Churchill's scientific adviser, Professor Frederick Lindemann, outraged on his behalf, called Inskip's promotion 'the most cynical thing that has been done since Caligula appointed his horse a consul'.[51] But Inskip proved far more influential than his critics could have imagined, his sharp legal mind slicing through the pieties of the bomber creed.

All too predictably, expansion schemes G and H soon proved insufficient in the face of German military growth. According to Sir John Slessor, the Air Staff's Director of Plans, the RAF in 1937 was 'at present totally unfitted for war'.[52] So the Air Staff came up with Scheme J. But this again gave a far higher priority to offence, envisaging a bomber force of some 90 squadrons, of which 64 would be heavy bombers. Inskip thought such an approach was misguided. In December 1937 he set out his views in an aide-memoire to Swinton. 'I cannot persuade myself that the dictum of the Chief of the Air Staff that we must give the enemy as much as he gives us is a sound principle,' he wrote. 'The *role* of our Air Force is not an early knock-out blow – no one has suggested that we can accomplish that – but to prevent the Germans from knocking us out.' The logical deduction, he claimed, was that to meet Britain's real requirements 'we do not need to possess anything like the same number of long-range heavy bombers as the Germans.' The first battles of Britain's air war, he believed, would take place not over the Rhine or the Ruhr but over the south of England, and the RAF's aim would be 'to knock out as many German aeroplanes as we can'. Once Britain had survived the first onslaught, it could go on the attack. But the nation had to be prepared for a long war.[53] The Air Staff were appalled at such arguments. 'The essential point is that an effective bomber force is a vital component in a successful defensive system,' wrote Newall to Swinton. In a poor misjudgement of what would happen in the Battle of Britain, Newall continued, 'It is doubtful whether any number of fighters we could provide could impose a rate of wastage upon the enemy which he could not make good in the absence of effective counter-action against his air force and their sources of supply.'[54] But Inskip had the weight of the Cabinet behind him. The primacy of the fighter was agreed. The Air Staff were ordered to come up with a less bomber-oriented plan, to be known as Scheme K.

The debate over air expansion preoccupied the Cabinet throughout the first months of 1938. With Germany seizing Austria in March and making aggressive noises against Czechoslovakia, there was now an imperative for urgent growth. Scheme K gave way to Scheme L, an even more ambitious programme which provided for the Air Ministry to accept as many aircraft as it could obtain over the next two years, up to a maximum of 12,000, with a front-line metropolitan strength of 2,400. As part of this expansion, the Spitfire contract with Supermarine was increased from 310 to 510 planes, despite the firm's chronic lateness with deliveries. In addition, the Fairey

Aviation company, which had built the Battle light bomber, was told that it would be required to manufacture 300 Spitfires at its Stockport factory in the near future. Richard Fairey assured the Ministry that he had the capability to fulfil such an order.

Much to the concern of the Chancellor, Sir John Simon, traditional prudence had now been all but abandoned in this deluge of expansion plans. 'Recent events in Europe, serious as they are, have done nothing to increase the financial resources of the country,' he complained.[55] But the War Secretary, Leslie Hore-Belisha, in a powerful speech to the Cabinet on 14 March, told his colleagues that the time for restraint was over: the government had to accept that 'we are now entering war.' Referring to the *Anschluss*, Hore-Belisha

> asked the Cabinet to realize that within half an hour three hundred German aeroplanes had arrived in Austria bringing with them the equivalent of three pre-war battalions of infantry with full equipment. We are up against new methods and a man who had gone a long way in the development of German armament. There would be a grave risk if our only reply to Germany's real effort was dilatory expansion. Our own air defence was terribly behind-hand. The Cabinet had been examining the question over months, but examination did not produce war material.[56]

In this climate of expansion, stretching the aircraft industry to the limit, the Air Staff remained aggrieved at the downgrading of bombers. Scheme L, wrote Newall, should provide 'a striking force of at least equal strength *at any given time* to that of Germany'.[57] But, much to his anger, the Inskip doctrine prevailed. Indeed, when Lord Halifax, the Foreign Secretary, asked in Cabinet at the end of April 'whether better value could not be obtained by providing more fighters and fewer bombers', he was assured by Swinton that 'the fighter programme would occupy the whole of the capacity of the industry available for that purpose.'[58] Newall subsequently wrote to Swinton to complain that the balance of the RAF between fighter and bomber strengths would now be badly skewed. 'By reducing our counter-offensive we shall inevitably put a greater strain on our fighters.'[59]

In a sense, Newall was right. The Inskip doctrine was based on a tremendous gamble: that, when war arrived, the RAF would have a fighter that could really challenge the Luftwaffe. In early 1938, as the Cabinet debated the expansion schemes, there was little sign of it. The Hawker Hurricane, it is true, had started to arrive in the front-line squadrons, but it had never been regarded as the equal of the Spitfire. And the February date that Supermarine had promised for the first delivery now slipped again. Yet again Swinton was forced to state at one of his progress meetings that 'he was afraid we were going to have serious trouble over this contract, which was one of the few matters in the aircraft programme on which we were likely to be open to serious criticism and he felt that no stone should be left unturned to improve the position.'[60] Swinton then met Sir Charles Craven to see if there was anything to be done. Craven was a mixture of reassurance and blame-passing. According to Swinton's account, Sir Charles

> agreed that the present position on the Spitfire contract was far from satisfactory and that the sub-contracting arrangements had been badly managed. He was doing his best to improve matters in this respect. He mentioned as a contributory cause the fact that the firm's main sub-contractors, General Aircraft and Pobjoy, were some distance from the Supermarine factory and this had thrown a considerable strain on the latter's drawing office which was not large.

But Sir Charles promised that he was 'paying particular attention to the Spitfire question at present', and claimed that Supermarine would soon be turning out twenty Spitfires a month.[61]

This was another example of exaggeration by Supermarine. But at least there was a hint of some movement forward. At the end of March, the company reported that thirty-five fuselages had been completed and sent to a larger hangar at the Eastleigh aerodrome, where the final assembly was carried out, but only four complete sets of wings had been received from the sub-contractors. 'The complete erection of these four aircraft is now in hand,' said Supermarine. The firm also revealed that it planned to supplement the output of the subcontractors by building some of the wings itself.[62]

But this news looked too late for Swinton. The pressure on him was now intense. The Air Ministry order for an extra 200 Spitfires only emphasized the current absence of the plane. A major debate in Parliament was looming in May as discontent over Britain's military weakness crystallized around delays in the air programme. Chamberlain had tried to lessen the anger by appointing the Sussex MP and Cabinet member Lord Winterton, the Chancellor of the Duchy of Lancaster, as spokesman for air policy in the Commons, thereby making the Air Ministry more accountable to MPs, but this was a political stratagem that did nothing for the Spitfire crisis. 'The real trouble', Freeman told Swinton at the beginning of April, 'appeared to lie in the chaotic state of the firm's sub-contracting arrangements. For example, there were 60 to 70 tailplanes lying at Shorts' works awaiting details and in several instances when the necessary parts had been received from the parent firm they would not fit.' Swinton now gave vent to his bitterness against Vickers: 'We had fallen in with Sir Charles Craven's desire that we should not interfere while he was investigating the position but time had elapsed and the situation had not improved. He [Swinton] felt that we could not let it go on any longer and that we must now step in and carry out an examination since we must have the aircraft.'[63]

Swinton had no time to carry out such an examination. A parliamentary row over the air estimates brought the crisis to a head, as two groups united to harry the government. One was the circle around Winston Churchill, deeply worried about the German menace and the inadequacy of Britain's response. The other was the Labour-led Opposition, which in 1934 had strongly opposed rearmament but had now taken up the cause. Political opportunism played its part in this change, but there is no doubt that Labour leader Clement Attlee, a distinguished soldier in the First World War, had genuine anxieties about planning for an air war. In January 1938 he had privately sent Chamberlain a list of fifty-six detailed questions about the Air Ministry's preparations, reflecting concerns about lack of innovation, limited productive capacity, and the failure to equip squadrons for immediate action.[64] On 12 May 1938 Labour opened the air-estimates debate, with Sir Hugh Seeley, the MP for Berwick, launching a fusillade against Winterton over the shortages of new types. After complaining about insufficient deliveries of the Hurricane, he continued, 'Take another machine about which I have asked questions: the Spitfire, which is supposed to be the more modern. Here again, we expected something. In March 1936 we asked, "Is it going into production?" We have been put off. What are the facts? Can the right honourable gentleman deny that there is only one machine, that is all?' In a feeble reply, Winterton, one of the most lightweight members of the Cabinet, tried to stonewall. 'I am not going to be led into particular figures,' he cried.

Winterton's embarrassing performance, in contrast to the mournful grandeur of Churchill's contribution during the debate, only further whipped up the storm. Chamberlain decided he had to act. He demanded the resignations of both Winterton and Swinton. It was a stroke of political realism, if not justice. Winterton accepted that he had to go, as he explained to Chamberlain's widow, Anne, after the war. 'I made a bad speech – or at least one that did not "come off" – when defending Swinton, the Air Ministry and Neville's administration,' he wrote.[65] But Swinton was bitter at the way he had been treated. He later complained, in one of his autobiographies, that Chamberlain had never given him 'active support' at the Air Ministry,[66] and in his letter of resignation he struck a melancholy note. 'What has hurt me most was saying goodbye to men who have not only been so loyal but who loved working with me. It is that, not outside criticism or attack, that really hurts.'[67] Lady Swinton, fiercely ambitious for her husband, felt his departure even more keenly. She collapsed in front of Anne Chamberlain, and felt compelled to write a letter of apology to the Prime Minister about the incident. 'The mental shock has jangled me badly,' she explained.[68] Within the Air Ministry, there was outrage. Lord Weir resigned as adviser immediately, while Freeman expressed his disgust: 'There can be few if any in the RAF who do not realize what a lot you have done for the service,' he told Swinton.[69] Churchill, who had played an indirect part in Swinton's downfall, put the issue in perspective nine months later: 'The press are such lackeys and do not seem at all to understand that up to the present whatever aeroplanes there are are due to you . . . If only you had been in the House of Commons, you could, I am sure, have fought your way through.'[70]

Swinton had paid the price largely because of Supermarine's failure to deliver. But his role in starting the Spitfire programme deserved more recognition than it received. His place at the helm of the Air Ministry was taken by the bespectacled lawyer and Methodist Sir Kingsley Wood. A confidant of Chamberlain's, he had served as Postmaster General and Tory party chairman. He was a competent administrator, but knew nothing about aircraft, lacked any charisma, and was a poor public performer. 'How silly the whole thing is. Here we are in the gravest crisis in our history, with a genius like Winston doing nothing and Kingsley Wood our Minister for Air,' wrote the National Labour MP Harold Nicolson in his diary.[71]

Ironically, the first production plane took to the air for flight trials on 14 May 1938, the very day of Swinton's resignation. Registered as K9787, it was flown by Jeffrey Quill. The plane performed largely as he expected. The only point he noticed was that in a high-speed dive, at over 450 mph, the ailerons became almost immovably heavy. At the time he did not think this was a serious problem, though later, after the experiences of combat, he came to regret not having done more about it, as he explained:

When we flew the first production Spitfire and dived it to 470 mph and found the ailerons so heavy, this was considered at the time to be quite a good thing. The technical people were rather afraid of things like aileron reversal and felt that if the ailerons became rock solid at very high speeds so much the better – it would stop the young buggers throwing the fighter around too much and perhaps pulling the wings off. With many others, I felt that in a war most combats – whether against bombers or fighters – would take place well below 400 mph and there the situation would be manageable, even if it was sometimes hard work. We knew there was a problem, but before the war nobody complained – the Spitfire had not yet been in a dogfight. Perhaps I should have shouted louder at the time. But I did not appreciate – and neither did anyone else at the time – that this might become a serious tactical limitation.[72]

Quill was hoping, with the appearance of K9787, that this would be the start of a regular flow of production Spitfires which needed to be tested. In fact he had to wait another two months before the second one appeared.

The resignation of Swinton had made little difference. The problems at Supermarine remained as bad as ever, despite assurances from the company that scores of fuselages had now been built. In Parliament another row erupted over the Spitfire, when Labour, in a debate on 25 May, called for an inquiry into Britain's air defences. 'Let me say a few words about fighters,' said Hugh Dalton, opening for Labour. 'We are informed that neither the Supermarine Spitfire nor the Hawker Hurricane have been delivered in any quantities. The Spitfire was shown three years ago at the Air Force display and an order for hundreds of them was given in 1936 but none has been delivered. An order for hundreds in 1936 and none delivered in 1938.' The debate had such significance that Chamberlain himself replied for the government. His defence was not entirely convincing. 'The Spitfire is the fastest fighter in service squadrons anywhere in the world. It is shortly coming into service.' This was too much for the Liberal leader Sir Archibald Sinclair, later to be Churchill's Air Minister for most of the war:

> The Prime Minister says that the Spitfire is the fastest fighter in the service of any country in the world. But it is not in the service of any country in the world. That is one of our complaints. In the face of these repeatedly falsified assurances of the Government – given, of course, in good faith – but assurances which they have failed to fulfil, can we doubt that it is our duty to our constituents to insist upon an inquiry, searching impartially into the causes of failure?

The demand for an inquiry was rejected, but the crisis lingered.

Sir Kingsley Wood, who had sharper political antennae than Swinton, thought that he might have the solution. During Swinton's time at the Air Ministry, the government, in its desperation to increase the aircraft industry's capacity for mass production, had built a number of so-called 'shadow' factories which mirrored the operations of their parent firms. Rolls-Royce, for instance, had opened a shadow factory in Crewe to help build the Merlin. Several other major manufacturers outside aircraft engineering had joined the shadow scheme: Austin the car-maker had a large contract for the Fairey Battle light bomber. Yet Britain's most famous mass-producer, Lord Nuffield of the Morris Corporation, had refused to participate. Two years earlier he had considered manufacturing aero engines, but he had fallen out badly with Swinton and had withdrawn his offer. Though Swinton's abruptness played its part, Nuffield's touchy, autocratic personality was largely to blame for the rupture. He argued over finance and the types of engine he should manufacture, then complained to the press that Swinton had treated him with insufficient respect. 'What an infernal nuisance these Captains of Industry are. They are temperamental almost to the extent of being female,' said Newall to Swinton.[73] Despite this, the Air Ministry never entirely gave up hope of luring Nuffield into its embrace. Morris was, after all, one of Britain's biggest industrial enterprises. In August 1937 Newall wrote to Swinton suggesting that a new approach be made. 'I appreciate the difficulties with regard to past history but I imagine we can surmount our own feelings in the matter and the public interest . . . I can't help feeling that the Nuffield organization is *too big* to be outside our fold in these dangerous days.'[74] There was, however, to be no rapprochement.

Swinton's departure revitalized the chances of a shadow scheme. One of Wood's first actions, on 19 May 1938, was to hold a meeting with Nuffield. The Air Secretary put forward a new plan, far bolder and more sweeping than anything discussed in the past. With little consultation, he proposed that Nuffield should build a massive new factory, which would begin its work by manufacturing 1,000 Spitfires. This vast order – almost double the total given to Supermarine, and more than three times that pledged to Fairey – belied Wood's reputation for caution. As *The Times* put it when the news was made public two months later, this was 'the largest single order for one type of aircraft ever placed in this country'.[75] It was estimated that the factory alone, which could be built wherever Nuffield wanted, would cost £2.5 million, and the bill for the 1,000 Spitfires would probably reach £7 million. Nuffield, duly flattered by this expression of confidence in his ability to run such a huge project, agreed. He then went to see Neville Chamberlain at Downing Street to cement the deal – another indication of its importance. In their briefing notes for the Prime Minister before the meeting, the Air Ministry warned that the plan was unorthodox in its scope and in its funding. It could not strictly be described as part of the official Scheme L programme for 12,000 new aircraft by 1940, since it was unlikely that all the 1,000 Spitfires would be built within the two-year period. Nevertheless, the order could be justified on long-term grounds, since 'it has always been contended that in order to be effective as a war potential a factory must plan and carry out an initial order and must be jigged for large scale production of a given type.'[76] And there was no type more badly needed than the Spitfire.

But Sir Kingsley Wood's compact did not attract unanimous praise, not even within the Air Ministry. Freeman pointed out that, in addition to the contract Supermarine for 510 Spitfires, Fairey Aviation had provisionally been promised an order of 300 Spitfires. 'All orders for fighter aircraft had already been allocated, and Lord Nuffield could only be given an order for Spitfires if the Fairey order for this type were cancelled. If this were done, Mr Fairey would be bound to cause trouble,' he warned.[77] Sir John Simon, already worried at the relentless increases in the air estimates, was dismayed at the informal, almost casual, nature of this initiative. In a letter which turned out to be highly prescient, he told Wood:

> There are two points about your conversation or arrangement with Lord Nuffield (I hardly know which term to use) to which I should draw your attention. The Treasury has a great responsibility in this matter and I myself only heard of the Nuffield project in conversation with the Prime Minister last Friday. It has necessarily never been mentioned in Cabinet or been the subject of any discussion or correspondence between yourself and me.

Simon's first point was that allowing Nuffield a completely free hand over the site of the factory 'could lead to very serious trouble' because of problems in acquiring skilled labour. His second concern was that the proposal fell outside the expansion scheme over which the Cabinet had agonized for so long.

> The arrangement with Nuffield, as it seems to me, cannot possibly be directed towards the fulfilment of the plan authorized by the Cabinet for he first has to construct this immense factory and then equip it and staff it. I imagine that the number of Spitfires he will actually produce by March 1940 will be a small fraction of this immense additional order. It is plain therefore that the Nuffield scheme is not really a further acceleration of the plan authorized so as to increase numbers but is in substance a provision for a later date.[78]

The excitement over what seemed like the first good news on the Spitfire programme since 1936 meant that the doubts of Freeman and Sir John Simon were swept aside. In the Commons, Wood was only too keen to celebrate this apparent triumph for the Air Ministry and the Spitfire: 'Since I saw Lord Nuffield he has undertaken to produce a large number of the best machines of any air force in the world, and we are making an immediate start in relation to our plans for buildings and factory provision.'[79]

The Nuffield scheme was soon under way. Oliver Boden, vice-chairman of the Morris Corporation, took charge, and a suitable site was found at Castle Bromwich in Birmingham. Already a sense of uncontrolled extravagance was creeping into the project. Though the land, owned by the Dunlop Rubber Company, was valued at £80,000, the government ended up paying £197,000 for it because of a legal mix-up over restrictions on its use. Few at the Air Ministry quibbled. Boden promised the delivery of at least 60 Spitfires a week when the factory was built, and Nuffield pledged his full commitment to the task. 'The magnitude of the undertaking to build the necessary factories, equip and organize them for a production output of 60 fighter machines per week is fully realized by me,' he told Wood in June. 'No effort is being spared to make the ultimate issue a successful one and the free hand which you have given me will help very materially to bring about the result we both desire.'[80] The mood of mutual self-congratulation was reinforced on 15 July when Wood, accompanied by Nuffield, visited Castle Bromwich and cut the first sod in a ceremony to mark the official launch of the 135-acre site. 'The new aircraft factory will be the biggest unit of its kind in the country,' reported *The Times* eagerly the next day. 'In Lord Nuffield the country has a great master of the mass production methods and he is to have free hand in the methods he adopts for the production of aircraft.' But there was one small anticlimax at the opening ceremony. A Spitfire was meant to reach Castle Bromwich in the mid-morning, but it failed to arrive because of technical problems. That non-appearance would become a metaphor for the early, calamitous, running of the Nuffield factory.

Two days later *The Times* declared that the Castle Bromwich order for 1,000 Spitfires was all the more vital because 'the delay in the production of the Spitfire has been one of the most disappointing features in the progress of the air programme.'[81] Disappointment was turning to despair at the Air Ministry. At the beginning of July, Freeman reported on a visit to Supermarine with the Ministry's new Director General of Production, Sir Ernest Lemon, who had been hired from the railway industry to sort out the aircraft companies. 'They found that production was seriously out of balance. There were 78 fuselages and just three sets of wings. He had ordered Supermarine to make additional jigs with all possible speed and General Aircraft had also been ordered to duplicate the wings.' Lemon added that 'the position was pitiful. Material was coming to the factory very badly and men were being taken off the fuselages owing to the lack of wings.'[82] Denis Webb later revealed that one of the causes lay in the way the equipment had been set up at Supermarine. 'Wings produced in the jigs at Woolston frequently failed to marry up with the fuselages.' Detective work pinned down the reason: 'It was traced to the state of the tide when the riveting and bolting up of the structure took place. The wing jigs had been erected on reclaimed ground on the side of the river and, in spite of the workshop having been built on massive piles, nevertheless there was a minute movement of the floor between high and low tide.'[83]

Finally, at the end of July, four Spitfires were completed and sent for testing at Martlesham, though Lemon warned sternly that, until the problems with the wings were resolved, 'a steady flow of production would not begin.'[84] More than two years after the prototype had first flown, and almost seven since the issue of Specification F7/30, the first Spitfire now went into service with the RAF. On the 4 August 1938 Jeffrey Quill delivered K9789 to 19 Squadron at RAF Duxford, a unit then equipped with the Gloster Gauntlet, the predecessor of the Gladiator. Suddenly, the sight of the modern Spitfire on the Duxford grass put the long wait into perspective. All those present at the plane's arrival could sense that a new era was dawning. As Quill later put it, 'The streamlined beauty of the K9789 standing alongside the biplane Gloster Gauntlets revealed how great had been the pace of change since the RAF's very first Gauntlet had been delivered in February 1935, just three and a half years earlier.'[85]

A week after its delivery, the plane was flown by Squadron Leader Harry Cozens, who, in a later interview, gave this surprising verdict on his first experience:

After flying the Gauntlet, my first impression of the Spitfire was that her acceleration seemed rather slow and the controls were a lot heavier than I expected. Thinking about it afterwards, I realized why: the Gauntlet took off at about 70 mph and was flat out at 220 mph; the Spitfire took off at about the same speed but could do well over 350 mph – in other words the speed range was much greater, and although the acceleration was in fact greater it took somewhat longer to reach its maximum speed. Moreover, as she neared the top end of her speed range, the Spitfire's controls became beautifully light.[86]

During these early weeks of the Spitfire in service, Sir Hugh Dowding, the head of Fighter Command, came to Duxford to speak to Cozens about the plane. His main concern was whether Cozens felt that the Spitfire could take on the Me 109. After more than twenty hours flying her, Cozens was convinced that she could – and indeed any other fighter:

But that was not to say she was perfect. For one thing the engines of those first Spitfires were difficult to start; the low-geared electric starter rotated the propeller blades so slowly that when a cylinder fired there was usually insufficient push to flick the engine round to fire the next; there would be a 'puff' noise, then the propeller would resume turning on the starter. Also the early Merlin engines leaked oil terribly; it would run from the engine, down the fuselage and finally got blown away somewhere near the tailwheel. Yet another problem was what we called the 'Spitfire Knuckle'; when pumping up the undercarriage it was all too easy to rasp our knuckles on the side of the cockpit.[87]

In fact Cozens had to wear a bandage on his right hand after flying the plane, because of 'Spitfire Knuckle'.

Flying Officer Arthur Banham, who was also based at Duxford, recalled a different sort of difficulty with that first Spitfire's undercarriage on one early-morning flight:

> There was a warning horn in the Spitfire – when you throttled back, this horn would come on to warn you that your undercarriage was not down. But you could cancel that if you wanted to. I made a long gliding approach to the aerodrome from a considerable height and this noise was annoying me considerably so I switched it off. And of course, at the critical moment, I came over the fence with my undercarriage firmly up. Fortunately there was a live wire in the duty pilot's office who fired a couple of red lights at me, and I realized at once what it was and I was able to pick up my engine, go round again and come down with the undercarriage down.[88]

It is one of the compelling features of the early Spitfire story that each step in the plane's development seemed to coincide with a milestone on the slide towards war. The maiden flight of the Type 224 took place exactly at the time of the first tentative steps towards rearmament in early 1934. The Air Staff's decision to go for an eight-gun fighter occurred just weeks after Hitler had boasted of air parity with Britain in the spring of 1935. The Spitfire's first flight took place in the very week that the Rhineland was remilitarized in March 1936. And the first delivery of a Spitfire into RAF service occurred just a month before the start of the Munich Crisis, which saw Britain and France dragged to the brink of war with Germany in defence of the integrity of Czechoslovakia, only for Neville Chamberlain to negotiate a humiliating peace deal that allowed Hitler to dismember the country without resorting to force of arms.

Yet the Spitfire's link to these milestones was not entirely coincidental, for the urge to drive forward the Spitfire programme was largely a response to the aggression ratcheted up by the Nazi regime. And in September 1938 there is little doubt that the perceived inadequacy of the RAF, as exposed in the dire shortages of modern fighters, played its part in the government's reluctance to go to war. By the end of September, with Hitler's bellicosity reaching new levels of hysteria, only five Spitfires had been delivered to 19 Squadron. It has been argued, most notably by A. J. P. Taylor, that the state of Britain's air preparations was an irrelevance to Munich, since Chamberlain never intended to fight in a 'faraway country' and only used military weakness as a cover for his determination to accede to Hitler's demands. Moreover, it is now known that, in the event of war, Germany had neither the means nor the intention to launch a bomber strike – the fabled 'knock-out blow' – against Britain. But there can be no dispute that the Air Staff were aghast at the possibility of having to take on the Luftwaffe with outdated equipment, and this certainly influenced the approach of the key politicians. 'It is probably not an exaggeration to say that it is our present inability to guarantee the security of this country against attack from the air – and that alone – which may compel us to withhold our support from the Czechs and hamstring our policy in Europe,' wrote Sir John Slessor at the height of the crisis.[89]

Slessor's view had been reinforced by a private discussion he had had with the renowned American aviator Charles Lindbergh, who in the autumn of 1938 had paid visits to the German and French air forces and aircraft industries before flying to Britain. Tellingly, Lindbergh had been to the Supermarine company in the company of Jeffrey Quill, who left this account:

> I met him at Eastleigh and showed him our erecting shop which was full of Spitfires in the process of final assembly. It was a fairly tatty old hangar with a big wooden truss roof. Lindbergh looked around the place, looked up at the roof and I could tell exactly what was going on in his mind. He'd been round these fine chromium-plated, modern factories in Germany and he was obviously thinking to himself, 'These bloody Brits are just playing with the idea.' What he didn't know was that we had a much superior aeroplane in the Spitfire. I bloody nearly said to him, 'You can think what you bloody well like . . . but you wait.'[90]

Quill was absolutely right about Lindbergh's opinion. The American told Slessor at dinner on 21 September that 'the only sound policy was to avoid war at all costs,' especially since Britain did not have 'the absolute minimum for defence' and 'the German air force could flatten cities like London, Paris and Prague.' Slessor sent a note of this startling conversation to Newall, the Chief of the Air Staff.[91]

Before he flew to Munich on 29 September, Chamberlain received a grim summary of Britain's air strength from Sir Charles Bruce-Gardener, who had become chairman of the Society of British Aircraft Constructors in 1937. In Sir Charles's version of events, when he had heard of Chamberlain's planned negotiations with Hitler,

> I took it upon myself to send him a piece of paper on which I wrote the numbers of fighters, bombers and all other types of aircraft that had been delivered during the month and the number expected the following month . . . The figures I sent to Downing Street showed how terribly weak we still were in the air and it is my opinion that when Mr Chamberlain went to Munich he had not a single, solitary card in his hand; he went there in the full knowledge that if war was declared, the equipment available for the RAF, both in types and numbers was far, far below that of the German air force.[92]

The reality was that, outside the small group of Churchill's supporters, there was little appetite within Britain or France for war in 1938 – hence the praise heaped on Chamberlain by both press and public when he returned from Germany claiming to have negotiated 'peace in our time'.

Sir Hugh Dowding, desperate for more Spitfires to be produced for Fighter Command, said 'Thank God' when he heard the news. 'It was very good that he did act in that way,' was his view of Chamberlain's approach.[93] This has become the classic defence of the Munich Agreement: that it bought Britain time to rearm. Allan Wright, one of the Spitfire heroes of the war and commander of 92 Squadron, said, 'One could see that Chamberlain in 1938 was playing for time. He couldn't possibly have gone to war . . . He did a very good job, under difficult circumstances.'[94] There are big holes in such an argument. Germany also gained time. The Luftwaffe was far stronger in May 1940 than in September 1938. The destruction of Czechoslovakia made the Reich much more powerful, in terms of both military confidence and physical resources. Yet it is undoubtedly true that the Munich crisis transformed the mood of Britain's political establishment. The desperate weakness of the nation's defences had been graphically exposed, and there was a new determination to make up for the years of neglect. All the hesitations now evaporated, as Sir Thomas Inskip recorded in his diary: 'The different atmosphere had its effect on Treasury representatives. It is easy to hark back and reflect on the objections to expenditure when war seemed far off. Now it is near, Treasury control disappears. That is the extravagance of war. No one can stem the tide.'[95]

In the Cabinet debates that followed Munich, air rearmament was the dominant theme. Yet once more the Air Staff tried to push the case for the bomber, Newall resorting to a sporting analogy: 'In war a bomber force acts as the most effective means of exerting pressure on an enemy. It is not enough to avoid losing a war. We have got to be able to win it and we can never win a war merely by protecting ourselves. A boxer cannot win a fight if he does no more than parry his opponent's blows.'[96] But this carried little weight with the politicians. What worried them was whether Britain could survive the early rounds. As a result, the thrust of the air programme was to be geared heavily towards fighters. In October Sir Kingsley Wood put forward a new plan, Scheme M, calling for 3,700 fighters, with immediate orders to be placed for half this total. 'We must make every effort to escape from the position in which we found ourselves during the recent crisis when we had less than one week's reserve behind the squadrons. This would have resulted in a rapidly declining scale of effort, especially in the fighter squadrons,' he wrote in his paper to the Cabinet. But he warned that, even with this renewed effort, the RAF would still be weak until late 1939. 'We shall still be re-engaged in the re-equipment of our fighter squadrons with Hurricanes and Spitfires, in the production of which, particularly the Spitfire, there have been serious setbacks of which my colleagues are aware.'[97]

Scheme M was the subject of a fierce debate within the government, not least because Newall continued to fight a rearguard action for the Trenchard doctrine, even to the extent of discrediting the Spitfire and the Hurricane. 'I am greatly concerned', he wrote to Wood, 'that we may be pressed into turning over further bomber capacity to the production of fighters which may well result at a later date in our having to accept a vast output of obsolescent, if not obsolete, fighters and at the same time deferring the re-equipment of the service with really powerful bombing aircraft.'[98] Again his views were ignored. The Cabinet met on 7 November for a final decision on Scheme M. Wood emphasized that the crucial lesson of Munich was that 'if we had had to engage in war in September, our position, so far as the air was concerned, would have been grave.' The only answer was 'a great increase' in the RAF, for which 'we must concentrate on our fighter strength,' increasing it by 30 per cent. Most of the Cabinet agreed, with Chamberlain making the case for the fighter on grounds of both defence and economy. 'The Prime Minister said he noted that one of these heavy bombers cost as much as four fighters . . . The loss of one of these machines would represent a far more formidable blow than the loss of a smaller machine. He could not help feeling that it would be more difficult to grass the whole covey of small birds than to bring down one large bird.' The Cabinet approved in principle to the full programme of 3,700 fighters, and gave Wood authority to place orders for half the total immediately. Meanwhile, bomber production was to be maintained only at a level to prevent dismissals from the aircraft factories.[99]

When Newall read the Cabinet minutes, he wrote alongside the bomber clause 'Christ!' underlined three times. It could almost have been a benediction for the death of Trenchardism. The question now was whether the Spitfire, after all the troubles of the last two years, would remain at the centre of the fighter programme.

4

'It was a bit like a love affair'

I N THE SUMMER of 1938, with war clouds gathering over Europe, the young Supermarine production worker Cyril Russell cycled to the Hambledon aerodrome in Southampton to watch an air display by the RAF, held to celebrate Empire Day. He paid his entrance fee, bought a programme, and stood on the grass to enjoy the aerobatics by RAF biplanes, which included one daring formation by three biplanes linked by ribbons. It was all thrilling stuff, taking place at speeds of up to 200 mph. Then, as the display drew to a close, he looked down at his programme and noticed there was one more event, listed as 'a surprise item'. Filled with curiosity, he moved to the front of the spectators. 'A mainly expectant crowd waited – for what we did not know,' he wrote later. 'Suddenly, and it was just that, with a rush and roar and seemingly at incredible speed, a Spitfire flashed very low in front of us all. Before it had reached the end of the airfield it went straight up like a rocket, rolled over and within seconds made another high-speed run before the crowd.' Its appearance, said Russell, 'brought home to the assembly there that day what vast changes were being brought about by this new generation of aircraft now being built – the fabric-covered biplanes looked almost prehistoric by comparison.'[1]

Russell's excitement was all the greater because of his working association with Supermarine. Professional pride overcame the frustrations of building the plane, struggling with the 'little beast' of panel 363 on the upper fuselage. But the wider British public were hardly aware of the struggle to produce the Spitfire, or the bitter recriminations and political arguments. What they saw, in the summer of 1938, was a masterpiece of design, a captivating emblem of modernism. In its sweeping curved lines, its incredible speed and manoeuvrability, its unique combination of grace and power, the Spitfire seemed as much a representative of a new age as the Empire State Building in New York or the Flying Scotsman train, both triumphant marriages of aesthetics and engineering.

In other ways the 1930s were a bleak decade – 'the dark valley' as the writer Piers Brendon called the period in his rich history of the era[2] – as brutalism, conflict and authoritarianism swept through Europe. The terrifying vision set out in H. G. Wells's 1933 novel *The Shape of Things to Come*, where mankind is subjugated by martial technology, appeared to be becoming a reality on the Continent as the Third Reich grew ever stronger. In such a context, a radical military plane like the Spitfire might have been regarded as another example of the sinister descent into an arms-fixated world where civilian populations were forced to live in permanent fear of the new armies of the air. But the Spitfire was never seen in such a light within Britain. This was not just a matter of simple patriotism, or of admiration inspired by the Spitfire's captivating appearance and speed. It was also because the fighter was the one tangible form of protection that the public seemed to have against the most frightening weapon of all: the bomber.

The fear of indiscriminate bombing campaigns was one of the most prevalent social attitudes of the 1930s in Britain, stoked up by gloomy government propaganda, populist literature, harrowing contemporary imagery of conflict, and memories of the First World War. Londoners could look back to the grim day of 13 June 1917, when a fleet of German Gotha bombers flew over the capital and dropped over 100 bombs, killing 162 people and injuring 426. The shock inspired by this single raid was greater than the endless daily reports of mass slaughter from the Western Front. The 1930s air offensives conducted by Japan against China and by Italy in Abyssinia reinforced this mood of anxiety, as did statements from politicians and warnings from officials: in 1939 the Ministry of Health calculated that 3 million hospital beds would be needed soon after the outbreak of war with Germany, while military experts asserted that 600,000 people would be dead within the first sixty days of any bombing campaign.[3] Science fiction and films frequently portrayed scenes of mayhem brought about by the terror from the air. The 1931 novel *The Gas War of 1940* by Miles – the pen name of the author S. Southwold – contained this description of an air attack on London:

> And then, in a moment, the lights of London vanished, as if blotted out by a gigantic extinguisher. And in the dark streets the burned and wounded, bewildered and panic-stricken, fought and struggled like beasts, scrambling over the dead and dying alike, until they fell and were in turn trodden underfoot by the ever-increasing multitude about them . . . In a dozen parts of London that night people died in their homes with the familiar walls crashing about them in flames; thousands rushed into the streets to be met by blasts of flame and explosion and were blown to rags.[4]

The Spitfire was a source of reassurance against these nightmares. Though the plane had hardly penetrated public consciousness in 1938, it was soon to become the most cherished symbol of heroic defiance against the bomber, its appeal only enhanced by its small size in relation to the offensive fleets. For

Britons living in the shadow of the Luftwaffe, the Spitfire captured the age-hold romantic British attachment to the courageous underdog pitted against the bully. As *Flight* magazine put it in a 1940 article explaining the aircraft's huge popularity, 'People are interested in the machines that protect them and not in those which attack the enemy in their turn and they are also taken by the name and the appearance and the performance of this remarkable little fighter.'[5] The author H. E. Bates, who served with distinction in the RAF, wrote during the war that the actions of the Spitfire pilot were

> a triumph of individuality; he flies alone in a high-powered piece of mecha-nism which is capable, in his hands, of evolutions at great speed, of great beauty and spectacular effect. He is engaged in a dangerous, apparently won-derful and often fatal occupation. Like the bull-fighter, he works near to and often in line with death . . . The coastal pilot is invisible, far out at sea; the bomber pilot is invisible, far out in darkness. The Spitfire pilot flies in the sun, turning his plane like a silver fish many thousands of feet up and fascinates the world below.[6]

And even in 1938, long before it had won glory in combat, the plane's repu-tation was spreading, if not among the civilian population, then certainly within the RAF. Its name was whispered with envy and anticipation among the crews of Fighter Command, eager to be able to fly in this wondrous machine.

That sense of enthusiasm was conveyed by Wing Commander H. R. 'Dizzy' Allen, who said the Spitfire was his inspiration for joining the air force. 'It was one of the loveliest aircraft ever designed, perhaps the superlative fighter,' wrote Allen. 'The Spitfire compelled me to apply for a commission in the RAF. I saw it in flight. I saw photographs of it and I fell in love with it. It turned me on. Nothing is perfect in this world, I suppose, but the Spitfire came close to perfection.'[7] Bob Doe had a similar feeling of adoration on his first sight of the Spitfire, when he was based at Leconfield in Yorkshire. 'One day a Spitfire landed on our airfield – we had a grass airfield then – and taxied over to our hangar. We walked over to this thing, we looked at it, we stroked it. Sat in it. I fell in love with it.'[8]

The first glimpse of the Spitfire always stood out in the memories of its pilots. Geoff Wellum, who left school at seventeen to join 92 Squadron, recalled:

> When I first saw it, I was struck by the line. Not a straight line anywhere. Beauty of line. It looked right. It looked like a fighter. It looked – it was – won-derful. It looked beautiful, beautiful little aeroplane. Oh yeah, I wanted to fly one. I was jolly lucky to do so too. Of course it was the highest bit of technol-ogy, it was right on. We were lucky to get on to Spitfires. Out of the whole of the course at flying training school only two of us went straight to a Spitfire

squadron, a fighter squadron. Many others went to Hurricane squadrons, but I went to a Spitfire. It was the latest and fastest thing, and a little bit daunting.[9]

Wilfrid Duncan Smith – described by Jeffrey Quill as 'one of the greatest British fighter pilots'[10] – had been inspired to take up flying when, as a boy on a shooting trip in Scotland, he saw a golden eagle soaring through the sky. He was reminded of that moment soon after he joined the RAF and saw a Spitfire landing at his base. One evening, out having a drink in a local pub, he was asked by his instructor what plane he would like to fly:

> Without hesitation I told him – Spitfires. It was my natural reaction for the simple reason that I had made up my mind from the first moment I saw a Spitfire, after it had landed one day at Woodley, that this had to be my aeroplane. It had been a thrilling first meeting, while the sheer beauty of line and the exciting power in flight reminded me of my golden eagle soaring up the mountainside with effortless ease after making his kill. Surely a dream come to life.[11]

Given that the Spitfire was so different from previous RAF fighters, flying it for the first time could be an intimidating, if exhilarating, experience for young pilots. Because there were no two-seater Spitfires in which instruction could be given, trainees could learn only by familiarizing themselves with the controls and then taking the plane up on a solo flight. Tom Neil of 249 Squadron described the rudimentary nature of this preparation:

> We flew Spitfires straight from biplanes. None of us had ever flown monoplanes before and suddenly we were faced with these fearsome aeroplanes called Spitfires. And the bloke said to me, 'This is a Spitfire; get in and fly it.' All the training you had was to sit in the hangar with a blindfold round your eyes and the Spitfire on trestles, and you felt round the cockpit trying to identify all the bits, pulling the wheels up and you put the flaps down etc. Half a day. Then you were introduced to your plane and told to get on with it, and that was that.[12]

Later on, pilots would have a less drastic transition, as they were taught on trainers such as the Miles Magister and the North American Harvard, which gave them the basic skills for monoplane flying.

The standard drill in the Spitfire was for the pilot to climb into the narrow cockpit, with his low-slung parachute forming a cushion in the bucket seat. He then attached the oxygen tube to his face mask, and plugged in the radio. The next steps were set out in this account from Bill Rolls, a young sergeant pilot from 72 Squadron, later to serve with distinction in the Battle of Britain and Malta:

I put my brakes on by the lever on the handle of the control column and looked out to the crew to see that they were on position on each wing tip and on the starter trolley. I primed the engine and then called out to the trolley man, 'Switches on, contact.' He pressed his button in the trolley and with a bang the engine started. The airman then pulled the cable from out of the cowl on the engine and closed the flap and then pulled the trolley clear of the aircraft.[13]

For Johnnie Johnson, the highest-scoring Spitfire ace of the war, it was always a thrill when 'the Merlin sprang into life with its usual song of power, a sound no fighter pilot will easily forget.'[14]

As soon as the engine started, pilots were desperate to get into the air because of the risk of overheating. Geoffrey Page, who was later shot down and badly burnt in combat, found this was his primary concern on his first flight:

A trickle of sweat ran down my forehead. Suddenly the powerful engine coughed loudly, blew a short stream of purply-white smoke into a small cloud and roared into life. Remembering that I had little time to spare before the temperature reached the danger mark of 110°, I waved my hands across my face. The waiting airman quickly ducked under the wing and pulled away the restraining chocks. Glancing down, I was alarmed to see that the glycol coolant temperature had risen from zero to 70°. Releasing the brake, I eased the throttle open and the surge of power carried the aircraft rapidly over the grass.[15]

One of the other big problems in preparing to take off in the Spitfire was the poor forward view – the issue that Dowding had raised at those early Air Ministry meetings in 1936. The only way to overcome the difficulty was to swing the plane from side to side to gain some idea of the path ahead, though this was made more complicated by the propeller torque, which tended to drag the plane to the left unless this swing were corrected by the rudder. As one of the great Spitfire aces Bob Stanford-Tuck put it, 'The main thing was the way we used to have to get used to taxiing the Spitfire because you could not see anything ahead with this great Merlin engine sticking out in front, so you went jinking along the whole way, rather than taxi smack into a petrol bowser or something like that.'[16]

Another awkward feature of the early Spitfire Mark I was the De Havilland propeller. This wooden two- or three-bladed airscrew was beautifully crafted and had two pitch options which, like the gears of a car, were meant to optimize its performance at different altitudes and speeds. But they also made life complicated for the pilot, who had to remember to set the airscrew in fine pitch for take-off, climbing and landing, and then select coarse pitch for normal cruising. Douglas Bader, the legendary veteran pilot who wore a pair of tin legs, having lost both his lower limbs in a pre-war flying accident, had a nasty experience at Duxford in March 1940 when he failed to select fine pitch for take-off. His plane refused to become airborne, crashed through a boundary hedge, and cartwheeled across a ploughed field, ending up as a complete write-off. Amazingly, Bader emerged without a scratch, though his tin legs were smashed beyond repair.[17] Later Spitfires resolved this difficulty by using a constant-speed, variable-pitch airscrew, which automatically adjusted the pitch so the engine would keep a constant speed of rotation.

The pilot's checklist for take-off was known by the initials BTFCPPUR: brakes, trims, flaps, contacts, petrol, pressures, undercarriage and radiator. Having completed this procedure, he then was cleared for take-off by radio from ground control and turned towards the runway. It was when the pilot opened the throttle fully, pushed the column forward, and began to speed along the ground that the Spitfire really showed its power. Dizzy Allen gave this description of an early struggle to handle the airscrew on a Mark I, registered LZ-X, as he prepared to take off:

> The Rolls-Royce Merlin engine developed over a thousand horsepower and I eased the throttle open gingerly on the grass airfield. As I tentatively gave her full boost, I felt the great tug of torque and had to wrestle with the aircraft to regain control . . . LZ-X lurched over the rough field gaining speed and I eased the stick forward only to be horrified by the immediate reaction which almost caused the propeller to dig into the grass. I over-corrected and she almost fell back on to her tail wheel . . . She was extremely sensitive fore and aft.[18]

David Crook in his 1942 book *Spitfire Pilot*, gave this description of his first experience in the plane:

> I taxied out on the aerodrome, sat there for one moment to check that everything was OK, and then opened up with a great smooth roar. The Spitfire leapt forward like a bullet and tore madly across the aerodrome, and before I realized quite what had happened I was in the air. I felt as though the machine was completely out of control and running away with me. However, I collected my scattered wits, raised the undercarriage and put the airscrew into coarse pitch, and then looked round for the aerodrome, which to my astonishment I saw was already miles behind.

For Geoffrey Page on his first flight, the final moments on the ground were filled with anxiety, as the glycol in his engine reached 109°:

> Opening the throttle firmly, I started the take-off run. The initial kick from the rapid acceleration drove the worry of the engine temperature away for a while. Working on the rudder hard with both feet to keep the sensitive little machine straight, I was too busy for other thoughts. Easing the stick forward, I was startled by the rapidity with which she responded to the elevator

controls. The long nose in front of me obscured the rapidly approaching hedge at the end of the airport, but by looking out at an angle I was able to get an idea of how far away it was. If the glycol boiled now at this critical stage, the aircraft would be enveloped in a cloud of white smoke that would prevent me from seeing the ground when the inevitable engine seizure and crash landing followed. Looking back into the cockpit again, I saw the hated instrument leering at me . . . 110° . . . Accompanying the feeling of fear was a new sound. The wheels had stopped drumming and a whistling note filled the air. The Spitfire soared gracefully into the air, thankful, as I was, to be away from her earthly bonds.[19]

Once the plane was in the air, climbing at 200 mph, the first task of the pilot was to retract the undercarriage, using the long handle on the right of the cockpit. This lever had to be pumped about twenty times with the right hand, while the left stayed still on the control column to guide the aircraft. It was almost impossible for an inexperienced pilot not to move both hands simultaneously, causing the plane to rise and dip alarmingly. 'You could always tell the chaps doing their first solo in the Spitfire, because the aircraft would be porpoising across the airfield,' says Peter Ayrest, who was on operational fighter duties for most of the war.[20] Geoffrey Page recalled that, barely 20 feet off the ground, he found his plane sinking towards earth as he tried to raise the undercarriage with the lever on the right of the cockpit. 'Being unused to the technique of keeping my left hand absolutely still while the right one moved forwards, I had inadvertently pushed the control column forward simultaneously with the first pumping stroke, thus causing the machine to dip suddenly.' In a state of near panic, he had to move swiftly to recover. 'Some trees flashed by alongside the aircraft as a frightened pilot hauled back on the stick and soon I found I was soaring skyward again . . . At this stage it was obvious that the Spitfire could handle herself better than I could.'[21] To indicate that the undercarriage was fully retracted, a set of warning lights in the cockpit would change from green to red. As a back-up system, there were also two small rods, one on top of each wing, which protruded vertically when the undercarriage was down and disappeared when the wheels went up.

Once this ordeal was completed and the aircraft had climbed to several thousand feet, the novice pilots began to experience the pure joy of flying the Spitfire – its speed combined with a wonderful responsiveness. 'To me she was my personal swallow,' wrote Dizzy Allen of his first flight. 'I rolled, I dived. I came up on the zoom and stall-turned her. She was as light as a feather on the controls, almost dangerously so. I put her into a dive and watched with satisfaction as the air-speed indicator build up to something over 400 mph, much the fastest speed I had then ever achieved.'[22] Bill Ash, who sacrificed his American citizenship to join a Spitfire squadron, wrote in his memoirs that as soon as he was airborne on his first flight all his trepidation disappeared. 'I felt like that man who runs marathons while wearing a deep-sea diving suit, suddenly released and allowed to run free almost weightless . . . In a Spitfire, making everything go well meant applying the gentlest, most subtle of guidance and letting the magnificent plane do the rest.'[23] Bill Rolls, whose previous aircraft had included the Hawker Hart light bomber, was astonished at the sensitivity of the aircraft when he was cruising at over 200 mph:

> I tried out the controls and was amazed how light they seemed and how responsive, almost immediate, they were to the slightest touch, either of rudder or elevator. Compared with the Hart, which up till then I had thought was the perfect machine, the Spitfire was like a greyhound, so sleek and fast. I climbed to 5,000 feet in no time at all and did various turns. I played with the controls to get the feel of them and waggled my wings from side to side, used the rudder and trimmer to see their response. It was magic. I felt that I was an integral part of the aircraft and that the wings were fixed to my arms and I could fly just like a bird. The cockpit was so small that there was no room to move and this made it feel as though you had it strapped on to you. I now tried some mild turns and the smoothness of them and the grace of the aircraft in performing the moves was unbelievable.[24]

This ability of the Spitfire to form a connection with the pilot, to make aircraft and man come together as a single unit, was often commented on by those who flew it. 'You're not flying an aeroplane, you've got wings on your back,' said Bob Doe. 'You are just flying. It's a dream. It's the most wonderful sensation I have ever known. That is the Spitfire. It is the only aeroplane I know where you don't climb into it, you strap it on.'[25] Pilot Officer James Goodson of 43 Squadron felt utterly at ease in the cockpit:

> Once you got used to the Spitfire, of course, you loved it. It became part of you. It was like pulling on a tight pair of jeans. It was a delight to fly. I used to smoke a cigar sometimes – against all rules and regulations – but if I dropped my cigar, instead of groping around on the floor, I'd move the stick a fraction of an inch, the Spit would roll over and I'd catch the cigar as it came down from the floor. That was the kind of plane it was. Everybody had a love affair with it.[26]

The same term is used by Nigel Rose, who joined the RAF in 1938 and had actually seen Spitfires being built in the late 1930s because his father was a manager at Vickers-Armstrong. 'It was a bit like a love affair. The Spitfire really was a wonderful plane. I mean even now when you see it on the box it makes you tingle a bit. It was so easy to handle. It had no vicious habits. You could stall it and it wouldn't whip into a spin like the Harvard would. The Spitfire was a little honey. And its reactions to the stick were very good, very sensitive.'[27]

More than forty years after his first flight, the memories of it still came flooding back to Wilfrid Duncan Smith 'as if they had happened yesterday, clear and exciting . . . The powerful slipstream clawing at my face; the snugness of the cockpit. I indeed felt part of the Spitfire, a oneness that was intimate.' The forgiving nature of the Spitfire was another of the qualities immediately seen by Duncan Smith on his first flight, after he had taken it up to 19,000 feet:

> I chanced some acrobatics and found the aircraft's response sweet and positive. One of the features of the Spitfire I discovered was how beautifully she behaved at low speeds and at high G close to the stall. With full power in a steep turn and at slow speeds she would judder and shake, rocking to and fro, but so long as she was handled correctly she would not let go and spin – surely a unique feature for a high-performance aeroplane.[28]

A key skill that Spitfire pilots had to learn was how to handle the phenomenon of 'blacking out', when those gravitational or G forces generated by sudden changes in speed or direction led to a loss of vision and movement. Brian Kingcome, the commander of the famous 92 Squadron at Biggin Hill, gave a good description of the effect of positive G, which usually occurred in a climb or sharp turn:

> When the stick is pulled hard back, as it constantly is in aerobatics and aerial combat, centrifugal force presses down hard, squashing you to the bottom of your seat. The harder you pull, the more you tighten your vertical or horizontal turn and the heavier the force you invoke until you become unable to move, your hands and feet growing too heavy to lift. Most dramatically, the blood is also forced down from behind the optic nerves, causing you to 'black out', which means a loss not of consciousness but of vision.

Kingcome pointed out that while tolerances to G varied, most pilots started to find their sight fading at about 4G – four times the earth's gravitational pull. Negative G, which pulled a pilot upward during a steep dive, was just as disturbing, yet it could work in favour of the pilot, claimed Kingcome, making it hard for the enemy to give chase. 'If you are blacked out the chances are that your opponent, unless he is Superman, will be as well, which will prevent him from being in the position to get a clear shot at you'[29] But Bill Rolls, who was otherwise thrilled with his first flight in a Spitfire, found this the hardest aspect to handle when he was practising his aerobatics: 'I had never blacked out in any of the aircraft I had flown in, so

I thought, The sooner I learn what to expect the better.' Rolls went into a dive by pulling the control column back. 'Then it happened. I felt a terrific pressure on my body . . . I did not black out but I did not like the feeling I had experienced. I was not quite prepared for such a quick reaction of my controls.'[30] There was one unfortunate bodily side effect of G pressure, as revealed by Flying Officer John Young of 249 and 603 Spitfire squadrons. 'You never hear a word about what happens as a result of the constant high G: haemorrhoids were quite common among fighter pilots.'[31]

But the aerobatics eventually had to come to an end, and any new Spitfire pilot was then faced with the daunting prospect of bringing the plane back to earth. Again he had to grapple with the poor forward view, something that was dealt with by taking a curved approach towards the landing strip. The undercarriage pump was easier to operate going down, because of gravity, though the pilot was aware that the undercarriage's narrow gap between its two wheels meant the plane had to be handled carefully. As a result of the experience of RAF test pilot Humphrey Edwardes-Jones, there was a horn in the cockpit of the early production Spitfire to remind the pilot to put down the wheels. It was triggered when the throttle was retarded to a certain point, ready for the landing approach, though some pilots turned it off because it tended to sound at too high an airspeed. On an embarrassing occasion at an Empire Day display at Hendon, one pilot from 19 Squadron, Sergeant J. A. Potter, completely forgot to lower his undercarriage and did a belly landing in front of a crowd of thousands. His furious commander fined him £5.[32]

The usual routine for the Spitfire pilot as he prepared to land was to radio ground control for permission to come in. When this was granted, he lowered the undercarriage until the green lights came on, opened the radiator to ensure the glycol temperature did not rise, switched the airscrew into fine pitch, and put down the flaps. Flight Lieutenant Godfrey Ball recounted how his first landing went almost to perfection, partly because he had practised his routines while flying in level cloud with reduced power to see how the plane reacted. 'It was such a clean aeroplane', he wrote, 'that it just seemed to slice through the air even without power.' So Ball felt at ease doing his final landing checks as he reduced the speed to 130 mph and began his descent:

> I refrained from putting down the undercarriage until almost at the end of the down-wind leg to prevent the glycol heating up. Everything went according to plan and I did the recommended curved Spitfire approach so I could keep the landing area in view as long as possible. When I was sure of making the aerodrome without having more power, I put down the flaps, re-trimmed the aircraft to keep a constant speed of 90 mph and floated gently to the ground.

The elevators were wonderfully light and effective and I was quite confident as I eased the stick back and felt all three wheels run along the grass together before I rolled to a gentle stop.[33]

The greatest expert on flying the Spitfire, Jeffrey Quill, argued that hardly any backward pressure on the stick was needed at all in landing the plane, another indication of its extreme sensitivity to its controls. 'In fact', he wrote, 'one of the reasons I believe that pilots liked the Spitfire was because one got a very brisk response about the longitudinal and lateral axes without having to thrash the stick around the cockpit as if one was stirring a pudding.'[34]

But others found a perfect three-point landing much more difficult to accomplish at the beginning. Johnnie Johnson, later the most assured of Spitfire pilots, almost had disasters on two of his first flights, when he was based at the RAF training unit in Hawarden in North Wales. He left this record of the initial one:

> Throttle back to circuit speed. Hood open. All clear ahead. Wheels down and curve her across wind. Now the flaps and the final turn into the wind. 120 mph on the approach and we are too high. Stick back and head over the side to judge the landing. Too high and in a semi-stalled condition we drop out of the sky to hit the unyielding ground with a hefty smack. As I suspected, my instructor had seen it all and was there when I switched off the engine: 'I saw the Spit get you into the air! And given a fair chance she would have carried out a better landing than yours! If you make a mess of your approach, open up and go round again. You've been told that in every plane you've flown.'

So the instructor took Johnson up in a Miles Master two-seater trainer to show him the correct way to complete a Spitfire circuit in a steady continuous turn, easing back on the column and closing on the throttle so the plane had a sinking sensation. Johnson thought he had understood the drill correctly, but four days later he was instructed to deliver an urgently needed package of maps to RAF Sealand, a training and maintenance base in North Wales:

> There was a stiff wind across the short, grass airfield and I aimed to be down close to the boundary fence so that I had the maximum distance for the landing run. I came over the fence too high and too slow and the fully stalled Spitfire dropped like a bomb. We hit the ground with a mighty crash and I had a little too much slack in the harness straps, for I was thrown violently forward and pulled up with a nasty wrench across the shoulders. For a few yards we tore a deep groove in the ground, then she slithered to a standstill in a ground loop which tore off one undercarriage leg and forced the other through the top of the port mainplane.

After Johnson had come to a halt and switched off the engine, a flight lieu-tenant strode over angrily and, looking him in the face, said, 'Don't you know the country's short of Spitfires?'[35] Johnson feared that another prang would mean his exit from operations. Fortunately for the future of Fighter Command, there were no more crashes in the weeks that followed.

The American Lee Gover, who joined the RAF out of his commitment to the Allied cause and was based for Spitfire training at RAF Llandow, had an even more challenging first flight, because of physical defects in his plane, though it did not have the same sorry physical consequences. He had just taken off when he was told by radio to land immediately because the base was becoming enshrouded in fog. But then he found his flaps would not lower, and he feared that the strip was too short for him to come in at speed. So he was ordered by the radio controller to find the nearby base of St Athan in south Glamorgan. As he recorded in his diary:

> The only problem was that I didn't know where the hell I was. I started down the coast at about 150 feet and 240 miles per hour. I soon spotted an airdrome and circled, then I dropped my wheels again and the damn things would go down but wouldn't lock. So what the hell – I made three passes at the field at about 20 feet and decided to slide it in, as the fog was getting really thick. On the way around the field it built up enough hydraulic pressure and the wheels snapped locked OK but still no flaps. I dug it in straight for about half a mile, cut the engine and stalled her down as much as possible. Well, she floated quite a bit and then settled down to a good landing. But having no air pressure and no brakes, I went about half a mile and was heading straight into a big four-motored bomber when I finally got her stopped and so ended my first ride in the Spitfire. I learned more on that ride and got more white hair than you can imagine.[36]

The innovative features of the Spitfire – such as retractable undercarriage, enclosed cockpit, four pairs of wing-mounted guns, engine with more than 1,000 horsepower generating speeds of over 350 mph, radio installation, ducted radiator, and fuselage of all-metal monocoque construction, in which the structural loads were carried by the skin – might have become standard for fighters by the middle of the Second World War, but they were revolutionary in the RAF of the late 1930s, used to biplanes and speeds below 220 mph. 'It was totally different to any other aircraft you'd flown, the speed in particular and the handling qualities,' said Cyril Bamberger, who flew with 610 and 41 Squadrons.[37] This sense of newness shines through a sales brochure produced by Vickers in June 1939 extolling the virtues of the Spitfire, 'the fastest mili-tary single-engined fighter in service'. The brochure explained that the plane was of exceptionally high performance, designed to operate day or night. Equipped with a Rolls-Royce fully supercharged engine, it incorporates all the experience gained in building a series of Schneider Trophy winners. The structure is of the all-metal stressed-skin type which has been developed by the Supermarine Company over a long period and results in a very robust construction of exceptionally low weight combined with a smooth outer skin essential for high speeds. Strong, manoeuvrable and outstandingly fast, the Spitfire is without question one of the most formidable and effective defensive air weapons in existence.[38]

For once, this was not just empty sales talk.

But, for all its virtues, it would be misleading to describe the Spitfire as a 'perfect' aircraft, as some have done. No man-made machine could ever attain such flawlessness. And the Spitfire certainly had some serious drawbacks, particularly in the early models. The Merlin II engine, for instance, had a tendency to go dead when the plane went into a sudden dive, because the fuel supply was temporarily cut by negative G. This was a serious defect in combat. Pilots of the Me 109, whose Daimler-Benz engine used fuel injection and therefore did not have the same problem, learned that they could often lose a Spitfire on their tail just by pushing the stick forward. On the prototype and the first Spitfires, the heaviness of the aileron controls at high speeds was another shortcoming – one that particularly concerned Jeffrey Quill, who said that it 'caused a severe restriction in lateral manoeuvres'.[39] One of Quill's fellow test pilots, Don Robertson, thought that the 'weakest point' of the early Spitfire was the 'relatively poor rate of roll' as a result of the ailerons becoming so heavy at high speeds. Robertson went on to explain the importance of this defect, when he wrote that, up to the war, 'the value of a very rapid rate of roll had not been fully appreciated, but when flying at very high speed, it is not possible to make any quick change of direction in the pitching plane due to the build up of G and the consequent black-out of the pilot. A quick roll or aileron turn in a vertical dive is a much more effective manoeuvre to throw off an enemy fighter in pursuit.'[40]

Nor was the Spitfire's standard armament of eight .303 machine guns particularly impressive by the time of the Battle of Britain. Because of increasingly effective armour plating on the German bombers, Spitfire pilots found that they could end up firing long bursts into the enemy aircraft without causing terminal damage. But the alternative of cannon, which had interested Ralph Sorley as early as 1934, had not been feasible before 1939, and the attempts to install such weaponry on the Spitfire in 1940 proved disastrous. Nevertheless, many in Fighter Command remained unhappy with the forced reliance on the Browning. 'If we'd had cannons in the Battle of Britain,' said John Bisdee, a

Cambridge graduate and member of 609 Squadron, 'then I believe that the defeat of the German air force would have been very much more complete than it was. A number of aircraft got back across the Channel with leaking glycol and so on from bullet wounds which would have undoubtedly been destroyed if we'd had cannons. Even one or two, given to people who were the best shots, would have had an enormous effect.'[41]

With only an 85-gallon fuel tank, in the fuselage in front of the pilot, the Spitfire had an extremely limited range. This did not matter so much in the Battle of Britain, fought over home territory, but it was to be a telling factor afterwards. In an attempt to increase fuel capacity for campaigns over France, the Low Countries and the Mediterranean, Spitfires were fitted with jettisonable 30-, 45- or 90-gallon tanks, but these were never a satisfactory solution, because the tanks were unreliable and increased drag. As a result, the Spitfire was never an effective escort for Allied long-range bombers over Germany. Instead, the American P-51 Mustang had to perform that role later in the war. It was the short range of the Spitfire that led to feelings of despair and derision among some US and Canadian pilots. Rod Smith of the RCAF recalled this exchange with his fellow Canadian Buck McNair, who was to fly 266 operational sorties over France and Malta, suffering serious injuries in the process. 'I met Buck one evening in the bar at Biggin. I had just checked out the Spitfire IXB and I said what a great aeroplane it was. Buck replied that he thought it was a fucking awful aeroplane.' McNair went on that the US 8th Air Force with its 'long-range Mustangs had far better range than our Spitfires and better long-range tanks'.[42]

Wilfrid Duncan Smith also saw this attitude when, one day in the summer of 1942, he and his section were forced to land at an American Flying Fortress base because their Spitfires were low on fuel. As he climbed out of his cockpit, he was informed by a US officer that nothing could be done until the Fortresses had been refuelled:

> We hung about for some time and not until an hour later did an enormous petrol tanker come along with a motley crew of American NCOs and airmen, or rather 'soldiers', hanging on to it. I doubt if any of them had seen Spitfires at close quarters before for they shrieked with laughter when they found that the Spitfire's fuel capacity was less than one hundred gallons. The crew chief drily remarked, 'Say Captain, you don't need our tanker – here, have my Zippo lighter – there's sure enough gas in it to take care of your Spitfire babies.'[43]

Before the advent of pressurized cockpits, the altitudes reached by the Spitfire indirectly led to another cause of complaint: the bitter cold to which pilots were subjected as they climbed to well above 35,000 feet. The cockpits neither were sealed nor contained any heating, so there was little protection against the sub-zero temperatures outside. Lee Gover's wartime correspondence contains vivid references to the near-Arctic conditions he occasionally had to endure, as in this letter of 6 December 1942 to his family in the USA: 'I went on a show this afternoon and damn near froze to death. I sure wish the Spitfire had a heater. In fact, my oxygen tube would freeze and when I'd squeeze it, ice crystals would blow into my mask and slap me in the face. Very refreshing when it's about 40 below, very.'[44] John Wilkinson, who joined the RAF in 1941, left in his papers a series of verbal snapshots of life as a Spitfire pilot. Among them was this account of the unsuccessful measures taken to protect against the cold:

> Since the Spitfire cockpit was so small we could not wear the heavy wool-lined leather jackets and trousers that the bomber crews wore. Consequently we dressed in a strange variety of clothing to keep warm. We did have electrically heated slippers in our flying boots, electrically heated waistcoats and gloves, reputed to be good to only minus 40° Fahrenheit. To describe my clothing: in addition to the electrically heated items, like most of us, I wore silk stockings, long woollen underwear, a wool sweater and wool battledress. My grandmother had knitted long stockings of heavy seamen's wool, without feet, to fit inside my flying boots and cover my legs and hips. On my hands first came thin chamois leather gloves, easier to remove if one got burned, then the electrically heated gloves and finally heavily lined gauntlets.[45]

For Ted Smith, a member of the 2nd Tactical Air Force, based in France from 1944, the chill added to the uncomfortable nature of flying the Spitfire. He wrote in his diary for 1 September 1944, 'Perhaps the only drawback to the Spitfire is the cockpit. It is bone-chillingly cold. Since you have no room to begin with, you can't even shift your buttocks. Your left hand is just cold enough to be almost painful. Your right hand, like both your knees, goes numb. You beat it against your knees, left right, left right, and when the blood comes back it is so painful you could cry.'[46] The cruel results of this physical distress were well described by Johnnie Houlton, a New Zealander with 485 Squadron. In March 1943 he flew from RAF Hornchurch on a raid over the Netherlands.

> We certainly experienced extreme discomfort in climbing to our assigned altitude of 30,000 feet. The cold gnawed deeply into the hands, knees and elbows in particular, and I can remember feeling almost grateful when the numbness suppressed the worst of the pain, but there was, of course, a price to be paid. On the homeward journey descending across the North Sea we were headed for Bradwell Bay to refuel before returning to base, and at around 6,000 feet feeling

began to return in the warmer air, accompanied by increasing pain, which by the time we landed became excruciating agony. Other escorting squadrons also put down at Bradwell Bay, and it was a bizarre scene as dozens of reasonably fit young men writhed on the ground and cried from the effects of the thaw. One pilot of a squadron which followed us virtually threw his Spitfire at the ground, to bounce sideways into a row of aircraft near the runway, demolishing his own and several other aircraft in the process.

Houlton led a demand from his squadron for the kind of electrically heated clothing worn in bombers, but he could not understand why 'no one thought to fit variable heat controls to the electrical supply points in the cockpit.'[47] The problem of cold was not confined to the pilots: at high altitudes the machine guns could also freeze up. To stop this happening, ground crews had to fit fabric patches over the ports, which came to have the secondary advantages of maintaining the smooth leading edge of the wing and of showing whether the guns had been fired or not.

Perhaps the Spitfire's greatest weakness, given its original purpose as a day and night fighter, was in its nocturnal role. When Specification F7/30 was drawn up, the Air Staff laid emphasis on the importance of the plane as a night fighter – the reason why a landing speed of under 70 mph was stipulated. But the Spitfire never fulfilled this objective. The long nose made visibility on the ground poor enough during the day; at night it was virtually non-existent. Moreover, the exhaust manifolds released jets of flame which further impaired vision. Without airborne radar, the pilot was flying blind. After the Battle of Britain, the failure of the RAF's premier fighter to operate effectively at night was to play a regrettable part in the downfall of Hugh Dowding. 'The Spitfire was a most objectionable aircraft to have to fly at night,' said Dizzy Allen:

> By day one could scan easily beyond the exhaust stubs; by night one would see only the whole apparatus of effluent left by the Merlin. At dusk as one took to the air, the previously invisible exhaust gases would begin to show in the form of blue flames. As night encroached, those blue flames would turn into fiery red flames and furthermore the exhaust-pipes would gleam bright red, showing the temperatures at which they had to work. All this was blinding on the final approach and landing, and when combined with the long nose of the Spitfire made the situation almost impossible.[48]

One attempted solution to the problem of the exhausts was to fit detachable metal hoods to the engine cowlings at night. To an extent they acted as shields against the flames, but they also had the effect of further worsening the forward view. Brian Kingcome described landing the Spitfire in the dark on a small airfield as 'a nightmare', made all the worse by the lack of any proper lighting because of the blackout. On a moonless night, being in a Spitfire was like 'flying in a barrel of Guinness', to use Kingcome's memorable phrase. He also wrote eloquently about the eerie feeling of being in a practice flight over East Anglia before the war, when the entire area was cloaked in darkness:

> I found myself in a lightless world . . . it had a most curious impact. For several seconds I felt divorced from all living things, entirely isolated, trapped in a small black suffocating hole in the air without hope of escape. The sensation lasted only a few moments, yet ever afterwards, whenever downcast and low in spirits, I found the same feeling returning and experienced the same sensation of entrapment in a black, all-enveloping void.[49]

Kingcome expressed surprise that there were not more night accidents at the beginning of the war. Yet the total was high enough for the Air Ministry, in December 1939, to rule that Spitfire units be largely excluded from night-fighter duties, except on bright moonlit nights. Typical of the incidents before this ruling was the experience of Sandy Johnstone, who commanded 602 Squadron during the Battle of Britain. In October 1939, at two o'clock in the morning, he was ordered to make a patrol of the Dumbarton area at 5,000 feet. In the murky gloom, his path along the airfield was defined by the headlamps of a Morris car parked by a corporal at the end of the strip, giving him 'two pinpricks of yellow light' to aim for. Once in the air, Johnstone soon realized that his sortie was a waste of time, since he could see nothing, 'with neither moon nor friendly star to guide me'. He decided he should land, and descended below 3,000 feet. Unable to distinguish any features on the ground, he let off a flare which lit up the local countryside. To his relief, he spotted what he thought was a large open field, big enough for a Spitfire landing. 'Realizing the flare would not last for ever, I wasted no time lowering the undercarriage and the flaps as we swept towards it, praying I could get down before the light went out. I suppose we were down to a few hundred feet before the awful truth dawned on me. It was no flat field I was aiming at – it was a ruddy great reservoir and it was coming up at an alarming rate.' Desperately trying to reverse his descent, he pulled on the stick and tried to pump up the undercarriage. But it was too late. Amid the sound of metal being torn apart, the Spitfire ploughed into the slope of a hill. Thinking the plane was about to blow up, Johnstone scrambled from it and then sat, bewildered and injured, on the hillside. The only sound filling the cold night air was the mournful bellow from the undercarriage horn, insistently telling him that the wheels were not locked in the down position. Finally convinced that the plane was not going to burst into the flames, Johnstone returned to the scene of the wreckage and settled himself in the cockpit to try to ward off 'the bitter chill'.[50] Eventually he was found by the warden of the reservoir and transferred to the Paisley Royal Infirmary. Unlike his plane, he was not found to have suffered serious damage.

The negative aspects of the Spitfire have occasionally led to claims that the plane's iconic status is undeserved, that the excellence of its fighting qualities and the revolutionary nature of its design have been exaggerated because of a mixture of nostalgia inspired by the Battle of Britain and the legacy of wartime propaganda, in which the Spitfire played a central role. This scepticism is seen at its most graphic in the long-running debate over comparisons between the Spitfire and the Hurricane, the other leading monoplane fighter at the start of the war. The Hurricane never received anything like the same praise or attention, but during the Battle of the Britain it actually shot down more German aircraft than the Spitfire. For supporters of the Hurricane, this is only a reflection of its superior worth. The plane might not be as beautiful as the Spitfire, but, they say, it had better visibility, could be produced and maintained more easily, had a tighter turning circle, and could be landed with less difficulty because it had a wider undercarriage with the wheels folding inwards. Above all, it has been argued that the Hurricane was a better combat fighter, because its thicker, straighter wings made it a more stable base for firing. On the Spitfire, the recoil from the Browning guns could suddenly knock almost 25 mph off the flying speed and lower the nose as if the landing flaps had been extended.[51] In contrast, recalled Douglas Bader, the Hurricane 'remained rock steady when you fired'.[52]

The Hurricane Mark I was a slightly larger plane than the Spitfire Mark I, with a wingspan of 40 feet and a length of 31 feet 4 inches, compared to a wingspan of 36 feet 10 inches and a length of 29 feet 11 inches for the Spitfire. Both were powered by the Merlin, and they weighed almost exactly the same, at approximately 6,200 pounds. But the wing loading on the Hurricane was lower – 24.1 pounds per square foot, compared to 26 pounds per square foot on the Spitfire – and this, some said, was why the Hurricane could out-turn the Spitfire. There was, however, no doubt that the Spitfire was much faster. Hurricane enthusiasts have claimed that the gap was only around 30 mph – significant enough in itself – but in truth the difference was above 40 mph in 1939, and widened considerably as the Spitfire developed. Tests conducted by Dowding at Fighter Command in July 1939 highlighted the disparity. In these trials, six pairs of Hurricanes and Spitfires took off from an airfield, with the Hurricanes 300 yards in front. At a given radio signal, the pilots were instructed to open their throttles fully and record their speeds once the Spitfires had overtaken the Hurricanes. The results showed that at 18,000 feet the six Spitfires reached an average 344.1 mph, compared to 302.8 mph for the Hurricanes. And, as Dowding admitted to the Air Ministry, this may have been a severe underestimate of the Spitfire's true potential, because the plane 'had not the time to work up to its full speed before overtaking the Hurricane'.[53]

But, for the Hurricane's defenders, speed was not everything. Frank Barber, who flew both types in the RAF, called the Hurricane 'an idiot's plane', which he meant as a compliment:

> If you couldn't fly it you really shouldn't be in the air. The undercarriage was so strong and so well constructed that you could drop them in very carelessly and get away with it. They would bounce and bounce. If you did that in a Spitfire the undercarriage would have poked through the wing! The Hurricane was also much stronger. From the cockpit back it was wood covered with fabric. You could shoot away great lumps without affecting its performance too badly. Do the same with a Spitfire – the monocoque construction would not take the punishment.

Barber was one of the few pilots who was not captivated by his first experience of the Spitfire. 'The first Spit I flew was a Mark I. It didn't impress me. It seemed tinny. Thinner wing. Looked very much more delicate than the sturdy, solid Hurricane . . . It certainly wasn't love at first sight. I preferred my Hurricane.'[54]

Like Barber, Paul Richey was another Hurricane veteran who was not impressed with his first experience of the Spitfire. Having fought in France and the Battle of Britain, he had to switch to operations in Spitfire Mark Vs in the spring of 1941. He had a deep affection for the Hurricane – 'I never hoped to fly a better fighter', he wrote – and he approached his first Spitfire 'with a certain amount of distaste. I had seen them flying and admitted I had seen few prettier aircraft. But on the ground, to my biased eye, the Spit looked knock-kneed, flimsy and rather silly. It lacked the air of robust strength of my beloved Hurry.' Richey's opinion did not change with his first flight. 'I flew three circuits and landings and some mild aerobatics, none of which I enjoyed. I found the elevators too sensitive, the ailerons too stiff, the nose too long and too high, the cockpit cramped and the vision restricted. The only thing I liked was the layout of the cockpit. The aeroplane flew all right but the thought of fighting in it I relished not at all! I taxied in feeling both disappointed and worried.' But Richey's combat record in the Spitfire – flying 61 missions in 1941, and destroying or damaging 8 Me 109s – proved that he overcame some of those concerns. He later wrote that he came to regard the Spitfire as 'a good compromise' between design and operational needs. 'It had its faults, like all aeroplanes, and it had very sensitive elevators . . . But the Spitfire made up for it in many other ways.'[55]

Pete Brothers, who joined the RAF in 1936 and became one of the most admired British fighter pilots, had this memory:

> At first I was flying the Hurricane, which was a lovely aeroplane, rugged, wide, stable undercarriage, particularly comfortable for rough ground. And a very good solid gun platform, and it could take a lot of damage. Later I was flying the Spitfire, which was a more delightful aeroplane to fly and control but had its disadvantages with a narrow undercarriage, which made it a little unstable on the ground, and it wasn't such a good gun platform.

Brothers maintained that the Spitfire's long nose also put it at a disadvantage when it came to firing at the enemy:

> The Hurricane's nose curved down slightly, the result being that when you were taking a deflection shot, in other words pointing well ahead of the target you were shooting at, with the Hurricane you could observe it the whole time. With the Spitfire, you could lose your target under the nose, so you couldn't see him. When you pressed the firing button, you hoped he was still there but, of course, you weren't sure he was.[56]

It was the heightened sensitivity of the Spitfire that disconcerted the American James A. Goodson, who achieved 32 victories in the war. 'The Hurricane was a much better gun platform,' he once explained. 'In the first few attacks I made, although I was right on top of the target, the Spitfire was jumping around such a lot. And if you got in the other fellow's slipstream, you had a terrible time. I missed three or four victories because the Spitfire was bouncing around. You had to get used to that.'[57]

In a controversial article in *Aeroplane Monthly* in February 1994, the distinguished fighter pilot and RAF commander Roland 'Bee' Beaumont also argued that at the start of the war the Hurricane was superior to the Spitfire. After admitting that the Spitfire was faster, he pointed to the Hurricane's steadiness, tightness of turn and manoeuvrability. He highlighted an occasion in November 1940, in which a pilot had landed at his base of Charmley Down near Bath with a brand-new Spitfire Mark II. With the encouragement of his fellow pilots, Bee Beaumont accepted the challenge of a mock dogfight:

> In his tightest turning with wingtip vortices, racking roll-reversals and everything he tried, I had no difficulty in staying in the slot behind his tailwheel. It must have been quite frustrating until he finally rolled out level and, still at full

power, started to draw away. That demonstration convinced us all that, for our job at the time, a Spitfire II could be nice but that our Hurricanes (and our knowledge of them) were, in the prevailing circumstances, much safer for us![58]

Many of the pilots who flew both planes did not go as far as Beaumont, but saw merits in each. Bob Stanford-Tuck's first reaction to flying the Hurricane during the Battle of Britain 'wasn't good':

After the Spit, she was like a flying brick – a great lumbering farmyard stallion compared with a dainty and gentle thoroughbred. The Spit was so much smaller, sleeker, smoother – and a bit faster too. It nearly broke my heart, because things seemed tough enough without having to take on 109s in a heavy kite like this. But after the first few minutes, I began to realize the Hurri had virtues of her own. She was solid, obviously able to stand up to an awful lot of punishment, just as well-powered as any other fighter in the world, with the same Merlin I knew and trusted so well . . . The controls were much heavier and it took a lot more muscle to haul her around the sky – and yet, you know, after that first hop, after I'd got the feel of her, I never seemed to notice this or any other differences any more.[59]

But, in the final analysis, it is mere sentimentality to pretend that the Hurricane was anything like the equal of the Spitfire. The plane may have performed courageously in the Battle of Britain, but there is little doubt that the struggle would have been won more easily if Fighter Command had been fully equipped with Spitfires. It is true that the Hurricanes shot down more Germans, but that is only because they made up two-thirds of Fighter Command's strength and were therefore certain to inflict proportionately greater losses. Moreover, precisely because of their slowness, Hurricanes were given the easier task of taking on the Luftwaffe's bombers, whereas the Spitfires had to deal with the fast, dangerous Me 109 fighters. And because of the methods used in its construction, including fabric, dope and wood, the Hurricane was at the peak of its development in 1940 and its production would not see out the war, whereas the Spitfire had massive scope for development. That is why its production was continually being improved and diversified right up to 1948.

In reality, the Spitfire proved itself in almost every theatre where it operated, whereas after 1940 the Hurricane was distinctly second class, often badly outmatched and outpaced. As Ken Plumridge, who joined the RAF in 1941, puts it:

I flew Hurricanes as well as Spitfires, but there's no comparison. The Spit was far, far superior. There were many times where if I'd flown a Hurricane I would have been shot down. But the Spitfire was superb. It was a wonderful, wonderful aircraft. The reason it was so good was because the moment you thought about moving, it moved – you didn't have to wait for it. The Hurricane had that nanosecond response time, which was fatal. If someone is pumping out nastiness, you couldn't afford the time.[60]

One of the greatest of all Second World War pilots, the New Zealander Colin Gray, gave this typically cogent assessment:

> As one who has flown both in action, I have no doubt that the Spitfire was superior by quite a margin. It was some 30 to 40 miles per hour faster, climbed quicker, and had a higher service ceiling. Being lighter on the elevators, it was quicker and easier to manoeuvre, and, contrary to general belief, it could out-turn a Hurricane. It was also more robust and could take more punishment. One particularly bad feature of the Hurricane was its vulnerability, because the main petrol tanks were situated in each wing root – often the first thing to get hit, especially when attacked from behind. In the Spitfire, the petrol tanks were in the fuselage just behind the engine. They were therefore protected from frontal attack.[61]

Tony Tooth, who fought with Spitfires in North Africa, had a brief spell on Hurricanes before he was in combat. 'The Hurricane was an aeroplane with a great reputation, well deserved, but there was absolutely nothing I liked about it! It was big, seeming much bigger than the Spit, and had an altogether clumsy feeling, being much slower and having slower reactions.'[62] Brian Kingcome was equally clear in his analysis, arguing that he would 'have had to award the supreme accolade to the Spitfire in any final judgement. The Hurricane was a solid, reliable, uncomplaining workhorse, but the Spitfire personified symmetry and grace. She was a thing apart, defying comparison. She was as relaxed, as elegant, as obviously effortless at home in her natural environment as a swallow and equally poetic in motion.'[63]

In August 1995 the Canadian former RAF pilot Rod Smith produced an acerbic, highly authoritative dismissal of the claims for the Hurricane's superiority. Writing in *Aeroplane Monthly*, he made a sweeping attack on the piece written the previous year by Bee Beaumont, calling it 'highly distorted' and riddled with 'surprising errors'. Smith, who flew Spitfires from 1941 until the end of 1944, said that 'not many realized how slow the Hurricane was', pointing out that in a dive the Spitfire was at least 70 mph faster – 'an astonishing difference'. Even at cruising speeds, Smith argued, a gap of 30 or more mph 'indicated obsolescence in the slower aircraft'. With its 'very blunt leading edge' and 'very thick wing', the Hurricane 'could never be in the same class as the Spitfire', he wrote: 'The Spitfire's wing, though the thinnest of all wartime fighter wings, was immensely strong. If a Hurricane pilot had ever dived to the speed a Spitfire could survive to (and he would have needed a booster rocket in the tail just to make a fist of it) he would have exchanged his mount's thick wings for some graceful feathered ones long before he reached it.'

Smith was equally sceptical of the belief that the Hurricane was better as a gun platform. 'I did some practice dog-fighting in a Hurricane and never found it the slightest bit easier to hold the sight on with than with a Spitfire. In fact, I would put it the other way round . . .The Spitfire was famed and beloved above all other types for its beautiful response to its controls. If you could hit with any aircraft you could hit with a Spitfire.' Smith further contended that the Hurricane's wartime record after the Battle of Britain was a sorry one. In 1941, for instance, a mere dozen Me 109s 'devastated Malta's Hurricanes without losing one aircraft', and 109s easily overcame Hurricanes in Greece and Crete. In conclusion, wrote Smith, the Hurricane was never a match for the 109s – unlike the Spitfire. 'The heart and essence of the achievement of Mitchell and his design team was in coming up with a fighter which, although weighing only a few hundred more pounds than the Me 109, had 40 per cent more wing area and yet unbelievably had no more drag, if as much. Hence the priceless gift of tighter turning with at least equal speed.'[64]

Perhaps the most compelling verdict came from the men who actually had to fight against the two planes: the pilots of the Luftwaffe. And there can be no dispute that the Spitfire struck far more terror into their squadrons than the Hurricane did. The warning 'Achtung Spitfeuer!' screamed by Germans over their radios in combat became one of the symbolic sounds of the Battle of Britain, reflecting the awesome reputation of the Spitfire and the growing fear it inspired in Axis crews. Adolf Galland, the leading German fighter ace, who first saw action in the Spanish Civil War, regarded the Spitfire as 'dangerous, on account of its armament, climb, manoeuvrability and the courage of its pilots', but, in contrast, he thought that 'the Hurricane was hopeless, a nice plane to shoot down.'[65] The Spitfire pilot John Dalley met Galland at a Luftwaffe reunion in 1974: 'He said to me, "We didn't hang around where the Spitfires were. We would not mix it with the Spitfires at high altitude because they were better than us." That's the amazing thing, that's what Galland said to me, "We tried to avoid mixing it." He knew the Spitfire was a superior plane.'[66]

It was a view shared by another Luftwaffe airman, Johannes Steinhoff. Though he held the Spitfire in respect, he said that for the RAF, 'The Hurricane was a big disadvantage to you, the rate of roll being bad – we were lucky to meet Hurricanes.'[67] German official reports bore out this opinion. An analysis made in July 1940 reported that over 60 per cent of the RAF's fighters were made up of Hurricanes, the rest Spitfires. 'Of the two models, the Spitfire is the better one.' The report went on to claim that, while both types were inferior to the Me 109, it was a different situation with other German planes such as the two-seater Me 110, which 'cannot compete with well-handled Spitfires in air combat'.[68]

Such was the German contempt for the Hurricane that a form of 'Spitfire snobbery' developed in the Luftwaffe, whereby pilots would always claim to have been shot down by a Spitfire, even if a Hurricane had been responsible. 'The Luftwaffe airmen often mistook Hurricanes for Spitfires,' wrote Peter Townsend, himself a Hurricane pilot during the Battle of Britain. 'There was the crew of the famous Heinkel which landed "in the sea" near Wick who swore a Spitfire had downed them when in fact it was a Hurricane. During the Battle of France, Theo Osterkamp seemed to see Spitfires everywhere. There were no Spitfires in France, only Hurricanes.'[69] When Hurricane pilot Eric Seabourne was shot down in 1940 by an Me 109, he ended up, badly burnt, in Hasler Hospital in Portsmouth. In the bed next to him was a German pilot. 'He was an English-speaker and he was creating because he had been shot down by a Hurricane, which he thought was much below his dignity. If it had been a Spitfire, it would have been OK, but not a Hurricane.'[70]

The charge that the Spitfire was less robust than the Hurricane has no evidence to support it. In fact, for all its technological sophistication, the Spitfire could be impressively resilient, able to sustain large amounts of damage and still bring its pilots home. During the Italian campaign in 1943, Wilfrid Duncan Smith had a dramatic insight into the Spitfire's ability to keep going even with the most grievous wounds. Having just downed an Italian Macchi fighter over Sicily, Duncan Smith was hit by an Me 109. 'There were two enormous bangs behind my back and the Spitfire seemed to double up with pain as the stick was wrenched out of my hand. I heard a high-pitched whine in my headphones and my radio went dead.' His Spitfire slid into a dive, and only with brute force did he manage to get it out of a spin. The elevator was jammed, his control wires were 'shot to bits', and he was rapidly losing height. 'I set course for Malta praying my Spitfire would hold together.' To his relief it did – an achievement which seemed all the more remarkable when he saw the damage to the plane. 'Cannon-shells had blasted a couple of large holes in the side. One had burst against the radio and armour behind my seat. Another, having made a hole the size of a football, had torn the control wires to shreds. The elevator was hanging on by one thread of frayed wire. Another cannon-shell had torn big pieces out of the elevator and rudder surfaces.'[71]

In his wartime diary for early 1945, Ted Smith recounted how he had landed back at his base after a mission over the Low Countries. On stepping out of the cockpit, Smith was breezily asked by one of the ground crew: 'We've been hit, sir. Are you aware?' To his astonishment, Smith saw three large holes in the fuselage, 'one of them large enough to put my head through'. Yet all he had felt over Holland was a mild bump in the aircraft. 'Look at this, Mr Smith, you're lucky to be alive,' continued the rigger. Smith went to see. 'My elevator cables were held together by one strand of wire. Beads of sweat appeared on my forehead, and I wiped them away.'[72]

In April 1944, John Wilkinson of 41 Squadron went through an incredible experience while on a fighter sweep over the Continent. He saw a German Fw 190, gave chase, and, when he was within range, opened fire. To his horror, the Fw 190 was carrying a bomb. 'There was an almighty explosion. I ducked down for maximum protection from my bullet-proof windshield and large engine. Although the outside air was very cold, I could feel the fiery heat on my neck between my collar and leather helmet. I could see the flaming fuel and wreckage engulfing my Spitfire.' But, as he emerged from the ball of fire, he was still in radio contact with his controller and was given directions so he could try to return to base. With 100 miles to travel, he climbed as high as he dared and then started back. Though his plane was badly damaged, his oil and pressure gauges seemed to be operating. So were the flaps and under-carriage, as he found when he reached his airfield and came in to land. Once safely on the ground, he discovered that 'one blade of my propeller had been split off longways; paint was burned off the fuselage, and part of the control-ling surfaces of the tail were missing. But most remarkable of all was that, while nothing had entered the huge radiator and oil-cooler air scoops under each wing, the edges of the scoops were riddled with holes. The hand of the Lord was indeed upon me.'[73]

R. A. Morton of 616 Squadron, based at Tangmere in Sussex, had just as fraught an ordeal when he was on escort duty for a bomber mission to Lille and was suddenly jumped on by a pair of Me 109s. 'The first thing I noticed was – nothing. The cabin was so full of smoke that I could not even see the instruments.' But he managed to force open his canopy so he could clear the smoke. Once he could see again, he surveyed the damage. 'One or two machine-gun panels were missing from my starboard wing, showing that a shell had exploded inside it, and there was a bullet hole on the top of the engine cover. The engine was sounding like a cement mixer. The radiator temperature needle was jammed against its upper stop, as was the oil tempera-ture indicator. The oil pressure needle had disappeared below the scale. Obviously damage to the radiator had caused the loss of all my glycol coolant.' Morton thought his only chance of survival was to head for the Channel, then bail out and hope to be picked up by an air–sea rescue operation. But somehow the Merlin refused to die. 'Against all reason that engine, the moving parts of which must have been near red-hot, kept going, not merely as far as the Channel, but clear across to Hawkinge, our emergency aerodrome. My circuit attracted all eyes and fortunately I made a copy-book approach – I didn't know, of course, that the cannon-shell in my right wing had blown that tyre to pieces, so that my landing was a series of ungainly hops, with a tight little circle at the end of it.'[74]

One of the reasons the Spitfires were so resilient was because of the work of the ground crews – or 'erks' as they were often known. They were responsible not just for the running repairs, but also for the daily checks, the refuelling, and the rearming. During the war they became remarkably proficient at their jobs, often working under the extreme pressure of an air raid or the urgent need to scramble for another sortie. Reloading the ammunition boxes and cleaning the guns, for example, was a complicated task, for the crew had to open 22 panels held by 150 turn-buttons, and then install 2,400 rounds – 300 for each of the eight Browning guns. As John Milne, an aircraftman at Duxford, recalled, the armourers' work 'could be arduous. Ammunition is heavy and loading the guns with it, tightly packed in the thin wings, was hard on the hands.'[75] Yet two armourers and two assistants could complete the routine in just three and a half minutes. 'To get the Spitfire back up in the sky as quickly as possible was very important to rigger, mechanic and armourer,' recalled E. A. Ellams of 611 Squadron:

> This team would practise the routine. Believe me, they were exciting times! During one of these 'panic' turnarounds, I was passing along the leading edge of the mainplane, the armourer was rearming and reloading the Browning guns when, as he was pulling back the striking pin with his toggle, it slipped and there was a round up the spout – the bullet passed by my face and I didn't even stop. When the 'kite' had taken off I said a prayer and broke into a sweat.[76]

And, even in this new age of advanced aeronautics, ground crews could be robustly practical, as John Wilkinson once discovered. Having taken off, he quickly found that the aileron of the left wing of his Spitfire was so heavy that he needed all the strength of both hands on the stick to keep the plane in level flight. When he landed, 'a mechanic came out to see what was wrong. When I told him, he said to stay in the cockpit. He got a hammer and a block of wood and proceeded to bang mightily on the trailing edge of the wing. I took off again and all was well.'[77]

Each Spitfire had its own flight mechanic, who checked on the engine, airscrew, and fuel and oil levels, and a rigger, who was responsible for the airframe, the undercarriage, the controls, and the air pressures for the pneumatic systems that operated the flaps, brakes and guns. Other operatives, not directly assigned to one particular plane, carried out various functional duties in their section. They included instrument-repairers, electricians, armourers and wireless men. The ideal official routine, once the Spitfire had taxied to the edge of the airfield, was for the crew to refuel it immediately, to stop condensation developing in the tank. The plane would then be pushed into a hangar, where the daily inspection would be carried out by the mechanic, the rigger and the rest of the crew. This included such steps as a check on the pressure in the air containers for the guns' pneumatic supply, which had to be at least 270 pounds per square inch. If it fell below that level, the guns would not fire. The ground crews also looked for any signs of damage on the surface of the plane, any leaks, any drop in the oxygen cylinder's pressure, and any malfunction in the instruments, wiring or lights. In the heat of battle, however, such a leisurely scrutiny was neither possible nor desirable. As Flight Lieutenant Duncan Stewart MacDonald, of 213 Squadron, recalled:

> The ground crews were marvellous the way they worked, the speed with which they managed to refuel and rearm. When you landed, the panels were off before you'd stop the aeroplane. You see it now in Formula One motor races – you see the driver coming in and the car's jacked up and the wheels taken off – that's how they worked. The ammunition was poured into the guns, the guns were cleaned, patches were put over the front of the guns, all the panels put back on, the aeroplane was refuelled – it was all done so quickly.[78]

Fred Roberts, an armourer based at 19 Squadron at Duxford, remembered one afternoon when Flight Lieutenant George Unwin came running into the hangar demanding his plane, which was up on trestles with its engine cowlings off, the guns unloaded, and the ammunition tanks removed:

> I am sure we must have broken a record for bringing a Spitfire to serviceability after the first shout from him! George was airborne in less than ten minutes and after the rest of the squadron with a straight take-off across the wind and no engine warm-up. I don't know if he caught up with them or took the Luftwaffe on his own, but it showed the courage of the man and the confidence he placed in us, his ground crew.[79]

Apart from the basic daily inspection routine, there were many other incidental duties for the ground crews. Their role in starting up the early Spitfires was crucial, as John Milne of 19 Squadron described:

It involved using a Trolley Ac, a two-wheeled enclosed low hand-cart containing accumulators. One starter trolley was shared between several aircraft so the crews became adept at high-speed trolley-pulling from one Spitfire to the next. The trolley had a thick cable which plugged through a flap in the engine cowling. Once the engine started, one of the crew pulled the cable out and took it away, being careful not to step back into the propeller.[80]

Next came the invigorating, if disturbing, task of lying across the tailplane to hold down the Spitfire while the pilot or the flight mechanic ran the engine at high revs, the violent slipstream leaving crews breathless. 'It was really hard going. There was nothing better for waking you up in the morning,' said Aircraftman Douglas Rattle of 19 Squadron.[81]

On one extraordinary occasion in February 1945 at Hibaldstow in Lincolnshire a Spitfire pilot, Flight Lieutenant Cox, ran up his engine with several 'erks' sitting on the tailplane. Among them was a member of the WAAF – the Women's Auxiliary Air Force – Margaret Horton. Suddenly Cox opened the throttle, began to race down the airstrip, and was airborne before Leading Aircraftwoman Horton had time to jump off. As the plane soared into the sky, she clung on for dear life, one hand gripping the elevator, her body stretched taut across the tailplane. Sensing there was something wrong with his plane but unable to see Horton hanging grimly from the rear, Cox radioed his base for advice. The controller, who had seen everything, told him to return to the airfield, but made no mention of Horton in case he caused a panic. Flight Lieutenant Cox duly landed, and was surprised to see Horton shakily putting her feet back down on the ground. 'Put yourself down for ten minutes' flying time,' he said with typical RAF dryness.[82]

Installation of new guns was another gruelling job. They had to be stripped and cleaned, and the feeds altered; then the old guns were removed and the new ones put in their place before the aircraft was taken to the firing butts, where the eight new guns were harmonized with the reflector sight, locknutted and test-fired. Alignment of the guns was necessary to ensure that that their firepower was concentrated at a certain distance; the Air Ministry recommended 400 yards as the point of maximum impact, though many pilots preferred the guns to be set so their bullets would converge at 250 yards. 'I spent days and days on my knees under the wings doing this work,' said Fred Roberts. 'We had to push the Spitfires to the butts and manually lift them on to the trestles for levelling before harmonizing, all hard work.'[83] The actual mechanics of harmonizing the guns have been described by the Spitfire test pilot Don Robertson: 'The aircraft was jacked up and placed on stands fore and aft with the fuselage datum at the angle it assumed in flight at the expected attack speed. Then, by removing the breech block, a small inverted periscope was inserted to allow the adjuster to see through the barrel to whatever the gun was aimed at and to adjust the mount to bring the gun into position on the chosen pattern.'[84]

Gun harmonization could sometimes lead to near-disasters, as Sandy Johnstone recorded in his wartime diary:

> Periodic alignments are carried out by the armourers, who first raise the machine into a flying position before using geometrical calculations to sight each gun in turn on pre-positioned markings on the door of the hangar. A couple of armourers were doing just that this afternoon when the bloke in the cockpit accidentally pressed the firing button, causing all eight Brownings to spew straight through the hangar door and blow the cap off an airman working on an aircraft inside. But the fusillade did not stop there; bullets continued into the clubhouse itself, passing through both walls of the kitchen and into the offices beyond.

One piece of molten led, 'spent but still very hot', flew straight on to the desk of a senior officer.[85]

John Milne had a particular dislike of one of his chores: pumping up the pneumatic shock absorbers for the undercarriage's legs. 'It was not the pumping that was hard, but dragging the heavy equipment around the airfield. It consisted of a long vertical pump arm, a pump, and a gauge to check the air pressure, all mounted on a large and heavy plank of wood, just like a railway sleeper. One needed a strong back to service the Spitfire.'[86] For all its wonderful reliability, the Merlin engine could also be a headache, especially when it had to be changed, as Flight Lieutenant Rob Collin, an RAF engineer who worked on Spitfires in North Africa, explained:

> A Merlin engine was a powerful beast producing 1,000 horsepower to pull it and the aircraft behind it through the sky. It also drove the vacuum pump for the pilot's blind-flying instruments, a hydraulic oil pump for the undercarriage and brakes and drove a generator for 24-volt electricity to charge the battery, this in addition to pumps for coolant, for the cylinders and the lubricating oil to stop the engine seizing up. One of the Merlin's troubles was that its position was at the front of the aircraft and another was that, if you thrashed it (as, for instance, in a dogfight) it leaked oil, which obscured the view from the windscreen of the pilot. It was a painstaking job to put together a leak-free Merlin.

Collin complained that installing a Merlin in the front of a Spitfire required 'a miniature version of the Forth Bridge to connect it to the airframe. Furthermore, the engine had to be totally enclosed by cowling which had to be easily removable for servicing. Rolls-Royce made no provision for affixing this cowling. It took two days to change an engine in a Spitfire.'[87] And E. A. Ellams felt that 'the Dunlop airbrakes were the weak part of the Spitfire. I must have spent hours of my time upside-down in the cockpit adjusting the air valves to synchronize the pressure with the rudder bar!'[88]

Because of its power, the Spitfire could occasionally be hazardous to the ground crews, as Joe Roddis, a flight mechanic with 234 Squadron, remembered, 'The pilots used to say that the Spitfire was the kindest aeroplane they'd ever flown. It would never do them any harm. But they were purely flying it. We sometimes got into situations where it could hurt you. But that was purely out of carelessness. We had an aircraft tip up on its nose and the prop flew off and cut a bloke in half.'[89] And Johnnie Houlton left this gruesome account of a tragedy that befell a crew working on a Mark XIV, one of the later models. In May 1944 a number of airmen from Houlton's 485 Squadron were grouped around a Spitfire as its engine started up in preparation for a bomber escort sortie. One of them, Flight Sergeant Frank Reeves, stood on the left wing tip:

> The engine involuntarily went from ticking over to 3,000 rpm and maximum power in one brief, roaring surge. The machine whipped nose-down over the chocks and the tail flicked high in the air, as I could see the fitter wrenching at the throttle in the cockpit. A great deluge of earth and debris exploded upwards as the four wooden propeller blades smashed into splinters against the ground, and two airmen were catapulted high in the air like helpless tumbling puppets. The stubs of the propeller blades clawed the Spitfire round to the left through an arc of ninety degrees, as the left chock held firm, but the right wheel pushed its chock clear. A body hurtled through the air out of the maelstrom, then the engine stopped dead, leaving a vibrating, shocking silence. I ran to the crumpled body, but Frank Reeves had died instantly.

The two other aircraftsmen were badly injured. 'To this day it is hard to reconcile that docile Spitfire with the instant monster which savaged its devoted attendants.'[90]

Such incidents were, thankfully, rare. Over the years of its service, the groundcrews came to hold the Spitfire in as much affection as did its pilots. Fred Roberts concluded that, despite 'cut fingers, numerous sore heads through bumping, wet trousers through kneeling in wet grass, leading to rheumatism in the knees, I still think of the Spitfire with a lot of love and will always say it was the greatest aircraft of its time'.[91]

5
'The Spitfires are wonderful machines'

∽∼

IN THE LATE 1930s, as tension between Britain and Germany increased, the arms race in the air took on a literal form. At an international flying meeting in Zurich in July 1937, the Germans boasted that a highly modified Me 109, winner of the Circuit des Alpes, was now the fastest fighter in the world, capable of reaching 379 mph. The Air Ministry was unwilling to let this claim go unchallenged. Supermarine, working with Rolls-Royce, was instructed to build a special high-speed version of the Spitfire which could break the world speed record for a land plane. The plane that the company came up with had a number of changes compared to the Mark I production Spitfire, including a reduced wing area, an absence of gun mountings and radio fittings, a streamlined skid instead of a tailwheel, a new windscreen, a four-bladed propeller, and a highly polished finish. Above all, the aircraft had an adapted Merlin II engine, based on the type used in the last Schneider Trophy winner and capable of 2,000 horsepower.

It was not until November 1938 that the racing Spitfire was finally ready. But by then the Germans had extended their lead. In June a Heinkel 100 had established a new record of 394 mph. Just as in the drive for rearmament, the British seemed doomed to be trailing. The Spitfire had slipped badly in its production schedule, and now it was losing in the quest for speed. By late 1938 the Air Ministry was starting to have its doubts about the entire venture. Worried about potential accusations that the government was spending energy and public money on little more than a vanity project, Sir Wilfrid Freeman, the Air Member for Production and Development, warned that in any public pronouncements the experimental research side of the work should be stressed. He also said that the Supermarine effort should continue only if there was a realistic chance of gaining the record: there was, he believed, no point on carrying on 'if the speed is on the borderline but not definitely such as to justify a whole hearted attempt to put up a really good show'.[1] A sense of despondency now crept into Supermarine. In December 1938 Sir Charles Craven of Vickers wrote of his regret at the government's loss of faith. 'I saw the specially prepared machine at Southampton ten days ago,' he told one of his fellow directors. 'I think the fear is that the Germans may be waiting for us to pinch the record from them and then slip in something that would pinch it back from us. I went to see Freeman last weekend and he felt that when we do get the speed record, we ought to take it by such a large margin that it would take some years for the Germans – or anyone else – to take it back again.'[2]

Supermarine had not given up entirely. In February 1939 the Speed Spitfire took off from Eastleigh and reached 408 mph. But more work was needed if a genuine challenge was to be mounted. Then in March any lingering hopes were extinguished by the news from Germany that an He 100 had attained the breathtaking speed of 463 mph, smashing not only the world land plane speed record but also the absolute world speed record, until then held by the Italian Macchi MC 72 seaplane at 440 mph. There was no chance that even the most streamlined and altered Spitfire of 1939 could go at anything like that pace. In fact the Heinkel's record for a piston-engined plane was to stand for thirty years, until it was beaten in 1969 by a Grumman Bearcat flying at 482 mph.

The Speed Spitfire project was now abandoned, though the elegant blue-and-silver plane was to survive right through war, used largely for testing new equipment. In the long term, the experiment proved useful in demonstrating to Joe Smith, Supermarine's chief designer, the Spitfire's far-reaching possibilities for development, particularly with the installation of a more powerful engine. In the immediate term, however, the failure of the Speed venture could have almost been a metaphor for the wider disillusion in government circles with the Spitfire itself in the late 1930s. The plane which had once promised so much only four years earlier now appeared to be second rate. The Germans were further ahead than ever, in both technology and numbers.

The inability of the Speed Spitfire to catch up with the Germans was matched by the inability of Supermarine to deliver the aircraft in sufficient quantities. Even after the first Spitfires had gone into service, in August 1938, troubles continued at the Supermarine works over the plane's production, particularly because of higher than expected costs and difficulties in recruiting skilled labour in Southampton. 'Owing to the inexperience of the main sub-contractors on this particular class of work,' wrote A. E. Marsh-Hunn, Supermarine's commercial manager, to the Air Ministry in October 1938,

> there have inevitably been abnormal initial costs in the preliminary develop-
> ment work and owing to the long delay in getting into production there has
> been an excessive amount of over-time and night-shift working and jigs and
> tools have had to be duplicated to accelerate production. Furthermore the
> recent desire to still further accelerate output, necessitating the recruitment and
> training of inefficient labour, introduces a further factor quite outside any of our
> original considerations.[3]

For more than two years the Air Ministry had endured a litany of such excuses. At a ministerial progress meeting in September 1938, there were reports that there might be further delays because Beaton's, one of the sub-contractors working on the wings, had 'only one set of tools'. Moreover, it was said that any modification to the wings to try to overcome the potential problem of guns freezing at altitude would further slow down production. Sir Cyril Newall, the Chief of the Air Staff, almost exploded with anger, declaring that if the Spitfire could not fire at the same heights as the bombers it would encounter then it would be 'useless as a fighting aircraft'. He insisted on the modification to the guns.[4] A report produced in September by Sir Ernest Lemon, the Air Ministry's Director General of Production and an acknowledged expert in industrial organization, reinforced the sense of gloom. 'In the difficult case of Supermarine,' he wrote, 'the real problem centres round the production of the Spitfire wings. These wings have been seriously set back from a variety of causes one of which, in my opinion, is the failure of the Supermarine Company to nurse and assist with technical advice the firms to which the wings were sub-contracted.'[5]

All patience was now running out with the Spitfire programme. What had been seen as the potential saviour of the RAF was an increasing source of irri-tation. An exasperated, dismissive tone crept into the discussions about it. Given the aircraft's cherished place in modern British history, it is remarkable to look at the papers of the Air Ministry right up to mid-1940 and see how little belief there was in the Spitfire. The excitement of the early 1930s, when Mitchell was at his peak, had entirely vanished, destroyed by production problems, rows with the Supermarine management, and disappointment over the plane's inability to achieve the speed once promised. From the middle of 1938 the Spitfire was no longer at the centre of the Air Ministry's thinking about future of Fighter Command. At least three other aeroplanes were thought to have greater long-term potential: the 360 mph, twin-engined Westland Whirlwind, whose prototype made its first flight in October 1938; the Bristol Beaufighter, another powerful, well-armed twin-engined machine; and a single-engine design from Hawker's, the Camm fighter, which eventu-ally evolved into the massive Tornado and then into the even more formidable Typhoon. Far from being regarded as the jewel in the crown of the Fighter Command, the Spitfire was seen by many as little more than a stopgap before the arrival of these potentially more successful types.

Such an attitude is all too apparent from the debates within the Air Ministry about the steps needed to meet the demands of the government's expanding fighter programme in the run-up to war. As early as February 1938 Sir Cyril Newall said that he 'would prefer the new fighters, the Camm and

Westland types, but as they would not be ready he was thrown back on the Hurricane and Spitfire, of which the latter was definitely the preferable type but was lagging behind in production'. Freeman agreed that the Westland would 'ultimately be our choice', but until it was available the RAF would have to rely on the Hurricane and Spitfire.[6] As a result, the Air Ministry had ordered another 200 Spitfires, on top of the original 310 contracted from Supermarines, but the lack of conviction about these orders was revealed in the lengthy deliberations over the future of the aircraft plants run by the Fairey company.

At first it had been conceived that Sir Richard Fairey would be asked to manufacture 300 Spitfires at his Stockport factory, but this had been superseded – despite the reservations of Sir Wilfrid Freeman – by the order placed in May 1938 for 1,000 Spitfires from the Nuffield factory in Birmingham. An argument now started as to which fighter Sir Richard's firm should build. In July 1938, at one of the Secretary of State's progress meetings, the Deputy Chief of the Air Staff, Air Vice-Marshal R. E. C. Pierse, graphically revealed the extent of official disillusion with the Spitfire, all but declaring it to be outdated before it had even gone into service. Pierse said that what the RAF needed was a cannon fighter, and the Westland machine was the answer. 'He would like to press very strongly that Fairey's should build the Westland fighter.' Sir Ernest Lemon agreed, adding that 'it would be a mistake to give Fairey's an order for an obsolescent type of fighter when they had the design staff to produce a better type.' The clear implication, as the Secretary of State for Air, Sir Kingsley Wood, pointed out, was that 'the Air Staff would regard the Spitfire as obsolescent by the time it could be put into production by Fairey's.' Sir Wilfrid Freeman, however, warned that the Spitfire, for all its problems, was now in production, whereas the Westland fighter had yet to be properly tested. At the end of the meeting it was agreed that, if the Westland model proved successful, then Fairey's should manufacture this type. If not, then Fairey's would be asked to produce an additional quantity of Spitfires.[7]

The successful initial trials of the Westland, powered by two Rolls-Royce Peregrine engines – a development of the Kestrel – further diminished the standing of the Spitfire. At a ministerial progress meeting in November 1938 Sir Cyril Newall, having again expressed regret at the lack of any cannon-gun fighters in the RAF, told Wood that 'he would like to place orders at once for the Westland fighter.' The first of this type, he said, 'had already flown and was expected to have a speed in the neighbourhood of 400 mph, which was a considerable advance on the Hurricane and Spitfire'. Freeman felt that, despite a satisfactory first flight of the Westland, it was too soon for such a step.[8] But Newall's scorn for the Spitfire could not be held back. At a progress meeting in December, he urged that the Nuffield factory, once it was operating, should be instructed to make the Westland fighter rather than the Spitfire. When other officials said that, even on the most optimistic timetable, the Westland could not be in production before 1940, he condemned such thinking as too conservative, arguing that there was no reason to delay until every drawing had been completed and every type of raw material ordered. Furthermore, he believed that the prime duty of the Supermarine factory was to assist in this process at the Nuffield plant, not continue to build the unwanted Spitfire. 'He thought that Supermarine's should concentrate on the manufacture of such parts for the Westland fighter and go on to the manufacture of other parts as the drawings and materials became available. By doing this it might be possible to reduce the size of the additional Spitfire order and to bring the Westland fighter into production at an earlier date.'[9]

But none of this could happen until the Westland prototype had proved itself and the Nuffield factory had been built at Castle Bromwich. The autocratic Nuffield, assisted by Oliver Boden of the Morris Corporation, had been given a free hand over the site and the erection of the plant. But, within a few months of Sir Kingsley Wood's well-received declaration in Parliament, it was obvious that all was not well with Castle Bromwich. As Wood reported in September 1938, 'he had received from a man who had recently visited the Nuffield factory a very unfavourable report on the progress that was being made. Other factories were being erected quickly and he could not understand why the Nuffield factory was taking so long.' He asked officials to see Boden to impress on him 'the importance of the early completion of the Nuffield factory'.[10] They soon reported back that 'Mr Boden was keen and pushing on with the factory, but a long time would elapse before the factory came into production.'[11] Newall had thought that Boden had little credibility as a manager when he first met him. 'He is old, looks flabby, is suffering from a swollen head and did not impress me at all as a mastermind or organizer,' he wrote.[12] One astute writer, the Biggles author W. E. Johns, had already detected a looming crisis. In the August 1938 edition of the magazine *Popular Flying,* Johns reflected:

> Viscount Nuffield's recent order for 1,000 Spitfires has sent me thinking. The brain behind the Morris concern may be an excellent one for producing large numbers. But Lord Nuffield has no factory. OK, he will build one and Sir Kingsley Wood has cut the first turf. That factory must take a year to build, then another six months to get busy, so no Spitfires for at least eighteen months. That's getting on for 1940. The Spitfire came out in 1936![13]

At the beginning of 1939, Whitehall's anxiety over the Nuffield factory was worsening, not just because of the lack of physical progress, but also because of the cost. Having originally been told by the Morris Corporation that the bill for the plant would be around £2 million, the Air Ministry was alarmed to learn that it had gone up to over £4 million. 'We were expressly warned not to press the issue in regard to the production of detailed estimates and plans owing to the difficulties of any trespassing on Lord Nuffield's "free hand",' wrote an angry official to the Permanent Secretary, Sir Arthur Street. 'I cannot but feel that we are laying up a crop of difficulties for ourselves in deferring action since we have not given the Treasury any considered figures or plans and the estimates are so far advanced as to make it difficult to effect any curtailment . . . The original estimate of £2 million always seemed to us grotesque but our doubts were silenced by the believers in "miracle working".'[14]

But further south, on the coast, the news was better. The Supermarine factory had at last resolved most of the subcontracting and production difficulties. Aircraft were at last starting to come out of the Southampton in significant numbers. All parts of the Woolston and Itchen works were operating to capacity. By the end of June 1939, 240 Spitfires had been delivered from the original order for 310 planes. There is little doubt that the sense of approaching conflict brought a new urgency to the shopfloor of Supermarine, helped by bonus earnings for overtime. In 1938 the average working week was 50 hours. A year later it had risen to 63 hours. The Supermarine manager Denis Webb, commenting on the increase in output after Munich, wrote, 'Neville Chamberlain's despised scrap of paper had given us a good return.'[15]

Yet Chamberlain had never viewed the Munich Agreement merely as a way of buying time. As he told the Cabinet in November 1938, he had always been 'trying to keep two horses abreast, conciliation and rearmament'.[16] For all his cold Midlands practicality, there was a part of him that genuinely believed his policy of appeasement could bring a lasting peace in central Europe. That naivety was cruelly exposed in March 1939, when the Third Reich occupied the remainder of Czechoslovakia, then began to menace Poland. Chamberlain's strategy was in tatters. The inevitability of war was recognized by almost everyone in government on 23 August 1939 when the Nazi–Soviet pact was signed, leaving Hitler free to attack Poland without having to worry about the eastern front. Once Hitler invaded, Britain would be forced to respond because of Chamberlain's guarantee to uphold the integrity of Poland. The assault duly started on 1 September, with German troops crossing the Rhine at 4.45 a.m. After much shameful dithering and talk of diplomatic conferences, the Prime Minister was finally forced by the majority of his Cabinet into declaring war on 3 September at 11 a.m.

In a gloomy, self-pitying broadcast to the British nation, he presented the epochal decision in personal terms, expressing his sorrow that all his work for peace had failed.

Britain was hopelessly ill-equipped to help Poland, possessing neither a strong expeditionary force nor an offensive air force – thanks largely to the policy that the government had adopted over the previous five years of focusing so much defence spending on fighter aircraft. But even with such limited capability as it had, Chamberlain's administration showed no willingness to make any gesture of attack against Germany. When one minister in the Cabinet suggested a bombing raid against Germany, Kingsley Wood reacted with outrage, saying that German private property could be put at risk. A mood of paralysing caution descended on the government. As the Spitfire pilot Brian Kingcome wrote, 'We had been expecting to hear the drone of approaching bombers at any moment from the time when Chamberlain finished broadcasting his warning to the nation. Yet nothing happened. A season of perfect weather, with blue unclouded skies and almost no wind, connived with the feeling of anti-climax. Meanwhile we itched to get airborne but no flying was allowed. A deep boredom set in.'[17] Alex Henshaw, who had applied to join Fighter Command but was recruited by Vickers as a test pilot, found the whole atmosphere 'disgraceful. Everyone was playing golf and tennis and people went on holiday and had their weekends off. The whole country was operating exactly as it was before the war. There was no urgency. It was dreadful.'[18]

The sense of inertia was captured in the diary of Air Commodore Sir Douglas Evill, one of the military representatives on the Supreme War Council. On 11 September, barely a week after the declaration of war, he wrote, 'A quiet day of routine.' The 12th was similarly 'a very dull day, without news and with little or nothing to do'. But behind this lassitude there was also a failure to grasp the Nazi government's ruthless long-term strategy: 'There can be little doubt that Germany must now make an effort to achieve a marked success against the Western powers, and to do so within the next few weeks,' he wrote on 12 October.[19] Neville Chamberlain was even more guilty of this kind of self-deception. 'My policy continues to be the same,' he told his sister Ida in October. 'Hold on tight, push up the economic pressure, push on with munitions production and military preparations with the utmost urgency and take no offensive measures unless Hitler begins it. I reckon that if we are allowed to carry on this policy we shall have won the war by the spring.' Chamberlain was almost as unrealistic about Britain's air defences. 'I am told that London is now the best defended place in Europe and no reasonably prudent air force would go near it. Our aerodromes and factories too would be formidable objects of attack and our fighter squadrons are just itching to give the German bombers the kick they believe they have in store for them. There is no doubt that in personnel and material, though not in numbers, we are superior to the Germans.'[20]

This was absurdly optimistic, especially on fighters. When war broke out, Supermarine had not even completed the original contract for 310 Spitfires, there was no sign of any productive activity at Castle Bromwich, and only 187 of the type were in front-line operational service, with a further 83 in maintenance units, undergoing testing or involved in training and other secondary duties. Before the war, Dowding had estimated that the absolute minimum number of squadrons that Fighter Command needed for home defence was 52, yet in September 1939 he only had 35 – and 4 of these had been sent to France to support the British and French armies, while 6 more had been put on a mobile footing. Even worse, much of Fighter Command's equipment was still made up of obsolete biplanes like the Gloster Gauntlet or obsolescent machines such as the Bristol Blenheim, too slow to be an effective fighter.

In this limited respect it was fortunate that the government had decided that the enemy should not be engaged. The long months of the so-called 'Phoney War' before the spring of 1940 provided more time for the build-up of Hurricanes and Spitfires. But the sense of inactivity was trying for many of the Spitfire pilots, who had joined the RAF for action. 'We are rapidly becoming bored with the war, for we seem to do little but sit around at dispersal these days, with occasional practice flights thrown in,' wrote Sandy Johnstone of 602 Squadron. In another diary entry, Johnstone complained that 'Sector control still insists on maintaining unnecessarily high states of readiness, thus keeping us on perpetual tenterhooks even though nothing much seems to be happening. We have also had a few false alarms, including one tonight when I spent a fruitless three-quarters of an hour being vectored all over Perthshire in pursuit of nothing in particular.'[21]

But the Spitfire was not entirely deprived of real action. At 11 a.m. on the morning of 16 October 1939 nine Ju 88 bombers took off from the north German island of Sylt on a mission to attack Royal Navy targets in the Firth of Forth. Having failed to score any real hits on the warships, the Ju 88s turned back for home. But as they climbed away, they suddenly found they were being chased by Spitfires from 602 (City of Glasgow) and 603 (City of Edinburgh) Squadrons. Horst von Riesen, a young lieutenant with the 1st Gruppe of Kampfgeschwader 30, gave this account: 'I knew that I would need all the speed I could possibly squeeze out of my Junkers if we were to escape. I pushed down the nose and dived for the sea. But it was no good.

The Spitfires, as we soon recognized them to be, had the advantage of speed and height from the start and they soon caught up with us.' Two of the Junkers were shot down in the Forth estuary – the first victories of the war for Fighter Command – but von Riesen managed to take his plane 7 miles out to sea before the inevitable happened: 'After a chase of more than twenty minutes there was a sudden "phooff" and my starboard motor disappeared from view in a cloud of steam. One of the enemy bullets had pierced the radiator, releasing the vital coolant and without it the motor was finished. There was no alternative but to shut it down before it burst into flames.' The Ju 88 remained airborne across the North Sea, but there seemed little hope that it could last the whole four-hour journey back to Sylt. Von Riesen's crew discussed whether they should return to Scotland and give themselves up. In a tribute to the fear that the Spitfire had instantly established in this first action, one of the men shouted over the intercom, 'No, no, never! If we go back there the Spitfires will certainly get us!' That was the view of most of the rest of the crew, including von Riesen himself: 'The thought of going back into that hornet's nest horrified us. We decided to carry on.' Somehow the Ju 88 staggered back to Sylt on one engine – not for nothing was it known as 'the wonder bomber'. Von Riesen concluded, 'So I survived my first encounter with Spitfires. It was not a pleasant experience.'[22]

The next day, 17 October, a Heinkel 111 on a reconnaissance sortie 25 miles off the coast of Whitby was shot down by three Spitfires from 41 Squadron in nearby Catterick. The Heinkel pilot and navigator managed to bail out and were rescued from the sea, thereby becoming the first German prisoners to be landed on English soil during the war. On 29 November in Lothian, Spitfires from 602 and 603 Squadrons shot down another He 111, the first Luftwaffe plane to be brought down on the British mainland. Sporadic incidents continued to take place over the coming months, such as the clash on 7 December when a group of He 111s were intercepted by Spitfires from 72 Squadron based at Drem in East Lothian. Willibald Klein, a rear gunner in one of the He 111s, described the action as the attack developed:

> In the other aircraft, on our left, the rear gunner was a very young man, very inexperienced, slack and slow; he hardly shot at all, so of course the Spitfires had great fun with him; they came so close that they hung on to his tail, riddling him before they turned away – and only then would he shoot. The machine was going slowly because of the hits, and as the battle progressed it was gradually pushed closer and closer to the sea until it was almost touching the waves. We stayed with it and when it finally ditched we were so low that the splash touched us.[23]

The last Klein saw of the crew was their heads bobbing in the icy sea. His own Heinkel managed to struggle back, badly damaged, to Sylt. On landing it was found to contain 350 bullet holes.

There were two lessons from these early skirmishes. First that the Spitfire was a formidable weapon, easily outclassing two of the German planes which formed the backbone of the Luftwaffe's bombing forces. Flying over Scotland and expecting to meet only a few Gloster Gladiators, the Germans had been shaken by the appearance of the Spitfires. 'Oh rubbish, the English defences are no good,' Klein's captain had said dismissively when first warned that Spitfires had been spotted.[24] This dangerous overconfidence was to continue right up until the end of the Battle of Britain. The second lesson was that Fighter Command had a potent defensive tool in the radar system, which had been first developed by the Scottish scientist Robert Watson-Watt in 1935 – the same year in which Mitchell produced the design of the classic Type 300 Spitfire. Again, the Air Ministry's embrace of radar – then known as Radio Detection Finding (RDF) – on the basis of a few experimental demonstrations at Orford, on the Suffolk coast, showed that the officials were not as hidebound as mythology suggests, though it should be said that, just as with the Spitfire, Dowding and Swinton were again the twin political driving forces behind the key decisions. By 1939 most of the eastern and southern coasts were protected by a chain of radar stations, with the result that Fighter Command did not have to mount standing patrols, which sapped fuel and energy. Instead, the Spitfires and Hurricanes could be guided directly to their targets by ground control, something which took the Germans completely by surprise. Indeed, it was not until late in 1940 that the importance of radar in Fighter Command's operations was recognized by the Germans.

A report by F. C. Broome of the Air Ministry, who completed a tour of the Spitfire squadrons at the end of October 1939, emphasized the excellent reputation the plane was rapidly building. 'The general impression is that the Spitfires are wonderful machines and that the Huns hate them,' he told Sir Charles Craven, though he felt that the armament and armour plating should be improved.[25]

But not all Spitfire interceptions were successful. On the foggy morning of 6 September 1939, just three days after war was declared, Spitfires of 74 Squadron, based at Hornchurch, were scrambled to tackle a flight of unidentified aircraft flying over the Essex coast and apparently heading for London. The Spitfires were led by Adolph 'Sailor' Malan, a hard, cold, but highly skilled pilot who had left his native South Africa to join the RAF in 1936. As the two sections of the squadron climbed through the sky, suddenly Malan caught a glimpse of the unidentified aircraft in the distance. 'Tally-ho,' he called out over the radio to the first section – the signal to attack. But almost as soon as he had uttered the phrase he realized that a terrible mistake was about to be made. The opposing aircraft were not the enemy at all: they were Hurricanes. Immediately Malan tried to change his orders. 'Friendly aircraft – break away,' he shouted. But it was too late. Two of the 74 Squadron pilots, Paddy Byrne and John Freeborn, pumped up by the thrill of their first combat, appeared not to have heard his words. Nor did they seem to see the RAF roundels and markings on the Hurricanes as they opened fire. Two of the Hurricanes were shot down, and one of the pilots was killed. Byrne and Freeborn were arrested as soon as they landed, and soon afterwards were brought before a court martial. Though they were acquitted, since it was difficult to apportion blame in the highly charged, confused atmosphere that reigned on that day, John Freeborn was bitter at the way he felt he had been betrayed by Sailor Malan, who appeared for the prosecution at the court martial. Freeborn, who claimed never to have heard the order to break off the attack, thought that Malan, ruthless and ego-driven, was trying to cover his own back, while Malan believed Freeborn had been irresponsible. They continued to serve together in the same squadron, but their relationship never recovered.[26]

The tragedy became known as 'The Battle of Barking Creek', and it had the indirect, long-term benefit of compelling the RAF to fit signal equipment in every plane, known as Identification Friend or Foe (IFF), which revealed to ground control whether an aircraft was hostile or not. But Barking Creek was by no means the only instance of friendly fire from Spitfires that year. Sandy Johnstone recorded in his diary how his 602 Squadron was scrambled on 21 December to take on a flight of German bombers apparently making a raid on the Royal Navy base at Rosyth on the Firth of Forth. Johnstone watched as six Spitfires took on 'what appeared to be twin-engined Dornier bombers looming indistinctly through the haze. The oncoming formation suddenly broke apart, aircraft swooping in all directions, trying to dodge the withering fire of the attacking fighters.' He was plunging into the melee himself when 'one bomber pulled up ahead of me in a steep climbing turn, presenting a full plan view of his underside. I was about to press the firing button when, to my utter horror, I saw RAF roundels clearly visible on the mainplanes. "Don't fire!" I shouted into the radio. "Don't shoot. They're friendly! They're friendly!"' It was too late: a pair of RAF twin-engined Hampden bombers had been sent crashing into the sea. One man had drowned; the others were rescued. A court of inquiry was held, which to Johnstone's surprise found in favour of the Spitfire pilots on the grounds that the Hampdens had drifted far off course in returning from a mission over the

German coast and had failed to give the correct signals to the RAF bases in a defended area. The Hampden crews showed what they thought of the decision as they left 602's airfield:

> Most of us came out to watch the departure. We continued watching while the Hampdens took off and climbed towards the north, forming up as they gradually gained height before turning back preparatory, we imagined, to treating us to a good old bullshit flypast. And flypast we certainly got, for, as the ten bombers dived towards us at full throttle, we watched in disbelief their bomb doors swinging open, whereupon hundreds upon hundreds of lavatory rolls rained down on us to spread far and wide all over the station.[27]

These tragic errors were due partly to inexperience, partly to a yearning for battle. John Freeborn of 74 Squadron later admitted that 'it was the excitement of war just declared and the resultant adrenalin surge' that led him to attack the Hurricanes without making a visual check.[28]

Inexperience, combined with the Spitfire's design, also led to a large number of accidents at night during the early years of the war. Between September and December 1939 there were no fewer than 60 serious nightflying accidents in Fighter Command, 38 of them fatal and most of them involving Spitfires.[29] Sandy Johnstone watched in dismay as one young sergeant took off from his base on his first night take-off, only to become totally disorientated. He flew 'straight into the ground at full throttle, creating a fireball that must have been visible for miles around'.[30] Bill Rolls, based at RAF Acklington, had a terrifying experience on one of his first night flights. He was patrolling the Northumberland coast in poor weather, with the Spitfire buffeted so badly that he found it hard to control. To his relief, he received the order over the radio to return to Acklington. He thought, judging by his instruments, that he was flying at around 2,000 feet when he began the descent towards the airfield, though he was surprised that from such a height he could see the lamps of the runway shining brightly:

> I decided to come in on a long approach on engine because of the bumpiness. I was about to lower my flaps when it happened. I felt a terrific bang on my head and heard the rending sound of metal; the aircraft pitched up into the air and I saw a blinding light go past me. I saw the front of the aircraft fall away and felt the bang as my right wing hit the ground and tore itself away from the fuselage. I was bouncing up the runway and then over to my left wing, which was torn off. I vaguely remember a howling wind as the fuselage went up the runway and a lot of noise but by then I was too dazed to care.

Though his Spitfire was a write-off, with wreckage strewn all over the runway, Rolls himself suffered only minor injuries. It was found that the accident was caused by faulty instruments, which had given him the wrong altitude. Within just four days he was back on patrol, a sign of his mental as well as physical strength.[31]

The large number of accidents was a severe drain on the already limited resources of Fighter Command, with production still not up to the level that Dowding wanted. He was to comment after the war, 'You see the main trouble was that we had such a tiny output of fighters.'[32] By late 1939 Dowding was battling on two fronts: one personal, the other relating to supply. Much older than any of his colleagues and never popular with them because of his perceived aloofness, his position as commander-in-chief of Fighter Command was insecure, with the threat of enforced retirement constantly hanging over him. Dowding, whose distant manner hid a sensitive ego, was already aggrieved at having been passed over for the post of Chief of the Air Staff in 1937, and the endless speculation from 1938 about his departure on the grounds of his age – though he was only fifty-seven at the outbreak of war – fuelled his antagonism towards the air establishment. He had been officially told that he was due to retire in June 1939, but the imminent threat of war led to the Air Staff asking him to stay at the head of Fighter Command until March 1940. Dowding took the opportunity to write a private memorandum expressing his anger at the way his case had been handled. 'I have received very cavalier treatment at the hands of the Air Ministry during the past two years,' he declared. He went on to complain about 'discourtesy' in the way that decisions had been made, and that his efforts to remedy the deficiencies of the RAF, such as through the development of radar and new fighters, had met with such resistance: 'This work has had to be carried out against the inertia of the Air Staff.' He further stated that he had been left out of policymaking, adding that that it was 'beyond question that my exclusion is deliberate and not inadvertent'.[33] But, having vented his annoyance on paper, he agreed to remain in his job until the spring of 1940.

As he revealed in that memorandum, one of Dowding's biggest irritations was his feeling that the Air Staff were reluctant to face up to the challenge of creating an effective home defence force. In particular, he argued, they refused to recognize the vital importance of the Spitfire, regarding his attachment to the plane as a kind of mild eccentricity. He cited, as an example, a meeting where he urged that bullet-proof glass should be fitted to the windscreens of Spitfires. To his amazement, the idea was greeted with laughter round the table, as if he had asked for something 'grotesquely impossible'. He retorted, 'If Chicago gangsters can have bullet-proof glass in their cars, I can't see any reason why my pilots should not have the same.'[34] He got his wish, and the

Spitfire canopies were fitted with a specially moulded form of Triplex, a thick sandwich of glass with an inner plastic layer.

But Dowding's overall perception was right: the Air Ministry's lack of belief in the Spitfire at the end of 1939 was all too obvious, despite its initial record of success against the Heinkel and Junkers bombers. With the benefit of historical hindsight, it is astonishing to find that just weeks before the outbreak of war the Air Staff were so indifferent to the future of the Spitfire programme that they not merely preferred to invest their hopes in the Beaufighter and the Westland and Camm fighters, but they even contemplated the sale of Spitfires abroad – this at the very time when Dowding was crying out for more fighters. Unlike Lord Swinton, Sir Kingsley Wood was not a strong enough minister to contradict this misguided thinking. Few would go as far as Sir John Reith, the head of the BBC, whose loathing for Wood was almost visceral. 'A self-seeking little cad' was one Reith diary description; 'a feeble little creature', 'a little swine', 'a little crook' and 'a little bounder' were others.[35] But most would agree that Wood was an unimpressive Secretary of State, unable to impose a clear direction or to provide strong leadership. Sir Henry 'Chips' Channon, the camp, gossipy Tory MP for Southend, commented on one of Wood's Commons speeches on air policy in October 1939, 'The House slept. He read it as if he was dictating to a typist.'[36]

With his limited strategic understanding, Wood could not counter the stance of his Ministry, which seemed determined to squander Mitchell's legacy. Even Sir Wilfrid Freeman, who with Swinton and Weir had been so instrumental in pushing forward the early development of the Spitfire, had come to see it as little more than a temporary cover for Fighter Command until better planes arrived. In a memorandum to the Chief of the Air Staff at the beginning of June 1939, Freeman demonstrated all too clearly that the Spitfire was not part of the Ministry's long-term thinking. In fact, as he revealed, the aim was to reduce production and promote sales overseas rather than burden the RAF with unwanted planes. 'Supermarine's will run out of their order for Spitfires in February or March 1940, and since it will be impossible to get a new aircraft into production at Supermarine's before September 1940, there is certain to be a six months' gap which we will have to fill.' The way to cut that gap next year, argued Freeman, was 'to reduce production to 30 aircraft a month' and to allow more foreign sales – something for which Vickers had been pressing in order to provide some security at the Southampton plant. He suggested that from October 1939 the Ministry should allow the release of Spitfires to meet foreign orders, starting with an average of four a month up to January 1940, rising to eight a month up to March. From then, sales abroad could 'take up the whole of the firm's output except that required to replace releases from Air Ministry contracts in the period from October 1939 to March 1940'. In effect, Freeman was arguing that, within a year, the production of the Spitfire at Southampton should be little more than a commercial export venture, supplying the needs of other air forces rather than the RAF.[37]

The need to reduce the Spitfire programme was said to be all the stronger because the Nuffield factory still had to begin work on its much-vaunted 1,000 order. There had been an attempt by the Air Ministry to encourage Lord Nuffield to switch production to Westland Whirlwinds, but the motoring magnate insisted on Spitfires, claiming that he was tooling up his factory and training a labour force, much of it inexperienced and female, specifically for the manufacture of that plane.

At a meeting of the Air Council's Supply Committee on 5 July, it was provisionally agreed to order another 450 Spitfires from Supermarine – a contract worth £2.3 million – on condition that at least 200 would be released for foreign orders. But, far from being any kind of vote of confidence in the Spitfire, this decision was merely a way of ensuring that Supermarine's books were kept filled, to stop redundancies and short-time working. A note of the meeting recorded that the main purpose of the order was 'to cover the gap between the end of the present contract for Spitfires and the earliest date at which production could begin of a new type. They should be given an order for the Beaufighter to follow on after this extended contract.'[38] The decision was confirmed in a letter to Supermarine on 9 August 1939, less than a month before the outbreak of war, which stressed that the order for 450 Spitfires was placed only 'on the understanding that you will be willing to dispose of at least 200 of them to Dominion and Foreign Governments'.[39]

The real debate at the Air Ministry in the summer of 1939 was not about the Spitfire, but about the merits of the Bristol Beaufighter, the Westland Whirlwind, and the Hawker Camm fighter. With a potential speed of 324 mph and four 20-mm cannon in its nose, the bulky twin-engined Beaufighter was the favoured choice for manufacture by Supermarine, largely because it was seen as more reliable and easier to build than the Whirlwind. In a note to the Chief of the Air Staff in July 1939, Air Commodore Robert Saundby, the Director of Operational Requirements, said that he had grave doubts about the Whirlwind from the viewpoints of both production and maintenance, because 'Westland's have complicated the design.' He warned that if Supermarine were instructed to make the Whirlwind rather than the Beaufighter, then it was possible that there could be serious delays. In that case, 'we would have to order more Spitfires to bridge the gap.'[40] Those words emphasize again how the Spitfire was seen in a negative light, as if it were an unattractive alternative to the other three fighters. Even after the start of the war, the assumption still remained that the Spitfire would be phased out after 1940, with Supermarine eventually turned over to the production of the Beaufighter.

But during the late autumn of 1939 that assumption had to change – not because of a sudden recognition of the Spitfire's combat qualities, but because the Beaufighter was 'abnormally beset by teething troubles'.[41] In November, Supermarine was told that it would have to plan to double its Spitfire output, while any idea of heavy foreign sales was to be abandoned. In response, Supermarine assured the Air Ministry that production levels could eventually be boosted to 100 planes per month. By January 1940 it was clear that neither the Whirlwind nor the Beaufighter would soon be coming into service with Fighter Command, while the Hawker Tornado – the Rolls-Royce version of the Typhoon – had also stalled badly as a result of problems with its Vulture engine. So the gap would have to be filled by the Spitfire. In a letter remarkable for its lack of any enthusiasm for the plane, Freeman explained to Newall, 'I realize that the Spitfire will not be as welcome as the Tornado but a fighter aeroplane of an economic sort will surely be useful for the Allies and for operations on fronts other than the Western Front.'[42] It is hard to imagine a more lukewarm endorsement of the Spitfire than the phrase 'a fighter aeroplane of an economic sort'.

In the same letter Freeman also tried to make an economic virtue out of production necessity. 'I must point out that the money we have spent on jigging and tooling the Spitfire in the Nuffield factory is prodigious. This has been made necessary by the need to use unskilled female labour in the manufacture of the Spitfire. If we change over at Nuffield's it will mean extensive jigging, perhaps costing as much as £2,000,000, in order that this female labour can be again made use of. The changeover to another type would certainly not be achieved in a period under eighteen months.' Freeman asked, therefore, that the Chief of the Air Staff agree to keeping the Spitfire in production. Newall did so, supported by the Air Council and Wood. Another 450 planes were ordered from Supermarine. The Spitfire had been granted a reprieve. The war was over before the question of ending production was to be raised again.

But even with these new orders, everything was not running smoothly at Southampton. Though production was up to 40 Spitfires a month in early 1940, many of the long-running problems still existed, such as the lack of floor space, the recruitment of labour, and difficulties with subcontractors and supplies of raw materials, especially light-alloy parts. Sir Charles Craven warned the Air Ministry that the goal of more than doubling Spitfire output would mean the recruitment of an additional 1,200 employees on top of the existing workforce of almost 3,000. 'The labour problem is so difficult that we have merely assumed it will be possible to obtain additional hands,' he wrote in January 1940.[43]

The high rate of Spitfire accidents, especially at night, also put pressure on Supermarine. At the beginning of March 1940 the company had delivered 538 planes, but only 246 were in front-line service. Of the remainder, 147 were in reserves, 45 were deemed unserviceable, and no fewer than 98 had either been written off or were undergoing repair, almost entirely as a result of accidental damage. 'The proportion of complete write-offs is rather high considering no machines have been lost in action,' stated an internal Vickers report.[44] Nor was there in the workforce any sense of the wartime drive that was to be so apparent later in 1940. Unreality and soporific detachment engendered by the Phoney War prevailed in parts of the Spitfire factory. Denis Webb complained of the 'odd attitude' of some of the men he was managing: 'It seemed as if they didn't mind a war being waged as long as it didn't affect them.' One day a German plane flew over the factory and was fired at by the anti-aircraft guns. A splinter from an anti-aircraft shell plunged from the sky, through the roof, and landed with a thud in the machine shop. There was a noisy commotion which led to Webb being summoned. 'I was speechless. I just did not know what to say. Was I supposed to laugh, cry or send a telegram to Hitler telling him to knock it off? In the end I said that if nothing worse happened in the next few years we would be bloody lucky. I ask you. What the hell was Management supposed to do about it?'[45]

The difficulties of Supermarine were nothing, however, compared to the chaotic paralysis that had engulfed the Castle Bromwich factory. What was meant to be the flagship of British aircraft production had become an expensive hulk still trapped in the dock. The first Spitfires were supposed to emerge from the Nuffield plant from April 1940, at a rate of 60 a week, yet not one had come close to being completed, even though, when war broke out, the Nuffield workforce of 6,235 men and women was more than double that of Supermarine. The Air Ministry was in despair over the lack of aircraft, the Treasury over the waste of public funds. As early as November 1938 the first doubts had been raised in Parliament about the project, when Garro Jones, the Labour MP for Aberdeen, had questioned Sir Kingsley Wood about the slowness in building the factory. Wood had replied that 'Lord Nuffield has shown a great deal of expedition in this matter' and claimed that parts of the factory might be available for production as early as February 1939.[46] Those words turned out to be hollow political rhetoric, as Nuffield's grand scheme became hopelessly bogged down. Throughout 1939 there was mounting concern over the management of the factory, as buildings failed to be erected and proper budgets failed to appear. Yet, mesmerized by Nuffield's reputation and intimidated by his manner, neither Wood nor his officials had the courage to challenge him, even when the estimated costs more than doubled to over £4 million.

A plaintive note at a ministerial meeting in May 1939 revealed the extent of this enfeeblement. Freeman reported that he had seen Nuffield and had 'gained the impression that he had no grip of the problem and knew none of the details. He was in no mood to be crossed and when the question of an approach to the Treasury was raised he said that if the Treasury would not approve the expenditure he would provide the money himself.'[47] A month later Wood had lunch with Nuffield and the Castle Bromwich manager, Oliver Boden. This time Nuffield's gripe was not about finance but about the technical support he had been given by Supermarine:

> Lord Nuffield and Mr Boden said that though they did not wish to make any complaints against Messrs Vickers, they could not help feeling that the condition of the drawings, etc. that were supplied to them for the manufacture of the Spitfire were very unsatisfactory and there had been constant modifications of these drawings ever since they received them. But for these modifications they would have got into production very much earlier.[48]

This moan about changes to the Spitfire's design was to become a constant refrain of Lord Nuffield's as he grew ever more defensive about the mismanagement of his plant. And it goes to the heart of why he was the wrong man to be entrusted with such a large and vital project. Lacking any understanding of the aircraft industry, he thought that planes could be mass-produced like motor cars. What he failed to appreciate was that the Spitfire was a far more complex piece of machinery than a Morris. The Supermarine engineer Eric Lovell-Cooper, who was later sent to Castle Bromwich, said that Nuffield's team 'used to draw everything out about four or five times full size, all the details, and they put every hole in accurately dimensioned, you know, to within a thousandth of an inch where it should be. The tools were made accordingly, they stamped the parts out and the parts were all perfect. Well, it might be all right for mass-producing motor cars but mass-producing aircraft is a very different situation. Ninety per cent of the holes in an aeroplane have to be matched up with the other holes and if you drill them separately they will never match! Their first attempts were absolutely hopeless.'[49] Moreover, Nuffield's protests about modifications were ill-conceived, for the Spitfire had to be in a constant state of redevelopment if it was to keep pace with modern technology. The

Spitfire type that the Nuffield factory had been instructed to build was the Mark II, whose main innovations included better armour protection for the pilot, an improved coolant tank, and a constant-speed airscrew, removing the necessity for the pilot to change pitch on take-off and landing. Perhaps the biggest change was the introduction of the more powerful Merlin XII engine, which was activated by a Coffman cartridge starter, an apparatus similar to the chamber of a pistol. With the Mark II, the 'erks' would not have to run around the airfields with their heavy trolley batteries. Yet Nuffield saw these improvements only as a further source of grievance.

The reality was that by the late 1930s Lord Nuffield was no longer the dynamic industrialist he had once been. He had always been a prickly, idio-syncratic individual, given to prejudices and whims, but now, in his sixties, his eccentricities had started to outweigh his talents. He was from a modest background, the son of an Oxfordshire draper, and he started in business at the age of sixteen by repairing bicycles, before moving on to the production of motor cars. By the end of the 1920s, thanks to shrewd marketing, skilful man-agement, and a name for reliable, good-value products, he was supplying a third of all motor cars in Britain. The next decade, however, saw both Nuffield and his company go into decline. Buttressed by his vast fortune, he dabbled in extremist politics, at one stage helping to bankroll Sir Oswald Mosley's neo-fascist New Party, the forerunner of the British Union of Fascists, while his chairmanship of Morris was 'arbitrary and often ill-informed', to quote one of his biographers, the historian Richard Overy.[50] He could justifiably claim to be Britain's greatest philanthropist, endowing a range of medical and educational foundations, including an Oxford college, but in his personal habits he was increasingly unconventional. Obsessed with his health, he drank large quantities of bicarbonate of soda, believing this was an antidote to his chronic wind, though it usually had the opposite effect, as the Morris executive Miles Thomas recalled: 'At the beginning of a business conversation he would take a liberal glassful and punctuate the progress of a subsequent talk with eruptive noises that we all came to regard as a normal part of the discussion.'[51] One of his peculiar party tricks was to throw osten-tatiously his own cigarettes on the carpeted floors of hotels and restaurants, knowing that they would go out as soon they were not being smoked, because they were made of special paper.

There is a sense that by the time Nuffield embarked on the Castle Bromwich factory he was a little unhinged. Intense, morbid and inarticulate, he was out of his depth in trying to deliver British history's biggest single aircraft order. As Robert Jackson, another of his biographers, has written, 'He was beginning to pay the price mentally. He was vague and could no longer grasp detail. He would not listen to his senior executives for more than a few minutes at a time, and whenever he went to London for a conference with ministries, he never troubled to read the briefs they had given him.'[52] The problem was compounded by the fact that the Castle Bromwich manager, Oliver Boden, was grossly overworked, since he also had to look after tank and car production by the Morris Corporation. On a typical day, Boden would start at 7 a.m. with a visit to the Spitfire factory, before going on to the Wolseley works in Birmingham where the tanks were built. He would then take a train to London for meetings at the Air Ministry or the War Office, before going on to the Morris headquarters at Cowley and then returning to his Birmingham home at 9 p.m. No one could put up with that schedule month in, month out. There was little surprise either at the Air Ministry or among colleagues when Boden dropped dead at the beginning of March 1940.

His sudden loss only worsened the sense of crisis hanging over Castle Bromwich. The Air Ministry wanted to appoint as his replacement Trevor Westbrook, the ill-tempered dynamo of the early Spitfire days, now in charge of Vickers production at Weybridge, but were warned by Sir Ernest Lemon that 'Lord Nuffield was prone to resent any outside interference.'[53] Nor was Nuffield willing to contemplate any other form of assistance from Vickers Supermarine, despite the urgings of the Air Ministry. His dealings with the company amounted to little more than a lament about 'the state of drawings which had been provided', though, after many tortured negotiations, Castle Bromwich did agree to supply some of their parts to Supermarine to allow the completion of Spitfires in Southampton.[54] This was only right, because, as the Supermarine manager Stan Woodley pointed out, Castle Bromwich's mismanagement meant that the factory had 'a large number of unbalanced sets of parts, with huge stocks of raw materials, many of which were in desperate shortage at Supermarine'.[55] The imbalance was also noticed by the Vickers director Alexander Dunbar, who visited Castle Bromwich on 8 March and saw that 'the detail departments – machine shop, press shop, sub-assemblies – are capable of much larger production than the wing and fuselage assembly.' There was, he wrote, 'a general slackness throughout the shops and one got the impression that employees were not really working because none of them knew what to do'.[56]

On 16 March, Sir Charles Craven arranged to see Nuffield personally to find out if there was any way that Vickers could help with the running of the Birmingham Spitfire factory. Afterwards Sir Charles sent Kingsley Wood a full account of the meeting, which lasted over two hours and again demonstrated Nuffield's distance from reality:

I was somewhat taken aback when Lord Nuffield assured me that he was not late in his deliveries of Spitfires and he thinks his people have done very well indeed in the progress they have made. This statement was so much at variance with what I have understood from you and Freeman that I felt I was on somewhat delicate ground. I therefore took the line that whatever was the situation today as regards the fulfilment of promises, there was undoubtedly a most urgent national need for increased production of Spitfires.

Nuffield then made the usual complaint about the modifications to drawings, which prompted Craven to tell Wood, 'the fact that Supermarine have been in regular production for many months proves that there can be no hold-up on this account.' Sir Charles then made a more general attack on Nuffield's operation:

I really think that a great mistake has been made in assuming that because the motor car trade are undoubtedly proper people to undertake mass production work, they can produce aircraft on the same lines . . . Lord Nuffield felt that we are constantly making alterations to the Spitfire now. This is, of course, the case, but as I explained to him, if anything arises as a result of the war to improve the fighting qualities or the safety of the machines, we must make the alterations at the first opportunity and not put off doing so until many hundreds of machines have been turned out.

Craven said he felt 'extremely sorry' for Nuffield, because he had 'lost a key man in Boden's death', but he concluded that 'Lord Nuffield, with all his enthusiasm and with all the success he has had in business during a very active life is today surrounded by "yes" men. His own life is going to be terribly overburdened with worries with all these people directly responsible to him.' Craven, however, could offer no solution to the impasse.[57]

Something had to change. And it soon did, in the most dramatic fashion, as the Phoney War came to an end and the Chamberlain government was gripped by a terminal crisis. For months after the fall of Poland there had been little overt aggression from Germany, prompting Chamberlain to remark on 4 April that 'Hitler has missed the bus.' The Führer had a habit of making the Prime Minister look foolish. Within four days Hitler had started a full-scale occupation of Norway and Denmark. The British military response to the invasion was shambolic, with Gloster Gladiators trapped in the Norwegian snow and the ill-equipped army issued with contradictory orders. Indignation at the government's mismanagement ran high in Parliament. After a highly charged debate, Chamberlain was forced to resign, having lost the confidence of his own party. He was succeeded by Winston Churchill at the head of a genuinely national coalition government. Churchill's arrival led to upheaval at the top of the Air Ministry. In came the Liberal leader Sir Archibald Sinclair as the Secretary of State for Air. It was the second time he had served under Churchill: during the First World War he had been Churchill's second-in-command in the 6th Battalion of the Royal Scots Fusiliers on the Western Front, when the great statesman was briefly in political exile after the Dardanelles disaster. It was often said that Sinclair never overcame his sense of inferiority and obedience in Churchill's presence.

Those were certainly not the characteristics of Lord Beaverbrook, the Canadian-born press baron Max Aitken, who was Churchill's most unorthodox, imaginative appointment. On 14 May Beaverbrook took charge of an entirely new department, the Ministry of Aircraft Production, whose creation reflected the importance Churchill attached to building up the strength of the RAF. In some ways Beaverbrook might have seemed an unlikely choice, since he had been a passionate appeaser throughout the late 1930s, and even as late as 1940 he wanted to persuade the Duke of Windsor to return from France and tour the country calling for peace with Germany. Only after the invasion of Norway had he given his whole-hearted support to Britain's war effort. Nor did his volatile personality lend itself easily to political administration. He had no time for paperwork, loathed committees, and despised routine. 'Organization is the enemy of improvisation' was one of his slogans. His small stature belied his manic, domineering energy. To many he was a man without principles, a kind of tyrannical elf. The puritan Lord Reith was even more repelled by Beaverbrook than by Wood. 'What a dreadful man he is; one of the worst I have ever met. Evil he seems,' wrote Reith in January 1940. When Beaverbrook was appointed Minister of Aircraft Production in May, he declared, 'My trust in God is not all it ought to be.'[58]

Many of those who worked with Beaverbrook at the Ministry found him despotic, unreasonable in his demands and discourteous in his manner. He used the telephone as an instrument of oppression. Sir Wilfrid Freeman, who became one of his chief officers at the department, was once about to take a flight when he was told that his transport had been grounded. When he asked why, he was told, 'Enemy approaching.' Freeman replied, 'Is that all? I thought it was a phone call from Lord Beaverbrook.'[59] Sir Charles Craven was another who was recruited for the Ministry. According to Denis Webb, on one occasion Craven was on the toilet when Beaverbrook rang his office. Craven's secretary said he was briefly unavailable because he was 'attending to the wants of nature'. Beaverbrook was furious and demanded that Craven come to the phone at once. The secretary, rather nervously, relayed this message to Sir Charles, who, with all the sarcasm he could muster, said, 'Tell his lordship that I can only deal with one shit at a time.'[60]

Yet for all his faults, Beaverbrook was exactly what the government – and the fighter programme in particular – needed in the early summer of 1940. Like much of the country, the aircraft companies had still failed to wake up to the reality of war. Beaverbrook's arrival was like a sudden electric shock to the system. It may have been unpleasant, but it was perhaps the only way to galvanize the industry into action. Just as in his role as proprietor of the *Daily Express*, Beaverbrook as minister was driven by a fixation with numbers. He treated manufacturing output in the same way as newspaper circulation, constantly trying to drive it upward. And the plane whose production he was most determined to raise was the Spitfire. With a clear-sightedness that others had lacked, Beaverbrook saw that the Spitfire and the Hurricane were going to be the prime RAF weapons in the coming air battles against the Luftwaffe. All the debates about other planes like the Whirlwind were an irrelevance.

As usual at the Air Ministry, where the flames of the Trenchard doctrine still flickered, there were doubts about this whole-hearted concentration on fighters. Air Chief Marshal Sir Philip Joubert de la Ferté wrote after the war, 'Lord Beaverbrook, to put it bluntly, played hell with the war policy of the RAF. But he most certainly produced the aircraft that won the Battle of Britain. What he did in the summer of 1940 set back the winning of the air war over Germany by many months. The bomber programme was disrupted to allow high-speed production of fighters.'[61] Others were far more enthusiastic about Beaverbrook's influence, most crucially Lord Dowding who wrote in 1943, 'The effect of Lord Beaverbrook's appointment can only be described as magical and thereafter the supply situation improved to such a degree that heavy aircraft wastage which was later incurred during the Battle of Britain ceased to be the primary danger.'[62]

In recent years there has been a wave of historical revisionism challenging the belief that Beaverbrook had any real effect on fighter production. The apparent increase was due to manipulation of figures, say his critics, and to his own shameless propaganda. Furthermore, argue his detractors, most of the decisions that led to increased fighter output had already been taken by the time he was appointed. This is hardly borne out by the official RAF statistics, which show fighter production rising from 256 planes in April to 325 in May, then to 446 planes in June and 496 in July as his influence started to bite. Spitfire production at Southampton rose from 124 planes in the first quarter of 1940 to 363 in the three months to September 1940, the target of 100 a month having been easily surpassed. And the argument also ignores the fact that Beaverbrook took a crucial decision right at the start of his term – one that was eventually to transform Spitfire production. As Alex

e plane that saved Britain. A Spitfire Mark I flying over Southampton, 1938.

The origins of greatness. The Supermarine S6 seaplane which wo the Schneider Trop in 1929, piloted by Flying Officer Dick Waghorn.

'A dog's breakfast.' Supermarine's first attempt at building monoplane fighter. Known as the Type 224, it featured cranked wings and trousered undercarriage.

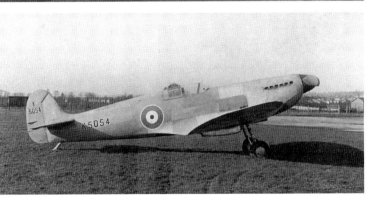

The birth of a lege The Spitfire protot in 1936. One Air Ministry official recalled the exciten after the maiden fli 'It really looked as we were going to h something which would match up to anything the Germ could build.'

Into service. 19 Squadron, based a Duxford, was the in the RAF to be equipped with the Spitfire.

above left: The genius behind the Spitfire, Supermarine's chief designer Reginald Mitchell. 'He was a curious mixture of dreams and common sense,' said one of his company's directors.

above right: Reginald Mitchell pictured with his wife, Florence, shortly before his premature death. He faced his fatal illness with remarkable fortitude.

right: Mitchell's successor as Supermarine designer, Joe Smith. He oversaw the development of the plane through an astonishing range of different types.

Scramble: Free
French pilots of the
RAF running
towards their plane
1941.

Spitfire Mark Is of
611 Squadron fly i
loose line astern ov
two other Spitfires
Digby, Lincolnshire

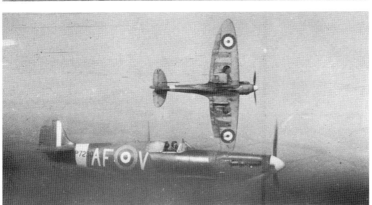

Two Spitfire Mark
from the Air Fighti
Development Unit.

Achtung Spitfeuer!
The view from a
German bomber's
gun as a Spitfire
passes.

'Hard on the hands' – ground crew servicing a Spitfire Mark XIV of 91 Squadron in West Malling, Kent, 1944.

Members of the Women's Auxiliary Air Force learnin to mount guns on a Spitfire 1941.

An armourer uses a periscope to adjust the .30 Browning guns on a Mark IXB Spitfire at Biggin Hill in Kent.

A Spitfire Mark IX of 140 Meteorological Flight is readied for a pre-dawn take-off.

bove left: The darkest hour
appeasement: Chamberlain
eets Hitler in September
*9*38. But the Prime Minister
as a surprising advocate of a
rong fighter defence force.

bove right: The eccentric
ess tycoon Lord
averbrook, Churchill's
inister of Aircraft
oduction during the height
the Battle of Britain, who
esided over a dramatic
crease in Spitfire output.
must have more planes.
on't care whose heart is
oken or pride hurt.'

iddle: Philip Cunliffe-Lister,
scount Swinton, Secretary
State for Air 1935 to 1938
d the political driving force
hind the creation of the
itfire. 'The most dynamic
inister I served,' said one of
s civil servants.

ight: Swinton's less effective
ccessor, Sir Kingsley Wood,
cretary of State for Air from
*9*38 to 1940. 'A feeble little
eature' and 'a self-seeking
d' was how the head of the
*8*C, Sir John Reith,
scribed him.

Study of a Mark XIV in flight. 'The bastards make such infernally tight turns. There seems no way of nailing them,' complained one German pilot.

Merlin-powered Spitfire Mark Is of 65 Squadron flying over Hornchurch, 1939. 'I looked at my squadron in formation behind and beside me, each Spitfire seemingly motionless in the still, cloud-free sky. I looked with affection more than pride. The sheer beauty of the Spitfire a poem of grace which contained a fighting man and an armoury of devastating destruction wrote one Spitfire squadron leader.

Henshaw put it, 'Beaverbrook was an unpleasant bastard. But he was the right man in the right place at the right time.'[63] Within three days of taking up his post, he had appraised himself of the disastrous position at Castle Bromwich and was resolved to act. Miles Thomas happened to be in Nuffield's office at Cowley in Oxford on 17 May when a call came through from Beaverbrook at the Ministry:

> They were both better in monologues than dialogues and from the Cowley end of the line it quickly became apparent that Lord Nuffield was vociferously defending his Castle Bromwich organization and making it abundantly clear that in his opinion the Minister of Aircraft Production could either have Spitfires or modifications but he could not have both. The moment of truth had arrived. Sarcastically, certain that he was putting the ace of trumps on the table, Nuffield shouted, 'Maybe you would like me to give up control of the Spitfire factory.' In a flash came the reply: 'Nuffield, that's very generous of you. I accept!' There was a click in the earpiece – the line went dead. Inwardly I breathed a sigh of relief. Nuffield's face was ashen. For a long time he did not say anything.[64]

Beaverbrook was straight on the line to Vickers, ordering the company to take over the running of Castle Bromwich. Stan Woodley recalled that he was sitting in his Southampton office 'when the phone rang and the General Manager Wilf Elliot looked up and said, "Woodley, have you got your car?" I said, "Yes." He said, "Right, go home and pack your bag. We're going to Castle Bromwich and I don't know when we're coming back."'[65] As soon as the Vickers team arrived in Birmingham, they saw the advanced plant and tooling but realized that there was no proper organization. So Elliot and Woodley sent for Supermarine chargehands and skilled men to break the bottleneck. Meanwhile Nuffield decided to challenge Beaverbrook's decision. He appealed to Churchill, and in typically gauche style mentioned the sums he had donated to the Tory party. 'I cannot interfere with the manufacture of aircraft,' replied the Prime Minister.[66] Bruised and beaten, Nuffield retired to sulk in his Oxfordshire retreat.

Soon after Vickers had taken over, Beaverbrook instructed Sir Richard Fairey, the distinguished aircraft manufacturer, to conduct a full investigation into Castle Bromwich. Fairey's subsequent report, which is contained on a microfilm in the Vickers Archive but has never been discussed in any Spitfire literature, provides a unique insight into the expensive shambles of Nuffield's organization. It should be remembered that Fairey had an axe to grind against Nuffield, because he believed his Stockport factory should have been manufacturing Spitfires; nevertheless, his study, sent to Beaverbrook at the end of June 1940, amounted to a powerful indictment not just of Nuffield, but also of parts of the Castle Bromwich workforce. 'It is, I regret to say, a picture of extravagance and an inability to understand the problems of aircraft production, coupled with an unwillingness to learn from those who do,' Fairey began. 'The state of affairs I have seen at Castle Bromwich is the exact reverse of that of other factories I have inspected on your behalf where output troubles have been primarily due to comparatively small companies with restricted finances having bitten off more than they can chew.' In contrast, at Castle Bromwich, he continued:

> Matters appear to have started with a blank cheque. Some £7 million of public money has been expended in a vast and extravagantly laid out plant, together with jigs and tools, with a large machine shop more than capable of the proposed output and huge stock of materials totalling 450 tons now on the premises. Much of this material has presumably been frozen there for some time. The machine shop is magnificent, comprising over 800 first-class machine tools, nearly half of which are perforce idle for want of equipment and skilled labour. For example, I saw the most perfect specimen of the Swiss jig borer costing some £14,000, just being erected. This machine should have completed its work six months ago.

Fairey went on to reveal further waste on buildings, expensive heating systems, and enormous steel hangars which could hold 200 Spitfires at a time. Records were hopelessly unreliable. 'I myself inspected a number of boxes of components and parts that had literally been raked out from under the working benches and for which no records existed.' Furthermore, Castle Bromwich had ignored the tooling work done by Supermarine and had instead started to design and plan its own tools, 'even altering the manufacturing limits of Supermarine drawings for reasons which are quite incomprehensible'. Fairey was also aghast to find that

> 350 of the total schedule of 7,000 parts had neither been ordered on the shops nor placed out elsewhere. The whole conception was not good since the reason for spending so much capital on tools and machinery should be to produce an even flow of parts in the numbers required. I inspected among other things a battery of six large presses standing idle and a pile of large press tools, mostly incomplete or awaiting rectification, for making various parts of the machine, such as tank ends, which had not yet gone into operation.

Fairey's harshest criticism, however, was reserved for the Castle Bromwich employees – which is interesting in the context of later mythology about the whole nation pulling together in the patriotic cause:

> Over-riding all these considerations and in my opinion the greatest obstacle to an immediate increase in output is the fact that labour is in a very bad state.

Discipline is lacking. Men are leaving before time and coming in late, taking evenings off when they think fit . . . In parts of the factory I noticed that men idling did not even bestir themselves at the approach of the Works Manager and the Director who were accompanying me.

Fairey mentioned that there had been a sit-down strike over a petty pay dispute the week before Vickers took over. 'The labour in the Midlands and the north is not "playing the game". They are getting extra money and are not working in proportion to it. In fact, in this particular factory there is every evidence of slackness. In my opinion it is management who are in need of rest far more than the operatives.' Fairey suggested that workers should be warned that if they were found guilty of indiscipline or laxity they would be liable for conscription. 'The labour are taking advantage of the services. In fact I maintain that without strong action on the labour not only will this programme not be achieved but that other factories will suffer.'[67]

Fairey's views on the workforce were not mere capitalist prejudice. The Supermarine engineer Cyril Russell had many colleagues who had been sent up to Birmingham to assist with parts and drawings, and he heard directly from them how 'there were a lot of squabbles over money',[68] how Castle Bromwich employees 'stopped work for financial greed', and how 'the project was "bugged" with industrial action (or inaction) which fell short of a complete factory shutdown but was fragmented into areas where the cumulative result ensured that no Spitfires reached the flight testing stage.'[69] To his anger, the management had frequently caved in to such pressure, with the result that those on the Castle Bromwich payroll earned much more than those at Supermarine. Russell even suggested that left-wing extremism might have been behind some of the disputes: in his view, the bottlenecks might have been 'orchestrated by politically motivated persons to delay the output of the aircraft that were so vital' – action which he believed 'bordered on treason.'[70] Apart from the complaint about general recalcitrance, however, there is no evidence for this in any of the archives.

Nevertheless, frustration with the workforce is all too clear from the correspondence of Alexander Dunbar, a tough accountant who became the overall managing director of Castle Bromwich in May 1940. 'We have been doing a bit of sacking this week and shall be doing a lot more before the end of the month,' he wrote to a Vickers director in July 1940:

Among other things we are cutting out time and a quarter payments for staff overtime and I have spent a lot of time today arguing with the chargehands. Yesterday it was the Draughtsmen's Union and last night it was the progress clerks but it's all in a day's work. Incidentally, we are sacking at least 60 Jig and Tool draughtsmen next week; we have tried to find out what they are doing but the answer's not a lemon . . . In the meantime we manage to build the odd Spitfire or two.[71]

The sheer technical idiocy of some of the early Castle Bromwich line workers was also revealed by another Supermarine expert, Bill Cox, sent up to the factory to help sort out production. Cox was talking to an elderly fitter about the stressed-skin construction of the Spitfire when the fitter replied, 'Make things with aluminium? Not bloody likely. That stuff is OK for pots and pans but we are going to make things to beat the Nazis. We'll use iron.' Cox also listened to a senior Castle Bromwich manager saying that 'the elliptical wing should be redesigned because the air would not know the difference between straight and curved leading edges.' So adamant was this manager about changing the design that Cox had to get on the phone to Joe Smith at Supermarine and warn him of the problem. Immediately, Smith contacted the Air Ministry and a civil servant was dispatched to Birmingham with the message that 'all drawings must be made to Supermarine's orders.'[72]

Beaverbrook was eager to show that Castle Bromwich was being turned around, so, with a characteristic showman's touch, he instructed the factory to build ten Spitfires before the end of June. But the new Vickers managers knew that, for all their sackings and the tighter discipline arising from the threat of military service, there was little chance of meeting this deadline, given the disarray of Castle Bromwich. So they resorted to a devious strata-gem. As Stan Woodley recorded, 'By shipping up from Southampton large numbers of finished components, including some fully equipped fuselages, and working round the clock, the magic ten in June were completed.'[73] The managers were given inscribed silver cigarette lighters to celebrate this achievement, though in reality it was little more than a piece of trickery. The ten in fact came from a consignment of Spitfires ordered by Turkey, which was cancelled due to escalation of the war. Instead of being shipped across the Mediterranean, they were taken out of their crates, modified to revert to standard RAF type, and shipped off to Birmingham.

Alex Henshaw had to test-fly the first of the ten, and the experience gave him a glimpse into the 'complete and utter shambles' of Castle Bromwich. As requested, he arrived early in the morning for the test, soon after sunrise, but to his annoyance he found that the Spitfire was not ready. 'I think there were at least twenty people standing round one solitary aircraft. It was utter chaos.' Henshaw was advised to go into Birmingham for some breakfast and return later in the morning. 'I came back and there was still chaos. This went on all day.' Finally, half an hour before sunset, the work was complete.

'They took the plane out on to the airfield and I got into it. Everyone was absolutely bushed. No hilarity, no joyous occasion, everyone just fed up. They were tired, frustrated and concerned because they didn't know how it would turn out, their first aircraft. But I took off for a fly and it behaved perfectly.' Remembering the glum faces he had seen on the ground, Henshaw decided he would liven up the spectators. 'I thought that they'd been working for days and all I had to do was hang around and fly the bloody thing.' So he launched into one of the daring aerobatic displays for which he became renowned, performing loops and inverted rolls before landing. The mood was now completely different. 'They were cheering, patting each other on the back and all embracing each other. I'll never forget that.'[74]

Even after the first Spitfires came off the Castle Bromwich production line, there remained tremendous problems at the factory, not least because the buildings had not even been completed. Two years after Sir Kingsley Wood had cut the first sod, parts of Castle Bromwich were still like a construction site. The architect overseeing the works, William J. Green, was an ineffectual manager, and his weakness was ruthlessly exploited by the contractors, led by an intractable foreman, a Mr Riley. So serious were the delays that Beaverbrook's department sent in a surveyor, A. J. Hill from Taylor Woodrow, to compile a report. Just as Sir Richard Fairey had done, Hill painted a picture of dangerous stagnation at Castle Bromwich. Work on the canteen and the main office block was 'almost at a standstill', while the architect had 'not shown any control over the contractors'. When Hill interviewed Riley the foreman he found him 'abusive and resentful'. Hill continued that Riley 'is bigoted, conceited, offensive and cannot be told anything that he thinks he knows already which, according to him, is everything'. Thanks to Riley's influence, contractors were refusing to work Saturday afternoons or Sundays. Hill concluded that his impression of his visit was that 'There was a total lack of organization and programming of the work. Co-ordination and construction and fitting out of buildings were completely absent. Meetings to discuss progress have been a waste of time.'[75]

Another difficulty was that, as Sir Richard Fairey had noted, the factory's recording procedures were in chaos, which also encouraged fraud and abuses within the workforce. J. E. Anderson, one of Vickers' experts, reported in July that the system was so 'poor' and riddled with 'inherent weaknesses' that the proper ordering of the work was impossible. 'The actual booking of operators' time on jobs is inaccurate and confused,' he wrote, which led to 'numerous cases of overpayment'.[76]

Gradually during the summer of 1940 the Vickers team began to transform the management of the factory, through the creation of efficient records, stores and production lines, as well as through the sacking of idle or troublesome employees. On 8 August, for instance, Dunbar told Craven, with a degree of relish, that he had just dismissed 184 staff, among them 'sixteen foremen whose experience and ability proved unsatisfactory'.[77] In the new climate of well-organized determination, output increased rapidly. In July, 23 aircraft had been produced; 37 followed in August. By the end of October 1940, 195 Spitfires had been delivered from Castle Bromwich. Beaverbrook wrote to Dunbar to say that he was 'very pleased with the improvement in the morale of the factory',[78] to which Dunbar replied, 'Castle Bromwich is a long way yet from being perfect but steady progress is being made in every way and I am confident that we shall justify the trust you have reposed in me.'[79] By February 1941 the Spitfire total from Castle Bromwich was above 600, proving that the factory had huge productive capacity provided there was effective management and a co-operative workforce. Eventually, over 13,000 of the type would be built at Castle Bromwich – more than half the total of all Spitfires produced.

The fiasco of the early years at Castle Bromwich, set out in Whitehall and Vickers files, has never been fully told before, perhaps because it does not fit in with the uplifting wartime narrative of British courage and unity. Moreover, Nuffield himself was anxious to downplay the mess over which he had presided: there is hardly a mention of the episode in any of his papers. He was, by all accounts, never the same man after being so ruthlessly ousted by Beaverbrook, and lapsed into a long, melancholy decline. 'He seemed to lose the vital force that drove him inexorably to greater and greater things,' wrote Miles Thomas.[80]

Yet in two crucial ways Castle Bromwich is a vital chapter in the Spitfire saga. First of all it destroys the myth, so sedulously cultivated by cheerleading propaganda, that a mood of patriotic endeavour was sweeping through Birmingham and the nation in early 1940. In the words of Cyril Russell, the truth was a tale of 'managerial weakness and ignorance, and an overdose of worker bloodymindedness'.[81] Second, the chronic delay in producing Spitfires had severe consequences for the fabric of Fighter Command. Given Nuffield's promise to make 60 planes a week, the contract for 1,000 Spitfires should have been easily fulfilled by the time the Battle of Britain reached its peak in September. If he had come anywhere near to meeting his pledge, the position of the RAF would have been transformed. Every squadron in the two front-line groups in the south of England could have been equipped with Spitfires, and there would have been enough for reserves and training.

The desperate tactics that Dowding had to use to protect his dwindling numbers would have been unnecessary. Much of the bitter controversy between his group commanders, caused by arguments over fighter resources, could have been avoided. The 'narrow margin' of the Battle was partly of Nuffield's creation.

6

'The days of easy victory were over'

———

'THE BEST DEFENCE of the country is the Fear of the Fighter,' wrote Dowding in September 1939.[1] Throughout the first months of the war, his dread was that Britain would become embroiled in a Continental conflict which would drain the resources under his command. Essentially insular in his outlook, he had cared little for the fate of Czechoslovakia in 1938, nor for that of France and the Low Countries in May 1940. The strength of the home fighter squadrons and his defence organization were all that mattered to him. In October 1939 he had warned the Air Staff, with some foresight, of the dangers of diverting fighter resources to France: 'The likely course which the war would take might well demand the use of all possible resources at home.'[2] The Chief of the Air Staff, Sir Cyril Newall, had appealed to him at the time to be more flexible: 'We must face facts, one of which is that we could possibly lose the war in France as much as in England . . . I am merely asking you to take the necessary steps so that if we are really in danger of losing the war in France through lack of fighters we shall not find ourselves unprepared.'[3] But Dowding had no faith in such an approach – not least because his visits to France had convinced him of 'the pathetic inefficiency' of the French air force, which lacked a defensive communications system like radar.[4] His personal assistant Flight Lieutenant Hugh Ironside later recalled that Dowding had been profoundly disillusioned with the French air force when he had visited an airfield in Lille in 1939. There the grass 'was at least knee-high and lined up along the side were a lot of incredibly old aeroplanes with skis in between the wheels'. Dowding and Ironside were taken to a large restaurant for a typically Gallic lunch with a lot of wine, which Dowding did not touch. After lunch, they were driven to an underground cellar which was, supposedly, the local air-force headquarters.

> We sat there for some considerable time and then the phone rang. The airman answered it and there were lots of 'Oui, oui, oui,' and then the airman put a red arrow on the blackboard. And this went on for an hour or so until the blackboard was covered in arrows of different colours. I don't think anybody knew what the hell it was all about. On the flight back, 'Stuffy' never said a word. He was absolutely silent. I think that's where he got his utter distrust of the French.[5]

The German attack on the western front, beginning on 10 May 1940, brought his anxieties to a head. Buckling under the onslaught of the 4,000-strong Luftwaffe, the French government appealed to Britain to send more fighters across the Channel. Churchill, whose instinct for military aggression was mixed with a romantic Francophilia, was sympathetic to the call. But Dowding was adamant that any further dilution of home defence would be calamitous. He feared that already too many Hurricanes had been dispatched to France over recent weeks, reducing Fighter Command's strength in Britain to 36 squadrons – far below what he regarded as an absolute necessary minimum of 52 squadrons. Now, with the prospect of demands for even more fighters, he decided he had to act. Against the background of relentless German advances through Belgium and at Sedan, on 15 May Dowding attended highly charged meetings of the Chiefs of Staff Committee and the War Cabinet at which he protested against the dispatch of further squadrons. According to some accounts, most notably those produced by A. J. P. Taylor and Lord Beaverbrook, there was an air of dramatic confrontation at the War Cabinet, with Dowding producing graphs of fighter wastage in France and even hinting at resignation if he was overruled. This is an exaggeration. The politicians and the military chiefs were inclined to agree with Dowding's stance, as Dowding triumphantly revealed to one of his fighter group commanders, Keith Park, in a letter written that afternoon: 'We had a notable victory on the Home Front this morning and the orders to send more Hurricanes were cancelled. Appeals for help will doubtless be renewed, however, with increasing insistence and I do not know how this morning's work will stand the test of time; but I will never relax my efforts to prevent the dissipation of the Home Fighter forces.'[6]

The next day, in order to strengthen his position, Dowding sent the Air Ministry a memorandum which reiterated the need for a home defence force of 52 squadrons and urged that the government provide an assurance that 'not one fighter will be sent across the Channel, however urgent and insistent the appeals may be.' His concluding paragraph was the most powerful:

> I believe that if an adequate fighter force is kept in this country, if the Fleet remains in being and if Home Forces are suitably organized to resist invasion, we should be able to carry on the war single-handed, if not indefinitely. But if the Home Defence Force is drained away in a desperate attempt to remedy the situation in France, defeat in France will involve the final, complete and irremediable defeat of this country.[7]

Churchill still longed to do something for France, and during his frequent flying visits there he sent back messages to the Cabinet pushing for more reinforcements. But the issue was fast becoming an irrelevance. The rapid sweep of the German invasion meant there were few French airfields from which British fighters could still operate. RAF operations were increasingly confined to sorties across the Channel from bases in Kent and Sussex. In any case, the focus on Britain's Fighter Command was misplaced. For all the hysterical appeals from the French government for more air support, l'Armée de l'Air was failing on an epic scale to utilize its own resources. According to the Czech pilot Miroslav Liskutin, who served in France and later flew Spitfires with the RAF, 'the defeatist attitude of many Frenchmen became completely unreasonable.' Around him, he witnessed 'an all-pervading madness. The behaviour of servicemen became so extraordinary that it defied all logic . . . They seemed overjoyed that "it is all finished."' Sabotage, he claimed, was frequent, as was mass desertion: 'French pilots parked their machines near a hangar and went home,' he wrote.[8] Moreover, at the end of the war it emerged that there were 1,700 French planes in the unoccupied southern zone suitable for front-line service, while in North Africa there were 2,648 modern French aircraft – more than the entire Hurricane and Spitfire fleet of Fighter Command.

It was the precipitous collapse of France that drew the Spitfires into their first intensive combat of the war. Until the middle of May 1940, Spitfire action had largely been confined to intercepting sporadic German raids or conducting patrols to protect British shipping, such as the occasion in April when Norman Ryder of 41 Squadron shot down a Heinkel 111 off the Yorkshire coast, but was himself hit by return fire and plummeted into the North Sea, the icy water knocking him unconscious. When he came round he was already sinking below the surface:

> I remember sitting in the cockpit and everything was bright green. I was very fascinated by the stillness of it all – it was amazing and I recall seeing a lot of bubbles running up the windscreen before my nose and parting as they got to the front. I sat there fascinated and not a bit afraid. The calm was so restful after the noise. The green colour around me was lovely but it turned to blackness before I got out.

Suddenly realizing the threat to his life, Ryder shook himself from his reverie and, after two attempts, managed to pull himself out of the cockpit. 'By now it was very black and I just saw the silhouette of the tailplane pass my face. I still had on my parachute which hampered my movement but I managed to paddle my way upward.'[9] By a stroke of good fortune, when he reached the surface he was rescued by a North Sea trawler, which had seen his fight with the Heinkel.

Dowding wanted to hold on to his Spitfires, still so limited in numbers, for the conflict over Britain that he knew was coming. But the plight of the British Expeditionary Force, cut off in Dunkirk, left him no alternative but to agree to provide cover in north-east France during the grim last week of May. Spitfires from squadrons in Kent, Sussex and Essex were in regular action. The evacuation from Dunkirk, beginning on the 27th, has become one of the British legends of the Second World War, synonymous with extraordinary self-discipline and self-sacrifice on the part of all three services as more than a third of a million men were taken from the beaches and harbours of the Pas de Calais. It was, to use Winston Churchill's phrase, 'a miracle of deliverance'.[10] Yet, at the time, the air over Dunkirk was thick with bitter recriminations against Fighter Command, which was perceived to have badly failed in its duty to protect either the soldiers or the vessels ferrying them back to England. 'Where was the RAF?' became one of the accusations from the troops.

The RAF pilots fiercely resented the charge that they had deserted the men on the ground. Throughout the long, hard days of Dunkirk, they flew sortie after sortie, preventing the Luftwaffe from roaming over the British lines at will. They believed they had made Operation Dynamo – the code name for the evacuation – possible. 'Frankly if it hadn't been for the RAF, the troops would never have got off,' said Pilot Officer Tony Bartley of 92 Squadron, which flew Spitfires from March 1940, 'because the German Air Force quit the beaches. We turned them back. I'm damned sure that Fighter Command had a lot to do with it.'[11] And some of the troops were only too grateful when they saw the Spitfires in action. Patrick Mace, a gunner with the Royal Artillery, who survived a hazardous journey to reach Dunkirk, recalled his first sight of the town: 'Behind us, stretching from Dunkirk as far as could be seen, was an immense bank of smoke, huge and impenetrable as a bank of clouds.' With daybreak, the Luftwaffe appeared. But so did the RAF:

> The sun had not been up very long when the first bombers arrived and they continued, without half an hour between waves, until eight o'clock in that evening. Our own fighters met and fought them, fight after fight, all through the day and it seemed to us planes fell like rain out of the skies. The noise of AA [anti-aircraft] fire and the cruel rap of the planes' machine guns, the distant crash of bombs into and around Dunkirk were in our ears all day.

Mace confessed to a sense of thrill at the battle overhead. 'I could not help a fit of shivering, half fear half excitement, as each fresh wave of planes came over. We lay as flat as possible, pulling our tin hats over our heads though no bombs fell very close. Once a Spitfire, shot down, roared clean over our heads, not a hundred feet up, with a German on his tail.'[12]

In the context of the Spitfire story, what was crucial about Dunkirk was not only that pilots gained hard experience in combat, but also that the plane proved itself a match for anything in the Luftwaffe, including the fearsome Me 109. All the expectations of its fighting qualities were fulfilled, making a mockery of the doubts that had been prevailing at the Air Ministry over the previous two years. Al Deere, who was in action for fourteen days at Dunkirk and downed six Luftwaffe aircraft, wrote that, as a result of his experience in fighting 109s, he was 'confident that, except in the dive, the Spitfire was superior in most other fields and, like the Hurricane, vastly more manoeuvrable'. He demonstrated this during an inland patrol over northern France one afternoon, when his squadron came under attack from Me 109s:

> As I pulled back violently on the stick into a steep turn, one fairly singed my eyebrows as it screamed past my port wing, the pilot endeavouring unsuccessfully to haul his aircraft around to attack me. Coming out of the turn, when it seemed safe to do so, I spotted an Me 109 diving away below me and gave chase immediately. He saw me almost at once and half-rolled for the deck with me after him. Down we went throttles fully open, engines roaring and each determined to get the last ounce out of his straining aircraft. From 17,000 down to ground level I hung to his tail, losing distance slightly in the dive, finishing up about 700 yards astern as he levelled out and set course inland. Inexplicably he began to climb again, from which I assumed he was not aware of my presence behind and below. He climbed, steadily but at full throttle, judging from the black smoke pouring from his exhausts, and I continued to close range until at about 15,000 feet I judged that I was now near enough to open fire. A long burst produced immediate results. Bits flew off his aircraft, which rolled slowly on its back and dived, apparently out of control, towards the scudding clouds below. I was taking no chances. I followed him down and continued firing until flames spouted from his engine. By this time, I had reached such a speed that my Spitfire was extremely difficult to control and the ground was uncomfortably close. As I eased out of the dive I was able to watch the Me 109 hit the ground just near the town of Saint-Omer and explode with a blinding flash.[13]

Alan Wright of 92 Squadron gained an instant understanding not just of the fighting capability of the Spitfire but also of its resilience when hit, as he took on an Me 109 on a sortie at 10,000 feet:

> Down we both went, each coaxing as much speed as we could out of our aeroplanes. The speed built up rapidly, the controls stiffened, the elevators were trimmed. It is remarkably difficult to move the nose around at high speed to get the sights steady on target and needs all one's strength and concentration. I fired several times and the range closed. The ground was clearly rushing towards us; in fact I can remember seeing houses, gardens and streets of suburbia. But I got the sights on again and pressed the gun button. His engine caught fire and his

dive steepened. As he was about to hit the ground there was an almighty bang in my cockpit. I thought the speed had been too much and my aircraft was breaking up. An unfamiliar smell and smoke filled the cockpit. We were going much too fast to manoeuvre, but heaving back on the stick I let the ground rush past and dragged the aircraft up and around. There was another Me 109 attacking me but I had no ammunition left. All I could do was to go on pulling on the stick as if to attack and then head off home, weaving and neck-twisting on the long journey back across the North Sea and able at last to count the fourteen bullet holes after landing back at Martlesham Heath.[14]

One wartime account, by Squadron leader B. J. Allan, demonstrated both the confidence that the Spitfire could inspire and the contemporary hostility towards the Germans, no doubt cranked up for propaganda purposes. Allan, on his first flight over Dunkirk, saw

a great black pall of smoke from Calais, drifting out in a long trail across the water. To the left another inky column showed the position of Dunkirk. There was something infinitely sad and terrible about the towering mass of smoke. I cannot describe just how I felt as I gazed fascinated on that dreadful scene but I know a surge of hatred for the Hun and all his filthy doings swept over me and I felt no mercy must be shown to a people who are a disgrace to humanity.

As he contemplated his feelings of detestation, his squadron came across a flight of Stuka dive-bombers:

We turned in behind them and closed the attack. The Huns flew on unheeding, apparently suffering from the delusion that we were their own fighter escort, until the leading Spitfires opened fire. Panic then swept the enemy formation. They split up in all directions, hotly pursued by nine Spitfires. I picked out one dive-bomber and got on his tail, staying there as he twisted and turned this way and that, trying to avoid the eight streaks of tracer from my guns. Finally he pulled up and stalled, rolled over and then plunged headlong towards the sea out of control. I felt happy! I had wondered what it would be like to shoot down an aircraft and bring it down. Now I knew and it was exhilarating.

Allan now came under attack from a group of Me 109s:

I pulled round in a tight turn, the aircraft shuddering just above the stall. I knew I could out-turn the 109s but I had very little petrol to play with now as well as being short of ammunition. Obviously it was time to get home. The leading 109 was firing short bursts every now and then. I remember I was cursing at the top of my voice. I was in a jam. I was frightened and I was furious at those Huns for making me frightened. Something had to be done and done quickly. I tightened the turn still more. The aircraft flicked as she stalled. I rolled over on my back and out of the reverse turn, a trick I had learnt at Flying Training School. This manoeuvre got me away from the Huns and I dived like hell for leather towards the sea, flattening out near the water, then opening the throttle wide.[15]

The Spitfire's effectiveness against the Messerschmitt was remarkable, given that its pilots had so little serious experience of combat, whereas many of the Luftwaffe crews had been involved in action back to the Spanish Civil War. In addition, the RAF squadrons had to fly at least 50 miles to France from their bases in southern England, which limited the time they could spend over Dunkirk, while they were also heavily outnumbered by the Germans. Nor did they have any effective radar – the key communications weapon of the Battle of Britain.

The head of fighter operations at Dunkirk was the forceful New Zealander Air Vice-Marshal Keith Park, the leader of 11 Group of Fighter Command, which covered the south-east of England. A First World War flying hero himself, and a former officer at Gallipoli, Park had not only a strong rapport with his pilots but also an instinctive gift for exploiting limited resources, as he was to prove in the Battle of Britain and Malta – though his critics, with some justification, were to accuse him of overcaution and a lack of creativity. Park's approach was to use 16 of the 36 squadrons of Fighter Command – the equivalent of around 200 aircraft – on rotating periods of heavy duty, with the other 20 squadrons kept in reserve. The absence of radar over northern France meant that he had to send his aircraft up in standing patrols, which could last only about forty minutes because of the restricted fuel capacity of the Spitfire and Hurricane. Such patrols could be appallingly wasteful, since there was no guarantee that they would be on target to encounter the Luftwaffe. And constant cover could not be provided without further diluting numbers. The Air Ministry's own official narrative of the air battle admitted that 'Fighter Command was required to meet, so far as was practicable with the available forces and bases, two virtually conflicting requirements over Dunkirk, continuity and strength.'[16] Yet, even in the face of these constraints, Fighter Command gave the Luftwaffe the first real challenge it had faced in the war. At the time, it was claimed that for every RAF plane lost, four Germans had been shot down. Such an assertion was to be typical of inflated wartime propaganda. Subsequent painstaking research by the aviation historian Norman Franks showed that the Luftwaffe lost 132 aircraft at Dunkirk, of which 35 may have been shot down by the guns of the Royal Navy. On the other side, the RAF flew 3,561 sorties, 2,739 of them fighter sorties, during which 99 fighters – 38 of them Spitfires – and 80 RAF pilots were lost. Even so, this is still a ratio favourable to Fighter Command, given that it was effectively operating over enemy territory.[17]

The memories of the Germans themselves are testimony to the uncompromising spirit of the RAF. On 27 May, when 64 German aircrew were killed, Major Werner Kreipe wrote in his diary, 'The enemy fighters pounced on us with the fury of maniacs.'[18] Kreipe later reflected, 'The days of easy victory were over. We had met the RAF head-on.'[19] In particular, the quality of Britain's fighters came as a shock after the easy victories over Polish, Belgian, Dutch and French air forces. As Ulrich Steinhilper put it in his memoir of his wartime career as a German fighter pilot:

> When we first saw the Hurricanes and Spitfires attacking our Stukas it was immediately clear that we were up against a very tenacious opposition . . . Our bombers pressed home their attacks but were constantly harassed by the RAF who inflicted substantial loses. I understand that it is a complaint of many British and French soldiers who were on the beaches that the RAF were nowhere to be seen. Believe me, they flew to their limit.[20]

The head of the Luftwaffe, Hermann Göring, had no appreciation of the combative quality of the RAF, hence his misguided promise to Hitler to wipe out the British Expeditionary Force from the air alone. One of his air-fleet commanders, General Albert Kesselring, thought that Göring had badly misread the situation at Dunkirk:

> I pointed out to Goering that the modern Spitfires had recently appeared, making our operations difficult and costly and in the end it was the Spitfires which enabled the British and French to evacuate across the water. Our battered and gradually reinforced formations strained every nerve to attain their objectives. The number of over-tired formations was higher than usual, with the natural result that the Spitfires steadily increased our losses.[21]

Yet little of this filtered down to the army on the shore or the Royal Navy on the Channel, struggling to cope with the German aerial bombardment. Admiral Sir Bertram Ramsey, who masterminded Operation Dynamo, submitted a report to the Admiralty two weeks after the evacuation was completed, one passage of which read:

> Rightly or wrongly full air protection was expected, but instead for hours on end the ships were subjected to a murderous hail of bombs and machine gun bullets . . . The Commanding Officers of many ships, while giving credit to the RAF personnel for gallantry in such combats as were observed from the ships, at the same time express their disappointment and surprise at the seemingly puny efforts made to provide air protection during the height of this operation.[22]

The same attitude of resentment existed in many of the lower ranks, as Second Lieutenant Norman Strother-Smith sarcastically recorded in his diary: 'Whenever German bombers appeared, sometimes the planes would come over and this morning at an odd time we saw some Spitfires – most of us had forgotten what they looked like.'[23] The heroic Al Deere had direct experience of this attitude when his Spitfire was badly hit by the rear gunner of a German Dornier 17 bomber and, with his aircraft engulfed in clouds of smoke from a punctured oil tank, he was forced to crash-land on a beach on the Belgian coast near Ostend. Badly wounded in the face, he managed to struggle by lorry and on foot to Dunkirk, where, after a long wait, he walked along a causeway and tried to get on-board a Royal Navy destroyer. Suddenly a voice barked, 'Where the hell do you think you're going? Get down from there and wait your turn.'

'I am an RAF officer,' replied Deere.

'I don't give a damn who you are, get down off there and fall in line with the rest.'

Deere explained that he wanted to get back to England as soon as possible to rejoin his squadron so he could return to give air cover over Dunkirk.

'For all the good you chaps seem to be doing over here you might just as well stay on the ground.'

This was too much for Deere, who told the naval officer, 'You have absolutely no say over what I do, and you can go to hell.' Deere still had to wait for the next ship. And even then he was given a frosty reception on-board by the soldiers.

'Why so friendly? What have the RAF done?'

'That's just it,' replied a young gunner lieutenant, 'What have they done? You are about as popular in this company as a cat in the prize canary cage.' Deere thought to himself ruefully, 'So that was it. For two weeks non-stop I had flown my guts out and this was all the thanks I got.'[24]

In a letter to his father, Tony Bartley, who had been flying Spitfires regularly over France, revealed the depths of the bitterness. 'The BEF have started stories that they never saw a fighter the whole time they were being bombed. The feeling ran very high at one time and some fighter pilots got roughed up by the army in pub brawls.'[25] Not all the RAF personnel were willing to put up with this abuse. One pilot, Ken Manger, was shot down in the crossfire of three Ju 88s but managed to parachute on to a beach near Dunkirk. When he reached the front of a queue waiting to board a destroyer, he was told by an army officer that 'all boats were for the army and not for the RAF.'[26] Manger, who had been a high-class amateur boxer before the war, threw a punch and sent the officer tumbling into the sea. He then calmly stepped on-board. The next day he was flying again.

The bad feeling was not confined to the army. Group Captain Bobby Oxspring, one of the select band of RAF fighter pilots who flew Spitfires operationally right through the war, recalled how in the summer of 1944 he was flying his Spitfire Mark XIV over Gravesend when, all of a sudden, 'the stick jumped violently in my hand and my Spit banked suddenly to the left. Thinking I'd fouled the cable I shat bricks until I found the aircraft still flying.' From his cockpit, Oxspring could see a large jagged hole in his port wing, but even with this damage he managed to land at Southend. It turned out that his plane had been deliberately fired on by a naval supply vessel on the Thames. 'The captain was a hairy old salt of the Royal Naval Reserve who, despite stringent regulations on opening fire in friendly waters, had been bombed at Dunkirk and had sworn that no aircraft would ever fly over his ship again. God bless the senior service.'[27]

Some of the army's scorn resulted from a lack of understanding at how the fighters had to operate. Under assault from the skies, the soldiers failed to realize that the Spitfires were usually trying to tackle the Luftwaffe bombers by patrolling inland rather than directly over the coast. Even when the soldiers did glimpse the RAF in action, they could not always appreciate the way that combat developed. Ray Morrant, a pilot shot down over Dunkirk, had this memory of watching the dogfights overhead as he sheltered with troops on the edge of the town:

> I saw one fully loaded bomber come down in the sea with a huge splash and an Me 109 explode in mid-air with a Spitfire on its tail – the pilot bailed out. I saw one Spitfire go for seven Huns. He got a great cheer from the troops. It was very interesting watching things from the ground as I could see the difficulties the fighters were up against. At times we could see Hun bombers bombing from the cloud, while our fighters were about half a mile away obviously unable to see them. The troops could not understand that one could see an aircraft in thin cloud above one, but from the air one could not.[28]

More disturbingly, some of the army personnel could not recognize the underside markings of planes belonging to their own side and therefore, full of indignation, viewed every aircraft as the enemy. The baronet Sir Archibald Hope was shot down on 27 May, belly-landed on the beach, and found his way to the nearest British unit. While he was there, a group of British fighters flew overhead at about 15,000 feet. To his surprise, the army took to their shelters. Hope told them there was no need to worry as the planes were RAF fighters. When asked how he knew, he replied that, for duty over northern France, the wings of the fighters were painted black and white underneath. This reply astonished the army. 'They said they had frequently seen aircraft with these markings and did not realize they were RAF.' Hope felt that this was 'an extraordinary failure by British intelligence in that at a unit as important as a brigade headquarters no one knew standard RAF markings'.[29]

Yet it would be unfair to put all the blame on the army, for there were also problems with the way in which the RAF used its fighters. In its first major combat, the Spitfire had proved itself a superb aircraft, while its pilots had demonstrated astonishing bravery against the dominant might of the Luftwaffe. But when it came to tactics at Dunkirk, Fighter Command was living in the past. Pilots were instructed to follow an approach that had been developed in the 1930s, when the Air Staff believed that there would be little use for the kinds of dogfight that had characterized the First World War. Unable to foresee that France would fall so quickly and Dutch neutrality would be ignored, the Air Staff thought that in any war the Luftwaffe would be forced to operate from bases in Germany, with southern Britain lying beyond the range of the German fighters. The primary task of the RAF's fighters would therefore be to shoot down unescorted bombers. To achieve this, they were instructed in a number of tactical manoeuvres which generally involved tight formations lining up in an orderly fashion and then taking it in turns to fire at the bombers. It was all very regimented – almost as if the RAF's aircraft were taking part in an aerial display. Indeed, so rigid was the Air Staff's mindset that the official manual on tactics set out five specific manoeuvres, known as the 'Fighting Area Attacks' (FAAs), to which the flight commander was meant to adhere in combat. So, in a certain operation, the commander might lead his flight towards the enemy, then call out over the radio a warning to prepare for 'Number Two attack'. His planes would move into their rehearsed positions in a 45-degree line angled away port or starboard from the leader. When about 400 yards from the enemy, the meticulously choreographed Number Two attack would begin, each plane following its pre-planned route towards its respective target in the enemy group of bombers.

The inflexibility of the Fighting Area Attacks was compounded by the RAF's use of the 'vic' formation, made up of three planes flying in a V, with the section leader in the centre and a wingman on each side. Like the FAAs, the vics might have seemed good on paper, but in practice they meant that the wingmen were constantly looking at their leader rather than searching the skies for the enemy. The Germans, because of their experience in the Spanish Civil War, had a far better, looser formation, based on the *Rotte*, or pair – two planes flying about 200 yards apart, with the rear plane covering the leader from quarter or astern attack. Two *Rotten* often combined to form a *Schwarm*, or flight, of four aircraft – a tactic eventually adopted by the RAF, where it would become known as the 'finger-four' formation, because it resembled the digits of an outstretched hand; the leader was effectively at the end of the second (longest) finger, his numbers two and three slightly behind on either side, backed up by the rear man, dubbed 'tail-end Charlie' or 'arse-end Charlie'.

Dunkirk might have revealed the fighting excellence of the Spitfire, but it exposed the woefulness of the Air Staff's theories. The legless wonder Douglas Bader of 19 Squadron shot down his first Me 109 in his Mark I Spitfire during the fighting over the coast, but he wrote that the FAAs 'struck me as absurd'.[30] The New Zealander Colin Gray left this description of one sortie which revealed the uselessness of the pre-war thinking:

> The FAAs were totally unsuitable for the type of combat we found ourselves in. We duly fanned out, each selecting a suitable bomber for attention, and this was when the escorting fighters arrived on the scene. Fortunately someone saw them coming and shouted over the R/T [radio telephone]: 'Break! Break! For Christ's sake break!' The result was chaos as we abandoned our primary targets and were forced to take violent evasive action. For the next few minutes I saw nothing but black crosses hurtling around in all directions. I managed to blast off all my ammo at a couple of 109s, both of which took spirited evasive action in their turn.[31]

To Bobby Oxspring, the Air Staff's Manual of Air Tactics was 'a criminal document – the whole formation sticks out like a dog's balls'.[32] Another Spitfire pilot, George Unwin of 19 Squadron, declared that 'our formation attacks were perfectly impressive for the Hendon Air Pageant but were useless for modern air fighting.'[33] And he was just as dismissive of the vics. 'Flying in threes turned out to be crazy. If you're flying in threes and you want to turn quickly, you can't without running into the other fellow. The Germans knew all this and they flew in twos. We had to pick it all up and reorganize our tactics accordingly.'[34]

Absence of radar meant that the Spitfires were often patrolling at the wrong height to tackle the Luftwaffe. Flight Lieutenant F. J. Howell wrote to his brother about a sortie on 31 May: 'With another squadron we flew over to Dunkirk about 2.30. The place was still burning furiously, a great pall of black smoke stretching 7,000 feet in the sky over Belgium. We again went to 20,000, with two squadrons below us at 10,000 feet. We never saw a single aeroplane within range and we learnt to our horror that eight blokes had been killed in a battle below us!' So, on the next patrol, Howell's flight was sent to 15,000 feet – only to find the enemy above. 'Here they bloody come, wave after wave of three bombers escorted by five 109s. How we all prayed for that extra 5,000 we had decided to do without. My heart gave a terrific thump I can tell you and we all went full throttle to get above them to 21,000 where there was a thin layer of cloud.'[35] Having gained more height, Howell managed to damage a Ju 88 and then downed a Heinkel, before returning to Kent.

The Spitfire's excellence at altitude encouraged commanders to push the pilots to fly as high as possible. 'In no time at all air fighting changed from the traditional pattern where one could see the ground to right on top where you couldn't see it at all. This is one of the reasons I'm sure the Army has often said, "Where are these fighter pilots?"' reflected Pilot Officer H. M. Stephen of 74 Squadron.[36] But Brian Kingcome, who shot down three Heinkels during the Dunkirk air battle, thought that the search for height became detrimental:

> As I sat in the relative safety of my Spitfire cockpit, it was the clouds that were the main problem. Our orders had sent us in at 30,000 feet, too high for the best of action, whereas the Hurricanes were patrolling at 15,000 feet. Needless to say we cheated and kept slipping down to see what was happening. Even then, though we ran into a few Germans, there did not seem to be the masses I anticipated. If the Hurricanes had been deployed at 5,000 feet and the Spitfires at 10,000, then between us we could perhaps have been more effective.[37]

The retreat from Dunkirk finished on 2 June. 'It was over as suddenly as it had begun,' wrote Tony Bartley. 'A decimated, bloody but unbowed squadron pulled out of the front line to lick its wounds and reform its ranks.'[38] For all the bruising it had experienced, the Spitfire had come triumphantly through its first ordeal. It showed that it was far more than just a thing of beauty: the plane had also dealt a powerful psychological blow to the Germans, while enhancing its own reputation in the RAF. Many of the doubts that had been so apparent in the previous two years now evaporated. As Jeffrey Quill put it later:

> It was at Dunkirk that the superior performance of the Spitfire Mark I in speed, rate of climb and manoeuvrability clearly demonstrated its true worth. This had a profound effect upon the attitudes of Fighter Command and the Air Ministry. It is probably fair to say that it was the operations at Dunkirk which established the Spitfire as the Number One Fighter in the Royal Air Force and resulted in decisions to produce as many as possible as fast as possible.[39]

Soon after the evacuation from the beaches, it was obvious that France would fall: its army was in tatters, its air force all but grounded. Within less than a fortnight the French government had collapsed. Marshal Pétain took power and asked for an armistice. On 22 June, France formally surrendered.

Britain would have to fight on alone. The Luftwaffe must inevitably be turned on the southern English coast. The Spitfire was one of the few rays of hope in this grim prospect.

But if the plane was to be a successful defender of Britain, not just the tactics for its use would have to be changed: it would also have to undergo several important technical adjustments to improve its performance. The most vital of these was the introduction of a new constant-speed, variable-pitch airscrew in place of the two-pitch propellers used on most of the Mark Is. By the summer of 1940 the Air Ministry was only too aware of the drawbacks of the two-pitch devices, which lowered the rate of climb, endurance and overall speed. The Mark II, being built with such painful delays at Castle Bromwich, had a variable-pitch airscrew built by Rotol, a joint subsidiary of the Bristol and Rolls-Royce companies, as did a limited number of bombers. For most of Fighter Command's Spitfire fleet, however, the De Havilland two-pitch was still used, partly because it was felt it would be prohibitively expensive and complex to convert all Mark Is.

A new impetus for change was provided by the capture of a fully intact Me 109 in May 1940. Immediately the plane was sent off for trials at the Royal Aircraft Establishment at Farnborough. The tests showed that the German fighter was far superior to the Hurricane 'in all respects with the exception of low-altitude manoeuvrability and turning circle at all altitudes'. The 109 was also better than a Spitfire fitted with a two-speed airscrew. But once a constant-speed propeller was installed on the Spitfire the match was far closer. The Farnborough report stated that the Spitfire was then 'only marginally slower than its German contemporary' below 20,000 feet. Overall, 'the Spitfire possessed a definite superiority in manoeuvrability at all altitudes as a result of its lower wing loading, and smaller turning circle, and a distinct advantage above 20,000 feet.'[40]

Dowding, with his usual technocratic drive, immediately ordered wider trials of the new propellor within Fighter Command. On 16 June, Air Vice-Marshal H. R. Nichol wrote to him saying that tests at Hornchurch demonstrated that the constant-speed airscrews offered a better take-off, a better climb, a higher ceiling, much greater manoeuvrability, increased diving speed, and increased endurance. This type of Spitfire, equipped with a constant-speed airscrew, he told Dowding, 'is the superior of any enemy aircraft yet encountered by our pilots at Hornchurch'. He therefore 'requested that the fitting of all Spitfires with these airscrews may now be considered a matter of supreme urgency'.[41] Even better news followed a week later, when a senior RAF engineer, A. R. Collins, reported that, as a result of investigations with the De Havilland company, no technical complications are foreseen in the conversion of Spitfire I airscrews . . . De Havilland's are fully aware of all that is involved in this conversion and can be relied upon to carry out the conversion on all aircraft in service. The De Havilland test pilot has already flown a Spitfire with a constant-speed airscrew at 35,000 feet, temperature −30°. The airscrew constant-speeded in a normal manner and there was no tendency to sluggish operation.[42]

On 22 June, Dowding ordered the conversion of all planes in Fighter Command, starting with the Spitfires because of their importance. As the Mark Is had De Havilland two-speed units De Havilland constant-speed airscrews were chosen for the conversion, rather than the Rotol ones currently being fitted to the new Mark IIs, because 'it is obviously undesirable, from the interchangeability and spares point of view, to have two different types of airscrew on the Spitfire Mark I if it can be avoided.'[43] This massive operation was conducted by De Havilland without a written contract but with an efficiency that had not always been seen in the Spitfire programme. From 24 June the company started to produce the airscrew conversion sets at its factory at the rate of twenty per day. The actual conversions began simultaneously at twelve Spitfire squadrons the following day, 25 June, led at each base by a De Havilland supervisory engineer, who worked with a hand-picked team of RAF fitters to carry out the job. The De Havilland experts often put in over fifteen hours a day as they moved from one squadron to the next. Within less than a month they had completed all the Spitfire modifications − a feat which few at the Air Staff would have thought possible, though this was just the kind of initiative that Beaverbrook so admired. By 15 August, 1,051 Spitfires and Hurricanes had been converted, the achievement executed at a rate of 20.2 aircraft a day. The pilots themselves were delighted with the change, as Sandy Johnstone recorded in his diary: 'Jeffrey Quill turned up with Supermarine's latest toy to try out. I flew this Spitfire for an hour yesterday afternoon and I found its variable-pitch, constant-speed airscrew a big improvement over the old push and pull device we've been using so far. It gives much more flexibility, besides a much smoother ride.'[44]

Apart from the airscrew, there were some other changes carried out to the Mark I as a result of the experience in France. An alloy cover was fitted over the main fuel tank in front of the cockpit to deflect rounds striking from a shallow angle; a 2-inch-thick layer of laminated glass was bolted on to the front windscreen to provide protection against head-on attacks; 73 pounds of armour plating was fitted behind the cockpit seat, including a quarter-inch piece of stainless steel behind the pilot's head; and the Sutton harness straps were lengthened to take account of this new armour. Rear-view mirrors were also installed above the windscreen − something that Sandy Johnstone welcomed. 'They should cut down the chance of a cricked neck every time one is embroiled in a dogfight,' he wrote in his diary.[45] Ammunition was improved with the introduction of the De Wilde incendiary bullet, which left no flame or smoke trace. As Al Deere explained, 'Its greatest value lay in the fact that it produced a small flash on impact thus providing confirmation to the attacking fighter that his aim was good.'[46] Despite the exotic name, De Wilde ammunition had actually been developed by a Brigadier Dixon of the Ministry of Supply: the story that it was produced by a Belgian company was only a cover to maintain its secrecy.

Another important lesson of Dunkirk was that harmonization of the Spitfire's eight guns to hit a target at 400 yards often brought disappointing results against German aircraft. Dowding had always been in favour of this range, partly because he felt it was the safest distance at which the pilots could fire and partly because he believed, as he wrote in July 1939, that 'it was by no means axiomatic that the closer the pilots got to the bomber the more bullets would hit it.'[47] But many leading airmen felt otherwise. They thought the 'Dowding spread', as it was known, was a recipe for caution rather destruction. Johnnie Johnson, the Allied top fighter ace in Europe during the war, wrote that the 400-yard range handicapped good marksmen 'who sometimes closed to excellent killing range only to find the area of lethal density was not particularly lethal'.[48] The best Spitfire pilots, like Al Deere and Sailor Malan, felt that 250 yards was the most effective distance, and had their guns refocused accordingly. Their success meant that this range became standard throughout Fighter Command.

In the context of shooting, another of the major advantages that the Spitfire had over previous fighters was the reflector sight, which replaced the ring-and-bead sight that biplane pilots had peered down as they tried to line up their targets. The former pilot John Vader, who flew Spitfires with the Royal Australian Air Force in the Pacific, described how the ingenious new mechanism operated:

> The reflector sight was a system of lenses which shone the image of a gunsight on to a small glass just behind the windshield inside the cockpit, the image intensity being adjustable for varying combat conditions. Thrown up by a lamp was a faint red circle with a dot in the centre. Running across the circle were two lines which could be adjusted inwards and outwards by turning a milled ring, graduated to represent the wingspan of various types of aircraft. When the enemy's wings filled the gap between the two lines it was within range.[49]

One of the great advantages of the reflector sight was that pilots could aim at their target while still flying normally. Furthermore, the internal lamp meant that accurate firing was possible in poor light, though Colin Gray thought that the sight's operation could be hampered by the long nose of the Spitfire: 'The reflector sight ring cut across the top of the engine so that as soon as one turned to follow a target it was lost to view beneath the engine . . . One was therefore left shooting at a point in space that could be up to forty yards ahead of where the target was last seen.'[50]

It is telling that the highest-scoring aces in the RAF were not just skilful, brave pilots: they were usually also gifted marksmen, with a naturally good eye and an instinctive understanding of the art of deflection shooting – firing ahead of a target to score a hit as it travelled into the bullets. Given that a bullet left the muzzle of a Browning gun with a velocity of 2,660 feet per second, delivered from a Spitfire that could be flying at over 300 mph against an enemy going at the same pace, this was a delicate skill to master. Impatient, determined and hard-nosed, Bob Stanford-Tuck, a flight commander with 92 Squadron from May 1940, was a keen sportsman and believed that game shooting improved his effectiveness as a pilot. His 30 victories in the Battle of Britain were strong evidence to support his theory. 'To see him shoot clay pigeons was an experience,' said John Ryder, an instrument man with his squadron. 'What an eye he had! No wonder he had such a large score in the air. Wherever he went there was always a mob of spectators. So far as we airmen were concerned, he was an "ace" on the ground as well as aloft.'[51] In a lecture in 1976 about the Spitfire, Stanford-Tuck made this revealing contribution:

Quite contrary to what the average person in the street would think, actual shooting was quite a precision business. I always looked upon it as that. Never fire very long bursts, spraying away. Wait until you are very close up to him and you know your built-in compensator says that is the position to shoot ahead of him as he is turning that way. When you have got everything dead right, and you are close and you know you are going to hit him hard, a two-second burst was all you required. Certainly you never had to continue. I am quite sure some of the pilots when they started, the youngsters who perhaps had little experience of combat, were guilty of locking their thumb on the firing button and squirting away as hard as they could go. But it was really a precision business.[52]

In the early summer of 1940 the most urgent need of the RAF was more fighter aircraft rather than improvements to existing types. The campaign in France had extracted a severe toll. Between 10 May and 20 June the RAF had lost 944 aircraft, of which 386 were Hurricanes and 76 Spitfires. On the final day of the Dunkirk evacuation, Fighter Command's resources were to be at their lowest point of the whole of 1940. Home defence was reduced to 331 Spitfires and Hurricanes, supported by 150 second-rank fighters such as

Blenheims and Defiants. If Germany had been able to mount an invasion across the Channel immediately after the fall of France, it is unlikely that Britain, with its army defeated and disarmed, could have put up prolonged resistance. Indeed, several German strategists urged Hitler to start precisely such an offensive, beginning with the use of airborne troops over the southern coast. The British Chiefs of Staff certainly expected an imminent invasion. On 27 May, at the height of Dunkirk, they discussed a paper which warned that Britain could hold out only as long as the Germans were denied air superiority. Yet the German High Command was in no rush.

This was largely for military reasons. For all their comprehensive victories in the west and in Scandinavia, the Germans had also suffered heavy losses in recent months. In the battle for France alone, at least 1,667 Luftwaffe planes were destroyed or damaged, while the Norway campaign had crippled a large part of the German navy, which would be vital in any attempt to secure the English Channel. The Reich's military forces, though flushed with triumph, needed to regroup – particularly because no plans had yet been drawn up for an attack on Britain. And after Dunkirk, the Germans appreciated that the British would be a sterner foe, at least in the air and at sea, than any previous opponents.

Hitler also had political motives for delay. Now that most of northern Europe was in his grasp, he was preoccupied with his long-term goal of defeating Russia, which was becoming increasingly bellicose in the east. To him, the idea that Britain, isolated and battered, could continue in the war was ridiculous. The years of Chamberlain's appeasement had convinced him that the government would not have the will to fight on. Britain, he believed, would soon come to its senses. But he had grossly underestimated the indomitable will of Winston Churchill, whose growling defiance and thunderous eloquence roused a new spirit of courage in the British nation. On 18 June – the day after Pétain formed his government – Churchill made one of his most memorable wartime speeches in the Commons: 'The battle of France is over. I expect that the Battle of Britain is about to begin. Upon this battle depends the survival of Christian civilization. Upon it depends our own British life, and the long continuity of our institutions and our Empire. The whole fury and might of the enemy must very soon be turned on us. Hitler knows that he will have to break us in this Island or lose the war,' ran one of the most stirring – and prophetic – passages. And he concluded with one of the greatest perorations in British oratorical history. 'Let us therefore brace ourselves to our duties, and so bear ourselves that if the British Empire and its Commonwealth last for a thousand years, men will still say, "This was their finest hour."'

The Nazi regime now saw that there was no chance of the Churchill government making any overtures for peace. On 30 June, Göring sent instructions to the Luftwaffe to prepare for a new offensive against Britain, which would include the destruction of industry, the disruption of supply lines, and the obliteration of the RAF's ground organization. 'So long as the enemy air force remains in being, the supreme principle of air warfare must be to attack it at every possible opportunity by day and by night, in the air and on the ground, with priority over other tasks.'[53] Two days later Hitler issued Directive No. 16, giving approval for an invasion: 'As England, despite her hopeless military situation, still shows no sign of willingness to come to terms, I have decided to prepare, and if necessary carry out, a landing operation against her. The aim of this operation is to eliminate the English motherland as a base from which war can be continued and, if necessary, to occupy completely.'[54] The attack, it was envisaged, would begin in August.

As both sides waited for the start of the onslaught, a strange lull descended, made all the more beguiling by the brilliant hot summer that arrived across western Europe. Instead of being plunged into intense conflict as they expected, the Spitfire pilots found they were carrying out largely routine work. H. R. 'Dizzy' Allen was disappointed to find himself performing convoy-protection work in the North Sea, which he felt 'wasted a great number of flying hours which should have been utilized in a fierce flying training programme'. Allen confessed that he was 'bored almost to tears', so, to gain some respite,

> I would fly as low as I dared, attempting almost but not quite to cause my propeller blades to flick the sea. The only distraction came via the radio in my Spitfire which, at that time, worked on high-frequency bands. This one would tune in on the waveband one preferred, and I preferred Henry Hall and the BBC Orchestra. I would listen to the hit tunes of the day, hour after hour, day in day out. And then what happened? They removed our HF radios and gave us VHF sets, which worked on set frequencies selected by pressing one of four buttons. This meant I could no longer tune in to Henry Hall. I nearly went mad.[55]

Bobby Oxspring of 66 Squadron felt enough ennui to challenge the Prime Minister when Churchill visited his base of RAF Coltishall in June. 'He asked how things were going and the main complaint to him was the lack of activity which, apart from Dunkirk, we had borne for nearly a year. His response to us was to be patient because very soon we would have as much as we wanted.' Yet Oxspring's duties were not totally without excitement. On 29 July, on patrol near Lowestoft, he led an attack on a Heinkel 111 at 15,000 feet: 'I misjudged the approach and had to close from dead astern to get into range. As we did so, the rear gunner opened fire, his tracers going to my right side and below. Closing in to about 400 yards, I let go with a long burst and then broke up and away to starboard. I didn't see any hits on the Heinkel but its rear fire had ceased.' Two other Spitfires followed up the attack, as the Heinkel tried to escape into some cloud at 8,000 feet. 'We picked him up again underneath the layer and expended the remainder of the ammo into him. He went down with both engines on fire to ditch into the sea. We stayed long enough to see two of the crew clamber out into their dinghy before the aircraft sank from sight.'[56]

A Heinkel 111 was also brought down by Sandy Johnstone flying his Spitfire at night, guided on to the target by the powerful beams of search-lights operated by an anti-aircraft base outside Edinburgh. From dead astern, Johnstone let fly 'with all eight Brownings, when my victim disappeared from view. At first I thought I'd blown it out of the sky until noticing my windscreen was covered in oil thrown back by the bomber.' Johnstone held the German plane in his sight, black smoke and flame pouring from its engine, until he saw it crash into the sea near Dunbar 'with a great splash, the beam from its landing light growing ever greener as the aircraft disap-peared below the waves. Strangely I felt no sense of elation; only a sudden feeling of loneliness.'[57]

If some of the Spitfire pilots did not feel overstretched in the days after the fall of France, the same can hardly be said of the Supermarine factory work-ers, whose diligence embodied the Churchillian mood of resolution in the national cause. By July 1940, all three Supermarine plants of Woolston, Eastleigh and Itchen were at full capacity seven days a week, with the day shift putting in 70 hours a week and the night shift even more, at 73.5 hours. The one-thousandth Spitfire was delivered from Southampton in August, and by the end of September 1940 the company had made 1,196 Mark Is. The Air Ministry was now so confident about the plane and the factory that in July an order for another 1,000 was placed.[58] The Supermarine manager Denis Webb, who had sometimes been critical of the workforce in the past, wrote, 'I still marvel at the way everyone adjusted to the change and slogged their guts out to achieve what they did.'[59]

On top of the inspirational quality of Churchill's rhetoric and the natural impulse towards patriotism at a time of crisis, the combustible force of Lord Beaverbrook also played a key part in driving aircraft production to new heights. Contemptuous of Whitehall protocol, indifferent to rank or Treasury rules, exhausting in his demands, and unorthodox in his methods, Beaverbrook devoted his energies towards the single goal of immediately building up the fighter strength of the RAF. As his biographer A. J. P. Taylor put it, 'He did not mind the accusation that he was sacrificing the future for the sake of the present. The present was all that mattered to him and unless that were secured there would be no future to sacrifice.' He had little time for either civil servants or the Air Staff; the latter were usually referred to as 'those bloody Air Marshals'.[60] Interestingly, the one air marshal whom Beaverbrook did respect was Sir Hugh Dowding. The career officer and the Canadian millionaire could not have been more different in character. Dowding was reserved, puritanical, cold to the point of frigidity, whereas Beaverbrook was amorous, extrovert, devious and unpredictable. But they both shared exactly the same outlook on the supreme importance of the fighter for the protection of Britain. Beaverbrook saw it as his central political duty to give Dowding what he needed, and nothing would stand in his way. 'I must have more planes. I don't care whose heart is broken or pride hurt or anything else at all,' he said.[61]

His ministerial empire was run like a personal autocracy rather than a branch of Whitehall. As soon as he arrived at his nascent department, he was disturbed by the quiet smoothness. 'It must be disorganized and unbalanced without delay,' he declared.[62] Widely known as 'the Beaver', he recruited his own staff for its headquarters, including key figures from the *Daily Express* and others from the aircraft industry, such as Sir Charles Craven and Trevor Westbrook from Vickers. To the outrage of the Air Ministry, he not only interfered directly with policy matters, but also requisitioned the Ministry's property. The Secretary of State for Air, Sir Archibald Sinclair, complained so vociferously about Beaverbrook's 'piratical tendencies' that Beaverbrook threatened to resign in July and had to be persuaded by Churchill to remain in post.[63] Even one of his own private staff, David Farrer, admitted that Beaverbrook possessed 'a ruthlessness bordering on sharp practice' – though Farrer also said that his boss had 'the quickest and sharpest brain I have ever known'.[64] The Tory politician Harold Balfour wrote of his approach:

> Any hen roost was robbed to produce just one more fighter. Risks were taken. Experimental units were robbed of test aircraft. Training stations had to give up service types. Factory management was bullied, praised, cajoled. Each week's effort was taken as the starting point of exhortation for a bigger and better next week. Bosses of great aircraft concerns learnt not to play golf on Sunday mornings but stand by the telephone, for this was Beaverbrook's favourite hour for telephone talk with these men.[65]

Speaking with his North Atlantic nasal twang, Beaverbrook could conduct multiple conversations simultaneously both over the phone and in person. He followed no routine and, apart from the War Cabinet, attended few committee meetings. 'Committees take the punch out of war' was one of his favourite sayings. Visitors to his offices were rarely provided with chairs, so they would not be inclined to dawdle.

A wonderful portrait of Beaverbrook in operation was provided by Jeffrey Quill, who was summoned for an appointment in August 1940 without any explanation being given as to the purpose of the meeting. Sir Charles Craven met him in the lobby and then ushered him into the Minister's presence:

> The Beaver was sitting at his desk conducting a telephone conversation in anything but a soft or mellifluous voice. To whom he was speaking I had no idea but this strange gnome-like little man was certainly making his wishes abundantly clear to whoever was on the other end of the line. He put the receiver down and Craven introduced me and Beaverbrook said, 'Ah, yes, Quill – good! I know all about you, young man, and I want to talk to you, but right now I'm too much engaged. Come to dinner at my house tonight at eight, Stornaway House – don't be late' – and with that the little man sprang to his feet and shot out of his office by another door. Sir Charles Craven looked at me and laughed and I said, 'Have you any idea what all this is about, Sir Charles?'
>
> 'Not much,' said Craven, 'I think it may be something to do with cannons in Spitfires.'

Quill confessed that he knew little about cannon in Spitfires, but recognized that he had been ordered, rather than asked, to go to dinner at Beaverbrook's Mayfair home. He duly turned up at the palatial residence, where there were several guests already drinking pre-dinner cocktails – among them the Minister for Information, Brendan Bracken. 'It was soon clear that they had even less idea than I had as to the reason for my presence. The Beaver was nowhere to be seen.' Eventually he turned up, accompanied by several acolytes, and dinner was served. But during the meal 'as Beaverbrook kept going in and out of an adjoining room to speak on the telephone or deal with secretaries we were left very much to our own devices.' The absences became longer as the evening wore on. By the time brandy and cigars arrived, Quill had given up all hope of finding out what Beaverbrook wanted or even where he was. 'A door into an adjoining room was standing open and from the other side of that door there was suddenly a loud and unmistakable snore. Brendan Bracken tiptoed in to investigate and we all peered in. Beaverbrook was in an armchair, a telephone on a table beside him, sleeping soundly.'[66] Quill never did find out the subject of Beaverbrook's urgent interest.

Beaverbrook's contribution to the increase in Spitfire production was enormous. Yet he played perhaps an even greater role in raising the profile of the plane in the national consciousness. Public recognition had been growing steadily in the weeks since Dunkirk, helped by BBC features such as the radio programme on 25 June entitled *Spitfires Over Britain*, which looked at the work of a home-defence squadron of Fighter Command. The broadcast carried a mock but convincing narration of a fictional incident in which three Spitfires attacked a section of Heinkel bombers near Newcastle. 'The two Spitfires flash down . . . 400 yards . . . 200 yards. The Heinkel's gunner is firing wildly. They've got him . . . cut him off like a whippet by anticipating a turn,' yelled the narrator in an exhilarated voice. That week's edition of the *Radio Times*, then the only broadcast listings magazine, stimulated further interest by carrying on its cover a dramatic photograph of three Spitfires hurtling across the sky. A month later, on 25 July, the BBC had the chance to broadcast a real commentary on a Spitfire dogfight when the reporter Charles Gardener, on another assignment, happened to witness a clash over Dover and made an instant recording of the scene. At a time when most radio programming was highly artificial and bound by script and studio, Gardener's verbal picture, aired shortly after he recorded it, was novel for the sense of instant excitement it conveyed through its jagged sentences:

> Oh, there's a terrific mix-up now over the Channel. It's impossible to tell which are our machines and which are the Germans. There's one definitely down in this battle and there's a fight going on – you can hear the little rattles of machine-gun bullets. [Sound of explosion] That was a bomb, as you may imagine. Here comes – there's one Spitfire, there are little bursts. There's another bomb dropping. The sky is absolutely patterned now with bursts of anti-aircraft fire and the sea is covered with smoke where the bombs have burst . . . There are about four fighters up there and I don't know what they're doing – one, two, three, four, five fighting right over our head now. There's one coming right down on the tail of what I think is a Messerschmitt and I think a Spitfire behind him.[67]

But, while the BBC generated a new awareness of the fighter, it was Beaverbrook's initiative that turned it into an icon, its very name redolent of British determination, its elliptical wings a source of intense national pride, its curved lines the moving embodiment of romantic Churchillian glory.

Beaverbrook's first attempt to involve the public in the war effort was not a huge success. At the end of June 1940 he suddenly grew concerned that Germany appeared to control much of the world's supply of bauxite, one of the vital raw materials for the manufacture of aluminium. With typical originality, he decided that the answer to this potential threat was a rallying call to the public. On 10 July he issued this call to 'The Women of Britain': 'Give us your aluminium. We want it and we want it now. New and old, of every type and description, and all of it. We will turn your pots and pans into Spitfires and Hurricanes, Blenheims and Wellingtons.' He went on to urge that women hand over pots, kettles, coat hangers, bathroom fittings and shoe trees to the local headquarters of the Women's Voluntary Service. There was a strong initial response – one pile of pots in a south-London borough rose more than a storey high – but the whole business had an air of unreality. There was already plenty of scrap aluminium available across the country, and donors were quickly disillusioned when they saw that shops remained as well-stocked with kitchen utensils as ever. Fraud also contributed to the disenchantment, with Beaverbrook's Ministry forced publicly to warn that 'unauthorized persons are collecting pots and pans.' Householders were told to give only to the WVS, not to 'any caller at the door'.[68] In any case, the amount produced was negligible, amounting to just one day's supply of the nation's needs.

Soon after this, Beaverbrook embarked on another appeal – one that was immediately to capture the public's imagination. At the end of June he had been asked by the mining millionaire Sir Harry Oakes how much it cost to build a Spitfire. Sir Harry, it seems, had been deeply impressed by the Spitfire's exploits over Dunkirk. Beaverbrook told him that it was about £5,000. Contrary to what has often been claimed in Spitfire literature that this was a severe underestimate, it was in fact pretty accurate. Though the first fifty planes were more expensive because of production difficulties and modifications, costing £8,783 each, in 1939 the Air Ministry had agreed a price with Vickers of £5,696 for each of the next 450, and by the beginning of 1940 Vickers was telling the Ministry that, because of economies of scale, future aircraft could be built for £4,725. Oakes duly sent off a cheque for £5,000 to the Ministry, and his generosity was praised in the press. In Wolverhampton, Alderman Morris Christopher, having read about the case, suggested that the local *Express and Star* newspaper start up a £5,000 Spitfire fund, for which he was enclosing a cheque for £50. Within a week the paper had raised over £6,000. Other towns and cities now took up the challenge, strongly encouraged by Beaverbrook, who used all his public-relations skills to boost the funds. To his delight, the Spitfire craze spread like wildfire. By the first week of August, £2.5 million had been raised.

The breadth of the funds' embrace was astonishing, from wealthy plutocrats to shopfloor workers, from widows in Ceylon to miners in Wales, from vast companies to the inmates of women's prisons. As the BBC put it in a private briefing for the Air Staff about the way the news of the funds should be covered, 'Some of the contributions have been really remarkable, for the places concerned are, comparatively speaking, poor and it must have been a great sacrifice on the part of individuals who made up the sums.'[69] The Spitfire had become the greatest catalyst for a single fund-raising drive in the twentieth century. When Beaverbrook received £5,000 from Captain Leslie Gamage, he replied, 'We shall instantly apply the money to buying a Spitfire. It is a fine machine, beloved by pilots. And you can be quite sure that it will be a terror to our enemies and a shield to our homes.'[70]

Some of the individual fund-raising activities showed an infusion of the Beaverbrook urge for innovation. In the borough of Bermondsey, for instance, 402,000 pennies were collected for Spitfires in door-to-door collections. One eight-year-old girl, Patricia Boncey, sent Beaverbrook a postal order for 15 shillings and explained that 'the money has been collected through an idea of my own. When my Mummy has taken me out and I have wanted to use a public convenience she has had to pay a penny. So I thought if we did the same at home it would help your fund. I hope to send you some more money when my box is full again.'[71] At the other end of the scale, the exiled Queen Wilhelmina of the Netherlands gave £500,000, Garfield Weston, the Canadian biscuit manufacturer and MP, £100,000, and the Nawab of Junagadh £15,000. Some of the corporate donations were equally impressive. The New Zealand Meat Producers Board, for example, gave £30,000, and the government of the Gold Coast in Africa £100,000. One of the more poignant gifts came from the American Fred Pearson, whose research foundation in Vienna had treated R. J. Mitchell in the last months of his life.

In return for these sums, the donors earned not just the gratitude of Lord Beaverbrook, but also the chance to have a Spitfire named after their district, company or country – or any other suitable title. Thus the people of Ely in East Anglia had their Spitfire called *Hereward the Wake*, after the local hero who had defended Britain against another invader 900 years earlier. There were no fewer than seventeen Spitfires named after places in Northern Ireland after an appeal by the *Belfast Telegraph* raised £85,000. Perhaps the most remarkable donation of all came from British prisoners of war held in the camp of Oflag VIB near the town of Warburg, where some 2,500 services personnel donated one month's pay to the fund. Described as a 'collection for charity', the money was deposited with the Germans and then sent by the Swedish Red Cross to England, where it was used to purchase a Spitfire called, appropriately, *Unshackled Spirit*.[72]

There was not universal approval for Beaverbrook's fund. Some of those in the RAF felt excluded by all the attention given exclusively to the Spitfire when they too were risking their lives in the national cause. One Hurricane pilot wrote anonymously to *The Times*, 'Why is it that we only hear of Spitfire funds? Why not a few Hurricane funds? We Hurricane pilots would really like to know. Perhaps the Spitfire has more sex appeal.' He had provided the answer to his own question. There were also occasional examples of criminals trying to exploit the public. In August 1940 Arthur Meachin, a building worker from Ilford, was sentenced to twelve months' hard labour for running fraudulent Spitfire appeals through a series of fake organizations including 'The Fighting Services Aid Association' and 'The Public War Aids Purchasing Fund', whose president was purportedly none other than Winston Churchill.[73] A few reactionaries, clinging to the Trenchard doctrine, thought that the Spitfire funds exposed the defensive mentality bred by the fighter. The MP E. H. Kealing complained that money should instead be raised for bombers: 'Our main objective is to win the war and that can only be done by attacking the enemy in Germany,' he said. This prompted a vigorous response from the detective writer Dorothy L. Sayers, the creator of the Lord Peter Wimsey novels. In a letter to the *Daily Telegraph*, she gave a compelling explanation of why the Spitfire funds had struck such a chord with the public: 'A fighter plane is, comparatively speaking, a very small machine and there is something irresistibly endearing about a very small thing that fights like hell . . . When a ferocious giant has been coming at one with a club, the impulse to send the hat round for Jack the Giant Killer is too strong to be restrained by any calculations of policy.'[74]

Some thought the entire business was based on sentimentality and a misunderstanding of public funding. One aggrieved member of the Athanaeum club, Mervyn O'Gorman, wrote to Air Chief Marshal Sir Philip Joubert de la Ferté of the Air Staff, complaining that the proposed Spitfire fund at his club was 'a sham':

> It won't increase the Spitfires by one iota. It is a presumptuous sham since the Athanaeum has no knowledge as to which group of fighters should be picked out. The notice sent by our General Committee exposes us to the risk of seeming ungrateful to the fighters should members properly reject this sham – which is no more than an invitation to tax ourselves. The Treasury can do that. It taxes where it will. There is no need for a Spitfire tax which does the RAF no good.[75]

To an extent, this has been the line taken by several historians since the war: that the funds were little more than a gigantic press stunt. 'The contributors never quite realized that money could not put Spitfires in the sky,' wrote Anne Chisholm and Michael Davie in their biography of Lord Beaverbrook, without explaining why not.[76]

There is something all too cynical about this argument. For the reality is that the money-raising was part of a huge national collective effort that *did* put thousands of Spitfires in the sky. In fact when the funds closed, in the spring of 1941, they had raised over £13 million, the purchase cost of roughly 2,700

Spitfires – more than double the entire Castle Bromwich first order. If that sum had not been raised, then the Ministry of Aircraft Production would have needed to have found it elsewhere in its budget. More importantly, the funds served both as a rallying cry for a nation in peril and as a powerful unifying force. Almost as much as Churchill's oratory, the Spitfire brought Britain together on the eve of one of the darkest ordeals in its history. Wars are not won by mere economic calculations, especially not in the modern era of total conflict. They are won by galvanizing the will of the civilian population.

The genuine inspiration that the Spitfire funds could provide was summed up in a painfully moving letter to Lord Beaverbrook from a father in South Wales, Mr H. H. Merrett from the small village of Michaelston-le-Pit, who had lost his son, an RAF pilot, during a raid:

> These tragic circumstances have served only to strengthen the determination of this little community to prove to the despicable enemy that we have set our hearts to rise to the greatest possible heights in assisting you and your colleagues in your admirable efforts to defend and feed the most sacred spot on God's earth. I cannot provide you with another gallant son. The one who has gone was our only son. But I want you to accept from the village of Michaelston-le-Pit the enclosed cheque for £5,000 to purchase a Spitfire, so that one of the growing number of lads from Britain and the Dominions, so anxious to defend us in the air, may be equipped with an instrument which, combined with that spirit of courage and fearlessness, will enable him – as his colleagues are doing – to take severe toll of those inferior beings attempting to destroy the morale of our people.[77]

7

'Achtung! Spitfeuer!'

O N 1 AUGUST 1940, Reichsmarschall Hermann Göring gathered his senior Luftwaffe officers to a conference at The Hague in Holland to discuss the final preparations for the air assault on Britain. He was in an expansive mood. The German triumphs in the west, in which the Luftwaffe had played a central part, had further bloated his oversized ego. The most powerful military leader in the Reich, Hitler's closest ally, and commander of the world's largest air force, he revelled in the power and trappings of his unique position. He had castles, hunting lodges and town houses across Germany, a retinue of personal servants, a large wardrobe of gaudy uniforms, and a personal train equipped with its own cinema and dining car and luxurious bedrooms for himself and his wife. His self-indulgent lifestyle was reflected in his heavy figure, though he had been a heroic pilot in the First World War and remained a passionate hunting enthusiast. If Himmler represented Nazism at its most clinically sinister, then Göring displayed its most extravagantly grandiose side.

The comparative lull after the fall of France had given him time to enjoy his pursuits. While Britain waited for invasion, Göring was a man of leisure through the last weeks of June and the first weeks of July, spending much of his time in Paris buying works of art. Many Luftwaffe pilots, too, welcomed the break after the intensity of the French campaign, though sporadic brutal fighting still continued around the English coast, mainly involving attacks by the Germans on British shipping. During July, Fighter Command lost 115 planes in total, including 33 Spitfires and 47 Hurricanes, while the Luftwaffe saw 218 planes destroyed, including 66 fighters. Flight Lieutenant F. J. Howell of 609 Squadron wrote to his brother in the army, in semi-jocular tones, about his dramatic experience in his Spitfire in taking on a Ju 88 bomber over the Hampshire coast on 18 July:

> I made an almost head-on attack at it. I don't think he liked that one little bit because he turned over and went split arse for the sea, releasing four large bombs and doing over 350 mph. I got in another attack and got his port motor . . . Just then I smelt a nasty smell! A horrid smell! I looked at the dials

and things and saw that the coolant temperature was right off the clock – about 180°C – and the oil temperature at 95° and going up. The bugger had shot me in the radiator! White fumes began pouring back into the cockpit, so that was not really good enough. The poor old motor began to seize up, groaning pitifully.[1]

Howell had to bail out at 5,000 feet over the water off Poole, and was rescued by a Royal Navy motor launch.

Convoy protection was a vital task in July, as the Germans probed the strength of air defences and sought to cut off Britain's supply lines through the Channel. It could be dispiriting work, alleviated only by the quality of the Spitfire, as Tubby Mayne, a veteran with 74 Squadron remembered: 'It wasn't so bad when you could find the convoy. But there were bad days even in the summer, looking for ships in low cloud and rain and damned great waves, green ones just below you. But the Spit and the Merlin engine, they were superb. They were what gave us confidence. You could get into that cockpit and shut the canopy and feel you were in a fortress and no one could get you.'[2] On the morning of 24 July, Al Deere's squadron was ordered off from Hornchurch to tackle a large raid by Dornier 17s preparing to attack a convoy in the Thames estuary. As soon as he spotted the German formation, he realized how formidable it was, with the Dornier bombers escorted by a large group of Me 109s. Deere admitted that 'an attack against such numbers was a frightening prospect', but he felt his squadron had no alternative other than 'to get among them' if the convoy was not to be obliterated:

A momentary buffeting as I hit the enemy bomber's slipstream, a determined juggling with the control column and rudder, a brief wait for the range to close and the right-hand bomber received the full impact of my eight Brownings. In a matter of seconds, in which time only a short burst was possible, I was forced to break off the attack for fear of collision. It was perhaps just as well, as the 109s were now all around us. In the next few minutes, a frenzy of twisting and turning. I managed quick bursts at three enemy fighters, as singly they passed through my line of fire, but without conclusive results. Suddenly the sky was clear and I was alone; one minute the air was a seething cauldron of Hun fighters, and the next it was empty.[3]

He returned to base after watching the convoy serenely wending its way down the Thames, oblivious to the struggle above.

The phenomenon that Deere described, of the sky suddenly turning from a mass of whirling planes into a silent void, would come to be recognized by all Spitfire pilots in combat. Hugh Dundas, who was only twenty in 1940 and became the youngest group captain in the RAF, put it well in his account of his first Spitfire dogfight, which took place over Dunkirk. 'At one moment it was all you could do to avoid collision; the sky around you was streaked with tracer and the thin grey smoke-trails of firing machine guns and cannons. The next moment you were on your own. The melee had broken up as if by magic. The sky was empty except for a few distant specks.'[4]

The strain on Fighter Command was heavy throughout July. Often more than 500 sorties a day were flown to guard the coast. On 19 July no fewer than 701 sorties were flown. And, just as at Dunkirk, the British fighters were often heavily outnumbered. But this was only a prelude. The real confrontation, involving the very fate of Britain's independence, was soon to start, as Göring explained to his Luftwaffe officers at The Hague. Hitler had just given orders that the Luftwaffe's grand attack against England should begin around 5 August, and that it should have achieved dominance in the air 'after eight or at the most fourteen days'. That having been accomplished, the invasion of Britain – Operation Sealion – would follow in mid-September. Göring was elated at having been entrusted with the responsibility of destroying the enemy. Theo Osterkamp, one of the leading Luftwaffe fighter pilots, left this record of the conference:

> Everybody of rank and name is present. Because of the good weather the fes-
> tival takes place in the garden. The Iron One appears in a new white suit. At
> first he praises extravagantly the lion's share of the Luftwaffe in the defeat of
> France. 'And now, gentlemen, the Führer has ordered me to crush Britain with
> my Luftwaffe. By means of hard blows, I plan to have this enemy, who has
> already suffered a decisive moral defeat, down on his knees in the near future,
> so that an occupation of the island by our troops can proceed without any risk.'

Göring went on to explain that he planned the attack in three phases: the first, lasting five days, would sweep over a large semicircle south of London; the second, over three days, would concentrate the assault within 50 to 100 kilometres of the capital; and the objective of the final five days would be the London area itself. 'That would irrevocably gain an absolute air superiority over England and fulfil the Führer's mission!'[5]

Osterkamp, having fought against the Spitfires and Hurricanes at Dunkirk, had grave doubts as to whether the British could be smashed within a fortnight. Göring caught his look of uncertainty. 'Well, Osterkamp, have you got a question?' Osterkamp replied that he feared the German High Command might have underestimated the strength of the RAF. Just as importantly, he warned that the Spitfire had proved to be as good as any German fighter. Göring reacted with fury: 'This is nonsense, our information is excellent and I am perfectly aware of the situation. The Messerschmitt is much better than the Spitfire because the British are too cowardly to engage your fighters.'[6] Göring's belief in the complete invincibility of the Luftwaffe meant that he would not tolerate dissent. Like Hitler, he thought that Britain was all but beaten – an outlook that sycophantic intelligence officers exacerbated by telling the Reichsmarschall what he wanted to hear. Göring's bouyancy was reflected throughout the German military and public. Osterkamp was in a minority. 'The situation as it presents itself against Britain is as favourable as it can be. What will happen when the German Air Force employs its whole strength against England? The game looks bad for England and her geographical and military isolation. We can face with confidence the great decisions to come!' said General Quade, the former commandant of the Luftwaffe Staff College, in July 1940.[7]

But Göring had underestimated the organization and resolution of Fighter Command – a persistent failing that was ultimately to cost the Luftwaffe dear. A study produced by his intelligence staff in mid-July showed little understanding of the RAF's front line, declaring, 'The German Luftwaffe is clearly superior to the RAF as regards strength, equipment, training, leadership, as well as air–geographic preconditions.' The German air force, the document promised, would be able 'to achieve decisive results, provided that the start date of major operations is set early enough to take advantage of the months with favourable weather'. German intelligence also underestimated the British fighters: 'Forty per cent are Spitfires and the rest are Hurricanes. Of the two models the Spitfire is the better one. In view of their still missing cannons and their fighting characteristics, both models are inferior to the Me 109,' though the analysis admitted that the twin-engined Me 110 'cannot compete with well-handled Spitfires in combat.'[8] The other point on which the study was correct was in its estimate of strength. 'There are about 900 fighters of superior quality, of which 675 are ready for action.' According to the authoritative work by Derek Wood and Derek Dempster, *The Narrow Margin*, this was highly accurate; Fighter Command had a total of 901 operational aircraft on 13 July. Another study estimated that there were 286 Spitfires in 19 squadrons and 463 Hurricanes in 25 squadrons, with Blenheims, Defiants and a few Gloster Gladiators making up the rest.

When it came to numbers, however, Göring and the Luftwaffe made two serious mistakes. The first was to underestimate the expansion in British fighter production in the summer of 1940. 'At present the British aircraft industry produces about 180 to 330 first-line fighters a month,' claimed German intelligence.[9] In fact, between 29 June and 2 August the industry turned out 488 Hurricanes and Spitfires, including 166 of the latter – well above the 100 a month that had been demanded of Supermarine at

Southampton. The influence of Beaverbrook had made itself felt. The second mistake was to exaggerate the losses that the RAF had suffered since Dunkirk. At the Hague conference, Göring claimed, with an ill-placed swagger, that Fighter Command now had fewer than 500 aircraft in its southern sector. In truth, thanks to the stepping up of production, Britain had far more fighter aircraft in the first week of August than at the end of Dunkirk. Indeed, there is a growing historical trend for demolishing the idea, so cherished in wartime propaganda, that the RAF was numerically outmatched at the start of the Battle of Britain. It can even be claimed, by some statistical juggling, that British fighter forces were larger than those of Germany in August 1940, since the combined total of the entire Fighter Command establishment outnumbered the Me 109s.

But this is to take revision too far. The imagery of David against Goliath can be overplayed, but so can the eagerness to rewrite history. The reality was that, on any count, the Luftwaffe in the summer of 1940 was a colossal instrument of war to use against Britain, with an establishment of 3,609 planes and a total serviceable force of over 2,600, including 1,200 bombers, 280 dive-bombers, and 980 fighters.[10] And it is wrong just to compare single-engined-fighter numbers, since the Hurricanes and Spitfires had to take on not only the Me 109s, but also the German bombers, which all had potent defensive armaments. Moreover, the Me 110, the twin-engined fighter which is so often ignored in the focus on the Me 109, could be an effective machine, capable of a speed of 350 mph and possessing four machine guns and two cannon; not for nothing was it known as *der Zerstörer*, 'the destroyer'. To play down the strength of the Luftwaffe is to do a disservice to the achievement of the British pilots.

Perhaps Göring's greatest mistake was to fail to appreciate the sophistication of the fighter defence organization which Dowding had developed throughout the 1930s. As the author Len Deighton wrote of the Reichsmarschall, 'He was not a fool but neither was he a military thinker. He took no interest in technology and he saw air combat merely in terms of shooting down as many as possible of the enemy's aircraft . . . Göring's concept of command, and his approach to the Battle of Britain, was crude in the extreme.'[11] Nor did Luftwaffe intelligence have any grasp of the way in which RAF operations were conducted: 'As formations are rigidly attached to their home bases, command at a medium level suffers mainly from operations being controlled in most cases by officers no longer accustomed to flying. Command at low level is generally energetic but lacks tactical skill.'[12] This was an ill-informed assessment of Fighter Command's defence system, which was by far the most advanced and intricate in the world. 'The war will be won by science applied to operational requirements,' wrote Dowding in 1940.[13] The brilliant effectiveness of the 'Dowding system', as it was called, demonstrated how he had put those words into practice.

Essentially, his scheme relied on a chain of radar stations, aided by the personnel of the Observer Corps, to pass on information about enemy activity to the Fighter Command control centre, which would then filter the reports down to a network of operations rooms. From there, local commanders would use the information to vector their fighter squadrons towards the German targets. The nerve centre of the entire system was the Fighter Command headquarters at Bentley Priory, an eighteenth-century country house at Stanmore in Middlesex, which had been bought by the RAF in 1926. Within this elegant building, a large two-level operations centre had been carved out of the basement and the main drawing room above.

During any battle, a flood of information would pour into Bentley Priory, arriving first in the Filter Room. There it would be assessed by the filterers, who had the crucial task of analysing and organizing all the incoming reports from radar stations, the Observer Corps and RAF bases. They would pass this data on to the operations room, where it would be plotted on a huge map table depicting the skies above Britain, thereby giving the senior officers a comprehensive visual picture of the progress of the battle. The plotting was done by airmen and WAAFs using counters which they moved around the map with long rakes as the action unfolded, looking 'like croupiers at some weird casino'.[14] Other staff would be continually on the radio-telephone, giving details of the plots to the local commanders, or would be verifying the 'pipsqueak' radio signals which identified whether a plane was friend or foe. It was exhausting, tense work, since the response of the squadrons depended on the dissemination of the correct information. Overseeing how the battle unfolded would be Dowding, standing in a gallery above the map table, at his side a bank of telephones with which to give instructions to his chiefs in the field. At any given moment, his elaborate communications system provided him with an excellent picture of what was happening in the air. 'I had no idea that the British could evolve and operate so intricate, so scientific and so rapid an organization,' said the American military attaché Raymond Lee after a visit to Bentley Priory.[15]

The decentralized structure of Dowding's organization was vital to its smooth running. He had divided Fighter Command into four geographical groups, each with its own operations room modelled on that at Bentley Priory. In turn the four groups were subdivided into a number of sectors, each again with its own operations room. Most sectors – which were based on key airfields like Duxford in Cambridgeshire or Biggin Hill in Kent – had two or three squadrons under their control, though some had as many as six. In some respects the sector controllers were the key link in the system, because they had direct authority over the dispatch of fighters. As the historian John Terraine put it, 'It was they who put the squadrons into the air, positioned them, fed them with essential information and brought them back again.'[16] Many of the pilots had a profound respect for their sector controllers, having learned to trust their decisions and rely on their guidance. One of the best-known was the Duxford sector controller, Group Captain A. B. Woodhall, known universally as 'Woody', whose calm, deep authoritative voice was a constant source of reassurance to his three Spitfire squadrons. Contrary to the beliefs of German intelligence about ground controllers, Woodhall was in fact a highly experienced pilot, having served long spells on fighters in the Fleet Air Arm and the RAF, and he had an intuitive understanding of fighter mentality. Wing Commander Peter Howard-Williams of 19 Squadron gave this tribute to him:

> If the three squadrons were late in the evening over London and got split up by enemy fighters, there would be a rush of requests over the radio for courses to steer for Duxford. Pilots were tired. It was getting dark. Fuel was getting short. Suddenly this most reassuring of voices would come over the R/T. Quietly and calmly he would give each pilot a vector to steer for home and it was always a relief to know that he had taken the trouble to go down to the Ops room to help everyone get back safely. He would sometimes throw in a remark like he would 'have a beer ready at the bar', thus demonstrating the calmness with which the whole very difficult operation was being conducted. Over the R/T he would always use his nickname, Woody, and we thought the world of him.[17]

The actual mechanics of using the VHF radio have been described by Nigel Rose of 602 Squadron:

> When we were airborne we wore headphones, of course, and had a microphone with the oxygen mask and we had our flying helmet, which came right over your head with earphones in a padded swelling on the side of the helmet. And then clipped to it, usually on one side, was a mouthpiece and oxygen attachment: the oxygen tube went down to a clip which you could turn on when you were at 15,000 feet and rising. And the microphone you had switched on all the time. You had the control box for your radio and with that you could switch to your own wavelength. And then, when you were airborne, within the squadron, you tried to keep silence as much as possible. This was the rule so as not to interrupt anybody shouting that something had been seen.[18]

The most basic unit of Fighter Command was the squadron, consisting of twelve aircraft, with four planes in reserve. The twelve were divided into two flights of six aircraft, which in turn were split into two sections of three fight-ers. Each flight was known as either 'A' or 'B', and each section was known by a colour: red, blue, green or yellow. As well as these codes, special RAF terminology was used in the radio communications between the controllers and the pilots during an operation. 'Bandits' meant German aircraft; 'angels' meant so many thousand feet in height; 'pancake' was the call to return to base; and the traditional hunting cry 'Tally-ho' signalled that the pilot had seen the enemy and was about to engage him.

Of the four Fighter Command groups, by far the most important was No. 11, which covered the south-east of England, where the brunt of the fighting would take place. The 11 Group commander – effectively Dowding's deputy – was a brave, resolute forty-eight-year-old New Zealander, Keith Park, who had been an Anzac commander at Gallipoli before he joined the Royal Flying Corps in 1917. Austere, efficient, some-what humourless, he was not unlike Dowding. They shared a similar outlook on the use of fighters in the Battle of Britain, seeking to protect their resources rather than go on the offensive. In particular, they both believed that Fighter Command's prime duty was not to become embroiled in dogfights, but to break up German bomber formations before they reached their targets. And they thought this could best be done by sending up small groups of well-directed squadrons rather than massed fleets. But, even if they shared objectives, Park was less remote than Dowding; he was deeply admired by most of the men in 11 Group, whose squadrons he regularly visited in his own Hurricane without any fanfare. 'He was right out of the top drawer as a leader. He knew what he was doing. He stuck to his guns. He led from the front. And he was a very fine officer commanding,' said Geoff Wellum.[19] Tom Gleave, another Battle of Britain pilot, thought that Park was an ideal leader for fighter operations: 'A very active man, physically and mentally, he was able to make decisions quickly. He did not flap or bluster, but he could be immovable if he thought he was right.'[20] But some of those at his own rank saw this stubbornness as a lack of intellectual capacity. 'Frankly I'm rather alarmed at finding what a stupid man he is,' said the RAF's Director of Plans, Sir John Slessor, later in the war.[21]

Second in significance as a fighter group was No. 12, which covered East Anglia, including the vital Duxford sector, the Midlands and much of the north. The commander was Trafford Leigh-Mallory, son of a Cheshire rector and brother of the mountaineer George Mallory. Large, ferociously ambitious, and aggressively minded, he had less experience of fighters than Park or Dowding, having spent much of his RAF career organizing training or army co-operation. 'He was not an easy man to know and was rather pompous, but I suspect this covered up for some shyness,' said James McCoomb, one of the pilots in 12 Group.[22] Leigh-Mallory's bitter opposition to Park, based on his belief that far more fighters and bigger wings should be sent up to tackle the Germans, was to lead to serious internal conflict when the Battle of Britain was at its most dangerous, giving rise to accusations of disloyalty that still echo today. Far less controversial were the other two group commanders: Richard Saul, in charge of 13 Group, covering the far north and Scotland, and Quentin Brand, whose 10 Group area encompassed South Wales and the West Country.

Contrary to what German intelligence believed, the Dowding system gave a great deal of responsibility to sector and group commanders. In fact, as the battle progressed, Dowding became open to the criticism that he exercised insufficient control over his commanders, diluting his role in directing the fighter effort. But there can be no dispute that his organization provided a crucial defensive shield for Britain. It compensated for the RAF being out-numbered. It averted the need for wasteful standing patrols, which, as Dunkirk had shown, reduced the effectiveness of the Hurricanes and Spitfires. Through the ceaseless flow of information, fighters could be directed to where they were most needed, with the Spitfires usually sent up as top cover to take on the Messerschmitt escorts, allowing the Hurricanes to take on the slower bombers.

What made the system even more proficient was that it took the Germans by surprise. They had no perception of the key role that radar played in the RAF, nor how the chain of stations was linked by radio and telephone to the Fighter Command operations rooms. The German military were certainly aware of radar technology, but, unlike Dowding, the commanders had failed to appreciate its potential in air combat. Nor did they understand the impor-tance of the radio traffic between the ground and the RAF crews, which they had been intercepting for weeks. One secret Luftwaffe report on 7 August reveals the disastrous extent of German ignorance. 'As the British fighters are controlled from the ground by radio-telephone, their forces are tied to their respective ground stations and are thereby restricted in mobility, even taking into consideration the probability that the ground stations are partly mobile. Consequently the assembly of strong fighter forces at determined positions and at short notice is not to be expected.'[23] Even towards the end of the battle, the German pilots still failed to comprehend how the RAF always seemed to be in the right place to meet them. Oberleutnant Ulrich Steinhilper thought it was down to his *Gruppe* always following the same rigid routine; he wrote of his exhaustion in October:

Running with the practised efficiency of the German state railways and just like passengers waiting for a scheduled service, the Spitfires would be on station waiting for the next wave. It was stupid to fly a schedule like this; it just handed us to the enemy on a plate. As we approached, the British would be climbing to their patrol height, by now well above our service ceiling, and then after waiting for us to turn, they'd come scything down through us.[24]

But the British were there not because of clever reading of Luftwaffe timetables, but because Fighter Command was watching every move by Steinhilper and his flight.

This was another of example of how, in 1940, the traditional British and German stereotypes were reversed. Supposedly so amateurish, the RAF was far more efficient in its organization than the Lutfwaffe. It was more professionally led, had a stronger command structure, and was better at exploiting technology. In its carefully constructed lines of communication and its complex interlocking networks, the Dowding system was almost a Teutonic achievement. Compared to Dowding with his detailed planning, Göring was recklessly slapdash. And it is telling that in the summer of 1940 aircraft production in Britain far exceeded that in Germany.

In a typically counter-intuitive remark, the historian A. J. P. Taylor once wrote that 'the Battle of Britain was won by Chamberlain, or perhaps by Lady Houston.'[25] That sounds absurdly flippant, yet it is true that Lady Houston's funds for the Schneider Trophy competition put Mitchell on the path to the Spitfire, while Neville Chamberlain, for all his calamitous errors in foreign affairs, was the political force behind the creation of a strong home defence. The Battle of Britain was precisely the conflict he had envisaged back in 1934, the Dowding system the ultimate expression of his defensive philosophy. A dying man in the autumn of 1940, Chamberlain lived long enough to see his policy vindicated before he succumbed to cancer in November.

But the system, no matter how efficient, would have been an irrelevance were it not for the courage of the men who flew the fighters. Dowding's technological umbrella could have evolved into British aerial equivalent of the French Maginot Line, which bred an ultra-defensive attitude that eventually slid into defeatism. That was exactly what the bomber enthusiasts feared could happen in the RAF because of the concentration on the fighter. It did not, however, because of the determination of the fighter crews. Angus Calder, in his book *The People's War*, argued that the Battle of Britain could be seen 'not as a struggle between men but as a contest between rival technologies. Had the superb planes and the excellent (though far from infallible) radar system not been in existence that summer, no commander, however sagacious, and no daring brotherhood of pilots, however well trained, could have resisted the

Luftwaffe.' But the very opposite point is just as valid: it was the daring brother-hood of pilots that ensured the success of the system. Yes, there was anxiety, sometimes even fear, but never the corrupting sense of resignation that can destroy the morale of any military force. Dowding, in one of his many tributes to his pilots, wrote that 'the brave man never lets his fear be seen, never permits his mind to dwell aimlessly on present or future dangers and never allows his actions to be influenced by his fears.'[26] This kind of steel was demonstrated not in bravado or bombast, but in cool stoicism in the face of the awesome challenge ahead. 'When the battle really began,' wrote the pilot Barry Sutton, 'I never saw anyone show he was frightened. "Frightened" is a bad word – we were keyed up, tensed. The moment of running to the aeroplane was the worst – the nearer you got to it, the less you thought about what was going to happen.'[27] Tubby Mayne, at thirty-nine one of the oldest Spitfire pilots in the Battle of Britain, put it like this: 'You just had a job to do and you did it.'[28]

As Mayne's words demonstrate, the pilots largely refused to adopt a heroic posture. Within Fighter Command, boasting was almost as great a sin as cowardice. The novelist H. E. Bates, author of *The Darling Buds of May* and himself a distinguished fighter pilot, wrote during the war that self-aggrandizement or 'shooting a line' was looked on as

> embarrassing, boring, comic, or in plain bad taste. The RAF has elected to speak even of its most exceptional achievements in terms of understatement. To treat the daily association with danger at if it were nothing more than a game of cricket has become almost the rule. Laconic, nonchalant, dry, indifferent, the RAF passes a common verdict even now on the most glorious moments of action with a couple of words. 'Good show,' it says, 'good show.'[29]

Despite this habit of understatement, the actions of many of the Spitfire pilots were truly remarkable in their bravery. The near-indestructible New Zealander Al Deere, who joined the RAF in 1937, had a series of adventures during the summer of 1940 that really belong in the realm of fiction. In the process of destroying 17 enemy aircraft in the four months from May to August, he was shot down 7 times, bailed out 3 times, collided with an Me 109, had one Spitfire of his blown 150 yards by a bomb, and had another explode just seconds after he had scrambled clear from its wreckage. His description in his 1959 autobiography of one dogfight over the Channel revealed his utter fearlessness, as well as the combat qualities and resilience of the Spitfire. His squadron were outnumbered six to one by Me 109s, yet Deere remained undaunted:

> Fastening on to the tail of a yellow-nosed Messerschmitt I fought to bring my guns to bear as the range rapidly decreased and when the wingspan of the

enemy aircraft fitted snugly into the range scale bars of my reflector sight, I pressed the firing button. There was an immediate response from my eight Brownings, which, to the accompaniment of a slight bucketing from my aircraft, spat a stream of lethal lead targetwards. 'Got you,' I muttered to myself as the small dancing yellow flames of exploding De Wilde bullets spattered along the Messerschmitt's fuselage. My exultation was short-lived. Before I could fire another burst two 109s wheeled in behind me. I broke hard into the attack, pulling my Spitfire into a climbing, spiralling turn.

Having escaped this menace, Deere soon came across another 109:

> He saw me almost immediately and rolled out of his turn towards me so that a head-on attack became inevitable. Using both hands on the control column to steady the aircraft and thus keep my aim steady, I peered through the reflector sight at the rapidly closing enemy aircraft. We opened fire together and immediately a hail of lead thudded into my Spitfire. One moment the Messerschmitt was a clearly defined shape, its wingspan nicely enclosed within the circle of my reflector sight, and the next it was on top of me, a terrifying blue which blotted out the sky ahead. Then we were hit. The force of the impact pitched me violently forward on to my cockpit harness, the straps of which bit viciously into my shoulders. At the same moment, the control column was snatched abruptly from my gripping fingers by a momentary but powerful reversal of the elevator load. In a flash it was over; there was clear sky ahead of me and I was still alive.[30]

With smoke and flame pouring from the Spitfire's nose, Deere tried to regain control, but the engine seized up and the propeller stopped: the blades had been bent almost double in the impact with the 109. Black smoke was now pouring into his cockpit, and Deere decided it was time to bail out. But the canopy was jammed. Feeling trapped, he had no alternative but to keep going in a gentle gliding descent, hoping to reach the English coast and open countryside. He could barely see because of the smoke, but somehow the broken Merlin managed to reach Kentish soil, where it came down in a cornfield and then exploded just after Deere had managed to escape. Badly cut and bruised, Deere was on operations the next morning.

Deere may have had 'an exceptionally efficient guardian angel', to quote a phrase of Dowding's,[31] but he was not unique. This kind of spirit pervaded Fighter Command, embodied in men such as Bob Stanford-Tuck, the ace of 92 Squadron, who had joined the RAF in 1935. His first operational duties were on Gloster Gladiators, before he transferred to Spitfires in May 1940. An exceptional marksman, Stanford-Tuck, like Deere, never relented in the battle against the Luftwaffe, despite two air collisions, several crash landings, and a plunge into the English Channel. One of his most astounding episodes took place when he flew in hard on a Ju 88, and, having just avoided smashing into its starboard wing, felt the impact of the rear gunner's cannon shells ripping through his engine. 'I can't understand why the engine didn't pack up completely, there and then. Somehow it kept grinding away. I was very surprised and deeply grateful for every second it gave me,' he said. Soon Stanford-Tuck's cockpit was engulfed in glycol fumes and the smell of burning rubber, making him vomit. Even with such heavy damage and personal discomfort, he hoped the plane might still make it to Kent. But, just as the Spitfire passed over Beachy Head, the engine exploded. 'A deep, dull roar like a blowlamp started down under my feet and up she went in flame and smoke.' As he pulled away his R/T lead and prepared to bail out, there was a loud bang and his face was covered in hot, black oil. He managed to escape, and parachuted down on to the estate of Lord Cornwallis, his blazing Spitfire crashing down several hundred yards away in open countryside. At the peer's home, he was given tea and a bath, but, despite the pleading of his lordship, who felt he should rest, Stanford-Tuck insisted on returning to Biggin Hill. 'Drop in for a bath any time, m'boy,' said Lord Cornwallis as the pilot was driven away.[32] Tuck was flying again a few days later. His crusade against the Luftwaffe did not end until he was shot down over France in 1942 and imprisoned in the notorious Stalag III camp, from where he escaped in January 1945.

Like many of the leading pilots, Stanford-Tuck was not an easy man. He had a facade of hard-drinking, hard-partying bonhomie, but behind that he could be intolerant and ruthless – traits that were heightened by combat. 'His throbbing impatience ruled out any possibility of careful consideration, of involved calculation. He was becoming a man with no half-tones in his register of thought and action – a man who at times could be ludicrously dogmatic,' wrote his biographer Larry Forrester of Stanford-Tuck during the Battle of Britain.[33]

Those characteristics could also be seen in the most famous RAF fighter pilot of them all, Douglas Bader, whose iron-willed stubbornness had enabled him to resume combat flying after losing both his legs in 1932, when he crashed a Bristol Bulldog. Indeed, Stanford-Tuck clashed badly with Bader over tactics and armament for the Spitfire – two strong-willed personalities unwilling to give ground. 'Christ he makes me so mad. Why does he have to be so obstinate?' said Stanford-Tuck to his fellow pilot Sailor Malan after one fighter conference on the Spitfire where Bader had said that cannon were a waste of time. 'Because if he wasn't so obstinate, he bloody well wouldn't be here,' replied Malan.[34] Bader certainly could give the impression of being cocky and obstreperous. One member of his ground crew at 242 Squadron in RAF Coltishall, David Evans, called him a 'bully' and 'an autocrat',[35] while the Spitfire pilot Peter Brown, who flew with Bader from Duxford in 12 Group, thought that his reputation as a fighter leader was exaggerated. Admitting that he was 'an extraordinary person with tremendous force of character', Brown complained that he had 'no understanding or acceptance of Fighter Command's defensive strategy', was guilty of 'poor airmanship', and had 'an arrogant and bombastic style'.[36]

Yet, as Malan intuited, Bader's flaws could not be divorced from the driving personality that made him a group captain despite his disability. The same impatience that would not tolerate life in a wheelchair forced him back up in the air. His noisy egocentrism grated with some, but was an inspiration to others. A balanced assessment comes from one of his squadron leaders in the Battle of Britain, H. W. 'Tubby' Mermagen, who saw that Bader had 'a total lack of humility' but was 'a fine Spitfire pilot' and 'an excellent flight commander'. Mermagen recalled, 'He used to come stomping into dispersal saying, "Come on chaps, get out of the way, I want a cup of coffee," barging everyone else aside, but the chaps loved him for it, he was a real morale booster.'[37] His natural aggression shone through everything he did. 'My first sight of Bader was sitting on the radiator of the Commander Officer's car holding a shotgun while the C.O. drove him erratically across the field in pursuit of rabbits,' said R. A. Morton, who served with Bader at Tangmere.[38] It is ironic that his tin legs, far from being a disadvantage, may actually have helped him in combat, because he could pull his Spitfire through far greater G forces than able-bodied pilots could tolerate and therefore he could execute tighter turns. Bader was the epitome of the Battle of Britain spirit, that sense of unconquerable valour when confronted with exacting odds. 'My personal debt to him is incalculable,' wrote Hugh Dundas, who flew with him in 616 Squadron during the battle. 'He showed me quite clearly by his example the way in which a man should behave in time of war . . . He was always, always looking for a fight . . . Here was a man made in the mould of Francis Drake – a man to be followed, a man who would win.'[39]

Bader's one-dimensional attitude to combat was a virtue in a time of crisis. A Spitfire pilot was once agonizing in front of a group of comrades about how he had shot down a Messerschmitt and then witnessed the pilot being burnt to death before he could bail out. Bader merely puffed on his pipe and said, 'Nobody asked the buggers to come over here.'[40] His feelings towards the Germans were not entirely diluted by the passage of time, though he had a professional respect for the Me 109 ace Adolf Galland. On one occasion he was invited by Galland as a guest to a Luftwaffe reunion in the Hofbrauhaus in Munich. With some reluctance, he eventually agreed to go, on condition he was not expected to be polite. He arrived at the beer cellar and then climbed up to the balcony, where he could see more than a thousand ex-Luftwaffe pilots below. Having surveyed the scene, he turned to a fellow RAF veteran and said, 'My God, I had no idea we left so many of the bastards alive.'[41]

Bader, Stanford-Tuck, Deere became the great names of the Spitfire battle, as did others like Colin Gray (a more extrovert New Zealander than the superhuman Deere), Brian Kingcome of 92 Squadron, Biggin Hill, and the South African Adolph 'Sailor' Malan, a former merchant seaman who had the toughness of a Boer farmer and the natural authority of a born leader. Brought up in an extremely tough Afrikaans school, he still bore the scars on his back from the beatings he suffered as a pupil. Yet he could also be sensitive. Archibald Winskill, a fellow fighter pilot, recounted this conversation after the war: 'I once asked him, as an old friend, "Were you ever frightened?" "Of course I was frightened," he said. "Right in the heat of the battle I went to my room and there were tears in my eyes." Even the toughest chaps felt the strain. It wasn't surprising.'[42] Full of loathing for the Germans, Malan pioneered some of the changes that were to improve dramatically the success of the Spitfires, including the abandonment of the useless 'vic' formations in favour of finger-fours, and the harmonization of guns at 250 yards. One of the keys to Malan's success as a fighter ace was his abnormally good eyesight: according to Dizzy Allen, 'He could have seen a fly on the Great Wall of China at five miles.'[43] It was Malan who devised the ten rules of air fighting, copies of which were pinned up in many Fighter Command stations. They included: 'Wait until you see the whites of his eyes'; 'Whilst shooting, think of nothing else, brace the whole of your body, have both hands on the stick, concentrate on your ring sight'; and 'Never fly straight and level for more than thirty seconds in the combat area.' His final, tenth, rule was 'Go in quickly – punch hard – get out!'[44]

It is interesting that so many of the top Spitfire pilots were essentially outsiders, whether from the Dominions like Deere, Grey and Malan, from Ireland like Paddy Finucane and Victor Beamish, or from modest backgrounds like Johnnie Johnson, the top-ranking Spitfire pilot of the war and the son of a Leicestershire police officer. Indeed, reflecting the plane's originality, few figures in the Spitfire saga could be said to come from the traditional English establishment. Mitchell was a shy locomotive engineer from Stoke; Ernest Hives, pioneer of the Merlin, was the twelfth child of a factory clerk; Beaverbrook was a maverick Canadian press baron and politician; and Jeffrey Quill hailed from an Irish family. It is one of the great myths of the Battle of Britain that the Spitfires were flown by dashing upper-class schoolboys. Only about 200 of the 3,000 pilots who fought in the Battle of Britain had been to a public school. The great majority were hardened RAF professionals or recruits from overseas: 42 per cent of all pilots were non-commissioned officers, while one-fifth of them were born outside Britain, including 141 Poles, 86 Czechs, 103 New Zealanders and 90 Canadians.

The courage of the RAF fighter pilots had been in evidence since the start of the war. But from August 1940 they faced their greatest test, as Germany embarked on the fulfilment of Hitler's order to subjugate Britain. On 6 August Göring assured the Luftwaffe: 'Within a short period you will wipe the British air force from the sky.' The German plan was to use two fleets based on the Channel coast, Luftflotte 2 under Albert Kesselring and Luftflotte 3 under Hugo Sperrle, the most experienced air officer in Germany, to attack three main targets: enemy aircraft, in the air and on the ground, British harbours and storage facilities, and the ground organization of the RAF around London. In addition, Luftflotte 5, based in Scandinavia, would make attacks on the north of England. The Nazi regime believed that it would take no more than four days to put most of the fighter defences of the south of England out of action – another example of Göring's ludicrous optimism. The start of the assault, known as *der Adlerangriff*, 'the Attack of the Eagles', was scheduled for 10 August, but bad weather in the Channel led to a postponement – an ominous sign for the German High Command. *Adlertag*, 'Eagle Day', finally took place on 13 August, though it was botched by inadequate communications. Because of poor weather, the Reichsmarschall wanted another postponement, this time until the afternoon, but the message was delivered too late to units of Luftflotte 2, which had already taken to the skies. What was meant to be a triumphant opening to the campaign ended dismally for the Germans. At the close of the day, the Luftwaffe had flown 1,485 sorties, but had lost 45 aircraft, compared to 13 losses for the RAF. A swift victory had already become a fantasy.

Spitfire pilot David Crook of 609 Squadron left a contemporary account of the mood on that opening day, as his flight was instructed to take on a German formation comprising Me 110s and 109s and Stuka dive-bombers over the English Channel: 'We were up at almost 20,000 feet in the sun and I don't think they ever saw us until the very last moment. The CO gave a terrific "Tally-ho" and led us round in a big semi-circle so that we were now behind them.' Crook saw a group of five 109s just below and immediately broke from his formation to attack the last of them. 'I gave him a terrific blast of fire at very close range. He burst into flames and spun down many thousands of feet into the clouds below.' Crook then returned to his base, where he awaited the arrival of the other Spitfires. Once they had all come back, 'we stood around in small groups talking excitedly, and exchanging experiences. It is very amusing to observe the exhilaration and excitement which everybody betrays after a successful action like this.'[45]

The pattern was repeated in the following days, as the Germans struggled to achieve the superiority which their commander had told them would be an easy task. On 15 August the Luftwaffe launched its most wide-ranging assault of the campaign. All three fleets went into action, including Luftflotte 5, which conducted two attacks from Scandinavia on the north of England and Scotland, expecting little opposition. To the Germans' surprise, their formations were torn apart by 12 and 13 Groups of Fighter Command, whose radar had plotted their course across the North Sea. Further south, the German bombers came under sustained punishment, though the Me 109s proved that they could hold their own against the Spitfires. Overall, this was a disastrous day for the Luftwaffe, which lost 71 aircraft, compared to Fighter Command's 29. The next day, 16 August, saw the Luftwaffe lose another 45 aircraft, compared to 8 for the RAF. There were, however, successful German raids on several airfields and radar stations, with Ventnor on the Isle of Wight being put out of action. Sandy Johnstone of 602 Squadron wrote in his diary this description of a raid by Stuka dive-bombers on Tangmere that day:

> We realized something out of the ordinary was up when scrambled from 'released' with no previous warning, but the cause was immediately clear when we scampered outside in time to catch sight of a string of Ju 87 dive-bombers screaming vertically down on Tangmere and releasing their bombs at the nadir of their dives. The noise rose to a crescendo as explosions from bursting bombs mingled with the din of Bofors guns firing from positions all around us and, even while we were hurriedly clambering into our flying gear and dashing out to the waiting Spitfires, large chunks of shrapnel and spent bullet cases were cascading down on us . . . The whole airfield became a cauldron of Spitfires fighting to get in the air through hell or high water. I shall never know how none collided. I got airborne in the middle of the melee and called the boys to form up over base at Angels Two. A Flight was already with me but B Flight was nowhere to be seen. But there was no time to wait for them as the air around us had become a kaleidoscope of whirling dervishes with dozens of aircraft swooping and diving in all directions. I felt like pulling the blankets over my head and pretending I wasn't there! I never imagined anything could be so chaotic.

Johnstone selected a gaggle of Me 110s and dived in to attack. 'I was momentarily taken aback when someone in the aircraft in front of me bailed out, until I realized he had come from the 110 I was firing at.' Later that evening, Johnstone surveyed the scene at Tangmere: 'I found the place a shambles, with smoke still rising from the smouldering buildings. Small groups of airmen milled around, many dazed and still deeply affected by the pounding they had received.'[46]

Two days later, 18 August, was tougher still for the RAF, as the Luftwaffe mounted three wide-ranging attacks along the south coast, including a daring low-level raid on the hangars of the training airfield at Brize Norton, where bombers destroyed 46 aircraft on the ground. But that day the Luftwaffe lost 71 planes – a rate of attrition much worse than anything Göring had expected. Far from winning the battle in a few days, as he had proclaimed he would, he had lost over 200 aircraft. The Stuka dive-bomber, which had caused such terror in the blitzkriegs in Poland and France, had proved a dismal failure and had to be withdrawn from action, while the Me 110's wide turning circle had left it vulnerable to the Spitfires. Shocked by the scale of the bomber losses, Göring ordered the 109s, the one truly successful type, to provide tighter escorts, which only further reduced their effectiveness. And he compounded his folly by demanding an end to the attacks on coastal radar stations, in the mistaken belief that these raids had been futile. In fact the temporary loss of the Isle of Wight station had caused serious disruption. An escalation of anti-radar operations might have paralysed the entire Dowding system.

For the next five days there was a brief lull in the combat, as the Germans conducted only scattered raids – though these could still cause serious damage, as Ulrich Steinhilper, a 109 pilot, wrote in his diary in describing an attack on RAF Manston:

> At first my heart was hammering in my chest, but when we pushed the noses of our aircraft down for the attack I calmed down. I aimed for a fuel tanker which was filling a Spitfire, then at two other Spitfires, one after the other. The tanker exploded and everything began to burn around it. My other two Spitfires began to burn on their own. Only now do I realize what power is given to a pilot with those four guns.[47]

But, in spite of such victories, the Luftwaffe had been taken aback by the ferocity with which the RAF fought. One fighter pilot, Hellmuth Ostermann of Staffel III of Jagdesgeschwader 54, commented bitterly after one fight, 'We could only watch as the Tommies knocked hell out of one of the bombers.'[48] Another German pilot, Helmut Wick, one of the great Luftwaffe aces, had this memory of a tense clash:

> I climb again, searching the sky. To the right, there is nothing, but I cannot believe my eyes when I look the other way. The sky is full of Spitfires, and just a few 109s. I get straight into the dogfight, but at once get a Spitfire on my back. At full speed I try to lose him. Now I have one Spitfire in front and

another behind me. Damn it! I dive vertically away to lose him, then climb again. Suddenly I see white trails shooting past. I look back. Yet another is behind me, sending his tracers past my ears like the 'fingers of the dead'. I will thank God if my mother's son can get out of this dogfight! I manage to out-climb the Spitfires try again to help my outnumbered comrades, but each time the Tommies come down behind me. Suddenly a 109 comes past very fast with a Spitfire behind it. This is my chance. I get behind the Spitfire and centre it in my Revi [reflector gunsight]. After a few shots it goes down.

Wick watched the Spitfire go into the sea 'with a great splash'.[49]

The same raw tension was also experienced by the Spitfire pilots during this first phase of the battle. Donald MacDonnell, commander of 64 Squadron at Kenley in Kent and winner of the DFC during the Battle of Britain, wrote an account of a fight in August with a 109 over Tilbury, an encounter he rightly described as 'a life and death joust': 'I spotted him in my rear mirror as I broke away from a flank attack on one of the bombers. I broke away hard and he crossed over me and I turned in, unsure where he was. We then met head-on, both firing but with his cannon shells luckily passing over my cock-pit. I don't think my head-on attack hit him. It was all too quick and impulsive.' MacDonnell and his opponent then began to circle each other warily, moving closer and closer. At one moment the Me 109 opened fire with his cannon. MacDonnell ducked and found himself below the 109 and turning fast:

> I pulled up with full boost and flattened out with him climbing and turning towards me. He then made his fatal mistake. He flicked into a half-roll and began a steep climb to my starboard and slightly astern. I pulled up and over and for a moment had him in my sights. I gave him a five-second burst and saw the tracer raking into him. He began to smoke and then went into an inverted dive. His cockpit canopy flew off and shortly afterwards the pilot fell out.[50]

MacDonnell watched as the pilot's parachute opened and the 109 plunged into a Kent field.

Dizzy Allen, another holder of the DFC, had his first successful Spitfire combat in August, when he took part in an attack on a Dornier 17, known as 'the Flying Pencil' because of its thin fuselage. His section was vectored to 25,000 feet to tackle the German plane, which was on a reconnaissance sweep. Once the section had seen the bomber, the leader went into the attack, then Allen put down his port wing and followed:

> The Dornier was very much larger in my gunsight than in the case of my pre-vious encounter with a Junkers bomber, meaning I was at much closer range. I pressed the gun button and nothing happened, so I hastily looked down and

found that it was still on *Safe*. I switched it to *Fire* and pressed it again. There was a noise similar to thin jute being torn apart by a giant and I saw tracer mixed up in the ammunition load hurtle in the direction of the Do 17.

Allen used up all his ammunition in the attack, as he watched the final moments of the plane:

> Smoke was pouring from one engine. Then, with horrifying gentleness, it slowly turned on its back and went into a vertical dive. I followed it down and saw it strike the sea with an awful disintegration, combined with a great plume of sea water, followed by a slick of oil, and then I saw yellow objects floating. These must have been the dinghies for the air–sea rescue operation. I felt sick, but a certain sense of exhilaration overcame that in short time.[51]

The key combat in the battle was not between the RAF fighters and the Luftwaffe bombers, but between the Spitfire and the Messerschmitt 109. This was to be one of the great rivalries of aviation history, not merely because of the dramatic backdrop of war, but because the planes were so evenly matched. The 109 had first flown in September 1935, six months before the Spitfire. Ironically, the prototype was powered by a Rolls-Royce Kestrel engine, the predecessor of the Merlin. As with Mitchell and the Spitfire, the 109 was Willy Messerschmitt's first combat aircraft; his previous pioneering work had been on the development of gliders. Again as with Mitchell, his central aim was to produce the maximum power within the most aerodynamic design. The result was this small masterpiece. The 1940 version of the Messerschmitt, the 109E, was capable of over 355 mph, similar to the Spitfire's maximum speed, and had much the same limited range, about 400 miles. The 109 was slightly smaller, with a span of 32 feet 5 inches, compared to the Spitfire's 36 feet 10 inches, and fully loaded it was about 700 pounds lighter than the Spitfire. Few would dispute that the Spitfire, with its curved lines and elliptical wings, was the more aesthetically pleasing. The Spitfire was also more manoeuvrable, and had a tighter turning circle. 'The Spitfire was a real shotgun,' said the German ace Adolf Galland. 'So when it was fighter against fighter, if you tried to shoot down the enemy while turning, the Spitfire was better. Also you had a better gunsight, not fixed like ours, which calculated the deflection automatically, whereas we had to do our own calculations.'[52]

The Me 109 had other disadvantages. Its undercarriage was even narrower than the Spitfire's, making it more awkward on the ground; 5 per cent of all 109s were lost in accidents. Unlike the Spitfire's, its more conventional wings did not give advanced warning of a stall. Its cockpit was even narrower, and its canopy more difficult to remove in an emergency. One German pilot, Walter Krupinksi, even argued, 'The Spitfire was a much better aircraft than the

Messerschmitt 109. The turning rate was fantastic compared with the 109. The climbing rate was also very good. The visibility out of the 109 was better than out of the Spitfire but what does that give? It's not so important, because you can handle your aircraft to see everything that's going on in the air.'[53]

Certainly, the very name 'Spitfire' inspired a greater sense of dread among the Luftwaffe pilots than the 109 ever did in the RAF. '"Spitfire on my tail," I hear this cry from 109 pilots on the radio quite often,' said Ulrich Steinhilper. 'From then it sometimes didn't last long until that voice didn't exist any more. "Spitfire on my tail" was usually a very bad surprise. And sometimes you panicked.'[54] But another Luftwaffe pilot, Hans-Ekkehard Bob, while believing in the superiority of the Spitfire, had little time for this attitude. 'I know my fellow 109 pilots were very fearful of the Spitfire. When the message "Watch out! Spitfire!" came everyone shuddered,' said Bob,[55] who recognized the strength of the Spitfire but felt he had the ability to deal with it:

> For me personally, my feeling was that I was in control of my plane and the Spitfire won't be a problem for me . . . The Spitfire was extremely manoeuvrable, albeit the 109 being still a bit faster, but you had to bring to bear all your skill and all of your feeling in order to be able to cope with the opponent in situations like that. During these aerial battles I managed again and again to outwit the Spitfire and to score air victories.[56]

The success of pilots like Hans-Ekkehard Bob was largely a result of two significant advantages that the 109 held over the Spitfire, which tended to balance out the other weaknesses. The first was that it could go into a sudden dive without losing power, because its Daimler-Benz DB 601 engine had fuel injection. In combat, this diving ability provided a vital escape route for the 109 pilot, who knew that the Spitfire could not give chase because the Merlin carburettors would suffer sudden fuel loss and the engine would temporarily cut out. The only way round this problem was for the Spitfire pilot to do a half-roll or even turn the plane on its back to restore the fuel flow. Any such manoeuvre both required aerobatic skill and wasted valuable time. The issue was highlighted shortly before the Battle of Britain, when in May 1940 the Royal Aircraft Establishment at Farnborough conducted tests on a captured 109. The pilot who flew the tests, Captain Hugh Wilson, later wrote of this 'outstanding characteristic which made us sit up and take notice. The great beauty of the fuel-injection engine was that you could push the stick hard forward and apply negative G without the engine stopping.'[57] But it was too late to change the design, and the Spitfire pilots had to deal with the consequences during the battle. Douglas Bader recalled the frustration of trying to follow the Me 109s in a dive:

Their engines went on running, but if we did it, the engine went dead. It all stopped, spanners came out of the bottom which the 'erks' had left behind and you stayed there watching while the Me 109 disappeared downwards. I remember a marvellous Director of Rolls-Royce called Bill Lappin used to come round and visit the squadrons and we always used to complain, 'Look for God's sake why can't we have something to keep the engine going?'[58]

The obvious question was why Rolls-Royce had not introduced fuel injection in the first place. The answer, said Sir Stanley Hooker, one of the Rolls-Royce engineers, was that the company had not recognized before the summer of 1940 that negative-G dives would be such an important part of combat. More importantly, it was believed that the Merlin's carburettors 'increased the performance of the supercharger and thereby increased the power of the engine'.[59]

A temporary solution was found, however, by a thirty-two-year-old scientist at the Royal Aircraft Establishment in Farnborough, Beatrice Shilling. An early pioneer of feminism and a keen motorcyclist, Miss Shilling came up with the brilliantly simple idea of installing across the float chambers of the carburettors a metal diaphragm with a hole punched through it. This 'restrictor orifice' stopped most of the fuel being flung to the top of the carburettors in a dive. Inevitably, within squadrons, it became known as 'Miss Shilling's orifice'; it operated until 1942, when the Bendix-Stromberg carburettor, which could cope with negative G, was introduced on the Merlin.

Just as troublesome for the RAF was the disappointing armament of the Spitfire compared to the Me 109, which carried two cannon in the wings and two machine guns in the engine cowlings. Some versions also carried a cannon firing through the airscrew hub. In contrast, Spitfire pilots during the Battle of Britain grew exasperated at the inability of the Brownings to inflict lethal damage. 'Though our Spitfires were quite capable of fighting the Me 109s,' wrote Wilfrid Duncan Smith, 'we felt we were outgunned. We desperately needed more punch. The eight .303 Brownings were devastating at close quarters but they were inadequate at longer ranges against enemy fighters, unless a hit was registered in the engine, petrol tank or cooling system.'[60] The Air Ministry had been well aware of the problem since 1935, when Squadron Leader Ralph Sorley had first investigated the use of Hispano cannon during a visit to Paris. He had found 'their mountings insufficiently rigid', which led to 'continuous trouble with stoppages', but admitted that 'the results obtained on a metal aircraft with a 20-mm solid shell were extremely attractive', while the cannon also had a 'longer range and a flatter trajectory'.[61] But, because of the impracticality of the sensitive cannon, the Ministry had opted for the Brownings.

But the build-up to war had intensified the search for stronger firepower – one reason why Air Chief Marshal Sir Cyril Newall was so much more keen on the cannon-armed Westland Whirlwind than on the Spitfire. Late in 1938 the Air Staff decided to look again at trying to fit cannon to the Spitfire, asking Supermarine to come up with a solution. Such a step, Supermarine was told, was necessary 'as an insurance against the ineffectiveness of .303 guns against armoured bombers'.[62] In January 1939 Joe Smith, the chief designer of Supermarine, proposed a scheme in which a 20-mm cannon could be installed in each wing – lying on its sides, with the gun barrel projecting 2 feet beyond the leading edge. 'It makes a good installation,' reported Ministry officials after visiting Supermarine, 'and although it will necessitate the removal of a portion of the web of the main spar – as the gun will have to pass through the main spar – Mr Smith does not anticipate any serious difficulty in providing adequate reinforcement at this point.'[63] Such optimism was badly misplaced. The issue would soon become one of the most vexing in Fighter Command.

In the autumn, the prototype of the cannon Spitfire flew, but it was soon obvious that all was not well. The cannon would not work at temperatures below 0°C, and could fire only solid shells, not explosive ammunition. Their sixty-round magazine was complex and inadequate, giving a firing time of just five seconds, compared to eighteen seconds for the eight-gun Spitfire. Even more ominous were the continual stoppages. Because of the way the guns had to be mounted on their sides within the thin wings, empty cartridge cases were continually becoming jammed in the breeches. Despite modifications carried out by Supermarine, the troubles continued when the cannon Spitfire underwent operational testing with 72 Squadron at Drem, near Edinburgh. In January 1940 Squadron Leader J. G. Munro submitted a worrying report which revealed that the difficulty with the empty cartridge cases bouncing back into the guns was still as bad as ever: the plane, he wrote, could 'not be completely successful for active service'.[64] The disturbing consequence of these chronic ejection failures was seen in action, when a raiding He 111 was tackled by a flight from 72 Squadron over Fife. Flying Officer G. V. Proudman, flying the cannon Spitfire as an experiment, opened fire at 12,000 feet at a range of 300 yards. After just one round his starboard gun stopped, then the port gun jammed after thirty rounds. Proudman put the stoppage down to 'a freak case'. It was to be far from that.[65]

More modifications were implemented throughout the spring, including the creation of a new deflector plate to try to ensure that empty cases travelled smoothly down the ejection chutes. Initially, this appeared to work. 'It seems that the problem of ejection stoppage has at last been solved, as 290 rounds have been fired through one gun, using the new deflector plate, and no ejection stoppage has occurred,' reported Proudman in April.[66] Impressed by this apparent breakthrough, the Air Ministry now ordered a limited production run of thirty cannon Spitfires, which would be delivered to 19 Squadron at Duxford. But Dowding, ever cautious and realistic, still had grave doubts as to whether the problems had really been resolved. When in July Sir Archibald Sinclair, the Air Secretary, urged him to commit 19 Squadron from 12 Group to front-line duties in 11 Group, Dowding replied that he was 'not at all keen' on sending up the cannon Spitfire against German fighters 'since it will be extremely badly equipped for that task' because of its unreliable armament. 'The existing cannon Spitfire is not an attractive type. The defects are that: it has only two guns; these guns were designed to operate on their bellies but have been mounted so they operate on their sides. This has led to technical difficulties. Each gun carries a drum containing sixty rounds, and it is impossible to re-load in the air.' Dowding concluded that no more two-cannon Spitfires should be manufactured beyond the current thirty, which would keep 19 Squadron going 'for some little time if it is not brought up against the Messerschmitts'.[67]

The real hope for the future, thought Dowding, was in a mix of cannon and machine guns; the one advantage of Browning machine guns was that, because of their wider spread, they did not require the same accuracy of fire as cannon. Such planes were starting to go into production at both Supermarine and Castle Bromwich in the late summer of 1940, usually featuring four Brownings and two cannon, though some, like the Mark IIC, had four cannon. With better mountings and a belt feed rather than a drum, their armament was more reliable.

Inevitably, Beaverbrook was at the thick of this development – not least because of his faith in cannon as an air weapon. And his method of motivating the Vickers management at Castle Bromwich was typically unorthodox, as manager Stan Woodley recalled. 'We were given a very tight programme when we started to work on this project. Lord Beaverbrook doubted our ability to meet the schedule. We said we would and Lord Beaverbrook bet us £100 we would not!' But, said Woodley, everything seemed to go wrong with the job. To avoid the risk of bombing, the work was transferred to a factory in Shropshire. But the county then suffered its worst flooding in forty years, with the factory being badly affected:

> The next morning I went to see what we could do and sent some of the men to find canoes. While they were doing that, being young and forthright, we pulled down a hoarding and I paddled through to make a reconnaissance in the shops. The jigs and fixtures were recovered and moved to another factory

on higher ground and a long way from a river. We produced the parts; we fitted the cannon to schedule and we received £100 from Lord Beaverbrook.[68]

But the improved cannon Spitfires were not ready for service by the time of the Battle of Britain. Meanwhile, the 19 Squadron Spitfires were living up to all Dowding's worst fears. Though he had managed to keep them out of 11 Group, their base at Duxford meant they were forced into regular action. And, despite all the technical changes, they were still plagued by stoppages – to the growing fury of the Duxford pilots. George Unwin recalled that once the jamming had occurred 'you couldn't clear the blockage in the air and once one cannon stopped it was like trying to fly a twin-engined aeroplane on one engine due to the pull exerted on the fighter from the other gun when it fired!'[69] It was found that the cannon Spitfire would often work satisfactorily in level flight, but almost as soon as it was in a dogfight and subject to rapid manoeuvres and high G it failed.

James Coward of 19 Squadron had a dramatic experience of cannon failure, when he went in to attack a formation of twenty Do 17s. He was shot in the leg by a rear gunner, but when he moved within range to fire, he discovered that his cannon would not operate. Cursing his armament, he flew under the Dornier, the top of his plane grazing the underbelly of the German bomber. The hood of his aircraft was ripped off, and the Spitfire spiralled out of control. At 22,000 feet Coward bailed out. To his relief, his parachute opened once he pulled the ripcord. 'The blood was pumping out of my leg. It was amazing how bright it was so high up. I thought I'd bleed to death so I used the radio wire from my helmet to put a tourniquet round my thigh. After that, I felt no pain, apart from the petrol that drenched me and was stinging my armpits and crotch.'[70] Fred Roberts, an armourer from Duxford, felt he and his colleagues were subjected to unfair criticism. 'We took a lot of stick from the pilots over these stoppages. We fitted various types of deflector plates. We altered the angle of the plate. We fitted rubber pads to dampen the force of the spent shell case, but none of these experiments worked.'[71]

At the beginning of September, the Duxford pilots were so incensed by the failures that they demanded the return of their Browning Spitfires. Wing Commander Woodhall wrote angrily to Leigh-Mallory, the commander of 12 Group, telling him that 'in the five engagements so far encountered, the port guns have fired 875 out of a possible 1,560 rounds with 15 stoppages. The starboard guns have fired 904 out of a possible 1,560 rounds with 11 stoppages. Until a modification is carried out to the existing wing, it would be useless to carry on with the present mounting of cannons in Spitfires.'[72] Squadron

Leader Philip Pinkham was just as vociferous: 'In all the engagements so far occurring it is considered that had the Unit been equipped with eight-gun Spitfires it would have inflicted far more severe losses on the enemy. It is most unfair that pilots should be expected to attack enemy formations of the size encountered at present with unreliable armament.'[73] Such words had a receptive audience in Dowding, who visited Duxford and promised the men they would have their Browning planes back. The hated cannon Spitfires were sent off to a training unit in North Wales in exchange for a dozen Mark Is.

The ineffectiveness of the cannon Spitfires was not just a source of frustration for 19 Squadron: it was also a major setback for Fighter Command, which turned out to be under-armed in the Battle of Britain against the 109. 'In a fraction of a second, I could bring down a Spitfire. If I could hit it twice, I could destroy it. The English had to score a great many hits with their machine guns to bring a plane down but they didn't need to shoot as accurately,' claimed the 109 pilot Hans-Ekkehard Bob.[74] Yet this was only indicative of the wider crisis that the RAF faced as the conflict reached its climax. From 24 August the battle entered a new phase, as the Luftwaffe concentrated its efforts on destroying Fighter Command on the ground. For the first time, cracks began to appear in the British defences. Airfields came under ferocious assault. Losses rose alarmingly. Numbers were depleted, pilots exhausted. Day after day, waves of massed German formations poured over the south-east of England, targeting 11 Group's bases. In one attack on Kent in the afternoon of 28 August, Fighter Command lost 20 Spitfires and Hurricanes, Al Deere being one of those shot down. He was forced to bail out and landed in a plum tree in an orchard near Canterbury. Between 29 August and 5th of September, 167 planes of the RAF's Metropolitan Force were destroyed.

The hammering of the bases and the fighters took its toll. Biggin Hill was hit so badly on 30 August that 39 personnel were killed. With all the telephone lines severed, control of the sector had to be transferred to Hornchurch. Fighter pilot Teddy Morris described the terrible scenes:

> Our flight was released for thirty minutes to get lunch in the mess. We had taken the first mouthful when the tannoy blared, 'B Flight 79 Squadron to Readiness Immediately.' We dashed to the door where a Humber shooting brake driven by a WAAF was pulling up. We all tumbled in and shot off to our dispersal. We were still in the hangar area when Rupert Clarke, who had been in the Norway fiasco, yelled out, 'Stop. Ju 88s. Into the shelter!' We all piled out and dashed up the steps of a bomb shelter which was luckily a few yards away. We had just made it when the ground shook from a near-miss and bombs were going off all round. When the All Clear sounded we climbed out into a world

of smoke, dust and damage. Where our Humber had been there was a large crater but no sign of the vehicle. A little later there was a shout from inside the hangar and there was our Humber; it had been thrown up some 60 feet and fallen through the roof, ending up on its back, a flattened wreck. Only a hundred yards away a bomb shelter with 40 WAAF had received a direct hit, killing most of them.[75]

The next day, 31 August, was also brutal, as over 1,500 German planes came over the coast; Hornchurch received over 100 bombs from a raid by Dorniers. The Spitfires of 54 Squadron based there desperately tried to get airborne in the chaos, as the explosions ripped through the airfield. Colin Gray made it into the sky amid the smoke and dust, but his fellow New Zealander Al Deere felt his plane overturn and then skate along the ground upside down at over 100 mph. Miraculously, he survived; the only physical damage he suffered was a scrape along his scalp where his head had been in contact with the ground. In *The Last Enemy*, Richard Hillary gave this description of the carnage at Hornchurch:

> Out of the corner of my eye I saw three Spitfires. One moment they were about 20 feet up in close formation; the next catapulted apart as though on elastic. The leader went over on his back and ploughed along the runway with a rending crash of tearing fabric. No. 2 put a wing in and spun round on his airscrew, while the plane on the left was blasted wingless into the next field. I remember thinking stupidly, 'That's the shortest flight I've ever taken.'[76]

There were four more waves of attacks on 1 September. Biggin Hill again suffered badly, its sector operations room reduced to a shambles, four Spitfires on the ground destroyed. Other stations like Detling near Maidstone, Hawkinge near Folkestone and Lympne to the west of Hythe in Kent were also badly hit.

Sandy Johnstone of 602 Squadron, which had moved down from Scotland to Westhampnett near Chichester, wrote in his diary soon after the Germans had intensified their attacks, 'It seems that Reichsmarschall Goering is throwing in everything to deliver the knock-out blow. Certainly the strain is beginning to show, for many are noticeably more short-tempered and twitchy and one wonders how much longer the lads can go on taking it.'[77] That twitchiness was recalled by R. A. Morton of 74 Squadron, which moved into Biggin Hill in late August:

> The atmosphere was decidedly gloomy. On arrival we found the station in a highly nervous state. A chink of light from an insufficiently blacked out window was not greeted with the usual 'Put that light out' but by a rifle shot aimed at the light. On my first evening in the mess I was astonished to see all the deep leather armchairs suddenly turn over, their late occupants peeping out from

underneath them. It appeared that everyone but me had heard what sounded like a falling bomb.[78]

A sense of draining fatigue hung over many of the Spitfire pilots, as Tubby Mayne experienced:

> By the end of August the squadron was flying four or five times a day and fighting most times it flew; at readiness from half an hour before dawn to half an hour after dusk and the nights were short. You lived on a razor's edge. Most people couldn't sleep soundly, you didn't unwind. And it was a wonder you had any digestive organs left. That kind of flying is hard on your insides anyway, and as for regular meals, if you picked up the teapot there always seemed to be a flap before you poured it.[79]

The telephone, ringing in the dispersal units to tell the men to scramble, became a symbol of this weariness. 'Telephonitis had us in its grip and the shrill bell was eating away at our nerve coverings, leaving the raw edges exposed. The click of the receiver being replaced followed by silence filled us with relief . . . Less and less time between flights was spent in idle talk,' wrote Geoffrey Page, who was shot down and horribly burnt during the Battle of Britain, but made a heroic recovery to fly Spitfires again.

> Sleep became the 'be-all' and 'end-all' in life. Climbing out of our machines we threw ourselves on the nearest piece of grass and were asleep within seconds of touching the ground. High-powered engines could be ground-tested near our sleeping figures without disturbing us. But the smallest tinkle of the telephone found us staggering bleary-eyed to our feet . . . Life became a nightmare, the centre of which was the telephone bell and the only sure escape was death.[80]

Dizzy Allen confessed that for the rest of his life he loathed the sound of a ringing phone.

The casualty rate during these dark days was appalling. Between 24 August and 6 September, one-quarter of Fighter Command pilots in action were lost. As Park reported to Dowding, the fierceness of the German assault was having 'a serious effect on the efficiency of fighter squadrons'.[81] Shortages of pilots had become more worrying than shortages of planes. Young, inexperienced men, with less than three weeks' training on the Spitfires, had to be thrown into the fray, many of them proving easy meat for the Germans. Bob Stanford-Tuck said in an interview after the war:

> Of course you had to be able to fly without thinking about it. It's like – what shall I say? – playing a piano. You can't be a musician while you still have to look at the keys. About the end of August, we were starting to get these boys as replacements who hadn't really finished their training. They still had to

think about flying their aircraft. It was pathetic to see them go down right away, in their first flight sometimes. You just didn't have to brood on that sort of thing or let others brood on it either.[82]

Some novices had barely any experience of firing their guns, even in practice, and had no idea of what would happen in combat. Ellis Aries of 602 Squadron was on his very first sortie, flying over the Sussex coast at 15,000 feet, when he saw more than 90 German planes. As the historian Richard Collier recounted, 'What looked like white glinting metal rods were stretching very slowly from them, describing a wide curve away from him, then accelerating towards him. It was as well that Aries broke radio silence to ask, "Why are they dangling little wires at me?" In the nick of time, a veteran screamed a warning, "Break you bloody fool, it's tracer." '[83] Dizzy Allen wrote that some of the pilots arriving at the bases could 'hardly ride a bicycle, let alone take their Spitfires into action. Shadowy figures came and went and one could see, not to be too dramatic, the look of death on the faces of some of them.' Allen witnessed one grisly moment when a new Spitfire pilot, only days after his arrival at the base, went into a vertical dive at full throttle after his oxygen supply appeared to have failed. 'His Spitfire exploded on impact with the ground and went on to form a very large crater.' The crushed remains of the pilot were dug out from under 30 feet of earth.[84]

Many within the RAF felt that Dowding and Park, far from holding the line, were actually exacerbating the crisis by sticking rigidly to their strategy of refusing to send up large fighter formations to engage the incoming German fleets, instead using squadrons in pairs. Their aim was to preserve their resources as far as possible in what could be a campaign lasting many months. Dowding feared that, like Admiral Jellicoe in the First World War, he was the man who could lose the war in a single afternoon if he gambled on winning one major confrontation. But, by allowing too many Germany bombers to get through to their targets, the approach was at risk of becoming counterproductive. One senior Polish pilot, Flying Officer W. Urbanonwicz, later the Polish air attaché in the USA, wrote acidly in one of his combat reports, 'Only two of our squadrons in the area – and a hundred Germans,' which, he said, meant the bombers had 'a free passage'. He continued, 'The English are a bit too cautious in restricting interception to one or two squadrons which cannot be effective, instead of, on such occasions, putting everything in the air and sweeping it clean.'[85]

The Polish fighter pilots were renowned for their unbridled, almost reckless, offensive outlook, motivated by their detestation of the Germans. And Fighter Command had senior figures who agreed with them – particularly those outside Park's 11 Group. Leigh-Mallory, commander of 12 Group, and his star Spitfire pilot Douglas Bader were embittered that they were seeing so little activity while 11 Group was being pummelled. Fighter Command's potential, they believed, was being squandered. What Leigh-Mallory wanted was large units of three squadrons or more joining in the air to provide a real threat to the Germans – an approach which became known as the 'Big Wing'. Dowding and Park dismissed the idea, saying that such 'Big Wings' would take too long to assemble and would lack flexibility. But to some 12 Group pilots this reflected excessive prudence. 'We weren't used as much as we should have been,' said George Unwin of 19 Squadron, adding that Park pushed 11 Group's fighters to the limit, though there were 'sixty serviceable aeroplanes up at Duxford, ten minutes' flying time away, and time and time again we were never used'.[86]

By the first week in September, the German strategy of pounding Fighter Command seemed to be working. For the first time, British losses exceeded those of the Germans. Many of the airfields were devastated. The communications system was stretched to the limit, the pilots shattered. 'It was no picnic,' remembered Colin Gray, 'despite what anyone might say later. I've seen Al Deere and others push away their breakfast when told to go up. Most of us were pretty scared all the bloody time. You only felt happy when the battle was over and you were on your way home. Then you were safe for a bit, anyway.'[87] To some of the Luftwaffe, there was a scent of victory in the air. 'The Englishman is a tough adversary,' wrote Ulrich Steinhilper to his mother, 'but he will eat humble pie yet.'[88] But the Germans were about to make a disastrous strategic error – one that would ultimately cost them the battle.

8

'Here come those last fifty Spitfires'

NO PRIME MINISTER has ever been more enthralled by the conduct of war than Winston Churchill. 'I am interested, geared up and happy. Is it not horrible to be built like that?' he once said of his excitement at the trumpet blast of military action.[1] His enthusiasm for war was reflected in his fondness for donning uniforms, some of them justified by his past army service, some of them acquired on a romantic whim. In 1940 he took to wearing an air commodore's outfit, though his attempts to acquire a pilot's licence in 1919 had ended in crash-strewn failure. His passion for military affairs meant that he was far more intimately involved with the detailed conduct of the war than any previous political leader, constantly challenging the military chiefs and putting up his own ideas. Some have condemned his approach as little more than amateurish micro-management.[2] But in truth he was a tremendous galvanizing force for the military – particularly in 1940, when the nation stood on the brink of catastrophe. The admirals, air marshals and generals knew that excuse-making, complacency and inefficiency would not be tolerated. 'Action this day' was the heading on a tide of written instructions that flowed out of Downing Street.

Churchill's interventionism was felt in Fighter Command throughout the summer and autumn. He bombarded the Air Ministry, Air Staff and Ministry of Aircraft Production with questions about numbers of aircraft, deployment of planes, accident rates, production levels, and training of pilots. Typical of his grip on detail was the concern he expressed in June about the time taken to refuel Spitfires. This was an issue that had been raised by Sailor Malan during an interview in Downing Street, and Churchill immediately fired off a minute to the Ministry. 'I am told that the refuelling of fighter aeroplanes could be much more rapidly achieved if there were more tankers on the aerodromes; and considering that an attack by waves would make every minute gained in returning the fighters to the air most precious, I should be glad if measures were taken at once to double or greatly increase the fuelling facilities,' he wrote to Fighter Command on 24 June.[3] Dowding replied that the situation was 'generally good' considering the losses in fuel tankers at Dunkirk. Each squadron, he explained, had four tankers, and, since only twelve machines were in use at any one time, there was one tanker for every three planes. 'It takes three minutes to refuel a Spitfire if two hoses are used.' The real bottleneck, he said, was in rearming rather than refuelling.[4]

Churchill was also involved in the press coverage of the Battle of Britain by US journalists, becoming annoyed at suggestions from the Ministry of Information that the RAF should spend time in providing direct evidence to challenge the scepticism of the Americans:

> The important thing is to bring the German aircraft down and win the battle, and the rate at which American correspondents and the American public are convinced we are winning, and that our figures are true, stands in a much lower plane. They will find out quite soon enough when the German air attack is plainly shown to be repulsed. It would be a pity to tease the Fighter Command at the present time when the battle is going from hour to hour and continuous decisions have to be taken about air raid warnings, etc. I confess I should be more inclined to let the facts speak for themselves. There is something rather obnoxious in bringing correspondents down to the air squadrons in order that they may assure the American public that the Fighter pilots are not bragging or lying about their figures We can afford to be a bit cool and calm about all this. The event is what will decide it all.[5]

Yet by far Churchill's greatest contribution to the Battle of Britain was not in military strategy, but on the rhetorical front. On 18 August – what became known as 'the Hardest Day' – Churchill drove with his Chief of Staff, General Sir Hastings 'Pug' Ismay, to the headquarters of 11 Group in Uxbridge to see the direction of fighter operations under the pressure of the German massed formations. On the way back in the car to Chequers, Churchill said to Ismay, 'Don't speak to me; I have never been so moved.' Caught up by the drama of the moment, he briefly fell silent and then continued, 'Never in the field of human conflict has so much been owed by so many to so few.'[6] Two days later, in the House of Commons, he repeated the phrase about 'the few' in one of his magisterial orations. The words soon became part of the Battle of Britain legend. In their poetic rhythm, they perfectly captured both the gratitude of the British people towards the fighter pilots and the sense of British defiance against the Nazi war machine. Along with his 'Finest Hour' speech, his tribute to 'the Few' was to resonate through history, fixing the heroism of the RAF for ever in the public imagination.

In the years and decades afterwards, the fighter pilots were proud to wear the label of 'the Few'. But at the time, in the spirit of RAF understatement, Churchill's speech was greeted with ironic humour. On several bases the joke went round that Churchill had actually been talking about the pilots' unpaid mess bills. Yet by the first week of September, a fortnight after the 'the Few' speech, jocularity was in short supply within Fighter Command. As the rate of attrition accelerated, the atmosphere grew increasingly strained. Some of the new pilots coming into the squadrons had only just mastered the art of landing, never mind the art of fighting. There seemed no sign of the Germans easing their assault. The strength of 11 Group was dwindling by the day. 'The incidence of casualties became so serious that a fresh squadron would become depleted and exhausted before any of the resting and reforming squadrons was ready to take its place. Fighter pilots were no longer being produced in numbers sufficient to fill gaps in the fighting ranks,' wrote Dowding.[7] On 7 September he told the Air Staff that the situation was 'extremely grave'.[8] The Luftwaffe was now coming close to achieving the air superiority that Hitler demanded. 'As a matter of historical fact,' wrote Spitfire pilot Dizzy Allen, '11 Group lost control over the air situation on about 1 September and the Luftwaffe could have covered the amphibious invasion – if Operation Sealion had ever been militarily feasible.'[9]

It was in the first week of September that Richard Hillary was shot down and badly burnt – the incident that would form the gripping centrepiece of his memoir *The Last Enemy*. But there were many other Spitfire pilots who went through similar experiences during this grim period of German intensity. William Walker, a pilot with 616 Squadron, based at Manston, recounted this tale of being attacked at the end of August when he was on patrol off the Kent coast at 20,000 feet:

> Suddenly there was a German on my tail. As you know, the Spitfire had this armour plating behind. Well, a bullet came through below the armour plating and straight into my ankle. At the same time, my controls were badly damaged. So I had no choice but to bail out. Everything was happening so quickly. I tried to jump, but I was pulled back because I was still plugged into the radio. So I had to take my helmet off and then jump. And it was dense cloud. I had no idea where I was or what was underneath the clouds. I pulled the ripcord straight away, but it took me ages to come down.

Walker then landed in the sea, where he blew up his life vest – known to all pilots as the Mae West, after the well-endowed blonde American actress. Eventually, after drifting in the cold water for some time, he was rescued by a fishing boat. Hauled on board, he was given a mug of tea mixed with whisky. 'I was on the brink of suffering from hypothermia really. The hot whisky and tea on my cold tummy left me in bloody agony.'

On his arrival onshore, Walker was first taken to Ramsgate hospital and then, because of the seriousness of his leg wound, to an RAF hospital near

London. On his way to the capital, he asked the ambulance to stop at Manston so he could visit his comrades. He immediately could see how ferocious a battering his station had endured. 'Of course there was no one there. We'd lost ten pilots in ten days. Five killed and five wounded. Terrible.' After some delay at the hospital he was seen by a surgeon, who immediately operated. 'When I came to, the surgeon was sitting on my bed. He said, "I think you'd like to have this," and he handed me the bullet. Then he told me, "You won't believe it but as we prized your ankle apart to get the bullet it actually shot out and hit the ceiling."' Bizarrely, Walker's leg wound was not dressed – a legacy of a dubious medical theory that became fashionable during the Spanish Civil War. 'They enclosed the whole wound with plaster and the idea was that the discharge would form a crust and it would heal. But it didn't work with me. My wound went on festering and festering, so all the plaster became soft. So in the end they had to make a hole and dress it properly. The only trouble was I smelled so awful. All the officers complained, so I had to be put in a private room.'[10] Following a spell of convalescence in Torquay, Walker recovered enough to go back on the duty with the RAF.

Spitfire pilots were usually anxious to reach dry land rather than ditch in the sea, because the plane had a reputation for sinking fast. Its heavy nose ensured that it went down like a stone, a process worsened by the way the radiator under the wing scooped up the water. And the speed of the descent under the surface made it difficult to escape from the cockpit. As the French Spitfire pilot Jacques Souviat, later a French air force general, put it, 'The Spitfire is an aircraft that doesn't ditch well. It doesn't know how to sit on the water after first contact with the waves. It dives and disappears.'[11] The German pilots were also better equipped for the English Channel than the RAF, who possessed no rubber dinghies during the Battle of Britain, and whose Mae Wests had to be inflated manually. 'Do you know, we were supposed to wait till we were in the drink and then unscrew the nozzle and blow up the thing with our own lungs? It's fantastic how primitive our equipment was,' said the Spitfire veteran Tubby Mayne.[12] In contrast, the German safety harnesses kept pilots afloat in the water without this effort, while the pilots also carried flare pistols and sea-dye and wore bright yellow skullcaps to make themselves more visible from the air. Moreover, the Luftwaffe had a much more extensive sophisticated air–sea rescue operation, including float planes, radio-equipped vessels, and rescue rafts anchored at various intervals along the Channel, whereas the British had just eighteen motorboats and a few Supermarine Walrus biplanes.

In seeking to avoid ditching, the pilots found the resilience of the Spitfire was again a blessing. So often a battered plane would manage to haul itself back to England, even after suffering major damage, as Nigel Rose of 602 Squadron recalled. On a flight over the Channel in the Battle of Britain, about 12 miles out to sea, he was hit by a Me 110:

> He made a nasty mess of my Spitfire. The trim was very strange, going up and down. So I put the hood back, undid my straps, and was just about to make my departure when I realized that the thing was still controllable. I thought it would be better to try to get back to land rather than get wet. I started to fly back. Unfortunately the shots had buggered up some of the instruments, and also the air bottle had given up, so there were no flaps or brakes. Getting it down at Westhampnett in Sussex was a bit problematic, because it was really just a couple of big fields put together and there wasn't much room for a long run on landing. I had to go round a few times, but I eventually got it down. I had to more or less close my eyes at the end. I came to a halt just in front of a briar hedge.[13]

The experience of being shot down over the south of England could be just as traumatic. A graphic description of such an occurrence during the first week of September was sent by Pilot Officer Robin Rafter in a letter to his mother from West Kent General Hospital. He began by explaining that he had been flying over Kent at around 25,000 feet on a 'lovely morning' on 5 September when he sighted a huge formation of Germans:

> I very nearly shot down a Spitfire by mistake, but then saw on my starboard side, underneath me, an Me 109. I got all fixed and started my dive on the Me 109 and was nearing it when I saw in my mirror a couple of 109s on my tail. Well, I took what evasion action I could, but found two a bit of a problem. I started to get away from them when my tail must have been damaged as all movement on my control column was to no avail, thus putting my machine out of control as far as I was concerned. Well, by this time I had a little piece of shrapnel in my leg, and probably owe my life to the fact that my machine was out of control as the Jerries evidently found difficulty in getting their sights on me as my machine was going all over the place. Luckily I was very high up and it then occurred to me to bail out. My oxygen tube had already become detached but I had great difficulty in undoing the pin of my harness to loosen myself out of my seat. I eventually got the pin out, but could not get out of the aircraft . . . The next part of my experience was rather a miracle. The machine's nose dropped violently thus having the effect of throwing me forward, the force so great that I went through the canopy, thus unknowingly injuring my head. You can't imagine my surprise. I was then at about 15,000 feet and floating about in the air rather like a cork.[14]

Rafter managed to pull the ripcord, and came to land in a field. From there he was taken to hospital and had surgery to remove the shrapnel.

Tragically, he was to be killed in an accident in his Spitfire Mark II only two months later.

Dizzy Allen wrote of the sense of fatigue during that early autumn of 1940 when 'Time was meaningless. Days meant nothing. I wouldn't have known if it had been a Sunday or a Wednesday.' During this hectic period, the pilots in the front line slipped into a weary routine, often starting an hour before dawn. Allen was invariably woken by his batman, carrying a mug of tea. He then crawled out of bed and had a shave, though he sometimes reserved that task for the battle climb. He threw off his pyjamas and put on his flying overalls and his RAF shirt, which had no collar attached:

> One turned the head with such frequency that a collar would have chafed the neck. Around my neck I wrapped the red silk scarf intended to alleviate the chafing, because the head was turned round so regularly to scan in the lethal area – a sector of about 15 degrees dead astern. The rear-view mirror was helpful but only about 60 per cent effective. This left a 40 per cent probability that one could be shot in the back before one saw the Germans coming in; that was an insufficient margin. It was up to me and no one else to ensure that I was in the right percentage. In this the scarf helped.

Allen claimed the scarf was actually the seventh veil he had snatched from a dancer at the Empire Theatre in Chatham. 'She had intended to remove only six veils but I was waiting in the wings and was quicker than she. My action nearly brought the house down because she wasn't even wearing a g-string.'[15]

Such erotic thoughts were usually far from the minds of the pilots in the early morning as they prepared for the first sortie. 'We forced down some breakfast and got shaken into wakefulness as we were transported to dispersal in a hard-arsed lorry,' wrote Bobby Oxspring of 66 Squadron.

> We arrived to the cacophony of Merlin engines being warmed up and tested all round the airfield by the reliable fitters. Having chalked up the allocations of pilots to aircraft and formation compositions, we donned our Mae West life jackets, collected our parachutes and helmets and trudged out to our aircraft. Detailed walk-round inspections such as are the mode today would have been an insult to our conscientious ground crews, many of whom had been up all night rectifying faults and repairing battle damage. A quick check on the tyres followed by a nervous pee on the rudder was quite sufficient.[16]

Pilots would then climb into the cockpit, where, in readiness for the scramble, they would arrange the straps of their safety harness, ensure that the oxygen supply was flowing through the mask, and check that the reflector sight was working and the firing mechanism was turned to *Safe*. On the early

autumn mornings, when pre-dawn mist soaked the aircraft in heavy condensation, the pilots would sometimes help the riggers to wipe down the
canopies. 'We had learned the hard way that unrestricted visibility was vital to
fighter pilots whose aggression and indeed survival depended so much on
clarity of vision,' wrote Oxspring.[17] Having completed their checks, the pilots
returned to their clubhouse or crew room in the dispersal area, where they
awaited the call to scramble.

As John Bisdee of 609 Squadron explained, there were three states of
standby:

> You might be on readiness, in which case it was a matter of pride that you were
> in the air in about two and half minutes at the most from the call. The next
> stage was fifteen minutes down from readiness, and thirdly there would be
> 'thirty minutes available', which gave you a chance probably to dash up to the
> mess and have lunch or something like that. But then the tannoy in the mess
> would say '609 Squadron to immediate readiness' and one would have to drop
> one's knife and fork and dash down to dispersal. There was a constant tension;
> one never knew when the tannoy was going to go.[18]

Those who were on readiness hung around dispersal, playing cards,
draughts or chess, talking or arguing, listening to music, or drinking more
tea as they waited for action. Periodically the phone would ring, jangling
their nerves, though often it would turn out to be some minor administrative matter, like news that the NAAFI cart was on its way. Eventually the
call to scramble would come through. The orderly listened to the controller,
put down the phone, and then bawled out the instruction, which would go
something like 'Squadron scramble, Dover, Angels Fifteen.' Dizzy Allen
recalled that there was 'always a sound and fury to a squadron scramble.
There was a crackle of Merlins starting up and the roar as the propellers
began to rotate, dust blowing from behind the Spitfires, white smoke bil-
lowing from the exhaust stubs, airmen running, pilots jog-trotting, starter
batteries being pulled out of harm's way, chocks being heaved away and
pilots roaring their engines as they moved out of line.'[19] John Bisdee gave
this description of the final moments before take-off:

> Your ground crew were sitting round your aeroplane more or less. You dashed
> up and put your parachute harness into your cockpit. You put on your helmet,
> connected up your oxygen, plugged in your radio and then you pulled the two
> main straps of your parachute harness across your chest. It all clipped up in the
> centre of your tummy and then generally your rigger put the shoulder straps in
> the aircraft across you. Now strapped like a turkey, off you went. Everything
> would be prepared beforehand and therefore it took almost a matter of seconds
> to put these things on.[20]

Taxiing to the take-off point on the grass airfield was almost as quick. Bobby Oxspring's account continues, 'Pausing to let the last aircraft get roughly in position, the squadron commander's upraised hand signal then came down and twelve pilots gunned their throttles speeding away in a wide formation.' At the height of the Battle of Britain, because of the urgent need to reach the enemy, the squadron leader would frequently give the order 'Buster', which meant the maximum speed attainable, though there was an emergency setting on the throttle which could give the engine a sudden additional boost for a few minutes. 'Struggling to gain every inch of height in the shortest possible time,' wrote Oxspring of a typical sortie,

> we gradually emerged out of the filthy brown haze which perpetually hung like a blanket over London. Suddenly, around 12,000 feet, we broke through the smog layer and a different world emerged, startling in its sun-drenched clarity. Long, streaming contrails snaked away above us from the Channel coast as the Messerschmitt high-flying fighters weaved protectively over their menacing bomber formations. Our radios became almost unintelligible as pilots in our numerous intercepting squadrons called out sightings, attack orders, warnings and frustrated oaths.[21]

The tight three-plane vic formations of Fighter Command had largely been phased out after the sorry experience of Dunkirk. Flights tended to adopt the less rigid 'finger-four' formation based on the German *Schwarm*, with the rearmost wingman acting as a defender – or 'arse-end Charlie' – to guard against attacks from the rear. Johnnie Johnson, who completed his training in August 1940 and, after a brief spell with 19 Squadron, joined 616 Squadron, praised this more open approach:

> Our squadrons had largely resolved the tactical inferiority which marked the beginning of the fighting. We had recognized the principle that two fighters constituted the smallest element which can fight and survive in the air. The vulnerable vic of three was fast disappearing and pilots who found themselves alone knew that there was no future in a hostile sky. Although some of our squadrons still clung to the line-astern formation, the individual sections of four aircraft were separated by greater horizontal distances and we were evolving a more flexible abreast style of fighting.[22]

The key aim of RAF fighter operations was to prevent the German bombers from hitting airfields and industrial centres, though in practice this meant that the Spitfires had to deal with the protective Me 109 escorts, while the more numerous Hurricanes headed for the bomber formations, because of the Hurricanes' 'inferior performance', to quote the phrase of Park's.[23] In the ensuing clashes, however, it was inevitable that squadron and flight cohesion broke up, as opposing aircraft were locked in individual combat. In *The Last Enemy*, Richard Hillary described one such sortie when his squadron was vectored to intercept twenty enemy fighters at 25,000 feet. As he flew towards the target, his radio picked up the German pilots talking to each other. Being multilingual, he threw in a few Teutonic insults across the airwaves after switching his radio to 'Send'. To his delight, this reply came swiftly back: 'You feelthy Englishmen, we will teach you how to speak to a German.' Moments later, Hillary saw the fighters below:

> One after the other we peeled off in a power dive. I picked out one machine and switched my gun-button to 'Fire'. At 300 yards I had him in my sights. At 200 I opened up with a long four-second burst and saw the tracer going into his nose. Then I was pulling out, so hard that I could feel my eyes dropping through my neck. Coming round in a slow, climbing turn, I saw that we had broken them up. The sky was now a mass of individual dogfights. Several of them had already been knocked down. One I hoped was mine . . . The next few minutes were typical. First the sky a bedlam of machines; then suddenly silence and not a plane to be seen. I noticed that I was very tired and very hot. The sweat was running down my face in rivulets. But this was no time for vague reflections. Flying around the sky on one's own at that time was not a healthy course of action.[24]

Even in such life-threatening situations, some fighters admitted to being thrilled at the excitement of combat, especially after the nerve-shredding tension of waiting on the ground. Gerald Stapleton, a twenty-year-old pilot with 609 Squadron, was so stimulated that he used to sing the Cole Porter classic 'Night and Day' as he climbed through the sky. 'You could see black dots in the sky and you'd think, "Oh Lord",' recalled Stapleton, universally known as Stapme. 'As well as aeroplanes, there would be anti-aircraft fire that would explode into black smoke. At that distance, you couldn't tell the difference between aeroplanes and the black smokes. It was still exhilarating, though.' Stapleton explained the best way to deal with a 109. 'If you could get underneath him and close and he didn't know you were there, then he'd had it. The rule is, get stuck in and get out, as quickly as you can.'[25] Taking on a German bomber posed different problems:

> Closing to a range of 50 yards was not a problem if the enemy was a fighter, but closing to within 50 yards of a bomber was daunting. The enemy aircraft seemed so massive. If you opened fire and hit the bomber, there was risk of damage to your own aircraft from the large amount of debris that flew back at you. Conversely, when we carried out head-on attacks, debris didn't pose a problem but it was vital you judged correctly the speed you approached the enemy bomber . . . There was a very real risk of flying straight into the enemy aircraft.[26]

But, performed properly, head-on attacks could be deadly, taking out the German pilots, causing bomber crashes as control was lost, and spreading terror through formations.

After each sortie, the Spitfires usually returned to their bases singly or in pairs. Sometimes several would be missing. By September the pilots had learned to accept death as part of the terrible cycle of the battle. 'You didn't have a lot of time to mope,' recalled Nigel Rose. 'I mean, you did feel sad, particularly when your friends didn't come back, chaps you knew pretty well and had flown with, were close to. That was sad, but you didn't have an awful lot of time to go into full-scale mourning over it. You were probably up on a flight thinking about other things.'[27] The pilots, often exhausted, would step out of their cockpits and walk back to the crew room in the dispersal area, where they would be debriefed by their commanding officer and would then have a meal. 'The high tension and excitement generated throughout the squadron gradually receded,' wrote Bobby Oxspring. 'Pilots' sweat-ridden shirts dried out and stomachs returned to normal. If this had been a morning show, we all knew that there could be at least two more formidable raids to contest before the day was through. Occasionally the activity called for five scrambles in the hours of daylight.'[28]

It was not just fighter pilots who were feeling the strain. The ground crews were also under relentless pressure as they kept the Spitfires in the air. 'That was our life, we were working all the hours of the day there,' said Dick Ashley, who was based at Hornchurch. 'The officers were bringing food round to us. When you couldn't keep your eyes open any more you used to kip out on a pile of blankets in one corner of the hangar.'[29] Conditions were tough, and in some places the men did not even have proper accommodation. John Milne, a fitter with 19 Squadron, recalled life at Fowlmere, the windswept satellite airfield near Duxford in Cambridgeshire, during the height of the Battle of Britain: 'We slept in bell tents, feet to the central pole. A mobile cookhouse accompanied us – one day it caught fire! We dug latrine trenches and spent most of our time out of doors. Nobody seemed to mind. Fowlmere later had Nissen huts, never popular, as condensation dripped down from the underside of the cold steel roof on to one's bedding.'[30] The armourer Fred Roberts, also based at Fowlmere, witnessed his worst event of the war during the first week of September, as a young pilot, aged just nineteen, tried to land his damaged Spitfire at the airfield. 'He went up on his nose on landing and the plane caught fire. We were there and we watched him burning. We couldn't do anything; we couldn't get near him. We hadn't got the fire-fighting facilities at Fowlmere and that sort of thing.'[31]

Yet as the crisis deepened at Fighter Command – particularly in 11

Group – the Luftwaffe failed to press home its advantage. Continued heavy attacks on Fighter Command's airfields and ground organization would soon have rendered the Dowding system inoperable, while bombing raids on the aircraft factories would have destroyed the ability to make up losses. The German failure was partly due to poor intelligence. Still unable to grasp the importance of radar, they made no sustained attempt to knock out the chain of stations along the coast. Nor was there any concerted effort to destroy the Supermarine factory in Southampton. In mid-August there was a series of sporadic raids in the area, but the Luftwaffe appeared to have little idea of the location of the Spitfire works, and instead the bombs fell mainly on the Thornycroft shipbuilding yards. Though in 1940 precision bombing was an impossibility, misleading information played a part. After the war, the Supermarine engineer Cyril Russell conducted detailed research on the Luftwaffe raids of August 1940 and discovered the actual maps used by German aircrews, showing shipyards marked as aviation works. 'How this "intelligence" was fed into the German system I do not suppose we will ever know,' wrote Russell, 'but this error gave us at least one or two more months' extra production time, just when it was most needed. It is even more remarkable when one recalls that, pre-war, a German mailplane used to alight on the river Itchen and used Supermarine's slipway for transferring mail and refuelling.'[32]

The Luftwaffe also suffered from inadequate equipment. Radio communications in its aircraft were nothing like as good as the RAF's, and the German air force lacked a heavy four-engined bomber, which could have inflicted more devastation on the industrial centres and airfields. Another crucial factor was the strain on the German pilots. Even though they had gained the upper hand over southern England by the beginning of September, they too had been worn down by the intensity of the fighting. Fighter Command had proved a more formidable opponent than any they had encountered on previous campaigns, the Spitfire a more formidable weapon. 'Utter exhaustion for the English operations had set in,' wrote Hellmuth Ostermann of JG 54; 'for the first time one heard pilots talk of the prospects of a posting to a quieter sector.' Describing a dogfight on 31 August, Ostermann continued, 'The Spitfires showed themselves wonderfully manoeuvrable. Their aerobatics display – looping, and rolling, opening fire in a climbing roll – filled us with amazement.'[33]

The German pilots took to calling the English Channel the 'dirty ditch'. A morale-sapping psychological syndrome called Kanalkrankheit, or 'Channel sickness', spread through the Luftwaffe fleets. Another German pilot, Gunther Rall of JG 52, wrote of the battle weariness:

In two months our strength fell from thirty-six pilots to four. We really wasted our fighters. We didn't have enough to begin with. We were tied to the bombers, flying slowly – sometimes with the flaps down – over England. We couldn't use our altitude advantage nor superiority in a dive. Of course the Spitfire had a marvellous rate of turn, and when we were tied to the bombers and had to dogfight them, that turn was very important.[34]

The resistance shown by the RAF perplexed the Germans. 'It is being said that the British are already on their last legs but when one hears what the operations pilots – and in particular the bomber crews – have to report, we're still a long way from victory. The losses suffered by our bomber crews must be terrible,' recorded Ju 88 pilot Peter W. Stahl in his diary.[35] For all their superiority in numbers, the Germans had the significant disadvantage of having to fight over enemy territory, which meant that every pilot shot down was either killed or held as a prisoner of war, whereas the British planes and fighter pilots could return to the fray. Indeed, by late August the RAF had developed a highly effective system for salvaging damaged aircraft, the Civilian Repair Organization (CRO), either using mobile crews to do the job at the airfields or sending the planes back to the factories if severely hit. This turned out to be a vital service. No fewer than one in seven of all Spitfires that fought in the Battle of Britain had undergone repairs. Interestingly, the CRO had a similar chequered history to Castle Bromwich, for it was initially managed by Lord Nuffield, who was given the grand title of Director General of Maintenance. Just as with the Spitfire factory, the motor baron allowed the organization to slide into chaos, but resented any attempt at interference. 'In the matter of procrastination and delaying decisions, the Nuffield Civilian Repair Organization could give points to any Government department,' wrote an exasperated Alexander Dunbar to Sir Charles Craven.[36]

Fortunately, the advent of the Churchill government in May 1940 meant that Beaverbrook took over the CRO as well as Castle Bromwich from the hapless Nuffield. His dynamism ensured that the organization was running successfully by the time of the Battle of Britain. He requisitioned stores, raided spares, and demanded that badly damaged Spitfires be cannibalized to make new ones. 'Better a stringency in spares and a bountiful supply of aircraft than a surplus of spares and a shortage of aircraft,' he said.[38] Fred Westacott, a Communist activist who worked in 1940 for a CRO contractor in Southampton, gave this picture of his job mending and servicing Spitfires:

It was hard work but extremely interesting and absorbing. Planes would come in straight from action, and after any mess (sometimes including blood) had been cleaned up, we had to repair them. We had to improvise a great deal, not having the machines and sophisticated tools of a factory, and I became an expert in repairing one particularly difficult part of the Rolls-Royce Merlin engine, for which I was later commended by an RAF boffin. We worked literally around the clock, often snatching a few hours' sleep curled up underneath the workbench. It was arduous but quite exhilarating. We were, of course, a prime target for German attacks. One incident I remember was during our midday break when we were sitting on the grass by the side of the runway eating our sandwiches. A low-flying plane suddenly appeared out of the clouds, roaring towards us, and we realized abruptly that it was an enemy bomber. I have never seen men move so fast. One bomb hit the runway, but another landed on a nearby school. Thankfully there were no pupils in it.[38]

Even with the obstacle of fighting over England, the Luftwaffe could probably have won a long-term war of attrition directed against Fighter Command. Sheer strength in numbers might have told in the end, given the way the RAF had become so overstretched. Between 24 August and 6 September, 295 RAF fighters had been destroyed and 171 badly damaged, against a total output of 269 new or repaired Spitfires and Hurricanes. Furthermore 103 pilots had been killed and 128 wounded. But Hitler and Göring were not interested in the long term. If Operation Sealion was to be launched in the autumn, Fighter Command had to be obliterated rapidly. Victory was being achieved too slowly, if at all. The cautiousness of Dowding and Park in refusing to commit all their fighters to one encounter was causing deep frustration. On 3 September at The Hague, Göring met his two chiefs, Albert Kesselring of Luftflotte 2 and Hugo Sperrle of Luftflotte 3, to discuss a change in tactics. Sperrle was in favour of continuing the attack on the fighter bases. Kesselring, however, felt that something more dramatic was needed. Ever since the Battle of Britain had started, he had favoured a massive sustained assault on London as the way to destroy British morale and orchestrate a decisive confrontation with Fighter Command. 'We have no chance of destroying the English fighters on the ground. We must force their last reserves of Spitfires and Hurricanes into the air,' he told Göring.[39]

Göring himself was all in favour of such a change. The idea of switching the focus of attack to London had been given new impetus by recent daring raids carried out on Berlin by Bomber Command, which had left ten people killed and had severely embarrassed the Reichsmarschall. These RAF raids had been in response to regular German attacks on British cities throughout August, including London, Liverpool, Portsmouth and Southampton. Over 1,000 British civilians had been killed, among them nearly 400 women and 140 children. But, until the Berlin bombings, Hitler had been opposed to a wholesale bombardment of the capital, believing that

Britain might still sue for peace. Now, on 4 September, he adopted a very different tone, threatening to unleash a new, more terrifying, onslaught against the British people. 'England will collapse. I know no other end than this,' he screamed in a speech in Berlin. 'And if people in England today are asking, "Why doesn't he come?" I reply, "Don't worry, he is coming."' Then, to hysterical cheers from his audience, he warned, 'We will eradicate their cities. The hour will come when one of us will go under, and it will not be National Socialist Germany.'[40]

The die was cast. Under the personal command of Reichsmarschall Göring, the Luftwaffe began its massed attack on London on Saturday 7 September. A gigantic formation of over 350 bombers, escorted by more than 600 Me 109s and Me 110s, filled 800 square miles of sky as it crossed the Channel and headed towards the capital. Fighter Command was stunned by the sheer size of the raid. As usual, the Group 11 sector controllers carefully vectored Spitfires towards the higher escorts and Hurricanes towards the bombers, only to find their fighters overwhelmed by the scale of the enemy forces. A flavour of the experience of facing this attack is provided by the diary of Sandy Johnstone, flying his Spitfire from Westhampnett in Sussex:

> 602 was naturally first to break through the haze although, when we did, I nearly jumped clean out of my cockpit. Ahead and above, a veritable armada of German aircraft was heading for London, Staffel upon Staffel for as far as the eye could see, with an untold number of escorting fighters in attendance. I have never seen so many aircraft in the air all at one time. It was awe-inspiring. They spotted us at once and, before we had time to turn and face them, a batch of 109s swooped down and made us scatter, whereupon the sky exploded into a seething cauldron of aeroplanes, swerving, dodging, diving in and out of vapour trails and the smoke of battle. A Hurricane on fire pulled up in front of me and span out of control whilst, to the right, a 110 flashed across my line of sight, only to disappear before I could draw a bead on it. Earphones were filled with a cacophony of meaningless sounds. A mass of whirling impressions – a Do 17 spinning wildly with a large section of airplane missing; pulling sharply to one side to avoid hitting a portly German as he parachuted past me with his hands raised in an attitude of surrender; streaks of tracer suddenly appearing ahead when I instinctively threw up an arm to protect my face.

Johnstone was soon running low on petrol. He began to head back to base, when he suddenly came under fire from three 109s. 'I let fly at the nearest, whose canopy shattered into a thousand pieces as he pulled away in an inverted dive, whereupon I banked steeply to meet the others head-on, only to find I was out of ammunition when I pressed the button. I don't know whether they were aware of my predicament, but they were certainly incensed by my impertinence.' The two remaining 109s locked on to Johnstone's tail. A frenzied chase ensued. 'I doubt if any Spitfire ever travelled so quickly when I dived near-vertically, foot on the throttle, weaving madly in a desperate attempt to shake off my pursuers.' It was not until he hauled out of a dive at 2,000 feet that he found he had finally lost them.[41]

The 7th of September was a hard day for Fighter Command, which lost 31 planes compared to the Luftwaffe's 39 losses. It was an even tougher one for London's East End. The attacks continued almost through the night, to 4.30 a.m. A total of 448 civilians were killed, and the docks were badly hit. Many in the RAF, including senior commanders, thought that this might be the final assault in advance of invasion. 'I remember very clearly the seven days starting on 7 September when our squadron stood-by at "readiness" with our Spitfires half an hour before dawn, awaiting a "scramble" to fly to the south coast to meet the invasion,' wrote Squadron Leader Peter Brown. 'It was a time of high expectation and high adrenalin. In 11 Group, Park had issued an order to his squadrons that, in the event of an invasion, pilots could expect to carry out eight sorties a day, landing mainly just to rearm.'[42]

Yet, far from being the harbinger of victory, the targeting of London was the beginning of the end for the Luftwaffe's campaign. The British public, not the fighter bases, were now required to bear the brunt of the attack. The squadrons in 11 Group had a chance to regroup. For the first time since early August they were not under bombardment. Damaged airfields and planes were repaired; communications were restored. Park himself admitted that when he saw the East End go up in flames 'I looked down and said, "Thank God for that" because I knew that the Nazis had switched their attack from the fighter stations, thinking they were knocked out. They weren't, but they were pretty groggy.'[43] The more far-sighted Germans recognized this. 'It was with tears of rage and dismay that, on the very point of victory, I saw the decisive battle against the British fighters stopped for the benefit of attacking London,' wrote General Theo Osterkamp.[44] Göring's blunder was compounded in the days immediately following 7 September, as the Luftwaffe slowed down its daytime activity, preparing for what it believed would be a final onslaught that would bring Britain to its knees. Again, German intelligence had badly misled the Reich's military. It was claimed that the RAF had little more than 100 serviceable Spitfires and Hurricanes. In reality, Fighter Command actually had more planes in the second week of September than it had had at the end of July.

It therefore came as a shock to the Germans that when, on Sunday 15 September, they launched their heavy offensive over southern England, they were met by large numbers of Spitfires and Hurricanes. The Luftwaffe expected to swat the last remnants of Fighter Command aside. Instead, German pilots found themselves in the middle of their hardest battle since the middle of August. 'Here come those last fifty Spitfires,' a Dornier Do 17 pilot sneered over his radio as his bomber group approached London, yet suddenly the sky was full of the roundels of the RAF.[45] All three waves of Luftwaffe planes which came over the coast between 11 a.m. and 6 p.m. were met by large RAF numbers and suffered crippling losses. At the time, the government claimed that 185 German aircraft had been downed – a gross exaggeration, for the real figure was only 56. Nevertheless, the Luftwaffe had undoubtedly suffered a decisive defeat, given that Fighter Command's losses totalled only 26.

That day, 15 September, became immortalized in history as Battle of Britain Day, the moment when the tide finally turned against the Germans. With the RAF gaining in strength, the Germans saw their hopes of air superiority vanishing. Even the German High Command, so prone to bombast, admitted that there had been 'great losses' during the combats of the 15th, with the result that 'the day's operations had been unusually disadvantageous.'[46] Göring raged against his commanders and his pilots, but he could not disguise the reality: the battle had been all but lost. Hitler spelled out the stark truth two days later, when he issued a directive on Operation Sealion postponing the invasion indefinitely. Britain, it seemed, had survived.

The air conflict was far from over, however. In fact the British public, especially in London, suffered more than ever as the Germans concentrated on night bombing, and the RAF, lacking an effective night fighter, was unable to offer any resistance in the air. But the risk of defeat for Fighter Command had passed. The sense of dejection within the Luftwaffe was well captured by Adolf Galland:

> Failure to achieve any noticeable success, constantly changing orders betraying lack of purpose, obvious misjudgement of the situation by the Command and unjustified accusations had a most demoralizing effect on us fighter pilots. We complained of the leadership, the bombers, the Stukas and were dissatisfied with ourselves. We saw one comrade after the other, old and tested brothers in combat, vanish from our ranks. Not a day passed without a place remaining empty at the mess table.[47]

Apart from the demoralizing losses suffered by the Luftwaffe on 15 September, perhaps the most significant aspect of the day's action was the employment of Leigh-Mallory's Big Wing from 12 Group. The wing, led by Douglas Bader, had operated three previous times since 7 September, but this was by far its largest and most successful action, with no fewer than five squadrons – 60 aircraft – working together, compared to Park's favoured method of just two squadrons. According to the glowing report that Leigh-Mallory sent to the Air Ministry of one combat on the 15th, the Big Wing – two Spitfire squadrons flying at 27,000 feet, and three Hurricane squadrons 2,000 feet below – took off before noon and engaged a fleet of Do 17s, escorted by Me 109s, just south of the Thames estuary:

> As the Hurricanes went in to attack the bombers, Me 109s dived towards them out of the sun, but as the Spitfires turned to attack them, the enemy fighters broke away and climbed towards the south-east, making no further effort to protect their own bombers, who were actually endeavouring to escape towards the west and the south. They did not all, however, manage to save their own skins in their precipitous flight, as the Spitfires were able to destroy a number of them before they got away.

Leigh-Mallory thought that the heavy damage inflicted on the Dorniers by the Spitfires and Hurricanes fully justified his Big Wing theory: 'In this engagement, the pre-arranged idea worked perfectly for there were sufficient numbers of Spitfires to attack the enemy fighters and prevent them from exercising their primary function of protecting their own bombers, which were destroyed by three Hurricane squads at their leisure.'[48] Bader himself relished this conflict: 'The finest shambles I've ever been in,' he said later.[49]

Leigh-Mallory's large army of critics, led by Park and Dowding, thought he was wildly exaggerating the efficacy of the Big Wing, and it is certainly true that, even by the optimistic standards of the RAF in 1940, the claims made for 12 Group could be absurdly inflated. Park and Dowding's dislike of the Big Wing was grounded in the belief that it was tactically naive, showed no understanding of the elaborate home defence system which had been constructed since 1935, was too cumbersome, and risked wasting scarce resources. Keith Park argued that the central problem was the time taken to get the Big Wing in the air. Whereas an individual squadron could be off the ground in less than four minutes, a wing of five squadrons or more could take more than twenty minutes to assemble. 'Owing to the very short warning received of enemy raids approaching the south of England, it would have been quite impossible to intercept enemy formations with Big Wings before they bombed their targets such as the aerodromes and aircraft factories,' he said.[50] Top pilots, including Johnnie Johnson and Al Deere, felt the same way. Dennis Armitage, who flew with 12 Group under Bader, summed up the feelings of many:

> There was plenty of organization and leadership but not enough enemy. The leading squadron might well get into action but very often the other squadrons would do very little. Personally I was not in favour of the idea; the

first problem was that we took so long to get to the job. By the time five squadrons had got off from Duxford and got down into the battle area, all we usually saw was the back end of the enemy disappearing over the Channel. So it was only Dougie Bader and the Poles in front who really got stuck into them if at all. It all seemed a lot of organization and not a lot of result.[51]

Dowding felt that the Duxford wing was indicative of Bader's misguided approach to fighter tactics. According to Dowding's analysis, Bader was trapped in a First World War mindset and, in his enthusiasm for old-fashioned dogfights, lacked a wider sense of responsibility towards Fighter Command. Showing his insouciance towards the Dowding system, Bader expressed his belief that 'If the controller will tell us where the bombers are in time – direction and height – we'll sort out the tactics in the air, get up-sun ourselves and beat hell out of them before they can bomb.' When this statement was reported to him, Dowding's one-word reply was 'Monstrous!'[52] Like others in the RAF, Dowding found Bader obstinate and uncooperative. As he put it, 'Bader suffers from an over-development of his critical faculties.'[53]

This kind of personal antagonism was another element of the Big Wing controversy, since Dowding and Park believed that Leigh-Mallory – motivated by spite, envy and personal ambition – was grossly disloyal, refusing to follow orders properly and undermining the overall defensive strategy through his promotion of Bader's freelance antics. All this, they believed, was because Leigh-Mallory wanted them sacked as a way of ensuring that he could take over 11 Group under the more congenial, attack-minded overall command of Sholto Douglas, the Deputy Chief of the Air Staff during the Battle of Britain. In fact Park claimed that Leigh-Mallory had openly said to him in February 1940 that he 'would move heaven and earth to get Dowding removed from Fighter Command'.[54] In Park's view, Leigh-Mallory's disobedience, which was in graphic contrast to the conduct of other commanders, was so serious that it assisted the German assault. In a letter to Dowding written in 1968, Park stated that

> throughout August and September 1940, on occasions when all my squadrons had been dispatched to engage the many German bomber forces, I called on No. 10 Group to cover some vital targets on my right with one or two squadrons. Brand always responded at once and on many occasions effectively intercepted the enemy, preventing them from bombing their target unmolested. In similar circumstances, I called on No. 12 Group to cover my fighter aerodromes north-east and east of London but Leigh-Mallory failed to respond. This resulted in North Weald, Hornchurch and Debden being accurately bombed whilst No. 12 Group wing was being dispatched, assembled and climbed in mass formation in the rear of my area.[55]

In another letter written at this time, to the actor Trevor Howard, who played Park in the film The Battle of Britain, the former 11 Group commander complained that 'frankly, I was more worried about this lack of co-operation than I was about out-witting the massed German raids.'[56]

Leigh-Mallory could also be dangerously territorial. After one fight over his area, he sent this message to Park: 'Full explanation required why 11 Group fighters have shot down enemy aircraft in 12 Group area.'[57] Peter Brown, another of the Duxford pilots, was outraged at his chief's attitude. He thought the failure of Leigh-Mallory to give whole-hearted support to Park was 'dishonourable and may well have caused higher fighter casualties in 11 Group . . . It seems that when his country was in great danger, ambition had replaced the loyalty expected of a senior commander.'[58]

For his part, Leigh-Mallory – and many of his fellow officers – felt that Park made insufficient use of 12 Group and fought the Battle of Britain as if it were his own personal contest against the Luftwaffe. Planes from 12 Group were often called too late into action, he argued, while the demand that they patrol over airfields rather than engage the enemy was a contradiction of the entire Dowding approach, which was meant to do away with standing patrols. It is undoubtedly true that there was a streak of vanity in Park, who was intolerant of any interference and saw himself as effectively in charge of fighter operations, particularly since Dowding exercised little direct control over daily tactics. Sholto Douglas wrote in his memoirs that, though Leigh-Mallory could be 'rather over-forceful', Park was 'rather inclined to resent, without even realizing it, the way in which squadrons from Leigh-Mallory's Group came into his area uninvited'. On one occasion, Douglas 'heard Keith Park complaining that No. 12 Group was "poaching". This sounded to me as if he were talking about a local shoot.'[59] Also, Leigh-Mallory had been on the receiving end of personal insults from Dowding long before the battle had begun. 'The trouble with you, Leigh-Mallory, is that you sometimes cannot see further than the end of your little nose,' said Dowding at a conference on fighter tactics in 1939 in front of several senior officers.[60]

It is grotesque that, at the moment when Britain was struggling for its very survival, the relationship between the three senior figures in Fighter Command should have been so clouded by petty rivalries and jealousies. All three men come out badly from the Big Wing row. Leigh-Mallory showed an arrogant contempt for orders; Park failed to marshal his resources effectively; above all, Dowding did not provide strong leadership, allowing the hostilities between his two top commanders to simmer. There was no need for the Big Wing to become a focus of such bitter controversy or dogma. If Park and Dowding had been more open-minded, they might have seen that there could be advantages to a large fighter formation on particular occasions, especially when the battle had grown more intense. Certainly the Germans who first encountered Bader's wing on 15 September admitted that they were shaken by it. 'The British are using new tactics. They are using powerful fighter formations to attack in force,' Theo Osterkamp reported to Göring, confessing that the RAF 'took us by surprise'.[61]

When it worked, the Big Wing brought confidence to the pilots, who found themselves in a more even battle against the Luftwaffe. 'I have the impression that 11 Group's squadrons have been to some extent affected by constant fighting against superior numbers,' wrote Douglas Evill, Dowding's Senior Air Staff Officer. 'It must be good for our fighter squadrons as a whole, and unhealthy for the Germans, for us to push in a three-strong Wing on occasions and reverse the position. I feel that Park should give more recognition to this fact and should endeavour to so organize things that he can deliberately use the strength of 12 Group's Wing as an effective way of dealing with a mass raid.'[62] Bobby Oxspring, at the centre of the battle on the 15th, wrote of the huge boost to morale that the Bader wing gave that day, when he watched a stream of bombers heading towards London: 'At that moment we witnessed the glorious sight of five squadrons from the Duxford wing come sailing into the raid. The impact of a further sixty Hurricanes and Spitfires charging in on the sorely harassed bomber force was too much. Bombs were jettisoned indiscriminately on south-east London and the raiders fled for home.'[63] It was Evill who in October gave the most balanced summary of the issue: 'It is quite useless to argue whether wing formations are or are not desirable; both statements are equally true under different conditions.'[64]

The Big Wing disagreement cast a shadow over the victory in the Battle of Britain, and it has been the subject of bitter dispute ever since, with most analysts taking the side of Park and Dowding. Yet, in its concentration on the detail of tactics, the quarrel has tended to obscure the far wider question of Dowding's overall handling of the battle. It is arguable that, after Eagle Day, on 13 August, his approach actually made Fighter Command's position far harder than it need have been, through his mixture of inflexibility, poor deployment of resources, obsession with structures, and unwillingness to take a decisive lead in organizing the RAF's response. At times, having delegated much of the crucial decision-making to Park, he seemed almost like a spectator as he watched the battle unfold at Bentley Priory.

Dowding was a brilliant technocrat, but he was no great leader of men or air strategist. Since 1931, he had given the RAF three crucial weapons for the fight against Germany: radar, the Spitfire, and a complex defence organization. Owing to production problems and the Castle Bromwich fiasco, the

Spitfire was not available in the numbers it should have been. Nevertheless, with the back-up of the Hurricane, the RAF should not have been brought to the brink of defeat in the first week of September. The impression often given, not least by Park and by Dowding himself, is that Fighter Command was stretched almost to breaking point in those dark days, but actually this was true only of 11 Group. The three other groups still had plenty of reserves, including Spitfires, but they were asked by Park to help only on an irregular basis. Fighting the battle should not have been a matter of issuing requests for assistance in moments of crisis. Given what was at stake, it was Dowding's duty to ensure that every Spitfire and Hurricane squadron had a central role, not merely an occasional supportive part.

Essentially, the Battle of Britain was fought not by Fighter Command, but by 11 Group. There was some truth in Douglas Bader's complaint that 11 Group 'seemed to be hogging the battle', keeping others on 'the ground while numbered squadrons had to engage a massed enemy'.[65] As the conflict went on through the late summer, the RAF became a victim of the rigid demarcation between groups. One of the key problems was that, in his operations room at Uxbridge, Park had only a map of his own sectors; therefore he had no overall picture of how the battle was progressing. In addition, large parts of 11 Group were too near the enemy once the Germans had been spotted on radar. So pilots in Kent and Sussex were often in the strange position of having to head north, away from the Luftwaffe, in order to gain height before turning for the attack, whereas those in the neglected 12 Group north and east of London could have gone straight on the offensive. All this could have been avoided if Dowding had taken charge of the battle from Bentley Priory, with its comprehensive maps and plots. Yet he failed to do so. Delegation of power descended into abnegation of responsibility. As the author John Frayn Turner put it, 'It was as though General Montgomery left a corps commander to fight the Battle of El Alamein and told him to call on other corps commanders if necessary.'[66] Even one of Dowding's most fervent admirers, Spitfire pilot Peter Brown, was forced to admit that 'a major weakness was that there was no one in authority in Fighter Command immediately below Dowding to co-ordinate overall battle tactics and to utilize all squadrons to best advantage to meet the very heavy and concentrated Luftwaffe attacks at that time.'[67] But this did not need the appointment of another officer: Dowding should have been doing the job himself.

By far the worst aspect of the group structure was the failure to ensure that the fighters, especially the Spitfires, were concentrated where they were needed most: in the south-east of England. Instead, even at the height of the Battle of Britain, Spitfires and Hurricanes were scattered all over the country.

It was nothing short of an absurdity that Dowding held almost half his fighter strength outside Group 11 throughout the conflict. At the beginning of the battle, no fewer than 21 of his Spitfire and Hurricane squadrons were in 12 and 13 Groups. A comparison by aircraft numbers graphically illustrates how badly the Spitfires were deployed. In 10 Group, covering the south-west, there were 63 Spitfires on 1 August, and 65 on 1 September; 12 Group, across the north of East Anglia and the Midlands, had 61 Spitfires at the beginning of August, rising to 77 at the start of September. Even 13 Group, in the north and Scotland, had 46 Spitfires in September. Yet in 11 Group, bearing the overwhelming burden of the fighting, the number of Spitfires rose from 96 on 1 August to only 97 on 1 September.[68] Even on 18 August, the 'Hardest Day' of the battle, there were Spitfires in far northern bases like Catterick and Acklington, and in Scotland at Turnhouse.

The traditional defence of the widespread dissemination of Spitfires is that Dowding had to guard against sudden German raids against the Midlands or the south-western coast. But this will not wash. First of all, radar meant that the Luftwaffe could mount no surprise attacks. Second, the Me 109s, because of their limited fuel capacity, could not have acted as escort on any bomber missions over such targets, while the longer-range Me 110s had, since Dunkirk, shown that they were no match even for the Hurricanes. Third, it was pointless to prepare for potential attacks in the future when the real and present ones were creating havoc.

A telling illustration of the folly over numbers could be seen on 15 September, the last real clash of the battle. On that day, Winston Churchill made one of his periodic visits to the headquarters of 11 Group to witness the action. At one stage, when the fighting was at its peak and every squadron was in the air, Churchill turned to Park and asked, 'What reserves have we?' To which Park replied, 'There are none,' an echo of the answer General Gamelin had given during the Battle of France to Churchill's question 'Où est votre masse de manœuvre?'[69] But Park's reply had far less justification than Gamelin's. For in reality there were large reserves throughout the south of England, but he was all too focused on his own group. In fact George Unwin, the 19 Squadron Spitfire pilot, described Park's statement as 'ridiculous . . . Park was at fault in many ways. I'm sure it was just personal pride. We were never called to help 11 Group on time. We were always called out too late and there's no excuse for it . . . He had sixty of us waiting – waiting ten minutes' flying away – and an awful lot of lives could have been saved, I think, and a lot more damage done.'[70]

Dizzy Allen, who rose to become an RAF wing commander himself, thought that the whole strategy of Fighter Command was deeply flawed:

'Given more competent handling of the fighter force in 1940, the Battle of Britain could have turned out to be a disaster for the Luftwaffe.' Allen said the idea that the Germans would regularly strike outside the south of England was 'nonsense'. The assumptions rested on the belief that the twin engine, long-range Me 110 was an adequate escort fighter even against the single-engined Hurricanes and Spitfires. Such conclusions merely indicated the paucity of intellect of those in high command. And, almost without question, these false premises underlay the poor deployment of the squadrons in Fighter Command.'[71]

Such sentiments were also held by senior figures in the Air Staff and the government, contributing to a mood of disillusion which was to lead, in November 1940, to Dowding's enforced retirement and Park's removal to other duties. To Dowding's supporters, both at the time and subsequently in the pages of history, his dismissal was an outrage, akin to sacking Wellington after Waterloo. He was, they argued, the ultimate architect of the triumph of the Battle of Britain, a man who should have been lauded by the government rather than treated in so shameful a fashion. He and Park were supposedly the victims of a disgraceful plot, led by Leigh-Mallory, to force them out of office, using the Big Wing row as a vehicle for undermining their reputations.

The conspiracy theorists have focused particular attention on a crucial meeting of the Air Staff on 17 October. Ostensibly this was held to discuss the lessons from the Battle of Britain for future fighter tactics, but much Spitfire literature portrays it as little more than a show trial in which Dowding and Park's critics united to destroy them. 'Meeting of Infamy,' was how it was described by the prolific author Dilip Sarkar, who has written over twenty books on the Spitfire. According to the pro-Dowding account, what is especially disturbing about this meeting is that Leigh-Mallory asked Douglas Bader to attend, though no other pilots were invited and someone of his junior rank did not usually take part in top-level policy discussions. The involvement of Bader – a noisy opponent of the Dowding strategy – has been seen as further evidence that the Air Ministry was determined to force out Dowding and Park. In his rather tortured letter to the actor Trevor Howard, Park summed up his view of the conspiracy:

> There was an intrigue by the Air Staff, Air Ministry and Leigh-Mallory which led to the sacking of Dowding after the battle had been won. As his chief operations commander I was also removed to make room for Leigh-Mallory. The specious argument about the Big Wing was used by the Air Staff and Leigh-Mallory as a pretext to get rid of Dowding in favour of Sholto Douglas. Bader, for whose bravery I have great admiration, was used by the conspirators as pretext to make room for Sholto Douglas and Leigh-Mallory.[72]

But the meeting of 17 October has been exaggerated in importance by Dowding's supporters. There were no sudden sackings, no dramatic changes in strategy, only a general support for greater use of wings. The key point agreed at the meeting was that, in the words of Sholto Douglas, 'Wings of three more squadrons were the proper weapon to oppose large enemy formations when conditions are suitable.'[73] The meeting did, however, reveal a growing sense of anxiety within the Air Staff over Dowding's hesitations about confronting the Luftwaffe in force, as well as his unyielding attachment to pre-ordained structures, tactics and procedures.

Yet there were several other, more significant, factors involved. The first was that Dowding's retirement had long been overdue. He had been in charge of Fighter Command for more than four years, a far longer spell than any other RAF commander, and his departure had been under discussion since mid-1938, when he was first told he would be relinquishing his command in August 1939. In March 1939 he was then asked to defer his retirement until July 1940. The outbreak of the battle led to yet another postponement, until the end of October 1940.[74] Though Dowding expressed his annoyance to Newall, the Chief of the Air Staff, about these constant changes, he could hardly claim that the call for him to retire from Fighter Command came as a surprise. It must also be said that Dowding was an extremely tired man by the autumn of 1940, having been working monumental hours for months on end, while also suffering from insomnia. Chic Willet, a member of his staff at Bentley Priory, recalled, 'The strain of the great problems and lack of sleep began to show. There were times when I saw him almost blind with fatigue; he obviously needed a long rest, he was becoming burned out.'[75] One particular cause of personal stress had been the fact that his son Derek had been a fighter pilot throughout the battle.

There was also the issue of Dowding's personality, for his stiff, cold manner meant that he enjoyed little popularity. His personal assistant in 1940, Flight Lieutenant Hugh Ironside, gave this insight:

> I really enjoyed working with him though he was very shy and difficult to engage in conversation. He was not a sociable chap – he hardly ever drank. His wife had died a long time ago and he lived with his sister and every few months they would have a sherry party. It was my job to get people to attend it. It was really gruesome. 'Stuffy' would have one sherry and he used to play ancient tunes on his ancient gramophone and after a time I found it difficult to get anybody to come.[76]

Dowding's traits of pedantry, aloofness and inflexibility worsened with the passage of time, creating more enemies. Similarly, Park was seen by Air

Marshal Sir Kenneth Porter, who worked daily with him throughout the battle, as 'an unlovable man, unnecessarily harsh and temperamental'.[77] Sholto Douglas, for example, felt after one meeting at the beginning of September that he had been treated with disdain by Dowding and Park, making him appear 'foolish' and little more than 'a music-hall turn'.[78] Douglas did not attend any more meetings at Bentley Priory after that experience.

None of this would have really mattered if Dowding – and to a lesser extent Park – had retained the faith of the political leaders. Dowding had never had any time for Sir Archibald Sinclair, the Air Secretary, whom he regarded as weak and unreliable. Indeed, according to Sinclair's biographer, Dowding developed 'a pathological hatred' for the Air Minister.[79] But for most of the Battle of Britain he had powerful support from those two great mavericks Churchill and Beaverbrook. In July 1940 Churchill had strongly argued against any attempt to shift Dowding, telling Sinclair, 'He is one of the very best men you have got.'[80] The position changed, however, in the autumn. This was partly because of a growing chorus of disapproval over fighter deployment and the Big Wing. Unfortunately for Dowding, the adjutant of Bader's squadron was Flying Officer Peter Macdonald, the Tory MP for the Isle of Wight. A strong critic of Dowding, Macdonald used his political connections to draw Churchill's attention to concerns about the failure to use 12 Group's planes effectively. Sinclair himself visited Duxford on 26 October and sent a report to Churchill outlining pilots' grievances that they were used too little and were never called into action until it was too late.

But even more influential was the growing concern over Dowding's inability to respond to the Germans' night-time bombing, which had begun in earnest on 7 September. Though not threatening Fighter Command, the Blitz was damaging the industrial infrastructure and the morale of the public, yet Dowding appeared to have no answers. To an extent this was hardly his fault, as the Spitfire, which had been envisaged as the RAF's premier night fighter, was not up to the job because of its poor visibility. As Colin Gray put it, 'Once it got dark the stub exhausts (of which there were six on each side of the engine) belched out a bright orange/blue flame, about a foot long, thus further limiting visibility. As one throttled back to land, this flame was embellished by a shower of sparks caused by exhaust back-pressure.'[81] But there was deep concern that Dowding lacked the imagination or the energy to come up with any solution. Churchill's scientific adviser, Frederick Lindemann, wondered whether 'everything is being done to cope with the night bomber,' and Churchill's Parliamentary Private Secretary, Eric Seal MP, told the Prime Minister that Dowding 'has a reputation of being very conservative and not being very receptive to new ideas'.[82] Churchill became so perturbed that he set up a special committee on night defence, under the chairmanship of Sir John Salmond, a former Chief of the Air Staff, to investigate the problem. Salmond quickly came to the view that Dowding had to go, and in league with the founding father of the RAF, Sir Hugh Trenchard – long an enemy of Dowding's – he worked behind the scenes to secure his dismissal.

Under the twin pressures of night bombing and fighter deployment, Dowding's position had become unsustainable. On 13 November he was summoned to see Sinclair, who told him that he was being relieved of his post, though the pill was sugared by giving him the job of leading a mission to the USA for the purchase of aircraft, this being an idea of Beaverbrook's to prevent Dowding being humiliated. On 24 November he left Bentley Priory for the last time. Before he did so, he sent this message to all units in Fighter Command:

> I cannot hope to surpass the simple eloquence of the Prime Minister's words, 'Never before has so much been owed by so many to so few.' The debt remains and will increase. In saying goodbye to you all, I want you to know how continually you have been in my thoughts, and that, though our direct connection may be severed, I may yet be able to help you all in your gallant fight. Goodbye and God bless you all.[83]

Churchill had played no direct role in Dowding's sacking; indeed, he had supported him longer than anyone else in the government. But, at the end, even he agreed that Dowding's tenure had run its course. Sir John Salmond later recorded that when he first told Churchill that Dowding should be dismissed, he 'practically blew me out of the room. After three weeks I met him again . . . Winston said I was right. Dowding had gone, "but it nearly broke his heart".'[84]

It nearly broke Dowding's own heart. He admitted that he felt 'unhappy and bewildered' at the decision.[85] His mission to America was a predictable failure, for he lacked the necessary diplomatic skills. With no further role to play in the RAF, he grew increasingly embittered and eccentric. He took up vegetarianism and spiritualism, causing some embarrassment at a Fighter Command dinner by telling the assembled pilots that he was in communication with their dead comrades. 'I am afraid that the reaction of most of us at the time was that "the old boy had gone round the bend,"' wrote Hugh Dundas.[86] He was also a follower of the creed of theosophy, whose beliefs include reincarnation. In 1950, after his long years of being a widower, his unorthodox faith led him to remarry; his second wife, Muriel Whitting, was a committed spiritualist. He himself became something of an evangelist for his beliefs, giving lectures and producing several books, including *The Dark*

Star and *God's Magic*. In his later years he became convinced that he had been a Mongol chief in a previous life, as he told Beaverbrook in a letter written in 1964. Even more bizarrely, in the same letter he claimed that both he and Beaverbrook had been chosen by divine will to save Britain in 1940:

> I am telling you this because I think it more than probable that your part in the battle was laid down by the Lords of Karma as a result of some action of your own in times long past. Looking back on my own life, I can see how events conspired to put me at the head of Fighter Command at the critical time, instead of Ellington as Chief of the Air Staff, as I had been told in 1935 that I should. I don't know if you, with your widely differing views, will think that is all nonsense but to me it is an integral part of my life. I think perhaps that the above will account for the way in which two such dissimilar characters as you and I were brought together and enabled to work harmoniously for the preservation of our dear country.[87]

After suffering badly from arthritis in his later years, he died in 1970.

Dowding's replacement at the head of Fighter Command was Sholto Douglas, the former Deputy Chief of the Air Staff. An RFC observer in the First World War, Douglas had been a senior figure in the Air Ministry since 1936, after years as an instructor. Much more offence-minded than Dowding, he believed that large fighter formations were the way to stop the Luftwaffe. He was expansive in appearance and authority as well as outlook. Bullish and barrel-chested, 'He seemed to take up the whole table,' said the Spitfire pilot Bill Rolls.[88] His aggression appealed to the politicians, who had wearied of Dowding's pessimism. But many pilots had far less trust in him than in Dowding, particularly in his understanding of the details of Fighter Command. 'Sholto Douglas was somebody I didn't really care for – he was very much a politician,' said Pilot Officer Tom Neil of 249 Squadron. 'I remember him coming to see us at North Weald and in the course of our discussion he said, "What do you think about flying a Spitfire?" I thought I'd misheard him. I said, "What?" He said, "How do you like flying a Spitfire?" We weren't flying Spitfires at all and I thought, "This man's mad, he really is."'[89]

The autumn also saw Park – described as 'another difficult customer' by Sir John Slessor, RAF's Director of Plans[90] – moved from his post at the head of 11 Group to take over Training Command. Like Dowding, he was embittered at the enforced change, especially because his arch enemy Leigh-Mallory took his place. To Park, this was tantamount to a reward for disloyalty, and a large section of pilots also saw it that way. 'We were livid. We couldn't believe it happened because we loved Dowding and Park. They won the Battle of

Britain. The others were just hangers-on. Leigh-Mallory was a very danger-ous piece of work,' said Flying Officer William David of 213 squadron.[91] The other major change was the retirement of the Chief of the Air Staff, Sir Cyril Newall, increasingly regarded as ineffectual by Beaverbrook and Churchill. He was replaced by the thrusting, demanding head of Bomber Command, Sir Charles Portal, who was to serve as head of the RAF for the rest of the war.

The names of Dowding and Park will for ever be remembered for their role in winning the Battle of Britain. Without the Dowding system, the RAF would probably have found it impossible to resist the Luftwaffe through the summer of 1940. But it is wrong to pretend that their demise was entirely the result of a sinister conspiracy by scheming rivals. The fact is that, by the beginning of September, they were losing the battle. Wrapped up in the 11 Group crisis, they failed to see the wider picture. It was almost as if the struc-ture was dictating strategy. As Alexander McKee put it in his ground-breaking history of the Battle of Britain, which is generally sympathetic to Dowding, the squadrons outside 11 Group were 'efficient and indeed exceedingly impa-tient for action', so 'the failure to use them fully partly justifies the criticism of undue caution.'[92]

Yet none of these controversies could detract from the one unalloyed tri-umph of the battle: the Spitfire. Unburdened by politics or personal disputes, it had become the ultimate symbol of Britain's struggle. Bathed in the warm glow of public adulation, it was now more than just an aircraft. It was an icon, a source of national pride. 'I looked at my squadron in formation behind and beside me, each Spitfire seemingly motionless in the still, cloud-free sky. I looked with affection more than pride. The sheer beauty of the Spitfire, a poem of grace which contained a fighting man and an armoury of devastating destruction,' wrote Squadron Leader Donald MacDonnell of one early morn-ing sortie over Kent, evoking exactly what the public felt about the plane.[93] People began to talk about 'the Spitfire spirit' – that unifying mood of resist-ance and heroism that swept through the country in the middle of 1940. One judge in London even complained that this attitude was so pervasive that it was leading to a rise in juvenile delinquency. 'Many escapades are due to a spirit of adventure that is abroad,' said Basil Henriques, president of the East London Children's Court. 'We want to encourage this Spitfire spirit but guide it in right and proper channels.'[94] The beautiful outline of the plane was now a vital element of propaganda and morale-boosting. Typical was the cover of a September edition of *War Weekly*, a boy's comic, which showed two Spitfires circling through the sky around a parachuting figure. 'Spitfires save parachut-ing pilot from the "Blighters"' was the banner headline across the cover.

The Spitfire funds were pulling in more money than ever during the height of the battle. 'We're all buying Spitfires, / As fast as we can buy, / Spitfires and Hurricanes, / For battles in the sky,' ran a little ditty in *Punch* on 25 September. *Flight* magazine reported that public enthusiasm for the Spitfire funds had reached a level of 'mass hysteria', in contrast to the calmness with which the bombing was accepted. 'Knowing nothing of performance figures they have instinctively chosen one particular type as the paragon of protective types and they have guessed correctly,' said the magazine.[95]

As the Spitfire legend grew, its pilots also basked in public acclaim: 'The public couldn't get enough of us. They were all over us. We could do no wrong. It was just like a pop star now. You were a star. Except for the army, who couldn't stand us after Dunkirk,' recalled Pilot Officer Roger Hall.[96] One young Londoner, Irene Thomas, later to be 'Brain of Britain', remembers how she was captivated by 'the Few':

> Our heroes were the fighter pilots who made repeated attempts to beat off the invaders . . . I can remember seeing a group of these young men walking along Oxford Street, with the crowds of shoppers making way for them. They wore dark glasses – reputedly so that their eyes would get used to the darkness – and wore the top button of their jackets unfastened. The names of fighter pilots were as familiar to us as the names of footballers now.[97]

Not everyone felt like this, however. The Spitfire pilot Kenneth Lee was shot down over Whitstable in Kent, and bailed out. He happened to land near a golf club, where he was taken to the bar to wait for the ambulance. 'I was in shirtsleeves, slightly bloodstained, but couldn't help hearing members at the last hole complaining that the distraction of the battle in the air was disturbing their putting, while once inside a voice demanded, "Who's that scruffy-looking chap at the bar? I don't think he's a member."'[98]

The Battle of Britain is the only conflict in British military history in which the victorious side is best remembered not by the name of its commander but by its prime weapon. The Spitfire belongs in the same pantheon as Drake, Henry V, Wellington and Nelson. Yet it is one of the curious aspects of the battle that there was no sense of victory once the Luftwaffe's day offensive was curtailed in October. This was partly because the Blitz was as intense as ever, with London severely hit and concern growing about Fighter Command's impotence in the face of the night-time bombing. Moreover, neither the RAF nor the British public could have known that Hitler had abandoned his plans for invasion. Many of the Spitfire pilots were unaware of any sense that they had conquered the enemy. Sandy Johnstone captured this in his diary, after Churchill had praised the RAF in a speech in the Commons on 5 November: 'It appears we have been taking part in a famous battle. He has been telling the people that they owe it to the pilots of Fighter Command for not being invaded in September. It's nice to know we have been of service, although, to be honest, it has not seemed like a battle to me: rather an extension of what we have been doing since we first came up against the Hun a year ago last October – only more so.'[99] Dowding himself wistfully commented after the war:

> It is a strange thing that even during the war there were very few people who realized the true significance of the Battle of Britain. Most of the battles of the war were fought as might be expected, in order to win the war, but that was not the case with the Battle of Britain, which was fought to prevent the country being invaded . . . The consequence was that when, about the end of October, the daylight fighting died down, the night attacks still continued and to the ordinary civilian, as well as the professional service man, there were no outward indications that the battle had been won at all.[100]

But the battle was undoubtedly a victory for the RAF. The Germans had set out to pulverize Fighter Command, and had failed to do so. German air supremacy was a more distant prospect in October 1940 than it was in July. The Luftwaffe, though undefeated, suffered a crippling rate of attrition. Figures for actual losses are notoriously difficult to compile, owing to excessive over-claiming by each side and difficulties of classifying whether aircraft were destroyed, damaged, or lost to enemy action or only to accidents. However, authoritative research by John Alcorn has estimated that Luftwaffe losses to fighter attack between 1 July and 31 October 1940 totalled 1,218 – almost exactly half of the 2,475 victories originally claimed by Fighter Command squadrons.[101] Alcorn's figure is close to the total of 1,318 Luftwaffe combat losses which the author Len Deighton put forward after extensive research in German records.[102] Deighton further estimated that Fighter Command lost 765 planes in combat – around 60 per cent of the German total – confirming the RAF's superiority in the battle. Around 35 per cent of the British losses were Spitfires, a pretty accurate reflection of their proportion in the Fighter Command fleet.

What was particularly interesting about Alcorn's research was that, through the depth of his statistical analysis, he proved that the Spitfire was a better fighter than the Hurricane, which may have shot down more German planes, but only because it made up around sixty per cent of the fighter fleet and was given the easier target of the bombers. Alcorn wrote:

> The 19 Spitfire units gained 521 victories, an average of just over 27 per squadron. The 30 fully engaged Hurricane units gained 655 victories, an average of just under 22 per squadron. On those figures, the Spitfire was 1.25

times more effective in action than the Hurricane. In combat, Spitfires and Hurricanes achieved victories in rough proportion to the numbers of these fighters engaged. However, the Spitfire units had an average victory-to-loss ratio of 1.8, compared with an average of 1.34 for fully engaged Hurricane units. Because the Spitfire units suffered lower attrition rates they could remain in action longer, an average of 19.9 days compared to 15.6 days for fully engaged Hurricane squadrons.[103]

This is in line with what the government was thinking towards the end of the Battle of Britain. At a meeting of Ministers on 14 October 1940, held to discuss the air war, it was agreed that 'the Hurricane is found not a match for the Messerschmitt. The Spitfire retains it superiority.'[104]

This is not to devalue the contribution of the Hurricane towards saving Britain in 1940. The reality is, however, that the Battle of Britain could have been won by the Spitfire alone, if it had been available in sufficient quantities. The same could not be said of the Hurricane. But in the end, at a unique moment in British history, they both played their part in the defeat of the Luftwaffe. It was the first setback for the Nazi war machine, and it started Hitler on the road that would ultimately lead to the downfall of his regime. After the war, the Commander-in-Chief of the German army, Gerd von Rundstedt, was asked in a television interview if the turning point of the conflict had been Stalingrad. 'Oh no, it was the Battle of Britain,' he replied. 'That was the first time we realized we could be beaten, and we were beaten, and we didn't like it.'[105]

9

'We kept the old organization going'

⌖

T HE GERMAN AIR strategy throughout the Battle of Britain had been deeply flawed, partly as a result of poor intelligence and Göring's lack of imagination. One of the most serious mistakes was the failure to take out the Spitfire factories at Supermarine and Castle Bromwich. The Southampton plant, on the south coast, was obviously the easier target, since it lay within the range of Me 109 escorts, though throughout the battle German bombers reached places as far afield as South Wales, Liverpool, Manchester and even Belfast Lough. If the Luftwaffe had conducted a sustained onslaught on the Supermarine works at Southampton in July and August 1940, before the Castle Bromwich factory was fully in production, the supply of Spitfires would have ground to a halt and Fighter Command would have been in desperate trouble.

As it was, the Germans conducted only a few irregular, ill-targeted raids on the two factories during the summer. In fact it was Castle Bromwich that was hit first, on 27 August. Though some machine tools were destroyed, only minor damage was done to the factory's infrastructure, and Beaverbrook reported to the Cabinet that 'the bombing had limited effect on the production of Spitfires.'[1] Beaverbrook was disturbed, however, by the vulnerability of the plant, and kept pressing the government to provide better air-raid and fighter protection at this factory, something that was to become a constant theme of his in the coming months. 'Nothing is further from my mind than to make complaints about Fighter Command,' he wrote at one stage to Portal, Chief of the Air Staff. 'I am well aware of their difficulties, but their burdens are added to if our factories are destroyed. It is their own babies we are asking them to look after.'[2] In contrast to the earlier complaints about the slackness in parts of the workforce, Alexander Dunbar, the Vickers manager of Castle Bromwich, wrote to Beaverbrook after the August raid to tell him of some of his employees' gallantry under fire – such as that of Miss Winifred Gilhooly, who was working in the factory's telephone exchange:

The exchange is a temporary one and protected only by sandbags but Miss Gilhooly, in spite of having just completed a 12-hour spell of duty, volunteered to remain throughout the night. Bombs fell on the factory and in the immediate vicinity for some hours but during the whole of this time Miss Gilhooly remained at her post and operated the service with customary efficiency. Hers was conduct worthy of the highest praise.[3]

It was not until 15 September that the Supermarine factory came under direct attack, previous German raids having been directed at the wrong part of the Southampton. This raid was carried out by eighteen Me 110s, each carrying two bombs. Only a few windows were blown out at the Woolston works, though nine people were killed in houses nearby. Cyril Russell had the traumatic experience of pulling a girl from the rubble of one demolished home: 'The whiteness of the skin and the limp limbs, plus the wide-open, unseeing eyes, told me the struggle had been in vain. I knelt there on one knee, cradling the poor soul in my arms, and unashamedly letting my own tears run down my cheeks to drop without hindrance on the pale face in my lap.'[4] There were far less tragic scenes within the factory. Denis Webb was unimpressed with the attitude of some of the staff on the night shift, again revealing how the 'Spitfire spirit' did not touch everyone during the Battle of Britain. Owing to the broken windows, wrote Webb in his memoir,

> we could not make the factory light-tight and so had to cancel the night shift. When this decision was made, men had already turned up by motor coach from Bournemouth. Some of them made it very clear to me that they thought we ought to have got ourselves organized better and phoned them before they left Bournemouth and so saved a wasted journey. There were a few occasions like this when some of us wondered if the war was worth winning.[5]

The raid on the 15th was only a precursor to a more serious assault on Tuesday 24 September, when a formation of over fifty Me 109s, converted into fighter-bombers, targeted Woolston. Cyril Russell had been cycling back to the factory after his lunch break when he heard the sound of a siren followed by anti-aircraft fire: 'I flattened myself into the gutter — and waited. The exploding bombs made the ground tremble and kick.' When the gunfire stopped, Russell knew the raid was over. He walked towards the factory, and was greeted by a picture of hell: 'In the roadway and into the tunnel under the railway embankment were dozens of people, like a disturbed ant-hill, rushing back and forth, digging, grabbing and pulling, all with frenzied speed.' Russell soon found that the impact of the bombs had blasted apart two of the air-raid shelters, as well as causing widespread casualties among those running for cover. 'Some poor souls had been blown up on to the railway embankment and lay like bundles of old clothing. Others had been blown into the embankment lower down and were buried, or partly buried, by the earth thrown up from the craters. Here and there a limb protruded or perhaps just the colour of the overall or the jersey could be seen.'[6] Russell then helped put the wounded into ambulances, which ferried them to hospital; at one stage Russell had to take over behind the wheel from a female driver who confessed that the sound of another air-raid siren made her too afraid to carry on.

Denis Webb had been caught right in the middle of the raid at Woolston, and later wrote this description: 'One of the shelters had been turned into a heap of soil and sand with arms and legs sticking out. I came across a young man who was just standing still and staring as if turned to stone. He was in complete shock so I led him to a first-aid post.' Just after doing this, there was another air-raid siren, so Webb joined other employees in one of the remaining shelters:

> I remember the horrible feeling of claustrophobia when huddled in there with thirty other frightened people as we felt the near-misses shake the ground and dirt fall from the ceiling. I think that a general panic was not far away but a works policeman, an ex-services chap, started singing a hymn which everyone took up. I am pretty sure no one was singing from any religious feeling but it distracted the mind, released some of the nervous energy and calmed everyone down.

After the all-clear sounded, Webb emerged from the shelter. He watched a lorry moving across the cratered earth, its journey providing a grim moment of gallows humour amid the devastation:

> A young man from the Supermarine Planning Department was shouting in a calm voice, 'Any more for the mortuary wagon?' We saw then that the floor of the lorry was covered with corpses, few of them showing any sign of injury. They had been just killed by the blast. In spite of everything, a burst of laughter rang out as one of the 'corpses' suddenly struggled to sit up, yelling, 'I'm not dead, it's my bloody leg that's broken.' So we gently hauled him on to a stretcher and into the first-aid room.[7]

The official report into the bombing put the death toll at 42, with 161 injured. Surprisingly, most of the Spitfire factory remained intact, though the gas and water had been cut off. Much worse followed two days later, on 26 September. As the German bomber formation appeared off the south coast, and the wail of air-raid sirens was heard in Southampton, nine Spitfires were scrambled to meet the invaders. But, as in the darkest days of the Battle of Britain, they were heavily outnumbered. The two successive waves of German planes, made up of 76 Heinkels and Ju 88s, accompanied by 60 Me 110 twin-engined fighters, could not be broken up as they continued on their lethal way towards their target by the river Itchen. Alexander McKee, who in September 1940 was a young writer living on the south coast, witnessed the drama in the sky:

> Above the Isle of Wight, there was a distant droning, increasing to the harsh uneven roar of an immense bomber formation coming in. Across that sound the whine of diving fighters suddenly rang like a trumpet scream and burst after burst of machine-gun fire echoed in the heights. A grey streak of smoke, a blaz-ing balloon, fell down slowly over Southampton, followed by a thunderous, long-drawn-out rumble, so many bomb detonations occurring simultaneously that it was all one ringing blow.

More than 70 tons of bombs fell on an area about a square mile in size, with the Spitfire factory at its centre; 55 people were killed, 92 injured. For the first time, widespread destruction was inflicted on the Supermarine buildings. McKee described the collapse of one structure on the site. 'Above an air-raid shelter was a store where Spitfire wings were stacked and painted; the store was hit, the ventilator which connected with the deep shelter blown open, and down it poured a rain of wing ribs, followed by a blazing tide of paint and dope, which flooded into the darkness of the shelter.'[8]

It was as if the Supermarine works had been smashed by an earthquake. There was not one roof left on any building; broken and collapsed walls were everywhere. Huge craters scarred the ground across the site; the railway line was a mass of twisted metal. The wrecks of near-completed Spitfires were strewn in the rubble. At Woolston, there was barely any of the factory left, merely 'a flat jumble of twisted girders', wrote McKee.[9] In fact the plant was never to be rebuilt: the ruins were turned into a training ground for com-mandos to learn street-fighting techniques. When Denis Webb saw the extent of the damage, he knew that 'it put paid to any idea of using Woolston or Itchen again.' There was, he found, a morbid atmosphere in the air: 'a curi-ous smell and aura hung around the place – a sort of witches' brew made up of violence, fear and death.'[10]

Castle Bromwich was now beginning to function properly, but the need for Spitfires was as desperate as ever, particularly because the government believed that the Lutfwaffe would maintain its air offensive right through the winter. There followed perhaps the most remarkable episode in the story of the Spitfire's production, as Supermarine's manufacturing operation was dis-persed right across the south of England, bringing in sites as diverse as bus stations and laundries. Inevitably, given the creative unorthodoxy of this stu-pendous task, the diminutive figure of Lord Beaverbrook was intimately involved, cajoling, hectoring and ordering. As soon as he heard of the devastating raid of 26 September, Beaverbrook went down to Southampton, accompanied by his lieutenant, Joe Cowley. His innate decisiveness was immediately on display. The day after the bombing, the fourth floor of the Polygon Hotel in the centre of the city was requisitioned by the Ministry of Aircraft Production to plan the dispersal. At the same time, the Supermarine design office and its precious Spitfire drawings were moved into a building at Southampton University, while the accounts and personnel departments took over 'Deepdene', a large private house in the north-east of the city.

But by far the most important task was to find new sites for actual production. The man entrusted by Beaverbrook with this job was the Supermarine works engineer Len Gooch. Though only thirty and far from the top rank of management, Gooch had instantly impressed Beaverbrook with his energy. He was, wrote Cyril Russell, 'the driving force behind the success of the Spitfire dispersal. While his seniors appeared bemused or temporarily stunned, Len grasped the problem.'[11] He first obtained a series of large-scale Ordnance Survey maps of Wiltshire, Hampshire and Berkshire, checked on transport links and local aerodromes, then sent out teams of men to find suitable premises in the chosen towns, ranging from Newbury to Trowbridge. Once a place had been requisitioned, jigs and machine tools were brought over from the shattered debris of the Supermarine factory. Even in the face of repeated explosions, most of these jigs had proved robust.

The new sites were generally chosen because they had wide concrete floors, high ceilings, well-sized access doors, and large areas uncluttered by pillars. Car showrooms, garages and bus depots were particularly suitable, though an intriguing variety of other premises were taken over by the Ministry, including rolling mills, warehouses, a strawberry-basket factory, a steamroller works, and even a stately home. At one stage Beaverbrook considered seizing one of the finest municipal buildings in England, as Russell recounted:

> There is one Beaverbrook story that Gooch told me personally. Discussing the dispersal with the 'Beaver' in the front-facing room of the Polygon Hotel, the Minister's eyes alighted on Southampton's Civic Centre complex, and, upon being informed that one large portion of it was the Guildhall, suggested that it should be commandeered to erect some of the jigs in. I understand that it took quite an effort to persuade the Minister that 'sprung' dance floors were not suitable for the purpose.[12]

Within six weeks of the bombing, no fewer than thirty-five separate units were turning out Spitfire parts. Acting on behalf of Beaverbrook, Gooch and his men had powers to requisition almost any property they wanted. Such authority was necessary, since several proprietors refused to enter into the wartime spirit and proved deeply uncooperative. Denis Webb encountered this kind of hostility when he sought to take over the Hants and Dorset bus depot in Southampton, which doubled up as a storage facility for the local fire brigade. As Webb recalled, the deputy town clerk refused to allow the trailer pumps to be moved out of the garage, 'on the grounds that they were of more importance to the town than "bloody Spitfires". My argument that "bloody Spitfires" in adequate numbers could make the trailers pumps unnecessary was not accepted. I told him he would be hearing from Lord Beaverbrook.' The Minister soon dragged the officious worthy into line, though the clerk left some piles of sandbags in the garage once the buses and pumps were cleared. 'We had to find out from him where we could dump the sand, it being anatomically impossible to put it where we would have liked.'[13] In Salisbury, the town's mayor also proved difficult about Supermarine taking over the local corporation's bus garage, so Beaverbrook had to send along Joe Cowley to sort out the problem. 'Tell me, Mister Mayor, I believe you are the patron of the local Spitfire fund?' began Cowley. 'Oh yes,' replied the mayor, beaming with civic pride. 'Well, may I suggest that you close that fund and start another to erect a statue to the Mayor who thought the Spitfire was not necessary.'[14] Capitulation followed: the Salisbury bus depot was in Beaverbrook's hands before nightfall. Denis Webb was surprised that some local residents objected to a dispersal workshop in their neighbourhood, on the grounds that it made them a more likely target for the Luftwaffe. 'Now I suppose we'll be bombed,' said one woman. 'Share and share alike, madam,' replied Webb.[15]

Len Gooch recalled that the most difficult move was shifting the production of the Spitfire wings' leading edges from Southampton to the Barnes Steam Roller works at Trowbridge, because the owner 'was not the easiest of people to get on with. He contended he could build any Spitfire products without the help of the company and he rejected very strongly this requisition.' He went to his local MP, and the matter eventually was taken to an arbitration panel, which decided to give Supermarine 75 per cent of the premises, the rest being kept for the steamrollers, 'which he regarded as more important than Spitfires!' As a result of this decision, a local building contractor had to build a high dividing wall between the Supermarine and the steamroller section. 'Looking back, the whole episode was like a Charlie Chaplin comedy,' said Len Gooch in 1976.[16]

By far the most luxurious site that Supermarine took over was the magnificent eighteenth-century colonnaded edifice of Hursley House near Winchester, home of the Dowager Lady Cooper. This imposing building, which was in dramatic contrast to the dingy offices where Mitchell had designed the prototype, was to play a crucial part in the Spitfire saga, for it was here that all the subsequent developments in the plane's design were conceived. From December 1940 the house became the headquarters of Supermarine, providing quarters for the administrative, drawing, design and laboratory staff. Despite the inconvenience, Lady Cooper proved far more accommodating than many public officials and businessmen. When the Supermarine team first turned up, she welcomed them with a spectacular floral model of the Spitfire in the entrance hall of the house. Sadly, she had to move out in June 1942 when the government decided that her private staff had become a security risk. In a plot worthy of a West End farce, an assistant cook had deliberately started a fire in one of the upper floors in order to distract attention from his attempt to break into Lady Cooper's safe in the basement and steal the family silver. Unfortunately for him, he was overcome by fumes from his own decoy fire. She and her retinue moved out to another of her residences nearby, but she was never to return. Vickers Supermarine remained at Hursley until 1958, when the house was taken over by the American computer giant IBM.

During the war, Hursley underwent a dramatic transformation. Its ballroom became a drawing office, its conservatory was used by the tracing staff, its linen room was turned into a laboratory and its wine cellar into a photographic room. Hangars were put up in stable yards and at one end of the 350-acre park, housing the experimental department which produced the prototypes of the Spitfire variants. An entertainment hall behind the stables was used as a machine shop, oil leaks ruining its fine parquet floor. Layers of heavily reinforced concrete walls and a roof were put round the garages and the coal store, now a document archive. By the middle of the war, so many staff were working at Hursley that special bus services had to operate from the neighbouring towns, with the buses hidden among the trees during the day so they would not be visible to the Luftwaffe. Various bedrooms on the first floor were occupied by Commander James Bird, the general manager of Supermarine, and other executives and secretaries. Unfortunately, during some refurbishment work the wallpaper of the Chinese Bedroom was thought to look shabby and was consequently given a coat of paint. The maintenance staff had not realized it was silk.[17]

The Supermarine dispersal was an astonishing achievement, which illustrated some of that mood of wartime defiance so well characterized by the Spitfire itself. In a classic British way, marrying ingenuity with necessity, a large number of this iconic plane were built not in some vast modern, high-tech factory, but in a mosaic of backyards, workshops and municipal depots. 'I am amazed how we achieved so much in such cramped and primitive conditions,' wrote Cyril Russell, who was part of a team assembling Spitfires in a tiny hangar at the High Post airfield in Salisbury. Originally used by a pre-war flying club, the hangar was so small that it could take only three Spitfires at a time, provided that the first two had their tailends pushed into the opposite rear corners so that the third could get its fuselage and tail between them. Russell left this description of the rudimentary nature of the assembly process, after the wings and fuselage had arrived at the airfield outside the hangar:

> Muscle power and a couple of 'skates' moved the fuselage inside, and the same manpower pushed the wing trolleys in. Then came the tricky bit. 'All under the wings' would go up the cry and all the men left whatever job they were doing so that a wing could be pushed over, freed from its trolley to be supported on the 12 to 15 men's backs. Once there, it would be shuffled into position until the front and rear root fitting were in correct alignment with their fuselage attachments and the fixing bolts driven home. This procedure would be repeated for the opposite wing.[18]

The hydraulic piping was connected and tests were done on the undercarriage, which was then lowered and locked so it could take the aircraft's weight on its wheels. The engineers carried out the rest of the fittings, including the guns, the cowlings and the propeller spinner. After a touch of paint, the plane was pushed outside, where further checks would be made and the engine run for the first time before it was test-flown. 'It was always a thrill to hear the cough and see the smoke come out of the exhausts as the engine burst into life at the beginning of its fateful journey into the wartime unknown,' wrote Russell.[19] It would take two and a half days to complete this operation at the High Post airfield, so, with three Spitfires on the go at any one time, six could be assembled every week.

This kind of intensive, back-straining work was conducted at sites throughout southern England from late September 1940. A complex network of micro-plants had been successfully created by Beaverbrook and Gooch, contradicting all the principles of industrial mass production that had been put forward since Henry Ford created his first assembly line. No fewer than 250 different subcontractors were involved in Spitfire manufacturing by 1942. At the end of 1944, Supermarine had 60 units, employing almost 10,000 staff, half of them female, compared to 2,880 at the start of the war. Altogether, 8,000 Spitfires were built in the southern region after the Southampton bombings – a feat for which Jeffrey Quill felt 'no words of praise are adequate.'[20]

Denis Webb believed that one of the keys to the dispersal's success was the way it mirrored the Supermarine works except over a far wider geographical area. 'Basically we kept the old organization going. In place of messengers taking job cards and drawings to the workshops we had motorcycle and side-car messengers doing it, and instead of parts being delivered to the central control and stores on hand trolleys, we had the parts delivered by a lorry which collected the parts from other workshops on the way.' Webb described one characteristic example of innovation. 'One of the main problems in building the fuselages was getting compressed air for the riveters. Sometimes we turned to compressors used by road contractors, running long lengths of hose into the workshops while the compressors roared away outside, to the discomfort of residents.'[21] A shuttle service operated between many of the local aerodromes and Eastleigh, where the final tests were carried out before the Spitfires were delivered to the squadrons.

It would be wrong, however, to pretend that the dispersal scheme resolved all Supermarine's problems. One of the many myths of the Spitfire story is that the bombings had little real effect on production. Typical is the claim made by the authors Derek Wood and Derek Dempster in their magisterial history of the Battle of Britain, where they stated that 'the Southampton facilities were dispersed to thirty-five sites and by the end of the year production was back to normal.'[22] This was far from the case. The first stage of dispersal was not even completed until early 1941, and it was not until 1942 that production levels passed their pre-bombing peak. The quarterly reports of the Supermarine company reveal the truth about the crisis in the aftermath of the raid. In December 1940 the Vickers directors were told that 'the continuity of production at Southampton has been seriously affected by the results of the enemy bombing action. The dispersal of production was proceeded with immediately, but temporarily the number of employees was considerably reduced and a considerable proportion were engaged in salvage work.' Indeed the total Supermarine workforce dropped from 3,660 in September to 3,079 in December. Further German attacks on Southampton in November and December 1940 hit dispersal operations, as telephone lines, gas supplies and electricity were cut off. 'Many of our employees suffered serious hardship due to bomb damage and difficulties with transport affected the number of hours which could be worked,' reported Supermarine.[23]

At the heart of Nazi Germany, Goebbels felt that the continued bombing of Southampton must inevitably destroy British morale. 'The city is one single ruin,' he gloated, 'and so it must go on, until England is on her knees, begging for peace.'[24] In fact in early 1941 Beaverbrook told Portal that Spitfire output in the south was down to 30 per cent of the level it had been in September.[25] As the Blitz continued, it was the labour question that presented the biggest headache for Supermarine, as the company struggled to find accommodation for skilled employees near the dispersal units: 'This has definitely resulted in a considerable retardation of production, particularly in the Salisbury area, to where it has been impossible to transfer skilled men up to the present.'[26] One solution was to put up huts around the Spitfire production sites, though this could be only a temporary measure until proper lodgings were found. Another effect of the Blitz was to discourage potential employees from working on the Spitfire, as Beaverbrook confessed to the Cabinet. 'It is now very hard to persuade staff in some centres to do night duty. The general effect has been to cut down the proportion of men employed on night work.'[27]

Yet it is a paradox of the Spitfire story that the dispersal, for all its problems, also made development of the Spitfire easier. Precisely because there was no longer a major, single production line, it was more simple for the company to introduce changes. Given the limited output from each site, Supermarine could refashion jigs and tools without serious disruption, since different sites could be geared towards different types. Jeffrey Quill later wrote of the dispersal scheme:

> It was the very antithesis of a monolithic structure, and the area managers had great scope for the exercise of their initiative and powers of improvisation. Therefore as new Marks of Spitfire had to be brought into production, often involving the most complicated modifications, such as, for instance, turning the leading-edge structure into an integral fuel tank for photo-reconnaissance aircraft, the southern region had the flexibility to get production going in the minimum time. Often there were several different Marks of the Spitfire in production simultaneously.[28]

The Spitfire's capacity for development was one of its greatest attributes, a reflection of the brilliance of Mitchell's aerodynamic design. Long before the Battle of Britain, Supermarine had been looking at the possibilities of improving the Spitfire's performance, mainly by increasing the engine's power and strengthening the airframe. But the Air Staff, under Sir Cyril Newall, had initially been reluctant to concentrate on an improved Spitfire programme, mainly because they hankered after the idea that the RAF's future lay with the twin-engined Westland Whirlwind and the two powerful versions of the new Hawker fighter, the Tornado and the Typhoon. By the spring of 1940, a litany of technical problems meant that none of these types looked like becoming a convincing successor to the Spitfire. The Tornado prototype had given a disappointing performance, especially in the climb, and never went into full production. The Whirlwind, with its Bristol Peregrine engines, turned out to be underpowered and less manoeuvrable than the Spitfire, while the early Typhoon, though an awesome beast in profile, was hopelessly unreliable, mainly because of its 24-cylinder Napier Sabre engine. Peter Jago, an RAF fitter, had experience of both the Spitfire and the Typhoon. He described the Spitfire as 'very straightforward, like Meccano', with its 'wonderful' Merlin engine. In contrast, the Typhoon had 'an abortion of an engine', which it was difficult to maintain. 'None of the studs, nuts and bolts were accessible – you couldn't even see them! You were feeling around corners and you'd got weirdly contorted spanners to get at them, giving it half a turn then choosing another spanner and giving it another bit of a turn! Oh it was shocking!'[29] When the Typhoon finally went into service, from 1941, more planes were lost through engine or structural failure in the first nine months of operations than through combat.

The failure of the Typhoon, Tornado and Whirlwind gave a new lease of life to the Spitfire. Joe Smith, the chief designer at Supermarine, had long believed that, for all the Air Ministry's doubts, the Spitfire would 'see us through the war' because of its development potential.[30] Similarly, the manager at Rolls-Royce, Ernest Hives, was dismissive of the idea that the Merlin could easily be superseded, as he explained to Wilfrid Freeman in July 1940:

> Consistently every few years we have been faced with some wonderful new engine, which was the last word in performance and efficiency, and that it was only a matter of time before Rolls-Royce would be out of business. There have been times when we have been so impressed with the information that we have believed it ourselves, but fortunately we have never believed it to the extent of dropping the substance and chasing the shadow.

In an obvious jibe at the Typhoon, Tornado and Whirlwind, Hives continued, 'It has been embarrassing at times because some of the senior technical officials at the Air Ministry have backed these projects to an extent far beyond what was justified and proved by subsequent events . . . We know the position as regards fighter aircraft and it is positively certain that the only machines we will have to fight the Germans with are the Hurricanes and Spitfires.'[31]

Towards the end of 1939, Hives had begun to upgrade the Merlin II engine to become the Merlin XX. Running on 100-octane fuel, it had 1,390 horsepower and a two-speed supercharger to provide improved performance at all altitudes. At the same time, Smith embarked on some modifications to the Spitfire Mark I to clean up its lines and accommodate the heavier engine. The fuselage was slightly lengthened; the tailwheel was made retractable; the undercarriage was strengthened and the canopy reprofiled to incorporate flat toughened-glass side panels in place of curved Perspex. The wings were clipped at each end, reducing their overall span by 6 feet. To cope with the extra power of the Merlin XX, a deeper radiator was fitted, and the fuel capacity was expanded by another 15 gallons. The Air Ministry was sufficiently impressed by the design to order a prototype, now named the Mark III. It was flown by Jeffrey Quill in March 1940, four years after Mitchell's original Spitfire had made its maiden flight. The Mark III's performance was judged 'satisfactory' in trials,[32] though the Air Ministry was still hesitant about the Spitfire's future. A letter sent by Sir Archibald Sinclair to Beaverbrook on the eve of the Battle of Britain again demonstrated how little real faith there was in the plane. Referring to the outcome of an Air Ministry conference held to discuss fighter development, Sinclair reported, 'In short-range fighters, it seems to me that the choice will probably lie between the Spitfire Mark III and the Hawker Typhoon. On the whole, after careful consideration of the factors involved, the general inclination at our conference was towards the Typhoon.'[33] The Battle of Britain – and Beaverbrook's passionate advocacy of the Spitfire – changed that attitude. In October 1940, after a few further changes had been made, the government ordered 1,000 of the Mark III. But it never went into production, having been overtaken by two events.

The first was the creation a new type of Rolls-Royce engine, far more powerful than the Merlin and with greater long-term potential. This was the Griffon, which used the technology of the famous 'R' power plant of Mitchell's Schneider-winning seaplanes in the early 1930s. With its capacity of 37 litres – 10 more than the Merlin – the Griffon led to a generation of much faster and heavier Spitfires in the final years of the war, resulting in a very different plane from the one that Mitchell had first designed. Yet work on the Griffon-powered Spitfire began as far back as October 1939. For most of the 1930s the Schneiderized 'R' type had been regarded as far too large for any fighter aircraft, but reconfiguration of its dimensions by Rolls-Royce meant that when the Griffon emerged, in 1939, its frontal area was only 7.9 square feet, compared to 7.5 square feet for the Merlin. Its installation in the Spitfire was now possible. For Supermarine, such an advance was ideal, because it could secure the long-term future of the Spitfire by overcoming the Air Ministry's prejudice in favour of aircraft then still at the experimental stage, like the Tornado and the Beaufighter, which it was planned that Supermarine would build. 'We had an idea', wrote Dunbar to Sir Charles Craven in October,

> that by fitting the Rolls-Royce Griffin [sic]* to the present Spitfires we should have a fast and easily manoeuvrable fighter with a top speed of 420 mph or per-

---

* Supermarine was obviously thinking of the Griffin, the mythical creature with a lion's body and eagle's wings, which is not a bad image for the Spitfire. The Griffon, a European vulture, was part of the Rolls-Royce birds-of-prey series, starting with the Kestrel.

haps 425 mph. This would be as good as a Hawker Tornado with a Vulture engine. I would like to see this machine go into production at Supermarine rather than have them turned over to the Beaufighters. But it would be unwise to raise the matter with the Air Ministry at present. The expressed policy of the Air Staff is, as you know, to have one fast single-engined fighter only and they appear to be satisfied that they have got what they wanted in the Tornado. Nevertheless the Griffin might be acceptable as it would enable Supermarine to continue without the expense and time involved in providing jigs and tools for a new fighter.[34]

Both Joe Smith of Supermarine and Ernest Hives of Rolls-Royce were enthusiastic. As he told Jeffrey Quill, Smith's support for the Griffon was based on his belief that 'the good big 'un will eventually beat the good little 'un.'[35] And Hives felt that the Griffon would mean 'a second power string for the Spitfire'.[36]

At the beginning of November, Craven wrote to the Air Ministry setting out the case for the Griffon Spitfire as an alternative to the Beaufighter. 'Our initial consideration of the Griffin Spitfire indicates that this will be a very satisfactory aircraft with an attractive performance and we hope to be in a position to submit a complete detailed specification before the end of the year.' Sir Charles added that once the Griffon was in production, in 1941, Supermarine could deliver 1,200 of the type, as opposed to the 550 Beaufighters set out in the Air Ministry's putative programme for 1941.[37] Sir Wilfrid Freeman was more supportive than Dunbar had imagined, the Spitfire having now been in action for several months and the development of other fighters plagued with difficulties. In May 1940 a formal contract was issued for the production of two prototypes, now known as the Mark IV. Development proceeded slowly after this, because of serious complications with the advanced technology of the Griffon engine. It was not until November 1941 that Quill first took a Griffon-powered Spitfire into the air. But he was impressed with the plane. 'The throttle needed to be handled judiciously on take-off but, once in the air, the aeroplane had a great feeling of power about it; it seemed the airborne equivalent of a very powerful sports car and great fun to fly.'[38] The one big difference he noticed was that, on the ground, the torque of the Griffon's engine, which rotated in the opposite direction to the Merlin, swung the plane to the right as opposed to the left with the Spitfires Mark I and II.

The progress towards the Mark IV prototype through 1940, albeit painfully gradual, took some of the urgency out of the development of the Mark III. But there was also a far more practical and pressing consideration behind the Air Ministry's abandonment of the Mark III programme. The Merlin XX engine was in short supply in the autumn of 1940 because its two-speed supercharger made it more complex to manufacture than the previous Merlins. The Ministry of Aircraft Production decided that priority had to be given to using it to upgrade the ageing Hurricane rather than pressing ahead with the Mark III. But at the same time the Air Staff knew they could not long continue with the original Spitfires Marks I and II while waiting for more supplies of the Merlin XX engine or the arrival of the Griffon, especially because the Luftwaffe was now using an advanced version of the Messerschmitt, the Me 109F. This new plane not only had a greater speed and rate of climb than the Spitfire, it could also out-turn the British fighter, something no previous German plane could achieve. For all its heroism in the Battle of Britain, the original Spitfire was now being outclassed.

Sholto Douglas, the head of Fighter Command, wrote in exasperation to Beaverbrook at the turn of the year about the inadequacy of his Spitfire and Hurricane fleet. 'I am concerned about the inferiority in the performance of our fighter aircraft compared with newer types of enemy fighters. The improved 109 not only outclimbs our fighters to about 25,000 feet but is faster at altitude and has a better ceiling. This confers the tactical initiative on the enemy.' Douglas then complained about the slowness in equipping all Spitfires with cannon and in developing new types like the Griffon. These delays, he said, were affecting the confidence of his men:

> Pilots invariably ask me, during my visits to squadrons, when they are going to get aircraft with better performance at higher altitude. If they do not get them, their morale is likely to be dampened and they may feel that we are drifting into a policy of quantity rather than quality. This, if true, would be disastrous as one of the most important lessons of last year was that quality will always beat mere numbers. I ask therefore, even if it means a substantial reduction in the production rate, that the fighter aircraft supplied to my command in the immediate future should be the highest powered and most heavily armed which the firms can turn out.[39]

A stop-gap Spitfire was urgently needed to tackle the 109F. In October 1940 Supermarine and Rolls-Royce came up with one in the form of the Mark V. The airframe was essentially the same as that of the Mark I, but it now incorporated a Merlin 45 engine, which offered more take-off power and greater effectiveness at high altitudes thanks to its single-speed supercharger. The other key change on the Mark V was the switch from fabric-covered ailerons to metal ones, thereby reducing their heaviness at high speeds and greatly improving the Spitfire's manoeuvrability. With hindsight it seems extraordinary that the Spitfire, for all its revolutionary qualities, should have fought the Battle of Britain with such relics of the biplane age on its wings, but, as Jeffrey Quill explained, before the war, 'bombers were considered the main threat so the Spitfire was to be a bomber destroyer and a high level of manoeuvrability, particularly in the rolling plane, was not regarded as an important factor.'[40] With the Spitfire production so troubled at both Supermarine and Castle Bromwich, the emphasis was just on getting the planes delivered: changing the ailerons was not seen as an issue of great importance. But the intense combat of Dunkirk and the Battle of Britain revealed the need for change. 'When you were diving at speed with fabric ailerons, the aircraft used to try to turn to the left and I hadn't the physical strength to straighten up,' recalled Cyril Bamberger of 616 Squadron.[41]

The installation of metal ailerons immediately led to a vast improvement in the Spitfire. In November 1940 Sandy Johnstone of 602 Squadron conducted trials of them and delivered this glowing report to Jeffrey Quill and Leigh-Mallory of 11 Group: 'The effectiveness of the new ailerons', he wrote, 'is so great that one has to fly the aircraft to believe it.' He went on to list the advantages, including 'lightness of the controls, particularly at high speeds, making for much greater manoeuvrability', and the reduction in effort 'to keep the control column straight'. Johnstone concluded that 'the adoption of this aileron would be a very popular move.'[42] This message was reinforced in January 1941 by a test report from 266 Squadron, based at Wittering in Cambridgeshire, which stated that the metal ailerons made the Spitfire 'much more pleasant and easy to handle at all speeds in excess of 140 mph'; other benefits were 'movement in the rolling plane extremely easy and smooth at all speeds' and 'accurate turns much easier to execute at high speed', which added 'greatly to the manoeuvrability of the aircraft'.[43] At the same time, full trials were held on the Mark V prototype, with its Merlin 45 engine. The successful results meant that the Air Ministry finally dropped the Mark III and instead decided to put the Mark V into production. 'This will meet the needs of Fighter Command . . . Its improved rate of climb and manoeuvrability at high altitudes is a distinct operational advantage,' wrote Portal.[44]

It is ironic that a plane intended merely as a stopgap should become the most produced Spitfire of them all, with 6,787 built in total. The Mark V's Merlin 45 engine was 25 per cent more powerful than the engine of the original Mark I, which meant that the plane had a higher ceiling, at 36,000 feet, and a faster climbing speed, reaching 20,000 feet in just six minutes. Having entered service in the spring of 1941, it equipped 44 Spitfire squadrons by the end of the year. As well as being the most heavily manufactured of all the Spitfires, the Mark V also had the most variants. When it first went into production there were two main versions: the VA, built at Castle Bromwich, which had the traditional eight Browning guns, and the VB, built by Supermarine and Westland, which had two cannon and four machine guns. But after just ninety-four VAs had been produced it was recognized that its armament was now plainly inadequate compared to the cannon, particularly because the jamming problems with the cannon had now largely been resolved. All production was therefore switched to the VB.

In October 1941, soon after the five-hundreth Mark V had been built, the VC appeared. This had what was called the 'universal wing', which could take three different arrangements of armaments, depending on squadrons' needs, whether it be four cannon, two cannon and four machine guns, or eight machine guns. The universal wing also had the benefit of a redesigned magazine and belt system, which increased the amount of ammunition per cannon from 60 rounds to 120. Apart from the wing, the only other significant change in the early Mark Vs compared to the Mark II was a raking forward of the undercarriage to improve stability on the ground.

In the coming years, no fewer than nine different variations of the Merlin 45 engine would be installed on the Mark V, such as the 50A, a special high-altitude version. A large number of later Mark Vs were also built with clipped wings, the tips being removed to improve low-level handling. A report after trials in October 1942 by the Air Fighting Development Unit, based at Duxford, found that the clipped-wing Spitfire was 'remarkably manoeuvrable in the rolling plane' up to 20,000 feet, though over 30,000 feet 'it feels barely in control.'[45] Though the clipped-wing Mark V had a slower rate of climb, it was almost 10 mph faster than an orthodox Spitfire below 10,000 feet. And, in keeping with this theme of variety, the Mark V was used not just as a fighter but in a miscellany of roles, including bomber, glider tug, floatplane, two-seater trainer, and reconnaissance aircraft.

In fact, by the end of the Battle of Britain, photoreconnaissance had become one of the most vital tasks of the Spitfire. The idea of using the Spitfire on such missions had first been suggested in August 1939 by the RAF intelligence expert Flying Officer Maurice 'Shorty' Longbottom, who argued that what was needed to photograph enemy territory was a fast fighter which could evade detection through speed and altitude. By stripping the guns and radio out of the Spitfire, extra fuel tanks could be installed which would give the plane the range to reach Germany. Longbottom estimated that a modified Spitfire could carry 240 gallons of fuel – three times as much as the fighter version.[46] But his proposal went against the conventional strategic wisdom of the time, which held that photoreconnaissance should be carried out by heavily armed bomber types which could defend themselves against attack. The experience of war soon proved the fallacy of such thinking. Bristol Blenheims flying unescorted over France in the first months of conflict suffered terribly. Out of 42 reconnaissance sorties made between 3 September and 31 December 1939, 8 failed to return and 20 produced no pictures.[47] An alternative was quickly needed. The way was now open for the Spitfire.

The RAF's Photographic Reconnaissance Unit (PRU), known by the deceptive name of the 'Heston Special Flight' and headed by Wing Commander Sydney Cotton, implemented Longbottom's proposal. Two Spitfire Mark Is were taken off the production line in Southampton and sent to Heston, where they were altered for their new experimental job. Cameras with 5-inch-focal-length lenses were placed in the wings where the Brownings would have been, looking down vertically to photograph a rectangular area below the aircraft. The planes were given an extra-smooth, highly polished finish to increase their speed, and then painted a pale shade of duck-egg green as camouflage. The first flight of the photoreconnaissance Spitfire – indeed the first ever flight by a Spitfire outside British territory – was made by Longbottom on the 18 November 1939 over the German city of Aachen near the Belgian border. Unfortunately he found it difficult simultaneously to navigate, take photographs and watch out for enemy aircraft, and so returned without any usable pictures of his target. But he had proved that his idea was practicable. Further sorties were more successful: in December, Longbottom managed to take some fine photographs of the Siegfried Line.

From then on, both the performance of the special PR Spitfires and their equipment steadily improved. In the PR Mark 1B, which first flew in January 1940, Type 24 cameras with 8-inch-focal-length lenses were installed, giving a far higher degree of definition.[48] In addition, the lead ballast in the Spitfire's rear fuselage, used to balance the weight of the propeller at the front, was replaced by a fuel tank, giving an extra 29 gallons capacity and an even greater range. Further expansions in fuel capacity followed in the next two types. The PR1C had a blister tank under the port wing, while the PR1D used the leading edges of the wings as additional tanks, bringing another 57 gallons on board, though this made it difficult to fly on take-off and led to its nickname 'the bowser', after the fuel tankers used by Fighter Command. The photographic unit's commander, Geoffrey Tuttle, said, 'You could not fly it straight and level for the first half hour or hour after take-off. Until you had emptied the rear tank, the aircraft hunted the whole time. The centre of gravity was so far back you couldn't control it.'[49] But it did the job, able to fly for over five hours and photograph sites as distant as Toulon on the southern French coast and Trondheim in Norway. Camera equipment was also radically upgraded. The introduction in April

1940 of the F52 camera, with a 36-inch-focal-length lens, meant that high-quality pictures could now be taken from 35,000 feet.

The photoreconnaissance Spitfires performed vital work during the Battle of Britain, soaring over France and the Low Countries to scrutinize German airbases and the build-up of the invasion fleet, ready for Operation Sealion. The information obtained was invaluable for Bomber Command, and it is estimated that about 10 per cent of the German barges and naval vessels were destroyed on the northern French and Belgian coasts. Even Dowding, who clung on to his Spitfires like a miser clings to gold, was willing to hand over several of the aircraft for reconnaissance purposes. The Spitfire's speed and manoeuvrability, enhanced by further developments after 1940, meant that it continued to be the RAF's essential reconnaissance plane throughout the war, operating in every theatre. It was particularly useful in photographing the results of the Allied air offensive over Germany from 1942, leading to improvements in bombing accuracy, and in assisting the Allied ground attack in France in 1944. In view of the Spitfire's justified image of heroic masculinity, there is a mild incongruity in the fact that many of the most successful PR Spitfires were painted a pale shade of pink – a colour that helped their camouflage against the sky, if not the rugged self-esteem of their pilots.

The technique of operating a reconnaissance Spitfire was well described by Pilot Officer Gordon Green, who was part of the photographic unit based in Cornwall:

> A great deal depended on being able to judge where the cameras were pointing. One flew alone to the general area of the target, then tipped the aircraft on its side to check one was properly lined up. Once that was done it was a question of holding the aircraft dead straight and level for the photographic run. Until one learned the art it was all too easy – if for example one had a bit of bank on – to come back with a lovely line of photographs of the ground a couple of miles to one side of the intended target.

Green stressed that

> the important thing with any photographic mission was to take the photos if one could and get them back to base. As the boss of PRU, Wing Commander Geoffrey Tuttle, often used to say, 'I want you to get home safely not just because I like your faces but because if you don't the whole sortie will be a waste of time.' So it was no use trying to play hide and seek with the Luftwaffe; if one had lost surprise during the approach to a heavily defended target, the best thing was to abandon the mission and go back another time when things might be better.[50]

But it was not always possible to get back to England, with the result that Spitfire PR work demanded as much courage as fighting. Jimmy Taylor of 16 Squadron, based in Belgium after the Allied advance, took his Mark IX over Germany in late 1944, unarmed, full of petrol, flying for five and a half hours to photograph airfields in the Rhine area: 'Halfway through the mission at 24,000 feet, the engine coughed and spluttered, smoke and flame came out of the exhausts. The flames stopped but the smoke became thicker and thicker, followed by black oil. Eventually the windscreen became covered and I could not see out.' In his blindness, Taylor desperately tried to drag back his Spitfire towards Brussels, losing height all the time and leaving a long black smoke trail through the sky. Any moment he feared there would be an explosion. He had no alternative but to bail out. He unplugged the oxygen mask and radio connections, and undid the straps of his Sutton harness. 'I raised the nose of the aircraft, turned upside down and fell out. Unfortunately either I hit the tail of the aircraft or the aircraft turned and hit me. I felt a severe blow in my midriff which seemed to cut me in half and certainly knocked me out. I recovered consciousness sufficiently to remind myself to pull the ripcord.'

Taylor landed in a field, and was soon surrounded by German soldiers. Showing amazing fortitude and ingenuity, he managed to escape by releasing the straps of his parachute, which then billowed into the German group. He ran into a nearby wood and then spent the next few days travelling across country in an attempt to reach Belgium, walking at night and resting in forests during the day, or occasionally hitching a ride on a railway goods wagon. But his remarkable adventure could not last. He was eventually picked up by the Germans in Doorn, and spent the rest of the conflict as a prisoner of war.[51] Squadron Leader Freddy Ball, another PRU stalwart, was more lucky when his engine failed while he was taking pictures over the Ruhr. His subsequent experience was yet another tribute to the resilience of the Spitfire:

> I could not see that there was anything I could do about it but necessity is the mother of invention and I found out that I could keep the engine going spasmodically by using the Ki-gas pump [which primed the engine]. I could not maintain height but at 150 mph on a slightly downhill path I managed to reach Dunkirk at 2,000 feet. At Dunkirk, I thought I might just reach the English coast but, pumping even harder and with no skin left on my hand, I crossed the English coast at 800 feet, a very happy chap. I thought I would have to put down on a mudflat or beach but I actually reached Eastchurch – just – and got my wheels down and on to the ground intact.[52]

Like the rest of the Spitfire range, the PR planes went through far-reaching changes during the war. Each major development in Spitfire type had its parallel in the reconnaissance field, from the early PR Mark 1A, through the four-bladed, Merlin-64-powered PRX, to the mighty Griffon-powered PRXIX with its five-bladed propeller, an engine of over 2,000 horsepower, an internal fuel capacity of 256 gallons, and a presssurized cabin. The PRXIX, wrote Quill, was an aircraft of 'spectacular performance'.[53] This was graphically demonstrated in February 1952 when a PRXIX flown by Flight Lieutenant Ted Powles, on meteorological duties with 81 Squadron in Hong Kong, managed to climb to 51,000 feet – unheard of for a piston-engined plane. For a while Powles was able to fly at this astonishing altitude without sending the plane into a stall, but when a warning light came on in his cabin, indicating that cabin air pressure was being lost, he had to go into a sudden dive. During this barely controllable descent, his airspeed indicator showed that he was travelling at 690 mph or Mach 0.94 – almost at the speed of sound. At this record-breaking pace the ailerons went into reverse and pulled the Spitfire out of the dive at 3,000 feet. In the mid-1930s, some experts at the Air Ministry had feared that the Spitfire could break up at speeds above 350 mph. Nearly two decades later it had attained almost twice that speed, yet Powles was able to land his plane without it suffering any damage. The aerodynamicist Sir Morien Morgan argued that this ability to reach such high Mach numbers was a tribute to Mitchell's design:

> Considering that he could have had little knowledge of Mach effects, Mitchell's decision to use such a thin wing was not only bold, but inspired. We now know that it was a close-run thing: had he made the wing a little thinner it would probably have been too weak and aileron reversal would have been encountered lower down the speed scale. And if that had happened, the Spitfire would have been just one more of those aircraft that did not quite make the grade.[54]

Back in 1941, the PR aircraft were showing the heights and range that the Spitfire could potentially achieve. As a result, the Air Staff sought to extend the range of mainstream fighter Spitfires through greater fuel capacity and their altitude through creation of pressurized cabins. The end of the Battle of Britain meant that, from 1941, the Spitfire was used in an increasingly offensive role over northern France and Belgium. The brief sorties and regular refuelling that characterized the combat of 1940 were superseded by longer missions on the Continent. It was obviously impossible to adopt the solution used by the photoreconnaissance aircraft, of replacing the guns and ammunition boxes with fuel tanks. So the alternative was to install special lightweight tanks underneath the fuselage – between the undercarriage wheels – which could be jettisoned, once they were empty, to reduce drag.

Tests were carried out on tanks made of laminated wood, welded steel and tinned steel, but eventually it was found that vulcanized fibreglass, made from chemically treated cotton rag, provided the best results. As was almost inevitable, there was a legion of teething problems with the tanks, which were generally made to hold 30 or 45 gallons, though some voluminous containers were built to handle 90 or even 145 gallons. At one stage the Ministry of Aircraft Production became so exasperated by the delays in deliveries that it threatened to end the contract with the tank manufacturer, the Vulcanized Fibre Company.[55] Moreover, the method of testing the installation of the tanks was extremely primitive, as Harry Griffiths, the Supermarine engineer, revealed: 'I remember when we had problems with the drop tanks we made a model from cardboard and constructed a crude wind tunnel using a hairdryer. The results showed that if we put hooks on the fuselage just to the rear of the drop tank trailing edge we solved the problem – on our cardboard model the hooks were drawing pins. I think this emphasizes the crudeness of our methods if judged by present-day standards.'[56]

By 1942 some of these difficulties had been resolved, and by December 1943 no fewer than 11,700 tanks had been dispatched. Yet the improvised nature of this approach was never entirely satisfactory. Not only did the tanks detract from the streamlined nature of the Spitfire, creating the kind of drag that Mitchell had sought to avoid, but they also proved unreliable, often interrupting the fuel flow from the main tank. Spitfire pilot Ted Smith, based with 127 Squadron as part of the 2nd Tactical Air Force, made this angry note in his diary in April 1945:

> We are getting very cross about the situations that call for drop tanks: We still haven't licked the problem of the occasional air lock. We are told *NOT* to switch drop tank *ON*, after take-off on 'mains'. Some of the boys say this is bullshit. Better to have the drop tank feeding fuel rather than gasping for air. An air lock usually lasts only a few seconds but it certainly leaves one close to panic when the engine is about to cut.[57]

Johnnie Johnson thought the use of drop tanks showed a dismal lack of long-term planning by the Air Ministry, explaining that all Spitfires suffered from 'the same fucking problem: lack of range. The tanks went some way to helping but it was really not good enough that the fucking Air Ministry had not the foresight to provide the specification for a long-range offensive fighter.'[58]

The early pressurized Spitfire also had mixed success. Before the Battle of Britain was over, the Air Staff had demanded a fighter for high-altitude operations, since it was feared that the Germans were about to put into production a new generation of high-flying bombers like the Junkers 86P. In April 1941 it was agreed to order a prototype of a pressurized Mark V, called the Mark VI, which was to have a ceiling of 41,000 feet. The Air Staff stated that they would need at least 350 of the model by the end of 1941. Jeffrey Quill first flew the prototype on 5 July 1941. He reported that the longitudinal and lateral stability were poor at high altitudes,* while the temperature in the cabin was uncomfortably high at low altitudes. Nevertheless, he believed that the plane could proceed, in view of the RAF's urgent need for a pressurized fighter.

The Mark VI had a number of important differences from the Mark V. The wing tips were extended to give greater efficiency at height, with the wingspan now reaching 40 feet 2 inches. A four-bladed propeller was attached to the Merlin 47 engine. And a special rubber-sealed canopy was installed to maintain the cabin pressure, though the pilot still had to wear an oxygen mask. Harry Griffiths recalled once more how unsophisticated the experimental production was at Hursley House:

> A Mark V was brought into the hangar at the stable yard and a small team, consisting of a project designer, an illustrator, and a small number of fitters and 'metal bashers', set about producing a pressurized cabin. The initial work was done with very few detailed drawings. As each item was made and fitted the illustrator sent sketches to the drawing office who made production drawings to pass on to the works. Sealing of electrical wiring and hydraulic pipes through the pressure-cabin walls was no problem, but special measures had to be taken to provide sealing for the moving control rods and cables to the ailerons, tail fins and elevator. The Trinidad Lake Asphalt Co. produced for us a water-base emulsion of pitch and rubber which could be brushed onto the inside of the seams and which, when dried, gave a good, flexible airtight seal.

Once the work was completed, Griffiths was told to sit in the cockpit with the canopy clamped shut and the air pressure was pumped up to an additional 2 pounds per square inch. 'As far as I know I suffered no ill effect other than to be deafened by the high-pitched noise of the blower. And, of course, ever since I have been able to boast that I was the first person ever to be pressurized in a Spitfire cockpit.'[59]

For the Spitfire test pilot Don Robertson, the experience of flying the Mark VI was unpleasant:

> The hood was held in place with four cam-type levers, the handles of which were pushed home with the pilot's elbows. It was rather like sealing oneself in one's own coffin and, although I do not suffer from claustrophobia, I did not

---

* Longitudinal stability allows the fuselage to be held horizontal in level flight. Lateral stability means that the wings can easily be maintained in a horizontal attitude. In *A Test Pilot's Story*, Jeffrey Quill defined longitudinal instability as 'the tendency of the aircraft to diverge away from the condition of steady flight if once disturbed'.

like it. There was also the danger of suffocation in the event of the failure of the mechanical pump. On coming down from altitude the interior of the wind-screen would mist up and the cockpit became unbearably hot.[60]

Another memory of the Spitfire's pressurized cabin emerges from the unpublished memoir of Flight Lieutenant J. Hall, who joined the RAF Volunteer Reserve in 1938 and later became part of the RAF's weather squadron, flying at high altitude to provide meteorological reports. What is particularly appealing about his recollection is the eulogy to the Spitfire. The weather-squadron Spitfire, Hall wrote, was

> quite fascinating to fly, no runway, no radio, no controller sitting on his throne, telling us what to do, we just had to use our own initiative and keep our eyes open. The Spitfires used to climb to 40,000 feet every day; mid-day. We didn't always make 40,000 feet but just had to keep going until the aircraft stalled. The canopy was bolted on like a diver's helmet and as the cockpit was rather small this gave a claustrophobic effect but it was forgotten as soon as we were air-borne. What a marvellous aeroplane. One had to be a bit careful taking off because the undercarriage was rather narrow and the enormous four-bladed propeller was going round one way with the wings naturally trying to counter-rotate. The real fun in flying the Spitfire was not to climb to 40,000 feet but to go low flying over the Norfolk countryside. With half-throttle we would be doing 240 mph and the lower you got the faster it seemed. It was like driving a very high-powered, high-geared sports car.

But Hall regretted the lack of armament on his 'met' Spitfire. 'Apparently some of our predecessors used to go looking for trouble instead of hurrying back home and so the Air Ministry decided we would hurry back sooner if they took our guns away! We were about as vulnerable as a virgin walking naked down Piccadilly.'[61]

As it turned out, the order for 350 Mark VI Spitfires was never completed, because the threat of high-flying German bombers did not materialize. In the end, only 97 were made, though the lessons of pressurization were applied to some later types. The thrust of Spitfire production for most of 1941 was con-centrated on the Mark V, whose main job at this time was to conduct fighter sweeps and carry out bomber-escort duties over northern France. This was part of the strategy conceived by Sholto Douglas and Leigh-Mallory, his 11 Group commander, to go on the offensive against Germany: 'We have stopped licking our wounds,' wrote Leigh-Mallory. 'We are going over to the offensive. Last year our fighting was desperate but now we are entitled to be more cocky.'[62] But such operations were disliked by most pilots, who saw them as dangerously pointless, putting lives at risk for no real gain. The

Spitfire squadrons had a taste of what it must have been like for the Luftwaffe crews during the Battle of Britain, flying over well-defended enemy territory against a tenacious opponent. The crucial differences were, however, that the Germans in 1940 had a far stronger, more deadly bomber force than the RAF had available in 1941; also, the Luftwaffe's attacks were geared towards the specific goal of attaining air supremacy in advance of an invasion, whereas Sholto Douglas had no tangible objective in mind beyond a desire to make trouble for the Germans.

After April 1941, when Hitler launched Operation Barbarossa against Russia, there was the additional aim of trying to help Britain's new Soviet allies by keeping German planes tied down on the western front, though the fighter sweeps failed hopelessly in this. At the start of the Russian campaign there were 300 German fighters in the west; by the end of July, despite the RAF offensive, the Luftwaffe felt able to withdraw around 100 planes from France. Meanwhile, Fighter Command was suffering. Between mid-June and the end of July – the period of the heaviest activity for squadrons – 123 fighter pilots and planes were lost.[63] Wilfrid Duncan Smith, one of the great Spitfire aces, wrote of this period, 'We were living all this time under constant tension with long, freezing sorties into hostile skies punctuated by moments of combat from which we returned wringing wet and exhausted.'[64] He argued that experience of fighting over France had a draining effect on morale:

> If you escaped by parachute or crash-landed, it was into a hostile world and final escape meant a trip to Spain via extreme hardship full of danger, perhaps by freezing to near death in the Pyrenees, perhaps starvation in a Spanish prison. Morale stems from self-confidence and self-confidence can only be instilled by leadership, superior tactics and equipment with which to fight the enemy on at least equal terms. I found therefore in the last weeks of the summer of 1941 morale at a low ebb because there is no doubt the Me 109s were able to pick off our fighter planes operating at extreme range, due to their superior performance and tactics which gave them space to operate. Coupled with this was the knowledge that no amount of fighting over France was going to win the war.[65]

There were various types of fighter operation over France. The ones that most reflected the spirit of Leigh-Mallory were known as 'circuses', in which formations of Spitfire wings, usually comprising three or more squadrons operating from Kent or Sussex bases like Biggin Hill and Tangmere, accompanied the RAF bombers on daylight raids over France and the Low Countries. The aim was not so much to inflict damage as to lure the Luftwaffe's fighters into the air, though the bombers loathed acting as bait. The Spitfire pilots were not thrilled either, given that they had to reduce their speed for the slow-moving Blenheims, making them more vulnerable to being bounced by the 109s.

In a combat diary he kept from the time of his being sent to 92 Squadron in April 1941, Neville Duke, one of the war's legendary Spitfire pilots, who later famously broke the world speed record with a Hawker Hunter jet, revealed his growing disillusion with Fighter Command's tactics. In one of his first entries, he wrote this appreciation of the Mark V: 'Wizard machines, equipped with two cannon and four machine guns, the new Merlin 45 engine, giving +12 boost on take-off and, although I haven't got my hands on one yet, they climb like monkeys.' His naive enthusiasm also shone through when he wrote, 'The ceiling is much better in these Spits – 38,000 feet is a cinch. The fight for height is, I think, the answer of the mastery of the air. The Hun is still above us but I believe we are on the right track. The cannons are another good thing; one is thus enabled to sit astern of a Hun and pump shells into it until pieces start falling off.' But his tune had changed after a couple of months in France. On 23 June he wrote of a circus accompanying Blenheims to Bethune:

> I was separated from the rest in the general mix-up and was attacked by five Me 109Fs near Le Touquet. One did a head-on attack; saw flashes from his guns and tracer whistling past. Gave him a burst and he skimmed just over me with white and black smoke coming from his engine. Claimed as a probable. Dog-fought with other four down to sea level. Hit by machine-gun bullets twice in the wing. Pretty warm time.

By August, the strain was beginning to tell. On the 7th he wrote, 'Lost squadron when jumped by some 109s and came back alone. Getting lots more opposition now. The German pilots appear to be pretty experienced blokes. Am getting a getting a little tired of circuses – am always getting shot at without a chance of shooting back.'[66]

Sergeant Jim Rosser of 72 Squadron described a sense of bewilderment on an early circus: 'We would cross the Channel in sections, line astern, climbing all the time. We always climbed into the sun, which was absolute hell; your eyes felt as though they were burning down into your head and within a few minutes you were saturated in sweat.' Rosser admitted that, on his first run, 'quite honestly I hadn't a clue what was going on. We flew in a sort of semi-circle over France, still in sections line astern, and then came out again. I never saw a single enemy aircraft but we must have been attacked because when we got home three of our Spits were missing.'[67]

One of the many brave Polish Spitfire pilots, Franciszek Kornicki, who flew with the Polish 303 Squadron, was struck by the toughness of the German response:

Sometimes they would attack in packs from several directions or would nibble at the edges or dive at terrific speed through the whole formation, starting from above the top wing, down to the Blenheims at 12,000 feet, firing at anything which might come within sight for a split second. It was all terribly fast, guns blazing all round, aircraft turning, diving and climbing in a series of individual dogfights, people getting hurt, aircraft being holed or exploding when hit by the big guns on the ground.[68]

Marginally more successful were the 'rhubarbs', which were small-scale, low-level raids, usually carried out by pairs of fighters using cloud cover, on ground targets like transport depots, goods vehicles, bridges, railways and gun installations. Peter Howard-Williams of 19 Squadron recalled that during 1941, 'I attacked alcohol distilleries, petrol lorries, wireless stations, gun sites and trains — it was very satisfying to see the steam shoot out of the boiler. But I should not exaggerate my prowess. Life in a fighter squadron generally consisted of 23 hours and 50 minutes of boredom with 10 minutes of sheer terror.'[69] That sense of terror came from the enemy defences, both in the air and through ground flak. Johnnie Johnson, one of the bravest men ever to fly a Spitfire, once called such raids 'bloody murder',[70] and said that he came to loathe them 'with a deep, dark hatred' since they 'usually yielded little more than a staff car'.[71] Squadron Leader Charlton Haw of 129 Squadron said of rhubarbs in a post-war interview, 'To my mind, the amount of damage did not warrant the risk. A lot of men were lost to light flak.'[72]

There were several other types of operation, including 'ramrods', which were another form of bomber-escort duties, 'Jim Crows', fighter patrols over the Channel, and 'roadsteads', low-level attacks on enemy shipping. Peter Howard-Williams described one such attack, in league with another Spitfire, on a German cargo ship off the French coast: 'We reduced speed to about 240 mph but continued our dive. I gave a long burst with cannons and machine guns at the rudder and steering gear and also at a gun which I could see mounted aft. I don't think they ever expected an attack from the direction of the coast and out of the sun.'[73] A few weeks after this Howard-Williams managed to catch a U-boat which had come to the surface. Peter Olver of 66 Squadron had a particular dislike of the maritime patrols. 'I recall some terrible times when the waves were not just three or four feet high, they could be several hundred feet high in the Atlantic . . . You couldn't be at nought feet like you were told, because you would be knocked into the sea. I hated it.'[74]

As Neville Duke's diary showed, there was some initial excitement over the arrival of the Mark Vs. Johnnie Johnson thought they were a big improvement in terms of armament and, more importantly, aileron control. 'In the air the difference in performance was quite remarkable, for the previous heavy stick pressures were greatly reduced and the rate of roll, at high speeds, was more than doubled. In other words, the lateral manoeuvrability of the Spitfire was improved tremendously with the introduction of metal ailerons.'[75] Winston Churchill, again showing his attention to detail, thought the Mark Vs were so good that he told Portal, the Chief of the Air Staff, that they should initially be kept in reserve until they could attack the Luftwaffe in heavy numbers. But Portal saw a virtue in giving the Germans an early surprise. On 7 March 1941 he wrote to Churchill telling of

> the advantage I expect to gain if the Germans treat all our Spitfires with greater respect after they have encountered the Mark V. The main point, as I see it, is that when the enemy finds himself in a position of advantage he may yet refrain from attack lest the Spitfires prove to be Mark Vs. A further point is that the confidence of the German fighter pilots will always be sapped by doubt as they commit themselves to a battle with Spitfires and the first requirement of success in an air battle is confidence in one's own superiority.[76]

Churchill remained unconvinced by this argument. 'It occurred to me that it would be a pity for the sake of using a few at a time to make the enemy a present of the knowledge of our spring fashions and that it would be better to wait until a really effective blow could be struck. In the last war the tanks were given away while we still only had a few.' Churchill also pointed out that it was illogical for Portal to argue that potential German wariness of the Mark V would be a gain for Fighter Command, since the whole aim of circuses was 'to bring the enemy to action in spite of his evasive tactics'. But Churchill said he would 'certainly not contest' whatever decision Portal took.[77]

Churchill had overrated the hitting power of both the Spitfire Mark V and Fighter Command. The campaign in northern France, Holland and Belgium turned out to be one of the more ill-conceived of the Spitfire's wartime adventures. Beyond providing experience for the fighter pilots, it achieved little. This is not to deny that the Spitfire pilots put up a tremendous fight in a hostile environment, as is shown by this combat report from Douglas Bader, who finally had his chance to lead his wing in battle after being kept on the sidelines for much of the Battle of Britain. Bader recorded that, on one sortie in July, he was flying over Gravelines at 14,000 feet when he intercepted an Me 109:

> I opened fire with a short one-second burst at about 150 yards. I found it easy to keep inside him on the turn and I closed up quite quickly. I gave him three more short bursts, the final one at 20 yards' range, as he slowed down very suddenly and I nearly collided with him. I did not see the result except one puff of white smoke halfway through. Squadron Leader Burton in my section watched

the complete combat and saw the Me 109's airscrew slow right down to ticking over speed and as I broke away the Me 109 did not half-roll or dive but just sort of fell away in a sloppy fashion quite slowly as though the pilot had been hit. Having broken away, I did not again see the Me 109 I attacked since I was engaged in trying to collect my squadron.'[78]

Johnnie Johnson wrote a lyrical account of a circus from Tangmere to Lille under Douglas Bader's leadership which resulted in a clash with 109s. As Johnson prepares to take off,

> the last few moments on the ground are full of tension . . . Vaguely I hear that the engine is perfect . . . The usual cockpit smell, that strange mixture of dope, fine mineral oil and high-grade fuel, assails the nostrils and is somehow vaguely comforting. I tighten my helmet strap, swing the rudder with my feet on the pedals, watch the movement of the ailerons when I waggle the stick and look at the instruments without seeing them, for my mind is racing on to Lille and the 109s.

As the Tangmere wing climbs towards France, much of the apprehension disappears: 'Although we are sealed in our tiny cockpits and separated from each other, the static from our radios pours through the earphones of our tightly fitting helmets and fills our ears with reassuring crackles. When the leader speaks, his voice is warm and vital, and we know full well that once in the air we are bound together by a deeper intimacy than we can ever feel on the ground.' That sense of intimacy is reinforced in combat, as the wing comes under attack from more than twenty 109s over Lille. 'The Messerschmitts come in close for the kill. At this range their camouflage looks dirty and oil-stained and one brute has a startling black-and-white spinner: In a hot sweat of fear I keep turning and turning and the fear is mingled with an abject humiliation that these bastards should single me out and chop me at their leisure.' But German overconfidence also gives Johnson his opportunity, as four Me 109s come roaring down at him: 'I see them in time and curve the shuddering, protesting Spitfire to meet them, for she is on the brink of a high-speed stall. They are so certain of my destruction that they are flying badly and I fasten on to tail-end Charlie.' Johnson gives him a burst of fire, but appears to cause little damage. He is then joined by Bader and another Spitfire pilot. The extra support gives him another chance to attack:

> The 109 is very close and climbing away to port . . . Time for a quick shot and no danger of losing the other two Spitfires if I don't get involved in a long tail chase. I line up my Spitfire behind the 109, clench the spade-grip handle of the stick with both hands and send short bursts into his belly at less than a hundred yards. The 109 bursts apart and the explosion looks exactly the same as a near

burst of heavy flak, a vicious flower with a poisonous glowing centre and black swirling edges.

After Bader has shot down another of the 109s, the sky suddenly becomes clear. The rest of the Messerschmitts have vanished. The Bader wing returns to Tangmere.[79]

Jean Offenberg, another courageous Tangmere pilot, was a native Belgian who joined the RAF in 1940 after the occupation of his country. In the journal he kept during 1941 he left several vivid descriptions of dogfights over France. One took place on 5 May over Cherbourg, when, just after shooting down a Heinkel, he saw a pair of Messerschmitts flying in from the east:

I turned north. An Me followed suit and I could see the black crosses on his wings. Flying at the same height, we converged on a point, almost head-on. I gave him the first burst and pulled hard on the stick to avoid a collision. Luckily the German had the bright idea of diving. I sped northwards. My good Spitfire behaved beautifully and the engine purred with a regularity that gladdened my heart. I was now being chased by two Mes, one on each flank. In my mirror I could see that they were not more than 500 yards ahead. I zoomed violently on a right-hand climbing turn and the moment the first appeared in my gonio* I let him have it and then without waiting banked to the left and fired at the second from 90°. Out of the corner of my eye I saw my Messerschmitt in a shallow dive with a trail of white smoke coming from his engine. He disappeared below my right wing. I thought it best to get away as quickly as possible from these waters and make for home.[80]

In another attack, on 22 June, Offenberg had been flying at over 20,000 feet above Dunkirk when he became involved in a series of dogfights which brought him down to about 1,200 feet. Just as he was levelling out over Gravelines, he came across another 109 hedge-hopping over the sand dunes:

What that cretin was doing was terribly dangerous in these waters. I set off in hot pursuit and easily caught up with him. I must be calm. My mask irritated me and I tore it from my face. 500 yards . . . 300 . . . 200 . . . and I gave him a short burst. I was terribly busy in the cockpit for with my left hand I was obliged to wipe my windscreen, which was covered with ice, while keeping my eye on an Me 109F who was cavorting about inland rather higher than ourselves. I broke away to the left to 100 yards and immediately got on his tail again. At 100 yards I opened fire . . . I was almost on top of him. I broke away, perhaps at 20 yards . . . Glycol streamed from the Me and covered my windscreen as I flew inward at altitude zero.

* Goniometer – an instrument for measuring angles and range.

Moments later one of the 109s he had been fighting earlier reappeared. Offenberg's extraordinary self-assurance was again apparent:

> I let him approach. I bet that Hun was singing his paean of victory over the radio. When he was at 300 yards, I banked violently to the left. My wing almost touched the water. He tried to follow me, firing as he went. My turn was too tight for him ever to get me. I saw his wings vibrating. In a moment he would be in a spin. I went on banking until I found myself facing north. Then I streaked away in a straight line a few feet above the water; this gives one an extraordinary sense of speed and power. The water beneath me passed at a giddy speed. The Me did not follow; he must have lost his nerve.[81]

Tragically, Offenberg, died in January 1942 when he collided with another Spitfire on a training exercise.

Overall, the Spitfires paid a terrible price for their missions over France. Squadrons took heavy punishment with little real damage having been inflicted on the enemy. Great Spitfire aces were lost in battle: the hardened Irishman Paddy Finucane was shot down over the Channel and drowned when his Spitfire sank immediately. Douglas Bader proved he was not indestructible when he had to bail out from his Spitfire in August, losing one of his tin legs in the process as he parachuted to earth, where he was taken as a prisoner of war, spending the next four years making life miserable for his German guards.

A similar experience was endured by the Canadian pilot Brian Hodgkinson, shot down in a fighter sweep over France in October 1941 when his squadron of Mark Vs was hugely outnumbered by 109s. The sky, recalled Hodgkinson, became 'a maelstrom of twisting and spiralling aircraft. We were totally out of formation, every man jack diving for his very life. It was absolute chaos.' Hodgkinson made a desperate effort to escape the Messerschmitts. 'Not even bothering to look behind me, I levered the spade grip of the control column hard to starboard and slammed on bottom rudder with all the force I could muster. The Spitfire responded obediently to the violent manoeuvre. As for me, it seemed that every "G" in the book was pulling my eyes from their sockets and rearranging the skin on my face.' Hodgkinson went into a screaming spiral, but still he could not evade the Germans, as a stream of bullets ripped through his aircraft. 'My instrument panel exploded in a shower of shattered glass and mutilated circuitry and the 1,500 horses of the Rolls-Royce Merlin coughed sickeningly and spluttered their last. Deprived of power in the rarefied atmosphere, my mortally wounded plane fluttered and yawed like a spent hawk.' Soon the plane was ablaze. 'Within seconds the merciless heat had begun to barbecue my feet and legs and the closed cockpit rapidly filled with the acrid fumes of burning metal. Coughing and choking, I reached up and fumbled for the latch to release the canopy.' At first the hood was jammed, but summoning up all his physical strength he managed to release it. Barely conscious, he bailed out at 31,000 feet, though the twisting and swaying of the parachute made him violently sick. At about 1,000 feet he saw an Me 109 heading straight towards him. Convinced he was going to be blown to pieces, 'I raised my right hand, as painful as it was, and saluted my about-to-be executioner.' But the German pilot, in a spirit of chivalry, did not open fire. Instead, he raised his hand in an answering salute. A few seconds later, Hodgkinson landed on the ground and passed out. He woke up to find himself in German custody.[82]

Squadron Leader Pat Gibbs of 616 Squadron was more lucky. His Spitfire was badly shot up over Le Touquet, but he managed to crash-land in a stubble field. He then embarked on an incredible journey through occupied France. This involved being sheltered by the resistance in Paris, a long train journey down the west coast using forged identity papers, and incarceration in a Vichy jail before crossing the Pyrenees by foot. Eventually, after reaching Gibraltar, he was flown back to England, three months after he had been brought down.[83]

Buck McNair, the heroic Canadian Spitfire pilot, had the misfortune to come down in the sea when on a circus in October 1941. Low on ammunition and ready to turn for home, he suddenly came under fire from a 109 that flew out of the sun before McNair could see him. 'He hit my engine and blew off the cowling. I got right down on the water and tried to out-turn him, but had to be careful as I didn't want to do a high-speed stall right above the sea. I could see and feel his heavy cannon shells hitting my aircraft, and every once in a while the rattle of machine-guns bullets hitting the machine too. The smell of cordite was getting ever stronger in the cockpit.' True to his reputation for extraordinary courage, McNair managed to get a shot at the Me 109 before his plane burst into flames. He struggled to 400 feet above the water, and then the Spitfire stalled. Even at this low height, he had no choice but to bail out, since there was little chance of survival if the Spitfire ditched in the sea. His parachute opened just at the moment he hit the water. He then managed to open up his dinghy, clambered on board, and started paddling towards England before he was picked up by a British rescue launch.[84]

McNair's time in his dinghy, however, paled beside that of John Carver, commanding officer of 118 Squadron. Carver's Spitfire was shot down on 13 March 1942 while escorting bombers over the Channel Islands. Using his paddle and living off the emergency rations in his escape kit, Carver travelled 33 miles towards England over the next fifty-eight hours, snatching a few moments of sleep at night curled up in the dinghy. Just seven miles off Portland, he was picked up by a cargo ship. His experience, one of the great solo survival efforts of the war, earned him the DFC, though he was killed in combat over France a few months later.[85]

The spirit of resilience, one of the powerful themes of the RAF's wartime experience, was never better captured than in an unpublished report by E. G. Brettell, a pilot who was badly injured over Saint-Omer in September 1941. His account, written soon after the incident, is remarkable for its honesty, its description of raw courage, its creation of atmosphere, and its testimony to human willpower and the strength of Mitchell's design. Flying at 13,000 feet, Brettell had seen two 109s and was determined to take them on. But, as he climbed in their direction, he quickly found himself in the centre of a large gaggle of Messerschmitts:

> I don't remember feeling frightened, only highly interested and thoroughly keyed up. I took a lot of evasive action and the Huns did a lot of inaccurate shooting, till it began to look as though I could float about all afternoon without being hit. I fired a short burst of half deflection at a 109E and knocked pieces from his radiator, releasing a storm of glycol and hoped the thing would catch fire and explode. I was very angry; I am always angry with the Luftwaffe and passionately desire its total annhilation. I tried to outclimb all the 109s into the sun, in order to start attacking from out of it. I have so often seen large German formations routed by very few English machines that it seemed worth trying and there would probably be one or two stooges who might give me a target.

But Brettell's plan did not work:

> In turning to fox a dual attack from the port side I gave a momentary opening for two more to close in behind me. Before I could rectify this, a series of loud metallic bangs occurred and large holes, appearing first in the starboard wing tip, swept straight inboard to the fuselage. Then there was a terrific bang inside the cockpit and something feeling like a steam hammer hit me on the back of the head . . . Complete darkness descended and I hadn't the energy to move a finger. I felt myself fading away, as though going under an anaesthetic. There was nothing left but pitch darkness and a pain behind my right ear. But a tiny corner of my mind, aloof from everything else, still seemed to be functioning and I remember thinking, detachedly, in the dark, 'So after all it has happened to me too . . . It's come to you, who have always told yourself there's some way out of every scrape. But there's no way out of this one, buddy, because you are quite blind and you haven't the strength to move a muscle and you are diving down towards the sea at an enormous speed with a lot of 109s on your tail, ready to polish you off very quickly if you show any signs of revival.'

But then consciousness and sight began to return. 'The darkness was no longer black. It was turning red. Very dimly, as though through ultra-dark red glasses, I began to make out the nose of the Spitfire, pointing straight down towards a dark red sea.' Seconds later Brettell regained full consciousness and recognized that the plane, for all the punishment it had taken, could still fly: 'I began to pull the Spitfire out of the dive, weaving all the time. She was mushy and sluggish, so that I knew the elevators had been hit.' But the Spitfire somehow kept going, while the shooting from the Me 109s on Brettell's tail grew increasingly wild. He took the aircraft down to 1,000 feet, struggling to keep control because of his injuries:

> There was blood all over the place, masses of it, pouring over my knees and unaccountably splashing the windscreen. I am not affected by the sight of blood, or at least not my own, but I knew I was losing rather a lot. The Spitfire was slow because of its injuries, which was annoying as a Mark V will normally leave a 109 at sea level. Two or three times when the Huns got too close I had to turn and mix it for a little while to stop them closing right in on my tail but we gradually approached England.

All the time Brettell was fighting to stay alert, with the blood still pouring from his wounds.

Within 8 miles of the English coast, the last of the Messerschmitts turned back to France:

> As I saw the 109s disappearing I remember thinking, 'Well, how many of you sods *does* it take to shoot a Spitfire down?' which was extremely foolish considering it has sometimes only taken one. So I made Hawkinge. I could feel myself getting weaker and weaker: I had to screw my willpower up for several seconds to lower the wheels and lower the flaps. As I held off to land I brightened up a bit, knowing the job was nearly done, and with infinite concentration made quite a decent landing.

He was immediately taken to Folkestone hospital, where he was given urgent blood transfusions and had surgery on his smashed head. There followed a long period of recuperation in Torquay before he could resume his duties.[86]

Brettell's ordeal had been a tribute to the Spitfire's ability, in the right hands, to match even the latest Messerschmitt. But the Germans had now produced a fighter in an entirely different class – one that make the Mark V look distinctly inferior. Johnnie Johnson described being on a mission in November 1941 when 'we were puzzled by the unfamiliar silhouettes of some of the enemy fighters, which seemed to have squarer wing-tips and more tapering fuselages than the Messerschmitts we usually encountered.' Some in Johnson's squadron said that these fighters had large radial engines;

LIBYA
Help them finish the job

of Britain's wartime resistance. A poster raising funds for the North African campaign.

A photo-
reconnaissance
Spitfire Mark IX
seen through a rol
of mesh, used in
making temporary
airstrips, Holland,
January 1945.

A clipped-wing M
XII, powered by t
mighty Rolls-Roy
Griffon engine, fly
over the Sussex co

The Sicily campai
1943. A Spitfire c
in to land on an
airstrip cut out of
wheat field, watch
by local farmers.

Spitfires of 242
Squadron in Cors
preparing for the
Allied invasion of
southern France,
1944.

near-tragedy.
Seafire, the
navalized version of
the Spitfire, goes
over the edge of the
carrier HMS *Hunter*.
Fortunately, the pilot
was rescued from the
water.

Spitfire Mark V,
flown by Squadron
Leader E. J. 'Jumbo'
Gracie, takes off
from HMS *Eagle* in
the Mediterranean,
bound for Malta.
The Spitfires'
defence of the island
in 1942 was to play
a crucial part in
turning the tide of
the war in the North
African theatre.

The Spitfire as
bomber. Armourers
loading up a Mark
IX in Normandy.

Above left: Sir Hugh Dowding, head of Fighter Command during the Battle of Britain. He saw the potential of the Spitfire earlier than any other RAF chief.

Above right: Keith Park, the New Zealander who commanded the vital 11 Group of Fighter Command in 1940. His pilots admired him; colleagues found him 'a difficult customer'.

Left: Trafford Leigh-Mallory who succeeded Park as commander of 11 Group. Critics saw him as excessively ambitious and conspiratorial

Right: A Spitfire manoeuvres into position to deflect a V-1 flying bomb from its target.

Middle: Inspection and servicing of a Mark XIV in the mud of Belgium.

Below left: The greatest Spitfire ace of them all, Johnnie Johnson, who achieved 38 victories during the war. He is pictured here with his devoted Labrador, Sally.

Below right: The great New Zealand ace Colin Gray. During the Battle of Britain, he shot down 14 Lutfwaffe planes, and probably destroyed or damaged another 14.

Left: 'Bright, alert and dominating' – the brilliant Supermarine test pilot Jeffrey Quill, whose advice to Spitfire engineers proved invaluable.

Below: The Castle Bromwich test pilot Alex Henshaw, pictured here with Winston Churchill. Renowned for his daring and aerobatic skill, Henshaw flew more Spitfires than any other man. 'His wizardry with his beloved Spitfires lives in my memory,' recalled one Castle Bromwich employee.

Above: George Unwin of
19 Squadron, stepping out
of his cockpit. He called
the Spitfire 'the perfect
flying machine'.

Right: The tough, ruthless
South African Adolph
'Sailor' Malan.

Last of the line. Three Spitfire Mark 22s flying over Castle Bromwich in March 1945. 'The classic lines had been replaced by forceful features,' wrote Alex Henshaw.

Israeli soldiers stand on the wreck of an Egyptian Air Force Spitfire shot down during the conflict of 1948 – the only time in history when Spitfires fought against each other.

others warned that they had a lethal mix of cannon and machine guns, all firing from the wing. 'Whatever these strange fighters were, they gave us a hard time of it. They seemed faster in a zoom climb than the Spitfire, far more stable in a vertical dive, and they turned better than the Messerschmitt, for we all had our work cut out to shake them off.'[87] The new fighters, described by Johnson as high-performing 'brutes', turned out to be Focke-Wulf 190s, the fast and fearsome plane designed by Kurt Waldemar Tank. With its large, 14-cylinder radial engine, the Fw 190 was capable of 389 mph, handled well, had a tight turn, and packed a savage punch.

If the Spitfire was to remain the RAF's key fighter, it would have to find a way of dealing with the Fw 190, which was delivered to the Luftwaffe in increasing numbers during the autumn of 1941. Some even thought that this new leap in German performance was bound to spell the demise of the Spitfire. In 1942, Dowding, now in disgruntled retirement, sent an extraordinary letter to Churchill declaring the Sptifire all but obsolete. The architect of the Battle of Britain wrote that

> it is not only in performance that the Fw 190 has the Spitfire beaten. It has superior hitting power as well. Performance and hitting power are the two basic essentials of the Day Fighter . . . The defence of the country is the keystone of war and it is once again in jeopardy. One may conjure a quart out of a pint pot but one can't get a gallon. The Spitfire has been moribund for two years and died when the Fw 190 made its appearance.[88]

Dowding should have known better. It was far too early to write off the Spitfire.

10

'No place for beginners'

THE LAST MONTHS of 1941 and much of 1942 were Britain's grimmest period of the war. Defeats and setbacks were experienced in almost every theatre, from northern Europe to North Africa. In the Far East, Singapore fell on 15 February 1942, when the Japanese conquered a numerically stronger British force. The surrender was described by A. J. P. Taylor as 'the greatest capitulation in British history'.[1]

Despite the excellence of its fighting qualities, the Spitfire was inadvertently caught up in this cycle of despair and failure. One of the most farcical humiliations occurred in February 1942, when a mixture of epic incompetence, complacency and poor communications allowed a flotilla of German warships, led by the battlecruiser *Scharnhorst*, to escape from the French Atlantic port of Brest and sail right up the English Channel and back to Germany. The German vessels had been holed up for months in Brest, subjected to continual assaults by Bomber Command. Yet when they moved out under the cover of darkness there was just one single RAF reconnaissance plane in the area, and it saw nothing. The first sighting was not actually made until just after ten o'clock on the morning of 12 February, when Bobby Oxspring, now in 41 Squadron, was carrying out a fighter sweep over the Channel. 'Banking into a turn we peered down through the rain and sighted a large oval of destroyers and smaller escorts in the middle of which were three larger ships in line astern; all were leaving creamy waves indicting that the force was moving fast. My first reaction that the Royal Navy was a bit off course was soon dispelled when we saw the flak guns on the deck firing at us,' he recalled. Oxspring climbed into a cloud and then, breaking the strict rule on radio silence, reported to base what he had seen. His radio message was intercepted by the German military, who expected that the RAF would imminently come down in large numbers on the convoy. But there was no reaction. Even when Bobby Oxspring landed at Biggin Hill and telephoned 11 Group headquarters, 'I got nowhere in conveying the seriousness of the situation.'[2]

Disgracefully, it was not until the *Scharnhorst* and the other German ships were in the Strait of Dover that the RAF finally went into action. Even then, response was pitifully inadequate. Based in England there were at least 242 planes from Bomber Command ready to take part, with potential escorts of almost 500 Spitfires and Hurricanes. In addition, Coastal Command had 36 torpedo-dropping Beaufighters on standby. But instead, partly because they still disbelieved the seriousness of the reports, the RAF and the Royal Navy decided to send along a section of ageing Fairey Swordfish torpedo-carrying biplanes, which would have looked more at home during the First World War than the Second. Known as 'Stringbags' because of their complex lattice of struts and spars, the Swordfishes were accompanied by Spitfires as cover. But it was a hopeless mix, since the Swordfish's maximum speed, around 100 mph, was only just above the Spitfire's stalling speed. 'The only way to hold them in view without spinning into the sea ourselves was to sweep behind them in large, loose figures of eight,' recalled Brian Kingcome of 72 Squadron, who was struck by the contrast between the huge German battlecruiser and the tiny, fragile biplanes, which he described as 'struggling museum relics'.[3] Also involved in the attack was 411 Squadron, led by Bill Ash, the American Spitfire pilot who had joined the RAF in 1940 through his abhorrence of Nazism:

> The Spitfires guarded the Swordfishes as best we could but the wall of German aircraft was keeping us busy from above and the waves of anti-aircraft fire blazing from below added to our sense of being trapped between a hammer and an anvil. Each of us was twisting and turning, trying to stay out of the thick of the red and green flak surging up while also engaging with the 109s, which were out in incredible force and had the advantage of altitude.[4]

The Swordfishes, led by Eugene Esmonde, showed bravery beyond comprehension as they flew straight into the flak of the German naval guns. It was all but a suicide mission: 'They were flying unswerving to certain destruction,' wrote Kingcome, 'and all we as their escort could do was sit helplessly in the air above them and watch them die.'[5] All six Swordfish crews were shot down. A few of the crew members were picked up by British rescue boats, but most of them were killed before they even hit the water. The German ships escaped through the Channel almost unscathed, though some were subsequently damaged by sea mines. In the aftermath of the disaster, Esmonde was awarded the Victoria Cross. The military establishment was rewarded with a secret inquiry and a cover-up for conduct far less gallant.

The military commanders proved equally culpable a few months later during the botched raid on Dieppe in August 1942, though again, as with the 'Channel Dash', the RAF pilots themselves emerged with great credit.

Operation Jubilee, the code name for the Anglo-Canadian landings on the French coastal town of Dieppe, was meant to take place in June, but bad weather led to its postponement until 19 August. Like the fighter sweeps over France, the Dieppe raid did not have a clear and realistic objective. It was aimed more at boosting morale, showing support for Russia by creating a diversion on the western front, gaining experience of landings, and generally harassing the enemy through the destruction of local defences, power stations and docks. But the Allies paid a high price for these limited goals. Of the ground force of 6,000 men, almost half were killed or captured. While the RAF's losses were small compared to this, amounting to just 53 men killed and 17 captured, 97 planes were destroyed, compared to total Luftwaffe losses of 48.[6] In their biggest operation since the Battle of Britain, the Spitfires bore the brunt of the air fighting, with 48 squadrons involved. During the exhausting day, 59 Spitfires were shot down and 31 badly damaged.

The main tasks of the Spitfires, organized by Leigh-Mallory from the headquarters of 11 Group, were to provide escorts for the bombers and defensive air cover for the landing forces. Many of them were flying almost continuous missions throughout the day between Britain and the French coast. Bobby Oxspring, with 72 Squadron, took off at six o'clock in the morning on his first sortie:

> Approaching the French coast we were greeted by an incredible spectacle. Ships of all sizes ploughed around the Channel Islands within a few miles of the beaches. Navy warships blasted off intermittent broadsides at inland targets, whilst around the harbour and beyond brilliant flashes and explosions erupted in every direction. Great palls of smoke drifted away with the wind, and at all heights in the restricted area squadrons of Spitfires swung up and down their allotted lines.[7]

For Johnnie Johnson, his first flight of the day was his most savage, for he became embroiled in a deadly chase with an Fw 190, which had already proved itself clearly superior to the Mark V. 'I asked the Spitfire for all she'd got in the turn; but the 190 hung behind like a leech and it could only be a question of time, and not much of that. Stick over and well forward and I plunged into a near-vertical dive – a dangerous manoeuvre, for the 190 was more stable and faster than my Spit in such a descent.' Johnson managed to escape by levelling out from the dive, ramming his throttle into the emergency position, and then heading straight for a Royal Navy destroyer, the Fw still in aggressive pursuit. The fighter pilots had been briefed not to fly below 4,000 feet over the shipping, otherwise the navy would open fire. Sure enough, flak opened up against Johnson from the destroyer, but he was going so fast he managed to avoid it. At the last moment he lifted his plane over the ship, by which time he had lost the 190. 'Either the flak had put him off or, better still, nailed him.'[8]

An equally tense encounter with an Fw 190 was recorded in the diary of Lee Gover, an enthusiastic American, who flew with 66 Squadron. His job in the late afternoon of the battle was to escort the Douglas Boston bombers which had been instructed to lay a smokescreen across the shore to cover the withdrawal of the commandos from Dieppe, the landings already having proved to be a disastrous failure:

> We went in at sea level and two of the Bostons were shot down right in front of me. I was about 250 yards from the shore and the German guns were spraying hell out of things. Large cannon shells were bursting all around, and cannon shells were hitting the water and shooting up tall columns of water . . . The beach was covered with fallen commandos. About 2 miles on the way home we were jumped by a gaggle of Focke-Wulf 190s. One was right on me and getting hits, so I pushed full left rudder and his bullets struck the water beside me. He turned and shot my number two straight into the sea. Then the third man in our threesome was shot down and I was now all alone. I weaved to beat hell and come home balls out. Saw three more pilots in the water in their little yellow dinghies. They sure looked lonely bobbing about in that mess.[9]

As always in combat, the physical toughness of the Spitfire was demonstrated at Dieppe. Miroslav Liskutin, who flew with his native Czechoslovakian 313 Squadron, had an incredible experience in the afternoon. Patrolling at 8,000 feet to protect the withdrawing Allied troops from German bombers, he caught sight of a Fw 190 and managed to get in behind it: 'A short burst from my guns caught his right wing, producing a spray of silvery sparks.' But then Liskutin came under fire from another Fw 190:

> I saw two glowing white rods appearing just above my head, accompanied by a rattling sound throughout my cockpit with the smell of cordite filling my cockpit . . . My reaction was quick and I think completely instinctive, to get out of his gunsight! I stepped on the rudder, applied full ailerons, throttled back the engine, and pulled back on the elevators. My Spitfire performed a violent flick roll. Never before had I experienced violence like it. Keeping the controls in extreme positions I continued deliberately with a spin.

The manoeuvre worked. Levelling out in cloud at 4,000 feet, Liskutin found that the Fw 190 had disappeared. But the ailerons of his Spitfire had been badly damaged. He discovered that he could stay in level flight only with full aileron deflection, which required an enormous physical effort. He did not think he could sustain this the whole way over Dieppe and then across the

Channel. 'Tiredness was overwhelming me and the pain in my arms felt unbearable. It was difficult to suppress thoughts about abandoning the aircraft because my physical state was becoming marginal.' Yet, determined to fall neither into German hands nor into the icy waters, he staggered on. Suddenly, when he was almost overcome by paralysing cramp, he remembered that the Spitfire carried a crowbar inside the cockpit door: 'Experimenting with the possible use of this tool, I found it could be placed against the side of the fuselage in such a way as to take up some of the unbearable strain. And it worked!' Liskutin now had the glimmer of hope that he could reach England. To his elation, almost anaesthetized by pain, he not only flew over the coast but found that his bullet-ridden plane could even keep going to his base in Redhill, Surrey. Without any flaps on the Spitfire, he had to touch down at 165 mph, but, with delicate handling of the brakes and some astute zig-zagging across the airfield, he landed perfectly, pulling up safely without any further damage.[10]

The Dieppe raid achieved none of its immediate objectives. The German defences in France remained as strong as ever, while the weakness of Allied inter-service co-operation and intelligence had been exposed. Yet, amid all the gloom throughout much of 1942, there was one outstanding success, a remarkable defensive triumph against the odds which ultimately would prove one of the turning points in the European war. And, just as in the Battle of Britain, the Spitfire was to play a central role in this victory.

By the spring of 1942 the island of Malta in the Mediterranean had been under siege for almost two years. Despite its small size and population, Malta had decisive strategic significance – 'the master key to the British Empire' was how Churchill described it.[11] For the Allies it was a vital link in the routes between Gibraltar, North Africa and the Middle East. For the Axis powers it represented a serious threat to shipping in the Mediterranean, particularly to the dispatch of reinforcements and supplies for Erwin Rommel's Afrika Korps. In the first two years of the war, Allied aircraft, destroyers and submarines based in Malta sank or damaged over half a million tons of Axis shipping.[12] With Germany occupied in the west and in Russia, the task of subjugating the island initially fell to the Italians. But their belief that this would be a straightforward operation for the Regia Aeronautica, the Italian air force, was badly mistaken. In terms of equipment, Malta's air defences were woefully inadequate, comprising just three Gladiator biplanes and a series of anti-aircraft guns. But these limitations were balanced by the determination of the Gladiator pilots. Having expected little resistance to their raids, the Italians were surprised to find the elderly biplanes, known affectionately by the Maltese people as *Faith*, *Hope* and *Charity*, putting up a fierce contest – so much so that Italian bombers had to be given fighter escorts. With the Italians shaken by their inability to achieve a quick victory, the RAF took the opportunity to reinforce the island's defences with batches of Hurricane fighters. Because of their limited range, the planes had to be flown from Royal Navy carriers sailing in the Mediterranean.

Exasperated by the failure of the Italians and the continuing damage to German supply lines in the Mediterranean, the Luftwaffe entered the fray in early 1941, building up its air fleets in Sicily, bombarding airfields, and using Stuka dive-bombers on the large Allied naval base in the Maltese capital of Valletta. 'Situation regarding air superiority has gravely deteriorated. It has completely passed into the enemy's hands. Enemy is obviously set on eliminating our fighters and has gone a considerable way to achieving this end,' warned Malta's governor Sir William Dobbie in a cable to Portal, Chief of the Air Staff.[13] Still the island managed to hold out, until in April 1941 the Luftwaffe was diverted from southern Italy to the Russian front. The assault was eased as the inept Italians took over once more. But the respite could not last long. In January 1942 Germany decided that the Maltese problem must be resolved. The presence of an Allied island fortress so near the Axis's southern flank had become intolerable, especially with the war in North Africa reaching a critical stage. A full-scale attack was now organized. As in the Battle of Britain, the Luftwaffe aimed to destroy the island's military infrastructure as a precursor to invasion.

Between 21 January and 24 February, the Germans flew nearly 2,000 bomber sorties over the island, accompanied by the deadly Me 109s. More than a thousand tons of bombs fell on the island in February. Outnumbered and outclassed, the valiant Hurricane squadrons were no match for this overwhelming force. As the Luftwaffe tightened its grip, the position of Malta became increasingly desperate. Convoys could not get through, nor could the navy operate from Valletta. Food supplies were rapidly dwindling. Dysentery, tuberculosis and polio were rife. The armed forces and the population were compelled to survive on brutally short rations, comprising little more than a few slices of bully beef and dried biscuits. The Colonial Secretary, Lord Cranborne, warned Churchill, 'Unless supplies can be substantially replenished over the next two months, the fortress will be within measurable distance of falling into enemy hands.'[14] But help was about to appear over the horizon.

For weeks, the RAF commander of Malta, the combative Air Vice-Marshal Sir Hugh Pughe Lloyd, had been appealing for Spitfires – the one weapon that could effectively challenge the Germans. At the beginning of February, Lloyd had only twenty-eight serviceable Hurricanes left. The government agreed that every effort must be taken to reinforce Malta's air defences by sending a squadron of Spitfires, despite some reluctance from Sholto Douglas to reduce his fighter and pilot numbers at home. But, as with the Hurricanes, there was the problem of the Spitfire's lack of range, for the island could not be reached by a normal Mark V Spitfire from bases in Gibraltar or Egypt. So the solution proposed was to fly the Spitfires, with specially adapted 90-gallon drop tanks, from an aircraft carrier, HMS *Eagle*, in the western Mediterranean. There were several postponements of this adventure because of poor weather and technical problems, which caused more irritation to Lloyd. 'Must have more fighters as soon as possible. Delay in Spitfires is annoying,' he telegraphed the RAF command in Egypt.[15]

Eventually, on 7 March, the sixteen Spitfires were ready for their 700-mile journey from the *Eagle*, off the coast of Algiers, to Malta. They had been brought by ship from Liverpool to Gibraltar in large wooden crates before being partially reassembled on the quayside by teams of expert RAF fitters. The operation was carried out under cover of darkness, for fear of German spies. With the help of a lorry-mounted Coles crane, the wooden boxes were taken apart, allowing access to the aircraft's two main parts, the fuselage and the wings (or 'mainplanes'). One of the fitters, S. J. Revell, who had travelled from England with the crates, recalled:

> The crane lifted the fuselage on a sling, pivoting on the tailwheel until a trestle could be positioned just aft of the bulkhead and the fuselage was then lowered on to the trestle. The mainplanes with supporting wooden frames were manhandled from the crate and, stripped of their supporting woodwork, were positioned adjacent to the fuselage. Then they were manhandled into position to allow a minimum number of root-end bolts to be inserted to secure the mainplane to the fuselage. With the mainplanes secured, the undercarriage was lowered and locked down.

The crane then hauled the Spitfire on to the flight deck of HMS *Eagle,* where the installation was completed of the other items: the propeller, rudder, elevators, armament, tailplane and 90-gallon drop tank.

The reassembly of the sixteen Spitfires took more than five nights to complete. Security remained a concern throughout. When fitting was being done on the flight deck, 'the Fleet Air Arm boys arranged some activity, such as ground-running Hurricanes, to camouflage the genuine bustle.'[16] The biggest problem was that the fuel flow in the drop tanks did not work properly because of damage caused during crating. Arthur Black, Supermarine's metallurgist, had to be flown out to Gibraltar to give emergency advice. The fact that Black turned up in full dinner dress, having been summoned out of a Supermarine function, was a measure of the urgency of his mission. With typical expertise, he immediately traced the fault to a defective transfer pipe and showed how it could be rectified.

Coming after a long sea passage around the Iberian peninsula, with poor accommodation on board, the delays added to a sense of frustration for some of the pilots. In Gibraltar the Australian pilot Sergeant Jack Yarra wrote caustically in his diary:

> The conditions are not fit for animals to live in . . . How the hell do they ever expect to win a war when they treat fighting men like cattle. This may seem rather hard but I am perfectly right and I am getting sick of seeing Churchill stick his bowler hat up on his cane so the populace hail him as their saviour and think we are winning the war. The sooner the people of England realize that we are losing this damned war so far, the better it will be for everyone.[17]

Part of his bitterness could be explained by anxiety. The Spitfires of the *Eagle* were not only the first fighters to be flown from outside British territory, they were also the first to take off from an aircraft carrier – a manoeuvre that required special skill on the part of the pilot, as well as a primitive temporary modification to the plane's wing. In order to get the necessary lift on take-off from the short strip of the carrier deck, the flaps were kept in a partially downward position by small blocks of wood wedged between the flaps and the wings. Once airborne, the pilots climbed to around 2,000 feet, dropped the flaps to allow the blocks to fall out, then quickly raised them again.

Despite the apprehension, all but one of the Spitfires took off successfully from the *Eagle* and reached Malta without incident. (The only pilot left behind was Jack Yarra, whose plane turned out to be unserviceable and he had to return to Gibraltar.) The Spitfires' arrival over the skies of the besieged island prompted an outburst of enthusiasm from a population which had been given precious little to celebrate in recent months, the public acclamation made all the greater by the lustre of the Spitfire's reputation from the Battle of Britain. As one reporter on Malta put it:

> There seemed to be a new sound in the air and it did not take the people long to identify the new aircraft which were zooming and hissing and whistling through the air. There they were, silvery streaks, skimming over the roof tops, climbing higher and higher and then diving straight to earth, vanishing behind the buildings, only to rise again at a speed never imagined possible before. The magic name was whispered from group to group; those who knew anything about them were showing off their knowledge.[18]

Flight Lieutenant Laddie Lucas, one of the pilots who had been under siege for weeks, left this description of the arrival of the first Spitfires at Takali, one of Malta's three airfields: 'Like small boys delving excitedly into their stockings at dawn on Christmas Day, so we rushed down to the airfield to touch and stroke our new toys. No Christmas or birthday morning in our short lives had ever produced such genuinely longed-for presents.'[19]

Yet this excitement, though understandable, was out of all proportion to the results that the Spitfires could achieve. The Luftwaffe was far too large for one single squadron to make much difference. Despite some strong resistance from the strengthened RAF, the bombardment remained savage. More Spitfires were desperately needed. On 27 March another squadron of Spitfires took off from the *Eagle*, among them one piloted by Jack Yarra. 'I was rather keyed up and my nerves were taut as stay-wires,' he wrote, 'but as soon as I opened the throttle I lost all my tautness and got that queer kick one always gets on the world's best fighter aircraft. The old Merlin sounded very sweet that morning as I raced down that little deck and lifted off the end.'[20]

There was nothing sweet about the combat zone into which the Spitfires were plunged, with the German attacks now more ferocious than ever. More bombs fell on Malta in March and April than on the whole of London in 1940. Over a thousand civilians were killed, and ten thousand homes were reduced to rubble. Convoys were still unable to reach the island because of the bombing, leading to a deepening crisis over supplies. Standing in queues for their meagre rations or at standpipes for their water, the people of Malta were struggling for their very survival. By the middle of April, the island appeared to be on the brink of starvation and defeat.

In the face of this crisis, the RAF resorted to cunning tactics to give the illusion of larger numbers. One brilliant trick was pulled off by Group Captain A. B. 'Woody' Woodhall, the hero of Duxford, who had taken over as controller in Malta and whose calm voice was a constant source of reassurance to the pilots. At one stage, when all the Spitfires were grounded for servicing, Woodhall decided to deceive the Luftwaffe into thinking that they were in the air. His ruse depended on knowing that the Germans were bound to pick up his radio messages. As Woodhall himself recorded:

> The Hun bombers came over in force with quite a large fighter escort. It happened that there were several fighter pilots with me in the Operations Room, one of whom was a Canadian with an unmistakable voice. I put him at the microphone at a stand-by radio set and proceeded to give him dummy orders. He replied just as if he was flying his fighter. This, we suspected, caused a cry of 'Achtung! Spitfeuer!' to go over the German radio. In any case, two 109s enthusiastically shot each other down without any British aircraft becoming airborne.[21]

But such deceit could be no substitute for real combat, and the pilots themselves knew it. 'A wave of depression set in,' recorded Paul Brennan. 'We felt impotent and helpless. There were so many targets and practically no air-craft with which to shoot at them. Most of us had to watch from the ground instead of fighting in the air, and we did not like it.'[22] The numbers of Spitfires coming off HMS *Eagle* were simply inadequate to make up for losses. Churchill recognized that drastic action was needed if Malta was to be saved. He decided on a personal appeal to US President Franklin Roosevelt, whose country had entered the war four months earlier, after Pearl Harbor. In a telegram of 1 April, Churchill wrote, 'Air attack on Malta is very heavy. There are now in Sicily 400 German and 200 Italian fighters and bombers. Malta can only now muster 20 or 30 serviceable fighters. We keep feeding Malta with Spitfires in packets of 16 loosed from the *Eagle* carrier from about 600 miles west of Malta. This has worked a good many times quite well but *Eagle* is now laid up for a month by defects in her steering gear.' Churchill further explained that other British carriers were either too small or slow to carry Spitfires:

> Therefore there will be a whole month without any Spitfire reinforcements. It seems likely from extraordinary enemy concentration on Malta that they hope to exterminate our air defence in time to reinforce either Libya or their Russian offensive. This would mean that Malta would be at best powerless to interfere with reinforcements or armour to Rommel and our chances of resuming offensive against him at an early date ruined.

Churchill therefore asked if Roosevelt would allow the use of the carrier USS *Wasp*, which could transport fifty or more Spitfires at a time. 'Instead of not being able to give Malta any further Spitfires during April a powerful Spitfire force could be flown into Malta at a stroke and give us a chance of inflicting a very severe and possibly decisive check on the enemy,' concluded the Prime Minister.[23]

Churchill's telegram further undermines the argument that he was a reck-less meddler, with no real grasp of military strategy. Without his crucial intervention, Malta might well have been lost and the entire conduct of the war in the Mediterranean would have been different. The President agreed to his request two days later. Forty-seven Spitfires were loaded on board the *Wasp*, docked on the river Clyde, on 13 April, and reached the western Mediterranean 35 miles north of Algiers a week later. The British pilots on board, used to cramped conditions and limited rations, were impressed with the American hospitality, which included ice cream and Coca-Cola, though there was no alcohol on board. On 20 April, the Spitfires lined up on deck ready for take-off. There was one moment of tragedy when a mechanic accidentally backed into a Spitfire's propeller and was cut to pieces. The pilot, a young Trinidadian, was ordered to fly on after an inspection had revealed no damage to his airscrew, a striking illustration of the harshness of war.

Despite this trauma, all the pilots managed to leave the ship successfully. They had been briefed for the journey by Squadron Leader E. J. 'Jumbo' Gracie, who had been on the first *Eagle* exercise. He told them that the best technique was to rev the engine up to 3,000 rpm on the brakes, then release them and select the emergency boost. Since the *Wasp*'s deck was longer than the *Eagle*'s, he promised that the take-off should be 'a piece of cake'. It was anything but that for Pilot Officer Michael Le Bas, whose experience could hardly have been more nerve-racking:

> The deck officer began rotating his chequered flag and I pushed forward my throttle until I had maximum rpm. His flag then fell and I released the brakes and I pushed the throttle to emergency override to get the last ounce of power out of my Merlin. The Spitfire picked up speed rapidly in its headlong charge down the deck but not rapidly enough. The ship's bows got closer and closer and still I had insufficient airspeed and suddenly – I was off the end. With only 60 feet to play before I hit the water, I immediately retracted the undercarriage and eased forward on the stick to build up my speed. Down and down with the Spitfire until, about 15 feet above the waves, it reached flying speed and I was able to level out. After what seemed an age but was in fact only a few seconds, my speed built up further and I was able to climb away. Nobody had told me about that in the briefing![24]

From radio interceptions, the Germans had advance warning of the arrival of the Spitfires from the *Wasp*. As the planes began to land, the airfields came under ferocious assault from 109s and Ju 88s. Sergeant Ray Hesselyn of 249 Squadron described the scene at Takali:

> I noticed one Spit with its wing tip sheared off. He was flying low down with a bunch of 109s above and was whistling around the circuit, waiting for a favourable moment to come and land. His damaged wing was plainly visible from the ground. About 18 inches of it was missing, and instead of the usual elliptical section of a Spit wing, it looked rather like the square-cut wing of a 109. Eventually the Spit came in but was hit. It went running past dispersal when the pilot whipped up his undercart, and skidded the aircraft along on its belly. It came to rest in a cloud of dust.[25]

John Bisdee of 609 Squadron thought that the Malta commanders had not thought through the preparations for receiving the planes, with refuelling, servicing and dispersal far too static: 'When we got there, the arrangements for meeting us were not very satisfactory and the aircraft were more or less in line being refuelled which was emphatically not a good idea.'[26] Thanks to the damage inflicted by the Germans over this and subsequent days, most of the Spitfires that arrived from the *Wasp* were soon put out of action. By 22 April, 9 had been destroyed on the ground, 26 damaged by bomb splinters and 8 destroyed in combat. Nevertheless, the few Spitfires that remained put up a courageous fight against the Luftwaffe, undaunted by the odds. Typical was this combat report on 21 April from the Australian Tim Goldsmith, describing being jumped by four 109Fs at 18,000 feet:

> I took evasive action, aileron turning down to about 6,000 feet and about 7 miles north of the Grand Harbour. Here one of the four enemy aircraft which had followed me down crossed my nose in a climbing turn to the left, at a range of 150 yards. I followed him round, opening fire with four cannons, observing strikes along the top of the mainplane and fuselage. After about two seconds, port cannons ceased firing, and I continued firing with starboard guns for two–three seconds. I then saw a large splash on the surface and the enemy aircraft was seen for a few seconds just under the water before disappearing.[27]

In a letter home to his wife, Squadron Leader Lord David Douglas-Hamilton, perhaps with a note of exaggeration, was full of praise for the mood of the pilots: 'You will have gathered from the press that we have raids every day and pretty heavy ones at that, but this place still holds out and it will continue to hold out . . . The boys here are simply marvellous – they have shot down masses of Huns for virtually no loss – it is a real honour to be with such chaps. My respect for the German pilots has gone down considerably – they are scared stiff of Spitfires!'[28]

Yet such optimism could not disguise the reality that Malta and its defences were taking a fearsome pounding. Courage alone could not make up for the lack of numbers in face of the overwhelming might of the enemy. Flight Lieutenant Tim Johnston was one of those on the receiving end of the Luftwaffe's firepower, when he was over Hal Far:

> Next instant, without warning, bang, bang, bang. I could hear and feel three cannon shells exploding at the bottom of my machine. I remember instinctively kicking on the rudder after the first explosion and feeling how futile it was as the other two followed in quick succession, as quickly as you can say three words, and then experiencing that sensation of insignificance and resignation that comes when you are suddenly overtaken by fate. I remember also that I realized that the aircraft was on fire.

Johnston then lost consciousness for a few seconds when his head hit the side of the cockpit. When he came to, he found the cockpit filling with flames:

My first thought was that this time it was certainly the end and that there must have been some mistake because I wasn't supposed to die . . . I can remember I noticed a curious smell. I don't know whether it was something burning or me being burnt; it was not so much unpleasant as entirely strange to me and it was this, not heat or pain, which was my most forcible physical sensation. I found out afterwards that my legs had been peppered with cannon splinters.

Even in his shattered state, Johnston had the strength to haul himself from his seat and bail out, before losing consciousness again just after pulling the rip-cord of his parachute. After falling to the ground, he was taken by the local Maltese to hospital.[29]

The sense of outnumbering the Spitfires shines through this report from the 109 pilot Walter Zellot, who was acting as an escort to the German bombers:

> I noticed a Spitfire firing at a Ju 88 from long range. I went right down behind the Spitfire and tried to chase it away with my machine guns. It would not break away and stayed behind the Ju 88, which kept shooting back. I could see that the Englishman was not hitting the bomber hard. I was close enough to fire at the Spitfire from a shallow left turn. At once, pieces flew off the aircraft. As he now saw me, he tried to get away doing a very sharp left turn, but while he was doing so I had the whole upper side of the aircraft in my sights. I did a right turn and was ready to fire again when I saw a parachute opening. The Spitfire tumbled over and crashed down in the sea. I then saw the parachute floating close to the oil slick which appeared in the water.[30]

The first *Wasp* mission could only be described as a failure, given the terrible losses endured by the Spitfires. Some pilots thought that Sir Hugh Lloyd was partly to blame for the inadequate preparations, which it was said exposed his wider lack of understanding of air defence. A functioning ground radar system, for instance, was only installed early in 1942, and many of the staff in the central operations had no proper grasp of how its information should be used. Lloyd's greatest concern, however, was that too many inexperienced pilots were being sent to the island, which he said was 'no place for beginners'.[31] It was a point with which the tough Canadian Buck McNair strongly agreed. On the day that the Spitfires landed from the *Wasp*, he watched as one them crashed into a dispersal bay, wrecking his own and another plane: 'It was heart-breaking. Another pilot had broken the tailwheel off his aircraft when he left the carrier. After he landed he began taxiing around. We cursed him and soon got him stopped, put a dolly under the tail so the machine could be pushed into position without bumping it to pieces. We had hungered so long and so much for new Spitfires it made us hopping mad to see them misused.' McNair admitted that some 'wonderfully fine pilots' had arrived, but there were others whom it seemed 'England was sending out just to get rid of them.' Interestingly, McNair; a highly experienced pilot himself, was disappointed in the Mark Vc. 'The first time I flew a Vc I noted how heavy it was and cumbersome. I was sure that it would not out-turn a 109, just knew it wasn't as fast. Generally speaking, fighter versus fighter, we were in a much poorer position with the Spitfire Vc against the 109 than we had been with anything before. We were all greatly disappointed.'[32]

Others thought it absurd that the Air Ministry had taken so long to provide the island with proper defences, when Spitfires were languishing idle in England or being wasted on useless fighter sweeps, the obsession of Sholto Douglas and Leigh-Mallory. Flight Lieutenant Godfrey Ball, itching for action in early 1942, was frustrated to be stuck at a fighter base in Northumberland, where the highlight of his spell was to organize mess dances. The whole atmosphere, he wrote, 'seemed like the Phoney War', yet 'at the same time Malta and the Middle East are crying out for fighter squadrons.'[33] No fewer than 75 fighter squadrons were kept in England in early 1942, something that Wilfrid Duncan Smith rightly described as 'a strange state of affairs'.[34]

By the end of April, the island could offer little real resistance to the continuing German onslaught. 'I could regard my task as accomplished. Our ascendancy at sea and in the air in the supply lines for Italy was assured,' wrote Albert Kesselring, the commander of the Luftwaffe forces in southern Italy.[35] Starving and battered, Malta was ripe for invasion, believed many in the German High Command. But Hitler prevaricated. Having experienced heavy losses in the invasion of Crete in 1941, he was reluctant to take the risk of another attack across the sea. Besides, Rommel's campaign in North Africa should be given priority in troop deployment, he argued, so the Italians would have to take the lead in any assault. It was to be another disastrous strategic blunder by the Führer, just as in the Battle of Britain Fighter Command had been saved by the switch in the attack to London.

At the very moment when Hitler was dithering, the British were planning a much larger reinforcement of the island's Spitfires. Recognizing the inadequacy of the first *Wasp* operation, the RAF reorganized the scheme. This time the *Wasp* was to work in tandem with the *Eagle*, thereby raising the number of planes sent to the island at one time to 64. In addition, more experienced pilots – many of them Battle of Britain veterans – would be used to spearhead the exercise. Meanwhile in Malta the ground arrangements for receiving the Spitfires were radically improved. Laddie Lucas, based at Takali, described what had to be done:

The nub of the thing was to refuel and rearm the aeroplanes in the minimum possible time on land: the need to get the aircraft off the ground again before the enemy could attack was paramount. The turn-around had to be treated like a pit stop in the middle of an international Grand Prix road race where every second counts. Where possible, Malta-based pilots had to be ready to take over the new Spitfires and get them airborne. To achieve this end, pilots and ground crews would be standing by in the sandbagged dispersal points at the immediate readiness to act. Petrol and ammunition would be available in each aircraft pen. Such serviceable aircraft as remained on the island would be airborne to cover the landings.[36]

The planning worked almost to perfection. The great majority of the Spitfires landed successfully from the *Wasp* and the *Eagle* and were swiftly in action against the Luftwaffe and Italian hordes. Michael Le Bas, who had flown on the first *Wasp* mission, recalled how he 'guided one Spitfire in and even before the pilot had shut down, men were clambering on the wings to load the cannon with their full complement of ammunition and the soldiers had started a human chain to pass up the petrol tins . . . Within fifteen minutes of landing, the Spitfire was ready to fight, and shortly afterwards I received the order to scramble.'[37] For the first time in the Battle of Malta, the defenders were able to put up significant numbers against the enemy. F. K. Rogers, a fitter with 185 and 69 Squadrons, stationed at the Hal Far airfield, kept a lively journal of his time on Malta, and some of its most compelling passages related to the arrival of the Spitfires at the beginning of May:

> The Spitfires were dispersed, re-armed and back in the air, with seasoned pilots, in record time. Our Axis friends got a shock and a big one and the first of many. Malta was back in business again. Malta was on the up, even if the rations were down. At last we are fighting back. It is very important to fight back because nothing is so soul-destroying as to have to sit there and take it and not be able to retaliate. We are enjoying our enemies' downfall, and excitement mounts as our Spits carve up the 88s and some 109s.

Rogers went on to describe the action he had seen from the ground:

> High in the sky the shells are bursting and now you can see them – Ju 88s this time – quite a number of them. They seem to be heading our way. The Spitfire guns and cannon are audible now, firing in short bursts mainly. They are amongst the 88s. The formations are breaking up. Some bombs are being jettisoned as the bombers turn and run. People are fighting for their lives up in that beautiful sky. An 88 is coming down in flames. Another with the engines streaming smoke is trying to dive away from the pursuing Spits. Fights are going on everywhere and some parachutes are drifting down, hopefully all enemy ones. The bombing attack is a shambles now. An 88

appears from the direction of Hal Far, going like hell, right over my lovely bay, with a Spitfire hanging on his tail, like a terrier, firing burst after burst into him. Not for long. The 88 loses height and disappears in an immense cloud of spray into the blue Med. The Spitfire pulls up in a jubilant roll and circles the spot.[38]

A new confidence swept through the squadrons as the advantage that the Axis had held for so long began to crumble. 'The Hun is getting a hiding,' said the New Zealander Ray Hesselyn of 249 Squadron. Hesselyn recorded how, in one of the fights on 10 May, he had dived to attack a Ju 88, only to come under fire from a Me 109, with cannon shells smashing into his port wing root and his cockpit. Fearless in the face of this battering, he managed to get on the tail of the Messerschmitt and opened fire from only 20 yards. 'My shells struck first on his starboard wing and, as he flew across my line of fire, travelled across his cockpit and then crashed into his port wing: Pieces flew off him in all directions. He seemed to be cut in half. His machine literally collapsed and went down in varying sizes'.[39]

Over Malta the Spitfires generally flew in finger-four formation, 200 yards abeam of each other, though in combat they would often break into pairs. The astounding bravery of the Spitfire pilots was shown in one incident the next day when another 249 pilot, Johnny Plagis, became separated from the rest of his section and then encountered eight Italian fighters. 'I thought my last minute had come and I decided to sell my life dearly. I flew straight at the nearest machine with the intention of ramming it. I did not fire a shot, but the Macchi pilot, suddenly realizing that his number might be up too, took violent evasive action, stalled and crashed into the sea.'[40]

Elated at the results of such action, Churchill telegraphed the US President, 'Many thanks for all your timely help. Who said that a wasp couldn't sting twice?'[41]

The combined *Wasp* and *Eagle* operation was the turning point of the battle. The Axis could no longer take air superiority for granted. Bombing missions were now more dangerous, dogfights more intense. The RAF ground crews, assisted by the army, had the chance to repair the airfields, strengthen the dispersal huts, and service the fighters. All the while, as the Maltese defences grew stronger, a steady stream of Spitfires came off carriers in the western Mediterranean. One Italian pilot, Ten Remo Cazzolli, captured the drama of being on the defensive against the RAF in a fight on 18 May:

There were many Spitfires and few Re 2001s, so when I ordered my pilots to break formation and engage, I found myself surrounded by Spitfires! As I opened fire, I saw before me in plan form, like a cross, a Spitfire. I took aim and fired, seeing a long black trail – possibly a sign that I had hit him. Suddenly there was a terrible noise like thunder and my engine stopped; it was the fire of 20-mm cannon, which overwhelmed my senses. I realized at once the situation and my face was covered in blood.

The cannon shell had jammed Cazzolli's canopy shut. Unable to escape, he felt his plane spiral out of control and plummet into the sea, though by a miracle he survived.[42]

The tide might have been starting to turn in the direction of the Allies, but life remained extremely tough in Malta both in the air and on the ground. Supplies from convoys were still struggling to get through, rations were more meagre than ever, and ammunition and other equipment was running dangerously low. In addition, fuel stocks were falling, limiting the sorties that could be flown. The task of refuelling planes was also extremely difficult. John Dalley, who flew a photoreconnaissance Spitfire, had nothing but admiration for the way the ground crews coped with the primitive facilities: 'My PR Spit took 216 gallons of fuel, yet most of the bowsers had gone so the planes were refuelled with 4-gallon cans. Lifting a 4-gallon can on to the wing and then pouring it into the tank through a funnel was hell, yet the men had to do this over fifty times for our planes. Absolutely incredible. They were shattered by the time they had filled an aeroplane.' Dalley lost 2 stone during his spell on the island because of the limited rations. 'We had no proper accommodation. Nearly everything I had I kept in my kit bag. We had no hot water, just the occasional cold shower.'[43]

One of the most debilitating aspects of life on the island was the widespread prevalence of a virulent form of dysentery known as the 'Malta Dog', which was contracted from contaminated water. 'To put it crudely, the definition of the "Dog" was being able to shit through the eye of the needle 50 feet away at least fifteen times a day. There was no relief from it,' said Pilot Office F. J. Sherlock of 185 Squadron.[44]

The unpublished journal of Spitfire fitter F. K. Rogers provides an insight into the hardships and risks faced by the RAF that summer:

> Like Cassius, we have a lean and hungry look. The rations are terrible, just two slices of bread a day and some biscuit duff, which is the mainstay of the diet. It can be flavoured, like mash. The tea is discoloured because the water is filled with chlorine. Some men think bromide is added to their tea to reduce their sexual longings and safeguard the local maidens. On our rations it is very debatable whether anyone could sustain an onslaught on the local ladies. One fitter joked, 'I hope they don't suddenly fly me home. My wife will divorce me on performance.'[45]

There was not much hope of a drink either. Often the only alcohol available was a local wine, officially called Ambete but nicknamed by the RAF 'Stuka juice'. According to the New Zealand Spitfire pilot Johnnie Houlton, this 'would turn the lips purple and had other devastating effects on the system'.[46] The heat and dust left its mark on the appearance of the crews. 'There is no toothpaste and little soap,' recorded Rogers, 'We have lost our regimented uniforms. Footwear is mainly open sandals made from aircraft tyres. We have patched-up shirts and shorts. We have no boot polish or razors. Our modern revamped airman now looks a bit of a sight, with his tyre footwear, bristling chin, long hair and assortment of bites, spots and open sores on his body.'[47]

The ground crews often had to service the Spitfires at night because of the risk of bombs, which added to the sense of exhaustion. But they were not always safe then, because the Germans and Italians conducted regular night raids, prompting the ghostly wail of the sirens – known on the airfields as 'wankers'. Rogers and his comrades went through a stressful incident one night when, after one such raid, an unexploded 500-pound bomb was found in front of one of the Spitfire pens. According to an army engineer, it was about to go off at any moment. The men were ordered to get round the Spitfire and push it to safety:

> We are off at the double, with many and varied remarks being bandied about. People's ancestries are questioned and trepidation is high. Someone leaps in the cockpit and releases the brakes. Chocks are heaved out of the way. There is no need for exhortation on this job. The Spitfire is practically airborne by the time we pass over the top of the bomb. Everyone is pushing like mad and round the back of the pen we go. There is now a solid wall between our precious plane and the bomb. The brakes are barely applied when, with an almighty bang, up goes the bomb and we are showered with dust and rubble. Within minutes, the army boys are filling in the bomb crater and rolling it flat for us to put the Spitfire back in its pen. All's well again.[48]

One of the most absorbing passages in Rogers's journal covered his experience of changing a damaged airscrew on a Spitfire, then testing the plane to see if the new propeller was working. The grandeur and power of the plane are clearly apparent from his description, as is the rudimentary nature of the equipment:

> The airscrew has a bullet hole through one of the blades. It has to be taken off with physical force. We have no equipment for heavy lifting. The army lads help and bring the replacement on the back of a 15-cwt truck. The driver reverses slowly up to the Spitfire. Four army lads jump on to the truck and I move it into position. I thank them and set to work to fit the rest of the mechanism, making sure the retaining nut is correctly tightened. This is achieved by

two big lads hanging on to a long tube on the end of the spanner and several good belts with a hammer, all technical stuff. Oh for a Rolls-Royce tool kit.

Once the new airscrew was installed, it was time for testing the engine. Chocks were put in place, and one of Rogers's colleagues, Taffy Owen, plugged the lead from a starter trolley into the aircraft to save its batteries. The engine cowlings were removed, then Rogers jumped into the cockpit and, after checking the fuel and the magneto switches, pressed the starter button:

> After a couple of healthy flicks, our Merlin bursts into life and as soon as it set-tles into an even running note Taffy removes the umbilical cord. I shut the cockpit door, put the seat to a good height and check all is well. The instru-ments glow softly. Flames are visible at the exhaust stubs in front of my face. The Spitfire is vibrating and pumping a little, as the slipstream hits the back of the pen wall and rebounds. The control column is now held hard back to keep the tail on the ground. Otherwise, she will nose over and my new airscrew will be shattered. Half-throttle and most of the checks are complete.

Rogers has one more task to perform: a full-power run, which required four men to sit on the tail to hold it down:

> With the Merlin bellowing at full revs, the slipstream blast is fierce and the lads will be blown flat across the tail surface and also showered with dust and any small stones that are lying about. Thumbs up from Taffy – the lads are in pos-ition – no time is wasted and the throttle is quickly opened fully. The Merlin responds immediately with a full-throated roar. The plane is alive. It is jump-ing about on the ground. A continuous flame licks back from its exhausts. Our Spitfire wants to get back into its natural element, but it is being restrained. All is well. I savour the moment briefly and close the throttle. The lads slide thankfully off the tail, tucking their shirts back in and trying to straighten their hair. I close the throttle, cut off the supply and the Merlin windmills to a halt. The exhausts cool and start to contract. Taffy and I cowl up the Spitfire and make her decent again. I close the cockpit hood and give her an affectionate pat.[49]

The battle remained bloody in June and July, but the growing numbers of Spitfires on the island meant that the RAF was no long engaged merely in survival. Attacks were now mounted on the Italian and Luftwaffe bases in southern Sicily, putting the Axis on the defensive for the first time. This new approach was overseen by Sir Keith Park, who took over from Lloyd as the island's air commander in July – a move that was welcomed by most RAF personnel because of his Battle of Britain experience and his knowledge of radar and ground control. 'He knows his stuff and has an offensive spirit.

Malta has got to start giving it back in quantity. Park wants the Germans shot down before they get to the island,' Rogers wrote in his journal.[50] In his special order of the day issued on his arrival, Park showed this spirit of aggression, which was in contrast to the defensive posture he had been forced to adopt throughout the Battle of Britain. His faith in the Spitfire was also re-emphasized:

> Our day-fighter strength has during June and July been greatly increased and the enemy's superiority in numbers has long since dwindled. The time has now arrived for our Spitfire squadrons to put an end to the bombing of our airfields by daylight. We have the best fighter aircraft in the world and our Spitfire pilots will again show their comrades on the ground that they are the best fighter pilots in the world.[51]

As in the Battle of Britain, Park was keen to maintain personal contact with his men, though instead of using a Hurricane he travelled between the airfields in an MG tourer or sometimes, when petrol rationing was at its most severe, on a bicycle. Just as in the Battle of Britain, he was far better at attracting the admiration of his pilots than of his senior colleagues: Lord Gort, the Governor of the island after replacing Sir William Dobbie in April, had difficult relations with him, though part of this stemmed from Gort's general contempt for the RAF ever since Dunkirk, where, as commander of the BEF, he had felt betrayed by the lack of air support. The Admiral of the Fleet Arthur Power, who visited Malta in 1942, was even more scathing about Park, describing him in his private diary as 'entirely insincere', 'an idiot' and 'very unsatisfactory to deal with'.[52]

But, for all such sneering, it was Park who emerged triumphant from the Battle of Malta, as he had done from the Battle of Britain. With the RAF holding its own, convoys were finally able to get through to the island, while Spitfire reinforcements were steadily coming off the carriers. The broken fortress, in danger of collapse in April, was defensively stronger than it had ever been by September. The Axis forces, on the verge of victory in April, were pursuing a lost cause by the start of the autumn. Every oil tanker and cargo ship that arrived in Valletta, every Axis bomber that was shot down, was a cause for rejoicing by the Maltese people and the British military personnel. F. K. Rogers gave this memorable description of his feeling on drinking a glass of beer for the first time in four months after the arrival of a convoy in August. 'It is magnificent. We have never tasted beer like this in our lives before. By the time we are halfway down the bottle we are in the best of spirits. What a glorious lovely day it is. God bless McEwan's.'[53]

Within the RAF, Malta was nicknamed 'the fighter pilot's paradise', because the sheer intensity of the combat provided so many opportunities for making kills. 'It all makes the Battle of Britain and fighter sweeps seem like child's play in comparison, but it is certainly history in the making and nowhere is there aerial warfare to compare with this,' wrote Flying Officer R. A. Mitchell at the height of the battle.[54] Malta appealed to the mavericks and the individuals, those fearless souls who refused to live by the rule book – men like Adrian Warburton, the pioneering photoreconnaissance Spitfire pilot, known universally as 'Warby'. He was so brilliant at his PR work that his commanders were willing to overlook his unconventional lifestyle, which including openly living with his girlfriend Christina Radcliffe, a glamorous dancer, though he was an – unhappily – married man. He also kept a marmoset monkey as a pet and had an addiction to aspirin.[55] 'Immensely brave, he delighted in taking fearful risks and would go out of his way to embarrass the enemy by the brazen impudence of his photographic reconnaissance missions,' wrote Wilfrid Duncan Smith.[56] F. K. Rogers, who ended up servicing the Maltese Spitfires' photographic unit, wrote of Warburton's gift for inspiring loyalty: 'He treats everyone with the same easy familiarity, rarely gives a direct order yet all the lads would do their utmost for him.'[57] On one reconnaissance mission over southern Sicily, Warburton flew so low that the Italian aircraft guns could not be depressed sufficiently to hit him. His aggressive spirit was shown in the way he insisted on mixing his photoreconnaissance duties with air fighting. 'He was totally unorthodox, a complete individualist with both courage and flair,' wrote one of his commanding officers, Group Captain E. A. Whiteley.[58] Warburton disappeared without trace flying over Italy in 1944.

Almost as idiosyncratic was the young Canadian George 'Screwball' Beurling, who arrived in Malta with a reputation for ill discipline, eccentricity and breathtaking flying skills. His nickname was derived from his habit of calling everybody and everything 'Screwball'. A lone hunter, disrespectful of authority, he always refused to accept a commission. His commanding officer, Laddie Lucas, recognized that behind Beurling's rebelliousness was a sense of inferiority, which called for encouragement rather than reproach. 'He was untidy, with a shock of fair, tousled hair above penetrating blue eyes. He smiled a lot and the smile came straight out of those striking eyes. His sallow complexion was in keeping with his part-Scandinavian ancestry. He was highly strung, brash and outspoken,' wrote Lucas. Under his CO's wise guidance, Beurling was transformed into the finest fighter ace of Malta, with a credited score of 26, revelling in the freedom he had been given and the large number of targets the enemy provided. His attributes were wonderful aerobatic skills, an instinctive feel for the Spitfire, excellent eyesight and judgement of distance, and unerring marksmanship. Lucas gave this account of Beurling's method:

I never saw him shoot haphazardly at an aircraft which was too far away. He only fired when he thought he could destroy. Two hundred and fifty yards was the distance from which he liked best to fire. A couple of short hard bursts from there and that was usually it. He picked his targets off cleanly and decisively, swinging his sight smoothly through them as a first-class shot drives partridges out of the sky. It was a fluent and calculated exercise.[59]

Beurling himself wrote the following report on his characteristically well-timed attack on two 109s which he saw over the Maltese coast at Fifla on 10 October:

I dropped in on them. I went down and down, clean under the starboard fellow, and rolled up under him, giving him a quick burst into the engine. He pancaked right smack down on his belly on the island and flipped over on to his back. The other fellow tried to circle away but I stayed with him. He turned out to sea, then whipped back across Fifla again. As he did I moved on to his starboard quarter and let him have it. The burst caught the gas tank and the 'ship' blew up; complete with pilot.[60]

Unlike Warburton, Beurling survived the war, only to be killed in an air crash flying from Rome in 1948.

As well as creating the reputation of men like Warburton and Beurling, Malta further cemented the legend of the Spitfire. Twice it had saved Britain from the brink of catastrophe. Twice it had thwarted the Luftwaffe from enabling the Axis powers to mount an invasion. Ronnie West, a Spitfire pilot who had been on tour in Malta and was later killed in a plane crash in England in 1943, delighted in telling a story which he had picked up from the RAF listening service in Malta. West explained that the RAF had intercepted the voice of a German fighter leader who was guiding his formation to attack the island soon after the first Spitfires had arrived from the *Eagle*. According to the RAF listener, the German said, 'Christ, Spitfires! We weren't told that there were Spitfires on Malta. Back we go.'[61] This may have been an exaggeration, but Squadron Leader Lord David Douglas-Hamilton – not a man prone to colourful overstatement – felt that the Germans were reluctant to 'stay and "mix it" in a straight fight, and they always knew they were in a fight if they stayed with our pilots.' Douglas-Hamilton recalled an occasion when six 109s were escorting Ju 88s over Valletta harbour in the days when the Spitfires were heavily outnumbered. 'One of our pilots shot the wing off their leader's plane and the remaining five just ran for it, back to Sicily, leaving the 88s a sitting target, which the pilots then dealt with. Had the Huns been really determined, none of us would have been able to land safely again in the days when relays of 109s kept us up circling the base long after a bombing raid had passed.'[62] After a dogfight in July, the German pilot Uffz

Horst Schlick admitted how difficult a well-flown Spitfire could be as an opponent: 'The Spitfire V was, admittedly, somewhat inferior in terms of speed, but climbed just as well as and turned far better than the Me 109. And there were thorough experts among the Tommies.'[63]

The last major Axis blitz on Malta took place in October. Overstretched by faltering campaigns in Russia and North Africa, battered by the Spitfires, Germany could no longer sustain the onslaught on the island. From now on, Malta, rather than being a place under siege, would be an launch pad for the Allies' attack on Italy. The Air Staff and Ministry may have been slow to react to the crisis, and indeed, as late as May 1942 Sholto Douglas was bleating that 'about 150 of my best Spitfire pilots are at present in Malta' and that he was 'in need of experienced pilots of this type at home' – a complaint that hardly reflects well on his strategic judgement.[64] But, thanks largely to Churchill and the military and air-force commanders, the necessary action was taken to create a Spitfire air force on the island. Between March and October 1942, in 13 carrier operations, 385 Spitfires were launched from carriers, and 367 reached the island. Those that failed to do so were generally either shot down or suffered engine failure, though one American deserted by flying straight to Algeria, claiming to have got lost. The most poignant deaths occurred when the carrier take-off went wrong. Johnnie Houlton had this grim experience when preparing to take off from HMS *Furious* in August:

> As one of the pilots ahead of me opened up for take-off, it was obvious, from the position of his elevators, that he was holding the stick hard back. I watched in horror as the Spitfire skidded across the deck to the left and plunged over the side, flipping over as it disappeared from sight. There was just a patch of foam to be seen as the ship raced by, and the unfortunate pilot must have gone down with his aircraft.[65]

As in the Battle of Britain, the actual losses incurred by each side were much closer than Allied propaganda at the time suggested. It has been estimated that during the Battle of Malta the Luftwaffe had 249 planes destroyed and another 50 damaged, while the Italians lost around 60. In return, 148 Spitfires and 45 Hurricanes were lost in the air, and a further 66 Spitfires had to make forced or crash-landings, mostly as a result of combat. A total of 120 British and Commonwealth pilots lost their lives, and 104 RAF ground personnel were killed – though this paled beside the 1,104 Maltese civilians who died in air raids. But the statistics only paint part of the picture. If the island had fallen, Rommel could have supplied and reinforced his Afrika Korps. The Eighth Army, Britain's ground force in North Africa, would have been exhausted and isolated. The outcome of El Alamein – and the war – could have been very different.

II

'That's no aircraft, that's a bleedin' angel'

⌐⌐

J OE SMITH, THE chief designer of Supermarine throughout the war, said in
1946, 'The hard school of war leaves no room for sentimental attachments
and the efficiency of the machine as a fighter weapon is the only criterion.'[1]
As Smith recognized, the Spitfire stayed in production for more than a decade
not because of some romantic affection inspired by the Battle of Britain, but
because it had proved itself time and again in combat. Moreover, its strength
and versatility offered tremendous scope for improvement without losing
sight of the essential brilliance of Mitchell's design. No other Allied aircraft
fighter was produced in such a wide range of variants. In the course of
producing 19 major different marks, almost 1,100 modifications were
incorporated in the aircraft between 1938 and 1945.[2] Jeffrey Quill once argued
that Smith's greatest achievement had been to 'devote the whole effort of the
Supermarine design department to developing the capabilities of the Spitfire
rather than devote effort to designing an altogether new aircraft which in any
case could not be in service for some years'.[3] As Smith himself put it, 'The
sound basic design of the aircraft with its outstanding simplicity enabled major
modifications to be incorporated without materially altering the original
conception. Although very few details remained unaltered by the time the
Mark 24 was built, the layout and basic design principles on which the aircraft
was based persisted throughout.'[4]

Smith and Quill were always full of praise for Rolls-Royce, which co-
operated closely with Supermarine throughout the process of development.
The company's inventiveness, quality of production and technical understanding of the Spitfire's needs were a crucial part of the plane's long success.
'I spent so many hours sitting behind Merlins and Griffons and bashing them
at full speed under rigorous test conditions and they so seldom let me down
that I may be forgiven for my opinion that Rolls-Royce were the greatest
engine firm in the world, bar none,' said Quill.[5] Like Smith, Ernest Hives, the
general manager of Rolls-Royce, pinned his faith on improvements to existing types. As he explained to Sir Wilfrid Freeman in June 1941, 'The only
thing to bank on for quantity production for next year is something that exists

today. This is not an original idea as far as Rolls-Royce is concerned – our whole policy has been framed round development of existing types rather than radical changes in design and there is no sign so far that we have come to the end of the possible improvements by development.'[6]

It must be said, however, that the impetus to keep developing the Spitfire did not stem solely from technical considerations. In a wartime economy stretched to the limits of capacity, the government had also to take account of finance and production. In practical terms, it was much cheaper and faster to keep turning out Spitfires rather than go through the expensive process of launching new types, and then rejigging factories and retraining workforces to build them. A study carried out by Vickers in 1951 graphically illustrated the gulf between the effort that had to go into designing the first Spitfire and that expended on all the subsequent marks. No fewer than 330,000 man-hours were put into the design and development of the Spitfire Mark I, yet the average man-hours used on each of the next most important fifteen marks was just 41,000. By far the most time-consuming of the later variants was the highly advanced Mark 21, though even this took only 165,000 man-hours. As M. M. Postan, the historian of British wartime production, wrote, the total of 620,000 man-hours used on the later fifteen models would have been 'barely sufficient to design two new aircraft of the Mark I type'. As Postan pointed out, the disparity was just as dramatic in terms of production: '800,000 man-hours were spent in jigging and tooling up the Spitfire Mark I. The average man-hours for jigging and tooling the other marks was 69,000.'[7] For the government and for Vickers, continuing with the Spitfire was the rational economic choice.

The Spitfire's versatility had been further demonstrated by the time the Battle of Malta ended. In addition to the Mark V with 90-gallon drop tanks, there was also a version with a phenomenal 170-gallon tank which could fly the whole way from Gibraltar to Malta. As the siege of the island ended and the RAF stepped up its operations in North Africa, playing an important role in El Alamein, Spitfires were modified with special Vokes filters on the air intakes to prevent damage from the heat and dust of the tropical climate. The Air Ministry was concerned that these tropicalized Mark Vs might have reduced effectiveness, but Jeffrey Quill, after testing them, assured the RAF that 'the loss of speed is at most 4 mph. We do not believe that the tropical air intake has nearly such a bad effect on performance as is general supposed. It is however very important that the filters be correctly and carefully fitted,' he reported.[8] The experience out in the desert of North Africa told a different story, however. The New Zealand ace Colin Gray described the Vokes filters as 'wretched. They cut down the boost pressure for high-level work alarmingly, so their performance other than at sea level was quite abysmal. These filters were a permanent fixture and could not be by-passed in flight by the pilot.'[9] Aesthetically the bulbous protrusion under its nose detracted from the graceful appearance of the Spitfire; Tony Tooth, who fought in North Africa, described it as 'the ugliest Spitfire'.[10] The Vokes filters, 'although vitally necessary', noted Godfrey Ball in his journal, 'did nothing to assist the performance of the plane and even less for its normally beautiful lines'.[11]

The preparation of the Spitfire for North Africa also required the installation of a tank of drinking water for the pilots. This led to another of those examples of improvisation that litter the Spitfire story, as Stanley Woodley, one of the Castle Bromwich managers, recalled:

> The tank for drinking water was designed like a petrol tank. It was a most difficult thing to make. It was riveted and it had some sort of jointing compound which produced a foul taste in the water – hopeless! We had a brain-wave. We sent everyone around the Birmingham district to look for hot water bottles and we found absolutely the ideal thing – a spun-aluminium hot water bottle. The manufacturer had a big stock and he went into production and so a hot water bottle went to war.[12]

Another instance of Supermarine's ingenuity occurred when the company wanted to test the effect of using dome rivets in place of flush ones, which gave a smoother finish but were more complex to install. 'So we set about seeing what would happen if dome rivets were used,' said the Supermarine engineer Harry Griffiths:

> Using tube of a propriety cellulose adhesive bought from the local ironmonger – there were no DIY shops in those days – we stuck split peas on the heads of all the rivets on the fuselage on one of the development aircraft. It is reported that the machine with all the split peas was 22 mph slower on flight test, so flush rivets continued to be used except in a few places where it was considered that dome heads would not affect the performance.[13]

The need to maintain a smooth surface on the Spitfire, thereby reducing drag, was emphasized by the government in its propaganda to the aircraft factories and services, through films, lectures and leaflets. At one stage the Air Ministry sent out a ditty entitled 'Keep It Clean', featuring a concerned Pilot Officer Vim, who bore no resemblance to any of the heroes of Fighter Command. A few verses give a flavour of the gruesome nature of this publicity:

> Sure enough 'twas a grim looking Spit,
> Battered and bent with a surface like grit,
> Vim checked it up and with dismay,
> Saw hopes of a gong pass swiftly away.

Guided by the book of rules,
They got to work with proper tools,
Beating out the bumps and dents,
Stopping up the surplus vents,
Filling in and rubbing down,
The slightest roughness raised a frown.

Cruising once more over France,
Speedy Vim now had more chance,
Sweeping in with belching guns,
Had the legs of all the Huns,
With a well directed squirt,
Damaged two and claimed a cert.

Forgive me if a moral shows:
Protect your steed from needless blows,
Train your crew to treat with care
Outside bits that meet the air;
Life and limb you may be riskin'
If you fly with damaged Spit skin.[14]

Yet the sentiment behind this patronizing dirge was not wrong. A clean finish could make a remarkable difference to a Spitfire's speed. A study carried out by the Royal Aircraft Establishment at Farnborough in 1943 showed that the average speed of a later production Mark V was actually lower than that of the Mark I, despite the improvement in the Merlin's engine power. The analysis by Farnborough suggested that the cause of the drop was 'shared between a further increase in equipment (amounting to 6 mph) and a deterioration in the finish (amounting to 9½ mph)'. The analysis 'confirms the suggestion that the Spitfire Vs deteriorated considerably in performance during their production'.[15]

Probably the most important technical development arising from Malta was the Spitfire's use as a fighter-bomber in the later stages of the siege. As the Allies went on the offensive in Italy, France and North Africa, this would become an ever more crucial role. In August 1942, Spitfire Vcs from 126 Squadron flew from Malta to southern Sicily with improvised racks underneath their wings carrying two 250-pound bombs. Bill Rolls was one of the pilots on the first bombing sortie and he later described the modification as 'a bit of a Heath Robinson arrangement. It was a 250-pound bomb which was hooked on to a Beaufighter bomb rack. It operated by pulling a piece of string in the cockpit which pulled two pins holding the bombs in the rack.' However, sometimes a bomb failed to be released, having become caught on one of the pins. In that case 'the bomb was likely to hit the ground when you landed and as the bombs were fused you can imagine the risks we took in trying out the bombs.' Rolls described how the mission was undertaken:

> The idea was that one squadron would fly with bombs and two or three squadrons would fly round us and that way the Germans would not suspect that there were twenty-four bombs ready for them. We would fly in formation over Comiso aerodrome and since sometimes the Germans did not want to waste their reserves just to go after fighters, we would then bomb the buildings, escorted by the fighters who shot up aircraft on the ground with cannon. It worked successfully as it took the Germans by surprise, but they soon got to know which Spitfires were carrying the bombs and went straight for us and most of us were glad when we finished bombing. After all we were fighter pilots not bomber pilots.[16]

Despite Bill Rolls's reservations, the Spitfire continued to act as a fighter-bomber right through the remainder of the war. It was particularly useful in weakening the supply lines of the German forces in northern France from 1943, and in destroying V-1 rocket bases in Holland. Typical of such operations was an attack in April 1944 by the New Zealander Johnnie Houlton, leader of 485 Squadron, on a railway line in Crécy. His account shows how technology and tactics had advanced since Bill Rolls's first venture. 'We carried one 500-pound bomb under the belly of the aircraft and the run–in was made at around 8,000 feet with the bomb carriers in echelon (angled slightly back from the leader). As we peeled off and dived, the momentary time-lag between each aircraft gave adequate separation in the dive.' The pilot, said Houlton, could fly very accurately to the point of bomb release:

> The usual practice was to then keep going on down to the deck and reform each section clear of the target area. Some of the targets were undefended but others had a respectable concentration of light flak guns which gave no encouragement to the Spitbombers to hang around looking at the damage. The German gunners usually held their fire until the aircraft were committed to the dive, probably not wishing to draw attention to their target area, in case we were just passing by.

Houlton also explained how the bomb system worked: 'The 500-pound bomb was carried on a removable rack beneath the aircraft and released by a battery-operated solenoid when a button on the control stick was pushed; while on the run-up to the target the bomb was "armed" by closing a switch on the instrument panel.' Yet, despite this greater sophistication, the life-threatening problem of unreleased bombs remained. Houlton himself once found that, after a mission to France, his bomb had failed to drop away, even 'after I had wrenched the aircraft around in a variety of violent efforts to dislodge it'. The guidance for pilots in such a predicament was to fly over the sea and then bail out, but Houlton felt this was too extreme a solution. So he flew back to his base. 'Instead of the usual three-point landing, which can cause a jolt, I "wheeled" the aircraft gently on to the ground with the tailwheel high and then felt a solid thud while the tailwheel kicked up a little higher – the bomb had dropped off as the wheels touched the ground, then bounced and dented the belly of the aircraft, right back near the tail.' Houlton's commanding officer gave him a lecture about the risks he had taken, then bought him a beer.[17]

Johnnie Johnson, who flew dive-bombing raids over France in 1944 and 1945, said that he was 'never crazy' about this work. One reason was that he found problems with accuracy, because it was hard to make allowances for deflection and the prevailing wind: 'The theory of dive-bombing was to put your aeroplane into a steep dive, aim it at the target and release your bombs about the same time as you pulled out of the dive. Unfortunately, the bombs did not possess the same line of flight as our Spitfires and if you aimed directly at the target, the bombs fell short.' Another reason was that Johnson felt that the two bombs under the elliptical wings ruined the classic look of the Spitfire. 'The Spitfire seemed to be intolerably burdened by her load and the ugly, big bombs were a basic contradiction of all the beauty and symmetry of the aeroplane.'[18]

It is a rich irony that for much of the 1930s the bomber enthusiasts were suspicious of the Spitfire because of its place at the centre of Dowding's fighter doctrine, yet from 1942 the plane itself saw service as an attack bomber. But 1942 was to see the Spitfire in an even more incongruous role: as a naval fighter. The Spitfire had, of course, been launched from aircraft carriers during the Battle of Malta, but that had been a unique exercise, with no question of the plane returning to the carriers. What the Fleet Air Arm, the Royal Navy's air service, wanted was a dedicated maritime combat aircraft, and eventually the Government decided that the Spitfire could be converted to this function. Mitchell had never envisioned the Spitfire operating from naval carriers; indeed, the plane was ill-designed for this purpose. Its undercarriage was too narrow and delicate for a rolling deck, its landing speed too high, its forward visibility too poor, its range too limited. Though the Sea Spitfire, as it was first called before the two words were combined, fought throughout the Mediterranean and the Pacific during the last three years of the war, it never entirely overcame its unsuitability as a naval plane. As David Brown, the historian of the Seafire, has argued, 'Even when the range and endurance qualities had been improved, there was still the problem of structural weaknesses. More thorough pilot training and general experience went far to reducing the rate of breakages, but the readiness of the Spitfire to suffer structural failure in the course of almost normal shipboard landings meant that attrition would always be higher than for any other individual fighter type.'[19]

In the opening years of the war, the Fleet Air Arm, the most neglected, unfashionable part of the Royal Navy, found itself without a decent front-line interceptor. Its front-line equipment included the obsolete Blackburn Roc, a turret fighter with a maximum speed of less than 200 mph; the Blackburn Skua, supposedly a dual-purpose fighter-bomber, though it was hopeless in either role; and the Fairey Fulmar, a two-seater, eight-gun fighter, the second onboard place being reserved for the navigator. The Admiralty, to be fair, was only too aware of this weakness, and had been pressing for its own Hurricanes or Spitfires. In fact, so desperate were the Admiralty chiefs that one commented, 'Any single-seat fighter is better than nothing.'[20] In November 1939 the Admiralty, with the approval of the Air Ministry, made a direct approach to Supermarine to see if it would be possible to have a navalized version of the fighter. Supermarine was willing to consider the idea, so Captain Matthew Slattery, a distinguished naval pilot, went down to Eastleigh and there, on the airfield, a space was marked out the same size as a carrier deck, and an arrester hook was installed on a Spitfire to simulate a sea landing. As Alexander Dunbar reported to Sir Charles Craven, the experiment had been satisfactory:

> Captain Slattery said that the Royal Navy needs a new fast fighter and to avoid delay consequent on bringing in a new design he would like to use the Spitfire. He said that there would not be any difficulty about the field of vision. The Spitfire as it stands, with a span of 37 feet, can apparently be accommodated in the lifts and hangars of existing carriers but for the new ships it would have to be equipped with folding wings.[21]

In response to Slattery's encouragement, Joe Smith came up with a design for a Spitfire with folding wings in January 1940. Yet, after initial hesitant support, the government became reluctant to progress the development of a Spitfire type for the navy. This was partly because energy and money had been invested in the Fairey Fulmar, and partly because Spitfire production had to be concentrated on Fighter Command. In March 1940 the First Lord of the Admiralty, Winston Churchill, who before the war had shown a misguided preference for the Boulton-Paul Defiant over the Spitfire, refused to sanction any more work on the Sea Spitfire. Churchill believed that the Spitfire was unsuitable for carrier operations, having too high a landing speed, and he had also learned from Sir Wilfrid Freeman that 50 folding-wing Spitfires would cost the equivalent output of about 200 ordinary Spitfires. 'I regard it as of very great importance that the production of Fulmars should be kept going,' he wrote.[22]

Churchill's decision may have been understandable in the context of the needs of home defence. But it meant that the navy was without a single-seater fighter throughout the dark early years of the war. In autumn 1941, with the inadequacy of the Fulmar all too obvious, the government finally relented and ordered proper maritime tests on a Sea Spitfire, essentially a Mark V with an arrester hook. The first such trial was held in January 1942, when Commander Peter Bramwell, of the Fleet Air Arm's Service Trials Unit, landed on the deck of HMS *Illustrious*, moored on the river Clyde. He reported that, though the forward view was poor, the aircraft itself was satisfactory. The Fleet Air Arm was now desperate to be supplied with the plane. Yet the needs of the RAF remained the priority for the government. The Air Ministry said that it was 'vital to build up stocks of fighters against possible continental operations in 1943', and offered 60 Hurricanes. The Admiralty was incensed. 'We must have more Spitfires . . . The Fulmar is obsolescent for modern warfare and the 60 Hurricanes would be purely stop-gaps.'[23] By mid-1942, with losses at sea mounting, the Ministry of Aircraft Production and the Air Ministry admitted that the Fleet Air Arm had a justifiable case. It was agreed that 250 Mark Vs should be adapted for naval use, while contracts were also placed with Westland and Supermarine for the production of over 400 Seafires during the next two years.

In September 1942, further trials were held on the naval Mark V to see if it could successfully land on a smaller deck than the *Illustrious*. They were carried out on HMS *Biter* by Captain Eric 'Winkle' Brown, one of the greatest of all test pilots – the only man to have flown every major combat aircraft of the Second World War. Because of the poor vision of the Spitfire, Commander Bramwell, in his first trial, had used a curving, steeply banked approach to land on the *Illustrious*. Brown, however, adopted a different method:

> I flew round the ship, turned on to my approach path and came in. As I closed the stern I swung the nose to starboard with the rudder and counteracted the swing by putting on slight opposite bank. In this way I made the Seafire crab in sideways, so that I had a view of the deck over the leading edge of the wing. I sank towards the stern. I was over the rundown at a speed very close to the stall. I took off the bank and kicked off the rudder as she sank on the deck. She made a good three-point touchdown and caught a wire.[24]

To Brown's horror, he found that he had landed on a completely empty deck, with not a batman in sight. And the wire that had caught his hook had actually been lying flat on the deck. It turned out that all the *Biter's* crew were at lunch below. Yet the incident proved, firstly, what a superb pilot Brown was and, secondly, that the Seafire could be landed even in the most difficult conditions.

The plane properly entered service with the Fleet Air Arm in June 1942, in 807 Squadron, and by the end of August, three other squadrons were equipped with it. The Seafire first went into action in November, taking part in Operation Torch, the Anglo-American landings in Morocco and Algeria which, combined with Montgomery's triumph at El Alamein, swept the Axis out of North Africa. Its main job in Torch was escorting the venerable Fairey Albacore biplane bombers in low-level attacks on airfields occupied by Vichy France. Little resistance was encountered, though Sub-Lieutenant G. C. Baldwin became the first Seafire pilot to make a kill when he shot down a French Dewoitine 520. Baldwin later said of his experience of the Seafire:

> Because the Spitfire was designed to have excellent air-to-air combat qualities, it was really very unsuitable for the rugged type of flying where none too experienced pilots threw it on to the flight deck and it had to be stopped in full flight by hydraulic arrester gear. In fact practically everything about the Spitfire from the purely naval point of view was the opposite of what was required. But the aircraft had that sort of charisma; everybody was determined to make it work, everybody loved working on it and flying it . . . Pilots fell in love with it, felt absolutely part of it, trusted it and its engine implicitly.

Baldwin described some of the physical consequences of carrier work for the Seafire's structure:

> We had a curious little expression about the Spitfire which summed up our problems on the deck. We used to say that it suffered from 'pecking, pintling and puckering'. Actually this was no joke, because 'pecking' was caused by the tail being thrown up as the aircraft caught the arrester wire, with the propeller then touching the flight deck. If it was a wooden propeller, pieces flew off in every direction. Believe it or not, this was cured by just taking a sharp knife and cutting three inches off the end of each blade with no noticeable loss of performance whatsoever. 'Pintling' was a phenomenon caused by the rather weak undercarriage. You could do a fairly reasonable but slightly rough landing and thereafter you could not get the undercarriage up when you took off, or once you had retracted it you could not lower it again. It was because the pintle in the undercarriage had become misplaced. 'Puckering' was if you made a successful landing but had a little bump which meant that the tail would drop hard on to the flight deck and the fuselage would bend just in front of the empennage [or tail unit]. Well, these were all difficult problems and they reduced serviceability considerably.[25]

In September 1943 the Seafire's reputation as a combat aircraft took a blow during the Allied landings at Salerno, where the invasion of mainland Italy began. Because Salerno was too far north from Sicily for land-based Spitfires to provide air cover, it was decided to give support from naval carriers, and 120 Seafires were put in five very slow ships. During the three days of the operation, few German or Italian planes were shot down, but 42 of the Seafires were lost or written off, including 32 wrecked in accidents. Another 39 were badly damaged in deck landings.[26] It was, said Baldwin, 'pretty disastrous'.[27] Captain Eric Brown described how the Seafires 'came roaring in at dangerously high speeds, tore their hooks out, bounced over the side, turned over, crashed into the deck park forward or hit the island [the carrier's equivalent to a control tower]'.[28]

As a result of Salerno, the Fleet Air Arm employed Jeffrey Quill as a pilot to advise on improvements to the Seafire and the best way to handle it, particularly on the approach to landing. Quill admitted that the experience was challenging: 'I had reached the stage where I felt I could land a Spitfire in my sleep on an aerodrome if need be, but I soon found that during a sortie from an aircraft carrier there was always at the back of one's mind . . . the consciousness that at the end of the sortie one had to get this damn thing back on the ship again.' The consequences of any error, Quill explained, could be

> immediate and dramatic. Failure to engage the arrester wire with the aircraft's hook mean an immediate crash into the cable barrier which separated the landing area from the forward deck park. Misjudging the approach speed, or getting a few feet off line, could result in a broken undercarriage and a damaged hook and a fair chance of going over the ship's side into the sea. The deck was 70 feet above the sea and it was extremely difficult to get out of a Seafire cockpit before it sank even if the pilot remained conscious after the impact. Not many pilots survived 'going over the side' in a Seafire.[29]

Quill's report, delivered in February 1944, recommended the use of a stronger undercarriage and more sophisticated arrester gear, including the installation of a hydraulic damper to eliminate hook bounce. Quill also argued that the best method of landing was to approach the ship in a gently curving left-hand turn with a well-controlled rate of sink, 'sneaking in, as it were, just in front of the Seafire's blind area astern of the ship'. This, he believed, could be done safely because of the Seafire's 'excellent lateral stability characteristics right down to the stall'. He rejected Winkle Brown's crab method as too dangerous for inexperienced pilots.[30]

Quill's efforts helped to speed up the introduction of radical improvements to the Seafire. By the end of the war, like the Spitfire itself, the Seafire had evolved into a formidable beast, powered by 2,000-horsepower Griffon engines and featuring intimidating weaponry, including cannon, bombs and projectile rockets. Altogether, 2,570 Seafires were produced in eight major different marks, ranging from the first Seafire Mark Ib – basically just an adapted Mark V – through to the Mark 47, which first flew just after the war and, fully loaded, weighed over 10,000 pounds – more than twice the weight of Mitchell's prototype. During its time in service, the Seafire became progressively more specialized for naval work. The Mark III, for example, had folding wings, thereby greatly enhancing the number that could operate from a carrier. And the Mark XVII, a Griffon-powered machine that first came off the production line in April 1945, featured an enlarged tail fin and a strengthened main wing spar for a stronger undercarriage. Winkle Brown, who had more experience of the Seafire than any other pilot, paid this tribute: 'Despite the innumerable changes, surprisingly little of the aesthetic beauty of the line had been lost – although, admittedly, the tail suffered somewhat – and none of the beautiful harmony of control.' Brown admitted that 'nobody could claim that the Seafire had been the ideal carrier fighter', but 'I never felt anything but exhilarated at the challenge it presented. It was an aeroplane that seemed tailor-made for the pilot and I cannot imagine any other aircraft that would have permitted the liberty of the crab-type approach that I and many other pilots used for the deck landing.'[31]

The Spitfire itself was also undergoing radical changes from 1942. The arrival of the Focke-Wulf 190 in September 1941 had meant that, for the first time, the Spitfire was decisively outclassed by the enemy. With a more powerful engine than the Merlin 45, the Fw 190 could outclimb and outrun the Mark V. John Freeborn of 602 Squadron even described the Mark V as 'a clod of an aeroplane'. It was, he said, 'underpowered because, quite simply, too much was hung on it'. The Mark II, he believed, 'handled better and went quicker', echoing the sentiments that Buck McNair had expressed with the arrival of the Mark V in Malta.[32] And the Mark V's limitations were evident not just in combat. The aircraft also suffered a worrying number of catastrophic technical failures. Normally so reliable, the Spitfire in 1942 began to put some of its pilots at risk.

According to Jeffrey Quill, at least 25 Spitfires – mainly Mark Vbs – were broken apart in the air because of disastrous mainframe or engine failures, almost always with fatal results. George Pickering, a distinguished Supermarine test pilot, was a victim of this curse. One who escaped was Denis Sweeting of 504 Squadron, who in September 1942 was flying at 24,000 feet above Scapa Flow. Suddenly his plane went into a vertical dive. Almost dazed by the savagery of the plunge, Sweeting 'pulled back on the control column with all my strength and blacked out. I kept heaving back and suddenly there was a tremendous explosion and everything was quiet and black.' At first Sweeting thought his Spitfire had hit the ground and he was dead, but then he sensed, in his blackness, that he was falling through the sky. He managed to open his parachute and, still temporarily blind, landed in a Highland peat field. It turned out that, in the sudden violence of his desperate manoeuvre to pull out of the dive, both wings were torn off, one of them slicing the tail section. Under massive G forces, Sweeting had been ripped out of his safety harness and ejected through the canopy, though, miraculously, his parachute had stayed intact.[33]

The American pilot Arthur Bishop was another who experienced near disaster, when he was flying a Spitfire Vb towards his squadron base in Redhill, Surrey: 'I had been in the air for about forty minutes, everything running smoothly, and was heading in the direction of the field at 1,000 feet when I was suddenly jolted by an explosion. The aircraft started to vibrate so violently that I couldn't read the instrument panel in front of me.' Bishop was flying too low to bail out. He tried to make it to the airfield, but smashed into two poplar trees. 'I shut my eyes and thought, I've had it; so this is what death is like. Then everything went blank.' But somehow the mangled plane crashed on its belly and came to a rest on the edge of the airfield. Bishop survived, without any serious injury. It seemed that the engine had blown a piston rod, which accounted for a large hole on the port side of the engine. Bishop was resentful when he was subsequently interviewed by an official from Rolls-Royce, who inclined towards blaming the crash on pilot error rather than engine failure. He was, said Bishop, 'a bowler-hatted little cretin. I didn't like him and the officious little bastard didn't like me.'[34]

Whatever the representative from Rolls-Royce might have thought, no aero engine could ever be infallible, and the Merlin 45 series seemed more prone to problems than other previous and later types. Alex Henshaw, the Castle Bromwich test pilot, who tested more Spitfires than any other man, suffered three Merlin engine failures in a row in 1942, one of which led to his crash-landing his damaged Spitfire on the gardens between the backs of two terraced streets in a Birmingham suburb. 'As the machine snaked off to the right the starboard wing caught a large oak tree and snapped off like a carrot,' wrote Henshaw:

> The nose then swung into the house whose cabbage patch I tried to take over; the engine tore a gaping hole, exposing the kitchen furniture to wholesale view. As the airscrew dropped on to the floor the port wing plunged into the soft ground and it also snapped off. The unrestricted fuselage then tore through everything in front of it and the earth, vegetables and debris flew up over the

cockpit in which I still remained in a terrifying crescendo. I prayed that it would all be over soon without too much pain.[35]

Typically, Henshaw was flying again the next day, despite severe bruising.

Perhaps even more worrying than the engine failures were the occasions when the Spitfire airframe disintegrated in mid-air. This phenomenon was traced to longitudinal instability in some Spitfire Vs, largely because their centre of gravity had been allowed to move towards the rear of the plane as a result of improper loading of extra equipment. The stability margins on the Spitfire had always been narrow, ever since 1936, as a deliberate policy. Jeffrey Quill explained that, when flying the prototype, he had

> tested the aircraft at an extended aft centre of gravity position at which it was violently unstable and quite unacceptable. Eventually we settled for an aft limit where the aircraft was slightly unstable which meant that at the normal service load the stability was just positive. That was how we sent it to Martlesham. This meant that the aeroplane was quite sensitive or tender fore and aft, but in fact this gave the aeroplane a certain feeling of liveliness and animation and a sense of finger-tip control which appealed to the pilots and seemed compatible with its lively performance and role as a fighter.[36]

But with the Mark V the margins were becoming too tight, especially if the ground crews did not follow the rule book from Supermarine on the correct installation of equipment such as signal cartridges and oxygen bottles, which led to the centre of gravity sliding backwards. Alex Henshaw, test-flying a Mark V in 1941, reported that 'the machine was handled at different heights at various speeds and was found to be longitudinally unstable. In the dive, the machine could not be trimmed out to fly hands off and required a load on the control column.'[37] The solution to this problem, put forward by the ever-resourceful Jeffrey Quill and one of the chief engineers at Supermarine, Alan Clifton, was to install bob weights on the elevator control system, which increased the stabilizing function of the elevators.

But this could only be a temporary, makeshift, answer. It was obvious that a new Spitfire was needed to overcome all the stability, combat and engine problems. In keeping with the quest for ever greater efficiency, Supermarine and Rolls-Royce were already working on a far more advanced version of the Merlin Spitfire – one that would revolutionize the plane's performance and secure its future for the rest of the war. The breakthrough came with the Merlin 61 engine, which featured a two-stage, two-speed supercharger, which dramatically increased both the plane's speed and its efficiency at high altitude. According to Sir Stanley Hooker, one of the design experts at Rolls Royce, the Merlin 61 was originally conceived to power high-altitude bombers.

Because it was at least 9 inches longer than the normal Merlin, the company did not initially think of using it on a fighter. 'It was Hives who first asked the question, "What would happen if we put this engine into a Spitfire?" This thought did not occur to any of us and, at the time, the extra length appeared to be a major obstacle, to say nothing of the extra radiator required,' explained Hooker in 1976.[38] The Rolls-Royce installation department at Hucknall in Nottinghamshire soon demonstrated that it would be feasible for the Merlin 61 to be fitted into a Spitfire, and Supermarine began work on two new types to accommodate this potent power plant. They were to be the Mark VII and the Mark VIII, the former with a pressurized cabin, the latter without but featuring a teardrop-shaped canopy which improved all-round visibility and a modified tailplane to improve stability.

While the redesign of the airframe was under way, however, the Air Staff were becoming increasingly anxious about the menace of the Fw 190. Between February and June 1942, Fighter Command lost 335 aircraft on fighter sweeps over northern France, most of them Spitfire Vs. So desperate was the situation that, on 13 June, Sholto Douglas was ordered to curtail such operations, which had become a pointless sacrifice. Given the time it would take for a major overhaul of the airframe to be completed, the air chiefs felt that they needed something more quickly to restore the balance against Germany. Another stopgap was demanded. The plane which emerged was to become perhaps the finest Spitfire of them all: the Mark IX.

The fighter pilot Paul Richey, who took part in the Battle of Britain and the sweeps over France, once described the Spitfire as a 'compromise'.[39] The word could not be more apposite for the Mark IX, which joined the new Merlin 61 engine to the Mark V airframe. Even the Air Ministry admitted in May 1942 that the Mark IX was only 'a lash-up installation' to 'tackle the enemy's new Fw 190s because the production of the Mark VIII airframe cannot be commenced before September'.[40] But this was no marriage of convenience. The 'lash-up' turned out to be a superb aircraft, eclipsing the Focke-Wulf and giving the Spitfire a new lease of life. Indeed, the Mark IX turned out to be far more successful than its potential successors. Whereas only 140 of the Mark VII were built and 1,654 of the Mark VIII, 5,710 Mark IXs were produced – by far second largest total, after the Mark V. Contrary to the early concerns of Rolls-Royce, there were barely any major changes needed to the plane's structure. All that was required was a lengthening of the nose by 9 inches, the fitting of a four-bladed Rotol airscrew to absorb the extra power, and the installation of a second radiator under the starboard wing, giving the underneath of the wings a symmetrical appearance for the first time. Jeffrey Quill knew he was on to a winner as soon as he tested the plane in April 1942. 'The performance and handling of this aircraft in its present form is quite exceptionally good at high altitude,' he reported after flying the Mark IX for a total of fifty-seven hours, 'and it is considered that this machine will be a very formidable fighter.'[41]

Sir Wilfrid Freeman, now effectively chief executive at the Ministry of Aircraft Production, displayed one of his rare but not unknown lapses of judgement when he moaned about the lack of innovation in fighter development, symbolized for him by the continued focus on the Spitfire programme. 'The mountain has again produced a mouse and substantially the same old mouse at that. If we persist in producing types inferior to those of the enemy, our defeat in the air is certain,' he complained.[42] Freeman could not have been more wrong. The Mark IX immediately impressed its pilots. When Jeffrey Quill brought the prototype over to Hornchurch, the charismatic and self-confident commander Group Captain Harry Broadhurst, one of the most experienced of all Spitfire leaders, decided he wanted to try it out. To the horror of Jeffrey Quill, who was watching his aerial progress on a radar plot in the sector operations room, Broadhurst took the prototype over the English Channel, just as a fighter wing from Hornchurch was about to engage the Luftwaffe above Lille. 'Goddamit,' said Quill, 'he's in my aeroplane! Do you realize that's the most important fighter prototype in the country right now – and, what's more, the guns aren't loaded.' The controller replied, 'Well, there's nothing I can do about it, but right now he seems to be well above 35,000 feet.'[43] Then the operations room heard two Spitfire pilots' voices over the R/T. 'Look at that aircraft up there, he must be as high as heaven,' said one. 'That's no aircraft, that's a bleedin' angel.'[44] To Quill's relief, Broadhurst landed soon afterwards. As he climbed out of the cockpit, he turned to Quill and said, 'It's a magnificent aeroplane. Get as many as you can, as quickly as possible. By the way, you might have told me that the guns weren't loaded.'[45] Quill bit his tongue.

As the Mark IX arrived in the squadrons, the pilots were fulsome in its praise, especially at the effect of the two-stage, two-speed supercharger, which gave it 'the kick of a mule', to use the phrase of Supermarine's Don Robertson.[46] The IX added at least 10,000 feet to the fighting altitude of the Spitfire, and 70 mph to its top speed. Brian Kingcome – by 1942 wing commander at Kenley – said that he could 'hardly believe the experience' the first time he flew a Mark IX:

> The effect was magical. I had expected an increase in power, but nothing to match the reality. To enhance the dramatic effect, the second stage cut in automatically without warning. One minute there I was, relaxed and peaceful, as I climbed at a leisurely pace towards 15,000 feet, anticipating a small surge of

power as I hit the magic number. The next minute it was as though a giant hand had grabbed hold of me, cradled me in its palm like a shot-putter and given me the most terrific shove forwards and upwards. The shock was so great that I almost bailed out. It literally took my breath away. It was exhilarating, a feeling that I could never forget. I yearned at once for a chance to demonstrate the astonishing new tool to the Germans.[47]

It was a view shared by other Spitfire pilots. Johnnie Johnson believed the Mark IX was 'the best Spitfire', with 'no bad flying characteristics like there was later with the Griffon-engined Spitfires'.[48] Squadron Leader Ron Rayner, based in Malta with 43 Squadron in 1943, described the IXs as 'marvellous, absolutely incredible. I remember that on my first flight in a Mark IX, an air test, I went up to 35,000 feet, just for the joy of experiencing what it was like to operate at high altitude. It was definitely a different aircraft altogether at high altitude compared to the Mark V. It really was quite something.'[49] In August 1944, Ted Smith, based with the 2nd Tactical Air Force at Thruxton, received his first IXB – whose supercharger kicked in at a lower altitude – and recorded in his diary, 'I flew my first IXB today. It is everything I hoped it would be. It has *power*. It is a kick up the arse, compared to the Mark V . . . It is a wonderful aerobatic machine. It will perform a full loop at 300 mph, and a half roll at the top at 340 mph. From the ground, the high whine of the supercharger is surely louder than any Spitfire ever built.'[50] Al Deere, another of the great Spitfire aces, believed that 'as an all-round fighter, the Spitfire IXB ···· ʋpreme, and undoubtedly the best mark of Spitfire produced, despite later and more powerful versions.'[51]

With the Mark IX, the Spitfire could restore the balance of fighting power in the air over north-west Europe. The sense of defensive anxiety evaporated. 'One of the greatest thrills', wrote Wilfrid Duncan Smith, 'was having twelve Spitfire Mark IXs in battle formation at 43,000 feet in the knowledge that no German fighter could touch us. Though it proved unnecessary to fly in formation at that altitude during operations, there was great satisfaction in recognizing, however, that our aeroplanes could out-climb anything the enemy could send to intercept us.'[52] From the spring of 1943, the tide began to turn decisively in favour of the RAF. A sortie at this time led by Johnnie Johnson, now in command of a Canadian wing at Kenley, was indicative of this new confidence, as he and his men bounced a formation of Fw 190s:

> I turned slightly to get directly behind the 190s and remembered to make the turn slow and easy so that our wingmen could keep well up. I put the nose down and had to fight back an instinct to slam the throttle wide open. We had to hit these brutes together. My own 190 was flying on the extreme port of the

enemy formation. We came down on their tails in a long, slanting dive . . .
Now it was up to the individual pilots to select their opponents and smack them
down. I missed the 190 with my first short burst and steadied the gun platform
with course stick and rudder. I fired again and hit him in the wing root just
behind the cockpit. The spot harmonization paid off and the cannon shells
thudded into him in a deadly concentration of winking explosions. He started
to burn but before he fell on his back I gave him another long burst. Then I
broke away in a steep climbing turn and searched the sky behind. Still nothing
there. Below me another 190 was falling in flames, and on the starboard a parachute had opened in full bloom.[53]

The Spitfire was not just on the offensive in combat over northern Europe,
it was also taking on limited bomber escort duties as the USAAF started to
mount daylight missions deep into Germany. Because of its restricted radius of
action, the Spitfire could not escort the Flying Fortresses the whole way to
Germany and back, so instead they provided cover between England and the
Dutch–German border, the main route taken by the bombers. Even with
drop tanks to increase the range, this was hardly ideal, and many Spitfire pilots
bitterly regretted that they could not provide more support, especially when
they saw the appalling losses that the Americans suffered as they heroically
ploughed through treacherous skies. Only with the arrival in December 1943
of the phenomenal Merlin-powered fighter the P-51 Mustang, with its range
of almost 2,000 miles, did the bombers have the proper escort they needed.
Nevertheless, the Spitfires did perform a useful function, boosting the spirits of
the US bomber crews and protecting the stragglers on the final stretch of
their journey home. As the French RAF ace Pierre Clostermann put it:

> You could imagine the blood pouring over the heaps of empty cartridges, the
> pilot nursing his remaining engines and anxiously eyeing the long white trail of
> petrol escaping from his riddled tanks. These isolated Fortresses were the Focke-
> Wulf's favourite prey. Therefore the squadrons detached two or three pairs of
> Spitfires charged with bringing each one back safe; an exhausting task as these
> damaged Fortresses often dragged along on a third of their total power, stretch-
> ing the endurance of their escort to the limit. In many cases it was only the
> moral support of the presence of a pair of Spitfires that gave them the courage
> to hold out to the end, to resist the temptation of bailing out and waiting for
> the end of the war in some Oflag or other.[54]

More effective, though, was the Spitfires' role in acting as an escort for the
US Bostons and Marauders on their missions to hit German ground targets in
France and the Low Countries. The Polish squadron leader Franciszek
Kornicki of 303 Squadron left this account of one such raid by 72 Marauders
on the industrial city of Lille in September 1943:

We were in the middle of a very large fighter escort. Just before we reached the target a group of about fifteen enemy aircraft approached our formation from behind and above and it looked as if they intended to dive through us to the bombers. I warned the squadron that as soon as they got a bit closer we should turn 180 degrees anticlockwise and meet them head-on as we had done on a training flight. Immediately the usual pandemonium started: guns blazing, aircraft turning, twisting, climbing, diving, and warnings and shouts over the R/T. After a while I wanted to get everybody together again and called them to join me at a certain altitude where I would circle to the left; to my surprise we reassembled very quickly and once again we were a force and not a team to be trifled with. By that time the bombers had disappeared from sight on their way home and it was time for us to do the same.[55]

One interesting incident in the RAF's war against the Focke-Wulf occurred in June 1942, when a German 190 pilot, Oberleutnant Arnim Faber, either through desertion or disorientation, landed his undamaged plane on Fighter Command's Pembrey base in South Wales. For months previously the RAF had been desperate to get hold of an intact 190 to analyse its performance. Highly secret plans had even been drawn up to launch a commando-style raid on a Luftwaffe base in northern France and seize one. Jeffrey Quill and Group Captain Hugh Wilson of the RAE at Farnborough were both willing to undertake the mission. But Oberleutnant Faber's bizarre generosity obviated the need for such a dangerous step. On hearing the news of the seizure of the 190, the Air Staff asked Wilson to go to Wales and fly it back to Farnborough, giving a guarantee that it would not be damaged. Wilson said it was impossible to give any such assurance, so the plane was dismantled and taken by lorry to the Royal Aircraft Establishment. When Wilson flew it, he made this comparison with the Spitfire:

> The 190 really was a delightful plane to fly, probably the finest propeller-powered fighter of the war. However, when we came to full analytical flying, its performance – as opposed to its manoeuvrability – had not much to offer compared to the Spitfire Mark IX and we were able to reassure Fighter Command in this matter. There was one aspect of the Fw 190 that I never really liked and that was the engine, which was very rough. It never gave me much sense of security, possibly because I was spoilt by flying behind those smooth British engines.[56]

A less edifying aspect of this curious episode was the punishment meted out to Oberleutnant Faber. In his unpublished memoir, Wilson recorded that when he first met Faber, 'I think in modern parlance he was a mixed-up kid. I found him extremely bumptious and not very helpful. He made sinister statements that the machine was fitted with an explosive charge for destructive purposes. I left with the impression that he was talking a lot of bull.' However, when he next saw Faber, who had then been transferred to army custody, he found 'a very different individual. He arrived in the room in tears and he had obviously been having the treatment. I think I found this meeting to be one of the most disillusioning events of the war. I was shaken to see how a man could so disintegrate and I realized that even the (so-called) chivalrous British were not at all beyond imitating some of the nasty things we heard about the Germans.'[57]

Such incidents were rare, however – particularly within the RAF, where there was a tradition of 'hard, clean, ruthless fighting in the air', to use a phrase of Laddie Lucas's.[58] A sense of mutual respect, even honour, prevailed between the fighter pilots of the RAF and the Luftwaffe, though the Poles and Czechs, filled with their visceral hatred for the Nazi regime, could be far less restrained. In his long experience of fighting, Laddie Lucas said he only once saw the moral code ignored. This happened during the peak of the Battle of Malta, when a pilot from 249 Squadron who had bailed out and was descending to earth below his parachute was blown out of the sky by a Messerschmitt. 'No discipline will hold the blind fury of a squadron which has witnessed such cruelty to a comrade,' wrote Lucas. Within a week, a Spitfire pilot had the chance to level the score when he came across the crew of a shot-down Ju 88 in a dinghy off the Maltese coast. Lucas was a witness to what happened next:

> My eye caught sight of a single Spitfire away to my left, at the bottom of a shallow fast dive, heading straight for the dinghy. A sustained burst of fire sent geysers of water creeping up on the tiny, inflated boat. Not content with one run, the pilot pulled up again into a tight climbing turn to the left and dived again. In war, one bad act will always beget another.[59]

By late 1943, it was a war that Germany was losing. The Nazi position in France was weakening. Germany itself was coming under increasing bombardment. The Allies were driving through Italy, having swept the Axis out of Africa. After the heroic defence of Malta, the Spitfires had played a vital part in the African campaign. The architect of the British air victory in the desert had been Arthur Tedder, who had taken over command of the RAF in the Middle East in May 1941 and proved himself the ideal leader: strong-minded, decisive and inspiring, he possessed 'one of the most brilliant minds in any of the services', according to the head of Bomber Command, Sir Arthur Harris.[60] Where Tedder was particularly creative was in working closely with the army, using his Spitfires and Hurricanes to full effect in combined operations.

Throughout the fight in North Africa, Tedder had been deeply impressed by the attitude of the RAF, noting this incident in the summer of 1942, after crated Spitfires had been arriving in Egypt. 'At one fighter aerodrome, I watched as a hundred men lifted a Spitfire bodily so as to get to the articulator beneath it. There was no crane available but they were determined not to lose the Spitfire. This was the spirit I had seen throughout the RAF in the western desert.'[61] Just as in Malta, it was the arrival of the Spitfires that checked the German advance and then helped to turn it back. As the German General von Waldau said of the RAF in July 1942, 'Combat effectiveness has been maintained and indeed increased by the assignment of new and excellently trained Spitfire squadrons from England. The employment of the Spitfires has given the enemy the confidence he needs to hold his own against our Me 109s.'[62] Led by the Spitfires, the RAF was crucial in the victory at El Alamein, which signalled the beginning of the end for German ambitions in North Africa. 'The continuing heavy attacks of the RAF who were practically masters of the air absolutely pinned my troops to the ground and made impossible any safe deployment or any advance according to schedule,' admitted Rommel.[63]

On 8 November, just days after the victory at El Alamein, Anglo-American forces landed in North Africa in Operation Torch, with carrier-based Seafires and Spitfires from Gibraltar providing air cover for the amphibious attack led by General Eisenhower. The assembling of the 118 Spitfires in Gibraltar, in foul weather, was 'a prodigious effort by the airmen responsible', involving 'the utmost haste and ceaseless activity', wrote Group Captain G. A. Bolland, one of those overseeing the task.[64] Within eighteen hours of Torch, Admiral Darlan, the representative of the Vichy government, had surrendered. Six Spitfire squadrons were soon operating from the Algerian airfield of Maison Blanche, and the first IXs began to arrive to handle the potential threat of Fw 190s over the Mediterranean. Bobby Oxspring, who had flown from Gibraltar with 72 Squadron, was one of those who spent Christmas in North Africa amid a tropical storm. A local Arab had sold them a large, elderly turkey for dinner, but, when cooked, it proved all but inedible: 'We couldn't get our teeth into the meat, which must have seen twenty summers.' The wine, very definitely *vin ordinaire*, was provided by the Foreign Legion and transported to the base in petrol cans. 'A mouthful of this pernicious gut-rot, flavoured with the fumes of 100 octane gasoline, was sufficient to recede the hairline untold inches. We huddled in our dripping tents, knocking back the witch's brew and toasted the health of faraway kin.'[65]

The first months of 1943 saw the Axis forces trapped in Tunisia. Their supply lines were gradually worn down by continual aerial bombardment, the Spitfires now holding complete air superiority over North Africa. 'We were operating all the time, attacking the Germans wherever we could find them,' recalled Peter Olver of 244 Wing, which by April comprised seven Spitfire squadrons.[66] The diary of Neville Duke, a Spitfire pilot in 92 Squadron, exudes confidence during these months. On 8 January 1943, for example, he described a fight with two Italian Macchi 202 fighters:

> We were well placed and in the sun – they never saw us until too late when they put their noses down for home but we were on them. The one I chased went down almost vertically from 10,000 feet to the deck, clocking 400 plus. Gained on him easily along the deck and drew smoke from him with a cannon shell in his radiator and oil cooler. He finally hit the ground and burst into flames after some more hits from my cannons which were working well this day![67]

As he grew more experienced, Duke's admiration for the Spitfire increased. 'I flew up to Sirte and had a look at the place,' he wrote on 5 January:

> I love just flying around doing nothing in particular. One minute nipping along the deck at nought feet and then, with just a gentle pull on the stick and a little more motor, soaring up for hundreds of feet, feeling the immense power that you have got just at your fingertips. Feeling that you are part of a fine machine, made by a genius. It is said that the Spitfire is too beautiful to be a fighting machine. I sometimes think that it is true but then, what better fighter could you want?[68]

Flight Lieutenant Godfrey Ball of 43 Squadron was also infused with optimism while on duty in North Africa, particularly when Spitfires replaced the squadron's ageing Hurricanes. 'I gloried in every minute I spent in the air with my beloved Spitfire. The possibility of action kept us on our toes and the good fortune of some of the pilots to encounter such things as the Italian Savoria Marchette 79, a slow wooden tri-motored aeroplane used as a torpedo bomber, made us all keen to take to the air.' Ball wrote this account of taking on a much more modern plane, the Ju 88 bomber, in March 1943 over the Tunisian coast:

> I was coming up nicely almost directly from behind, maybe ten degrees off, but if anything a shade below his height. I was almost within range, but I wanted to get really close, for everyone I had spoken to on the subject insisted that to get in really close was the only sure way of getting a 'kill'. At that moment he must have spotted me. The Ju 88 banked steeply to starboard in towards me. I banked with him and the range closed rapidly. I started firing as my gunsight creased his tail and I drew the bead along his fuselage, canopy and starboard wing. I could see strikes on the wing and the engine nacelle and then I had to break upwards in a steep climbing turn to starboard lest I collide with him. As I banked over almost to an inverted position I could see him

diving almost vertically with a long stream of black smoke flowing out from his starboard engine. Already he had an incredible lead on me but I just changed my over-banked climbing into a sort of half-roll and followed him down. The Spitfire is a reluctant diver and had to be trimmed very nose heavy to make the dive steep. I will never know what speed I reached. I daren't take my eye of the Ju 88 lest I lose it; it was going down steeply and at great speed. If it hadn't been for the black plume I would have had trouble keeping it in view.

The Ju 88 plunged through a cloud and then, according to ground control, disappeared off the radar screen, presumably having crashed into the sea, though Ball pulled out of his dive before he reached the cloud and so witnessed none of this. When Ball landed, he found that he had been going so fast in the dive that 'the camouflage paint on my Spitfire's wing tips and the leading edge of the tailplane had been stripped off. They glistened as brightly polished duralumin!'[69]

The increasing sense of self-confidence abroad was mirrored at home in the burgeoning production and servicing operation for the Spitfires, which by the end of 1943 had reached a size and sophistication far beyond anything that Mitchell – or the exasperated Lord Swinton – could ever have imagined. On the south coast, the Supermarine dispersal scheme was operating with remarkable smoothness, given the mosaic of different locations involved. At the outbreak of war, Supermarine had a workforce of 2,879. By September 1943 the number of employees had risen to 9,115. In that quarter, the company delivered 362 Spitfires from its southern plants, compared to 124 in the first three months of 1940.[70] The turnaround at Castle Bromwich was even more dramatic. Having been gripped by paralysis on the eve of the Battle of Britain, the factory now had one of the highest outputs in Europe. In June 1943 the workforce at Castle Bromwich totalled almost 14,400, and the plant turned out 320 Spitfires that month – more than the entire first Supermarine contract, which had taken almost three years to complete and had dragged the government into crisis.[71] Eric Holden, one of the Castle Bromwich inspectors, felt this rapid growth in production was a tribute to the Birmingham workforce, once it was under the well-organized management of Vickers: 'People worked tremendously hard. I can remember talking to a foreman and he fell asleep on my shoulder. We got up to over 300 planes a month. It was a stupendous achievement. I used to walk out on to the tarmac and think, Those couldn't all have come out of this plant.' Because of the demands of the armed services, more than 40 per cent of Castle Bromwich's workforce was female, though Holden felt that this was a benefit: 'There were lots of girls in the factory and I must say that they were amazing. They were marvellous at riveting. My experience was that once they had been shown the required skill, they were more quality conscious than the men.'[72]

Megan Rees, from South Wales, was one of those riveters, starting work at the factory when she was only twenty:

> I worked on the starboard wings of the Spitfires. The wings of the Spitfires were built vertically in jigs. I once drilled through my little finger and went to first aid with the bit of the drill still in my finger and holding the drill steady in my other hand. I then progressed on to marking the position of the holes. You had to be very accurate. When things had to be riveted together you worked in pairs, one person operating the riveting gun and another with an iron block underneath the hole being riveted to take the pressure. It was very noisy and there was a lot of vibration.

Rees recalled that she was allowed to smoke 'all day. We smoked Craven "A" and Senior Service. I was forever putting the cigarette down, so that most of it went up in smoke. There were no restrictions on smoking even though paint spraying was taking place in the area. It seems strange now but smoking was a way of life then.' The hours were extremely long – sixty-three a week over seven days – and there was the ever-present danger of air raids: by the end of the war 200 bombs had been dropped on Castle Bromwich, with 11 people being killed and 55 injured.

> We worked one of two shifts, starting at 6 a.m. and 6 p.m. When on the night shift, at 9 p.m. we would put our gas masks and clothes ready at the end of the jigs so that we could grab them when the sirens went off. We would have to run to the air-raid shelters. The shelters were underground and huge. There were benches each side for sitting. There were no bunks for sleeping. The men used to play cards down one end of the shelter. There must have been some lighting, but there were no facilities for making a drink or anything to eat. Each block had a restroom, and there was a big canteen. The radio programme *Workers' Playtime* used to come to the factory. Throughout the war I just remember being so very tired working long hours, but you just got on with doing what had to be done. I was too tired to do anything but work and sleep, but I will always have a special place in my heart for the Spitfire.[73]

Dorothy Bailey was another female employee, beginning as an eighteen-year-old seamstress sewing fabric for the Spitfire's rudder: 'Where we worked was called the Dope Room. After we had done our sewing, they would put the parts in the dope to make the fabric go brown and waterproofed. It was a filthy liquid – the smell was always atrocious, like rubber. My mother always knew when I came home because she could smell my bag when I put it down on the chair.'[74]

The hero of the Castle Bromwich workforce was the fearless test pilot Alex Henshaw, who during his time with Vickers flew more than 2,000 Spitfires – around 10 per cent of the entire output in the country during the war. What made him so popular with the workforce was the unique mix of courage and aerobatic skill which he showed during the Spitfire demonstrations at Castle Bromwich for the factory's regular stream of visitors. Few other pilots had the nerve to perform the daring manoeuvres that he frequently carried out, demonstrating his complete mastery of the aircraft. 'He has a reputation for technical accomplishment and calculated recklessness which has made him a crew-room legend,' said a profile in the *Birmingham Evening Mail* in 1945.[75] One Castle Bromwich administrator, Lillian Sherman, explained Henshaw's appeal:

> Alex was a great guy and gave us office wallahs something to think about. His wizardry with his beloved Spitfires lives in my memory. He used to dive so low over the factory that he often broke parts off the porcelain ridge tiles from the glass roof which would then skelter down the roof whilst we sat hunched up expecting the crunch which, of course, never came. He used also to taxi down the main drive of the factory and send us wenches into panic as he airily moved on, making rude gestures as he passed. He was a great favourite with us all.[76]

A flavour of his dazzling talent in the cockpit of a Spitfire can be gleaned from this description of one of his displays in 1941:

> In a few minutes he was off again, roaring past the hangars and then climbing over our heads like a hawk against the grey ceiling. There was a moment of stillness and suspense and then he was putting the machine down into a power dive at more than 400 mph. Suddenly the machine is rushing at you like a thunderbolt and you have to dig your heels into the grass so as not to duck or run in that second when he is flattening out over your head.[77]

Born in 1912, the son of a wealthy businessman, Alex Henshaw always possessed an adventurous nature and a passion for flying. Early in 1939 he made a record-breaking solo return flight from England to Cape Town in a Percival Mew Gull, landing at Gravesend 4 days and 10 hours after he had first taken off. He was so exhausted that he was on the verge of collapse, and had to be lifted from the tiny cockpit. His buccaneering outlook continually rebelled against officialdom. His war was waged as much against the rule book as against Germany. On one occasion he grew fed up with a pompous Air Ministry civil servant using his own Castle Bromwich office for long phone calls to

Whitehall. So he secretly rigged up his phone to a wireless set. The next time the official tried to ring London all he heard was the sound of dance music.

In the early years of the war, Rolls-Royce grew exasperated at some of his daring aerobatics, particularly his enthusiasm for flying upside down. 'We cannot believe that there is any necessity to indulge in this type of flying and if carried out may result in engine trouble,' Rolls-Royce warned the Castle Bromwich management in December 1940.[78] In January, a senior Rolls-Royce sales representative, Bill Lappin, again found cause to complain after a visit to Castle Bromwich: 'It came to my notice that Henshaw and his assistant are regularly fooling around with Spitfires and flying them inverted across the aerodrome at low altitude . . . It cannot help being risky from the engine reliability point of view as they must run with no oil pressure.'[79] According to Alex Henshaw, when the Castle Bromwich directors put the accusation to him, 'I replied with some emphasis that I tested all aircraft to a detailed specification prepared by Supermarine's design office. I did this to the best of my ability and if there were those who found this unsatisfactory I could resolve the situation by giving them my resignation. The meeting ended very quickly.'[80]

It was Henshaw's anger at bureaucracy that gave him one of his finest moments. In September 1940 the Lord Mayor of Birmingham told him that, as part of the local Spitfire fund-raising drive, he would have to give a display right over the city centre. Henshaw was furious not only at the peremptory demand but also at the distraction from his hectic flight-testing schedule at the peak of the Battle of Britain, as well as the potential danger to the public. 'I was bloody angry, very angry. I thought, How bloody stupid to ask me to put my own life at risk and those of all the other people.' So he decided to teach the civic leader a lesson. He raced his Spitfire low down the main street, barely 100 feet above the ground, rolling the plane as he went, before flying in an inverted position level with the top of the City Hall. So awesome was the sight that he brought the centre of Birmingham to a standstill. When he landed at Castle Bromwich, the Chief Constable was waiting for him. Henshaw was told that he would have to make a statement to the police. 'I'm not going anywhere and I'm certainly not making a statement. I suggest you get in touch with your lord mayor,' he replied. That was the end of the matter.[81]

His innate distrust of political authority meant that he 'regretted' all his later life having accepted the CBE, though he was a huge admirer of that other maverick Winston Churchill, who saw him in action at Castle Bromwich in 1941. He also, of course, adored the Spitfire, from the moment he first flew it:

I realized at once it was the best monoplane I had ever flown. I knew it was an exceptional plane to fly. The Spitfire changed with the Mark IX. Up to the IX, it still retained the Spitfire qualities. But when you came on to the more powerful plane, yes, as a weapon of war it was superb. But from a flying point of view my favourite would be the Mark V with metal ailerons. It had enormous power. It could take off in less than 200 yards and you could bring it up in a vertical loop, get it over at that angle, then you could actually do rolls and moves at low levels.[82]

Alex Henshaw was always publicly appreciative of the Castle Bromwich workforce for its efforts on Spitfire production. Yet, though the majority of employees did labour heroically, it would be wrong to pretend that the spirit of self-sacrifice was universally in evidence. In his epic work *The Audit of War*, the historian Correlli Barnett revealed the extent of trade-union intransigence within British industry, including aircraft manufacturing, throughout the war. Trivial and parochial disputes regularly disrupted production, though officially all the wartime stoppages in the aircraft industry were illegal, since strikes had been banned under the Essential Work Order of 1940. One particularly grotesque example occurred in 1942 at the sheet-metal factory run by Hawksley's in Gloucester, where the workers went on strike because one employee would not 'go slow' and earned 7s. 9d. an hour by piecework when the union restricted earnings to 4s. 6d. an hour.[83] Between July 1942 and December 1944 the total number of man-hours lost to strikes in the aircraft industry was 4.1 million, with disputes running at the level of ten a month in mid-1943.[84] Castle Bromwich was not exempt. The legacy of the early days still lingered. In December 1942, as the Mark IX was introduced, the Vickers board was told that, at the Birmingham factory, 'this quarter has shown a serious development of unauthorized strikes which, particularly in December, has had a most adverse effect on production. The tendency to "direct action" has steadily increased and the union organizers seem unable to stop it.' One of the causes of the unrest had been the introduction of a new rota system, which had to be suspended because of the severity of opposition.[85]

The problem was so serious that the government had to intervene. Ben Smith, former London cab driver, Labour MP and deputy to Sir Stafford Cripps, the left-wing Secretary of the State at the Ministry of Aircraft Production, was sent to Birmingham one stormy night to resolve the dispute, as senior Castle Bromwich manager of the time Bonar Dickson, head of aircraft production, described:

> We were changing over to a new series of engines and there was a quibble over piecework rates which led to a stoppage. Sir Stafford Cripps was then Minister

and I remember thinking of him as a man too ready to give in to the workers on such matters. I was determined not to stand down, although there was only one thing to aim at – getting production going at the earliest possible moment. Mr Ben Smith set out from the Ministry at 9 p.m. expecting to arrive at my house about midnight. But it was a terrible night. Trees were being blown over in the gale, and of course it was a blackout and road conditions were very bad. He did not arrive until 3 a.m. and was too tired to talk. He had a brandy and went to bed. The next morning he met the men while I looked on apprehensively. To my delight he tore into them and pulled no punches, with the result that they all agreed to go back to work on Monday morning and allow their grievances to be settled by arbitration. Spitfires were back in production.[86]

Even after this settlement, concern remained about the quality and attitude of the Castle Bromwich workforce. Another Vickers report, in 1943, complained that:

the standard of male and female labour has steadily deteriorated over the last six months, as many of the individuals find movement from firm to firm comparatively easy because their health gives an ever ready reason for release if they are discontented. Many men recruited from the north have obtained their release, the largest percentage on health grounds although they were examined by the local Ministry of Labour doctors and pronounced fit to do heavy manual labour before they were brought down to Castle Bromwich.[87]

Such criticisms of the trade unions and parts of the workforce continued to be heard for the remainder of the war. Managers grew exasperated with 'protracted negotiations' about overtime rates for clerical workers, and the failure by union committees to provide 'any examples of suggestions to improve production', since they were 'mainly centred on working conditions'. The year 1944 saw further claims that the 'standard and class' of recruitment was 'very low', making it 'extremely difficult for certain departments to carry on', while the trade unions had mounted 'very strong opposition' to any changes in the skilled-rate payment system. Shortages were another problem: 'We are now taking on men to do work which could satisfactorily be done by women but as few women are available, we have no alternative.'[88]

Nor was Castle Bromwich unique in this respect. At South Marston, one of the Spitfire dispersal sites, it was reported to Vickers that there was 'a serious absentee problem' in 1943.[89] Cyril Russell, the Supermarine operative, was occasionally disappointed with the recalcitrant or self-serving outlook of some of his colleagues. When engaged on Spitfire assembly at High Post in Wiltshire, he discovered that some of the armoury employees, who were on a special incentive scheme, were manipulating repair records so they could work 'a fiddle from the accumulated time they had'.[90] A trade-union member himself, Russell was even more enraged when he was once asked to deputize for his official branch convener at a Vickers consultative meeting. At the height of war, the petty-mindedness of other union representatives appalled him:

> I sat and listened, expecting to hear either justifiable grievances or proposals from the shop floor that would aid or increase production. To my surprise – and may I add my growing annoyance – all that came forth were piddling little complaints about the shortage of loo rolls here and no soap there, cold meals in the canteens, bad lodgings, underpayment of bonuses and a whole host of trivial matters, all of which should have been and could have been dealt with by the foreman.

One of the Vickers managers, Vernon Hall, listened patiently to this catalogue, but at the end of the meeting, when Hall asked if there was any other business, Cyril Russell could not hold his tongue: 'In my iciest voice, and restraining the factory language that was in my mind to use, I told my so-called representative colleagues just what I thought of their whingeing and whining complaints, and apologized to Mr Hall for his having to sit through such drivel.' When Russell finished, there was 'a stunned silence' and then the meeting broke up 'in unaccustomed disorder'.[91] Russell was never asked to deputize again at a works meeting.

But it would be wrong to exaggerate the importance of this kind of trouble. In such a huge Spitfire workforce, operating under long hours under pressure, there was bound to be occasional friction. The very fact that grievances were so trivial points to a general mood of unity rather than any widespread discontent. As the Ministry of Aircraft Production pointed out, the hours lost in strikes in the aircraft industry, even at their peak in mid-1943, never amounted to more than 0.5 per cent of the total hours worked.[92] It is a tribute to the Castle Bromwich workforce that on 24 November 1944 the ten-thousandth Spitfire rolled off its production line.

12

'I say, Miss, you must be good on instruments'

BY 1944 THE Spitfire was a global phenomenon. Almost abandoned by the Air Ministry in 1939, declared by Downing to be obsolescent in 1942, the plane now had an international reach on a scale that was never to be achieved by any other British aircraft in history. It was fighting with the RAF over Italy, France, the Low Countries and the Mediterranean, as well as in the Far East, Burma and the Pacific. And the Spitfire's operations were not confined to the RAF. The plane was supplied to other Allied or neutral air forces as diverse as those of Russia, Portugal, Australia and Turkey.

When Russia was first invaded in 1941, the British agreed to send the Red Air Force 200 Hurricanes. No Spitfires could be spared. If they were unavailable for Malta, they were certainly not going to be shipped across the Baltic. In October 1942, however, two squadrons of RAF Spitfires were temporarily sent to Russia to carry out photoreconnaissance duties in support of British bombers which were helping to protect Soviet convoys. Seeing the PR Spitfires in action, the Russians were quickly impressed. With the Germans advancing relentlessly to the Caucasus, the Russian ambassador to London, Ivan Maisky, sent Churchill this note: 'I must inform you that our position in the Stalingrad area has changed for the worse since the early days of September . . . We are short of fighters with which to cover our forces. Even the bravest troops are helpless without air cover. What we particularly need are Spitfires.'[1] Churchill, with his instinctive geopolitical understanding about the importance of Stalingrad, agreed to send a batch of Mark V fighters. On 8 October he telegraphed directly to Stalin, 'We will send you as soon as possible by the Persian Gulf route 150 Spitfires, with the equivalent of 50 more in the form of spares to be sent as they become available.'[2] As if to underline the efficacy of the gesture, the Foreign Office telegraphed Moscow a week later, 'Please convey following from Prime Minister to Premier Stalin. "I should have added that the 150 Spitfires are all armed with 2 cannons and 4 machine guns."'[3] Because of the pressures of Malta and North Africa, however, the Spitfires did not reach the Soviet air force until March 1943, when they were handed over to the

Russian mission at Basra, Iraq, the RAF roundels being immediately replaced by red stars.

One Russian pilot, Senior Lieutenant Anatoli Ivanov, used to flying the Polkarpov 1-16 fighter, gave this rather dismissive initial reaction to the Spitfire in the Soviet press:

> The Spitfire was simple to fly and tolerant of mistakes but it was not anything special. The 1-16 had been much more demanding. The Soviet fighters had a significantly better performance. The sole advantage of the Spitfire was the fact that it was very light and, with its powerful engine, it climbed well. This would give us the advantage of height. Its worst feature was that the guns were mounted in the wings, the distance between the cannon was nearly 4 metres, so when attacking the enemy from close range the concentration of fire power was low.[4]

Such remarks have to be seen within the context of chauvinist anti-Western propaganda, which held that no foreign machines could match Soviet designs. Even so, Ivanov could not deny the thrill when he flew his Spitfire into combat against the Luftwaffe over the Black Sea port of Novorossiysk in June 1943, taking on a formation of Heinkel 111s:

> Now I had plenty of altitude. The leader of the Heinkels seemed to have seen neither my aircraft nor that of my wing man . . . I went down steeply and sneaked in behind the leading Heinkel. 'Cover me, I'm going in to attack!' I commanded Ragozin my wing man . . . The nose of my Spitfire was pointing at the belly of the fascist. I opened fire, turned away just in time and saw an explosion. The Heinkel began to tilt and two parachutes fell clear. I felt great. I had knocked down my second enemy of that day.[5]

For the rest of the war, despite some negative comments in the press, the Spitfires continued to prove useful to the Soviet Union, especially when the Mark Vs were replaced by the Mark IXs. Towards the end of 1944, whole production lines from Castle Bromwich were reserved for shipment to Russia. By April 1945 a total of 1,331 Spitfires had operated in the Red Air Force.

Other countries also benefited from Mitchell's aircraft. Portugal, concerned about a possible invasion from Spain's Franco regime, acquired 48 Mark V Spitfires in October 1943. For most of the war, until March 1945, Turkey maintained a stance of strict − some might say cynical − neutrality between the Axis and Allied powers, symbolized by its import both of tropicalized Spitfires and Focke-Wulf 190s. Britain's closest neighbour, Eire, still nominally a Dominion under the Crown, kept its neutrality right up to VE Day. The only two Spitfires that arrived in Ireland during the war did so as a result of crash landings, leading to the internment of their pilots.

At the other end of the Commonwealth spectrum was Australia, one of Britain's most loyal allies from September 1939. Australian pilots had fought heroically in the Battle of Britain, and in 1941 there were two RAAF squadrons in England, equipped with Spitfires. But when the war opened up in the Far East, planes and men were urgently needed back in Australia. From February 1942 the port of Darwin on the northern coast came under bombardment from the Japanese air force, and similar attacks continued throughout the year. The RAAF – equipped only with outdated American P-39s and P-40s – was unable to mount an adequate response. Churchill had agreed in May 1942 to send three squadrons of Spitfires, but, though the personnel reached Australia quickly, there were long delays over dispatching the planes. In another illustration of the growing international reputation of the Spitfire, the Australian Prime Minister, John Curtin, felt compelled to write to Churchill, 'There is a most urgent need for the three squadrons and the personnel will be idle until the equipment arrives. We wish to emphasize that the air strength of Australia without the Spitfire squadrons represents a great wastage of personnel and equipment because of the superiority of the Japanese fighter aircraft over the American types ... Our air power will be greatly enhanced by Spitfires.'[6] In response, Churchill stressed the pressures of the unfolding crisis in North Africa, but promised that planes would soon be sent.

It was not until the middle of January 1943, however, that the Spitfires finally did arrive. They fought tenaciously against the Japanese, shooting down twenty-four enemy aircraft by May, and the Spitfire Vc's maximum speed of 365 mph exceeded that of the Japanese Zero at around 350 mph. But, because they had seen heavy action elsewhere, the planes proved vulnerable and unreliable. Gun stoppages were particularly common. A sense of disillusionment over the famous fighter spread through the Australian air force, as shown by this revealing letter sent by Major General R. H. Dewing, the head of RAF liaison in Australia, to Churchill's Chief of Staff Sir Hastings 'Pug' Ismay after a visit to one of the squadrons:

> When I talked to them, officers of the squadron were almost bitter about the aircraft they had to use. They are far from the latest type of Spitfire and the machines themselves have done an amount of flying which at home would put them on the scrapheap. As you probably know the squadron lost rather heavily through the pilots, in their enthusiasm, pursuing the Japanese too far out to sea. General Headquarters released their losses without any explanation so that the initial impression was given that they were shot down by the Japs. The moral of the story seems to be that if and when the United Kingdom is sending material contributions to this theatre, someone ought to ensure that the thing is handled to enhance prestige.[7]

The Air Staff recognized that more had to be done. With the Axis in retreat throughout Europe from mid-1943, the British government could afford to be more generous. It was agreed to send 40 of the Mark VIII – the more advanced version of the Merlin 61 Mark IX – in November, followed by 22 of the latest tropicalized Spitfires every month. 'A splendid contribution' was the verdict of the Australian Foreign Minister, Bert Evatt, in a telegram to Churchill.[8] As in Europe, the Spitfires helped to turn the tide from late 1943, as the Japanese campaign lost its momentum and the RAAF went on the offensive over the Pacific.

The Spitfire was also a truly international aircraft in the sense of the range of nationalities that flew it from the United Kingdom. Poles, Czechs, and Belgians were all prominent in the Battle of Britain, as were pilots from throughout the Dominions. In fact the Poles, who continually proved to be the most accurate marksmen in RAF gunnery contests, shot down 7 per cent of all the enemy aircraft destroyed in the battle.[9] This overseas influence continued to grow from late 1940, with the RAF developing separate squadrons for foreign nationals, such as the Belgian 349 and 350 Squadrons, or the Norwegian Spitfire units, 331 and 332. And Free French pilots made up no fewer than ten squadrons within the RAF by the time of liberation. Miroslav Liskutin, a pilot with the Czech 312 Squadron for most of the war, was one of the many foreigners who was thrilled with the experience of the Spitfire. Having escaped from France in 1940, he was sent the following year to a Spitfire operational training unit (OTU) in Grangemouth, Scotland, where he was overwhelmed by the sight of the planes on his arrival at the base: 'A pleasant green field with a very large fleet of beautiful Spitfires. For some unexplained reason, these aircraft were neatly parked in rows, as if awaiting an inspection, and were not dispersed as required by wartime regulations. This was the first time I had seen RAF aircraft so assembled. It looked absolutely beautiful! I felt emotionally uplifted.' A few days later Liskutin felt even greater excitement, when he had his first flight in a Spitfire. 'It was a wonderful and unforgettable experience. Everything was so pleasant and so easy. It felt perhaps even nicer than I hoped it would be. For me it was a confirmation of love at first flight! It was the start of a happy partnership in war and peace.'[10]

Liskutin had an eventful four years of war in his Spitfire, battling with Fw 190s over the English Channel, escorting bombers over France, dive-bombing sites in Normandy after D-Day, and carrying out reconnaissance missions over Nazi-occupied Holland in late 1944. One particularly dangerous Dutch sortie involved photographing Flushing harbour. So risky was it that Liskutin later admitted that it became 'deeply engraved on my memory'. To take the necessary pictures, he had to make a low-level pass over the harbour, weaving between the cranes and the anti-aircraft fire:

> Shells exploded all around me and tracer bullets seemed to have created a momentary smoke-cage which enveloped my aircraft. I heard the sound of bullets and splinters of shrapnel tearing through the skin of my aircraft. The overpowering smell of cordite filled my cockpit and it seemed to have a created a strange, stimulating sensation. I clearly remember that it was actually quite unnerving but, at the same time, it was as though I was watching the whole show as a spectator. The chances of getting out alive were minimal but I viewed it with extraordinary equanimity.

Yet he was able to return and land his plane, which, to his astonishment, had sustained only a few bullet holes in the wings and the tailplane.[11] Incidents like this only deepened his admiration for the Spitfire.

On another occasion in 1944 he was on a ground-strafing mission over Caen after D-Day when he flew straight through a line of poplar trees. The airscrew chewed up one tree; the left wing sliced through another. Yet, despite the grave damage, his Spitfire remained flyable and he was able to coax it to the English coast. But as he approached Portsmouth the glycol temperature shot up, going off the scale at over 150°C. 'Fire in the engine seemed imminent, or the engine may seize up, or it may explode. The tension was mounting with every passing minute of flying in this unthinkable state.' But, with his characteristic fortitude, Liskutin hung on until he reached his base of Appledram in west Sussex. As he went into the curving approach, throttling back and putting the undercarriage down, the engine shut down completely, though he was still able to glide in and make a normal landing. 'The hardy Merlin took a terrific scourging but survived long enough to get us safely home. The local Rolls-Royce representative was dancing around with obvious pride and satisfaction. This is reliability in extreme adversity.'[12]

By 1942 there were enough American volunteers in the RAF to form three separate 'Eagle' squadrons, nos. 71, 121 and 133, using a mix of Hurricanes and Spitfires. Opposition to Nazism and the excitement of flying in combat were among the motivations for signing up. Lee Gover, an air enthusiast from Redwood City in California, said that the chance of experiencing the Spitfire added to his decision to fight in 1941. 'England's struggle in the Battle of Britain sure made me figure that I was going to war pretty soon.' When Gover heard that one of his friends 'was in an Eagle squadron and flying Spitfires, I started to think seriously about joining the RAF myself. I knew that I had plenty of flying experience but couldn't qualify for Army or Navy pilot training since I hadn't gone to college. And flying the Spitfires, wow!' On his arrival in England, his expectations of the plane were fulfilled. He described in his diary one training flight in which he tested the Spitfire's aerobatic qualities, going up to 31,000 feet, rolling it on its back, and then going into a dive before pulling out at 25,000 feet. 'I was doing a true ground speed of 480 mph, which is pretty damn fast in any man's army. Then I did spins, slow rolls, loops and lazy eights. Finished up with some cloud flying. Boy, the oxygen sure works swell in Spitfires, and she just screams at that speed. What an airplane!' Gover's uncomplicated approbation continued right through his training:

> The Spitfire cockpit was really something. It was all business. At first I thought it was pretty cramped, since the sides were only a couple of inches from your shoulders and you only had an inch or so of headroom with the canopy closed, but it was actually quite comfortable . . . I was also awed by the size of the engine. It seemed to stick out in front of the cockpit for yards and yards . . . I never ceased to be impressed with how smooth the engine was. There was none of the vibration and shaking that I had come to expect on most planes that I had flown.[13]

Like Liskutin, Gover was a heroic aviator, his years of war filled with daring missions. One of the most nerve-racking occurred in September 1942. Flying 25 miles inland over Holland on escort duty for a formation of Boeing B-17 Flying Fortresses, he became detached from his squadron. Immediately six Me 109s began to approach him:

> I saw the Germans and tried to figure out how to get by them. I remembered my dad always told me that if a fight was going to happen, strike the first blow as hard as you could and you have the other guy mentally whipped. I had about 3,000 feet of altitude on them, so I put the Spitfire into a shallow dive and built up all the speed I could. I dove right for them with all guns blazing. I gave a little left rudder and then a little right rudder so my bullets would spray them and maybe make them scatter. Sure enough, they broke every which way as I went through them. I just kept going, since my engine was not running.

Gover made it home with 3 gallons of petrol and no ammunition.[14]

Later in the war, like many Eagle pilots, he flew in the American fighter the P-47 Republic Thunderbolt, a gargantuan machine that packed a 2,700-horsepower engine. The Thunderbolt was so large that its wing tip was higher than the Spitfire's cockpit, though it had none of the Spitfire's elegance and manoeuvrability. 'I have always been puzzled', wrote the Spitfire pilot Godfrey Ball, 'as to why, when some genius like Mitchell designed an aeroplane as perfect as the Spitfire and the Spitfire was still capable of being developed to perform any of the myriad roles demanded of a fighter, that the resources of the Allies should be dissipated to make such an expensive and unnecessary experiment as the Thunderbolt. It looked like some historic frilled lizard. And being in its huge cockpit was like sitting in front of a theatre organ.'[15] One of the answers was that the Thunderbolt had a far great range than the Spitfire, being able to penetrate deep into Germany. A former Eagle pilot, Ervin Millar, recalled:

> So, reluctantly, we had to give up our beautiful little Spitfires and convert to the new juggernauts The war was moving on and we had to move with it. The change to the Thunderbolt might have been necessary militarily but my heart remained with the Spitfire . . . She was such a gentle little aeroplane, without a trace of viciousness. She was a dream to handle in the air. I feel genuinely sorry for the modern fighter pilot who has never had the chance to get his hands on a Spitfire; he will never know what flying was really like.[16]

With America entering the war after Pearl Harbor, the three Eagle squadrons were eventually subsumed within the USAAF. Before the transfer took place, the Spitfire Mark IXs of 133 Squadron took part in one of the most wretched fighter episodes of the war. They were ordered to provide a covering patrol for B-17s attacking the German airfield of Morlaix on the Brest peninsula, but on their way over the Atlantic they were driven off course by freak weather conditions and ended up over the Bay of Biscay. Hopelessly lost, they tried to return northward, and when they sighted land they thought they had reached Cornwall. Filled with relief, they searched for an airfield at which to land. As they slowed on their descent, the sky was filled with exploding shells. What they had believed was Cornwall was in fact the port of Brest, one of the most heavily defended cities in German-occupied France. The Spitfire squadron was cut to ribbons. Most planes were shot down. A few managed to limp from the scene, but their pilots were forced to bail out because of damage or lack of fuel. One escaped; the rest became prisoners of war.

The disastrous Morlaix raid was not only tragic for the pilots who lost their lives or freedom, it was also a setback for the Allies, since the Germans had been handed a number of almost intact versions of the Mark IX, thereby revealing the technology of the Merlin 61. 'It dramatically shortened the margin of time in which we were able to enjoy the huge advantage of our two-stage blower,' wrote Brian Kingcome, whose own 92 Squadron had taken part in the exercise but had made it back to England.[17] Despite this, Spitfires were to remain a key part of the Americans' air arsenal right up to VE Day, more than 1,000 serving in USAAF colours.

The American influence on the Spitfire could also be seen in the production of the Packard Merlin 266, a version of the Merlin 66 engine built under licence by the Packard motor company based in Detroit. At the peak of the war demand for the Merlin was so great – not just for Spitfires and Hurricanes, but also for the Lancaster bomber – that Rolls-Royce could not meet all the need. So an agreement was reached between the British and American governments to increase supply by manufacturing the engine in the USA. Initially, in 1940, Henry Ford had shown an interest in building the Merlin under licence, but with the fall of France he grew convinced that Britain would soon be defeated and his enthusiasm for the project disappeared. But the Packard venture proved highly successful, with over 25,000 Merlins turned out by the Detroit plant and shipped to England. Indeed, a new type of Spitfire, the Mark XVI, was created just to accommodate the Packard Merlin 266, which provided exceptional performance at low altitudes. Altogether, 1,053 Mark XVIs were built.

The involvement of Canada as well as the USA could be seen in the training of Spitfire pilots. At the start of the war, all RAF instruction had been provided within Britain: through training schools, through the officers' academy at Cranwell – the RAF's equivalent of Sandhurst – and through the two voluntary wings of the service, the RAF Volunteer Reserve and the Royal Auxiliary Air Force, which tended to attract well-connected university graduates. Fully qualified RAF flyers would then be sent to an operational training unit to learn how to handle their chosen aircraft type. But the network of domestic schools and OTUs could not cope with the burden of producing enough pilots for war, so an Empire Training Scheme was established, with centres throughout Canada, New Zealand, Australia, Rhodesia and South Africa. At its peak in mid-war, the scheme was turning out 11,000 pilots a year. From 1942, the USA, with its vast resources, also assisted in pilot training.

Tony Tooth, who later fought in North Africa in Mark Vs, earned his wings at the Dallas School of Aviation in Texas, where the No. 1 British Flying Training School was based. 'The flying proved very enjoyable and at times very exciting. Apart from learning how to get the aeroplane off the ground and down again, there were important skills like navigations, formation flying, and aerobatics that are vital for a military pilot to master. The reason for this is that a military pilot has to be able to make an aircraft do anything that it is physically capable of,' he said. Having qualified, he returned to England and was sent to a Spitfire OTU at Heston, where Sailor Malan and Brian Kingcome, both Battle of Britain aces, were instructors. Tooth found Kingcome 'wonderful' and 'particularly helpful', though he thought Malan could be 'standoffish and not very welcoming.' Tooth and his colleagues learned on an ancient Mark I – 'a very old and battered one that had some-how survived the ungentle hands of generations of students. Despite being so old and clapped out, she was definitely a Spitfire and therefore a vast leap for-ward for me and an unbelievable thrill. I was actually flying a fighter!'[18]

It was common for hardened Spitfire pilots, like Malan and Kingcome, to be given spells as OTU instructors after stiff tours of duty. Some took their responsibilities more seriously than others. Tough-minded Godfrey Ball was sent out as a senior instructor to an OTU in Cairo after fighting in North Africa, Malta and Sicily, and was disappointed at the attitude of some of his fellow instructors in Egypt, who, unlike him, had not seen intense combat. When, as part of his course, he said that all instructors would have to demon-strate to the trainees how to recover from an intentional spin in a Spitfire, he encountered some opposition:

> The reaction to my order did not really surprise me. Many pilots did not par-ticularly enjoy flying. They had joined as pilots for a variety of reasons: glamour, extra pay and privileges, and better chances of promotion. In Fighter Command, unless you got caught up in battles like the Battle of Britain or Malta, you didn't really have to stick out your neck if you didn't want to. The number of old-fashioned dogfights where violent manoeuvres were required was minimal. It was usually a case of being jumped by enemy fighters or jump-ing some of theirs. Many admitted to me that they had never done another spin after their dual ventures at training school.[19]

But Ball insisted, particularly because many of his graduates would be sent to the Far East to fight against the Japanese.

One of the highlights of Godfrey Ball's spell in Cairo was when he had a chance to fly a special Mark V belonging to the chief instructor, Wilf Sizer – an experience which, for Ball, demonstrated the full glories of the Spitfire. To make it fly as fast as possible, Sizer's Spitfire, fitted with a Packard Merlin engine, had had all its surplus equipment removed, including armament, armour plating, camera gun, and gunsight. All the joints had been smoothed to eliminate any drag, and the airframe's finish had been left unpainted, the aluminium having been polished to a high sheen. 'The whole magnificent creature appeared like a sparkling jewel under the desert sun,' wrote Ball. One day, after much persistence, Ball persuaded Sizer to let him fly it. The result was an impassioned eulogy to Britain's most famous fighter:

> I had hardly opened the throttle to take-off power before I was airborne. I was at the peak of my Spitfire flying ability at that time and in perfect flying prac-tice. I was able therefore to appreciate to the full the startling performance and surprising agility of this perfected example of Mitchell's creation, unfettered by

apprehension and unlimited by fear. It was joy, sheer joy, to be at the controls of this dazzling wonder. I had raised the undercarriage when I was a foot or so from the ground, but the incredibly steep angle I had to assume to hold normal climbing speed was staggering and as I rocketed up I thought of the aptness of the American simile describing the climb of a high performance aircraft as being like 'a home-sick angel'.[20]

The impressive scale of the RAF's late-wartime international effort for the Spitfire was mirrored in an increasingly large and sophisticated organization at home, encompassing training, production, development, transport and maintenance. The Supermarine prototype had been produced in a dingy office, with the back-up of a few RAF pioneers. By 1944 the Spitfire was at the centre of a massive structure that ensured the delivery of planes and pilots to the front line. It was not, thankfully, managed with the same iron-willed, ruthless efficiency as the Nazi war machine, but it still far exceeded anything that could have been envisioned in the 1930s. One Free French Spitfire pilot, Jacques Souviat, left this interesting description of the late-wartime RAF:

> In the enormous organization that was the RAF, many things seemed illogical and shocked our French backgrounds. Each time we received the same explanation, 'Yes, but it works!' and it was true. Everything was based on pragmatism and the confidence reciprocated in general, called the 'team spirit'. Our second impression was that, while the vast RAF machine turned without any apparent effort, its wheels had been perfectly oiled, there was no panic or nervousness among the 'high-ups'. The cool British temperament was very much to the fore.[21]

Manufacturing and ground crews were obviously two of the vital elements of the structure that supported the Spitfire. Factory staff and RAF riggers and fitters often spoke of their feelings of pride and duty towards the plane. 'I felt honoured to be a member of Alex Henshaw's team, working with a dedication that no one can dream of today,' said one Castle Bromwich worker.[22] Sidney Sexton, a mechanic who was mentioned in dispatches in 1945 for his work on Spitfires in the Far East, recalled that 'the one thing I felt was that I was given responsibility, a lot of responsibility, but I liked Spitfires and that was that. I enjoyed working on them. I would do anything for them. The servicing I did was 100 per cent. The rigger and I were always polishing because we were told that pilots could get another 4 mph that way.'[23] Nigel Rose of 602 Squadron was full of praise for the ground crews: 'They were terrific chaps, they really were. You get a lot of nice things said about them and they are all true. Directly you landed and taxied in, they were swarming all over the thing and they regarded any action that you'd been in as part of their job, which was great.'[24]

The work was exacting in its demands. Every day the ground crew would have to carry out 155 individual inspections of each Spitfire, including 'testing the pneumatic system; cleaning the air intake; examining the coolant, fuel and oil system for leaks; cleansing and lubricating the Coffman starter breech; checking the brakes, undercarriage and the movement of the control surfaces'.[25] After every thirty hours, a minor inspection was done on each Spitfire, which involved overhauling the plane and checking it for any visible signs of wear. More infrequent were the major inspections, for which the plane was pulled apart and its entire structure analysed. And after every 240 hours of flying the Merlin engine was due to be changed. But, as always, it would be foolish to think that conscientiousness was universal. Sexton remembered that on one occasion a Spitfire was taxiing across the airfield ready for take-off when oil started pouring out of the plane. 'I ran across the field and stopped the pilot. It turned out that someone had checked the oil and then forgotten to put the cap back on.'[26]

An intriguing, non-romanticized picture of life in a Spitfire ground crew comes from the unpublished memoir of Ted Sadler, who joined the RAF as an aircraftman in 1941 and saw how selfishness and carelessness existed even at the height of war. Sadler began his wartime career with basic training in Blackpool, which, on top of instruction in metalwork, riveting, fabric repairs and the maintenance of hydraulic and pneumatic systems, also involved a twice-weekly trip to the local baths for a shower, a swim and a medical inspection for venereal disease. 'It was interesting, to say the least, as everyone was required to stand naked in front of the Medical Officer, with arms and legs spread, while he shone a torch into our joints.' After qualification as a fitter, he was posted to RAF Benson in Oxfordshire, where, on his first day, the mechanic designated to 'show me the ropes' refused to do so – 'I ain't bloody well telling you nothing. You get more pay than me' – though he later relented.[27]

As he gained experience, Sadler was surprised at some of the slipshod workmanship. If screw holes, for instance, on the airframe did not match those on an oil-cooler fairing, then this method was occasionally used: 'Firstly all those screw holes that did line up were fixed in place. Secondly, those holes which did not quite line up were forced into position with an ice-pick. Thirdly, those screws that would only go part of the way were sawn short, filed to a point and forced in. Any screws left were stuck in with glue.' Another time, a fellow airman accidentally kicked over one of the undercarriage indicators on the wing, a short piece of cane which rose vertically as the undercarriage was lowered. 'Go on, mate, do us a favour, I don't want to drop in the shit,' said Sadler's colleague. So Sadler found an old piece of wood and, using his pocketknife, carved it in the shape of an indicator. He then glued this to the broken end of the real indicator. But the pilot took off before the glue had time to set. Almost immediately, the hand-carved stick blew away in the slipstream. Sadler was hauled up before the sergeant and, having refused to betray his mate, was told that his recommendation for promotion had been withdrawn.[28]

Sadler's enthusiasm for the Spitfire also landed him in trouble. His main job at Benson was servicing photoreconnaissance Spitfires, which were camouflaged in white, light blue and pink. 'The lighter coloured ones were known as "dicers" because the pilots "diced" with death, unable to defend themselves,' recorded Sadler, who wrote that, such was his adoration of the Spitfire, 'I used to lean on the tailplane with my arm resting on the fuselage just in front of the fin and look along the graceful lines of *my* Spitfire, to admire it and feel proud of my part in keeping it serviceable and airworthy.' Sadler decided one day to give his Spitfire an extra shine with a mixture of oil and petrol before it took off on a mission to France. When the plane landed, Sadler bounded up on the wing, hoping to bask in the congratulations of the pilot.

'Who cleaned this kite?' asked the aviator.

'I did, sir,' replied Sadler, beaming.

'Well, don't bloody well do it again. It shines like a sixpence up a sweep's backside. I've been chased by every Hun over France.'[29]

In addition to the RAF ground crews, there were also maintenance units throughout the country staffed by civilian operators and run by the Air Ministry. These units carried out installation of equipment, modifications, servicing and repairs before the Spitfires were sent to their designated squadrons. Sid Denney, a skilled electrician, worked at RAF Lyneham in Wiltshire for most of the war, specializing in wireless engineering:

> When the Spitfires first arrived at Lyneham, the Marks I and II, they had very primitive wireless equipment. All the controls were manually extended to the pilot in the cockpit. And the radio equipment was only HF, high frequency, and the aerials were literally a wire which came out behind the pilot's head, through a short mast and into the tail. Of course, after a while we moved to VHF, electronically controlled, and the mast gave way to big aerials.

Denney explained his role:

> The Spitfires would arrive empty, and all the wireless equipment would be held in one central depot at Lyneham and then would be dispatched to the various sites for installation. And I was on B site. The wagon would arrive with all the gear, and it was a big part of my job to sort it out. Then, when it was installed, we would make sure it was working properly by testing it out: call the control tower, make sure it was two-way, that sort of thing.[30]

It was while he was working at RAF Lyneham that Sid Denney met his wife, Eileen, who had been working as a rigger there since 1940. In 2006 they celebrated their diamond wedding anniversary during an event at RAF Duxford to mark seventy years of the Spitfire. 'He never stood a chance,' joked Eileen when looking back on when they met. Eileen Denney was only seventeen when she started working on Spitfires at Lyneham, her youth meaning that she was ineligible to serve in the WAAF. As a rigger, she performed a wide range of tasks: patching up holes, checking the hydraulics of the undercarriage, holding on to the tailplane when the engine was run, and painting the roundels and squadron numbers on the airframe. 'The Spitfires were wonderful planes. We just loved them,' said Eileen. 'They just got better and better, and with each new type that came in we would all crowd round and have a look at it. Mind you, I remember the Seafire. That could be dangerous. It had a spring-loaded hook, and you were warned not to go behind the hook in case there was someone in the cockpit about to test it.' Eileen was proud to be a female pioneer in a masculine world, though she regretted some aspects of discrimination. 'What did upset us girls was that when anybody did anything on the plane you had to sign a form, and I wasn't allowed to do that, even though I had done the work. It was only in the last year of the war that we were allowed to sign our own forms.' The one task she could not perform was taking out the pilot's seat when the plane came in for servicing. 'The seat had armour plating on the back, so there was no way I could do that. Someone had to get the seat out for me and then put it back afterwards.'[31]

Women also played a prominent part in the Air Transport Auxiliary, which had the crucial task of ferrying Spitfires from the factories and maintenance units to the squadrons. The ATA had been set up just before the war as a result of an initiative by the Imperial Airways director Gerard D'Erlanger, who saw that civilian air services could provide logistical support for the RAF. The Chamberlain government was enthusiastic – again belying its reactionary reputation – and D'Erlanger became the ATA's first chairman. During the war the ATA undertook 57,826 Spitfire or Seafire ferry flights. Men with a love of flying but barred from joining the RAF because of age or physical considerations found a welcome niche in the ATA. One of the more extraordinary was Charles Dutton, who had only one arm, yet made 541 flights in Spitfires and even force-landed one without damage after total engine failure. Explaining how he managed in a Spitfire, Dutton once said:

I trim the aircraft and set the friction nuts very tight on the throttle and boost levers. I open up with the control column between my knees and, if I've got the friction nuts right, the throttle and boost don't creep back on me. I take my only hand off the throttle block and transfer it to the stick until I am airborne. Then once again I put the stick between my legs, put up the undercarriage, throttle back to climbing revs and boost, then take the stick again for a climb.[32]

Like so many others, Hugh Bergel fell in love with the Spitfire instantaneously, though, as he later confessed, he almost made a mess of his first flight 'While running it up on the ground, I was worried by something in the engine's behaviour and when I looked out of the cockpit the whole front end was oozing steam. I had been caught out by the Spitfire's liability to overheat very quickly on the ground. There was nothing to do but switch off, go and have lunch, and hope that I hadn't caused a leak in the coolant system.' Bergel's second attempt was more successful:

> At last I was in the air in the aeroplane which then seemed – and still does – to be the most beautiful mechanical object ever made by man. I had been told to be aware of its exceptional sensitivity to the controls; I found it rather to be exquisitely responsive. They said that the forward view before me from the cockpit was very poor; true there was a long, flat nose stretching out before me but I could see all I wanted to see. I looked at those superb little elliptical wings and listened to the sweet sound of the Merlin (a Merlin always seemed to run more sweetly in a Spitfire than in any other airframe) and I realized once again the saying that 'what looks right is right' had been proved to be true.[33]

But it was the ATA's women who created the biggest impact, partly because the idea of women flying still seemed so novel in 1940, despite the pioneering journeys of Amy Johnson, who was herself killed in 1941 on an ATA trip over the Thames estuary. Of the 1,318 pilots who served with the ATA during the six years of war, 166 were women, though by 1944 about a fifth of the ATA's flying crews were female. Diana Barnato Walker, the glamorous daughter of a millionaire racing driver, became one of the most renowned ATA pilots, flying 260 Spitfires during the war, from the Mark I right through to the Griffon-powered Mark 21. 'They all flew beautifully,' she said, 'with that Spitfire characteristic of it feeling as if it were part of you. The Mark I was really light on the controls; the Mark V gave a fluttering feeling in flight, while the Mark IX had become more stable. All the PR Marks were lighter to fly. I didn't like the sound of the Griffon engine, not at all as comforting or glorious as the Merlin.'[34]

One of the more difficult aspects of the job of ATA pilots was that they had to fly without radio contact, often at a low level in poor weather, having never been trained on instruments. Diana Barnato Walker went through an ordeal when she had to fly a Spitfire Mark IX from Hanworth in Middlesex to Cosford in Staffordshire, and ran into dense cloud almost as soon as she had taken off: 'The options were now few. I couldn't bail out because I was wearing a skirt! The wartime black stockings were a bit short and left off just above my knees. My wartime panties, made out of silk from old parachutes, didn't come down to meet my stockings so there was a large gap of me in between. And anyway, the chute straps chafed the insides of my legs.' She had, however, passed the airfield of Little Rissington earlier, and she decided to try to make for it. As she descended rapidly, she glimpsed it through the bottom of the clouds:

> It looked more like a pond than a landing ground as the rain cascaded down. I landed – splosh! And at once wondered whether the Spitfire would go up on its nose. But I skidded through the puddles and eventually came safely to rest. A tall RAF man came out of a Nissen hut with a camouflaged rain cape over his head. As he came up to the aircraft I got out on to the wing – and my knees collapsed. 'I say, Miss, you must be good on instruments.' I did not want to disillusion him.[35]

Jackie Moggridge, a South African pilot with the ATA, admitted frankly that she was terrified by the thought of her first flight in a Spitfire, which she had to deliver from Oxford:

> When I arrived, they were running it up and there were sparks and flames coming from the exhaust of the huge Rolls-Royce Merlin engine. I was absolutely petrified and I thought, 'I'm never going to manage this!' It looked so vicious. I got in and followed all my notes and held my breath. It was fast and it flew like a bomb when I took off. It was so powerful that I had to start with my foot full on the rudder to the side opposite to the way the propeller was rotating – otherwise it would have done a right-angle turn before I took off. But once it was flying, it was just like a Tiger Moth.

Moggridge also made a discovery about a certain piece of equipment that could occasionally be necessary on longer trips. 'I pulled a thing out from under the seat that looked like a tube with a funnel at the end. "What's this?" I asked the engineer. "That's only for the gentlemen pilots," he explained.'[36]

The hectic pace of wartime production was captured in an incident experienced by Ann Welch when flying from High Post in Wiltshire. She had already made five trips one day when, at half past eight in the evening, she was asked to ferry another plane. The Spitfire was still on its initial test flight as she arrived. 'It landed. The pilot got out, I got in. I taxied out to the end of the airfield, turned around and the entire spinner assembly fell to the ground. I got out, picked it up, packed it back, they fixed it and off I went.'[37]

Many involved with the Spitfire frequently expressed their high regard for the courage, skill and diligence of the female personnel not just in the ATA, but also among the civilian ground crews, communications staff, and production-line workers, as well as those in the WAAF, which was over 100,000 strong after 1941. Cyril Russell, based at the Supermarine dispersal site of Keevil in Wiltshire, was in awe of the performance of one ATA woman, who, in taking off, lost one of the legs of her Spitfire's undercarriage when the port wheel struck a granite boulder on the edge of the airfield. She calmly took to the air, then swung the plane round and glided in again. 'She made the best single-wheel landing I've ever seen, cutting her throttle at just the right moment.' The Spitfire balanced on one wheel, 'then the port wing went down slowly, until its tip took some of the strain and the whole aircraft slewed to a halt. When I reached the aircraft everything was switched off and a young unflurried woman was busy shaking out her hair, having just removed her helmet and goggles. Calm and brave, she remains in my memory epitomizing Britain's women at war.'

Jacques Souviat, of 329 Squadron, showed a classically Gallic appreciation of the feminine spirit at his base, where he encountered women drivers, mechanics and flight controllers:

> The courage of these young ladies gained our admiration, for to see them sitting on the wings of aircraft at our dispersal, or with the huge pipes of pouring petrol under their arms in order to refuel the aircraft, was tremendous. Also to see two or three holding on to the tail of a Spitfire in the freezing back-blast caused by the propeller impressed us all. You only had to see their hands, blackened with oil and often bloodied, turning a screwdriver or spanner, and all with a smile, to warm to them.[38]

For all such fine words, there was undoubtedly a strong element of physical attraction in the wartime enthusiasm for the female ATA pilots. The combination of the curved lines of the Spitfire and a curvaceous young woman in uniform was irresistible for most men, especially in the highly charged, adrenalin-soaked atmosphere of RAF bases. There was an almost palpable sense of excitement running through an airfield when a beguiling female pilot arrived, as Ted Featherstone, an RAF mechanic at Millom in Cumbria, recalled of one occasion when he guided a Spitfire into the dispersal area:

> I didn't know the gender of the pilot as I marshalled the aircraft into the allotted space near the Control Tower, placed the chocks in front of and behind the wheels, and then made to climb on the wing to see if I could be of any help with the straps, etc. From my ground-level viewpoint, I saw the helmet

come off, the head give a shake and the blonde hair come streaming out in the breeze. I was very impressed with everything that happened after that, including the swarms of young officers who seemed to come from every corner to view this ATA phenomenon. Where had they been hiding? I was right out of the scene, of course, but I would dearly like to have been part of it.[39]

Even the stern Poles could be diverted from their crusade against Nazi Germany by the allure of a female aviator. In his private memoir, Franciszek Kornicki wrote fondly of the day in 1943 when 'a Spitfire was delivered by a lady ferry pilot – slim, very attractive and speaking Polish. It was Second Officer Jadwiga Pilsudska, daughter of the great Polish statesman Marshal Josef Pilsudski. We were bowled over by the event. I drove her by the longest possible route to the 303 Squadron mess for lunch, where the squadron leader and his warriors looked after her with gentle and tender attention.'[40] Diana Barnato Walker admitted that the men were 'rather flirtatious. One Commanding Officer made sure I stayed overnight by having the plugs removed from the aircraft I was to fly back in.'[41]

It was not just the ATA pilots who stimulated such yearnings. All sorts of WAAF personnel, from telephonists to couriers, could fire the passions of eager young men. Typical was this comment from the Czech pilot Miroslav Liskutin when he was based in Catterick, Northumberland: 'The parachute section was staffed with some of the prettiest girls I have ever seen. It almost looked as if somebody had succeeded in selecting a team of beauty queens to help with morale.'[42] Similarly, when women arrived at Bentley Priory to staff the operations room from September 1939, the mezzanine gallery quickly became packed with officers transfixed by the scene below. Before the Battle of Britain began, some in the Air Staff were concerned that this influx of pulchritude might undermine the smooth functioning of the Dowding system. 'Owing to the limitations of space in the Filter Room,' wrote Wing Commander J. N. T. Stephenson to the Air Ministry Establishment Committee, 'the filterers are working not only close to the WAAF plotters but have constantly to lean over them and push past them. It so happens that many of the young women are extremely attractive and with equal and similar attraction on the other side they cannot fail to make some claim on the attention of the men filterers working with them.'[43] Another officer reported, with a mix of concern and salacity, 'I must say that when I visited the present Filter Room I found the WAAFs more attractive than the plotting table and I feel that, unless we limit the field to eunuchs, we should be unlikely to find filterers who could give to their work the individual attention that is vitally necessary.'[44] As it turned out, the arrival of the German bombers was to focus minds and reduce the sexual charge.

When it came to gender symbolism, there was a paradox at work with the Spitfire. It was the most masculine of planes: tough, fast, powerful, intimidating, aggressive. Yet, because of its beauty, pilots tended to think of it in female terms, speaking of the Spitfire as 'a goddess' or 'a princess' or 'a lady'. Other planes and vehicles were also referred to as 'she', of course, but with the Spitfire the attitude went far beyond mere nomenclature. The devoted intimacy between man and machine was almost like a physical relationship. Spitfire pilots talked about falling 'in love' with the plane. Some, like Gerald Stapleton, even described their connection as similar to 'a marriage'.[45] In one passage in his autobiography, Dizzy Allen wrote quite openly that the Spitfire 'turned me on'. He continued the comparison: 'Women of the utmost beauty can be faulted, so could the Spitfire. In certain of her mannerisms she was nearly as awful a bitch as the loveliest woman I ever met, who was on a par with Browning's mistress, smooth marbly limbs and all – but they were nothing like as cold as marble.'[46] War hero Freddie Lister, DSO and DFC, leader of 127 Squadron, was even more explicit when he spoke about the plane in 1985:

> The Spitfire was a lady in every definition of the word. And of all the World War Two aeroplanes, she remains the *only* lady, every line of her – the beautiful ellipse of the wings, the unmatched grace of her tail unit, the unmistakable sit – as she banked in a steep turn – displaying that feline waist . . . She was sensitive to the touch, and if you treated her right, she would take care of you. And if you didn't treat her right – she gave it back to you in full measure. She let you know that she was a lady, and she would not forgive you easily if you gave her brutish treatment.[47]

But there was another, more tangible, manifestation of the Spitfire's sexual chemistry. This could be found in the desire that Spitfire pilots aroused in women. 'We were having a high old time,' said Frank Baker, who flew Spitfires and Hurricanes in the Battle of Britain. 'When you have got a pair of wings on your chest, the women just flock to you! You could walk into any Palais de Danse, look about and say right!'[48] What is remarkable about the Spitfire pilots' accounts is how uninhibited and forward many of the women of the 1940s appear. The idea that it was only in the 1960s that sexual liberation began is flatly contradicted by some of these tales, like Dizzy Allen's memory of a liaison with a blonde RAF batwoman called Gertie, who did a lot more than just perform his chores. 'She used to bring me cocoa before she retired and it began to dawn on me that the buttons on her shirt were tending to fall away.' Soon so many buttons had been lost that Allen detected that she was not wearing a bra: 'It followed that Gertie had one special shirt for me and others she wore for the purpose of going on parade.' One evening, after

Gertie had stoked the fire and given him his cocoa, Allen felt bold enough to ask her if he could help her in any way. After some inconsequential talk about household tasks and meals, Allen said, 'Well, Gertie, what I meant when I asked if I could assist was, can I help you to get your knickers down?'

'No need for that, sir, I don't wear any,' she replied, lifting her skirt above her head to prove her point. It was the start of a brief but intoxicating affair.[49]

If Allen is to be believed – and he won the DFC, became a wing commander and the Queen's Messenger – the case of Gertie was just one example of a mood of sexual freedom sweeping through parts of Britain in wartime, as traditional moral boundaries were dissolved. Though surveys in the mid-1940s showed that less than half of couples had sex before marriage, national service gave many women a new sense of independence and self-confidence, and RAF pilots began to be counted among their prime targets. Allen claimed that when he was based in Cornwall, in 1941, large throngs of women from London would arrive by train eager for trysts with the dashing airmen of his squadron, 'the girls staying for only one week . . . Love, at this period, never entered my head. I was only there, so to speak, for the fornication. But not only did we enjoy this pleasant little interlude. So did the girls. Almost to a woman they returned to the trials and tribulations of living in London refreshed in mind and body.'[50]

But, according to the American Spitfire pilot Lee Gover, the atmosphere in London could be just as unrestrained. It appears that for a virile young pilot with a powerful libido there were plenty of opportunities for entertainment, especially because traditional domesticity was being eroded by the social flux of war. 'Met two beautiful gals in the subway as I was on my way out to dinner,' Gover wrote in his diary for 1 March 1942. 'They gave me their apartment number and I went over there later. Having a grand old time but it sure is wicked.' Gover never ceased to be amazed at how open the 'gals' were, undermining the image of British prudery and diffidence: 'You have to beat the women off with a club', read one diary entry. The stylish exoticism of America seemed part of the appeal for free-minded London women. 'Boy, what a night. I really got around. That old USA on the sleeve does all right. The phone woke me up this morning. It was one of the gals from last night. They don't give up,' read another entry. One night in a London pub Gover met a woman called Rose, who had a husband serving out in the Middle East. But she felt unencumbered either by her marital arrangements or by the present boyfriend she had in tow: 'She was there with another guy. I guess she was attracted to me because she got up, came over and opened my greatcoat to see if I had wings. When she saw them, she dumped the other guy, fortunately without getting me in a fight, and I had her . . . The first night I met her we went to her apartment and, wow, did I learn some things.' The feeling that lives had to be lived to the full, because death could arrive at any moment, only added to this frenzied climate. Another evening Gover became intimate with a brunette, 'a very frightened young lady who had no idea what tomorrow might bring'. They ended up at her flat, where 'we spent a long time making love and finding peace, comfort and release in each other's arms. The war and all the upheaval it had brought seemed far away for a few hours.'[51]

The renowned Spitfire pilot Peter Howard-Williams recalled this regular disconcerting scene when stationed at the remote Norfolk base of Horsham St Faith – now Norwich airport: 'The Spitfires were lined up, with only a ditch and a hedge separating them from the main road. When we got the order to scramble, several airmen would appear from a ditch, pulling their trousers up as they began to start the aircraft. The girls would then appear and rejoin the large crowd who gathered by the road, especially at weekends.'[52]

Yet there was a less seamy, more uplifting side to the interplay of the sexes, for the presence of women on the bases helped to raise the spirits of the men. One WAAF sergeant, Hazel Bowling, serving as a waitress in the mess at Lympne in Kent, recalled this incident, which captures a sense of wartime chivalry:

> I sometimes felt that we weren't doing anything worthwhile, till one evening a pilot came into the dining room.
>
> 'Why so solemn, Sergeant?'
>
> 'You're all doing something important and we're just down here,' I blurted out.
>
> He replied, 'Up there, coming back, we think the girls will be there to greet us, so don't dare say you're doing nothing.'[53]

13

'Too much power and too much performance'

⌒⌒

SINCE THE START of the war, the Spitfire had been in a near-continuous state of change, and this was a process that had its drawbacks. 'Almost every design change introduced in the course of developing the aircraft's performance was in some way detrimental to the flight handling,' said Jeffrey Quill in a lecture after the war, adding that 'The Supermarine philosophy was to concentrate primarily upon the maximum combat performance. I took the view that we were trying to produce the most effective possible fighting machine, not the most elegant flying machine. Consequently there were times when the handling qualities of the Spitfire left something to be desired, but still, most pilots loved the aeroplane.'[1]

The greatest leap in design was the introduction of the 12-cylinder, 2,000-horsepower Griffon-powered range of Spitfires, which added another 10 litres to the engine capacity but, as a consequence, took away some of the plane's beauty and aerobatic elegance. 'To me this was the end of the line: the engine had outgrown the airframe,' wrote Wilfrid Duncan Smith.[2] Since 1939 Supermarine had been working on the development of a Spitfire with a Griffon engine, called the Mark IV. Though it had proved relatively straightforward to install the larger engine, there were difficulties in modifying and strengthening the airframe. It was not until late 1941 that the prototype first flew. Meanwhile the Merlin had been dramatically upgraded with the two-stage, two-speed blowers of the 61 series, thereby reducing some of the urgency of the Griffon programme. The Spitfire IX, perhaps the most successful of all types, led to a specialized photoreconnaissance version, the PRXI. Serving in Europe, the Far East and Africa, this became the main RAF reconnaissance aircraft in the later part of the Second World War, with a total of 464 built. Some were also used as high-speed couriers.

It was in a PRXI that the highest wartime speed in a Spitfire was achieved. During tests conducted at Farnborough in April 1944 to analyse the handling of an aircraft close to the speed of sound, Squadron Leader 'Marty' Martindale climbed at 340 mph to a height of 40,500 feet, then put his PRXI into a dive.

At one stage he recorded a true airspeed of 606 mph – Mach 0.89. Then, just as he was thinking of pulling out of the dive,

> there was a fearful explosion and the aircraft became enveloped in white smoke. I incorrectly assumed that a structural failure had occurred as I knew this to be a danger. The aircraft shook from end to end. I knew I could not bail out at such a speed so I sat still. The aircraft was doing nothing startling. The screen and hood were now quite black and I could see nothing. Automatically I eased the stick back. After a time I discovered by looking backwards through a chink in the oil film that I was climbing. The airspeed was obviously falling as the noises were dying down. I realized instantly that I could now bail out and opened the hood. It had not jammed.

But, as he prepared to leave, Martindale realized that he had the aircraft under partial control, though the engine had broken completely. So he pointed his plane towards the base, and, despite the blackness which still engulfed the windscreen, he managed to glide back to Farnborough, making a perfect three-point landing. It was a reflection of his skill that he had managed to survive, for the entire propeller and reduction gear had broken away, one of the connecting rods had pushed its way out of the crankcase, and the entire engine had shifted sideways. But the camera survived, showing that the record had been achieved.[3]

From the middle of the war, because of different stages of development, specification and orders, the numbering system for the Spitfire marks had lost all logical cohesion. Just as the Mark V arrived before the Mark IV, the IX before the VIII, so the PRXI went into service long before the Mark X. The Mark X was basically a pressurized version of the PRXI with a slightly more powerful Merlin engine. It did not come off the production line until 1944, and was not successful, largely because pilots 'complained that the vision through the thick Perspex was poor'.[4] Only 16 were built. The last Merlin reconnaissance Spitfire was the PRXIII, a specialized low-level plane. By the time it went into service, in April 1943, it had already been superseded by other types and just twenty-six of the PRXIII were manufactured.

For all the success of the Mark IX as a fighter against the Fw 190, the plane was less effective at lower altitudes – a weakness that assumed a new importance in the autumn of 1942 when the Luftwaffe adopted the tactic of launching low-level nuisance raids against targets on the south coast. A new fighter was needed, and the Griffon Spitfire prototype, for all the slow pace of its development, was reconsidered by the Air Ministry – though not with much enthusiasm, since renewed hopes had also been invested in the latest version of the massive Hawker Typhoon. Moreover, some engineers at Rolls-

Royce were concerned that heavy official backing for the Griffon might inhibit the development of the Merlin. But the performance of the Griffon Spitfire could not be ignored. In front of Air Ministry officials in July 1942 at the Royal Aircraft Establishment at Farnborough, Jeffrey Quill flew it in competition against the Typhoon, which the Air Staff believed could become the fastest fighter in the RAF, and the captured Fw 190. Given that Quill's prototype was based on a Mark III airframe married to a largely untested Griffon engine, with a two-speed, single blower, there seemed little hope that the Spitfire could catch the other two aircraft. But, as so often before, the Spitfire defied the sceptics.

The contest required the three planes to race at 1,000 feet between the RAF airbase at Odiham in Hampshire and Farnborough. The Typhoon was in the middle, with Quill and Captain Hugh 'Willy' Wilson, in the Fw, on either side. As Quill described it:

> All went according to plan until, when we were about half-way between Odiham and Farnborough and going flat out, I was beginning to overhaul the Fw 190 and the Typhoon. Suddenly I saw sparks and black smoke coming from the Fw 190s's exhaust and at that moment Willy also saw it and throttled back his BMW engine and I shot past him and never saw him again. I was also easily leaving the Typhoon behind, and the eventual finishing order was, first the Spitfire, second the Typhoon and third the 190. This was precisely the opposite result to that expected or indeed intended. It certainly put the cat among the pigeons.[5]

Eight days after this triumph, the Air Ministry urgently ordered the production of the first Griffon-powered Spitfires, eventually known as the Mark XII. To tackle the low-flying German raiders, the Mark XII was built with clipped wings, improving its lateral manoeuvrability at high speeds. Capable of a maximum speed of 400 mph at 18,000 feet, it had a four-bladed Rotol Jablo propeller and an armament of two Hispano cannon and four .303 Brownings. It first went into service with 41 Squadron in February 1943, and Squadron Leader Tom Neil, DFC, who had flown in the Battle of Britain with great distinction, recorded this memory of his first flight in it:

> Once in the air, the XII behaved much as any other Spitfire except that the engine was a good deal rougher than the Merlin – it grumbled rather than buzzed – and the beat of the big four-bladed airscrew was very pronounced. It was about 30 mph faster than the Mark V, for the same engine settings, and the nose waved about like a terrier's tail with any change of power. This tendency to fly sideways, given half a chance, was a characteristic of all Griffon-engined Spitfires (bar one) and detracted from the aircraft's performance as a gun platform. In moments of stress, a pilot could hardly be expected to fiddle about with the rudder bias, with the result that the aircraft was seldom properly in trim.[6]

The New Zealand ace Colin Gray was disappointed with the type: 'I thought this must be an improvement on the Spitfire IX but its performance was not any better.'[7]

The Mark XII was only an improvised aircraft, aimed at meeting a specific need. At higher altitudes its performance was significantly inferior to that of the Merlin-powered Mark IX, and it had a poor rate of climb, being handicapped by its single-stage supercharger. It is, of course, one of the common threads of the Spitfire story that the interim types, like the Mark V and the 'lashed-up' Mark IX, so often proved to be better than the supposedly more refined versions that were planned as their successors. But this was not the case with the Mark XII. Only 100 were built, and it was phased out by September 1943. A more advanced Griffon type was required if more radical progress was to be made.

The obvious answer was to develop a two-stage, supercharged Griffon, similar to the Merlin 61, and in August 1942 Rolls-Royce was given the order to produce just such an engine, though there were some delays in development because of other pressures on the company. The first prototype of the new Griffon Spitfire flew in January 1943, and immediately demonstrated its awesome capabilities, doing 445 mph at 25,000 feet with a rate of climb of over 5,000 feet per minute, its power enhanced by its five-bladed Rotol propeller. Jeffrey Quill reported to the Air Ministry in March 1943 that 'it is thought by all the pilots who have carried out the tests that these aircraft show considerable promise as fighting machines. In speed they have an extremely good performance from ground level to 40,000 feet.' The only complaints were about the 'lack of directional stability' and the 'large changes of directional trim', but overall 'the general impression gained is extremely favourable.'[8]

During the summer, Quill also tested a Griffon Spitfire with a massive six-bladed contra-rotating airscrew, made of two three-bladed propellers on concentric shafts turning in opposite directions and controlled by a constant-speed unit. The virtues of this device were that it converted even greater amounts of power into thrust and it eliminated torque on the ground during take-off and in manoeuvres in the air. The defect was that it was extremely complicated mechanically, and was prone to sudden failure. Only towards the end of the war was a reliable contra-rotating airscrew developed.

After successful trials in early 1943 of the new two-stage Griffon 61 Spitfire – now named the Mark XIV – the plane should have rapidly gone into production. But there were now more delays to accommodate a further refinement of the Griffon engine. It was not until January 1944 that the first XIVs arrived in service – starting with 610 Squadron, based in Exeter.

Altogether 957 Mark XIVs were built, the last substantial production run of any Spitfire type.

Because of the prodigious energy generated by the 2,025-horsepower engine, many pilots initially found the Mark XIV difficult to handle. On the ground the high torque tended to swing the plane heavily to the right, while in the air even the smallest push of the throttle led to a dramatic surge in power. As Jeffrey Quill put it, with its 'tremendous power, increased propeller solidity, and increased all-up weight, it was a good deal more of a handful for the pilot than previous fighter variants and so required more attention to flying than its predecessors'.[9] This point was reinforced by Bobby Oxspring, who in 1944 had risen to the rank of wing commander in 24 Wing of the 2nd Tactical Air Force. Admitting that pilots 'who relaxed or were careless caused some hair-raising incidents', Oxspring recalled the time when an Australian called Red Bloomer, who had just returned from France after being shot down and evading capture, was 'so anxious to get airborne again that he took off in a XIV without adequate briefing. The aircraft leapt off with a gigantic swing which with full rudder he could not hold, then headed at a right angle away from the runway towards the hangars. After his wheels missed the tops of the buildings by inches, it took those of us who witnessed his hairy exhibition a considerable time to get our toes unknotted.'[10]

Don Healey of 17 Squadron, who served out in Madura, India, during the Burma campaign, described the Mark XIV as 'a hairy beast to fly and took some getting used to. I personally preferred the old Mark Vs from a flying standpoint . . . Even with full aileron, elevator and rudder, this brute of a fighter took off slightly sideways!' The extra weight of the Mark XIV, at 8,475 pounds fully loaded – nearly 3,000 pounds heavier than the Mark I – meant that extra height had to be allowed when performing loops, as Healey learned when watching the Battle of Britain ace Squadron Leader Ginger Lacey in action:

> He attempted to do a loop from what he thought was an adequate starting height over Madura one afternoon. At the bottom of the loop he cleared the ground by barely four feet and upon recovering back at the field Lacey looked ten years older than when he took off. He immediately gathered us around and told us in no uncertain terms not to attempt a similar manoeuvre with anything less than a 4,000 foot reading on the altimeter.[11]

Despite these difficulties, in terms of performance the Mark XIV was the ultimate Spitfire that saw significant action during the war. Its growling power and explosive speed made it invaluable in a wide range of roles, from shooting down German rockets to carrying out hard-hitting armed reconnaissance missions over France. To Jeffrey Quill, it was the finest of the breed: 'I thoroughly enjoyed flying it and found its performance exhilarating. I think that, all in all, it really was the best of the fight variants and I think it is the one of which I feel the most proud.' The handling problems for inexperienced pilots were, he felt, an inevitable consequence of technological progress: 'If pilots had to work a bit harder and concentrate a bit harder in the flying, it was better than sending them to war in an aircraft of inferior performance.'[12] Quill's was a verdict with which many RAF pilots agreed. Flight Lieutenant Ian Ponsford, who fought over Germany in 1945, believed that

> the Spitfire XIV was the most marvellous aeroplane at that time and I consider it to have been the best operational fighter of them all as it could out-climb virtually anything. The earlier Merlin Spitfire may have had a slight edge when it came to turning performance but the Mark XIV was certainly better in this respect than the opposition we were faced with. The only thing it could not do was to keep up with the Fw 190D in a dive. It could be a bit tricky on take-off if one opened the throttle too quickly as you just couldn't hold it straight because the torque was so great from the enormous power developed by the Griffon engine. One big advantage that we had over the Germans was that we ran our aircraft on advanced fuels which gave us more power. The 150-octane fuel that we used was strange-looking stuff as it was bright green and had an awful smell – it had to be heavily leaded to cope with the extra compression of the engine.[13]

The armament was formidable as well, comprising either four 20-mm cannon, or two cannon and four machine guns. There was also a carrier for either a 250-pound or 500-pound bomb. It is a measure of how far the Spitfire had advanced that the Fw 190, the scourge of Fighter Command in 1942, should be thoroughly on the defensive three years later. Ian Ponsford had a vivid recollection of carrying out an armed reconnaissance mission over Kremmen in April 1945 when his section came across a group of eight Fw 190s. Despite being outnumbered, the Spitfires managed to break up the Fws, shooting down two, and claiming one as a probable and another as damaged:

> The nearest 190 to me was turning pretty tightly and was firing. He passed very close to me and slightly below and I was able to look down into his cockpit. He can't have been more than a few feet below me, still firing, and I clearly saw the pilot with his black helmet, looking up at me! I think he must have stalled his aircraft as he fell away and I had no difficulty in getting on to his tail and firing with cannon and machine gun. His aircraft was well-peppered with strikes and he dived away at a steep angle with smoke pouring out. He just kept going down.[14]

The Mark XIV had a greater fuel capacity than any earlier fighter Spitfire – up from the usual 85 gallons to 115 – which meant that it had a wider radius of action, even though its fuel consumption was higher than that of previous types. Wing Commander Pete Brothers, who headed the Culmhead Wing in 1944, appreciated this increase in range as he led fighter sweeps over France. 'On these missions we hit anything that took our fancy – vehicles, trains and airfields, mostly,' he recalled. Like Jeffrey Quill, Brothers saw the Mark XIV as 'the real performer thanks to its Griffon engine. It was truly an impressive machine, being able to climb almost vertically – it gave many Luftwaffe pilots the shock of their lives when, having thought they had bounced you from a superior height, they were astonished to find the Mark XIV climbing up to tackle them head-on, throttle wide open!' Brothers left this memorable description of a typical ground strafing in France, showing both the firepower of the Mark XIV and his own tactical skill:

> On one of these sorties one of my pilots spotted a flak train steaming along below us. I acknowledged his call, but proceeded to fly along on the same course, thus giving the enemy the impression that we hadn't seen them. After flying on for a further 20 miles, I gave the order to drop down to the deck and turn back in towards the train. At that height all you could see was the smoke from the engine, and we waited until the train vanished into a thick wood before we lined up for our single attacking pass. We timed our approach perfectly and as the engine emerged from the wood, I squared it up in my gunsight and gave it a broadside of cannon. The other pilots followed suit and by the time the deadly flak batteries had emerged from the wood we were on our way, having left the engine a hissing wreck.[15]

The Griffon Spitfires could trace their lineage back to the Schneider winner of 1931. But there was another version of the Spitfire which had an even greater affinity with Mitchell's seaplane. During the ill-fated Norwegian campaign of 1940, the RAF suffered badly from a lack of airfields. The Air Ministry therefore decided to look at converting a number of Hurricanes and Spitfires into floatplanes, which could operate from the Scandinavian fjords. Tests were carried out on a scale model of a Mark I fitted with floats, and the initial results were satisfactory, but before the prototype could make its first flight the disastrous campaign was over and all energies had to be focused on production for the Battle of Britain. The start of the war in the Far East against Japan in 1941 led to a revival of the idea, since it was felt that a floatplane might be useful in an environment filled with islands and lagoons. So a Mark V was fitted with a set of floats designed by Supermarine, the conversion being carried out by Folland Aircraft of Southampton. Jeffrey Quill flew the plane in October 1942, and later recalled that 'it was a very successful experiment. The floats were very good. In fact it would have been rather surprising if they were not since they were designed by Supermarine. The plane handled beautifully in the water and it was great fun to fly. The drag of the floats was surprisingly low.'[16]

After the initial flights, Quill handed the Mark V floatplane over to his Supermarine colleague Don Robertson for further testing on the river Hamble. 'Although highly secret,' wrote Robertson, 'one could hardly fail to hear it flying round the Hamble area as it made a strange sound like an organ due to the open end of a cross-tube used to locate the axle of a pair of launching wheels.'[17] Robertson then decided to take the plane out on to the open sea between Southampton and Poole – a move that was almost to end in disaster. Because it was only 80 miles from the German aerodromes in occupied France, this part of the south coast was heavily defended by anti-aircraft batteries. Before Robertson took off, warnings were broadcast to all the gun sites that the distinctive floatplane would be in the vicinity, but few of these units appeared to pay much attention:

> When over the Royal Poole Motor Yacht Club I suddenly noticed some red tracer shells coming from a Bofors gun emplacement just ahead of me. Having no radio and thinking that perhaps an enemy aircraft was about, I hastened to get out of the way. To my surprise, other guns opened up, obviously aimed at me! The red tracers seemed to come quite slowly towards me rather like a catch in the deep field at cricket, but were travelling fast as they came close.

Robertson managed to escape the flak by heading further out to sea, though when he tried to return over Christchurch the Bofors opened up again 'with a grand firework display'. He then dived down 'at full power to tree-top level' and flew inland over the New Forest, 'where I knew I should be too low for them to take aim'. Robertson was able to land on Southampton Water without the plane being damaged.

News of the incident travelled quickly. That night, Robertson and his wife, Ella, were at a drinks reception hosted by the anti-aircraft regiment on the Hamble.

'I bet your husband was scared stiff this afternoon by his unfortunate experience,' said the commanding officer to Ella.

'Not at all. He realized that if your men couldn't recognize a Spitfire after three years of war, there was little chance of them being very good shots.'[18]

In January 1943 the Mark V floatplane was dismantled and taken up to the Marine Aircraft Experimental Establishment near Glasgow for its service trials. Two more floatplanes were converted, and then, in October, all three were shipped out to Egypt rather than the Far East, the plan being to use them against the German transport planes operating around the Greek islands. But by the time they arrived in Alexandria the Luftwaffe had control over the entire Aegean Sea, so they could not be put to any use.

In 1944, with the war in the Pacific growing more intense, there was a third attempt to develop a successful floatplane, this time using a Mark IX. But tests carried out in July by the Supermarine pilot Frank Furlong showed that the plane was directionally unstable and had a tendency to 'waddle' from side to side during high-speed runs before lifting off from the water. It was also found that water was entering the engine via the tropical intake filters. The problems were never resolved. The experiment was abandoned, and so the floatplane – physically the most direct descendant of the Schneider S6 – never saw action.

Back on land, the Griffon Spitfires had arrived to supplement the fleets of Mark Vs and Mark IXs which were fighting with increasing confidence throughout Europe as the might of the Axis crumbled. Mussolini had fallen in July 1943 after the Allied invasion of Sicily, in which the Spitfire played a crucial role in destroying ground defences and providing air cover for landings. 'It was a magnificent sight,' Wilfrid Duncan Smith wrote of the Sicilian invasion. 'The shallow waters were packed with amphibious craft and infantrymen while further out a grey shield of warships formed a protective arc, the red flashes of their guns stark against the dawn sky. Our Spitfires were stepped in layers from 10,000 to 20,000 feet, waiting to pounce on any formations that dared to interfere with the operations on land and sea.'[19] The Axis planes put up little resistance on the first day of the landings, but the next morning Duncan Smith was involved in a hectic dogfight when an Italian Macchi 202 got on his tail:

> Knowing my Spitfire's capabilities so well, I pulled her up sharply in corkscrew turns into the sun as steeply as I could. I expected to hear and feel the unwelcome bangs of exploding shells in my fuselage but nothing happened until suddenly I felt my Spitfire shake violently and the next instant we were spinning – I caught her after a couple of turns and getting control again looked for the Macchi. Sure enough there he was, slightly to one side and below me asking to be shot down. My first burst caught him in the cockpit area and wing root and he went up in flames, shedding bits as he winged over and dived into the high ground over Noto. He must have thought he had got me when he saw me spin.[20]

Patrolling in his Spitfire on 1 August 1943, Squadron Leader Michael Doddington of 249 Squadron recorded the damage wreaked on Sicily: 'A surprising sight. There is very nearly a continuous stretch of aerodromes, each one smothered in bomb craters and smashed Hun and Italian planes.'[21] Despite the Allies' air superiority, the cruel realities of war were brought home to Brian Kingcome, commanding 244 Squadron, when one of his Spitfire pilots came down just inside British lines during the Sicilian campaign. He survived the crash, but was trapped inside his burning cockpit. 'A group of soldiers did their best to free him until they were driven back by the flames, and the pilot, powerless to escape the agonizing death he saw roaring implacably towards him, implored them to shoot him. Faced with the alternative of turning their backs and leaving him to burn, one finally levelled his rifle and fired. It was a terrible responsibility and an act of supreme moral courage.'[22]

The Spitfires kept up the pressure throughout the hard campaign on the Italian mainland, as the Germans, battling ferociously on the ground, retreated northward. The Salerno landings, in which the Seafires were ravaged by accidents on their aircraft carriers, were also tough for the two advanced squadrons of Spitfires trying to operate from a narrow landing strip on a bridgehead established by the army, particularly because they had to dodge fire not only from the Germans but also from the British artillery. 'Our 25-pounders were banging away absolutely non-stop, firing, of course, directly across our runway and approach. I calculated that there must be almost as much metal as fresh air in the sky through which we had to fly when taking off and landing,' said Hugh 'Cocky' Dundas, leader of the Spitfire squadrons.[23] But after three days the Allies broke through and began the conquest of the peninsula.

For the last months of 1943 and the first part of 1944, the Spitfires met only intermittent resistance from the overstretched Luftwaffe. Their main job was support for Allied ground forces through heavy-bomber escort, strafing, bombing, and fighter reconnaissance, most notably in the Anzio landings and in the exhausting siege of the fortified hilltop town of Cassino, which finally fell in May 1944 after continual Allied bombardment had shattered the German supply lines and all but reduced the place to rubble. The way was now open to Rome, which was taken on 4 June.

During this period Teddy Morris of 250 Squadron, based in Poretta on the north-east tip of Corsica, played a variety of roles in his Spitfire VIII, the advanced version of the Merlin-61 Mark IX – 'easily the best fighter I have ever flown, superior to the 109F in all respects', as he recorded in his private journal of his war in Italy. The sense of the RAF being in command of the skies shines through his account, such as in this passage:

> We escorted a number of highly successful bomber attacks but the most spectacular was the attack by 36 Marauders on the Liguri marshalling yard, which produced an enormous explosion. It was decided on photographic evidence that it was an ammunition train. Our most effective armed reconnaissance attack was against a division found on the coast road south of Pisa early in the

morning. Intelligence recognized it as the Hermann Goering Division on its way to reinforce the resistance being put up by the Germans south of Rome. To the Corsica wing it was the perfect strafing target spread along 30 miles of coastal road, trying to hide in any wooded cover. The two wings kept it under constant attack throughout the daylight hours, leaving burning vehicles every few miles. The remnants of the vision were too late to take part in the battle which decided the fate of Rome.[24]

Admiration for the Spitfire VIII was also felt by Roger Henshaw White, who took part in the Italian campaign with 92 Squadron. In his wartime diary, he recorded how on 23 July, after the fall of Rome, he went over the mountains to Ancona, north-west of Florence, using 'one of the youngest Mark VIII's I had flown – nothing in its trim or engine power had been stretched as yet so it felt incredibly responsive to every breath, let alone manual movement'. Like so many other pilots, he thought of his Spitfire in feminine terms, calling her 'Charlie Girl'. On 22 September he wrote how he was having her 'completely repainted' by a cellulose expert from High Wycombe to improve her condition. He was pleased with the results. The next day he 'went up to Maintenance to see the finished Charlie Girl in broad daylight. She is very beautiful now and we'll keep her well-scrubbed.' White also basked in the pleasure of flying Charlie Girl in the evening over the pastoral Italian landscape, bathed in the mellow glow of fading sunlight:

> We bombed the road north of Prato again and since we had been free of any opposition we enjoyed a line-astern chase all the way home in a golden world of cloud and sunset blend. As a 'thumbs-up' to the troops, we banked over those in our bomb line so that they could witness our silhouettes through the cockpit canopy, in a wide-sweeping turning-climb so that no one could harm us, we hoped. Behind our lines, we dropped to hedge height and our tail-chase had taken us to watch the cows being led from milking to their pastures, when suddenly the aerodrome appeared immediately in front of us.

But there were more serious moments, and White left this account of attacking a train near Bologna amid anti-aircraft fire. What makes this diary entry particularly interesting is its description of how the use of cannon affected the Spitfire's flight:

> Going from west, back to the east, we saw a stationary train and engine about 3 miles east again. It looked a cinch so we all spread out and waited our turn. A lot of 40-mm flak had been waiting for us too, but it wasn't very accurate. The train load comprised eight open trucks and eight flat-tops, with motor transport and two tanks on them. I concentrated on the engine and on my third run every shell went right home; it really was perfect air-to-ground

firing. In air combat, the deceleration effect of the cannon is so short-lived that one's automatic tensing of muscular control – to aim and fire accurately – tends to pull the stick just that fraction to compensate. In this prolonged air-to-ground firing the deceleration effect is so much more marked that the nose drops quite fast and has to be corrected. Perhaps I have got used to it by now.[25]

The battle for Italy, brutal though it often was, paled in scale of conception beside the liberation of France and the Low Countries, the centrepiece of the Allied strategy for defeating Germany in the west. In preparation for Operation Overlord, the invasion of Normandy in June 1944, the Spitfires were given two key tasks: first, to help establish complete air supremacy over northern France and, second, to weaken the German defences. All this was a far cry from the desperation of Sholto Douglas's fighter sweeps of 1941, which had so badly sapped the morale of Fighter Command to no useful purpose, especially when confronted with the Fw 190. Now the Spitfire squadrons had clear objectives and superior equipment. The organizational structure had changed too, reflecting the growing importance of army support as pioneered in North Africa by Arthur Tedder, who became Eisenhower's second-in-command for Overlord, with Leigh-Mallory in charge of combined air forces. In November 1943, Fighter Command was renamed by its 1936 title, Air Defence Great Britain, and many of its squadrons were transferred to the Allied 2nd Tactical Air Force. The name change, however, turned out to be a psychological blunder, and the title of Fighter Command was restored in late 1944.

The softening-up of German defences took place throughout the early months of 1944, with dive-bombing and ground-attack missions against enemy armoured vehicles, trains, depots and troops right across northern France by Spitfire IXs, VIIIs, and XVIs, often using 90-gallon drop tanks to penetrate far inland. Pilot Officer Ken 'Paddy' French, one of the many Irishmen serving in the RAF, went on regular dive-bombing sorties in the build-up to D-Day and left this description of how the techniques improved. At first the method used was:

> to fly over the target at 10,000 feet and when we saw it appear behind our wing we would turn over on our back, going into a steep dive at the target. When you reached a height of 2,000 feet you would pull out of the dive and count three seconds before releasing the bomb, then pull back hard on your stick to climb away from any ground fire. At this point I always blacked out because of the G force but the plane would keep climbing and you would come round again. As you can imagine, this was rather haphazard and accuracy could not be guaranteed. We later developed a much better technique which was highly

effective. We would come right down low and fly the plane directly at the target and at the last second release the bomb so that it would go into the target and at the same time you would lift the plane over the top. You couldn't really miss.[26]

Yet, for all such improvements in methods, the Canadian pilot Arthur Bishop, who also took part in D-Day, felt that the Spitfire was never suitable for the bombing role – particularly not compared with the US Thunderbolt or the Hawker Typhoon, which had finally come into service and was proving invaluable as a ground attacker:

> Unlike the Typhoon and the Thunderbolt, which were built for dive-bombing and rocket-firing and were powered with air-cooled engines, the Spitfire had a liquid-cooled in-line engine. The basic difference was that the former could sustain substantial damage, while in the case of the latter, a single bullet or a small piece of shrapnel slamming into the radiator or piercing one of the line feeds could put the Spitfire right out of business. Nevertheless, to invoke the idiom of the day, 'We pressed on regardless'.[27]

Indeed, because of their air-to-ground qualities, the Typhoons were described by the legendary French Spitfire pilot Pierre Clostermann as 'the stars of the RAF during the Normandy landings . . . It is no exaggeration to say that it was in great part due to them that the operations of June, July and August 1944 went ahead without disastrous setbacks'.[28]

A sense of anticipation spread through the Allied forces as D-Day approached. Though the actual date was a closely guarded secret, the colossal build-up of forces – Eisenhower joked that it was only the barrage balloons over southern England that prevented the island from sinking – meant that everyone involved knew the invasion was imminent. On the evening of 5 June, the air crews were briefed for the mission the following morning. Johnnie Houlton described the scene at his base:

> The Briefing Officers uncovered their maps of the Normandy coast, then laid out the broad outline of the entire operation. We were shown the sites of the five landing beaches, the airborne assault areas, the shipping lanes and the general tactical plan; all balanced against the forecast weather. As we listened, the vanguard of 5,000 ships and 287,000 men was already on its way across the Channel, the great forward move which had been fought for over the last four years since Dunkirk. I remember the stillness in the briefing tent; the awareness that, right then, history was in the making; and I had a vivid sense of concentrated will for success going out to the soldiers and sailors of the invading force.[29]

Overlord was the most complex military operation in history. Bobby Oxspring recalled that the briefing alone took two hours to complete, and the order form which rolled off the teleprinter at his base was 28 feet long.[30] Geoffrey Page, now in command of the Spitfires of 132 Squadron, based at Ford on the Sussex coast, recalled that he could not sleep that night, such was his anxiety. So he rose from his bed 'and stood outside the tent listening to the never-ending drone of the night-bomber force winging overhead. The last phase of the softening-up process was being completed.'[31] In preparation for D-Day, the Spitfires, like all other aircraft, were painted with black and white stripes along their fuselages and wings for ease of recognition.

Nine Spitfire squadrons provided the initial cover for the first troop landings on 6 June. Altogether, 14,674 sorties were flown by Allied aircraft that day, utterly overwhelming the Luftwaffe. The scene off the Normandy coast was described by Bobby Oxspring, who flew regular patrols over the Channel. 'Dense clouds of smoke poured from destroyers laying screens around the main fleet as explosions erupted inland signifying intense battles in progress with the enemy. Above all, swarms of Allied aircraft were either patrolling or heading across the coast on tactical strikes. It was a spectacle the like of which could never be repeated.'[32] Arthur Bishop said that:

> four things stand out in my memory: the crowds of landing craft and troop and supply ships with cable balloons rising above them, the broken gliders strewn across fields like smashed wooden matchboxes, the smoke rising from small fires here and there, and the lack of Luftwaffe interference. Our biggest danger that morning was collision with other Allied aircraft. Bombers, fighter-bombers, reconnaissance aircraft and artillery and navy planes were all crammed into that crowded airspace below the clouds.[33]

The Germans were so shaken by the epic scale of the attack that there was little airborne resistance, though Johnnie Houlton claimed the first kill for a Spitfire, taking out a Ju 88 by using his new gyro gunsight:

> Most pilots were sceptical of the new instrument and preferred to use the conventional type of sight, which was still incorporated on the screen of the new sight. Normally one would open fire only at ranges below 250 yards but I adjusted the gyro sight on to the target at 500 yards with a deflection angle of 45 degrees, positioned the aiming dot on the right-hand engine of the enemy aircraft and fired a three-second burst. The engine disintegrated, fire broke out, two crew members bailed out, and the aircraft dived steeply to crash on a roadway, blowing apart on impact.[34]

In the days that followed the Normandy landings, the Luftwaffe became more organized and the Allied fighters encountered more aerial activity. But now able to operate from makeshift landing strips, they were more powerful than ever. The Fw 190s and Me 109s, for all their spirit, were now engaged in a losing struggle, especially as more Allied reinforcements came pouring over the Channel, along with ground crews and radar communications. 'From dawn to dusk Allied fighters ranged far behind enemy lines,' said Geoffrey Page, 'attacking any legitimate targets that moved along the roads. Seldom did my squadron and I return to our airstrip with our guns unfired. Rising columns of smoke bespoke of the funeral pyres of lorries and armoured cars. Only heavily armour-plated tanks could withstand the attacks of Spitfires but these soon fell prey to the deadly rocket-firing Typhoons.'[35]

Two events were symbolic of this Allied superiority. One was the extraordinary achievement of Squadron Leader Wally McCleod of 83 Group in shooting down two of the once-feared Fw 190s on one mission with just thirteen rounds from each of the cannon of his Spitfire IX – only about a tenth of his ammunition. The other was Johnnie Johnson's thirty-third kill of his Spitfire career, beating the record held by Sailor Malan. The Spitfire's old adversary the Me 109 was the victim as Johnson and his section made a surprise attack out of the sun, covered by another section. 'This was perfect teamwork,' wrote Johnson of his record-breaking victory. 'I could pay undivided attention to the Hun below and I hit his ugly yellow nose with a long steady burst. Thick black smoke poured from the Messerschmitt, but he continued to fly and darted for the protection of the cloud.' But Johnson remained on his tail, and the cloud layer was too thin to give the German any security. 'The 109, conspicuous by its trailing banner of smoke, was some 800 yards ahead and I closed in for the kill.' By now, however, the Messerschmitt was out of control, mortally wounded by Johnson's previous strike. It smashed into the ground at 200 mph, 'hit a dyke, tore into a stout hedge and pitched into the air once again. The wings and the tail were torn apart. The fuselage twisted as it fell to the earth, where it disintegrated into a thousand pieces.'[36]

In an attempt to halt the Allied advance in the west, Germany began launching unmanned V-1 flying bombs – known as doodlebugs – at southern England, bringing indiscriminate slaughter and fear to the civilian population. Hurtling on their deadly journeys at over 400 mph, the V-1s were a terrifying new weapon which could have undermined the Allies' advantage were it not for the courage of the RAF's fighter pilots. The Hawker Tempest, the explosively fast successor to the Typhoon, was vital in blowing the V-1s out of the sky, but the Spitfires, with their high speed and power, also played a crucial part. Bobby Oxspring, who was one of those deputed to take on the V-1s, described the best approach for dealing with these missiles:

We found the ideal tactics . . . to be crucially governed by the range at which we fired. Over 250 yards usually hit the flying control system of the craft which would dive to the ground still with an active warhead. Often a range of 150 yards or less almost always clobbered the warhead, which could severely damage the attacking fighter. The ultimate lay in accurate shooting between 200 and 250 yards, which provided a reasonable certainty of exploding the warhead in the air without undue danger to the fighter.[37]

The experience of a V-1 blowing up in front of a pilot could be intimidating, but, as Spitfire pilot Tom Slack explained, the only way to cope 'was to fly through the blast and not turn away, which would expose the belly of the air-craft to all the flying metal'.[38] As John Dalley remembered, after flying through the explosion the Spitfire would be 'completely black, couldn't see through the windscreen or anything. It was a horrible sight. And it took a gang of people twenty-four hours to get the black sticky smoke off the aero-plane. The ground crew were not always best pleased with the pilot.'[39]

The pilots taking on the V-1s showed incredible bravery, sometimes to a heroically suicidal extent. One Free French aviator, Jean Maridor of 91 Squadron, fired and hit a target in the tail control, sending it into a dive. But then, to his horror, he saw that it was heading straight for a military field hos-pital. So, with a remarkable sense of selfless sacrifice he deliberately rammed the warhead, blowing up both the V-1 and himself.

As well as courage, tackling the doodlebugs required rare aerobatic skill – especially at night, since the Spitfire was such a difficult plane to fly in the dark. One night in July 1944 Frank Mares of 310 Squadron was vectored by ground control to intercept a V-1 heading for London. He quickly saw the flame of the bomb racing through the sky and, 'While shouting "Tally-ho", I stood the air-craft on its nose, spiralled through 180 degrees, the throttle opened to its fullest extent, lined the flame in the gunsight and pressed the button. While the can-nons loudly responded, the roar of the Spitfire engine began to cough, then gave up in silent protest.' With his engine suddenly failing, Mares felt powerless. But

just as I was beginning to despair, the engine regained its senses, roared into life and I was able to continue the pursuit of the, by then, distant flame. Both man and machine revitalized, the cannons spitting out their venomous message, I was willing shells towards their target. Just as I was declaring my mission a fail-ure, there was a blinding flash and a terrific explosion, which preceded some very severe turbulence. My feeling was one of gleeful satisfaction as I reported my success to Flying Control.[40]

The V-1 killed over 900 civilians and injured about 35,000, though the Tempest and the Spitfire soon gained mastery over it. But from September

1944 Hitler unleashed an even more sinister weapon, the V-2, a rocket carrying a 1-ton warhead, which travelled to a peak altitude of about 50 miles above the earth until it ran out of fuel, then plunged towards its target at the speed of sound. The V-2's technology was the forerunner of that used in the NASA lunar programme, and there was nothing Mitchell's plane could do against such a futuristic brute in flight. The only way to deal with the V-2 was to try to locate and destroy its launching sites in Holland before the rockets were fired at London. Packard Merlin Spitfire XVIs of 12 Group were given this job, and they enjoyed a degree of success – helped by the Dutch resistance, which fed intelligence to the RAF about the sites. The future BBC presenter Raymond Baxter of 602 Squadron was one of those involved in these missions. In his autobiography, he explained that the bombing raids on the V-2 sites, known as 'Big Ben' sites, were conducted in sections of four or more, with Spitfires carrying a single 500-pound or two 250-pound bombs:

> If you were leading, you flew over your target so that it passed under your wing, just inboard of the roundel. You would then count, 'One and a thousand, two and a thousand', roll on your back and come down like that, with every aeroplane following doing the same thing. So, ideally, it was a stream of four aeroplanes together. We bombed individually but obviously did not drop bombs until the leader had pulled away. And that was the trick. It all depended on how good the leader was because if he was too far away, and his dive wasn't steep enough, the other dives would tend to be flatter and flatter which made the bombing inaccurate and was also dangerous. The desired angle of dive was 70 to 75 degrees, which feels vertical. Ideally we would start at 8,000 feet, drop the bombs at 3,000 feet and then pull out, maintaining low level to clear the area. We never bombed at random, only when we were sure we had identified the pinpoint target.[41]

But such raids could not be the complete answer, and it was only when the Allies drove the Germans out of Holland that the V-2 attacks finished.

Baxter described the Mark XVI – which was basically the Mark IX with an American-built Packard Merlin engine – as 'easily the most offensively optimized Spitfire I ever flew'.[42] But even with the Allies in the ascendancy and new fighter types like the Hawker Tempest in service, Supermarine did not abandon the quest for ever greater improvements in the Spitfire. An advanced version of the Griffon-powered XIV was in development from late 1943, eventually emerging as the Mark XVIII, with strengthened wings and main undercarriage, and marginally greater fuel capacity. But the first example did not come off the production line until after VE Day, and only 300 were built. There was also the record-breaking PR XIX – in terms of extreme performance, the most successful Spitfire of them all, capable of a maximum 460 mph – an increase of more than 100 mph over the Mark I. The Mark 20 was not a new type at all, merely a redesignation by the Air Ministry of the old Mark IV, the first and unlamented Griffon prototype, though, as with so many bureaucratic exercises, this relabelling succeeded only in creating yet more confusion in the already chaotic numbering system.

The next step, however, was more radical and significant. Supermarine recognized that the increasing power of the Rolls-Royce Griffon meant a modified airframe was needed. So Joe Smith's design team stiffened the wings, particularly by strengthening the main spar booms, while the fuselage was reinforced by replacing the duralumin longerons with stainless-steel units. The underside of the mainplane was made smoother by installing fairing doors for the undercarriage wheels, and four Hispano cannon were provided in the wings. In addition, fuel tankage was increased, the undercarriage legs were lengthened, and a larger, five-bladed propeller was fitted to cope with the 2,400-horsepower engine. But the array of changes – for which Castle Bromwich was already retooling and rejigging in mid-1944 – had made the new version of Mitchell's masterpiece increasingly difficult to handle. Jeffrey Quill later commented:

> From the first time I flew the Spitfire 21 it was clear that that we had a bit of a hot potato. There was too much power and too much performance for the aeroplane as it was and what was needed were much larger tail surfaces – both horizontal and vertical. But this could not be done quickly and the great production sausage was already rolling. Therefore the immediate problem was to make the handling of the Mark 21 in the air reasonably tolerable so that the aeroplane would be operationally viable, pending the happy day when a much larger tailplane would become available. So we tried all sorts of expedients – different sorts of tabs, and anti-balance tabs etc.[43]

Quill believed that, though he and Joe Smith had still not got the handling right, their modifications had made the plane acceptable, particularly 'in view of the spectacular performance which the aeroplane provided as an air combat fighter'.[44] But this was not the view that the Air Fighting Development Unit took, having tested the plane at Wittering. Its report read, 'Although the Spitfire 21 is not a dangerous aircraft to fly, pilots must be warned of its handling qualities and in its present state it is not likely to prove a satisfactory fighter.' The report concluded dramatically, 'No further attempts should be made to perpetuate the Spitfire family.'[45] Quill thought that this was an absurdly dogmatic judgement 'The AFDU were quite right to criticize the handling of the Mark 21, although their first report over-did it a bit in my opinion. Where they were terribly wrong was to recommend that all further development on the Spitfire should cease. They were quite unqualified to make such a sweeping judgement.'[46]

Quill's fellow test pilot Alex Henshaw was inclined to agree, though his first response to the sight of the Mark 21 had been negative: he feared

> the genius passed on by Mitchell had died. The beautiful symmetry had gone; in its place stood a powerful, almost ugly fighting machine. The classic lines had been replaced by forceful features and I had to push my emotions to one side and remind myself that this was not a pretty toy, it was a fighting machine designed to enter a battle yet to be won and it would go into that battle with all the strength we could muster.

Nor was Henshaw impressed with the take-off. 'The powerful torque needed a great deal of rudder to control it and the port wing dipped badly until the machine was well under way.' He also felt that the plane suffered from longitudinal instability – a perennial complaint with Spitfires. But other aspects in the air were much more attractive. It climbed to 40,000 feet in just ten minutes, and had 'a tremendous lightness of control' at high speeds. Henshaw said he 'revelled in aerobatics at speeds that would have been impossible before'.[47]

The damning verdict from the AFDU was premature. With some modifications to the controls, the Mark 21 was deemed acceptable for the RAF, and in January 1945 it entered service with 91 Squadron, based at Manston in Kent. Its first sorties, however, were low-level strafing and fighter-reconnaissance operations – something that Jeffrey Quill found absurd, given that it was designed for altitude performance: 'It is incomprehensible how the Ops. Staff at Group headquarters can have perpetrated such a gross and idiotic misuse of an aeroplane which was essentially an optimized medium and high altitude air combat fighter, but this sort of thing, I regret to say, was all too prevalent.'[48] A total of 121 Mark 21s were built before the end of the war led to the cancellation of more orders. The early lessons with handling were learned, and an upgraded version appeared in March 1945 as the Mark 22, which had the long-awaited larger tailplane and a teardrop canopy. Most of the 264 Mark 22s produced went into service after the war.

The final variant in the long line was the Mark 24, the very last Spitfire to enter service with the RAF. The only differences between this and the Mark 22 were a change from a pneumatic to an electric gun-firing system, the installation of racks under the wings for rocket projectiles, and the creation of large fuel capacity through an additional fuel tank in the rear fuselage. The first Mark 24 arrived at the Maintenance Unit at RAF Lyneham in April

1946, and the very final one on 24 February 1948 – almost exactly a dozen years since Mitchell's prototype had first flown.

There was just one other Spitfire version which deserves a mention, if only for its eccentricity. This was the so-called Mark XXX, which was actually a Mark Vc modified to carry beer barrels across the Channel to the thirsty troops in northern France after D-Day. The beer was provided by the Sussex brewers of Henty and Constable, and one 18-gallon beer barrel was fitted underneath each wing using an adapted bomb rack. Jeffrey Quill, who was involved in this important project, later joked, 'We were a little concerned about the strength situation of the barrels but on application to Henty and Constable we were astonished to find that being flown on the bomb racks of a Spitfire was a case that had not been taken into consideration in the design of the barrels.'[49]

Soon after the Normandy landings, the German jet-powered Messerschmitt 262 made its first appearance, pointing the way to an aeronautical revolution that would spell the end of all piston-engined planes soon after the war. At 540 mph, the 262's maximum speed was far in excess of that of any other Second World War fighter, and the plane caused consternation among Allied pilots when they first encountered it. 'Suddenly we were outmoded and outdated,' said Johnnie Johnson.[50] One Free French pilot, Henri de Bordass of 329 Squadron, was so shocked to find a 262 directly in front of him when flying over Enschede that he forgot to press his firing button.[51] But the 262 was less manoeuvrable than the Spitfire, which was sometimes able to get the better of the German jet in combat. In February 1945 Flight Lieutenant F. A. O. Gaze of 610 Squadron wrote this combat report of a patrol over Holland:

> I did an orbit at 13,000 feet to clear off the ice on the windscreen and sighted three Me 262s in vic formation passing below me at cloud-top level. I dived down behind them and closed in, crossing behind the formation, and attacked the port aircraft, which was lagging slightly. I could not see my sight properly as we were flying straight into the sun, but fired from dead astern at a range of 350 yards, hitting it in the starboard jet with the second burst, at which the other two aircraft immediately dived into cloud. It pulled up slowly and turned to starboard and I fired, obtaining more strikes on the fuselage and jet, which caught fire.[52]

The Me 262 descended through a cloud, and as Gaze dived after it he could see it crash to the ground. Once more, even against turbine technology, the Spitfire had proved its class.

For all its breathtaking speed, the 262 arrived too late and in too small numbers to have any serious influence on the conduct of the war. By the autumn of 1944 the Allies were in an utterly dominant position, as demonstrated in a broadcast for the BBC by Richard Dimbleby on 24 October 1944, commenting on the Allied air offensive over Germany: 'Today, as the great broad stream of Lancasters and Halifaxes crossed the frontier of Germany, there was not a single aircraft of the Luftwaffe to be seen, only the twisting and criss-crossing vapour trails of our own Spitfires and Mustangs protecting us above and on the flanks.'[53] The consequences of Allied supremacy were seen at their most graphic in late August 1944, when the 2nd Tactical Air Force trapped the retreating German army in the Falaise Gap on the edge of Normandy. The German ranks were torn to shreds by strafing, rocket-firing and dive-bombing Typhoons and Spitfires. More than 10,000 soldiers were killed in the process. Johnnie Houlton, who flew a number of sorties over Falaise, recalled that 'it was a very hot day, and we could smell the stench of the battle area long before we reached the killing ground.'[54] Paddy French witnessed the scene shortly afterwards: 'The aftermath of the fighting in the Falaise Gap was horrendous – we had witnessed it from the air but down here was the reality. Mile upon mile of destruction, quite literally the death of an army. As far as you could see, burnt out lorries and tanks and the bodies of soldiers and horses lying about everywhere.'[55]

On the other side of the world, in the Far East theatre, the Spitfire was again shifting the advantage in favour of the Allies and against the Axis. For a time, in 1944, it looked as if the Japanese might overrun Burma and then launch an invasion of British imperial India, but Spitfire Mark Vs and Mark VIIIs, which had been arriving in Burma in significant numbers since September 1943, helped the British army to turn back the Japanese at the Battle of Kohima. Operating from jungle clearings, the Spitfires conducted lethal strafing operations against the enemy troops, as well as protecting the transport planes bringing in supplies to the British ground forces. Whereas the Hurricanes had been overwhelmed by the Japanese fighter planes, like the superbly manoeuvrable, radial-engined Mitsubishi Zero and the fast tactical fighter the Nakajima Hayabusa – known to the Allies as the Oscar – the Spitfire proved a match for both. Don Healey, who fought with 17 Squadron in Burma, said that the Mark VIII had two great virtues in combat against the Japanese: first, 'you could outclimb them if you could maintain a sustained ascent' and, second, 'if you had the height you could outdive them as well, as the Mark VIII weighed almost twice as much as any enemy likely to be encountered.'[56]

Just as in northern Europe, the fighting against an implacable foe could be brutal, but by early 1945 the Japanese were in full-scale retreat. A picture of this harsh but ultimately victorious campaign is provided by the journal of Flight Sergeant N. 'Dobbie' Dobbins, who flew with 607 (County of Durham) Squadron. The conditions in the jungle were extremely oppressive, with water supplies limited, the heat scorching, and the risk of Japanese attacks ever present. One night in April 1945, at a makeshift airfield in a narrow clearing near Kwetnge, Dobbins and his comrades were warned that the Japanese might be closing in:

> The place stank of death and I felt a shade sick. All around was dense jungle. The majority of us had only a knife and a revolver. I remember crouching in a ditch with three other guys and I was scared. Everything that cracked appeared as though there were hundreds of Japs out there and, as it was a pitch-black night, you couldn't tell friend from foe. My heart was pumping that fast that I thought anyone would be able to hear it.[57]

A few days later Dobbins's squadron moved to Kalaywa. 'What a hole,' he commented. 'There was no water. All the wells either had dead bodies or had been poisoned. Unless you have been in a blazing sun with a temperature of 100° to 108° you will never know what hell it is to go without water.' That night the airstrip came under fire from Japanese troops, though the British soldiers and airmen managed to hold them off.'[58]

But Dobbins's mood quickly changed as the squadron went on the counter-attack, hitting the Japanese who were evacuating Rangoon. Dobbins himself was relieved to be on fighter-reconnaissance missions rather than waiting anxiously in the jungle. On 1 July, for instance, he came across a flotilla of Japanese boats trying to cross the river Sittang: 'I dived down on the boats with our cannons and machine guns blazing. I have never seen bods leave a boat so quick. Some of them bought it where they sat and as the boats were sinking we went down only using the machine guns and let the Japs have the lot.' Further up the river, he then saw a large camouflaged boat. 'Just as I was diving on it, a number of Japs ran from the near side of it, so I opened up with cannons and machine guns and knocked the hell out of them.' A real feeling of visceral loathing for the enemy comes through Dobbins's diary, as in this entry for 28 July, when he was on a bombing and strafing mission over the town of Pa-an. 'I managed to drop my bomb from 300 feet smack among four buildings. When it burst, three of the buildings had all their sides blown in and believe you me what a hell of a mess it was. To sit up in the sky and watch twelve 500-pound bombs blast on a city is a wizard sight, more so when you know the joint is full of Japs. I should imagine about 2,000 Japs were killed.' Of another attack on the river Sittang, Dobbins wrote that the Japanese 'never stood a chance. Even though two of them stood up and fired, we knocked the hell out of them. A cannon shell must have caught one bod right in the guts for he was blown into the air for the matter of 30 feet. I saw two Japs swim and reach the bank but before they could climb out I nipped down and gave them a load of cannon and machine-gun bullets. They will never return to Japan.'[59]

As Dobbins gloried in death by the banks of the Sittang, the Allies were on the verge of victory in Europe. In the new year the Germans had launched their last onslaught to challenge the Allied advance, the Luftwaffe using 800 aircraft to bombard Allied airfields in Belgium and France. A total of 144 planes of the 2nd Tactical Air Force were destroyed, many of them Spitfires, but the Germans lost 300 aircraft, 56 of them to Spitfires. From then on the German retreat gathered pace, as the Spitfires and other planes tore mercilessly into the enemy, hitting everything from troops to transport. This vivid description by John Wilkinson of 41 Squadron is typical of the destruction of the German war machine in the spring of 1945:

One pleasant although cold afternoon, four of us flew our Spitfire XIVs deep into enemy territory, where we attacked any target of opportunity, fulfilling our official squadron motto, 'Seek and Destroy'. One of our prime ground targets was trains. This particular afternoon we came across a freight train . . . Picture, if you will, diving down towards a railway engine, while scanning the area for anti-aircraft guns and watching for enemy fighters. I released the safety catch and switched on the camera gun to record the action. I am looking through the gyroscopic gunsight in front of the bullet-proof windshield and over the length of the powerful engine, the propeller spinning so fast there is no obstruction to the view. I manoeuvre to place the dot of my gunsight on the cylinder that drives the wheels – this is the hardest part for the Germans to replace. I press the gun button and feel the powerful rumble as the shells and armour-piercing bullets speed on their destructive path. The spread of shells also hits the boiler, which provides a satisfyingly spectacular explosion and plume of steam. Having destroyed the engine, I then raked the freight cars with cannon and machine-gun fire.[60]

On 24 March 1945 Ted Smith, flying his Mark XVI over the Rhine as part of the 2nd Tactical Air Force, recorded in his diary:

I realized, quite suddenly today, that this may be the beginning of the end. Now that we are over the Rhine, there seems little to stop us . . . All the stories coming back from captured Germans are stories of horror, from the air – and this means us. The Huns can hardly get a truck or a staff car on the road without the fear that any one of our fifty-plus squadrons will swoop in from the sky, raking it with cannon and point-fives – or blasting it with 60-pound rockets.

A few weeks later, on 16 April, Smith learned that the Germans called the Allied fighter-bombers *Terrorflieger* – 'terror flyers'. 'Whatever they call us is well justified,' he commented. 'The only time the German army can move is dusk to dawn. They can hardly get a motorbike moving in daylight without Spitfires zooming down from the sky.'[61]

Less than a month later the war in Europe was over. On 7 May the Germans signed an instrument of unconditional surrender at Eisenhower's headquarters. On 2 September Japan formally capitulated to General MacArthur. It was perhaps fitting that it was a Seafire, operating over Tokyo Bay on 15 August, that shot down the last aircraft of the Second World War before peace was declared.[62]

The day before VE Day, Bobby Oxspring climbed into his Spitfire for a joyful sortie of aerobatics. 'I had reason to celebrate. I could scarcely believe that I was still in one piece after six years of war and still flying my faithful Spitfire.'[63]

Epilogue

'IN JANUARY 1946, the day came for my last flight in a Spitfire,' wrote Alex Henshaw in his autography, *Sigh for a Merlin*:

I climbed into the cockpit with the casualness of very long habit – no words were spoken – just a glance and the chocks moved away and the Griffon roared into life. As I climbed steeply from the airfield I reflected back over the years to my first flight from Castle Bromwich in a Mark II. I wondered if there had ever been a closer attachment and understanding between man and machine than had developed in the constant and often demanding association that had been my life for six years and four months. The Spitfire over those years had grown up and matured; its vigour and aggression had increased – I had grown older.

Then, as he climbed through the sky, his mind went back to the summer of 1940, when he had first arrived at Castle Bromwich, 'when so little had been produced and so much was expected from the works that now lay below me. We had kept our morale, we had produced our weapons and finally we had won our battles.'

But there was no sense of elation as Alex Henshaw landed, no enthusiasm in the wake of victory gained. Instead there was a sense of loss as 'I drove away, leaving that lone Spitfire on the vast, empty expanse of tarmac.' The glorious, exhausting chapters of the Spitfire's narrative were over. The heroic deed had been accomplished. Britain had been saved, the tyrant conquered. The new era of the jet engine was beckoning. Yet it was not quite the end of the Spitfire story. For, even in post-war age of advancing technology, the Spitfire was to linger on for more than a decade, performing useful roles, sometimes going into action, and always serving as a reminder of the RAF's heroism.

When the war ended in Europe, in May 1945, the latest marks of Spitfires were still coming off the production lines, albeit in far fewer numbers. Indeed, with jet propulsion still in its infancy, Supermarine, with the government's encouragement, was still looking for ways to extract more performance from piston-engined fighters. The final two Seafire types emerged after the war: the Seafire 46, with a Griffon 61 engine, contra-rotating propeller and larger tailplane; and the Seafire 47, with folding wings and a new type of supercharged engine. The Seafire 47, which had its maiden flight in April 1946, was the more successful of the two, and was to see action briefly in the 1950 Korean War. A total of 89 Seafire 47s were built, and the last of them served with the Royal Navy Volunteer Reserve until 1954.

The Spitfire also provided the inspiration – and the fuselage – for the Supermarine Spiteful, which was meant to be the successor to Mitchell's fighter. Under development from 1942, the Spiteful used part of the Mark XIV airframe, but had a radically different wing. In place of the thin, classical sweeping curves of the ellipse, the Spiteful's laminar wing was thicker and had straight edges and clipped ends, giving it a far stubbier, squat appearance – an effect enhanced by the wider undercarriage, which folded inward. But the ellipse had been the secret of Mitchell's success, and the Spiteful's laminar wing, far from reducing drag as had been predicted, actually worsened performance. It could also be dangerous, because its innovative use of rods to control the ailerons sometimes led to jamming. The Supermarine test pilot Frank Furlong was killed in September 1945 when the Spiteful prototype dived straight into the ground. With development plagued by troubles, the first jets now in service, and a new Labour government looking to make defence savings, the Spiteful programme was radically cut from an original order for 800 to just 24 in December 1946. In the end, only 19 were built, 13 of which were sold for scrap in less than a year. A naval version, known as the Seafang, was ordered in May 1945, but again it was overtaken by jet technology and only 16 were built, though a development of the Spiteful with a jet engine – called the Attacker – did go into naval service as the first carrier-based jet fighter.

When the war ended, the RAF had no fewer than 5,864 Spitfires – far more than it needed in the age of demobilization. The cutbacks that followed in home-based, front-line squadrons were dramatic and immediate: by Battle of Britain Day in 1946 just two Fighter Command squadrons were equipped with Spitfires. There was, however, a revival after the government decided to re-establish the Royal Auxiliary Air Force as a volunteer reserve, with 13 of its 20 squadrons using the Spitfire. When the RAAF was formally placed under the control of Fighter Command in February 1949, it meant that 221 Spitfires were being used in home defence. And, because of financial constraints on jet production, the RAF's home-based Spitfires were not finally phased out as front-line fighters until 1951. Even then the plane continued in a back-up role with the RAF, serving in the civilian Anti-Aircraft Co-operation Units until

1954. And three photoreconnaissance XIXs were retained in the civilian-operated Temperature and Humidity Flight until 1957, providing meteorological data to the Central Forecasting Office in Dunstable.

But even the resurrection of the Auxiliaries and the tenacity of Bedfordshire meteorologists could take up only a fraction of the vast supply of post-war Spitfires. So a large number of those not wanted by the RAF or the navy were sold to foreign air forces, which again reinforced the Spitfire's international reach. The Belgian government, for instance, took delivery of 132 Mark XIVs between 1948 and 1951. Thailand purchased 30 Mark XIVs in 1948, Holland 55 Mark IXs, Eire a squadron of Seafire Mark IIIs and 6 Mark IX trainers, and Burma 20 de-navalized Seafire Mark XVs. One of the odder deals was the sale by the Soviet Union of some of its Spitfires to the People's Republic of China – the kind of arrangement that Beaverbrook would have liked to have negotiated at his peak. And by far the most controversial overseas transaction was the shipment in 1948 of 59 Spitfires by Czechoslovakia to the newly created state of Israel. This had the bizarre consequence of creating a situation where, for the only time in history, Spitfires ended up fighting against each other on opposing sides, for the Royal Egyptian Air Force had received 37 Mark IXs in 1946, and two years later, when the British Palestinian mandate expired, Egypt went to war against the fledgling Israeli nation, immediately sending its Spitfires into action. But Israel, now armed with its Czech Spitfires, was a formidable adversary as it struggled for its independence. In an air battle over Negev on 21 October 1948, Jack Doyle, a Canadian pilot with Israel's 101 Squadron, shot down an Egyptian Spitfire – the first kill by the Israeli air force.

But it was not the first Spitfire to be downed in the war. In an implausible twist, Spitfires of the RAF were also involved in this conflict. When the fighting started, the British were still in Palestine organizing their withdrawal. Two RAF squadrons, equipped with fighter-reconnaissance Mark XVIIIs, were present on a base at Ramat David to provide airborne protection. On 22 May 1948 a squadron of Royal Egyptian Air Force Spitfires dive-bombed this base, setting fire to two of the RAF Spitfires. A couple of hours later the Egyptians were back, but this time the RAF was ready, The British Spitfires were quickly scrambled, and one of the Egyptians was blown from the sky, another crashed in the desert, and a third was brought down by anti-aircraft fire. The following day the Egyptian government made an unconvincing announcement claiming that the incident had been caused by 'regrettable navigational error'.[1]

Yet this was not the last time that RAF Spitfires were dragged into the bloody mire. On 7 January 1949, with the Arab–Israeli War reaching its climax, a group of RAF Mark XVIIIs was on a reconnaissance mission over the Suez Canal Zone, where Britain had treaty rights to maintain a military presence. Suddenly the RAF came under attack from Israeli Spitfires, having allegedly violated Israeli airspace on the country's southern border. Three Mark XVIIIs were shot down, and, when several Hawker Tempests were sent to investigate after the Spitfires failed to return to their base, one of them was also hit by the Israelis. What was remarkable was the stoical response of the British government, though in the RAF the attitude was one of 'stunned dismay',[2] particularly because two pilots had been killed, another had been badly injured, and one had been taken prisoner by the Israelis. Some pilots even wanted to take action against Israel. It was only when the war ended, in July, that the tensions were eased.

The Middle Eastern conflict was both disturbing and unique. Never before or since did a set of circumstances contrive to put the Spitfire at the centre of a tripartite clash. But the Spitfire's fighting days were not over. In the Far East, for three years from 1948, Spitfires were used by the British government of Malaya as part of a counter-guerrilla campaign against Communist insurgents demanding independence. The Spitfires, based in two front-line squadrons in Singapore, flew some 1,800 sorties, carrying out bombing, rocket and strafing attacks on suspected insurgent camps in the jungle – though it was doubtful if they achieved much beyond trying to boost the government's morale. 'It was all rather loose and inconclusive,' recalled Flying Officer John Nicholls of 28 Squadron. 'Guerrilla fighters make the maximum use of available cover. They travel light, move fast and seldom concentrate. Operating in dense jungle, they are extremely difficult to find.' Besides, as Nicholls admitted, the Spitfire was now becoming obsolescent. 'The ineffectiveness of the Spitfire in these operations illustrates the sort of problem we had using an interceptor designed thirteen years earlier to bomb such difficult targets . . . We were really asking too much from the Spitfire.'[3] In a throwback to the Spitfire's glory days, the final flight in Malaya, on 1 January 1951, was led by Wing Commander Wilfrid Duncan Smith, hero of the Battle of Britain, Malta and Italy. This was to be the last time that the Spitfire would fly on combat duty. It was appropriate that the last page in its operational history should be written by a man who had flown the aircraft with such distinction.

Another military campaign against Communism – this one in Korea – saw the last action by the Seafire. During July 1950, twelve Mark 47s carried by HMS *Triumph* took part in the United Nations operations against the North Korean forces which had occupied South Korea. Initially deprived of land bases, the UN could operate only from aircraft carriers, and the Seafires undertook 115 ground attacks and 245 offensive patrols, hitting road, rail and

port installations, providing cover for coalition vessels, and striking
Communist junks suspected of minelaying. But, just as in the Second World
War, the Seafire was prone to accidents on deck landings, and within barely
a few weeks it had to be withdrawn from the combat zone. It was not the
most uplifting end to the plane's career.

Concerns about Communism in the early 1950s had also led to the
strengthening of the RAF base in Hong Kong with a Spitfire squadron, aimed
at deterring any Chinese aggression. And it was from Hong Kong that the very
last official flight of the Spitfire in RAF or Commonwealth service took place,
on 21 April 1955, in a special fly-past to honour Queen Elizabeth's birthday.
The Spitfires were Mark 24s which had previously belonged to 80 Squadron.
Those taking part in this ceremony were well aware of its historic significance
as the Spitfires in the colony took their bow before going into retirement.
Geoffrey Cairns, the adjutant and chief instructor who led the fly-past, recalled:

> We were conscious that this was going to be the last flight of the Spitfire in
> service. That is why I arranged to have a film made of the event, borrowing a
> cine camera from a rich Chinese gentleman. The film was taken from the
> back of a Harvard. It could be awkward with the Mark 24 as it was a bit of a
> handful, especially if there was a crosswind, but it all went smoothly. The other
> pilots were all volunteers, because it was an Auxiliary unit, but at that time
> everyone in Hong Kong had to do some national service because of the
> Chinese threat. Because I was the leader I had to get the timing just right, but
> it was fine. And that was that.[4]

Well, not quite. The Spitfire had one more duty to perform for the RAF.
In 1963 the government was concerned about trouble flaring up in Indonesia,
whose air force was equipped with American Mustangs. And the strategists
wanted to find out how the RAF's latest Mach-2 fighter jet, the Lightning,
would engage with the Mustang, particularly in the use of heat-seeking missiles. Unfortunately the RAF had no Mustangs, but it was suggested that, in
terms of performance, a Spitfire had many of the same qualities. So a mock
dogfight was arranged at the Central Fighter Establishment at Binbrook, in
Lincolnshire, where the commander was John Nicholls, who had fought in
Korea as well as in the Malaysian campaign. Because of the Lightning's potential vulnerability to the Spitfire's more manoeuvrable dogfighting game, said
Wing Commander Nicholls,

> in the end we evolved a type of attack which was the antithesis of all I had
> learned from my own operational experience of fighter-versus-fighter combat
> in Korea. Instead of trying to get above the enemy and diving on him to
> attack, we found it best to use the Lightning's very high power-to-weight ratio

to make a climbing attack from behind and below. From that angle the field of view from the Spitfire was poor, there was a good chance of achieving surprise and the infra-red source gave the best chance of missile acquisition.[5]

With that, more than thirty years after Mitchell had sat down to design a plane to meet Specification F7/30, the Spitfire saga, at least within the RAF, had come to end. The legend, of course, lives on, and will always endure as long as Britain still cherishes its history and its past. It is a testament to the continuing appeal of the plane that, more than seventy years after the prototype first flew, there is a thriving market in Spitfire restorations. It has been estimated that around fifty Spitfires, lovingly returned to their original glory, are flying today, a larger total than when the aircraft retired from RAF service in the 1950s. The Spitfire will remain immortal, an enriching symbol of national identity and freedom, a tiny, vulnerable but heroic creature that inspired fear in the world's darkest tyranny. The Spitfire pilot Bill Rolls was once injured during the Battle of Malta and ended up in a Valletta hospital. In the ward with him was a Ju 88 pilot who had been shot down earlier – coincidentally, by Rolls's squadron. The two men ended up talking. 'He told me that the most terrifying thing that had happened to him so far was the sight of twelve Spitfires all firing cannon and machine guns and coming head on at his formation. He said that all the front gunners had frozen stiff with fear and could not fire their guns at us. It was a terrible sight, and the look on his face spoke for itself.'[6]

But it was a wonderful, glorious sight for the British, and for all those struggling against the yoke of German oppression. The spirit of defiance which the Spitfire so perfectly embodied was once summed up by the most famous RAF pilot of them all, Douglas Bader, in a remark during a symposium held in 1976 at the University of Southampton to mark the fortieth anniversary of the Spitfire's maiden flight:

> The Battle of Britain was won by the whole of the British nation. It was won by the people who took the bombing on the ground, and one remembers nostalgically, almost with tears in one's eyes, the various pictures that appeared in the press. I remember one of a tobacconist's shop outside Victoria station which had been bombed the afternoon before, but in the morning there was a trestle table outside and a notice which said, 'Business as Usual' and a grinning cockney standing beside it. These are the people that we so seldom see, our own people, the people we love, our own compatriots who took it. If they had not taken it, if they had not fought, if they had not built the aeroplanes and the ammunition and everything else, we could not have fought. We were the glamour boys up there and had something to fight back with, that was the difference. I want to say it here in this place with the memory of R. J. Mitchell. This is what mattered. It was a united effort by everybody.[7]

Notes

Fuller details of works cited in short-title form and the location of papers cited may be found in the Bibliography.

Introduction

1. W. G. G. Duncan Smith, 'The Spitfire at War' (1976), Quill papers, 94/38/1. An edited version of this account subsequently appeared in Duncan Smith's autobiography, *Spitfire into Battle*.
2. Haining, *The Spitfire Log*.
3. Levine, *Forgotten Voices*.
4. Allen, *Battle for Britain*.
5. Rolls, *Spitfire Attack*.
6. Ball papers, 85/19/1.
7. Caine, *Spitfires, Thunderbolts and Warm Beer*.
8. Militärarchiv-Bundesarchiv Freiburg, RL2 II/1424.
9. Galland, *The First and the Last*.
10. D. Robinson, *Invasion 1940*.
11. Lecture to the Warton branch of the Royal Aeronautical Society, Quill papers, 94/38/1.
12. McLean interview with J. D. Scott, Nov. 1959, Vickers Archives, 701.
13. Minutes of Secretary of State's progress meeting, 16 Feb. 1937, Swinton papers, 3/15.
14. Aide-memoire on air policy by Sir Thomas Inskip, 9 Dec. 1937, National Archives, AIR 8/226.
15. 7 July 1940, Chamberlain papers, NC18/1/1164.
16. Crossland, 'Britain's Defence and the Munich Crisis'.
17. 9 July 1932, National Archives, AIR 20/167.
18. Note to the Deputy Chief of the Air Staff on 'delays with new aircraft to specification F7/30', 15 Feb. 1934. National Archives, AIR 2/167.
19. Dobbins papers, 83/41/1.
20. Scott, *Vickers*.
21. Henshaw, *Sigh for a Merlin*.
22. Offenberg, *Lonely Warrior*.
23. 'Forty Years of the Spitfire'.

Chapter 1: 'The supremacy of the monoplane'

1. Hoare, *Wilde's Last Stand*.
2. H. F. King, 'Sires of the Swift'.
3. Ibid.
4. Scott, *Vickers*.
5. Webb papers.
6. Mitchell, *R. J. Mitchell*.
7. Ibid.
8. Ibid.
9. Contribution to lecture on Spitfire, 4 Mar. 1986, Royal Aeronautical Society Southampton Branch, Davis papers, AC93/14/15.
10. Mitchell, *R. J. Mitchell*.
11. Webb papers.
12. Quill, *Spitfire*.
13. J. Smith, 'R. J. Mitchell'.
14. McLean interview with J. D. Scott, 9 Nov. 1959, Vickers Archives, 701.
15. Russell, *Spitfire Odyssey*.
16. Mitchell, *R. J. Mitchell*.
17. Note by Jack Davis, Feb. 1986, Davis papers, AC93/14/15.
18. J. Smith, 'R. J. Mitchell'.
19. Mondey, *The Schneider Trophy*.
20. J. Smith, 'R. J. Mitchell'.
21. Webb papers.
22. Ibid.
23. J. Smith, 'R. J. Mitchell'.
24. Lovell-Cooper to Jack Davis, 8 Feb. 1977, Davis papers, AC93/14/18.
25. Griffiths, *Testing Times*.
26. Webb papers.
27. H. F. King, 'Sires of the Swift'.
28. Mondey, *The Schneider Trophy*.
29. *Flight*, Aug. 1922.
30. Ibid., Sept. 1925.
31. Mondey, *The Schneider Trophy*.
32. Mitchell, *R. J. Mitchell*.
33. Ibid.
34. H. F. King, 'Sires of the Swift'.
35. Mitchell, *R. J. Mitchell*.
36. McLean interview with J. D. Scott, 9 Nov. 1959, Vickers Archives, 701.
37. Webb papers.
38. Eric Lovell-Cooper to Jack Davis, 8 Feb. 1977, Davis papers, AC93/14/18.
39. Smithies, *Aces, Erks and Backroom Boys*.
40. Wallis interview with J. D. Scott, 28 Sept., Vickers Archives, 701.
41. Saward, *Victory Denied*.
42. Mondey, *The Schneider Trophy*.
43. Mitchell, *R. J. Mitchell*.
44. *Time*, 27 Nov. 1933.
45. Baker, *From Biplane to Spitfire*.
46. Quoted in Budiansky, *Air Power*.

47. Terraine, *The Right of the Line*.
48. Brooke-Popham to Newall, 8 July 1927, National Archives, AIR 20/167.
49. 30 Sept. 1932, National Archives, AIR 20/167.
50. Undated Air Ministry paper, 1931, National Archives, AIR 20/167.
51. May 1930, National Archives, AIR 20/169.
52. 13 July 1931, National Archives, AIR 20/167.
53. Divine, *The Broken Wing*.
54. Morgan and Shacklady, *Spitfire*.
55. McLean interview with J. D. Scott, 9 Nov. 1959, Vickers Archives, 701.
56. Handyside interview with J. D. Scott, 28 Sept. 1959, Vickers Archive, 701.
57. Clifton interview with J. D. Scott, 13 Oct. 1959, Vickers Archive, 701.
58. Shenstone to J. D. Scott, 29 Jan. 1960, Vickers Archive, 377.
59. Price, *Spitfire: A Documentary History*.
60. Report to the Air Ministry, 30 July 1933 AIR 2/2850.
61. R. Cowlin to Supermarine's resident technical officer, 24 Oct. 1933, National Archives, AIR 2/2850.
62. Flying Operations to Deputy Chief of the Air Staff, 15 Feb. 2004, National Archives, AIR 2/167.
63. Price, *The Spitfire Story*.
64. Webb papers.
65. Mitchell, *R. J. Mitchell*.
66. Webb papers.
67. Smithies, *Aces, Erks and Backroom Boys*.
68. Scott-Hall to the Air Ministry, 20 Feb. 1934, National Archives, AIR 2/2850.
69. F. E. Collin to Flight Lieutenant Potts, 26 Feb. 1934, National Archives, AIR 2/2850.
70. 'Forty Years of the Spitfire'.

Chapter 2: 'I don't want anything touched'

1. Winterton to Neville Chamberlain's widow, 28 Feb. 1951, Chamberlain papers, NC11/1/93.
2. Quoted in Terraine, *The Right of the Line*.
3. Hyde, *British Air Policy between the Wars*.
4. Ibid.
5. Entries for 6 Apr. 1933 and 15 Dec. 1934, Pownall, *Chief of Staff*, vol. 1.
6. Entry for 4 Dec. 1933, Pownall, *Chief of Staff*, vol. 1.
7. M. Smith, *British Air Strategy between the Wars*.
8. Kershaw, *Making Friends with Hitler*.
9. Entry for 26 June 1934, Pownall, *Chief of Staff*, vol. 1.
10. 28 July 1934, Chamberlain papers, NC18/1/881.
11. Kershaw, *Making Friends with Hitler*.
12. Wright, *Dowding and the Battle of Britain*.
13. Ray, *The Battle of Britain*.
14. Ibid.
15. Wright, *Dowding and the Battle of Britain*.
16. Ibid.
17. Sinnott, *The Royal Air Force and Aircraft Design*.

18. Note by Flying Operations, 15 Feb. 1934, National Archives AIR 2/167.
19. Memorandum from Operational Requirements to Deputy Chief of the Air Staff, 25 Apr. 1934, National Archives, AIR 2/167.
20. Sinnott, *The Royal Air Force and Aircraft Design*.
21. L. V. Meadowcroft to Supermarine, 4 Sept. 1934, National Archives, AIR 2/2850.
22. Harvey-Bailey, *Hives*.
23. Ibid.
24. Price, *Spitfire: A Complete Documentary History*.
25. 'Forty Years of the Spitfire'.
26. Price, *The Spitfire Story*.
27. Price, *Spitfire: A Documentary History*.
28. 'Forty Years of the Spitfire'.
29. Ibid.
30. Dowding, 'The Real Story of the Spitfire'.
31. Shenstone to J. D. Scott, 29 Jan. 1960, Vickers Archives, 377.
32. Ibid., 4 Mar. 1960.
33. Vickers Archives, 701.
34. National Archives, AIR 2/2850.
35. Air Ministry to Mitchell, 26 Nov. 1934, National Archives AIR 2/2824.
36. Draft notes of Air Ministry conference, 5 Dec. 1934, Supermarine papers.
37. Sorley, 'Eight Guns for a Fighter'.
38. 'Factors Involved in the Conception of the Eight Gun Fighter', memorandum, 6 May 1945, Sorley papers, AC72/19/16/2.
39. The phrase appears in the draft of his 1957 *Times* article, though it was deleted from the printed text.
40. *Les Ailes*, 704 (13 Dec. 1934).
41. Sinnott, *The Royal Air Force and Aircraft Design*.
42. 28 July 1933, National Archives, AVIA 8/167.
43. 1 May 1935, National Archives, AIR 2/2824.
44. Note by Chief of the Air Staff, 4 June 1935, National Archives, AIR 46/119.
45. 4 May 1935, National Archives, AIR 2/2824.
46. Dowding to the Deputy Chief of the Air Staff, 5 May 1935, National Archives, AIR 2/2824.
47. Morgan and Shacklady, *Spitfire*.
48. Griffiths, *Testing Times*.
49. Morgan and Shacklady, *Spitfire*.
50. Webb papers.
51. Kershaw, *Making Friends with Hitler*.
52. Entry for 23 Apr. 1935, Pownall, *Chief of Staff*, vol. 1.
53. Speech to the Darlington Mechanics Institute, *Air Review*, Dec. 1934.
54. Kershaw, *Making Friends with Hitler*.
55. Minutes of Sub-Committee on Air Parity, 13 May 1935, National Archives, CAB 27/518.
56. Report of Sub-Committee on Air Parity to Cabinet, 17 May 1935, National Archives, CAB 27/518.
57. Minutes of Secretary of State's progress meeting, 30 July 1935, Swinton papers, 270/4/1.
58. Ibid., 22 Oct. 1935.
59. 26 Nov. 1935, National Archives, AVIA 10/20.

60. Minutes of Secretary of State's progress meeting, 6 Feb. 1936, Swinton papers, 270/4/2.
61. Webb papers.
62. Haining, *The Spitfire Log.*
63. Webb papers.
64. Price, *The Spitfire Story.*
65. Webb papers.
66. Quill, *Birth of a Legend.*
67. Supermarine papers, C99/736/34.
68. Levine, *Forgotten Voices.*
69. Minutes of Secretary of State's progress meeting, 10 Mar. 1936, Swinton papers, 270/4/2.
70. Ibid., 17 Mar. 1936, Swinton papers, 270/4/3.
71. Forrester, *Fly for Your Life.*
72. Henshaw, 'A Tribute to Jeffrey Quill'.
73. Quill, *Spitfire.*
74. Ibid.
75. Minutes of Secretary of State's progress meeting, 31 Mar. 1936, Swinton papers, 270/4/3.
76. Furse, *Wilfrid Freeman.*
77. Quill, *Birth of a Legend.*
78. Ibid.
79. Edwardes-Jones, interview with Dr Alfred Price, in Price, *The Spitfire Story.*
80. Accounts of this conversation are in both Mitchell, *R. J. Mitchell,* and Price, *The Spitfire Story.*
81. Quoted in Mitchell, *R. J. Mitchell.*
82. Quill, *Spitfire.*
83. *The Times,* 19 June 1936.
84. Quoted in J. W. R. Taylor and M. Allward, *Spitfire.*
85. J. Smith, 'R. J. Mitchell'.
86. Mitchell to W. H. Beaton, 20 Mar. 1937, Mitchell papers, AC72/24/9.
87. Mitchell, *R. J. Mitchell.*
88. 16 Mar. 1937, Mitchell papers, AC72/24/10.
89. 16 Mar. 1937, Mitchell papers, AC72/24/11.
90. 20 Mar. 1937, Mitchell papers, AC72/24/11.
91. Mitchell, *R. J. Mitchell.*
92. Quill, *Spitfire.*
93. Mitchell, *R. J. Mitchell.*

Chapter 3: 'A disgraceful state of affairs'

1. 8 Aug. 1935, Weir papers, 19/10/11.
2. 12 Aug. 1935, Weir papers, 19/10/11.
3. Report on the handling trials of Spitfire K5404, Martlesham Heath, Sept. 1936, National Archives, AIR 2/2824.
4. Minutes of Secretary of State's progress meeting, 16 June 1936, Swinton papers, 270/4/3.
5. Ibid., 22 June 1936.

6. Ibid., 16 June 1936.
7. Ibid., 28 July 1936.
8. Ibid., 19 Jan. 1937.
9. Ibid., 7 Feb. 1937.
10. Ibid., 10 Feb. 1937.
11. 'Forty Years of the Spitfire'.
12. Russell, *Spitfire Odyssey*.
13. Axell to Jack Davis, 10 Mar. 1984, Davis papers, AC93/14/19.
14. Webb papers.
15. Verney's report after a visit to Supermarine, 30 Apr. 1936, National Archives, AVIA 10/8.
16. Price, *The Spitfire Story*.
17. Russell, *Spitfire Postscript*.
18. Ibid.
19. Webb papers.
20. Newton's unpublished memoir, Davis papers, AC93/14/16.
21. Supermarine quarterly report, Mar. 1937, Vickers Archives, 722.
22. Smithies, *Aces, Erks and Backroom Boys*.
23. Supermarine quarterly report, June 1937, Vickers Archives, 722.
24. Griffiths, *Testing Times*.
25. Quill, *Spitfire*.
26. Webb papers.
27. Russell, *Spitfire Odyssey*.
28. Webb papers.
29. Dixon to Jack Davis, 11 Mar. 1977, Davis papers, AC93/4/20.
30. Webb papers.
31. Quill, *Spitfire*.
32. Minutes of Secretary of State's progress meeting, 16 Feb. 1937, Swinton papers, 270/4/3.
33. 17 Feb. 1937, Weir papers, 19/2/22.
34. Minutes of Secretary of State's progress meeting, 23 Mar. 1937, Swinton papers, 270/4/3.
35. Ibid., 20 Apr. 1937.
36. Statement by Sir Cyril Newall, ibid., 27 Apr. 1937.
37. Minutes of Secretary of State's progress meeting, 14 Sept. 1937, Swinton papers, 270/4/3.
38. Supermarine quarterly report, Dec. 1937, Vickers Archive 722.
39. 29 Nov. 1937, Vickers Archive 866.
40. Minutes of Secretary of State's progress meeting, 16 Jan. 1938, Swinton papers, 270/4/3.
41. Ibid., 12 Feb. 1938.
42. Minutes of CID, 24 Feb. 1938, Weir papers, 19/1.
43. 1 Mar. 1937, National Archives, AIR 6/45.
44. M. Smith, *British Air Strategy between the Wars*.
45. Swinton, *Sixty Years of Power*.
46. Cross, *Lord Swinton*.
47. Ibid.
48. Report on visit to Germany, May 1937, Evill papers, AC74/8/34.
49. Weir to Swinton, 14 Mar. 1938, Weir papers, 19/19.

50. The opinion of Sir John Slessor, the Air Staff's Director of Plans, quoted in Hyde, *British Air Policy between the Wars*.
51. Manchester, *The Caged Lion*.
52. Terraine, *The Right of the Line*.
53. 9 Dec. 1937, National Archives AIR 8/226.
54. 11 Dec. 1937, National Archives AIR 8/226.
55. Memorandum by the Chancellor, 4 Apr. 1938, National Archives AIR 8/237.
56. Minutes of Cabinet, 14 Mar. 1938, National Archives AIR 8/237.
57. Note by the Air Staff on Scheme L, 4 Apr. 1938, National Archives AIR 8/237.
58. Minutes of Cabinet, 27 Apr. 1938, National Archives AIR 8/237.
59. 29 Apr. 1938, National Archives AIR 8/226.
60. Minutes of Secretary of State's progress meeting, 22 Feb. 1938, Swinton papers, 270/4/3.
61. Ibid., 1 Mar. 1938.
62. Supermarine quarterly report, Mar. 1937, Vickers Archives, 722.
63. Minutes of Secretary of State's progress meeting, 5 Apr. 1938, Swinton papers, 270/4/3.
64. 14 Jan. 1938, Weir papers, 19/1s.
65. 28 Feb. 1951, Chamberlain papers, NC11/1/933.
66. Swinton, *Sixty Years of Power*.
67. Swinton to Chamberlain, 20 May 1938, Chamberlain papers, NC7/11/31/263.
68. 20 May 1938, Chamberlain papers, NC7/11/31/259.
69. 17 May 1938, Swinton papers, 2/8.
70. Churchill to Swinton, 24 Feb. 1939, Swinton papers, 2/10.
71. Entry for 17 May 1938, Nicolson, *Diaries and Letters*, vol. 1.
72. Price, *The Spitfire Story*.
73. 29 Aug. 1936, National Archives, AIR 19/1.
74. Ibid., 23 Aug. 1937.
75. *The Times*, 16 July 1938.
76. Briefing for the Prime Minister, 23 May 1938, National Archives, AIR 15/3750.
77. Minutes of Secretary of State's progress meeting, 24 May 1938, National Archives, AIR 6/36.
78. 24 May 1938, National Archives, AVIA 15/3750.
79. Hansard, 25 May 1938.
80. 28 June 1938, National Archives, AIR 19/1.
81. *The Times*, editorial, 18 June 1938.
82. Minutes of Secretary of State's progress meeting, 5 July 1938, National Archives, Air 6/62.
83. Webb papers.
84. Minutes of Secretary of State's progress meeting, 26 July 1938, National Archives, Air 6/64.
85. Quill, *Birth of a Legend*.
86. Price, *Spitfire: A Complete Fighting History*.
87. Ibid.
88. Levine, *Forgotten Voices*.
89. Internal Air Ministry memorandum, Sept. 1938, Slessor papers, AIR 75/2.
90. Levine, *Forgotten Voices*.
91. 24 Sept. 1938, Slessor papers, AIR 75/2.

92. Bruce-Gardener to Mrs Anne Chamberlain, 1954, Chamberlain papers, NC11/12/1.
93. Wright, *Dowding and the Battle of Britain*.
94. Davidson and Taylor, *Spitfire Ace*.
95. 15 Sept. 1938, Inskip papers, INKP 1.
96. Paper from Chief of the Air Staff, Nov. 1938, Slessor papers, AIR 75/2.
97. RAF Expansion Scheme M, 25 Oct. 1938, National Archives, AIR 8/250.
98. 4 Nov. 1938, National Archives, AIR 8/250.
99. Minutes of Cabinet, 7 Nov. 1938, National Archives, AIR 8/250.

Chapter 4: 'It was a bit like a love affair'

1. Russell, *Spitfire Odyssey*.
2. Brendon, *The Dark Valley*.
3. A. J. P. Taylor, *English History 1914–1945*.
4. Quoted in Terraine, *The Right of the Line*.
5. *Flight*, 26 Sept. 1940.
6. Haining, *The Spitfire Log*.
7. Allen, *Battle for Britain*.
8. Davidson and Taylor, *Spitfire Ace*.
9. Ibid.
10. Duncan Smith, *Spitfire into Battle*.
11. Ibid.
12. Davidson and Taylor, *Spitfire Ace*.
13. Rolls, *Spitfire Attack*.
14. Johnson, *Wing Leader*.
15. Page, *Shot Down in Flames*.
16. 'Forty Years of the Spitfire'.
17. Dibbs and Holmes, *Spitfire*.
18. Allen, *Battle for Britain*.
19. Page, *Shot Down in Flames*.
20. Interview with the author.
21. Page, *Shot Down in Flames*.
22. Allen, *Battle for Britain*.
23. Ash, *Under the Wire*.
24. Rolls, *Spitfire Attack*.
25. Davidson and Taylor, *Spitfire Ace*.
26. Levine, *Forgotten Voices*.
27. Interview with the author.
28. Duncan Smith, *Spitfire into Battle*.
29. Kingcome, *A Willingness to Die*.
30. Rolls, *Spitfire Attack*.
31. Levine, *Forgotten Voices*.
32. Quill, *Birth of a Legend*.
33. Ball papers, 85/19/1.
34. Lecture to the Warton branch of the Royal Aeronautical Society, Quill papers, 94/38/1.
35. Johnson, *Wing Leader*.
36. Caine, *Spitfires, Thunderbolts and Warm Beer*.

37. Davidson and Taylor, *Spitfire Ace*.
38. Brochure in the Quill papers, 94/38/1.
39. 'Forty Years of the Spitfire'.
40. D. Robertson, *Those Magnificent Flying Machines*.
41. Smithies, *Aces, Erks and Backroom Boys*.
42. Franks, *Buck McNair*.
43. Duncan Smith, *Spitfire into Battle*.
44. Caine, *Spitfires, Thunderbolts and Warm Beer*.
45. Wilkinson papers, 03/32/1.
46. E. A. W. Smith, *Spitfire Diary*.
47. Houlton, *Spitfire Strikes*.
48. Allen, *Battle for Britain*.
49. Kingcome, *A Willingness to Die*.
50. Johnstone, *Spitfire into War*.
51. Oliver, *Fighter Command 1939–45*.
52. Bader, *Fight for the Sky*.
53. Dowding to Harold Balfour, Under-Secretary for Air, 25 July 1939, National Archives, AIR 2/2824.
54. Smithies, *Aces, Erks and Backroom Boys*.
55. Richey and Franks, *Fighter Pilot's Summer*.
56. Davidson and Taylor, *Spitfire Ace*.
57. Kelly, *Hurricane and Spitfire Pilots at War*.
58. Beaumont, 'Hurricane Testing'.
59. Forrester, *Fly for Your Life*.
60. Interview with the author.
61. Gray, *Spitfire Patrol*.
62. Tooth papers.
63. Kingcome, *A Willingness to Die*.
64. Rod Smith, 'In Defence of the Spitfire'.
65. McKee, *Strike from the Sky*.
66. Interview with the author.
67. McKee, *Strike from the Sky*.
68. Report of Luftwaffe High Command, 16 July 1940, Militärarchiv-Bundesarchiv Freiburg, RL2 II/935.
69. Townsend, *Duel of Eagles*.
70. M. Parker, *The Battle of Britain*.
71. Duncan Smith, *Spitfire into Battle*.
72. 22 Jan. 1945, E. A. W. Smith, *Spitfire Diary*.
73. Wilkinson papers, 03/32/1.
74. Morton papers, 86/61/1.
75. Milne papers, X303/4645.
76. Sarkar, *Bader's Duxford Fighters*.
77. Wilkinson papers, 03/32/1.
78. Levine, *Forgotten Voices*.
79. F. Roberts, *Duxford to Karachi*.
80. Milne papers, X303/4645.
81. Levine, *Forgotten Voices*.
82. Vader, *Spitfire*.
83. F. Roberts, *Duxford to Karachi*.

84. Burns, *Bader*.
85. Johnstone, *Spitfire into War*.
86. Milne papers, X303/4645
87. Collin papers, 06/76/1.
88. Sarkar, *Bader's Duxford Fighters*.
89. Levine, *Forgotten Voices*.
90. Houlton, *Spitfire Strikes*.
91. F. Roberts, *Duxford to Karachi*.

Chapter 5: 'The Spitfires are wonderful machines'

1. Price, *The Spitfire Story*.
2. Craven to Sir Robert Micklem, 3 Dec. 1938, Vickers Archives, 410.
3. Marsh-Hunn to A. C. Boddis, Air Ministry, 14 Oct. 1938, Vickers Archives, 339.
4. Minutes of Secretary of State's progress meeting, 22 Sept. 1938, National Archives, AIR 6/58.
5. 5 Sept. 1938 National Archives, AIR 6/54.
6. Note of discussion on Aircraft under Scheme K, meeting held in Secretary of State's room, 21 Feb. 1938, National Archives, 6/52.
7. Minutes of Secretary of State's progress meeting, 26 July 1938, National Archives, AIR 6/54.
8. Minutes of Secretary of State's progress meeting, 23 Nov. 1938, National Archives, AIR 6/62
9. Minutes of Secretary of State's progress meeting, 6 Dec. 1938, National Archives, AIR 6/62.
10. Ibid., 22 Sept. 1938, National Archives, AIR 6/58.
11. Ibid., 27 Sept. 1938.
12. Newall to Swinton, 29 Aug. 1936, National Archives, AIR 19/1.
13. Quoted in Russell, *Spitfire Postscript*.
14. Peters, Air Ministry, to Sir Arthur Street, 2 Jan. 1939, National Archives, AVIA 15/3749.
15. Webb papers.
16. 7 Nov. 1938, National Archives, AIR 8/50.
17. Kingcome, *A Willingness to Die*.
18. Interview with the author.
19. Evill papers, AC74/8/4-6.
20. 8 Oct. 1939, Chamberlain papers, NC18/1/1124.
21. Johnstone, *Spitfire into War*.
22. Price, *Spitfire: A Complete Fighting History*.
23. McKee, *Strike from the Sky*.
24. Ibid.
25. 8 Mar. 1940, Vickers Archives, 410.
26. Cossey, *A Tiger's Tale*.
27. Johnstone, *Spitfire into War*.
28. Cossey, *A Tiger's Tale*.
29. B. Robertson, *Spitfire*.
30. Johnstone, *Spitfire into War*.
31. Rolls, *Spitfire Attack*.

32. Dowding, 'The Real Story of the Spitfire'.
33. Wright, *Dowding and the Battle of Britain*.
34. Ibid.
35. 4 Oct. 1937, 5 Apr. 1932, 27 June 1939, 28 Oct. 1938, Reith, *Diaries*.
36. Entry for 10 Oct. 1939, Channon, *Chips*.
37. 7 June 1939, National Archives, AVIA 10/8.
38. Air Staff paper, 5 July 1939, National Archives, AVIA 10/219.
39. J. L. Cotton, Air Ministry, to Vickers Supermarine, 9 Aug. 1939, National Archives, AVIA 10/210.
40. 5 July 1939, National Archives, AVIA 10/219.
41. B. Collier, *The Defence of the United Kingdom*.
42. 19 Jan. 1940, National Archives, AVIA 10/219.
43. Craven to Freeman, 4 Jan. 1940, National Archives, AVIA 10/219.
44. Alexander Dunbar to Sir Charles Craven, 9 Mar. 1940, Vickers Archives, 410.
45. Webb papers.
46. Hansard, oral answers, 16 Nov. 1938.
47. Minutes of Secretary of State's progress meeting, 25 May 1939, National Archives, AIR 6/67.
48. Air Ministry note, 16 June 1939, National Archives, AIR 15/3749.
49. Smithies, *Aces, Erks and Backroom Boys*.
50. Entry in the *Oxford Dictionary of National Biography*. Overy was the author of *William Morris: Viscount Nuffield* (1976).
51. M. Thomas, *Out on a Wing*.
52. Jackson, *The Nuffield Story*.
53. Minutes of Secretary of State's progress meeting, 26 Mar. 1940, National Archives, AIR 15/3749.
54. Secretary of State's Office to Air Staff, 13 Mar. 1940, National Archives, AIR 15/3749.
55. S. P. Woodley, 'Production of Spitfire at the Castle Bromwich Shadow Factory', contribution to 'Forty Years of the Spitfire'.
56. Dunbar to Sir Charles Craven, 8 Mar. 1940, Vickers Archives, 410.
57. 18 Mar. 1940, National Archives, AIR 19/1.
58. 13 May 1940, Reith, *Diaries*.
59. Davie and Chisholm, *Beaverbrook*.
60. Webb papers.
61. A. J. P. Taylor, *Beaverbrook*.
62. Ibid.
63. Interview with the author.
64. M. Thomas, *Out on a Wing*.
65. S. P. Woodley, 'Production of Spitfire at the Castle Bromwich Shadow Factory', contribution to 'Forty Years of the Spitfire'.
66. A. J. P. Taylor, *Beaverbrook*.
67. 29 June 1940, Vickers Archives, R26.
68. Russell, *Spitfire Postscript*.
69. Russell, *Spitfire Odyssey*.
70. Russell, *Spitfire Postscript*.
71. Dunbar to Sir Frederick Yapp, 20 July 1940, Vickers Archives, 416.
72. Memories of Bill Cox, Davis papers, AC93/14/16.
73. S. P. Woodley, 'Production of Spitfire at the Castle Bromwich Shadow Factory', contribution to 'Forty Years of the Spitfire'.

74. Interview with the author.
75. Report to the Ministry of Aircraft Production, 13 July 1940, National Archives, AVIA 15/3749.
76. 20 July 1940, Vickers Archives, 416.
77. Transcript of telephone conversation, Vickers Archives, 416.
78. 27 Oct. 1940, Vickers Archives, 416.
79. 28 Oct. 1940, Vickers Archives, 416.
80. M. Thomas, *Out on a Wing*.
81. Russell, *Spitfire Odyssey*.

Chapter 6: 'The days of easy victory were over'

1. Ray, *The Battle of Britain*.
2. Flint, *Dowding and the Headquarters of Fighter Command*.
3. Ibid.
4. Ibid.
5. Levine, *Forgotten Voices*.
6. Orange, *Park*.
7. Terraine, *The Right of the Line*.
8. Liskutin, *Challenge in the Air*.
9. Jackson, *Spitfire*.
10. Hansard, 4 June 1940.
11. Levine, *Forgotten Voices*.
12. M. Brown, *Spitfire Summer*.
13. Deere, *Nine Lives*.
14. Franks, *The Air Battle for Dunkirk*.
15. Allan, *Spitfire*.
16. Quill, *Birth of a Legend*.
17. Franks, *The Air Battle for Dunkirk*.
18. C. Bowyer, *Fighter Command*.
19. Richardson and Freidin, *The Fatal Decisions*.
20. Steinhilper and Osborne, *Spitfire on My Tail*.
21. Kesselring, *Memoirs*.
22. Orange, *Park*.
23. M. Brown, *Spitfire Summer*.
24. Deere, *Nine Lives*.
25. M. Brown, *Spitfire Summer*.
26. Franks, *The Air Battle for Dunkirk*.
27. Oxspring, *Spitfire Command*.
28. Franks, *The Air Battle for Dunkirk*.
29. Ibid.
30. Bader, *Fight for the Sky*.
31. Gray, *Spitfire Patrol*.
32. D. Robinson, *Invasion 1940*.
33. Sarkar, *Bader's Duxford Fighters*.
34. M. Parker, *The Battle of Britain*.
35. Wood and Dempster, *The Narrow Margin*.
36. Franks, *The Air Battle for Dunkirk*.

37. Kingcome, *A Willingness to Die*.
38. Franks, *The Air Battle for Dunkirk*.
39. Background notes on the Spitfire for Thames TV, Quill papers, 94/38/2.
40. Terraine, *The Right of the Line*.
41. National Archives, AIR 2/2824.
42. Collins to Fighter Command, 22 June 1940, National Archives, AIR 2/2824.
43. Fighter Command memorandum, 20 June 1940, National Archives, AIR 2/2834.
44. Diary entry, 19 July 1940, Johnstone, *Spitfire into War*.
45. Diary entry, 4 June 1940, ibid.
46. Deere, *Nine Lives*.
47. D. Robinson, *Invasion 1940*.
48. Ibid.
49. Vader, *Spitfire*.
50. Gray, *Spitfire Patrol*.
51. Forrester, *Fly for Your Life*.
52. 'Forty Years of the Spitfire'.
53. Terraine, *The Right of the Line*.
54. Ibid.
55. Allen, *Battle for Britain*.
56. Oxspring, *Spitfire Command*.
57. Diary entry, 26 June 1940, Johnstone, *Spitfire into War*.
58. Vickers quarterly reports, June and Sept. 1940, Vickers Archives, 197 and 198.
59. Webb papers.
60. A. J. P. Taylor, *Beaverbrook*.
61. Beccles, *Birth of a Spitfire*.
62. Ibid.
63. De Groot, *Liberal Crusader*.
64. Lucas (ed.), *Wings of War*.
65. Balfour, *Wings over Westminster*.
66. Quill, *Spitfire*.
67. M. Brown, *Spitfire Summer*.
68. Ministry of Aircraft Production Bulletin No. 32, 11 July 1940, Beaverbrook papers, BBK/D/39.
69. BBC to Air Marshall Joubert de la Ferté, 7 Aug. 1940, Joubert de la Ferté papers, AC71/14/4/3.
70. Spitfire-fund file, Beaverbrook papers, BBK/D/41.
71. 1 Feb. 1941, Beaverbrook papers, BBK/D/41.
72. J. W. R. Taylor and M. Allward, *Spitfire*.
73. *The Times*, 27 Aug. 1940.
74. M. Brown, *Spitfire Summer*.
75. 12 Sept. 1940, Joubert de la Ferté papers, AC71/14/4/1.
76. Chisholm and Davie, *Beaverbrook*.
77. Beccles, *Birth of a Spitfire*.

Chapter 7: 'Achtung! Spitfeuer!'

1. Wood and Dempster, *The Narrow Margin*.
2. Interview, *Sunday Times*, 17 July 1960.
3. Deere, *Nine Lives*.
4. Dundas, *Flying Start*.
5. D. Robinson, *Invasion 1940*.
6. Townsend, *Duel of Eagles*.
7. Overy, *The Battle of Britain*.
8. Report of Luftwaffe High Command, Section 1c, 16 July 1940, Militärarchiv-Bundesarchiv Freiburg, RL2 II/935.
9. Deighton, *The Battle of Britain*.
10. Terraine, *The Right of the Line*.
11. Deighton, *The Battle of Britain*.
12. Ibid.
13. Wright, *Dowding and the Battle of Britain*.
14. Wood and Dempster, *The Narrow Margin*.
15. M. Parker, *The Battle of Britain*.
16. Terraine, *The Right of the Line*.
17. Howard-Williams papers, 96/58/1.
18. Davidson and Taylor, *Spitfire Ace*.
19. Ibid.
20. Orange, *Park*.
21. Ibid.
22. Townsend, *Duel of Eagles*.
23. Deighton, *The Battle of Britain*.
24. Steinhilper and Osborne, *Spitfire on My Tail*.
25. Chisholm and Davie, *Beaverbrook*.
26. Introduction to Deere, *Nine Lives*.
27. McKee, *Strike from the Sky*.
28. Interview, *Sunday Times*, 17 July 1960.
29. Haining, *The Spitfire Log*.
30. Deere, *Nine Lives*.
31. Forrester, *Fly for Your Life*.
32. Ibid.
33. Ibid.
34. Ibid.
35. Sarkar, *Bader's Duxford Fighters*.
36. P. Brown, *Honour Restored*.
37. Sarkar, *Bader's Duxford Fighters*.
38. Morton papers, 86/61/1.
39. Dundas, *Flying Start*.
40. Davidson and Taylor, *Spitfire Ace*.
41. Levine, *Forgotten Voices*.
42. Ibid.
43. Allen, *Battle for Britain*.
44. Haining, *The Spitfire Log*.
45. Crook, *Spitfire Pilot*.
46. Johnstone, *Spitfire into War*.

47. Steinhilper and Osborne, *Spitfire on My Tail*.
48. C. Bowyer, *Fighter Command*.
49. Deighton, *The Battle of Britain*.
50. MacDonnell, *From Dogfight to Diplomacy*.
51. Allen, *Battle for Britain*.
52. McKee, *Strike from the Sky*.
53. Levine, *Forgotten Voices*.
54. Ibid.
55. Ibid.
56. Davidson and Taylor, *Spitfire Ace*.
57. Wilson papers, KCLMA GB99.
58. 'Forty Years of the Spitfire'.
59. Ibid.
60. Duncan Smith, *Spitfire into Battle*.
61. 'Factors Involved in the Conception of the Eight Gun Fighter', memorandum, 6 May 1945, Sorley papers, AC72/19/16/2.
62. Report of Air Ministry meeting, 12 Dec. 1938, National Archives, AIR 2/3532.
63. Report of Air Ministry, 5 Jan. 1939, National Archives, AIR 2/3532.
64. 30 Jan. 1940, National Archives, AIR 2/3532.
65. 5 Feb. 1940, National Archives, AIR 16/132.
66. Report on trials of the Cannon Spitfire, 4 Apr. 1940, National Archives, AIR 2/3532.
67. 24 July 1940, National Archives, AIR 2/3532.
68. S. P. Woodley, 'Production of Spitfire at the Castle Bromwich Shadow Factory', contribution to 'Forty Years of the Spitfire'.
69. Dibbs and Holmes, *Spitfire*.
70. M. Parker, *The Battle of Britain*.
71. F. Roberts, *Duxford to Karachi*.
72. 1 Sept. 1940, National Archives, AIR 2/3532.
73. 2 Sept. 1940, National Archives, AIR 2/3532.
74. Levine, *Forgotten Voices*.
75. Morris papers, 99/7/1.
76. Hillary, *The Last Enemy*.
77. Diary entry, 24 Aug. 1940, Johnstone, *Spitfire into War*.
78. Morton papers, 86/61/1.
79. Interview, *Sunday Times*, 17 July 1960.
80. Page, *Shot Down in Flames*.
81. Overy, *The Battle of Britain*.
82. Interview, *Sunday Times*, 17 July 1960.
83. R. Collier, *Eagle Day*.
84. Allen, *Battle for Britain*.
85. McKee, *Strike from the Sky*.
86. M. Parker, *The Battle of Britain*.
87. McKee, *Strike from the Sky*.
88. Steinhilper and Osborne, *Spitfire on My Tail*.

Chapter 8: 'Here come those last fifty Spitfires'

1. Toye, *Lloyd George and Churchill*.
2. Corrigan, *Blood, Sweat and Arrogance*.
3. Churchill to Dowding, 24 June 1940, National Archives, CAB 120/294.
4. 2 July 1940, National Archives, CAB 120/294.
5. 21 Aug. 1940, National Archives, CAB 120/294.
6. Glancey, *Spitfire*.
7. Wright, *Dowding and the Battle of Britain*.
8. Ray, *The Battle of Britain*.
9. Allen, *Battle for Britain*.
10. Interview with the author.
11. Sampson, *Spitfire Offensive*.
12. Interview, *Sunday Times*, 17 July 1960.
13. Interview with the author.
14. Sarkar, *Courage and Sacrifice*.
15. Allen, *Battle for Britain*.
16. Oxspring, *Spitfire Command*.
17. Ibid.
18. M. Parker, *The Battle of Britain*.
19. Allen, *Battle for Britain*.
20. M. Parker, *The Battle of Britain*.
21. Oxspring, *Spitfire Command*.
22. Johnson, *Wing Leader*.
23. Memo to sector controllers, 5 Sept. 1940, quoted in Ray, *The Battle of Britain*.
24. Hillary, *The Last Enemy*.
25. Davidson and Taylor, *Spitfire Ace*.
26. Ross, *Stapme*.
27. Davidson and Taylor, *Spitfire Ace*.
28. Oxspring, *Spitfire Command*.
29. Smithies, *Aces, Erks and Backroom Boys*.
30. Milne papers, X303/4645.
31. M. Parker, *The Battle of Britain*.
32. Russell, *Spitfire Odyssey*.
33. Bekker, *The Luftwaffe War Diaries*.
34. Deighton, *The Battle of Britain*.
35. 25 Aug. 1940, Stahl, *The Diving Eagle*.
36. 20 Apr. 1940, Vickers Archives, 410.
37. Deighton, *Fighter*.
38. Westacott, *Shaking the Chains*.
39. Bekker, *The Luftwaffe War Diaries*.
40. Townsend, *Duel of Eagles*.
41. Johnstone, *Spitfire into War*.
42. P. Brown, *Honour Restored*.
43. Deighton, *The Battle of Britain*.
44. Townsend, *Duel of Eagles*.
45. R. Collier, *Eagle Day*.
46. Townsend, *Duel of Eagles*.
47. Deighton, *The Battle of Britain*.

48. Report on wing patrols sent up by 12 Group, 17 Sept. 1940, Leigh-Mallory papers.
49. Townsend, *Duel of Eagles.*
50. Wright, *Dowding and the Battle of Britain.*
51. Levine, *Forgotten Voices.*
52. Wright, *Dowding and the Battle of Britain.*
53. Ibid.
54. Orange, *Park.*
55. 2 July 1968, Bader papers, X002-9343/004.
56. 22 July 1968, Bader papers, X002-9343/003.
57. Deighton, *Fighter.*
58. P. Brown, *Honour Restored.*
59. Douglas, *Years of Command.*
60. Ray, *The Battle of Britain.*
61. Burns, *Bader.*
62. Dunn, *Big Wing.*
63. Oxspring, *Spitfire Command.*
64. Terraine, *The Right of the Line.*
65. Brickhill, *Reach for the Sky.*
66. Turner, *The Bader Wing.*
67. P. Brown, *Honour Restored.*
68. M. J. F. Bowyer, *The Spitfire 50 Years On.*
69. Jenkins, *Churchill.*
70. Davidson and Taylor, *Spitfire Ace.*
71. Allen, *Battle for Britain.*
72. 22 July 1968, Bader papers, X002-9343/003.
73. Sarkar, *Bader's Duxford Fighters.*
74. Wright, *Dowding and the Battle of Britain.*
75. Flint, *Dowding and the Headquarters of Fighter Command.*
76. Levine, *Forgotten Voices.*
77. Ray, *The Battle of Britain.*
78. Orange, *Park.*
79. De Groot, *Liberal Crusader.*
80. Flint, *Dowding and the Headquarters of Fighter Command.*
81. Gray, *Spitfire Patrol.*
82. Flint, *Dowding and the Headquarters of Fighter Command.*
83. Ibid.
84. Ray, *The Battle of Britain.*
85. Wright, *Dowding and the Battle of Britain.*
86. Dundas, *Flying Start.*
87. Ray, *The Battle of Britain.*
88. Rolls, *Spitfire Attack.*
89. Levine, *Forgotten Voices.*
90. Orange, *Park.*
91. Levine, *Forgotten Voices.*
92. McKee, *Strike from the Sky.*
93. MacDonnell, *From Dogfight to Diplomacy.*
94. *The Times,* 8 May 1941.
95. *Flight,* 26 Sept. 1940.
96. Levine, *Forgotten Voices.*

97. M. Brown, *Spitfire Summer*.
98. Ibid.
99. Diary entry, 18 Nov. 1940, Johnstone, *Spitfire into War*.
100. Undated note, Dowding papers, AC71/17/58.
101. Alcorn, 'Battle of Britain Top Guns', Sept. 1996.
102. Deighton, *Fighter* and *The Battle of Britain*.
103. Alcorn, 'Battle of Britain Top Guns', Sept. 1996.
104. National Archives, AIR 19/1.
105. Davidson and Taylor, *Spitfire Ace*.

Chapter 9: 'We kept the old organization going'

1. Memo to the War Cabinet, 27 Aug. 1940, Beaverbrook papers, BBK/D/34.
2. 24 Feb. 1941, Beaverbrook papers, BBK/D/329.
3. 12 Sept. 1940, Vickers Archives, 416.
4. Russell, *Spitfire Odyssey*.
5. Webb papers.
6. Russell, *Spitfire Odyssey*.
7. Webb papers.
8. McKee, *Strike from the Sky*.
9. Ibid.
10. Webb papers.
11. Russell, *Spitfire Odyssey*.
12. Ibid.
13. Webb papers.
14. Ibid.
15. McKee, *Strike from the Sky*.
16. 'Forty Years of the Spitfire'.
17. 'Hursley Park: World War II and the Spitfire', paper written for IBM by D. Len Peach, Sept. 1988, RAF Museum, Hendon.
18. Russell, *Spitfire Odyssey*.
19. Russell, *Spitfire Postscript*.
20. Quill, *Spitfire*.
21. Webb papers.
22. Wood and Dempster, *The Narrow Margin*.
23. Report to directors, Dec. 1940, Vickers Archives, 199.
24. Overy, *The Battle of Britain*.
25. 24 Feb. 1941, Beaverbrook papers, BBK/D/329.
26. Report to directors, Mar. 1941, Vickers Archives, 200.
27. 24 Dec. 1940, Beaverbrook papers, BBK/D/34.
28. Quill, *Spitfire*.
29. Smithies, *Aces, Erks and Backroom Boys*.
30. Morgan and Shacklady, *Spitfire*.
31. Harvey-Bailey, *Hives*.
32. Alexander Dunbar to Sir Charles Craven, 6 Apr. 1940, Vickers Archives, 410.
33. 30 July 1940, Beaverbrook papers, BBK/D/21.
34. 23 Oct. 1939, Vickers Archives, 410.
35. Quill, *Spitfire*.

36. Ibid.
37. Craven to Sir Arthur Street, Permanent Secretary, Air Ministry, 1 Nov. 1940, Vickers Archives, 410.
38. Quill, *Spitfire*.
39. Undated but probably Jan. 1940, Beaverbrook papers, BBK/D/29.
40. Levine, *Forgotten Voices*.
41. Ibid.
42. 20 Nov. 1940, National Archives, AIR 2/2824.
43. 5 Jan. 1941, National Archives, AIR 2/2824.
44. Price, *The Spitfire Story*.
45. Report of the Air Fighting Development Unit, 14 Oct. 1942, National Archives, AIR 2/2825.
46. Price, *The Spitfire Story*.
47. J. W. R. Taylor and M. Allward, *Spitfire*.
48. Darling, *Merlin-Powered Spitfires*.
49. Price, *The Spitfire Story*.
50. Ibid.
51. Taylor papers, 91/26/1.
52. Kelly, *Hurricane and Spitfire Pilots at War*.
53. Quill, *Spitfire*.
54. Glancey, *Spitfire*.
55. Brown papers, MISC 171/2624.
56. 'Forty Years of the Spitfire'.
57. E. A. W. Smith, *Spitfire Diary*.
58. Sarkar, *Johnnie Johnson*.
59. Griffiths, *Testing Times*.
60. D. Robertson, *Those Magnificent Flying Machines*.
61. Hall papers, 6/51/1.
62. Dunn, *Big Wing*.
63. Dundas, *Flying Start*.
64. Duncan Smith, *Spitfire into Battle*.
65. W. G. G. Duncan Smith, 'The Spitfire at War' (1976), Quill papers, 94/38/1.
66. Duke, *War Diaries*.
67. Jackson, *Spitfire*.
68. Kornicki papers, 01/1/1.
69. Howard-Williams papers, 96/58/1.
70. Sarkar, *Johnnie Johnson*.
71. Johnson, *Wing Leader*.
72. Audio tape of 1993 interview with Charlton Haw, Liddell Hart Archives, KCLMA/GB99 Haw.
73. Howard-Williams papers, 96/58/1.
74. Darlow, *Five of the Few*.
75. Johnson, *Wing Leader*.
76. National Archives, CAB 120/294.
77. Churchill to Portal, 7 Mar. 1941, National Archives, CAB 120/294S.
78. Combat diary, 4 July 1941, Bader papers, 023173.
79. Johnson, *Wing Leader*.
80. Offenberg, *Lonely Warrior*.
81. Ibid.

82. Hodgkinson, *Spitfire Down.*
83. Pitchfork, *Shot Down and on the Run.*
84. Franks, *Buck McNair.*
85. Pitchfork, *Shot Down and in the Drink.*
86. Brettell papers, 98/30/1.
87. Johnson, *Wing Leader.*
88. 8 Sept. 1942, RAF Museum, Dowding papers, AC71/17/48.

Chapter 10: 'No place for beginners'

1. A. J. P. Taylor, *English History 1914–1945.*
2. Oxspring, *Spitfire Command.*
3. Kingcome, *A Willingness to Die.*
4. Ash, *Under the Wire.*
5. Kingcome, *A Willingness to Die.*
6. Franks, *The Greatest Air Battle.*
7. Oxspring, *Spitfire Command.*
8. Johnson, *Wing Leader.*
9. Caine, *Spitfires, Thunderbolts and Warm Beer.*
10. Liskutin, *Challenge in the Air.*
11. D. Austin, *Churchill and Malta.*
12. Ministry of Information, *The Air Battle of Malta.*
13. D. Austin, *Churchill and Malta.*
14. Douglas-Hamilton, *The Air Battle for Malta.*
15. Shores, Cull and Malizia, *Malta.*
16. Revell papers, 67/400/1.
17. Cull and Galea, *Spitfires over Malta.*
18. Ibid.
19. Ibid.
20. Shores, Cull and Malizia, *Malta.*
21. Ministry of Information, *The Air Battle of Malta.*
22. Cull and Galea, *Spitfires over Malta.*
23. Churchill papers, CHAR 20/73.
24. Price, *Spitfire: A Documentary History.*
25. Shores, Cull and Malizia, *Malta.*
26. Smithies, *Aces, Erks and Backroom Boys.*
27. Shores, Cull and Malizia, *Malta.*
28. Douglas-Hamilton, *The Air Battle for Malta.*
29. Cull and Galea, *Spitfires over Malta.*
30. Shores, Cull and Malizia, *Malta.*
31. Cull and Galea, *Spitfires over Malta.*
32. Franks, *Buck McNair.*
33. Ball papers, 85/19/1.
34. Duncan Smith, *Spitfire into Battle.*
35. Kesselring, *Memoirs.*
36. Lucas, *Five Up.*
37. Price, *Spitfire: A Documentary History.*
38. Rogers papers, 91/1/1.

39. Cull, Malizia and Galea, *249 at Malta*.
40. Ibid.
41. 11 May 1942, Churchill Papers, CHAR 20/74.
42. Cull and Galea, *Spitfires over Malta*.
43. Interview with the author.
44. Franks, *Buck McNair*.
45. Rogers papers, 91/1/1.
46. Houlton, *Spitfire Strikes*.
47. Rogers papers, 91/1/1.
48. Ibid.
49. Ibid.
50. Ibid.
51. Ministry of Information, *The Air Battle of Malta*.
52. Orange, *Park*.
53. Rogers papers, 91/1/1.
54. Douglas-Hamilton, *The Air Battle for Malta*.
55. Spooner, *Warburton's War*.
56. Duncan Smith, *Spitfire into Battle*.
57. Rogers papers, 91/1/1.
58. Lucas (ed.), *Wings of War*.
59. Lucas, *Five Up*.
60. Shores, Cull and Malizia, *Malta*.
61. Sampson, *Spitfire Offensive*.
62. Douglas-Hamilton, *The Air Battle for Malta*.
63. Cull and Galea, *Spitfires over Malta*.
64. 2 May 1942, National Archives, AIR 2/2824.
65. Houlton, *Spitfire Strikes*.

Chapter 11: 'That's no aircraft, that's a bleedin' angel'

1. J. Smith, 'The Development of the Spitfire and Seafire'.
2. Postan, Scott and Hay, *The Design and Development of Weapons*.
3. Background notes on the Spitfire for Thames TV, Quill papers, 94/38/2.
4. J. Smith, 'The Development of the Spitfire and Seafire'.
5. Lecture to the Warton branch of the Royal Aeronautical Society, Quill papers, 94/38/1.
6. Harvey-Bailey, *Hives*.
7. Postan, *British War Production*.
8. Quill to Lieutenant Commander Bryan Kendall, RAF Wittering, 8 June 1943, Quill papers, 94/38/1.
9. Gray, *Spitfire Patrol*.
10. Tooth papers.
11. Ball papers, 85/19/1.
12. 'Forty Years of the Spitfire'.
13. Griffiths, *Testing Times*.
14. Ibid.

15. RAE technical note no. Aero 1273: 'Note on Speeds of Production Spitfires', National Archives, AVIA 6/10393.
16. Rolls, *Spitfire Attack*.
17. Houlton, *Spitfire Strikes*.
18. Johnson, *Wing Leader*.
19. D. Brown, *The Seafire*.
20. Morgan and Shacklady, *Spitfire*.
21. 18 Nov. 1939, Vickers Archives, 410.
22. Morgan and Shacklady, *Spitfire*.
23. Ibid.
24. E. Brown, *Wings on My Sleeve*.
25. 'Forty Years of the Spitfire'.
26. Sweetman, *Spitfire*.
27. 'Forty Years of the Spitfire'.
28. E. Brown, *Wings on My Sleeve*.
29. Quill, *Spitfire*.
30. Ibid.
31. E. Brown, *Wings of the Navy*.
32. Cossey, *A Tiger's Tale*.
33. Mitchell, *R. J. Mitchell*.
34. A. Bishop, *Winged Combat*.
35. Henshaw, *Sigh for a Merlin*.
36. Note on longitudinal stability, Quill papers, 94/38/1.
37. Report by Alex Henshaw on the Mark V, 26 May 1941, Quill papers, 94/38/1.
38. 'Forty Years of the Spitfire'.
39. Richey and Franks, *Fighter Pilot's Summer*.
40. Note by J. D. Breakey, Director of Operational Requirements, Air Ministry, 28 May 1942, National Archives, AIR 2/2825.
41. Report on Spitfire R6700, 18 Apr. 1942, Quill papers, 94/38/1.
42. Furse, *Wilfrid Freeman*.
43. Quill, *Spitfire*.
44. Duncan Smith, *Spitfire into Battle*.
45. Ibid.
46. D. Robertson, *Those Magnificent Flying Machines*.
47. Kingcome, *A Willingness to Die*.
48. Sarkar, *Spitfire*.
49. Ibid.
50. E. A. W. Smith, *Spitfire Diary*.
51. Dibbs and Holmes, *Spitfire*.
52. Duncan Smith, *Spitfire into Battle*.
53. Johnson, *Wing Leader*.
54. Clostermann, *The Big Show*.
55. Kornicki papers, 01/1/1.
56. Wilson papers, KCLMA GB99.
57. Ibid.
58. Introduction to Douglas-Hamilton, *The Air Battle for Malta*.
59. Ibid.
60. Terraine, *The Right of the Line*.
61. Tedder, *With Prejudice*.

62. Terraine, *The Right of the Line*.
63. Tedder, *With Prejudice*.
64. Bolland papers, 2/34/1.
65. Oxspring, *Spitfire Command*.
66. Darlow, *Five of the Few*.
67. Duke, *War Diaries*.
68. Ibid.
69. Ball papers, 85/19/1.
70. Quarterly report to Vickers Board, Sept. 1943, Vickers Archives, 213.
71. Ibid., June 1943, Vickers Archives, 210.
72. Interview, *Birmingham Post*, 21 Feb. 1994.
73. Interview with the BBC West Midlands, 2004.
74. Interview, *Birmingham Post*, 21 Feb. 1994.
75. *Birmingham Evening Mail*, 5 Dec. 1945.
76. Ibid., 29 Aug. 1989.
77. *Sunday Express*, 8 Dec. 1941.
78. Lappin to Alexander Dunbar, 23 Dec. 1940, Henshaw papers, AH2/25.
79. Internal Rolls-Royce Report by Lappin, 1 Jan. 1941, Henshaw papers, AH2/25.
80. Note by Alex Henshaw on the above correspondence, written in 1985, Henshaw papers, AH2/25.
81. Interview with the author.
82. Ibid.
83. Barnett, *The Audit of War*.
84. Government paper, 'Production through the War', National Archives, CAB 102/406.
85. Quarterly report to Vickers board, Dec. 1942, Vickers Archives, 206.
86. McIlroy papers, X002.
87. Report to the Vickers board, June 1943, Vickers Archives, 209.
88. Reports to the Vickers board, Mar.–Dec. 1944, Vickers Archives, 211–13.
89. Report to the Vickers board, June 1943, Vickers Archives, 211.
90. Russell, *Spitfire Postscript*.
91. Russell, *Spitfire Odyssey*.
92. Government paper, 'Production through the War', National Archives, CAB 102/406.

Chapter 12: 'I say, Miss, you must be good on instruments'

1. B. Robertson, *Spitfire*.
2. Churchill papers, CHAR 20/81.
3. Prime Minister's Personal Telegram no. T1349/2, 18 Oct. 1942, Churchill papers, CHAR 20/81.
4. Price, *The Spitfire Story*.
5. Ibid.
6. 30 June 1942, Churchill papers, CHAR 20/77.
7. 10 Aug. 1943, Liddell Hart Archives, Ismay 4/10/1.
8. 3 Sept. 1943, Churchill papers, CHAR 20/117.
9. Len Deighton, *The Battle of Britain*.
10. Liskutin, *Challenge in the Air*.

11. Ibid.
12. Ibid.
13. Caine, *Spitfires, Thunderbolts and Warm Beer*.
14. Ibid.
15. Ball papers, 85/19/1.
16. Price, *Spitfire: A Complete Fighting History*.
17. Kingcome, *A Willingness to Die*.
18. Tooth papers.
19. Ball papers, 85/19/1.
20. Ibid.
21. Sampson, *Spitfire Offensive*.
22. Letter from V. Jollife of Doveridge to the *Birmingham Evening Mail*, 24 Jan. 1990.
23. Interview with the author.
24. Ibid.
25. Taylor and Allward, *Spitfire*.
26. Interview with the author.
27. Sadler papers, 6/11/1.
28. Ibid.
29. Ibid.
30. Interview with the author.
31. Ibid.
32. Walker, *Spreading My Wings*.
33. Bergel, *Fly and Deliver*.
34. Walker, *Spreading My Wings*.
35. Oliver, *Fighter Command*.
36. Levine, *Forgotten Voices*.
37. 'Forty Years of the Spitfire'.
38. Sampson, *Spitfire Offensive*.
39. Featherstone papers, 95/20/1.
40. Kornicki papers, 01/1/1.
41. Glancey, *Spitfire*.
42. Liskutin, *Challenge in the Air*.
43. Flint, *Dowding and the Headquarters of Fighter Command*.
44. Ibid.
45. Davidson and Taylor, *Spitfire Ace*.
46. Allen, *Battle for Britain*.
47. Introduction to E. A. W. Smith, *Spitfire Diary*.
48. Smithies, *Aces, Erks and Backroom Boys*.
49. Allen, *Battle for Britain*.
50. Ibid.
51. Caine, *Spitfires, Thunderbolts and Warm Beer*.
52. Howard-Williams papers, 96/58/1.
53. Bowling papers, X002-5779/01.

Chapter 13: 'Too much power and too much performance'

1. Lecture to the Warton branch of the Royal Aeronautical Society, Quill papers, 94/38/1.

2. Duncan Smith, *Spitfire into Battle*.
3. Price, *The Spitfire Story*.
4. *Spitfire 70*.
5. Quill, *Spitfire*.
6. Caygill, *Ultimate Spitfires*.
7. Gray, *Spitfire Patrol*.
8. 25 Mar. 1943, Quill papers, 94/38/2.
9. Background notes on the Spitfire for Thames TV, Quill papers, 94/38/2.
10. Oxspring, *Spitfire Command*.
11. Dibbs and Holmes, *Spitfire*.
12. Background notes on the Spitfire for Thames TV, Quill papers, 94/38/2.
13. Caygill, *Ultimate Spitfires*.
14. Ibid.
15. Dibbs and Holmes, *Spitfire*.
16. 'Forty Years of the Spitfire'.
17. D. Robertson, *Those Magnificent Flying Machines*.
18. Ibid.
19. Duncan Smith, *Spitfire into Battle*.
20. Ibid.
21. Doddington papers, 77/85/1.
22. Kingcome, *A Willingness to Die*.
23. Bader, *Fight for the Sky*.
24. Morris papers, 99/7/1.
25. White, *Spitfire Saga*.
26. French papers, 06/76/1.
27. A. Bishop, *Winged Combat*.
28. Clostermann, *The Big Show*.
29. Houlton, *Spitfire Strikes*.
30. Oxspring, *Spitfire Command*.
31. Page, *Shot Down in Flames*.
32. Oxspring, *Spitfire Command*.
33. A. Bishop, *Winged Combat*.
34. Houlton, *Spitfire Strikes*.
35. Page, *Shot Down in Flames*.
36. Johnson, *Wing Leader*.
37. Oxspring, *Spitfire Command*.
38. Slack, *Happy is the Day*.
39. Interview with the author.
40. Darlow, *Victory Fighters*.
41. Baxter and Dron, *Tales of My Time*.
42. Dibbs and Holmes, *Spitfire*.
43. Note to Dr Alfred Price, Quill papers, 94/38/2.
44. Ibid.
45. Price, *The Spitfire Story*.
46. Note to Dr Alfred Price, Quill papers, 94/38/2.
47. Henshaw, *Sigh for a Merlin*.
48. Note to Dr Alfred Price, Quill papers, 94/38/2.
49. Lecture to the Warton branch of the Royal Aeronautical Society, Quill papers, 94/38/1.

50. Johnson, *Wing Leader*.
51. Sampson, *Spitfire Offensive*.
52. Glancey, *Spitfire*.
53. Haining, *The Spitfire Log*.
54. Houlton, *Spitfire Strikes*.
55. French papers, 06/76/1.
56. Dibbs and Holmes, *Spitfire*.
57. Dobbins papers, 83/41/1.
58. Ibid.
59. Ibid.
60. Wilkinson papers, 03/32/1.
61. E. A. W. Smith, *Spitfire Diary*.
62. 'Forty Years of the Spitfire', contribution from Commander R. H. Reynolds.
63. Oxspring, *Spitfire Command*.

Epilogue

1. M. J. F. Bowyer, *The Spitfire 50 Years On*.
2. Caygill, *Ultimate Spitfires*.
3. Dibbs and Holmes, *Spitfire*.
4. Interview with the author.
5. Price, *Spitfire: A Complete Fighting History*.
6. Rolls, *Spitfire Attack*.
7. 'Forty Years of the Spitfire'.

Bibliography

Unpublished Sources

Air Ministry papers (National Archives, Kew)
Armstrong, Flight Sergeant T. I. F. (Imperial War Museum) – logbooks
Bader, Douglas (RAF Museum, Hendon)
Ball, Flight Lieutenant Godfrey (Imperial War Museum) – memoir
Beaverbrook, 1st Baron (House of Lords)
Bolland, Group Captain (Imperial War Museum) – 'A Guy from Coastal Command'
Bowling, Sergeant Hazel (Imperial War Museum) – memoir
Brettell, E. G. (Imperial War Museum) – 'Report on Receipt of Injuries', 22 Sept. 1941
Brown, D. F. (Imperial War Museum) – 'The Story of the Fibre Jettison Tank'
Buck, G. F. (Imperial War Museum) – logbooks
Cabinet papers (National Archives, Kew)
Chamberlain, Neville (Chamberlain Archives, Birmingham University)
Churchill, Sir Winston (Churchill Archives, Cambridge)
Collin, Flight Lieutenant Rob (Imperial War Museum) – 'War Years'
Davis, E. J. (RAF Museum, Hendon)
Dennis, Group Captain D. F. (Imperial War Museum) – logbooks
Dobbins, Flight Sergeant N. (Imperial War Museum) – 'The Burma Campaign'
Doddington, Squadron Leader Michael (Imperial War Museum) – journal
Dowding, 1st Baron (RAF Museum, Hendon)
Evill, Air Chief Marshal Sir Douglas (RAF Museum, Hendon)
Featherstone, E. (Imperial War Museum) – memoir: 'A Worm's Eye View of the RAF'
Freeman, Sir Wilfrid (National Archives, Kew)
French, Flying Officer J. K.G. (Imperial War Museum) – memoir
Gordon-Marshall, P. E. (Imperial War Museum) – memoir
Hall, Flight Lieutenant J. (Imperial War Museum) – memoir
Haw, Squadron Leader Charlton (Liddell Hart Archives, King's College London) – transcript of interview: 'RAF Memories'
Haworth, Captain Michael (Imperial War Museum) – 'Some Memories of World War II'
Henshaw, Alex (RAF Museum, Hendon)
Howard-William, Wing Commander Peter (Imperial War Museum) – memoir
Inskip, Sir Thomas (Churchill Archives, Cambridge)
Ismay, General Sir Hastings, (Liddell Hart Archives, King's College London)
Joubert de la Ferté, Sir Philip (RAF Museum, Hendon)
Kingcome, Brian (Imperial War Museum) – 'Notes on Suggested Improvements to the Spitfire, 1940'

Kornicki, Franciszek (Imperial War Museum) – memoir: 'The Struggle'
Kucera, Wing Commander Jiri (Imperial War Museum) – memoir
Leigh-Mallory, Air Chief Marshal (RAF Museum, Hendon)
McIlroy, A. J. (RAF Museum, Hendon) – 'A Pretty Toy: Memoirs of the Journalist A. J. McIlroy'
McIntyre, Air Commodore K. J. (Imperial War Museum) – logbooks
Mileham, Denys Edgar (Imperial War Museum) – letters to family
Militärarchiv-Bundesarchiv Freiburg (Freiburg im Breisgau)
Milne, John (RAF Museum, Hendon) – memoir: 'Life at Duxford'
Ministry of Aircraft Production papers (National Archives, Kew)
Mitchell, R. J. (RAF Museum, Hendon)
Morris, Edward James (Imperial War Museum) – 'RAF Memories'
Morton, R. A. (Imperial War Museum) – memoir
Quill, Jeffrey (Imperial War Museum, Southwark)
RAF Escape and Evasion Accounts, 1944–5 (Imperial War Museum)
Raven, Flight Lieutenant F. H. (Imperial War Museum) – logbooks
Revell, S. J. (Imperial War Museum) – 'Reinforcing Malta with Spitfires'
Richey, Wing Commander Paul (Imperial War Museum) – logbooks
Robinson, Squadron Leader F. A. (Imperial War Museum) – logbooks
Rogers, F. K. (Imperial War Museum) – 'Malta: The Blitz and the Siege'
Sadler, Ted (Imperial War Museum) – 'My War'
Saundby, Air Marshal Sir Robert (RAF Museum, Hendon)
Slessor, Marshal of the Air Force Sir John (National Archives, Kew)
Sorley, Air Marshal Sir Ralph (RAF Museum, Hendon)
Southwell, Group Captain John (Imperial War Museum) – logbooks
Stapleton, Air Vice-Marshal Frederick (Imperial War Museum) – logbooks
Supermarine (Southampton Hall of Aviation)
Swinton, Philip Cunliffe-Lister, Earl of (Churchill Archives, Cambridge)
Taggart, Flight Lieutenant P. H. (Imperial War Museum) – memoir
Taylor, Flight Lieutenant Jimmy (Imperial War Museum) – memoir: 'One Flight Too Many'
Tooth, Tony (private) – memoir
Vickers (Cambridge University Library)
Vine, Sergeant Pilot Bill (Imperial War Museum) – memoir and logbook
Webb, Denis (Vickers Archives, 508, Cambridge University Library) – memoir: 'Never a Dull Moment'
Weir, 1st Viscount (Churchill Archives, Cambridge)
Wilkinson, John F. (Imperial War Museum) – 'My Experiences in WWII as an RAF Pilot'
Wilson, Group Captain Hugh (Liddell Hart Archives, King's College London) – memoir
Young, Wing Commander M. J. B. (Imperial War Museum) – logbooks

Published Sources

Adeney, Martin, *Nuffield: A Biography* (1993)

Alcorn, John, 'Battle of Britain Top Guns', *Aeroplane Monthly*, Sept. 1996 and July 2000

Allan, Squadron Leader B. J., *Spitfire: The Experiences of a Fighter Pilot* (1942)

Allen, Wing Commander H. R. 'Dizzy', *Battle for Britain* (1973)

Andrews, Allen, *The Air Marshals* (1970)

Andrews, P. W. S., and Brunner, Elizabeth, *The Life of Lord Nuffield* (1955)

Arthur, Max, *Lost Voices of the RAF* (1993)

—— *Forgotten Voices of the Second World War* (2004)

Ash, William, *Under the Wire* (2005)

Austin, A. B., *Fighter Command* (1941)

Austin, Douglas, *Churchill and Malta* (2006)

Avery, Max, with Shores, Christopher, *Spitfire Leader: The Story of Wing Commander Evan 'Rosie' Mackie* (1999)

Bader, Douglas, *Fight for the Sky* (1973)

Bailey, Jim, *The Sky Suspended: A Fighter Pilot's Story* (1964)

Baker, Anne, *From Biplane to Spitfire: The Life of Air Chief Marshal Sir Geoffrey Salmond* (2003)

Balfour, Harold, *Wings over Westminster* (1973)

Banks, Air Commodore F. R., 'Memories of the Last Schneider Trophy Contests', *Journal of the Royal Aeronautical Society*, Jan. 1966

Barnett, Correlli, *The Audit of War* (1986)

Baxter, Raymond, with Dron, Tony, *Tales of My Time* (2005)

Beaumont Roland, 'Hurricane Baptism', *Aeroplane Monthly*, Jan. 1994

—— 'Hurricane Testing', *Aeroplane Monthly*, Feb. 1994

Beccles, Gordon, *Birth of a Spitfire: The Story of Beaverbrook's Ministry and its First £10,000,000* (1941)

Bekker, Cajus, *The Luftwaffe War Diaries* (1964)

Bergel, Hugh, *Fly and Deliver* (1982)

Best, Geoffrey, *Churchill and War* (2005)

Bingham, Victor, *Merlin Power* (2003)

Bishop, Arthur, *Winged Combat* (2002)

Bishop, Edward, *McIndoe's Army* (2001)

Bishop, Patrick, *Fighter Boys: Saving Britain 1940* (2004)

Black, Naomi, 'Decision-Making and the Munich Crisis', *British Journal of International Studies*, Oct. 1980

Bond, Brian, 'Dunkirk: Myths and Lessons', transcript of lecture at the Royal United Services Institute, Feb. 1982

Boot, Henry, and Sturtivant, Ray, *Gifts of War: Spitfires and Other Presentation Aircraft in World War II* (2005)

Bowman, Martin, *Scramble: Memories of the RAF in the Second World War* (2006)

Bowyer, Chaz, *Fighter Command 1936–1968* (1980)

Bowyer, Michael J. F., *The Spitfire 50 Years On* (1986)

Brendon, Piers, *The Dark Valley: A Panorama of the 1930s* (2000)

Brew, Alec, *The Turret Fighters* (2002)

Brickhill, Paul, *Reach for the Sky* (1955)

Brown, David, *The Seafire* (1973)

Brown, Captain Eric 'Winkle', *Wings of the Navy* (1980)
—— *Wings on My Sleeve* (2006)
Brown, Michael, *Spitfire Summer* (2000)
Brown, Squadron Leader Peter, *Honour Restored: The Battle of Britain, Dowding and the Fight for Freedom* (2005)
Budiansky, Stephen, *Air Power* (2003)
Bungay, Stephen, *The Most Dangerous Enemy* (2000)
Burns, Michael, *Spitfire! Spitfire!* (1986)
—— *Bader: The Man and His Men* (1990)
Cabell, Craig, and Thomas, Graham A., *Operation Big Ben* (2004)
Caine, Philip D., *Spitfires, Thunderbolts and Warm Beer* (2005)
Cairns, John C., 'Great Britain and the Fall of France: A Study in Allied Disunity', *Journal of Modern History*, Dec. 1955
Calder, Angus, *The People's War: Britain 1939–45* (1969)
Caygill, Peter, *The Darlington Spitfire* (1999)
—— *Spitfire Mark V In Action* (2001)
—— *Ultimate Spitfires* (2006)
Channon, Sir Henry, *Chips: The Diaries of Sir Henry Channon*, ed. Robert Rhodes James (1967)
Charmley, John, *Churchill: The End of Glory* (1993)
Chisholm, Anne, and Davie, Michael, *Beaverbrook: A Life* (1992)
Clarke, Peter, *The Cripps Version: The Life of Sir Stafford Cripps* (2003)
Clayton, Tim, and Craig, Phil, *Finest Hour* (1999)
Clostermann, Pierre, *The Big Show* (1951)
Collier, Basil, *The Defence of the United Kingdom* (1957)
Collier, Richard, *Eagle Day: The Battle of Britain* (1966)
Colville, John, *The Fringes of Power: Downing Street Diaries, 1939–1955*, (1985)
Connolly, J. V., 'Aircraft Production', *Journal of the Royal Aeronautical Society*, Jan. 1966
Coombs, L. F. E., *The Lion Has Wings* (1997)
Cooper, Duff, *The Duff Cooper Diaries 1915–1951*, ed. John Julius Norwich (2005)
Corrigan, Gordon, *Blood, Sweat and Arrogance and the Myths of Churchill's War* (2006)
Cossey, Bob, *A Tiger's Tale* (2002)
Crook, D. M., *Spitfire Pilot* (1942)
Cross, J. A., *Lord Swinton* (1982)
Crossland, John, 'Britain's Air Defences and the Munich Crisis', *History Today*, Sept. 2004
Cull, Brian, with Galea, Frederick, *Spitfires over Sicily* (2000)
—— *Spitfires over Malta* (2005)
—— with Malizia, Nicola, and Galea, Frederick, *249 at Malta* (2004)
Curtis, Lettice, *Her Autobiography* (2004)
Darling, Kevin, *Griffon-Powered Spitfires* (2001)
—— *Merlin-Powered Spitfires* (2002)
Darlow, Stephen, *Victory Fighters: The Veterans' Story* (2005)
—— *Five of the Few* (2006)
Davidson, Martin, and Taylor, James, *Spitfire Ace* (2003)
De Groot, Gerard, *Liberal Crusader: The Life of Sir Archibald Sinclair* (1993)
Deere, Air Commodore Alan C., *Nine Lives* (1959)
Deighton, Len, *Fighter: The True Story of the Battle of Britain* (1979)
—— *The Battle of Britain* (1980)
—— Len, *Blood, Tears and Folly* (1993)

Dibbs, John, and Holmes, Tony, *Spitfire – Flying Legend* (1996)

Divine, David, *The Broken Wing: A Study in the British Exercise of Air Power* (1966)

Douglas, Sholto, *Years of Command* (1966)

Douglas-Hamilton, Lord James, *The Air Battle for Malta: The Diaries of a Fighter Pilot* (1981)

Dowding, Hugh, 'The Real Story of the Spitfire', *The Star*, 13 Sept. 1951

Downing, Taylor, and Johnson, Andrew, 'The Spitfire Legend', *History Today*, Sept. 2000

Drake, Billy, with Shores, Christopher, *Fighter Leader* (2002)

Duke, Neville, *The War Diaries of Neville Duke 1941–44*, ed. Norman Franks (1995)

Duncan Smith, Group Captain W. G. G., *Spitfire into Battle* (1981)

Dundas, Hugh, *Flying Start* (1988)

Dunn, Bill Newton, *Big Wing: The Biography of Air Chief Marshal Sir Trafford Leigh-Mallory* (1992)

Dutton, David, *Neville Chamberlain* (2001)

Eden, Anthony, *Facing the Dictators* (1962)

Fearon, Peter, 'The Formative Years of the British Aircraft Industry, 1913 to 1924', *Business History Review*, winter 1969

——— 'The British Airframe Industry and the State, 1918–35', *Economic History Review*, May 1974

Feiling, Keith, *The Life of Neville Chamberlain* (1946)

Flack, Jeremy, *Spitfire* (1996)

Flint, Peter, *Dowding and the Headquarters of Fighter Command* (1996)

Fopp, Michael, *The Spitfire V Manual* (2003)

Foreman, John, *Fighter Command War Diaries* (1998)

Forrester, Larry, *Fly for Your Life: The Story of Bob Stanford-Tuck* (1956)

'Forty Years of the Spitfire', proceedings of Royal Aeronautical Society symposium, 6 Mar. 1976

Franks, Norman, *The Greatest Air Battle: Dieppe, 19th August 1942* (1979)

——— *The Air Battle for Dunkirk* (2000)

——— *Buck McNair – Spitfire Ace* (2001)

Furse, Anthony, *Wilfrid Freeman: The Genius Behind Allied Survival and Air Supremacy* (1999)

Galland, Adolf, *The First and the Last* (1954)

Gibbs, Air Marshal Sir Gerald, *The Survivor's Story* (1956)

Gilbert, Martin, *Churchill: The Wilderness Years* (1981)

——— *Winston S. Churchill* (vols. 4–8 and companion vols., 1975–88)

Glancey, Jonathan, *Spitfire: The Biography* (2006)

Gray, Colin, *Spitfire Patrol* (1990)

Griffiths, Harry, *Testing Times* (1992)

Haining, Peter, *The Spitfire Log* (1985)

Halfpenny, Bruce Barrymore, *Fight for the Sky* (1986)

Harvey-Bailey, Alec, *The Merlin in Perspective: The Combat Years* (1983)

——— *Hives: The Quiet Tiger* (1985)

Haslam, Group Captain E. B., 'How Lord Dowding Came to Leave Fighter Command', *Journal of Strategic Studies*, June 1981

Hayward, James, *Myths and Legends of the Second World War* (2003)

Henshaw, Alex, *Sigh for a Merlin: Testing the Spitfire* (1979)

——— 'Spitfire: A Test Pilot's Defence', *Aeroplane Monthly*, Sept. 1995

——— 'A Tribute To Jeffrey Quill', *Aerospace*, Apr. 1996

——— 'Testing Times: The Castle Bromwich Spitfires', *Journal of the Friends of the Fighter Collection*, summer 2002

411

'The High Performance Spitfire Trainer', *Flight*, July 1947

Higham, Robin, 'Quantity versus Quality: The Impact of Changing Demand on the British Aircraft Industry 1900–1960', *Business History Review*, winter 1968

Hillary, Richard, *The Last Enemy* (1942)

Hoare, Philip, *Wilde's Last Stand* (1997)

Hodgkinson, Brian, *Spitfire Down: The POW Story* (2000)

Hooton, Ted, *Spitfire Special* (1972)

Hornby, William, *Factories and Plant* (1988)

Houlton, Johnnie, *Spitfire Strikes: A New Zealand Fighter Pilot's Story* (1985)

Hunter, Ian, *The Collected Correspondence of Winston Churchill and Archibald Sinclair, 1915–1960* (2005)

Hyde, Montgomery, *British Air Policy between the Wars* (1976)

Ivie, Tom, and Ludwig, Paul, *Spitfires and Yellow Tail Mustangs* (2005)

Jackson, Robert, *The Nuffield Story* (1964)

—— *Spitfire: The History of Britain's Most Famous World War II Fighter* (2003)

Jenkins, Roy, *The Chancellors* (1998)

—— *Churchill* (2001)

Johnson, Air Vice-Marshal Johnnie, *Wing Leader* (1956)

—— et al., *Heroes of the RAF* (1960)

Johnstone, Air Vice-Marshal Sandy, *Spitfire into War* (1986)

Joubert de la Ferté, Sir Philip, *The Forgotten Ones: The Story of the Ground Crews* (1961)

Kaplan, Philip, *Two-Man Air Force* (2006)

—— and Collier, Richard, *The Few: Summer 1940, the Battle of Britain* (1989)

Kelly, Terence, *Hurricane and Spitfire Pilots at War* (1986)

Kershaw, Ian, *Making Friends With Hitler: Lord Londonderry and Britain's Road to War* (2004)

Kesselring, Albert, *Memoirs* (1953)

King, H. F., 'Sires of the Swift: A Forty Year Record of Supermarine Achievement', *Flight*, Oct. 1953

King, Martin, 'Spitfire PRXI', *Journal of the Spitfire Society*, spring 2006

Kingcome, Brian, *A Willingness to Die* (1999)

Levine, Joshua, *Forgotten Voices of the Blitz and the Battle of Britain* (2006)

Lewis, Geoffrey, *Alice – But Not Through the Looking Glass: Memories of a Spitfire Pilot* (2006)

Lewis, Peter, *The British Fighter since 1912: Sixty Years of Design and Development* (1974)

Liskutin, M. A., *Challenge in the Air* (1988)

Lockwood, Bruce, 'Riding the Griffon', *Aeroplane Monthly*, Mar. 2007

Lucas, Laddie, *Five Up* (1978)

—— (ed.), *Wings of War: Airmen of All Nations Tell Their Stories, 1939–1945* (1983)

Lyall, Gavin (ed.), *Freedom's Battle: The War in the Air* (1968)

MacDonnell, Donald, *From Dogfight to Diplomacy: A Spitfire Pilot's Log, 1932–58* (2005)

McKee, Alexander, *Strike from the Sky* (1989)

McRoberts, Douglas, *Lions Rampant: The Story of No. 602 Squadron* (1985)

Manchester, William, *The Caged Lion: Winston Churchill, 1932–40* (1988)

March, Peter, *The Spitfire Story* (2006)

Ministry of Information, *The Air Battle of Malta: The Official Account of the RAF in Malta, June 1940 to November 1942* (1944)

Mitchell, Gordon, *R. J. Mitchell: Schooldays to Spitfire* (1986)

Mondey, David, *The Schneider Trophy* (1975)

Morgan, Eric, and Shacklady, Edward, *Spitfire: The History* (1987)

Morpurgo, J. E., *Barnes Wallis: A Biography* (1972)
Morton, Karenza, 'Spitfire Legend: An Interview with Gordon Mitchell', *Southampton Daily Echo*, 23 Apr. 2005
Nicolson, Harold, *Diaries and Letters*, ed. Nigel Nicolson (2 vols, 1966–7)
Nixon, Frank, 'Engine Developments during the Past Half Century', *Journal of the Royal Aeronautical Society*, Jan. 1966
Offenberg, Jean, *Lonely Warrior* (1970)
Ogley, Bob, *Biggin on the Bump* (1990)
Olejnik, Robert, 'Achtung Klein Indianer: A Luftwaffe Pilot Remembers', *Aeroplane Monthly*, Sept. 1980
Oliver, David, *Fighter Command 1939–45* (2000)
Orange, Vincent, *Park: The Biography of Air Chief Marshal Sir Keith Park* (2000)
Overy, Richard, *The Air War 1939–45* (1980)
—— *The Battle of Britain* (2000)
Oxspring, Group Captain Bobby, *Spitfire Command* (1984)
Page, Geoffrey, *Shot Down in Flames* (1999)
Parker, Matthew, *The Battle of Britain* (2000)
Parker, R. A. C., 'British Rearmament 1936–39: Treasury, Trade Unions and Skilled Labour', *English Historical Review*, 96 (1981)
—— *Chamberlain and Appeasement* (1993)
Pitchfork, Graham, *Shot Down and on the Run* (2003)
—— *Shot Down and in the Drink* (2005)
Postan, M. M., *British War Production* (1952)
—— Scott, J. D., and Hay, D., *The Design and Development of Weapons: Studies in Government and Industrial Organization* (1964)
Pownall, Lieutenant General Sir Henry, *Chief of Staff: The Diaries of Lieutenant General Sir Henry Pownall*, ed. Brian Bond (1972)
Price, Alfred, *Spitfire: A Complete Fighting History* (1975)
—— *Spitfire: A Documentary History* (1977)
—— *The Hardest Day: The Battle of Britain, 18 August 1940* (1979)
—— *The Spitfire Story* (1982)
—— *Late Marque Spitfire Aces 1942–45* (1995)
—— *Late Marque Spitfires* (2000)
Quill, Jeffrey, *Spitfire: A Test Pilot's Story* (1983)
—— *Birth of a Legend: Spitfire* (1986)
Ray, John, *The Battle of Britain* (1994)
Reader, W. J., *The Architect of Air Power: The Life of the 1st Viscount Weir of Eastwood* (1968)
'A Real Thoroughbred: The Vickers Supermarine Spitfire – its Ancestry and Evolution', *Flight*, Sept. 1940
Reith, John, *The Reith Diaries*, ed. Charles Stuart (1975)
Richards, Denis, *Portal of Hungerford* (1977)
Richardson, William Holt, and Freidin, Seymour, *The Fatal Decisions* (1956)
Richey, Paul, *Fighter Pilot* (1941)
—— with Franks, Norman, *Fighter Pilot's Summer* (1993)
Ritchie, Sebastian, *Industry and Air Power* (1997)
Roberts, Andrew, *The Holy Fox: The Life of Lord Halifax* (1991)
Roberts, Fred, *Duxford to Karachi: An RAF Armourer's War* (2006)
Roberts, Leonard, *War Diaries* (2003)

Robertson, Bruce, *Spitfire: The Story of a Famous Fighter* (1960)
Robertson, Don, *Those Magnificent Flying Machines* (1984)
Robinson, Anthony, *RAF Fighter Squadrons of the Battle of Britain* (1987)
Robinson, Derek, *Invasion, 1940* (2005)
Rolls, William T., *Spitfire Attack* (1987)
Ross, David, *Richard Hillary* (2000)
—— *Stapme: The Biography of Squadron Leader Basil Gerald Stapleton* (2002)
Rudhall, Robert, *Battle of Britain: The Movie* (2000)
Russell, C. R. R., *Spitfire Odyssey* (1985)
—— *Spitfire Postscript* (1994)
Sampson, Wing Commander R. W. F., *Spitfire Offensive* (1994)
Sarkar, Dilip, *Through Peril to the Stars* (1993)
—— *The Battle of Britain: The Photographic Kaleidoscope* (2000)
—— *Johnnie Johnson: Spitfire Top Gun* (2 vols, 2004–5)
—— *Bader's Duxford Fighters* (2006)
—— *Missing in Action – Resting in Peace* (2006)
—— *Spitfire – Courage and Sacrifice* (2006)
Saward, Dudley, *Victory Denied: The Rise of Air Power and the Defeat of Germany, 1920–45* (1985)
Scott, J. D., *Vickers: A History* (1963)
Sebag-Montefiore, Hugh, *Dunkirk – Fight to the Last Man* (2006)
Shenstone, Beverley, 'Hindsight is Always One Hundred Per Cent', *Journal of the Royal Aeronautical Society*, Jan. 1966
Shores, Christopher, and Cull, Brian, with Malizia, Nicola, *Malta: The Spitfire Year 1942* (1991)
Sinnott, Colin, *The Royal Air Force and Aircraft Design, 1923–1939* (2001)
Slack, Tom, *Happy is the Day: A Spitfire Pilot's Story* (1987)
Slessor, Sir John, *The Central Blue: Recollections and Reflections* (1956)
Smith, E. A. W., *Spitfire Diary* (1988)
Smith, Graham, *Taking to the Skies: The Story of British Aviation, 1903–1939* (2003)
Smith, Joseph, 'The Development of the Spitfire and Seafire', transcript of lecture at the Institution of Civil Engineers, 1946, published in *Journal of the Royal Aeronautical Society*, Jan. 1947
—— 'R. J. Mitchell: Aircraft Designer', *Journal of the Royal Aeronautical Society*, May 1954
Smith, Malcolm, *British Air Strategy between the Wars* (1984)
Smith, Richard, *Hornchurch Eagles* (2002)
—— *Al Deere: The Authorized Biography* (2003)
Smith, Rod, 'In Defence of the Spitfire', *Aeroplane Monthly*, Aug. 1995
Smithies, Edward, *Aces, Erks and Backroom Boys* (1990)
Sorley, Air Marshal Sir Ralph, 'Eight Guns for a Fighter', *The Times*, 14 Sept. 1957
Spick, Mike, *Allied Fighter Aces* (1997)
'A Spitfire Score', *Flight*, Jan. 1946
Spitfire 70 – Flypast magazine special annual (2007)
'Spitfire Twelve', *Flight*, Apr. 1944
Spooner, Tony, *Warburton's War* (1987)
Stahl, Peter, *The Diving Eagle: A Ju 88's Pilot's Diary* (1984)
Steinhilper, Ulrich, and Osborne, Peter, *Spitfire on My Tail* (1990)
Stewart, Graham, *Burying Caesar: Churchill, Chamberlain and the Battle for the Tory Party* (2000)

Stokes, Doug, *Wings Aflame* (1998)

'The Supermarine Spitfire XIV', *Flight*, Sept. 1944

Sweetman, Bill, *Spitfire* (1980)

Swinton, Lord, *I Remember* (1948)

—— *Sixty Years of Power* (1966)

Taylor, A. J. P., *Beaverbrook* (1972)

—— *English History 1914–1945* (1965)

Taylor, John W. R., and Allward, Maurice, *Spitfire* (1946)

Tedder, Arthur, *With Prejudice: The War Memoirs of Marshal of the Royal Air Force, Lord Tedder* (1966)

Terraine, John, *The Right of the Line* (1985)

'This is the Spitfire', *Flight*, Sept. 1940

Thomas, Gil, *Shoulder to the Sky* (1956)

Thomas, Hugh, *The Spirit of the Blue: Peter Ayerst: The Fighter Pilot's Story* (2004)

Thomas, Miles, *Out on a Wing* (1964)

Townsend, Peter, *Duel of Eagles* (1970)

Toye, Richard, *Lloyd George and Churchill: Rivals for Greatness* (2007)

Turner, John Frayn, *The Bader Wing* (1981)

—— *The Battle of Britain* (2004)

Vader, John, *Spitfire* (1969)

Wade, Squadron Leader T. S., 'Two Spitfires in One', *Aeroplane Monthly*, May 1947

Walker, Diana Barnato, *Spreading My Wings* (1994)

Wellum, Geoffrey, *First Light* (2002)

Westacott, Fred, *Shaking the Chains* (2002)

White, Roger Henshaw, *Spitfire Saga: With a Spell on Wellingtons* (1981)

Wood, Derek, and Dempster, Derek, *The Narrow Margin* (1961)

Worley, Brian, 'Fighter Fundamentals', *Aeronautics*, 1940

Wragg, David, *RAF Handbook 1939–45* (2007)

Wright, Robert, *Dowding and the Battle of Britain* (1969)

Acknowledgements

I owe thanks to a great many people. First of all, I am in the debt of those former Spitfire pilots and ground crew who were kind enough to give me personal interviews: Peter Ayrest, Geoffrey Cairns, Ken Coop, John Dalley, Sidney and Eileen Denney, Laurie Frampton, the late Alex Henshaw, George Morgan, Dennis Nichols, Ken Plumridge, Nigel Rose, Sidney Sexton, Ernie Unstead, and William Walker. Tony Tooth generously gave me a copy of his private memoir of wartime flying. The late Harry Griffiths, the Supermarine engineer and chairman of the Spitfire Society, was extremely helpful in putting me in touch with these heroic figures, as was Tracey Woods, the media manager at the Imperial War Museum in Duxford. With regard to the archive material used, I am grateful for all the assistance shown me by the staff of the Imperial War Museum in Southwark, the National Archives in Kew, the Neville Chamberlain Archives in Birmingham, the Cambridge University Library, the British Newspaper Library in Colindale, the Churchill Archives Centre, the House of Lords Records Office, and the library of Southampton Hall of Aviation, run by David Whatley and David Hatchard. I want to put on record my particular gratitude to the staff of the RAF Museum in Hendon, including Peter Elliott, the senior keeper of the Department of Research, and Peter Devitt and Hugh Sidaway, who were unfailingly co-operative and full of sound advice. But I must make particular mention of Daniel Scott-Davies, the curator of the Alex Henshaw Collection, whose generosity and phenomenal grasp of Vickers history opened up new avenues of research for me.

Other research, especially on journals, was performed with great thoroughness by Alannah Barton, while Wendy Love did an excellent job of transcribing the tapes of interviews. For assistance with the photographs, I am indebted to John Wells of Cambridge University Library, Peter Elliott and Andy Renwick of the RAF Museum, Laura Clouting, Thomas Easton and

Louise Oliver of the Imperial War Museum, Anna Bond of the Science Photo Library, Helen Trompeteler of the National Portrait Gallery, the Corbis Picture Agency, the Vintage Magazine Company and Matthew Fry of the Hulton/Getty archive. I am particularly grateful to Frank Sanders for his generosity in sending me examples from his own private collection of Seafire photographs. And Sarah Quill, daughter of the legendary test pilot, kindly gave me permission to use photographs from her father's estate.

On the production side, I am indebted, as always, to all at John Murray, especially Roland Philipps, Rowan Yapp, Lucy Dixon and Caroline Westmore. My copy-editor, Bob Davenport, was a Trojan of diligence and meticulousness and my agent, Georgina Capel, provided wise advice and support. On the personal side, I would like to thank Christopher and Cathy Foyle for their epic hospitality and support during large parts of the research. And finally I must pay tribute to the tolerance, kindness, wisdom and patience of my wonderful wife, Elizabeth, who kept me going during the long hours of research and writing over the last year. This is my seventh book, and, despite the upheaval they have all caused in our lives, she has never given me anything but encouragement and devotion.

Index